History of the Electric Automobile

Battery-Only Powered Cars

Ernest Henry Wakefield, Ph.D.

Published by:
Society of Automotive Engineers, Inc.
400 Commonwealth Drive
Warrendale, PA 15096-0001
U.S.A.
Phone: (412) 776-4841
Fax: (412) 776-5760

Library of Congress Cataloging-in-Publication Data

Wakefield, Ernest Henry, 1915-
    History of the electric automobile : battery-only powered cars / Ernest
Henry Wakefield.
        p.   cm.
    Includes bibliographical references and index.
    ISBN 1-56091-299-5 : $49.00
    1. Automobiles, Electric--History 2. Automobiles, Electric--Batteries--
History. I. Title.
TL220.W343 1993
629.25'02--dc20   93-32254
                                                                              CIP

ISBN 1-56091-299-5

SAE Order No. R-122

Gustave Trouvé,

who in 1881 first assembled an electric vehicle

Courtesy: H. Munn & Co.

To Ann and John

and

their late mother,

Hilda Gertrude Overholt Wakefield

Those who cannot remember the past
are condemned to repeat it.

—George Santayana

Table of Contents

Contents

Foreword

The lure of the electric powered vehicle for personalized transportation has been a recurring enigma to automotive engineers for over a century. Like the undulating surge of electrical power itself, the interest in electric vehicles rises and falls with changes in the world's economic status and concerns about the availability of fossil fuels and environmental health.

Since the late 1800s, more than 300 companies in the United States alone, and many others throughout the world, have espoused the quiet power, ease of control, and cleanliness of electric automobiles for personal and commercial applications.

In the early 1900s, the electric vehicle was the overwhelming favorite to lead America's transportation revolution. But as the motor vehicle ventured beyond city limits, it soon was apparent that the "silent servant" had an all too severe problem of limited range, weight, and price.

The electric storage battery was its Achilles heel, and despite millions of dollars invested in over a century of research and development, the "miracle" battery is yet undiscovered. However, the promise and excitement of electrically powered personal transportation is as alluring and alive today as it was a century ago.

The past century of electric vehicle development has finally been recorded. It is a story well documented by one of the leading authorities on electric vehicles. Dr. Ernest H. Wakefield has spent a lifetime in the electrical and nuclear engineering fields.

As an electrical engineer, educator, lecturer, author, inventor, and entrepreneur for the past half century, Dr. Wakefield is eminently qualified to chronicle the history of the electric vehicle. In this volume, the development of the electric vehicle throughout the world is recounted.

The early development of the storage battery in France including the efforts of Gaston Planté and Camille Faure in the mid-nineteenth century and the glory days of the electric car in America are highlighted. Included are the pioneering efforts of Riker, Baker, Trouvé, Ayrton, Perry, Baker, and Woods, the evolution of the batteries, the chargers, the controllers, and modern day trials of new alternating-current drive concepts. The developmental history of the electric car is indeed well documented by Dr. Wakefield.

Today, in a world of transportation focused on responding to demands for environmental, economic, and ecological progress and zero emission vehicles, the alluring, elusive, and enduring electric finally stands on the threshold of success after a long, arduous journey.

James A. Wren
Patent Department
American Automobile Manufacturers Association

About the Author

In his teen years Dr. Ernest Henry Wakefield authored a weekly newspaper column. With an enlarging world and education, B.A., M.S. (Fine Arts), and a Ph.D. (Electrical Engineering) from the University of Michigan, by being employed by General Electric Co. and Westinghouse Corp., by teaching electrical engineering at the University of Tennessee, by volunteering into the U.S. Army, by military training at Camp Crowder, Missouri, with stints at MIT in radar and the University of Chicago in physics, and by being assigned to the Physics Division of The Manhattan Project (Atom Bomb) at the University of Chicago, he still writes.

After WWII he founded and operated a world class nuclear instrument company with factories in Skokie, Illinois and Berkeley, California, manufacturing both for the domestic and export markets. Later he employed many persons in the Philippines and Haiti in local fabrication. Then he independently discovered the concept of frequency and pulse-width modulation for changing direct-current to variable frequency three-phase alternating-current, a technique now being widely applied in electric vehicles. To employ this concept he designed and built electric cars. In this period Dr. Wakefield continued his writings on transportation authoring *The Consumer's Electric Car,* 1977.

Travelling in 56 and lecturing in more than 20 foreign countries, participating for more than 40 years as a visitor both in the African and in the Physics Programs at Northwestern University, Dr. Wakefield continues his writing.

Dr. Wakefield has written about the nuclear field, editing and authoring *Nuclear Reactors for Universities and Industry,* 1957; on entrepreneurship and many economic papers on Third World nations: African, Southwest Pacific, as well as the Caribbean.

In history he has recently completed editing fifty booklets bearing text and etchings entitled *Wakefield's American Civil War Series.* Among them are *The Battle of Mobile Bay,* 1988. He has written *The Lighthouse That Wanted To Stay Lit,* 1992, and also on genealogy for writers who have access to a word processor.

In fiction Dr. Wakefield wrote *The Treasure of Fisherman's Reef,* 1953. Using his forty-year experience in nuclear energy, he has also chronicled the chance of nuclear winter, and has written a three volume love story.

Preface

This book is the story about electric automobiles. In anticipation of oil shortages and increasing air pollution in American cities the U.S. Congress passed over a Presidential veto the *Electric and Hybrid Vehicle Research, Development and Demonstration Act* of 1976. By nomenclature the Congress differentiated between battery-powered electric vehicles and those vehicles which might have both battery-power as well as other means of propulsion. This particular book is devoted to the history of the battery-only powered electric vehicle and its components. A second volume is being written that covers the development of the many multi-powered electrics including battery-powered plus: a spring, an internal combustion engine, a flywheel, solar cell powered, and fuel cell vehicles and their unique constituents. As batteries, controllers, and electric motors are common to both classes of vehicles, their development is in this volume only.

While probably no person has exact knowledge, qualitatively speaking possibly equal time has been spent on each of these two paths of personal transportation. Presently intense work is proceeding on battery-only powered vehicles with possibly less emphasis on multi-powered electric cars. Both approaches have a rich background; however, no one knows which system will be followed in the near and distant future.

To many the romance and nostalgia of electric cars and electric carriages have an almost mystical interest. Furthermore, with electricity being such a clean and versatile fuel that is so widely used, a perennial question is asked: why not employ it for personal transportation? Because no book chronicles the history of electric vehicles, the author collected this information and placed it in book form for its preservation. Fortunately, the author has been, for more than a third of a century, an integral part of the emerging electric vehicle industry in conception, design, construction, marketing, financing, and interpretation. This book, in treating the past of this long nascent industry, is an attempt to bring clean air to metropolitan cities worldwide. Hopefully objective and correct, the authorship has been a labor of love.

Electric cars have resulted from a happy arrangement of mechanical, electrical, magnetic, and chemical laws which, operating in perfect order, yield personal transportation. This book describes and illustrates the application of these natural laws to vehicles, to battery chargers, to batteries or other sources of energy, to controllers, to motors, to transmissions, to wheels, and identifies some pioneers who were responsible for their applications. Considering the range of physical principles embodied in an electric vehicle, no one can be an expert on all phases of their elements. The present volume can only touch on much of the technology. However, the serious student should be able to secure an introductory grasp on the principles of electric vehicles from this book and its Notes, Appendices, and Further Readings list.

History of the Electric Vehicle: Battery-Only Powered Cars is structured into five sections. There is a brief introduction indicating how the knowledge for electric vehicles was gained through earlier centuries, particularly the period beginning with the quantitative experimentation with electrical phenomena. These innovations were finally assembled as an electric vehicle system in 1881. Then the first two electrical vehicles, which were developed in France and England, are explored first, followed by early electric vehicle development in America. With this introduction, a critical comparison of gasoline, steam, and electric powered systems is undertaken. Then turning to the vehicles themselves, the development of the electric battery charger, the motive power batteries, the controller, and direct-current electric motors are briefly discussed. In design, the motorcars of this period were wagons or carriages which closely copied horse-drawn vehicles. Small wonder they were called horseless carriages.

The second section demonstrates improvements in electric vehicles from 1900 to 1935. Beginning in 1902 the automobile adopted its present conformation, engine forward. Personal cars also gained a closed-in body during the early years of this time span, serving to protect passengers from the weather. The era was a period which saw the flowering and demise of the commercially produced over-the-road electric car. Yet the decade from 1902 to 1912 was one of the most productive and fruitful in design of personal cars and industrial trucks. And it was also an era of high mortality of companies. One could succeed, and one could fail.

Steel-tired, wood-fabricated wheels yielded to solid rubber-tired, then pneumatic-tired, wire-spoked wheels which in turn became pressed all-steel design as well as cast aluminum. From the component with the greatest single problem—punctures, tires became a paragon of reliability. The chassis was transformed from a wagon to a well-engineered assembly. The body metamorphosed from a horseless carriage to its present configuration. Wick lamps became acetylene, then filament, now gaseous-discharge. Brakes proceeded from wheel rim-friction to an axle-based contracting cylinder, then finally to disc-type. Drive power-transfer passed from linked chain to the concept of the earlier conceived differential. Smooth friction surfaces adopted roller-bearings. Lubrication changed to high-technology, petroleum greases and liquid. All these improvements, and many more, transpired to place the Western World on wheels. As if to match, many nations began major road-building programs that continue today.

The third section of the volume covers the dead period for electric vehicles (1935 to 1955) and prepares the reader for the transition and rebirth. This section critiques why the manufacture of electric cars ceased and presents reasons for the dominance of the internal combustion engine-powered vehicle.

The fourth section describes the innovative, modern electric drive systems that were devised internationally in the early 1960s. Employed is solid-state electronics, 3-phase A-C power, and more exotic batteries. The period demonstrated new electric drive systems. This segment also shows advances, which continue at this writing, to vehicles that reach road-testing.

The fifth section of *History of the Electric Automobile: Battery-Only Powered Cars* contains ten appendices, a glossary, and an index. Finally, for more than a century, from 1881 through the present, nearly all seers who have predicted the role of electric vehicles in personal transportation have been wrong. This book records what actually happened in America and throughout the world.

Acknowledgements

In writing this book the author owes a debt of gratitude to the late Claud Erickson, formerly Manager of the Lansing, Michigan Electric Power Board, for originally interesting me in the history of electric vehicles. I also owe an obligation to Janet Ayers, Engineering and Science Librarian; Mary Roy, Mary McCreadie, Renée McHenry, Dorothy Ramm, Librarians, Transportation Center; Marjorie Carpenter, Interlibrary Loan Librarian; and Maude M. Kelso, Periodical Supervisor; and to all of Northwestern University. Also, I wish to thank the staff of the University of Illinois Library, Champaign-Urbana, for their many courtesies.

For help in the technical phase, I thank my good friend Dr. Gordon J. Murphy, Professor of Electrical Engineering and Computer Sciences, Northwestern University; and my peers who were instrumental in the revival of the electric vehicle industry in the 1960s and 1970s: Dr. Paul D. Agarwal of General Motors; Robert R. Aronson of Electric Fuel Propulsion; Robert F. Beaumont of Sebring-Vanguard Company; Wayne E. Goldman of Electromotion, Inc.; Paul R. Hafer of Battronics, Inc.; Robert S. McKee of McKee Engineering Corporation; Mark J. Obert of the American Motors Corporation; Wally E. Rippel of California Institute of Technology; Dr. Lewis E. Unnewhehr of the Ford Motor Company; and Dr. Victor Wouk of Petro-Motors, Inc. And surely there were others.

Thanks is also extended to those who have patiently reviewed elements of the book (Dr. John B. Ketterson, Professor of Physics, Northwestern University; and Dr. Paul A. Nelson, Deputy-Director of the Electrochemical Division, Argonne National Laboratory, who contributed to Chapter 11 on batteries and fuel cells) and those who reviewed the entire manuscript (Mary Irwin, Editor of the University of Michigan Press; Dr. Alan L. Kistler, Professor of Mechanical Engineering at Northwestern University; Ralph A. Ocon, science writer of Sarasota, Florida; William H. Shafer, spokesman for Commonwealth Edison Company on electric vehicles (ret.); Dr. Gene E. Smith, Professor of Mechanical Engineering of the University of Michigan; James Wren, Manager of the Patent Department, Motor Vehicle Manufactures Association; and others). All of these people helped improve the work.

In preparing the electrical and multi-powered vehicle glossary, I received help from the late John Bardeen, Nobel Laureate, University of Illinois, Urbana; the late Lewis Erwin, Professor, Mechanical Engineering, Northwestern University; Douglas A. Fraser, Thayer School of Engineering, Dartmouth College; and William B. Rever III, Product Manager, Crystalline

Division, Solarex Corporation. The following reference books were used extensively: *The International Dictionary of Applied Mathematics*, New York: D. Van Nostrand, (1960); *IEEE Standard Dictionary of Electrical and Electronic Terms*, Ed., Frank Jay, New York: Institute of Electrical and Electronic Engineers, Inc. (1984); *McGraw-Hill Dictionary of Scientific and Technical Terms*, 3rd ed., Ed., Sybil P. Parker, New York: McGraw-Hill, (1984); Automobile Advertising Supplement to *The New York Times*, May 13, 1990; Stephen Stanley Attwood, *Electric and Magnetic Fields*, New York: Wiley, (1949).

For technical aid in preparing the book, I wish to salute Dr. Peter Roll, Vice President for Information Services, the University Microcomputer Support Group; Joel D. Meyers, Assistant Dean, Robert R. McCormick School of Engineering and Applied Science; Robert T. Schreiber and Ms. Mildred Wiesser, both of the Center for Manufacturing Engineering; and Frances Glass-Newmann of the Program of Master of Management in Manufacturing; and all of Northwestern University, Evanston, Illinois. All have been most helpful. In addition, I wish to thank Ruth L. Barrash for placing onto computer disks all that is read below and for much more. Likewise, I would compliment Apple Computer, Inc. for aid in additional computer service.

I wish to thank the many industrial and utility companies who, in their early funding when dollars were hard to come by, encouraged my own continued interest in designing and building electric vehicles in this emerging industry. These organizations are listed in Chapter 24.

Prologue

The Growth of Appropriate Knowledge Before the Electric Car

Before an electric vehicle could be developed there had to be a suitable drive system carried in a vehicle whose wheels were serviceable. Below are related the developments in electricity, of the bicycle/tricycle, a vehicle which was the genesis of the electric car, and of rubber-bearing wheels before the advent of the electric car. Only in a society which permitted free scientific thought and an easy exchange of information could the transformations cited below flower. Based on this early work, Chapter 1 and later chapters chronicle the international growth of electric vehicle knowledge and the cars which resulted. Events related in this book had an early beginning as is seen below.

Status of Electricity Before the Electric Car

The unique properties of natural magnets or lodestones were known to the Ancients. And as early as 1000 A.D. European navigators were using suspended magnets for guiding their ships, enabling them to more safely sail in open water rather than being limited to visual coastal sailing. The earliest studies on a natural magnet were made by Petrus Marcourt in 1269 at the time of the unsuccessful seventh Christian Crusade. Shaping a lodestone into a sphere, he sequentially located a magnetic needle at various points on its surface marking its pointings. Connecting these directional markings the meridians formed joined at two points. Thus Maricourt is credited with the concept of two poles for a magnet.

In England, William Gilbert, physician to Queen Elizabeth, published his book *De Magnete* in 1600. Gilbert showed not only was the earth a magnet, but that friction between certain substances could induce static electricity. Gilbert also differentiated between magnetism and electricity. From this healer we also obtained the word 'electricity.' For bodies which exhibited electric features he called *electric* after *elektron*, the Greek word for amber, a substance which, when rubbed with fur, charged both items. Thereafter, Otto von Guercke constructed the first friction-electric machine in 1660, a coaxially rotating glass plate on which an item such as fur might be pressed. Such a device might be used to charge conducting spheres between two of which, separated by an air-gap, a substantial voltage difference could exist. Carrying on

Gilbert's experiments, Stephen Gray in England discovered electrical conductors in 1729 and showed electrification is identified with surfaces and not with volumes. In 1733 Charles Francois de Cisternay Dufay described two types of electrical forces: an attractive force and a repulsive force. Continuing advancements in science, Ewald George von Kliest and Peter von Musschenbroek in 1745-1746 independently discovered electricity could be stored in a glass bottle if containing copper wire or mercury. On discharge small animals were killed.[1] From this experiment Grolatt created at the University of Leyden what became known as the Leyden jar, an object which today is recognized as an electrical condenser.

The American Benjamin Franklin in 1752 not only identified lightning with electricity, demonstrating a spark from it would ignite alcohol, just as would a spark from a friction machine, but introduced the plus (+) and minus (-) sign to electricity. In addition, Franklin, always conscious of public opinion, proceeded to popularize electric phenomena, thus gaining support for science. Acting on Franklin's suggestion, Joseph Priestley, an English chemist, showed that when a hollow conducting vessel is electrified no electric forces act on objects in the interior, a concept known today as electrical shielding. From this experiment and others, Priestley deduced the inverse square law applied to electric charges, noting the similarity with Newton's 1680 discovery of the inverse square law applicative to gravitation. In 1769 James Watt significantly improved the efficiency of the steam engine, a prime mover which would be so important to the later developed electric generator. Advances on Priestley's discoveries were made by Henry Cavendish, Charles Augustin Coulomb, and by Siméon-Denis Poisson toward the end of the 18th century and in the early 19th century. Poisson applied mathematics to electric and magnetic fields. Coulomb's invention of the torsion balance in 1777 enabled him to quantify electric charges, establishing Coulomb's Law in 1785.

In what is now Italy, Luigi Galvani, a professor of anatomy in Bologna, observed that probes of different metals, when applied to a frog's leg, caused the muscles to twitch. Galvani published his work in 1791 incorrectly identifying the energizing force as *animal electricity*. Learning of these experiments Alessandro Volta of Pavia in 1794 properly assumed the results were caused by a reaction between two different metal probes and the frog's body fluid. Continuing his experiments Volta in 1800 placed between plates of copper and zinc a sheet of blotting paper steeped in salt water. This assembly was the first electric battery, one of the greatest discoveries of all time. See Chapter 10. Issuing from Volta's *pile* (battery) was a *continuous* flow of electricity, whereas before Volta's battery a current flowed only while the charged body was discharging. Volta also found if his batteries were placed in parallel a greater current could be drawn, and if placed in series a greater voltage was obtained. Writing of his work in 1800 to Sir Joseph Banks, president of the Royal Society, within ten days William Nicholson and Anthony Carlisle observed water could be separated into hydrogen and oxygen by an electric current. The science of electro-chemistry had been born. Almost immediately Sir Humphrey Davy isolated the elements potassium and sodium, and in 1801, placing many batteries in series he was able to create the first incandescent carbon-arc light source. The carbon-arc led to Sir William Crooke's gaseous discharge tube, and later to the fluorescent lamp. Davy, besides being a scientist, was a teacher offering regular free Sunday night lectures in London.

---

[1] The first capital punishment electric chair was provided with alternating-current. Isaac Asimov, *Asimov's Biographical Encyclopedia of Science and Technology*, Garden City: Doubleday, 1964.

One of Sir Humphrey's wisest acts was the appointment in 1813 of Michael Faraday as his assistant.[2] Faraday, a bookbinder and son of a blacksmith, Fig. P.1, had attended one of these lectures, had carefully written up the notes, provided illustrations, bound the lecture in booklet form, and presented the volume to the Master. As a result Faraday was hired as an assistant. His initial task was to wash laboratory bottles, but then, Sir Humphrey, making a European trip, invited Faraday, giving him the opportunity to visit the scientific greats and to see their laboratories. Making his way Faraday has been identified as one of the truly great experimentalists of all time. Only a few of his developments are here described. He not only discovered both self- and mutual-induction between elements of conductors carrying an electric current (an independent observation made by the American Joseph Henry), but also in 1821 achieved a rotational force by using the properties of magnetism and electricity, a discovery which eventually led to the electric motor. See Fig. 12.6. In addition, Faraday laid the basis for

Figure P.1. Michael Faraday (1791-1867) in an 1830 engraving by J. Cochran. Scientific American, October 1991, p. 129.

---

2 John Meurig Thomas, *Michael Faraday and the Royal Institution: The Genius of Man and Place*, New York: Am. Inst. of Physics, 1991.

alternating-current (AC), the transformer, telegraphy, and the ubiquitous induction motor. Alternating-current electric power is now employed all over the world, and is the emerging preferred power source for the modern electric car. Faraday also published in 1844 his concept of magnetic and electric lines of force whose importance will be described later.

In 1820 Denmark's Hans Christian Ørsted observed a pivoted compass-needle would swing to be at right angles to a conductor carrying current, rotating 180 degrees when being over the wire to being under. And in the same year the French physicist André-Marie Ampère demonstrated two wires conducting direct-current in the same direction attracted each other, while if the flow were in the opposite direction they repelled. In 1824, using the principles of Faraday, Dominique Francois Arago demonstrated induction by rotating a copper disk beneath which was a coaxial compass needle. The latter, too, followed the rotation. William Sturgeon in 1825 constructed the first electromagnet, a length of iron wrapped with an insulated current-carrying wire, noting the magnetic field was enhanced by the iron. He went on to invent the galvanometer in 1836. In 1827 George Simon Ohm, a German, published the results of his experiments on current flow in an electric circuit in which different resistances were successively placed. Here was the origin of Ohm's law relating current, resistance, and voltage, mastered by every sophomore physics and engineering student today: $V=IR$, where V is voltage, I the current, and R the resistance.

Competition to Create a Motor/Generator

Noting Faraday had obtained rotary motion by the proper physical relation of a magnet and a current-carrying wire, the Frenchman Hippolyte Pixii on 3 September 1832 demonstrated an operating electric motor before the *Acadamie des Sciences* in Paris. This public demonstration was the first of an electric motor. Also in 1832, Karl Friedrich Gauss determined a set of measurement units for magnetic phenomena, and in 1833 he established an electric telegraph.

Reading of Faraday's experiments, Thomas Davenport, an American, constructed the first electric motor to perform useful work, driving a lathe, in 1836. See Fig. 12.9. Gradually the importance and versatility of electricity was receiving ever-widening appreciation. In 1838, under the auspices of Czar Nicholas I, Moritz Jacobi, a German born physicist, operated an electrically powered paddle-wheel boat on the Neva River before the Russian city of St. Petersburg in cooperation with W. R. Grove of England.[3]

Supplementing the practical problems of using electricity, cited both above and below, were a host of scientists clarifying physical phenomena in the middle of the 19th century: Franz Ernst Neumann, Wilhelm Eduard Weber, H. F. E. Lenz, Sir William Thomson, better known as Lord Kelvin, James Prescott Joule, Herman von Helmholtz, Sir George Gabriel Stokes, and Gustav Kirchhoff, all names familiar to today's scientists and engineers. In 1856 Weber and his assistant Rudolph Kohlrausch determined the ratio of electric and magnetic units. The very next year, 1857, Kirchhoff and Weber's experiments showed that electrical disturbances on a wire proceeded with the speed of light. Thus by 1860, only one year before the American Civil War, electromagnetism and optics were seen to be linked.

---

[3] W. R. Grove, *On a New Voltaic Combination, Philosophical Magazine*, 13 pp. 430-31, 1838.

Faraday's experiments greatly impressed all scientists in Europe and in America. How to build an electric motor/generator capable respectively of yielding or producing substantial power? Pixii had been a pioneer, now in the middle-half of the 19th century a platoon of scientists and engineers independently sought to develop these elixirs of electricity, rotating machinery and light sources into commercial products. For a motor/generator the question was how best to arrange the three necessary physical elements: copper wire, magnetic iron, and resistance. Aug Guerront by text and figures highlights this rampant pursuit as described in the text under *Further Readings*. Only a few of the many are chronicled here. Stohrer created a hand-crank generator in 1843.[4] Sir Charles Wheatstone placed the first electromagnet on a direct-current generator in 1845.[4] Later, he also developed the Wheatstone Bridge, a device for precisely measuring a resistance. Rumkorff built a hand-crank generator.[4] In 1862 a carbon-arc source, replacing an oil lamp, was installed in a lighthouse on the south coast of Kent, England; likewise at the port of Havre, France in 1863, using a DC generator assembled by Hippolyte Pixii. For lighting buildings based on Davy's work, Paul Jablochkoff enclosed the

Figure P.2. *Antonio Pacinotti's ring-type motor/generator. Scientific American Supplement, Vol. XIV, No. 357, Nov. 4, 1882, p. 5696.*

---

[4] *Scientific American*, Vol. XIV, No. 357, Nov. 4, 1882, pp. 5695-6.

carbon-arc with a hollow cylinder of kaolin,[5] which, becoming incandescent, the now-translucent clay broadened the emitted spectrum thus offering a more pleasing light. With this luminous source Jablochkoff offered his newly constructed "ecliptic" DC generator. Charles F. Brush in America used carbon-arcs for city street lighting, thus mitigating the gloom of city streets.

The Italian, Antonio Pacinotti, invented the ring direct-current motor in 1861 and demonstrated it at the University of Pisa as illustrated in Fig. P.2.[6] Ring-type electric motor/generators became standard. Pacinotti is an unsung hero, for, in addition to the above, he was the first to report a generator is also a motor, a concept later announced by Gaston Planté.[7] Pacinotti's call to military service purloined from him this glory. Wilde constructed a DC machine in 1864. Impressed by Faraday's lines of force concept the Englishman James Clerk Maxwell in the same year, 1864, published his elegant set of electromagnetic equations which synthesized into a unitary concept electricity and magnetism. De Romilly created a DC machine in 1866. Almost at the same time was a similar machine constructed by William Ladd in 1867. Weston would also create an operating DC machine.

Finally in 1869 a Belgian, Zénobe Théophile Gramme constructed the first direct-current electric motor which could perform work at a rate greater than one horsepower, (about 3/4 of a kilowatt). This machine, like the others above, if rotating mechanical power were applied, would yield electricity. If, instead, an electric battery were placed across its output wires, rotational mechanical power would be delivered. Thus Gramme's *dynamo*, as earlier announced by Pacinotti, could be operated both in the generator or in the motor mode. See Fig. 10.6. Furthermore, Gramme was the first to connect the force of steam, already a major source of power used in trains, in road steam-wagons, and in industry, to his electric generator, as demonstrated in Fig. P.3. With this development delivery of large amounts of electric power, in contrast to the limited power from a battery, could be contemplated. Supplementing the above Sir William Siemens and brother Friedrich, born in Germany but opting to be Englishmen because of more favorable patent laws, developed the Double T Iron Armature Machine motor/generator in 1870.[8] In addition, the brothers contributed greatly to increasing the efficiency of steam heating as a prime mover for an electric generator. The first industrial use of generators was to electroplate nickel and silver for the jewelry trade.[9]

Of historical interest, during the Civil War Confederate personnel in New Orleans attempted to build a battery-powered submarine using an electric motor. While unsuccessful, Confederate electric-contact torpedoes, now called mines, proved terribly destructive of Union gunboats.[10] This information indicates how innovative Southern experimenters were during the American government's supreme political test, the 1861-65 War Between the States.

---

[5] *Scientific American*, Nol. XLVII, No. 20, June 11, 1882, p. 310.

[6] Antonio Pacinotti, *Descrizione di una Machinetta Electromagnetica, Il Nuova Cimonto*, 99 pp. 378-384, 1863.

[7] Gaston Planté, *Recherches sur l'Electricité*, Tr. Paul Bedford Ewell, London: Whittaker, 1887.

[8] *Scientific American Supplement*, Vol. XIV, No. 357, Nov. 4, 1882, pp. 5695-6.

[9] J. Hamel, *Colassale Magneto-electrishe Machine zum Versibern und Vergelden, Jour. fuer practische Chemie*, 41 pp. 244-5, 1847.

[10] John Coddington Kinney, *Farragut at Mobile Bay, Battles and Leaders of the Civil War*, New York: The Century Co., 1888.

Figure P.3. Zénobe Théophile Gramme's steam-engine driving two identical generators. Scientific American Supplement, Vol. XIII, No. 327, April 8, 1882, p. 5207.

Later, in 1879, Thomas Alva Edison in America, using a split bamboo for a filament, and Joseph W. Swan in England perfected the electric filament lamp. The former initiated the electrical infrastructure for a direct-current generating distribution system at his Pearl Street station in New York City.[11] The initial commercial installation of electric lights, however, was on shipboard. In 1879, the steamer *Jeanette* of the deLong Expedition was fitted out at the expense of newspaper tycoon, James Gordon Bennett, to explore the Arctic seas around what is now Russian Wrangel Island.[12] In this marine application the generator and lighting system served well for two years when the ship was crushed in the ice. Also in 1879 the California Electric Light Company was established in San Francisco. And on January 12, 1882, a British electric system, built on the Holborn Viaduct in London, provided electricity for 3000 incandescent lamps. The system employed Edison jumbo generators which were powered by steam engines manufactured by Armington & Sims. It might be noted: the incandescent lamp is probably the most ubiquitous complex electric device in existence.[13]

The Frenchman Gustave Trouvé operated an electric-powered outboard motor boat on the Seine River in Paris in 1881, almost surely the first outboard motor boat. At the same time Trouvé drove the first electric propelled vehicle on the streets of the City of Light. And de Meritsen would create two compact DC machines in 1882, one type of which is shown in Fig. P.4. Finally, the brothers Albert and Gaston Tissandier in 1883 flew an airship powered by an

---

[11] *Scientific American*, Vol. XLVII, NO. 20, Sept. 10, 1882, p. 176.

[12] *Ibid.* Vol. XLII, No. 16, Oct. 14, 1882, p. 244.

[13] The author's father installed the first electric lights in Cleveland, at the Society for Savings Bank in 1882. The lighting fixtures were manufactured in the author's great uncle's factory in Newburg, Ohio.

electric motor. The 30 by 10 meter diameter airship, filled with 1060 cubic meters of hydrogen, had a still-air speed of 10 kilometers per hour. Thus, the electric motor was the first power source, after steam, to propel man on land, on water, and in the air, 1881-83.

Parallel with the above described rotational machines and electric sources of light were experiments with Volta-type batteries, a subject more thoroughly covered in Chapter 10. Soon two basic types of batteries were available, primary and secondary batteries. Volta's battery was a primary battery, as was C. H. Wilkinson's "plunge battery" of 1804.[14] In operation one plate was consumed; the other changed. Georges LeClanché, a French chemist and electrician, made an early alkaline primary battery. A primary battery, as is known, cannot be easily recharged. Soon secondary batteries were developed which could be recharged by a direct-current electric generator. One of the most successful secondary batteries developed was conceived by the

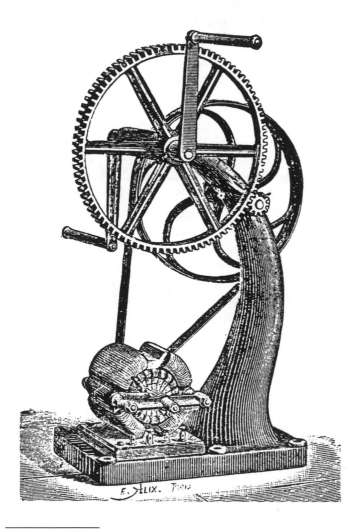

Figure P.4. This two-man generator by De Meritens in 1882, one year after the first electric car, gives some indication of the manpower required to generate electricity. The gearing and belting indicate a generator turned at high speed.

---

[14] C. H. Wilkinson, *On the Means of Simplifying and Improving the Galvanic Apparatus*, Nicholson's Journal, 8, pp. 15, 1804.

French chemist, Gaston Planté in 1859. His improved lead-acid battery, described in Chapter 10 as are other batteries, is used everywhere today. It was Planté's battery and a modified Siemens' motor which powered the first electric car.

The Genesis of Alternating-Current Motors/Generators

At the University of Graz in Austria, a Croatian-born student, Nikola Tesla, experimenting with Gramme's electric dynamo in the early 1880s conceived of a revolutionary idea. He would employ three sinusoidal alternating-currents in a novel way. Each would be electrically displaced from the other by 120 electrical degrees and, if properly wound on selected poles of an iron stator, a rotating electro-magnetic field would be created. If a conducting iron bobbin were suitably placed on a coaxial shaft within the stator, induced forces would provide a 3-phase alternating-current motor, one now known as an induction motor. If instead of the electrically isolated bobbin there were substituted one properly wired and provided with a DC current through two slip-rings, and rotating mechanical power applied to the shaft on which the bobbin turned, 3-phase electrical power would be generated. Here was the grand concept of Gramme's dynamo all over again except, with a different design, the machine is operating in the AC mode.

Tesla developed the above described ideas, and taking international patents, proceeded to Paris where he sought employment at the Paris Edison works.[15] With a letter of reference and his drawings, Tesla emigrated to America in 1884 seeking employment in Edison's New Jersey factory. As Tesla presented his 3-phase power concept to Edison, the great inventor would scarcely listen to the young man. Discouraged, Tesla sought George Westinghouse, the successful inventor/manufacturer of air-brakes for railroad trains in Pittsburgh. Recognizing Tesla's genius, Westinghouse bought the former's patents for one million dollars (at least twenty million 1990 dollars) and a royalty on each machine of one dollar for each kilowatt, a handsome payment. Tesla and Westinghouse, together and with others, developed the infrastructure for an AC power system just as Edison had previously done for DC power. The many advantages of Tesla's concept of 3-phase power, over a DC system, were soon recognized, and its use became universal. For detailed description of the 3-phase AC generator, 3-phase transformer, elements of a squirrel-cage 3-phase induction motor, and an AC synchronous motor, the reader is referred to books in electrical engineering listed in the Section of Additional Readings. These elements are the principal infrastructure of Tesla's 3-phase power system.

While at the time of the first electric car (1881) the investment in electric power was small, in America as in other industrial countries, the provisions for generation and distribution of 3-phase electric energy is today the single greatest capital investment in the country. And every transmission line seen today, anywhere in the world, may be considered a monument to Tesla's genius.

In 1881 at the Paris Exhibition, electrical engineers and scientists standardized on terminology to encourage easy and exact communication. The units agreed upon were: Ampere, Faraday, Gauss, Henry, Ørsted, Ohm, and Watt. These terms, taken from the names of early

---

[15] Nikola Tesla, *Experiments with Alternate Currents of High Potential and High Frequency*, with biographic data, New York: W. J. Johnson, 1892.

electrical experimenters, designated respectively: current, capacity, magnetic flux, magnetic inductance, magnetic intensity, resistance, and power, enabled most electrical phenomenon to be numerically described. As Lord Kelvin warned: Unless you can place numbers on a concept you really don't understand it.

Later, Professor S. P. Thomson in a lecture October 7, 1882 at the University of Bristol, spoke of a "friendly wire always ready to bring the power." He then speculated that "before the Electric Age is over our knives will be polished, our coffee roasted, our shoes shined, our vehicles driven, our potatoes pared, and our mincemeat chopped by the self-same agency that will bring light into our dwellings."[16]

Development of the Bicycle and Tricycle

The development of the electric car came sufficiently late in the 19th century as to benefit from the availability of rather well developed bicycles and tricycles. Of the two types of cycles, the two-wheeled version had the earlier origin. On a good road, compared with walking, a person uses only one-fifth the energy in traversing an equal distance, and at perhaps five times the speed.[17] A bicycle is capable of carrying ten times its own weight, a factor unique in any type of transportation even today.[18] Compared with preparing a horse for riding or drawing a buggy, the time required to place a bicycle or tricycle in operation was smartly reduced. Moreover, with the light weight of a bicycle they became relatively inexpensive.

The antecedent of the bicycle was called a *Draisienne* or *Hobby-Horse*. As shown in Fig. P.5, it consisted of two wheels interconnected by a crossbar on which was mounted a seat. The rider propelled both the vehicle and himself by foot-action. The bicycle was invented by Nicephore Niepce of Chalons, France in 1816.[19] Baron Saverbrun improved the machine in 1818. As the price was high, the vehicle could only be used by the wealthy, including the British Prince Regent. The first true bicycle was built in 1839 by Kirkpatrick MacMillan of Scotland, a blacksmith. He modified the *Hobby-Horse* by adding a crank, pedals, driving rods, a seat, and handlebars. Figure P.6 shows its method of operation. In 1846 Gavin Datzell improved upon MacMillan's machine. These two men were the pioneers of the bicycle.

Twenty years passed with little improvement until Pierre Lallement, an employee of M. Michaux of 29 Avenue Montaigne, Paris, brought forth a bicycle with a rotary crank. This vehicle could be commercially purchased at the above address for 200 francs ($50.00). Just before the Franco-Prussian War of 1871 an extraordinary craze developed for these velocipedes. As the Coventry Sewing Machine Company was making small numbers of the *Michaux* for the English market, their French agent placed an order for 500. To handle this surge of orders, the company was reconstituted as the Coventry Machinists Co., Ltd; later the Swift Cycle Co., Ltd. Before the Michaux bicycles could be shipped the War started, and the company, faced with this inventory, created a market in England. These bicycles bore two nearly equally sized wheels,

---

[16] University College of Bristol archives, 1882.

[17] C. F. Caunter, *The History of the Development of Cycles*, Part I, London: Her Majesty's Stationery Office, 1955.

[18] *Encyclopaedia Britannica*, Chicago: *Encyclopaedia Britannica*, v. 3, p. 544, 1959.

[19] *Oxford English Dictionary*, Oxford: The Clarendon Press, 1970, p. 855.

Figure P.5. A French Draisienne or Hobby-Horse: 1818. C. F. Caunter.

Figure P.6. MacMillan's modified Hobby-Horse. C. F. Caunter.

with the larger in front on which the driving cranks and pedals were placed. Bicycles of this style were heavy, possessed wooden wheels with iron tires, and had a massive iron backbone. For their riding ability they came to be known as *boneshakers*.

With demand for the machines rising, more makers offered improvements. The heavy wooden wheels gave way to lighter ones of metal, bearing wire spokes. With rubber becoming ever more common and cushioning desirable, solid rubber tires were glued onto the rims. To enhance stability of the two-wheeler, the tricycle was developed in 1850 as shown in Figs. P.7 and P.8. And it would be the three-wheeler which would be the basis for the first personal electric vehicle.

Figure P.7. Starley Royal Salvo tricycle: 1880. C. F. Caunter.

Fig. P.8. Butler Omnicycle Tricycle: 1879. Probable genesis of the first English electric vehicle. C. F. Caunter.

All bicycles and tricycles illustrations courtesy Her Majesty's Stationery Office, 1955.

In parallel with electrical and bicycle experiments cited above, the American, Charles Goodyear, was investigating the properties of the exudation of a tropical plant *Hevia brasiliensis*, given the name *rubber*, for it could be used to erase or rub-out a pencil mark on paper.[20] Goodyear learned in 1843, after many painstaking experiments, how to vulcanize rubber.[21] If rubber, he found, were combined with sulfur and with lead oxide in the presence of heat, it could be resilient, non-sticky, and be formed into lasting, useful articles of commerce such as a hose or tubing.

In 1845 Robert W. Thomson invented and tested the pneumatic tire, but because of inadequate marketing knowledge, manufacturing ceased. A Scotsman, James Boyd Dunlop, practicing veterinary medicine in Ireland, used inflated rubber-tubing on his son's tricycle, and thus reinvented the pneumatic tire in 1888 just in time for the explosive increase in bicycle use.[22]

---

[20] *Oxford English Dictionary*, Oxford: The Clarendon Press, 1970, p. 855.

[21] Bradford K. Pierce, *Trials of an Inventor: Life and Discoveries of Charles Goodyear*, New York: Phillip & Hunt, 1866.

[22] Arthur du Cos, *Wheels of Fortune*, London: Chapman Hall, 1938, p. 56.

Capitalizing on this craze, two brothers, André and Edouard Michelin in France, who had a firm manufacturing bicycle tires in Paris, learned the technique of bolting pneumatic tires onto the rim of a wheel of a vehicle.[23] Both Dunlop's first use of pneumatic tires and Michelin's fastening of tires on rims are shown in Chapter 27. The Paris-Bordeaux-Paris automobile race of 1895 described in Chapter 15, a watershed in the industrial world's perception of the motorcar, confirmed the advantages of the pneumatic tire.

With the above early history of electricity, bicycles/tricycles, and rubber tires the succeeding chapters describe the development of electric-powered vehicles domestically and internationally. In both America and Europe the initial electric cars would be based on the tricycle. The industrial world was waiting.

Notes

Listed below are additional readings of interest to the historical scholar. While the scientists listed are in chronological order, the numbering system is unrelated to the references in the Prologue.

1. von Guericke, Otto. *Experiments Nova Magdeburgica* (Jansson, Amsterdam, 1672), book 4, p. 147.
2. von Kleist, Hugo. Letter to Dr. Lieberkuhn, November 4, 1745; J. G. Kruger, *Geschichte de Erde* (Luderwaldischen, Halle, 1756).
3. Franklin, Benjamin, *Philos. Trans. R. Soc. London* 47, 565 (1751-1752).
4. Galvani, Luigi. *Bononiensi Scientiarum et Artium Instito Atque Academia Commentarii* 7, 363 (1791).
5. Volta, Alessandro. *Philos. Trans. R. Soc. London*, Part 2 90, 403 (1800).
6. Pixii, Hippolyte, *Ann. Chimig Phy.*, Vol. 50 (1832), p. 322; and Vol. 51 (1832), p. 76.
7. Faraday, Michael, *Experimental Researches in Electricity*, London: R. & J.E. Taylor, 1939–55.
8. Tesla, Nikola. *Lectures, Patents, Articles*, Nikola Tesla Museum, Beograd, 1956.
9. Ampère, André-Marie. *Essai sur la Philosophie, des Sciences*, Paris: Bechelier, 2 v., 1838-43.
10. Ohm, Georg Simon. *Das Grundgesetz des Electrischen Stomes, Akademische Verlags Gsellschaft*, mbh, 1938.
11. Pecqueur, Onesiphore. *Des Amélirations Materièlles dans leur Rapports avèc la Liberté*, 2nd. ed., Paris: Gosselin, 1843. (Discovery of the differential gearing for vehicles.)
12. Maxwell, James Clerk, *An Elementary Treatise of Electricity*, Ed. by William Garnett, Oxford: Clarendon Press, 1881.
13. Hertz, Heinrich Rudolph. *Electric Waves*, Tr. D.E. Jones, London: MacMillan, 1893.

---

[23] *Scientific American Supplement*, Vol. XL, No. 1023, Aug. 10, 1895, p. 16343.

CHAPTER 1

The First Two Electric Vehicles

France and England were the first nations to develop the electric vehicle. With the principle demonstrated, the entrepreneurs of neither nation pursued this revolutionary form of transportation with vigor. It was a curiosity of an electrical engineer in France in 1881, and it was a toy of two professors in England in 1882.

Until 1895 few Americans devoted attention to what would be known as the automobile. Those inventors who did had products which were crude and impractical. There was little public interest to replace the horse as a means for personal transportation in local travel. Those few pioneers who offered practical means for mechanical locomotion were forced to curb their impatience, and await the public's show of livelier interest. Fortunately that time would quickly arrive. In an incredibly short period public sentiment for the automobile changed from indifference to enthusiasm. What ignited the fuse was the second automobile race. The first, Paris to Rouen, an event of June 1894, placed more inventive minds at work, but the public was passive.[1] The race from Paris to Bordeaux and return, however (a distance of 705 miles completed in 48 hours and 53 minutes, for an average speed of 14.4 mph, including fueling stops, repairs, and all), caused the informed citizens of all industrialized nations to clearly recognize the time for the self-propelled personal vehicle had, indeed, come. All levels of the public discussed this feat. The newspapers everywhere carried the news. From city to hamlet to country, the race results sped.

As E.P. Ingersoll, editor of *The Horseless Age,* editorialized, "Where before there was one inventor evolving a self-propelled vehicle, there were now more than a score." The *Chicago Times-Herald* offer of prizes for a motorcar race between Chicago and Evanston and return on November 28, 1895 further impelled this program.[2] Here was an opportunity for scores of inventors to finish their vehicles and to participate in the first motorcar race staged in America. With such widespread impetus probably no mechanical device was developed as quickly as was the motorcar. *The Horseless Age* stated that between July 1 and November 1, 1895 "no less than 300 different types of motor vehicles" were under construction.[3] From all this applied ingenuity a better means of personal transportation would emerge. The clatter of hoofs on city streets

---

[1] *The Horseless Age*, Vol. 1., No. 1, Nov. 1895, pp. 1-2.
  Also, *Electrical Engineer*, Vol. XIX, No. 350, Jan. 16, 1895, p. 55
[2] *The Horseless Age*, Vol. 1, No. 12, October 1896, p. 53.
[3] *Ibid.*, Vol. 1, No. 1, November 1895, p. 8.

would cease; the horse as man's drudge would rest; the streets, freed from droppings, would be cleaner; the flies and other insects, with breeding areas absent, would be less prevalent. A new era of transportation, based on mechanical power, would emerge, and the electric car would be a part of this colorful pageant.

In England Sir David Salomons, motor enthusiast and Mayor of the city of Tunbridge Wells, himself an equestrian, spoke of "the bloodless revolution" in the forthcoming displacement of horses.[4] While from Paris, it was reported that "over 20,000 names are already counted in (the) membership rolls of the Touring Club of France."[5] But let us start at the beginning. What were the first electric vehicles like? Who were the individuals to initiate them?

With Faraday's experimental work of 1825-1831 laying the foundation for the development of both the a.c. and d.c. electric motors and generators, the next five decades were spent by a host of experimenters perfecting these two classes of machines. A Belgian, Zenobe Theophile Gramme, in 1873 finally achieved a design of motors and generators which approached today's performance.[6] At this time the thinking among the growing body of electrical experimenters was almost wholly devoted to the problems associated with illumination, generation, and distribution of power for the new wonder of electric lighting. The source of light might be the arc lamps of Brush, of Jablochkoff, or of the filament lamps of Edison, Swan, or Maxim.[7] In his experimental work Gramme observed that an assembly of copper, iron, and insulation, if mechanical power were applied, was itself a generator of electricity which could charge a battery. Conversely, if mechanical power were no longer furnished, the assemblage would receive electricity from the recently charged battery, and convert the electricity into mechanical power. Thus a motor and generator were one and the same piece of equipment depending on type of power applied, a phenomenon Pacinotti earlier observed.[8]

Trouvé's Electric Tricycle

While Davenport in America first used an imperfect electric motor for operating a lathe in 1835,[9] and Moritz Jacobi, a visiting German in Russia,[10] used a primitive electric motor to power a boat in 1838, in each case a primary battery was the source of power. The battery would consume its active elements. It was M. Gustave Trouvé of France who first applied the rechargeable lead-acid secondary battery, invented by Gaston Planté in 1859, and the improved d.c. electric motor to personal land transportation. At the anticipated International Exhibition of Electricity held in Paris, August to November 1881, Trouvé displayed an operating boat, a working electric tricycle, and his motor-powered model dirigible. Trouvé, therefore, was the

---

[4] *Ibid.*, Vol. 1, No. 2, December 1895, p. 6.

[5] *Ibid.*, p. 9.

[6] Elihu Thompson, *Electricity During the Nineteenth Century, Smithsonian Institute Annual Report*, 1, 1900, p. 333.

[7] David Porter Heaps, *Report on the International Exhibition of Electricity Held in Paris, 1881*, Government Printing Office, Washington, 1884, p. 287.

[8] Aug Gueront, *The History of Magneto & dynamo Electric Machines, Scientific American Supplement*, Vol. XIV, No. 357, November 4, 1882, p. 5697.

[9] *Scientific American Supplement*, Vol. XIV, NO. 359, November 18, 1882, p. 5728.

[10] Ernest H. Huntress, *Moritz Hermann von Jacobi, (1801-1874)* AAAS Proc. (79) Jan. 1951, pp. 22-23.

first to provide an outboard motorboat, the first to operate an electric vehicle, and his motor was the first to propel a model dirigible, all electrically powered.

Of this epochal event, the operation of the first electrically powered vehicle, it was indeed fortunate to be recorded by a literate eyewitness, Abbe Moigne, who wrote:[11]

"I had just crossed the Palais Royal and arrived on the Rue de Valois, when my attention was drawn by a man who was on a tricycle and arrived at full speed. I would have left immediately if, upon the approach of the tricycle, I had not heard a few exclamations uttered by passers-by who said: 'Of course it is steam or electricity which propels it.' Upon hearing the word 'electricity,' I paid closer attention to the vehicle which was going by me at that precise moment and it was easy for me to notice that, in fact, the 'soul' of the movement was indeed electricity, because I immediately recognized the small motor which had been presented and demonstrated by its inventor during a social gathering given by Vice Admiral Mouchez in the Paris Observatory. However, I did not recognize M. Gustave Trouvé, the famous electrical engineer, as being the person who was on the tricycle, but I soon heard he was standing apart and that from a window in the Hotel de Holland, he had followed all phases of the experiment. Let me tell you a few words about it.

"The tricycle had two steering wheels and a simple, large propelling wheel, the latter being, I believe of English manufacture, and appearing quite heavy. Placed beneath the axle joining the two small wheels were two small, Trouvé motors, the size of a fist. These motors were communicating movement by means of two link chains each of which engaged its respective sprocket gear on either side of the big propelling wheel.

"Behind the seat and sitting on the axle, a rough, newly fashioned wooden box contained six secondary batteries. These accumulators were quite similar to those of M. Gaston Planté and actuated the motors. To the left of the seat was a brake lever easily reached by the conductor. On the lever was an electrical switch by which the driver could easily stop or start immediately.

"Here is, as succinctly as possible, the portrait of the electrical tricycle on 8 April 1881, which, seen from the back, vaguely resembled the cart of the ancient salesmen. Let me add that this tricycle, of English engineering, in fact, was very heavy, about 55 kgs. The total weight of the vehicle, with batteries and driver, could reach 160 kgs and the effective power produced by both motors corresponded to 7 kilogrammeters per second (1/10 hp)."[12]

As the author has not found a drawing of Trouvé's electric tricycle, and the most lucid description of the event appears above, there is good reason to believe that Trouvé mounted two electric motors on the axle between the two trailing steering wheels of a Dublin tricycle, illustrated in Fig. 1.1. As is seen below, the pinions of these two motors were linked by chain to sprocket gears on either side of the large wheel. Whereas in the Dublin, the two steerable wheels were in front, it appears from Moigne's description that Trouvé employed the two

---

[11] Georges Barral, *Histoire d'un Inventeur, Gustave Trouvé*, Georges Carre, Editeur, Paris, 1891, pp. 610.

[12] Translation, courtesy of Molly Mitchell, University of Illinois, Urbana, Illinois.

Figure 1.1. A Dublin Tricycle: 1876. Her Majesty's Stationery Office. C. F. Caunter.

steerable wheels in sequential fashion, for Moigne says: "Behind the seat and sitting on the axle, a rough newly fashioned wooden-box contained six secondary batteries." These words place the large driving wheel in front.

Of the Dublin tricycle Caunter writes:[13] "The Dublin tricycle had a large rear driving wheel, and two small steering wheels placed in front and mounted in separate forks. The rear wheel was driven by wooden treadles, by means of which, cranks, attached to the wheel spindles, were rotated through a system of connecting rods and pivoted levers." Reinforcing the claim for the Dublin tricycle is Moigne's reference "this tricycle, of English engineering...." Of all the tricycles, and there were few, the Dublin appears the best candidate. We may assume, therefore, the illustration shown is the type vehicle Trouvé modified to be the first electric vehicle ever assembled.

As interesting as the first electric vehicle would be at the International Exhibition of Electricity, dominated as it was by equipment associated with lighting, the electric tricycle was scarcely recorded. The official U. S. Army observer, David Porter Heaps, Major, Corps of Engineers, U.S.A., wrote of the application of motors:

"M. Trouvé has obtained remarkable results compared with the weight of the apparatus. A tricycle weighing 120 pounds was driven by means of a motor and six

---

[13] C. F. Caunter, *The History of the Development of Cycles*, Part I, Her Majesty's Stationery Office, London, 1955, Plate IVm, p. 11.

Planté secondary batteries. The total weight of the vehicle, rider, batteries, and motor was 350 pounds. The motor, weighing 11 pounds, propelled the vehicle at the rate of 7 1/2 miles an hour.

"M. Trouvé has also applied the motor to a small boat...the batteries...are placed amidships and the motor is mounted on the rudder....In large boats the motor would be placed direct on the screw shaft. On the lake in the Bois Boulogne the speed attained was 10 feet per second (six mph) with a four-blade screw. The boat was 18 feet long and 4 feet wide. The weights were as follows:

Weight of boat	176.0 pounds
Weight of batteries	52.8
Weight of motor	11.0
Weight of three passengers	528.0
Total	767.8

"The motor has also been applied to the propulsion of toy boats and to a model balloon devised by M. Tissandier.[14] These applications to both boat and balloon, though of not much practical value, are of interest as illustrations of electricity as a prime mover. The motor may and probably will find many applications where very small powers are required."

While the Tissandier brothers would construct and together fly in their balloon powered by batteries and an electric motor in 1883, the application of electricity to lighter-than-air craft was short lived. Not so the use of electric power drives in boats, for it was the combination of batteries and the electric motor which led to the great success of the submarine. Figure 1.2 shows M.Trouvé in his boat,[15] while Figs. 1.3 and 1.4 illustrate his motor and its method of mounting.[16] Surely Trouvé qualifies as the inventor of the outboard motor, and the first outboard motor was electric. It appears that Trouvé provided motors for both the boat and the tricycle. So to Trouvé of France belongs the honor for having first combined the rechargeable secondary battery and the electric motor for personal land transportation. While Trouvé is not referenced in Asimov's *Encyclopedia*,[17] nor in Dunsheath's *History*,[18] he is nevertheless, the Edison of France. Not only did he design and build the motor shown above, but in addition he devised the Trouvé Bichromate Sealed Battery and the Trouvé Dry Battery. This era was a time when nearly all parts of an apparatus had to be hewn from raw products, and Trouvé had the means and the ability to bring forth these two types of personal transportation. His training was directed such "that his fingers, to use Dumas's apt words, should possess at once the strength of the Titans, and the delicacy of those of fairies."[19]

---

[14] See Chapter 12.

[15] *Scientific American Supplement*, Vol. XIV, No. 362, December 9, 1882, p. 5767.

[16] David Porter Heaps, *Report on the International Exhibition of Electricity Held in Paris, 1881*, Government Printing Office, Washington, 1884, p. 287.

[17] Isaac Asimov, *Asimov's Biographical Encyclopedia of Science and Technology*, Doubleday & Company, Garden City, N.Y. 1964, pp. 662.

[18] Percy Dunsheath, *A History of Electrical Engineering*, Faber & Faber, London, 1962.

[19] *Scientific American Supplement*, Vol. XIV, No. 362, Dec. 9, 1882, p. 5767.

Figure 1.2. Trouvé's electric boat competing in the regatta at Troyes, August 6, 1882. Scientific American.

Of this extensive work in personal transportation Trouvé himself modestly wrote:[20]

"I had the honor of submitting to the Academy, in its session of July 7th, 1880, a new electric motor, founded on the excentricity of the play of a Siemens' coil. By successive studies, which have permitted me to reduce the weight of all the parts of the motor, I have succeeded in obtaining the following results, which appear to me worth of notice:

"A motor, weighing 5 kilos., impelled by 5 Planté secondary elements, procuring an effective work of 7 kilogrammetres per second (1/10 horsepower), was placed on the 8th of April on a tricycle, the weight of which, including the rider and the batteries, reached 160 kilos., and impelled it at a rate of 12 kilometres per hour (7 mph).

"The same motor placed on May 26th upon a boat 5 1/2 metres in length by 1.2 metre in width, and containing three persons, gave it a speed of 2 1/2 metres per second (5.7 mph) whilst descending the Seine to Pont Royal, and 1 1/2 metres on returning. The motor was worked by two batteries, each of six bichromate elements and the propeller was a screw with three blades.

---

[20] Gustave Trouvé, *The Telegraphic Review & Electrical Review*, Vol. IX, No. 206, September 1, 1881.

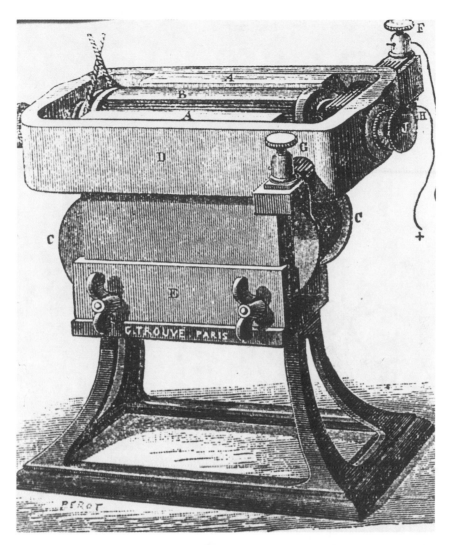

Figure 1.3. A period electric motor by Gustave Trouvé. The diagram indicates it is a separately excited d.c. motor. The two poles are illustrated by A, the armature by B, the field windings by C. U.S. Government Printing Office.

"On June 26th I repeated the experiments on the calm water of the upper lake in the Bois de Boulonge, with a screw of four blades of 0.28 meter in diameter, and twelve flat Bunsen elements, of Rhumkorff's modification, charged with 1 part hydrochloric acid, 1 part nitric acid, and 2 parts water, in order to reduce the escape of hypo-nitric vapours.

"The speed at the outset, as measured by an ordinary log, was exactly 150 metres in 48 seconds, or rather more than 3 metres per second; but after working for three

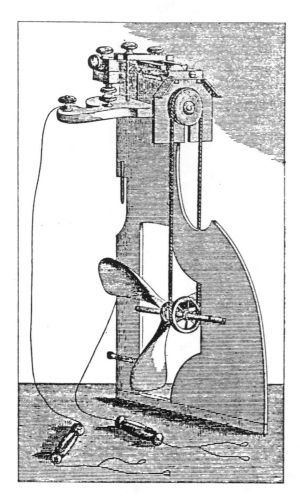

Figure 1.4. Trouvé's electric motor and outboard propulsion for small craft. U.S. Government Printing Office.

hours it fell to 150 metres in 55 seconds. After five hours' action the speed was still 2.3 metres per second, as the 150 metres were traversed in 65 seconds."

What were the origins of this modest and most remarkable inventor?[21] M. Trouvé was born in 1839 of distinguished parents in the village of La Haye-Descarte, in the valley of the Vienne River, some 40 miles due south of Tours. For schooling his rather affluent parents dispatched him 30 miles to the town of Chinon, to the northwest. There he entered the Écoles des Arts et Métiers, and afterwards proceeded to Paris to labor in the shop of a clockmaker. Shortly, Trouvé established his own facility. His enterprise almost immediately asserted itself for he soon fabricated a small lamp assembly to illuminate cavities within the human body. This new mode of illumination was ably adopted for hazardous areas within mines and powder mills. During the Franco-Prussian War he developed a portable telegraph of which his hermetically sealed battery, mentioned above, was an integral part. Devoting considerable time to perfecting the electric motor, he had the distinction of excelling in applying electric propulsion both on land

---

[21] Georges Barral. *Histoire d'un Inventeur, Gustave Trouvé.* Georges Carré, Editeur, Paris, 1891, p. 610.

PROFESSOR W. E AYRTON, F.R.S.   PROFESSOR JOHN PERRY, M.E.

Figure 1.5. Professors W. E. Ayrton and John Perry in England assembled the second electrical-powered personal vehicle, a tricycle, in 1882. Scientific American.

and on water. In addition, M. Trouvé developed a pendulum escapement, an electric gyroscope at the request of M. Louis Foucault, of pendulum fame, the electro-medical pocket case, an electric bit to curb unruly horses, the universal caustic holder, and contributed many important improvements to magnets. For our purpose Trouvé is the father of electric vehicles. With France in the vanguard could England, but a Channel away, be far behind?

Ayrton and Perry's Electric Tricycle

Professors William Edward Ayrton and John Perry, long time associates, both of whom are shown in Fig. 1.5, almost surely attended in 1881 the International Exhibition of Electricity in Paris from nearby London. In 1882 these collaborators demonstrated a tricycle shown in Fig. 1.6.[22] The vehicle was both electrically propelled and electrically lighted by means of lead-acid batteries. The latter are seen on the lower platform. With the ten cells illustrated the system would have a nominal 20 volts. Power flowed from the Faure-type batteries to the 1/2 horsepower direct-current motor shown mounted beneath the driver's seat. This motor had an efficiency from 30-40 percent depending on load and speed.[23] The shaft of the motor terminated

---

[22] *Scientific American*, Vol. XLVII, No. 22, Nov. 25, 1882, p. 343.
[23] *The Telegraphic Journal & Electrical Review*, Vol. XII, No. 304, Sept. 22, 1883, p. 217.

Figure 1.6. Ayrton and Perry's electric tricycle of 1882. Scientific American.

in a pinion gear with 12 teeth which engaged the larger geared wheel with 240 teeth. The motor turned, therefore, 20 times faster than the large 44-inch wheel. Speed of the vehicle was controlled by the number of cells in series, varied at will by the operator through the technique of voltage switching.[24]   An Ayrton and Perry motor of this era is shown in Fig. 1.7.[25]

Vehicle braking is by a friction block applied to the rim of the left wheel. Steering of the tricycle is achieved by moving the lever on the right forward or backward. By a rigid rod the action can deflect the rear wheel as understood in the illustration. Lamp L-L of four candlepower, each yielding 50 lumens, lighted the ammeter on the right which read current to the motor, and the voltmeter on the left which gave voltage at the terminals of the motor. The product of these two readings, amperes and volts, yields, of course, power flow to the motor. Power for lighting arose from two of the motive power cells. The weight of the motor was given

[24] Ernest H. Wakefield, *The Consumer's Electric Car*, Ann Arbor Science Publishers, Inc., Ann Arbor, Michigan, 1977.

[25] *Scientific American Supplement*, Vol. XIII, No. 335, June 3, 1882, p. 5340.

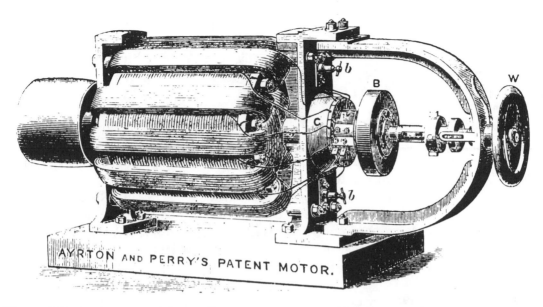

Figure 1.7. An Ayrton and Perry direct-current motor of 1883. Scientific American.

as 45 pounds, while a battery weight of 150 pounds was said to yield an energy storage of 1 1/2 kilowatt-hours. Speed of the vehicle was given as nine miles per hour.

With a rider, and the vehicle advancing slowly, the electric tricycle exerted a force of 33 pounds as measured by a spring balance held by a person attempting to retard the motion. Assuming the tricycle to have had a total weight of 370 pounds, estimated by detailing each part, then the ratio of battery weight to curb weight of the vehicle was about 40 percent. Assuming that batteries from this era had a specific energy ratio of 50 percent of present batteries, this first vehicle would have had a range at a constant speed of nine miles per hour of 10-25 miles on hard roads, assuming 70-100 watt-hours per mile. These numbers also include the rather less efficient motors of this time.

Almost as soon as driven, Ayrton and Perry's electric tricycle was shown to be in violation of the so-called "Red Flag" laws of the Island Kingdom, for in a letter by "Chancery Lane."[26]

"Sir: What is the use of an electric tricycle? The Locomotive (Roads) Act, Sec. 3, enacts that 'every locomotive propelled by steam, *or any other than animal power*, on any turnpike, road or public highway, shall be worked according to the following rules and regulations amongst other, namely: Firstly, at least three persons shall be employed to drive or conduct such locomotive; secondly, of such persons while any locomotive is in motion one shall proceed such locomotive in motion on foot by not less than 60 yards, and shall carry a red flag constantly displayed, and shall warn the riders and drivers of horses of the approach of such locomotives and shall signal the driver there of when it should be necessary to stop, and shall assist horses, and carriages drawn by horses, passing same.

---

[26] *The Telegraphic Journal & Electrical Review*, Vol. XI, No. 258, Nov. 4, 1882, p. 353.

"And by Section 4, the speed at which such locomotive shall be driven along a highway is limited to four miles per hour, and through a city, town, or village to two miles per hour. Is this how electric tricycles are proposed to be driven? That a tricycle is a locomotive within the meaning of the act of Parliament if driven by other than animal power has been recently decided by the Queen's Bench in the case of Parkyns v Preist, 7 Q B D , 313.

Yours, etc.

October 31, 1882.   Chancery Lane."

What Professors Ayrton and Perry thought of the letter, or the Act of Parliament which evoked it, is unknown, but another five years would pass before a second electric vehicle would appear on English roads, an account of which is recorded in Chapter 6. This "Red Flag" Act was revoked only in 1896,[27] and throughout that relatively late period the King's highways were largely limited to horses and horse drawn liveries and conveyances. This Act is one of the best documented examples of government regulation limiting progress, for by 1896 France was alight with the personal automobile. England had shown less progress, particularly in gasoline-powered cars.

At the time these two engineers gave the world the second electric vehicle Ayrton had already achieved recognition. He was a Fellow of the Royal Society, author of two books, *Practical Electricity: A Laboratory Lecture Course*, and *Manuals of Technology*,[28] recognized for his advancement of the science of electromagnets. Perry, on the other hand, was Professor of Electrical Engineering at Finsbury Technical College, and during his lifetime would produce seven books: *England's Neglect of Science, Applied Mathematics, Calculus for Engineers, Discussions on Teaching Mathematics, Spinning Tops, Spinning Tops and Gyroscopic Action*, and *The Steam Engine and Gas and Oil Engines*. Both men were consultants to the Faure Electric Accumulator Company, a corporation inaugurated on July 10, 1883 with a nominal capital of one million British Pounds ($5,000,000) to exploit the Faure lead-acid battery.[29] Together Ayrton and Perry had in 1879 produced the first portable ammeter, in 1881 invented the direct reading ohmmeter, and in 1883 brought forth the first solenoid type ammeter.[30]

While Ayrton was senior and the better known, he and Perry were primarily pragmatic engineers when electrical phenomena in England were dominated by scientists such as Lord Kelvin and James Clerk Maxwell, the former an experimental physicist, the latter a mathematician. As the paths of the electrical engineers departed from the physicist these two long-term partners were among the first to forge the profession of electrical engineering together with Swan and Crompton in England, Seimens in Germany and in England, Gramme in Belgium, Pacinotti in Italy, Edison, Tesla, and Westinghouse in America, and Trouvé, Deprez, Planier, and De Marittens in France. That engineering could be a remunerative profession is attested. On the death of Professor Ayrton in November 1908, after living 61 years, he left a gross estate to his wife and two daughters of £43,590, a sum of $215,000 at the then rate of exchange.[31]

---

[27] *The Horseless Age*, Vol. 1, No. 6, April 1896, p. 9

[28] Card File, Northwestern University Library, Evanston, Illinois, USA

[29] *The Telegraphic Journal & Electrical Review*, Vol. XIII, No. 312, Nov. 17, 1883, p. 389.

[30] Percy Dunsheath, *A History of Electrical Engineering*, Faber & Faber, London, 1962.

[31] *The Electrical Review*, Vol. 64, No. 1625, Jan. 15, 1909, p. 103.

Trouvé in France, Ayrton and Perry in England. These three pioneers in Europe guided electric propulsion of the personal vehicle, when the horse, the mule, the donkey, and the oxen were almost the only alternate sources of power. The remarkable gasoline-fueled, internal combustion automobile was still in the future. As original as were these three innovators, without those experimenters, theoreticians, and mathematicians who earlier laid the foundation in electricity and magnetism, they could not have succeeded. With such activities on the roads of France and England, what happenings were afoot in America?

CHAPTER 2

The Horseless Carriage in America, 1890-1898, Part 1

An electric powered tricycle had been assembled in France in 1881, and a somewhat larger vehicle of the same type had been fabricated in England in 1882. While thought could cross the Atlantic Ocean in a few seconds in the Eighties, for the submarine cable had been laid electrically connecting the two continents,[1] three official observers from America had attended the International Exhibition of Electricity in Paris in 1881.[2] Edison's display of lighting equipment had been the largest at the Conference,[3] still, nine years would elapse before a precursor of the electric car would be operating in America.

Other than the first few electric vehicles assembled, the first ever, the dominant characteristic of this era's early conveyances were indeed horseless carriages. Their style was directly identifiable with a farm wagon, a delivery wagon, a surrey, a phaeton, a victoria, or a stanhope. Onto these vehicles the early electric car builders placed batteries, an electric motor, a means of controlling the current to this motor,[4] and mechanically connecting it to the drive wheels of the vehicle. The pinion gear on the motor shaft might either directly engage a larger sprocket rigidly fastened to the drive wheel, or would be connected by an endless linking chain. As the presently known differential was not employed, there would be either dual-drive motors, or a single motor engaging a "balance gear," a primitive type differential.[5]

Another characteristic of the dominant design through the year 1895 was the presence of wooden-spoked wheels. While the earliest vehicles were equipped with iron-tired wheels, hard rubber was soon introduced not only to increase the quality of the ride, but also to cushion

---

[1] A submarine cable had been laid connecting England and America on August 5, 1858, largely through the efforts of Cyrus Fields. "Dramatically splicing the cable in mid-ocean, four ships from England and America unrolled the cable as they steamed for home, the *Niagara* and the *Gordon* for Trinity Bay in Newfoundland, the *Agamemnon* and *Valorous* sailing for Valentia, Ireland, which were the two terminals. The cable had a length of 1950 miles, and over two-thirds was laid in water over two miles deep." President James Buchanan exchanged greetings with Queen Victoria on August 16, 1858. Isabella Field Judson, *Cyrus W. Field, His Life & Work*, Harper & Bros, NYC 1896, p. 332.

[2] David Porter Heaps, Major, Corps of Engineers, U.S.Army; Hon George Walker, Commissioner-General; Prof. George F. Barker, Commissioner-Expert. *Annual Report, Smithsonian Institution*, Government Printing Office, Washington, 1882, p. 44.

[3] *Scientific American Supplement*, Vol XII, No. 309, Dec. 3, 1881, p. 4919.

[4] To limit current to the motor on start-up, and thus to allow a more uniform increase in speed, the batteries were successively connected to yield 12, 24, 36, and 72 volts, for example.

[5] *The Horseless Age*, Vol. 2, No. 5, March 1897, p. 7-8.

vibration which could cause the friable lead-oxide on the battery plates to disengage and to fall to the bottom of the cells. Of this period, also, the front and rear wheels might be of different diameters. As the vehicles became heavier and their speeds greater, the lateral forces on the wheels, particularly on cornering, became excessive and would induce wooden-spoked wheels to collapse. To provide greater wheel strength the spokes of wood were replaced with spokes of wire. The geometry of the latter delivered stresses more uniformly over the circumference of the wheel. The wire-spoked wheel, while observed on some of the more advanced designs in this section, is an important characteristic of the vehicles in Chapter 8. Presently used in bicycles, this invention by C. S. Mott in November 1896 was most important, for it permitted automobiles to travel safely at high speeds.[6] The importance of this invention is underestimated.

The characteristics of electric vehicles, as represented above, the names of the inventors and of the promoters, the vendors, the trends of the industry, in short, all causing the electric carriages to be ushered in, were described in the journals of the day. Prominent among the media would be the venerable *Scientific American*, and its companion, the *Scientific American Supplement*. While the above were established journals, *The Horseless Age* would address specifically this new industry. Edited and owned by E. P. Ingersoll, the journal, initiated in November 1895, would faithfully register the incisiveness of the publisher, providing a leavening effect. A reproduction of the now rare title page of Vol. 1 No. 1 of the journal is Fig. 2.1.

Other journals of the day recording newsworthy events of electric cars would be *The Electric Engineer, The Telegraphic Journal & Electrical Review, L'Electricité, Les Mondes, La Nature, La Petite Republique Française,* the *McClure Magazine*, and others. While the last decade of the century would be known in song as the 'gay nineties,' and the era in both America and Europe when the bicycle was supreme, personal transportation, too, was being born, and prominent in early American electric personal vehicles would be Andrew L. Riker.

Riker's Electric Tricycle

The first American to construct an electric vehicle would be Andrew L. Riker of Brooklyn, New York, in 1890. His electric tricycle is illustrated in Fig. 2.2.[7] It would be the beginning of a series of distinguished electric vehicles by this innovator. Riker, it appears, was captivated early in life by the thought of applying electric power to personal transportation. His first vehicle was a tricycle of 1890 imported from England, seen in Fig. 2.3. In his first vehicle Riker fabricated his own 1/6-hp motor, about equal in power to the one on Trouvé's tricycle. A motor at this time was not an article of commerce. The speed of Riker's vehicle on good roads was given as 8 mph with a rate of battery drain equal to four hours of operation. His tricycle would have had a range of about 30 miles, as the weight of his vehicle was given as 150 pounds.

The batteries, four cells yielding a nominal eight volts, were located in the box behind the driver. Such a small motor and low voltage source would require no controller for current limit. Moreover, he might kick-start his tricycle. While not clear from the photograph, he may have

---

[6] George S. May in his *A Most Unique Machine* (William B. Eerdman's Publishing Co., 1975) relates the importance of C. S. Mott both to the automobile industry and to its integration in the Detroit area.

[7] *The Horseless Age*, Vol. 2, No. 1, November 1896, p. 9.

THE HORSELESS AGE.

A MONTHLY JOURNAL

DEVOTED TO THE INTERESTS OF THE MOTOR VEHICLE INDUSTRY.

VOL. I. NEW YORK, NOVEMBER, 1895. No. 1.

THE HORSELESS AGE.

E. P. INGERSOLL, Editor and Proprietor.

PUBLICATION OFFICE:

157-159 WILLIAM STREET, NEW YORK.

SUBSCRIPTION, FOR THE UNITED STATES AND CANADA, $2.00 a year, payable in advance. For all foreign countries included in the Postal Union, $2.50.

ADVERTISEMENTS.—Rates will be made known on application. When change of copy is desired it should be sent in not later than the fifteenth of the month.

COMMUNICATIONS.—The Editor will be pleased to receive communications on trade topics from any authentic source. The correspondent's name should in all cases be given as an evidence of good faith, but will not be published if specially requested.

Address all correspondence, and make all checks, drafts, and money orders payable to
THE HORSELESS AGE, 157-159 William Street, New York.

Salutatory.

—o—

WE PRESENT to the trade and the public the first number of the HORSELESS AGE, a journal which will be published monthly hereafter in the interest of the motor vehicle. The appearance of a journal devoted to a branch of industry yet in an embryonic state, may strike some as premature, and the somewhat desultory character of this number may provoke criticism in some quarters. But those who have taken the pains to search below the surface for the great tendencies of the age, know what a giant industry is struggling into being there. All signs point to the motor vehicle as the necessary sequence of methods of locomotion already established and approved. The growing needs of our civilization demand it; the public believe in it, and await with lively interest its practical application to the daily business of the world.

In such a condition of expectancy the chief want is news. Not only those directly concerned in the perfection of the new vehicle, but the reading public as well, wish to be informed of the progress of this great mechanical movement; to know the forms or styles in which the new vehicle is to appear, and to examine the claims that are offered, no less than the facts that are accomplished. To satisfy this demand is the work to which the journalist should bend his energies. Criticism, at such a time, may properly be left to the mechanical expert or the intending purchaser. His chosen task is to collect the materials upon which an intelligent judgment may be based.

At this formative period of the motor vehicle industry, exact data are difficult to obtain. All over the country mechanics and inventors are wrestling with the problems of trackless traction. Much of their work is in an unfinished state; many of their theories lack demonstration; but enough has already been achieved to prove absolutely the practicability of the motor vehicle. What is here presented, however, is merely an earnest of what is to come.

The second number of the HORSELESS AGE will contain a detailed account of the *Times-Herald* contest, which is to be held at Chicago on November 2nd, and many new illustrations. In succeeding numbers, topics of importance to the trade will be taken up for discussion. Several projects bearing broadly on the future development of the industry are now under editorial consideration, and will be announced in due time.

The Horseless Age.

—o—

It has a fascinating sound, and ere the close of 1895, the idea will have been proved as practical as the sound is fascinating.

It is often said that a civilization may be measured by its facilities of locomotion. If this is true, as seems abundantly proved by present facts and the testimony of history, the new civilization that is rolling in with the horseless carriage will be a higher civilization than the one we now enjoy.

Figure 2.1. The First Issue of the First Journal Chronicling The Horseless Age.

Figure 2.2. The first electric vehicle in America was assembled by Andrew L. Riker in 1890. Courtesy: The Horseless Age.

Figure 2.3. The Rudge Rotary tricycle of 1880 was one of the most successful of the single-driving tricycles. Riker is seen to have borrowed this principle for his first electric vehicle. Courtesy: Her Majesty's Stationery Office, London. C. F. Caunter.

had two speeds forward. From the reproduction, the two-pole motor, seen against the large wheel, drove by friction contact against the hard rubber tire. From the calculations below it appears that the batteries contributed slightly more than one-half the vehicle weight.[8] Whether knowingly or not, Riker's first vehicle had a ratio of battery weight to curb weight of the vehicle similar to electric automobiles designed by computers nearly a century later. Riker, as will be developed, became one of the best electric car designers of the early period. While Riker was the first, others would follow.

---

[8] Energy = power × time = $\dfrac{1/6 \text{ hp}}{\text{motor efficiency}} \times 4 \text{ hr} = \dfrac{1/6\ 746}{0.5} \times 4 = 992$ watt-hours ≈ one kwh.
A battery containing one kwh of energy in 1890 weighed about 100 pounds.

Morrison's Electric Surrey and Derivatives

An idea whose time has come can have multiple births in several regions. The earliest electric vehicle constructed in Midwestern America, 1891, was by William Morrison, illustrated in Fig. 2.4.[9] This vehicle was subsequently purchased by J. B. McDonald, President of the American Battery Company of Chicago in 1892. The carriage was built for the Chicago Columbian Exhibition scheduled to open in 1892, but was delayed until 1893. Morrison's was the first electric vehicle seen on the streets of Chicago.[10]

Morrison's vehicle had been assembled in Des Moines, Iowa. Power was furnished by 24 storage batteries placed beneath the seats to yield 112 amperes at 48 volts. Each cell weighed 32 pounds, giving a total battery weight of some 770 pounds. Charging time was given as ten hours. Receiving this flow of power was a 4-hp motor with a Siemen's armature, a type, as was quoted, "which facilitated easy replacement when burned out."[11] This motor was geared to the rear axle as indicated. Forward steering was provided by a gear coupling to the pivoted forward axle, while the speed of the vehicle was controlled by voltage switching of the battery cells. Morrison claimed 13 hours of continuous running time, a seemingly high figure,[12] and a top speed of 14 mph. For the Exhibition the carriage would be shown by Harold Sturges and John A. Qualey.

As will be cited below, Sturges, who was in 1896 the president of the Sturges Electric Motocycle Company, could foresee that Morrison's wagon had a future.[13] Sturges, having demonstrated Morrison's electric wagon at the Fair, had a second electric vehicle built by the Sturges Electric Motocycle Company of Chicago. This electric surrey is shown in Fig. 2.5.[14]

Sturges' surrey originally bore three seats, but the third was removed to provide more battery space. Likewise modified were the wheels. The iron rims were removed and solid rubber tires substituted to mitigate the mechanical shock to the friable battery plates. The

---

[9] *Scientific American*, Vol. LXVI, No. 2, Jan. 9, 1892, p. 18.

[10] *The Horseless Age*, Vol. 1, No. 1, November 1895, p. 24.

[11] The 'burned-out armature' indicated that the need for current limitation on start-up was not fully understood. The article later states 'no rheostat is used.' That is the specific reason he 'burned out' his armature. *Author.*

[12] Either a printing error, or an exaggeration.

[13] William Morrison is authoritatively quoted as being the first American builder of an electric carriage. Andrew L. Riker is cited in *The Horseless Age* as having said he had an electric tricycle in 1890, which would be one year earlier than Morrison's claim. This author is willing to give the honor to Riker for the following reasons: 1) on the eastern seaboard he was exposed to European developments, while Morrison was in Des Moines; 2) the Riker electric tricycle is a reasonable derivative of the French and English electric tricycles of 1881-82; 3) Riker was a careful and competent engineer who became the best early builder of electric vehicles. In addition, his company offered electric generators for lighting installations. Hence his 1890 claim carries credence; 4) in the quotation we are given from Morrison, that his vehicle "has run continuously 13 hours," appears hyperbolic; and 5) to an electrical engineer Morrison's phrase, earlier cited, "which facilitated easy replacement when burned out," indicates he really didn't understand the theory of electric motors. This author is satisfied that Riker and not Morrison probably built the first electric vehicle in America.

[13a] In the new *Encyclopaedia Britannica*, Vol. 2, p. 518, Ken W. Purdy writes, "Invention of the storage battery, by Gaston Planté of France in 1859-60, and its improvement by Camille Faure in 1881, made the electric vehicle possible, and what was probably the first, a tricycle, ran in Paris in 1881. It was followed by other three-wheelers in London, 1882, and Boston, 1888. The first American battery-powered automobile, built in Des Moines, Iowa, in 1890, could maintain a speed of 14 miles (23 kilometers) per hour."

[14] *The Scientific American*, Vol. LXXIV, No. 7, Feb. 15, 1896, p. 105.

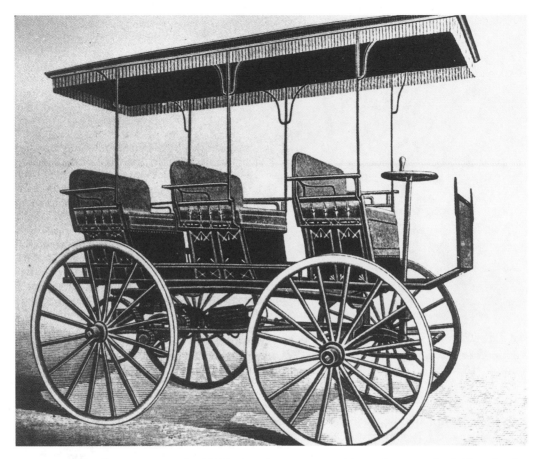

Figure 2.4. William Morrison's 1891 electric surrey could reach a speed of 14 mph. It appears to have been the first 4-wheel electric vehicle built in America. Courtesy: H. Munn & Company.

vehicle bore 36 battery cells with a capacity of 250 ampere-hours. Speed control was by voltage switching to yield a speed from 3 to 10 mph. For hard roads the range was given as 70 miles. In *The Chicago Times-Herald's* Chicago-Evanston race of 1895 the Morrison-Sturges entry ran 13 miles in the snow of six inches. While not finishing, the surrey's owners were recompensed with a $500 stipend.

The batteries in the Sturges' machine contained about 15 kilowatt-hours of energy at a useful discharge rate. The reporter, probably relating what he had been told, was overly generous in giving a range of 70 miles for this vehicle, probably by a factor of two. The fact that six inches of snow dropped the range to 13 miles provides credence to an exaggeration.

For the 1895 *Chicago Times Herald* Chicago-Evanston and return race Sturges' vehicle was typical of the electric carriages of the day. Three additional years would introduce a substantial change in the chassis and in the body. A 53-mile race in snow, and with a single battery charge, was too far then as now (1993) for an electric car. While the winner was a Duryea gasoline-powered wagon, the next year would have an electric vehicle surpassing the Duryea.

Figure 2.5. The Sturges' Electric Motor Wagon of 1895 bore a battery system of 36 cells, giving a nominal voltage of 72 volts from 250 ampere-hour battery. Courtesy: H. Munn & Company.

An early electric vehicle, as seen from Fig. 2.6, is the electric wagon developed in 1894 by Dr. H. C. Baker and J. R. Elberg of Kansas City.[15] Primitive in some respects, even for its time, an innovative feature was its braking method. The motor was placed in reverse. As cited below, this is a modern day technique utilized by operators of fork-lift trucks. The Baker & Elberg wagon weighed some 3000 pounds. Batteries were of the chloride type activating an electric motor bearing a shaft pulley. A rawhide belt linked the pulley to a flange on the inside of the rear wheel. An ingenious lever permitted detachment of the driving belt, allowing the motor to run while disengaged. Control of the wagon's speed was by voltage switching. Reversing was permitted. A forward speed of 15-18 mph was claimed. The stated range was 50 miles.

As one reads the above, it is apparent that while this wagon is contemporary to the vehicles of both Riker and Woods, its design is far more diluvian. For power transfer from the motor to the wheel, Baker and Elberg relied on a friction contact. Riker and Woods both were employing a chain drive, while Morris and Salom were using meshing steel gears. Both methods would be more efficient and more positive than the friction drive. For the first time, to brake a vehicle, the concept of "current reversal" is mentioned. Today this technique is know as plugging. Plugging can most easily be achieved on a shunt-wound motor. Without significant improvements the Baker & Elberg vehicle could not compete in the marketplace with the vehicles of Riker, Woods, or Morris & Salom as will be seen in the next sections.

---

[15] *The Horseless Age*, Vol. 1, p.32, 1895.

Figure 2.6. The Baker & Elberg Electric Wagon of 1894 Courtesy: The Horseless Age.

Riker's Four-Wheel Electric Vehicles

A still young Mr. Riker is seen on a four-wheel vehicle, the wheels equipped with wire spokes. This illustration, Fig. 2.7,[16] may be the first electric vehicle on which all four wheels had wire spokes, a construction which became general with the transitional electric vehicles described in Chapter 8. The vehicle had a dual motor drive, with each motor from a pinion driving its own large sprocket gear rigidly mounted to its respective rear wheel. Riker's four wheeler also appears equipped with pneumatic tires. This second Riker vehicle, a distinct improvement over his earlier one, serves to illustrate the engineering growth of this young man. As will be seen in Chapter 3, Riker developed advanced electric carriages, and his growth in vehicle design is the best known to demonstrate the evolution of early electric cars by one maker.

Riker was an entrepreneur, for at this time he had appointed himself president of the Riker Electric Motor Co., of 45 York Street, Brooklyn. Riker's second electric vehicle was experimental. He was learning. The combination weighed 310 pounds, carried one person at a reputed speed of 12 mph for a period of four hours on one battery charge. To avoid a differential, Riker had two 1/2 hp motors each weighing 24 pounds, each geared to a rear wheel.

---

[16] *The Horseless Age,* January 13, 1896, p. 19.

Figure 2.7. Andrew L. Riker's First Four-Wheel Electric Vehicle, 1895. The significance of this vehicle was that from the first it was conceived as having electric propulsion. Courtesy: The Horseless Age.

The battery weighed 135 pounds. In a country road test Riker reported an average speed of 15 mph. The reader is invited to view how Riker, being conscious of weight, milled out his two large gears into a spider-web frame.

Riker was aggressive in this electric field. Besides his electric car business, he was offering electric generators for lighting purposes.[17] In addition, he was writing about electric vehicles,[18] but in a less scholarly manner than was C. E. Woods, who shall be discussed in Chapter 5. Riker, however, shall next be discussed as an automobile racing enthusiast in Chapter 15; for, in order to continue his electric vehicle promotion, Riker would participate in the first automobile race ever held on an oval track.

Did Riker appreciate at the time the industry he had ushered in? For shortly, the electric vehicle would be used in a commercial way, and Morris & Salom would show the way.

---

[17] *The Electrical Engineer,* Vol. XVII, No. 315, May 16, 1894, p. 442.

[18] Andrew L. Riker, *The Electric Automobile, Scientific American Supplement*, Vol. XLIX, No. 1277, June 23, 1900, pp. 20470-72.

Morris & Salom Electric Vehicles

In the early 1890s inventors like Riker and Morrison placed on the city streets electrical contraptions in which only they and their friends would ride. From such modest beginnings the nucleus of a corporation, later to be highly financed, appeared. In a Philadelphia shop, two electrical engineers would form a lasting partnership. In 1894 Henry G. Morris and Pedro G. Salom organized a firm called the Electric Carriage and Wagon Company. The two would produce most serviceable vehicles. Their first carriage they chose to call the Electrobat, Fig. 2.8, stating it was a compound word, the termination "bat" being derived from the Greek word "bainein," meaning "to go," hence a conveyance deriving its power from electricity.[19] Their first vehicle, converted from a delivery wagon of the day, with large rear wheels and smaller, steerable front wheels, was considered a success.[20]

The first Electrobat, a joint effort, ran on the streets of Philadelphia in 1894. Morris was a mechanical engineer, while Salom was an electrician. Total weight of their vehicle was some

Figure 2.8. The First Electric Wagon of Morris & Salom - 1895. The Horseless Age.

---

[19] *The Horseless Age*, Vol. 1 No. 2, Dec. 1895, p.15; *Scientific American*, Vol LXXIII, No. 20, Nov. 16, 1895, p. 315.
[20] *The Horseless Age*, Vol. 1, No. 12, Oct. 1896, p.47.

4250 pounds, with a battery contributing 1600 of the total. The latter consisted of 60 chloride accumulators of 100 ampere-hours. As electric motors had by this time become articles of commerce, power was from a 3-hp General Electric motor capable of delivering 9-hp for a short time. As the weight was 300 pounds, design had progressed to yield 1-hp/100 pounds. Speed control was by voltage switching. Steering was by a suitable hand wheel with a geared 5th wheel riding on ball-bearings, which engaged the front wheel axle.

For the Chicago-Evanston race, Morris and Salom would appear with an Electrobat weighing only 1600 pounds.[21] This race, with its six-inch snow, the two partners wisely refrained from entering. But they did win a consolation prize for appearing. Assisting in the assembly of this second vehicle was Hiram Percy Maxim, who shall be discussed later. Morris and Salom were pure Adam Smith entrepreneurs, as will be seen, and Barrows, too, was of that noble and job-creating breed.

Barrows Tricycles

In 1895 when Riker had developed his electric four-wheeled bicycle, Charles A. Barrows of Willimatic, Connecticut, had designed an electric tricycle with a combination forward drive and steering wheel. This forward wheel, while possessing one hub, had two sets of spokes and rims with solid tires. Secured between the two sets of spokes was a large sprocket linked by chain to the small pinion of the motor. The gearing had a speed reduction of 14 to 1, a ratio about midway between that of Ayrton and Perry's tricycle and Tissandlier's electric drive system for the elongated balloon. The driving batteries were in two 24 x 8 x 8 inch boxes, supported by the bifurcated post with the box ends supported by a rod. The battery, which gave a reported 30 volts at 25 amperes, weighed 100 pounds, and was capable of 50 amperes, thus yielding as much as 2 hp. The weight of the vehicle was 300 pounds. Speed could be varied from a crawl up to 20 mph, it was reported. Each wheel was independently journalled whereby all extra friction on curves was avoided. Steering was achieved, as seen in Fig. 2.9, with a handlebar.

Figure 2.9. The Barrows Electric Tricycle of 1895. Courtesy: The Horseless Age.

[21] *The Horseless Age*, February 24, 1897, p. 14.

As the electric power was from primary batteries, it was said that with one filling of the electrolyte the vehicle could travel 100-150 miles. Sufficient electrolyte could be stored, it was claimed, to run some 500 miles. As will be seen in Chapter 11, discussing modern advanced batteries, it would be nearly 90 years in the future that primary batteries would be again considered for powering electric vehicles.

In electric vehicle design, Barrows was persistent and innovative. In a second vehicle, shown in Fig. 2.10,[22] the same general style tricycle was employed, but Barrows had learned. He had switched to friction drive with two pulleys on the ends of the motor shaft bearing on the forward tires. Riker had used this technique on his first vehicle, then on his second proceeded to direct gear coupling. Barrows increased the separation of the two front wheels to give greater stability and to enhance the vehicle's ability to carry additional batteries. This time Barrows employed 16 secondary cells assembled by T. D. Dunce, of New York City. The set was capable of a discharge rate of 24 amperes for 2 hours and 40 minutes. A 2-hp Riker motor weighing 79 pounds provided driving torque to the friction pulleys, one to each forward wheel. It appears Barrows' vehicle might have had a range of 25-30 miles on good roads. Control was by one handle and curb weight was 500 pounds.

Figure 2.10. The Barrows Electric Tricycle of 1896. If the steering handle is depressed, the small motor wheel makes a friction contact with the forward drive wheel. Raising the handle removes the contact wheel from the tire, while lowering the brake-block to the rubber. Courtesy: The Horseless Age.

---

[22] *The Horseless Age*, Vol. 2, No. 4, Feb. 1897, p. 14.

Close examination of the picture indicates that to stop the vehicle, the driver lifts his steering tiller, the motor pulley is disengaged from the tire surface, and at the same time the brake-bar, at the other end of the lever, is applied to the tire. There is indeed an economy of action in this single tiller used to steer, to start, and to stop the vehicle.

Barrows was captivated by the three-wheel vehicle concept, and to execute his belief he would inaugurate the C. H. Barrows Company to manufacture electric tricycles.[23] The one shown in Fig. 2.11 was for family use with the forward wheel being an "electric horse." The 2-hp Riker motor was powered by 24 battery cells, with the 500 pounds of battery distributed both forward and aft. The motor's 2 1/2-inch pinion gear was direct coupled to a 28-inch steel gear bracketed to the rim of the forward wheel. This motor was seen to be more powerful than the one used by Ayrton & Perry's 1882 tricycle, but the gear ratio was smaller. The control, by voltage switching, gave 3-speeds forward, and two in reverse. Maximum forward speed was stated to be 12 mph. Steering of the vehicle was by a handle bar. Typical of all Barrows' vehicles, to apply the brakes, the handle was raised. This action served both to electrically disconnect the motor and to engage a friction brake. Range for the tricycle was given as 30-40 miles. Battery interchange was possible, a subject to be illuminated below. With the coming of Barrows' vehicle the efficiency of ball-bearings was gaining in credence, and pneumatic tires were winning more adherents.

The three-wheeler would prove a less successful avenue for personal transportation. The four-wheel vehicles, then and now, were to offer the main path of development. Barrows'

Figure 2.11. Another 1897 Model of the Barrows Tricycle. Courtesy: The Horseless Age.

---

[23] *The Horseless Age*, Vol. 2, No. 10, Aug. 1897, pp. 5 & 15.

dream, like Abraham Lincoln's store in New Salem, would "wink out." While Barrows was pursuing the three-wheel vehicle, Riker, Woods, and Morris & Salom were using four wheels. Three wheels would prove to be an unsuitable solution.[24] Progress, however, counts dead-ends as well as throughways. And Riker, technically competent as he was, would eventually be merged out of business. Of the early electric vehicles only Woods, with his Woods Electric Vehicle Company, and the Detroit Electric would be manufactured into the 1920's.

At the time Barrows, Riker, and Morris & Salom were creating new styles of personal transportation, two inventors working together in Massachusetts were active. The city was Boston.

The Holtzer-Cabot Electric Brake

Through communication with friends across the Atlantic, a wealthy Bostonian wished for an electric car, a Brake, modeled after one in England, and capable of seating six or seven persons. For this Back Bay resident, the Holtzer-Cabot Electric Company assembled the electric Brake shown in Fig. 2.12. Its design should be compared with the electric carriage fabricated by Walter Bersey of Westminster illustrated in Fig. 6-5.

Figure 2.12. Holtzer-Cabot's 1895 Model Electric Brake. The Horseless Age.

---

[24] Three-wheeled vehicles, subject to less government regulations, are now a choice for innovative vehicles.

The batteries were in the body of the vehicle. For access, the two rear seats, hinged forward, were thrown over the front seat. Forty-four, 250 ampere-hour chloride cells were provided at a nominal discharge rate of 25 amperes. Aboard were about 20 kilowatt-hours of energy. The cells were arranged in four groups of 11 each and were connected to the motor in a series, parallel controller providing speeds of 5, 8, and 15 mph, with no intermediate resistances. The lever beside the bicycle-type steering-staff operated the controller. To reduce friction the wheels were provided with ball-bearings. Steering was arranged at the hub of the front axle, heavy crank levers being geared to the steering shaft. To lock the wheel at any angle, the user could adjust by foot pressure a tooth-segment with spring latch.[25]

The 7 1/2 hp motor was 4 pole, series-wound, and weighed 450 pounds. Speed at full load was reported to be 250 rpm, at a motor efficiency of 89 percent. To provide for different wheel speeds on cornering, the motor pinion engaged an intermediate gear, the shaft of which was divided and connected through differential gearing. An intermediate shaft drove the rear wheels by two sets of chains, one of which is visible in the illustration. Notice should be taken of the friction-brake on the steel tire of the right rear wheel. As the reader can observe, here is the horseless farm wagon; it illustrates the mental baggage each of us carries when faced with designing a new product. While the Brake above was 4-wheeled, the 3-wheeled concept was not dead, as is seen in the next section.

With electric vehicles now considered by some as an acceptable alternate means of local transportation in America, after five years of experimentation, the entrepreneurial mind discovered a means for commercially exploiting the horseless carriage. They would be used as taxis in New York City as developed in Chapter 4.

---

[25] *The Horseless Age*, Vol. 1, No. 12, Oct. 1896, p.37.

CHAPTER 3

Background for the Electric Horseless Carriage

Civilization was awaiting the motorcar, and its rapid adoption indicated its superiority over the horse-drawn carriage. As is often true during immaturity of an invention, there were competing systems. For personal travel at the turn of the century there were carriages powered by steam, by gasoline, and by electricity.[1] It is to electric vehicles and their mentors this book relates, together with the major elements that compose the electric drive system: the battery charger, the motive power batteries, the controller, and the traction motor. All of these components were first assembled in 1881 when the first electric vehicle was operated.

A Comparison of Power Systems in the 1890s

Of the above three types of power systems, steam had been the first applied to transportation. Nicholas Joseph Cugnot, a French artillery officer, had operated a heavy tram on the roads of France in 1769. His vehicle was oriented to military use as a tug for pulling cannons. Its modest boiler produced too little steam, necessitating frequent stops to build up pressure. The earliest use in Britain of steam in road transportation had been by Richard Trevithick, an English mining engineer, who placed several steam-driven carriages on London streets in 1801. The continually perfected steam engines, growing ever lighter and capable of increased speeds, became a particular success. These road engines travelling on good highways were often faster than a train locomotive on rails. Figures 3.1 and 3.2 illustrate British steam carriages of the middle 1860s. Progress on such vehicles was halted by a Parliament-passed Bill discriminating against them, a story detailed in Chapter 1.

On the continent Leon Serpollet in France developed a flash boiler in 1889 enabling steam to be raised and the vehicle placed in motion in two minutes, thus enhancing safety and simultaneously reducing start-up time. One steam carriage completed the watershed Paris-Bordeaux-Paris race automobile race in 1895.

In America the Stanley twins, Francis E. and Freelan O., built a number of lightweight steam automobiles. With their success in 1897, in order to commercially produce their vehicles, they moved from their hometown in Lewiston, Maine, to Newton, Massachusetts. At about the same

---

[1] *Three Types of Automobiles, The New York Electrical Society*, March 22, 1900.

Figure 3.1. Holt's Steam Carriage of 1867. Scientific American.

time Ransom Eli Olds produced his first automobile. It was steam-powered and driven from his barn in Lansing, Michigan. To record steam cars Edward W. Staebler has written of his steam automobile trip from Toledo, Ohio to Ann Arbor, Michigan in 1901.[2] There were many champions for this source of power and one fortune, as is well known, was spent on its development in the 1970s by William P. Lear, an outstanding aeronautical engineer and holder of many patents.[3]

Figures 3.3A through 3.3C illustrate an 1899 steam Locomobile with a curb weight of 550 pounds,[4] a lightness which would only be matched by an electric automobile produced by the Cleveland-based Baker Electric Company, as will subsequently be learned. The Locomobile was fueled with gasoline in contrast to coal for the British steam carriages. The boiler had a surface area of 42 square feet from which steam could be raised from a cold start in five minutes. The steam passed to a 5-hp two-cylinder engine capable of turning at 400-500 rpm. The rotation of the rear axle was by a chain linking the engine-shaft 12-tooth gear with the 24-tooth sprocket on the compensating gear-box to the rear axle. The Locomobile was said to have had a

---

[2] F. Clever Bald, *Horseless Carriages in Ann Arbor*, Michigan Historical Collections, Bulletin #6, December 1953.

[3] Andrew Jamison, *The Steam-Powered Automobile*, Bloomington: The University of Indiana Press, 1970, pp. 85-97.

[4] *Scientific American*, Vol. LXXXII, No. 4, Jan. 27, 1900, pp. 54-55.

Figure 3.2. Catley & Ayres' Steam Wagonette, 1863-67. Scientific American.

"wonderfully rapid acceleration" to gain a top speed of 10-12 mph. A foot-pedal operated a band-brake. Stopping could also be effected by reversing the engine. The gas tank is seen forward. The 240-pound pressure boiler is under the rear; the water tank of 15 gallons is before the boiler. A mirror permitted the driver to keep his eye on the water gauge.

Where the piston steam engine can be uniquely traced to one person, Thomas Newcomen in 1712, the internal combustion engine as now conceived has, by court decision, been classed as a social invention. Several persons at different times were responsible for its development. Two types of engines concern us: the two-cycle variety, used today in motorcycles, lawnmowers, and outboard motors, the so-called Brayton type, and the four-cycle version, very early applied to the automobile. The latter is the Otto cycle design. Karl Benz and Gottlieb Daimler each independently in 1885 constructed a vehicle powered by an internal combustion (IC) engine, the former using a tricycle, the latter a type of bicycle. Benz used the modern spark-ignition to ignite the compressed gasoline-vapor and air; Daimler used the hot-tube method, a system also employed by Hiram Percy Maxim in America in 1893. It would be in France, however, the IC engine automobile would have its initial success under the guidance of René Panhard and Émile Lavassor. At the century's end France was the largest builder and exporter of motorcars.

In America the Duryea brothers, J. Frank and Charles E., would initiate the commercial production of the gasoline-powered car in 1893. Their entry, seen in Fig. 3.4, in the Chicago-Evanston-Chicago Thanksgiving race of 1895, won easily over a Benz car, the single other

Figure 3.3A. *On the Road.*

Figure 3.3B. *The 4-Horse Power Engine.*

Figure 3.3C. The Locomobile — Sectional View, Showing Location of Engine, Boiler, and Tanks.

Figures 3.3A, 3.3B, & 3.3C: The reader will discern this steam road carriage is of American origin by its descent from the tubular frame of the bicycle. Note gasoline tank forward; water tank and condenser to the rear. On November 16, 1901 S. T. Davis drove his steam car one mile in one minute 39 seconds (36 mph = 60 kph). Scientific American, Vol. LXXXV, No. 22, Nov. 30, 1901, p. 347.

Figure 3.4. Charles E. Duryea in the 2-cylinder, IC-powered, pneumatic-tired Duryea won the Chicago Times-Herald race on 28 November 1895. His brother Frank drove the car in the race. The Horseless Age.

finisher.[5] The Duryea had an average speed of 7 1/2 miles per hour, when allowing for repairs. Duryea's pneumatic tires were among the first used in America. They were manufactured by the Hartford Rubber Works, a subsidiary of the Pope Manufacturing Company, about which more will be discussed below.[6]

It was, however, the Paris-Bordeaux-Paris race of June 11, 1895 "which set the inventive world alight" with the merits of powered road travel. Of the 22 cars which started, eight gasoline-fueled and one steam-powered completed the course, the winner in an elapsed time of 48 hours and 48 minutes for an average speed of 14.4 mph! In this challenge the lightest vehicles fared best, generally speaking. The weight of powered carriages was shown to be an important factor. M. Charles Jeantaud, in an electrically-powered vehicle completed in three months, entered this race using the principle of battery interchange, a technique discussed below. While his surrey had suffered a hot rear bearing due to poor lubrication, he had experienced no failure on his way to Bordeaux. This record would coin the reputation of electric vehicles for reliability.

---

[5] *The Horseless Age*, Vol. 1, No. 2, December 1895, p. 18.

[6] Joseph Nathan Kane, *Famous First Facts*, 3rd ed., New York: H. W. Wilson Co., 1964.

Table 3-1 presents the relative advantages of these three sources of propulsion as compared with a horse and buggy. It would be the two underlined factors in this Table which led to the eventual dominance of the IC-powered car, imperceptibly in the 1890s, but strongly after 1902 and today, nearly a century later.

With energy cost of slight importance in 1895, and consequently efficiency of motive power of less concern, the factors which spelled success for the IC engine were: energy density of the fuel, and achievable range of the vehicle with that fuel.[7] The steam car required water every ten miles, the electric car a battery charge every 30 miles. And the horse and buggy had neither speed nor range. In the Age of Touring, conceived at the end of the 19th century, the convenience of the IC-powered car with its extended range was unequalled. The subsequent emergence of the exhaust muffler to the IC engine, invented by Hiram Percy Maxim after he left the vehicle field, and the application of the electric starter in 1912, conceived by Clyde J. Coleman in 1899 and perfected by Charles Franklin Kettering,[8] assured the dominance of the gasoline-fueled automobile. Be that as it may, the electric car, as will be revealed, possessed merit.

World Conditions at the Genesis of the Automobile

To better assess the environment for the literate citizen of America, England, France, and Germany, what were the conditions in 1881, the year in which the first electric vehicle was assembled and operated?

As tersely related by the historian Albert Guerard in the 1950s, "The pattern of world power was being influenced by the ongoing decay of the Turkish Empire, which would permit Russia to expand to the south; the principle of self determination of a people, which, while life to France and to England, would be death to the Austro-Hungarian Empire, and anathema to the Russian and Turkish Empires, each containing unassimilated races; and the rising power of the Germanic People, now the most powerful nation in Western Europe. During this period France herself was energetically recovering from the humbling experience of occupation as the aftermath of the Franco-Prussian War of 1871. The Empire under Napoleon III had been replaced by the Third Republic in 1878. Surprising even the best informed, France had paid off her indemnity of one billion dollars to Germany, and was, indeed, more economically sound than was victorious Germany."[9]

In 1880 England, and her empire, was essentially at its crowning, achieved with an electorate of only eighteen percent of those citizens over 20 years of age.[10] With a navy greater than any other two national fleets, much of the world enjoyed a *Pax Britannica*. But on the continent of Europe, under the new conditions of battle created by railways, modern techniques of mobilization and increased firepower, Britain was in no condition to intervene alone. Yet the

---

[7] G. D. Hiscox, *Horseless Vehicles, Automobiles, and Motor Cycles Operated by Steam, Hydro-Carbon, Electric & Pneumatic Motors*, New York: Munn & Co., 1900, 400 pp.

[8] John Buist Sadler, personal communication, February 1992.

[9] Albert Guerard, *France, A Modern History*, Ann Arbor: The University of Michigan Press, 1959.

[10] *Encyclopaedia Britannica*, Vol. 17, Chicago: Encyclopaedia Britannica, 1959, p. 320.

Table 3-1. Categories Comparing Types of Road Transportation in 1895

Vehicle Type	Fuel for 1 hp-hr.[a]	Weight/hp in Pounds	Control	System Durability	Efficiency Source	Maintenance	Range Miles	Start-Up Time	Noise	Fumes	Speed mph
Steam	6# coal[b] 40# water	200	steam valve	good	10%	modest	10 water	2 minutes	little	little	40
Gasoline	1 ounce[b] gasoline	185[d]	carburetor	fair	15%	modest	150 gasoline	5 minutes cranking	very noisy	much	20
Electric	220#[b] batteries	70[e]	voltage switching	excellent	50% with battery	little	30 charge	immediate	almost none	none	25
Horse	12#[c] oats	1000	bridle	good	70%[f]	considerable	15 with buggy	15-30 minutes	little	much	walk

(a) One horsepower-hour = 3/4 kilowatt-hour
(b) *Scientific American Supplement*, Vol. XL, No. 1023, 10 August 1895, p. 16343.
(c) Personal communication.
(d) John B. Rae, *The American Automobile*, Chicago Press, 1965. p. 33.
(e) *Scientific American Supplement*, Vol. XL, No. 1030, September 28, 1895, p. 16459.
(f) Thomas Edison, *The New York World*, Sunday, November 17, 1895.

Island Kingdom was producing nearly a third of the world's output of manufactured goods, being overly specialized in coal mining, in iron and steel, and in textiles. "The price of this prominence was a large scale decline of agriculture, a migration of country residents to the cities, a substantial importation of food, and a crumbling of village society. At the center of this web of domains, colonies, and countries to whom Britain exported capital as well as goods, was the London money market. In 1881 the Liberal Party had just defeated the Conservatives, Gladstone was Prime Minister, and Queen Victoria was on the throne."[11]

For America in 1880 the center of population was a few miles southwest of Cincinnati, Ohio, and Washington would be the territory next to become a state in 1889. A presidential term ending, the new president inaugurated and assassinated, 1881 was one of the two years in which the nation had three presidents: Hayes, Garfield, and Arthur. The period was a time of looking inward and toward western expansion. To paraphrase President Calvin Coolidge, it was a time "when the business of America was business." Agriculture and industry were all growing as more land came under cultivation, and as ever greater volumes of iron, steel, coal, lumber, fired clays, and oil were needed to build a nation. Household names taken from the press were Vanderbilt, Carnegie, Frick, James J. Hill, Leland Stanford, and Rockefeller. The national debate was on the power of trusts and the institution of the Civil Service. The time was one of healing the wounds occasioned by the recent War Between the States. But it was the economic strength of the North which characterized the nation.

The Seemingly Indispensable Horse

One of the most salient features of the Twentieth Century has been the emergence of the personal automobile and the resulting mobility given its occupants. Other than the United States Constitution, possibly no event has so influenced America. Now the motor car is universally considered as petroleum-fueled, but at the end of the Victorian Period, 1901, steam-powered, electric-powered, and gasoline-powered vehicles were all in contention. Before this time, at least in the Western World, power for immediate travel was, apart from the long trip made by train or ship, almost invariably provided by the horse. For example, Colonel Robert E. Lee, U. S. Army, summoned from Texas to Washington, D.C. by Lieutenant-General Winfield Scott at the behest of an alarmed President Abraham Lincoln in 1860, rode a horse from bivouac to bivouac, travelling with aides to the Mississippi River, there to take a steamboat to Cairo, Illinois, and then by train to Washington, D.C.

At best, with a wagon, surrey, or carriage, the beast was good for probably fifteen, or at most twenty miles per day. As American cities were smaller then, any personal vehicle with a range of fifteen or more miles was tolerable. In cities on the Continent, in England, and likewise in America, the horse-drawn taxi, usually a hansom or a coupe, was prevalent, all utilizing the wheel and axle. In Russian cities, with their longer winters, while the *droshky* and the berline were used as wheeled conveyances for hire, sleigh taxis were also common.[12]

---

[11] K. B. Smellie, *Great Britain Since 1688*, Ann Arbor: The University of Michigan Press, 1962, p. 207.

[12] Fyodor N. Dostoevsky, *A Raw Youth*, Constance Garnett, Translator, New York: McMillan, 1916.

The presence of a horse, as any person who has sustained one knows, requires a substantial effort. The purchase of oats for feeding, and the procurement of water for drinking; the cooling and currying; the removal of packed debris from the insteps of each of the four hoofs; the securing and the storage of straw and the preparation of bedding; the cleansing of the stables and the disposal of the wastes; the bridling and harnessing of a sometimes intractable animal; and the wiping and cleaning of the harness. The hitching of a horse to a rig for even a short trip was a major task. Then there was the shoeing, requiring the services of a farrier. In addition, a horse, a mammal like man, was subject to disease and other forms of discommode. These difficulties have been recently reported: "Equine influenza occurs widely in many parts of the world, and is particularly troublesome in race horses and riding horses."[13]

Therefore, to own a horse and carriage necessitated several hours a day in preparation for its use. To overcome these tasks was the goal of the inventors of mechanically powered personal vehicles. Successful efforts to employ horseless means for personal transportation need await Nicholas-Joseph Cugnot, a Frenchman, utilizing steam in 1769; Gustave Trouvé, a Frenchman, by means of electricity, in 1881; and by Carl Benz, a German working in France, employing the internal combustion engine in 1885.

---

[13] M. M. Kaplan and R. G. Webster, *The Epidemiology of Influenza, Scientific American*, Vol. 237, No. 6, December 1977, p. 88.

CHAPTER 4

The Electric Car's First Commercial Application

It would be the partners Morris and Salom, earlier referred to, who would make the first commercial use of electric vehicles anywhere in the world. In their second generation of the Electrobat, three models of which are described below, the partners believed they had assembled the alternate for the horse and cab, namely an electric taxi. Edison's invention of the incandescent lamp in 1879 and its speedy adoption, the rapid growth in the use of electric tram cars, the application of the electric motor to an ever growing number of industrial practices, caused all who were associated with the new electric industry to be optimistic. If one would seek a parallel today, it might be in solid state electronics in which the number of discrete devices used has doubled 11 times in the last 17 years.[1] That the taxi application for electric vehicles had merit was as effectively reasoned then as it would be today, if argued:[2]

> "They (Morris & Salom) are not attempting at present to fill individual orders for carriages in various parts of the country, as they consider such a scheme impracticable, but are confining their attention to building a number of electrical hansoms and coupes for public service in New York City and Philadelphia. When they have demonstrated the commercial success of a system of this kind, they believe it will be an easy matter to establish stations in every large city of the Union, where a private individual who desires a carriage can have it properly charged and cared for. An indiscriminate putting forth of such vehicles they regard as unwise, because it would be impossible for them to send a skilled engineer out with every carriage they sold, and the average layman knows nothing about the electric business."

The failure to heed this 1896 dictum of organized fleet operation and eschewing individual vehicles caused an electric utility-based committee in 1972 to initiate the disastrous Edison Electric Institute electric truck purchase discussed in Chapter 24. Dr. Victor Wouk has noted this unfortunate choice.[3] Fortunately the 1896 reasoning is being followed today by the U.S. Department of Energy in initiating fleets of electric cars under the Electric & Hybrid Research,

---

[1] Robert N. Noyce, *Microelectonics*, Scientific American, Vol. 237, No. 3, September 1977, p. 67.

[2] *The Horseless Carriage*, Vol. 1, No. 11, September 1896, p. 18.

[3] Victor Wouk, *Two Decades of "High Performance" EV Fleet Operation*, Eighth Electric Vehicle Symposium, Washington, D.C., 1986.

Development and Demonstration Act of 1976 discussed below.[4] Morris and Salom would carry out their plans for establishing a fleet of electrical taxis, and their concept was to influence strongly a number of persons.

Morris & Salom's Electrobats

The originators of the Electrobat, Morris and Salom, brought out a series of electric cars, one of which is shown in Fig. 4.1.[5] The largest of Morris and Salom's Electrobats was brilliantly colored black and red, and seated two persons. Large, wooden wheels, equipped with pneumatic tires, were forward, while similarly equipped smaller steering wheels trailed. The turning radius was 20 feet. A much lighter vehicle than their first, the present one had a weight of only 1650

Figure 4.1. A two-motored, rear-wheel steering Morris & Salom 1895 Electrobat. The first commercial electric vehicles anywhere, hansom cabs based on this model were used in New York City in 1897. The wood spokes indicate the design was pre-1896. Courtesy: The Horseless Age.

---

[4] *Commerce Business Daily*, November 3, 1977.
[5] *The Horseless Age*, Vol. 1, No. 2, Dec. 1895, pp. 15-17.

pounds. Batteries were four sets of 12 cells each, with a capacity of 50 amperes per cell. The energy carried may be calculated to be some five kilowatt-hours. Utilizing the principle of battery switching, the vehicle had four forward speeds and one in reverse provided by two Lundell 1 1/2-hp motors.[6] Maximum speed was given as 20 mph, and range was cited to be 25 miles, a figure more reasonable than similar ranges given by earlier vehicle builders. Reflecting specialization in construction, the carriage work was by Chas. S. Caffrey Co. of Camden, New Jersey.

Seen in Fig. 4.2, standing beside the smaller Electrobat, is almost surely Hiram Percy Maxim, who shall be discussed later. Maxim, son of the famous inventor of the rapid-fire gun, an aeronaut and designer of early aircraft, was introduced to electric vehicles by Morris and Salom. He, with others, would assemble the Electrobat which would be entered in the *Times-Herald* Chicago to Evanston and return race already alluded to. Maxim would subsequently join the engineering staff of the Pope Manufacturing Company, a firm to contend with in 1900, and one discussed in Chapter 8.

This more modest Electrobat, styled as an electric road wagon, was a harbinger of vehicles. The chassis was of cold-drawn tubular steel throughout; the spoked wheels were of bicycle

Figure 4.2. Morris and Salom were the first to market several different electric vehicles at the same time, thus anticipating today's automobile manufacturing practice. The photo shows a smaller Electrobat in 1895. Courtesy: The Horseless Age.

---

6 *The Lundell Motor, The Electrical Engineer*, Vol. XIX, No. 372, June 19, 1895, pp. 555-6.

design equipped with pneumatic tires, and furnished with ball-bearings. The gearing and general operation of the vehicle was said to be similar to the larger model. Its speed was some 20 mph, and complete with batteries, it had a reported weight of 1180 pounds, a figure believed at the time to be the lightest of the electric vehicles. It would be Walter Baker, an electric engineer, who later, in 1902, would introduce electric vehicles weighing less than 600 pounds.

Showing remarkable fecundity in electric vehicle design, the partners, Morris and Salom, assembled a two-place electric buggy toward the end of 1895, shown in Fig. 4.3.[7] Known as the Crawford Wagon,[8] it had four bicycle wheels equipped with pneumatic tires, and was driven by two small electric motors, powered by batteries placed under the operator's seat. At the time of development Morris and Salom showed pioneering leadership in designing a lightweight vehicle, in employing uniformly-sized wheels, and in early appreciating the higher weight-carrying capability and superior cornering ability of the wire-spoked wheel. It appears this modified stanhope was one of a kind, and it was of a general style which would be popularized by the Baker Electric Vehicle Company in 1902. Walter Baker, a Case School of Applied Science graduate engineer, in solving the turning problem which caused the above partners to employ two motors, would use but a single motor and a differential as we now know it.

As competent as was the engineering of Morris & Salom, their entrepreneurship in establishing the first electric taxis in New York City was also a step to be admired.

Figure 4.3. A Two-motor Morris & Salom Electric Road Wagon of 1896. A company inaugurated by these partners was the first to apply the automobile to commercial pursuits, a New York City taxi fleet of electric hansoms established in 1897. Courtesy: Scientific American.

---

[7] *The Horseless Age*, Vol. 1, No. 3, Jan. 1896, p. 24.
[8] *Scientific American*, Vol. LXXIV, No. 7, February 15, 1896, pp. 105-106.

Electric Taxis in New York City

In showing at the same time three different styles of Electrobats, Morris & Salom anticipated the concept of a complete line of vehicles which became standard practice in the mature automobile industry. The records indicate that these partners were not only mechanically and electrically capable, but, in addition, they were enterprising. Their first electric vehicle a success, they reasoned that electric taxis would be cheaper to operate than horse-drawn cabs. In addition, by having all their vehicles in one area, the problem of servicing was greatly simplified.[9] C. E. Woods, earlier cited, would write a book that would be published in 1900. In it he made a cost comparison between an electric taxi and a horse-drawn cab.[10] Morris and Salom may have themselves made a similar study, but Woods had his published.

"The next question of interest and vital importance is to know by what means the electric vehicle can be made to work more economically and more advantageously than the horse-drawn vehicle. Two or three very terse and simple comparisons will be drawn to illustrate this point. Taking first the ordinary cabs, as drawn by horses, and based on the average rates established by all liveries of fifty cents for the first mile and twenty-five cents for each additional mile, the horse vehicle will cover about five miles in one hour and is good for about four hours' work per day, making a possible twenty miles and six dollars revenue as an average. The same cab, to make further earnings or mileage, must have another horse attached to it, twenty miles per day being all that one horse can possibly do. Short trips in the centers of large cities will sometimes run the earnings up to seven or eight dollars per day.

"Now a look at what the electric cab can do. An average speed of nine miles per hour would give it thirty-six miles in four hours. It would earn in that time, on a mileage basis of fifty cents for the first mile and twenty-five cents for each additional mile, two dollars and fifty cents per hour, or ten dollars for four hours, at a cost not to exceed two cents per mile for electricity, or seventy-two cents, and twenty-five cents an hour for the driver, or one dollar, making a total cost of one dollar and seventy-two cents for operating expense of running only.

"The horse cab will have earned in the same time, on twenty miles, six dollars, at a cost of eighty cents for the horse and one dollar for the driver, figuring the latter on the same basis of twenty-five cents per hour. Thus the electric cab has, in the same length of time, sixty-six and two-thirds percent greater earning power, and at about three and one-half percent less cost.

"Now here's a look at other conditions. The first cost of electric cab is $3,000, as against $1,200 for a good cab, horse and harness, or almost three times as much. The depreciation of the latter is about thirty-three and one-third percent, while the depreciation of the former is not to exceed twenty percent. But as yet, by no means has it reached the earning capacity of an electric cab per day. After using it four hours in the morning, we can charge, say from 12 noon until 1:30 in the afternoon, and then

---

[9] *The Horseless Age*, Vol. 1, No. 11, Sept. 1896, p. 18.

[10] C. E. Woods, *The Electric Automobile: Its Construction, Care and Operation.* Herbert S. Stone & Company, 1900, pp.10-12.

See also: G. C. Sever and R. A. Fliess, *Cost/Ton Mile for Horses and for Electric Vehicles, Scientific American,* Vol. LXXXI, No. 4, July 22, 1899, p. 52.

have until 5:30 to make another thirty-six miles. Then by charging from 5:30 until 7, the cab has thirty-six miles more for the night's work. Further comparison here would be superfluous so far as cabs go."

Morris and Salom would have agreed with the later economics as expressed by Woods, for they planned to introduce electric taxis into New York City on November 1, 1896.[11] Their vehicles were coupés and hansoms as illustrated in Figs. 4.4 and 4.5. Like all *Electrobats*, these vehicles, bearing only a different body, had the same chassis and were steered by their rear wheels. The vehicles, with front-wheel drive, had a range, it was stated, of 20-30 miles. The coupé and hansom cabs were each equipped with two 1 1/2 hp Lundell Motors and 44 chloride lead-acid cells yielding a nominal 88 volts. There would be 12 *hansoms* and one coupé.[12] In March 1897 the editor of *The Horseless Age* would write:[13]

"The metropolitan newspapers have had a great deal to say lately about the electric hansoms which the Electric Carriage & Wagon Company are now plying for hire in New York City. About a dozen of these cabs are at present in regular service, no difficulty having been experienced in procuring the necessary license from the Board of Alderman. Many of the chappies and men-about-town are availing themselves of the opportunity to try the sensations of riding in a horseless vehicle, which sensations they are describing privately in the clubs and publicly in the columns of the press. Even the aristocracy has been bold enough to overcome

Figure 4.4. Morris & Salom's Coupé of 1896; Front Drive, Steerable Rear Wheels. A-frame, wire-spoked wheels are a hallmark of a post-1895 vehicle. The Horseless Age.

---

[11] *The Horseless Age*, Vol. 1, No. 11, Sept. 1896, pp. 17-18.
[12] Census Reports, Vol. X, *Manufactures*, Part IV, Washington, D.C.: United States Census Office, 1902, p. 165.
[13] *The Horseless Age*, Vol. II, No. 5, March 1897, p. 5.

Figure 4.5. The lower vehicle, a hansom, became the first machine powered taxi ever introduced. A fleet of 13 were placed in operation on Manhattan in 1897 by the builders, Electric Carriage & Wagon Company of Philadelphia, a partnership of Morris & Salom. The Horseless Age.

convention and step into the horseless cab. A scion of one of the wealthiest families took his bride to ride in one of them the other day as an incidental diversion of their honeymoon, thereby establishing a precedent which will encourage others of high station to make use of the new vehicle for trips matrimonial or otherwise. Some of the views expressed are decidedly narrow and prejudiced, as is universally true when any new idea is presented for public approval, but that the judgement of the people is in the main favorable is proved by the statement of the company that the cabs are in almost constant demand and that more will be put in service soon. For the enterprise they have shown in being the first to introduce motor cabs in the streets of New York this company is entitled to great credit and will no doubt reap commensurate profit."

For those of us living today who have always known of automobiles, what comments were being written in the metropolitan newspapers? Fortunately there have been saved some columns from the *New York Journal* titled, *A Chappie and a Horseman Try the New Horseless Carriage.*[14]

"In search of a new sensation not inconsistent with a proper observation of Lent, I went yesterday and rode in a horseless carriage. I don't regret the experiment. After the first flush of the thing, and barring the familiar aspect of the dashboard, the harness and the horse, it was not unlike riding in an ordinary hansom, for all the

---

[14] *The Horseless Age*, Vol. 2, No. 5, March 1897, pp. 15-16.

carriages in the place that I went to are built on the hansom plan, which is to say that they are the homeliest vehicles that were ever invented.

"But it is in that first sensation that you get your novelty. It is as though you were being served with a "high ball," without the ball. There is a sense of incompleteness about it. You seemed to be sitting on the end of a huge pushcart, propelled by an invisible force and guided by a hidden hand.

"There is also a seeming brazenness to the whole performance. I dreamed once that I walked down Fifth Avenue in my pajamas in the full tide of the afternoon promenade, and I almost died with shame before I awoke. Yesterday I had something of the same feeling as I sat there and felt myself pushed forward into the very face of grinning, staring and sometimes jeering New York. But it wore away after a while. Gradually I felt that I did not need the protection of a horse in front of me. I returned the wicked glances of the bicycle ladies on the Boulevard, and when I got back to Fifth Avenue I was almost as much at home and felt almost as devilish as the other chappies whose faces were glued to club windows, and whose eyes were riveted on the beautiful river of femininity that sweeps in counter currents along our main throughfare of fashion.

"The fellow who sold me the horseless carriage said that there was no call for such vehicles from the clubs, a statement that I do not doubt. Your club chappie likes novelty, but he doesn't want the whole world to watch his indulgences in that direction. He has a reputation for conservatism that he must preserve. He will ride in a horseless carriage by and by, but it will be when to do so will attract no more attention than to ride a bicycle. I know two or three chappies who have tried the horseless carriage, but it has been after dark and along streets where the electric lights were not too bright.

"I believe that I am the first representative of dudedom who has ever ridden in a horseless carriage in the garish glare of day. I congratulate myself that I survived the ordeal. At one time I thought the nasty little boys who throng the unaristocratic avenues where I went first to avoid my acquaintances were going to stone me. They ran after me and hooted and cast pebbles and otherwise evinced derisive hostility to such a degree that I begged the motorman to make haste to the Boulevard where I hoped to find protection among the many other strange and curious things that swarm there on wheels. I was right. Only the horses paid any attention to us on the Boulevard. Elisha's chariot of fire wouldn't create the slightest ripple of excitement on the Boulevard.

"On Fifth and Madison Avenues surprise was expressed by an aristocratic elevation of the eyebrows, except among my personal acquaintances, whose startled faces indicated their fear that I had gone mad. The horseless carriage will have to be improved before it becomes popular in chappiedom. There must be some sort of guard in front to keep clubmen from tumbling out on their way home after 3 A.M. There must be some sort of a screen for Summer night driving in the Park. As the vehicle is now constructed there is altogether too much publicity about it. The chappie's dearest prerogative is his privacy and he is going to preserve it, horse or no horse.

Cholly Knickerbocker"

Cholly Knickerbocker complains of the electric hansom, "There is a sense of incompleteness about it. You seem to be sitting on the end of a huge pushcart, propelled by an invisible force and guided by a hidden hand." Figure 4.6 shows a hansom cab and horse of which Cholly was long familiar in a remarkable picture by Alice Austen taken in Union Square at Broadway and Fifteenth Street, in 1896. What Cholly misses, of course, is viewing the moving rump of Dobbin, and his swishing tail. Cholly continues, "There must be some sort of guard in front to keep clubmen from tumbling out on their way home at 3 A.M."[15]

Riding along with Cholly was Francis Trevelyan, a surely less blasé New Yorker than was Cholly. As together these two "dudedom" reporters weighed 425 pounds in an era when corpulence was a mark of affluence, Morris & Salom's hansom was out of balance. Francis' free comments are interesting, for they recapture a bygone era.

> "Cholly Knickerbocker may like it, for it certainly catches the eyes of the girls, and it may perhaps suit the other chappies, or even the hardened frequenters of the bargain counter, but - and this is a most important "but" - I do not think the motor cab will ever be anything more than a fad. New York is a blasé city, and already, except where fashion reigns, or the other extreme, the tenement house population, holds

Figure 4.6. A Horse-drawn Hansom Cab in New York City - 1896. Staten Island Historical Society.

---

[15] John A. Kouwenhoven, *The Columbia Historical Portrait of New York*, Doubleday & Co., Garden City, N.Y., 1953, pp. 428 & 430.

sway, the horseless cab attracts little or no attention. Still, in its present usual form-that of a hansom cab sawed off short of the dashboard and stuck on in front of a truck - it gives the occupant a hopeless sensation of being perpetually shot through a chute, with the pleasing possibility of being utilized as a battering ram in a collision with a cable car or a runaway team.

"There is absolutely no comparison between the exhilarating thrill of driving a fleet footed trotter or stylish stepper and the sitting cooped up at the mercy of the individual who is in charge of the electricity. Electricity, by the way, is the motive power generally used for these automobiles, and the only power that has been used here for the hansom cab style of conveyance. This leads up to a point that is quaint. The horseman knows that his horse has a limit of endurance, but he also knows that the animal's powers can be husbanded if necessary. On the other hand, when you start for a trip - it can scarcely be called ride or drive - in a motor cab, you have to order your stored electric force to suit the length of your journey, which might be rather awkward under such circumstances as missing your way on a country road.

"Another point that provokes a smile, even from the trussed travelers on a horseless hansom - for one needs to be undersized to fit them as at present constructed - it is that wheelmen seem to dislike the apparatus even more than horses. The horses, especially when they are well-bred trotters, regard it rather curiously, but on the whole contemptuously; but in the bosom of the average cyclist it seems to arouse derision, scorn and contempt. An occasional cab horse, doing his level best under the lash, may not see the strange machine till close to him, and in the excitement of the moment endeavor to cut a somersault, but as a rule the New York horses are already accustomed to this new, strange thing, especially those that would seem most likely to be scared, the well fed occupants of private stables. The wheelmen sneer at the contrivance, spurt by it to show their contempt for its traveling powers and then slow up again to get another chance to cast a glance of unaffected disgust.

"Viewed simply and seriously as a means of locomotion, the motor cab has fewer disadvantages than would seem probable at first sight. When I had the pleasure of appearing before the public side by side with Cholly Knickerbocker the cab was certainly carrying top weight - some 425 pounds. Some excuses might therefore have been made for it, especially as the weight in front was not counterbalanced by any great avoirdupois on the part of the - engineer, jehu, electrician or whatever one should call the man in charge. Nevertheless, the cab was well under control, stopping or slowing without delay or spurting along directly it was called upon. It "steered" well, too; nor were ruts, holes, or car tracks any apparent obstacle, the driver having to take no greater care to avoid them than he would have if he had had a horse between the shafts.

"The chief trouble with the motion of the cab is that on smooth going, such as asphalt, the thick rubber tires do not give sufficient fulcrum to keep the vehicle moving steadily. The consequence is what would be called "weaving" in a horse, an irregular wobbling from side to side. This is not at all apparent on cobblestones, and over these there is far less jarring than would be expected.

"Still, whatever merits these motor cars may have, it is difficult to imagine that they will ever hold the affection of any one who has ever sat behind a free-going roadster.

Francis Trevelyan"

As the description of the hansom cabs would indicate, with the two portly individuals in the front seat, the vehicle would be nose heavy, a feature which would enhance any wobbling to which Mr. Trevelyan referred. In addition, these Morris & Salom cabs all were steered by their rear wheels, a concept that mitigates against straight line driving.

The Economics of New York Electric Taxis

Cholly Knickerbocker and Mr. Trevelyan having presented a firsthand account of their initial ride in an electric vehicle, what were the economics of this earliest powered cab system in New York City? Fortunately we have an account, which while not completely quantitative, provides some conclusions.[16]

"Philadelphia, Pa., Aug. 3, 1897.

Editor, Horseless Age:

Dear Sir: The results of the operation of our station in New York, which was put into operation March 27, 1897, and which we believe is the first and only one in the world, are as follows:

Total mileage to Aug. 1st	14,459
Average mileage for 12 hansoms	1,215
" " " 10 " (in actual service)	1,446
Average mileage per day per vehicle	11
Total number of passengers carried	4,765

"The total number of accidents and delays of all kinds since the introduction of the service to Aug. 1 was 40, or about one for every 360 miles, which we think will compare favorably with the record for horse service.

"When the novelty and difficulties of the service are considered and the necessity of employing comparatively inexperienced drivers, this record becomes quite remarkable and demonstrates at once what perfect control the driver has over the vehicle, and the future reliability of the service.

"While we do not care to publish the actual receipts and expenditures for conducting the service, we would say that the results have been so satisfactory as to warrant the organization of a new company with a large capital stock for the purpose of manufacturing and operating electric motor vehicles of all styles, and that the construction of 100 additional electric hansoms will be begun within the next thirty days.

Yours very truly,
Electric Carriage & Wagon Co.
Morris & Salom"

---

[16] *The Horseless Age*, Vol. 2, No. 9, July 1897, p. 12.

Using the information presented in the above letter, the economic study on taxis by Woods, given above, and some accounting, how profitable was this first taxi venture? Let us assume one-half of the miles travelled produced revenue, the vehicles cost $3,000 apiece, depreciation is 20 percent per year, a driver would be paid two dollars per day, fare is fifty cents for the first mile and twenty-five cents for the second mile, electricity is two cents per mile:[17]

With probable income of $3,600 and expenses of $5,800 it appears that the first four months of operation, at best, could be no more than a break-even economy. But as will be seen, a promoter enters.

From the vantage point of the author it appears that the Electric Carriage and Wagon Company was suffering from a problem of cash flow. Morris & Salom had built at least four experimental electric cars, and now had 12 hansoms. The first four must have cost some $20,000, the next 12, $40,000. For their entry into electric vehicle exploitation they must, for a minimum, have expended $60,000. New York offices, garage, and other arrangements, which were located at 1684 Broadway, would have brought this sum to at least $100,000.[18] And after four months their income had been only $3,000-$4,000, hardly a bonanza. It appears that Morris and Salom decided to cut their losses and sell their company together with their taxi rights in the Empire City. And the above letter was a means of enhancing the company's probable selling

Table 4-1. Income and Expense Statements for New York City Taxis			
INCOME			
Miles providing fare:	14,459/2 =	(about)	7,200
Miles per passenger:	7,200/4,765 =	(about)	2
Fare collected:	4,765 (50¢ + 25¢) =	(about)	$3,600
EXPENSES			
Running expense			
Electricity	14,459 (2¢ per mile)	(about)	$288
Drivers	10 at $2.00 per day, 120 days		$2,400
Depreciation			
12 vehicles at $3,000	20 percent per year, 4 months		$2,400
Supervision	20 percent of gross		$720
			————
		(about)	$5,800

---

[17] W. F. Shafer of Commonwealth Edison Company (ret.) of Chicago has been commuting with a small electric vehicle of his own assembly for over five years. He reports a non-depreciation cost of 20¢/mile. Personal communication, March 30, 1982. (See appendix J).

[18] *The Horseless Age*, Vol. 3, No. 7, Oct. 1898.

price. The letter is detailed, yet the results are vague. The clue to poor business is the average mileage per day. Only 11 miles. Yet C.E. Woods in his economic study of electric vehicles for taxis, cited above, and written about the time of Morris and Salom's taxi venture in Manhattan, speaks of 108 revenue miles per day. In actual practice it appears that Morris and Salom had no more than about ten percent of Woods' generous figures.

That Morris and Salom were out of funds is further bulwarked, for, as will be cited later, when William C. Whitney and P.A.B. Widener later ordered 200 taxis, they did not return to Morris & Salom as a source, but went to the well established Pope Manufacturing Company. One can easily surmise that Morris and Salom shrewdly bargained with Isaac L. Rice, Rice with Whitney and Widener, and the latter with Colonel Pope. In the end, it was Pope who was damaged. He was the last monkey on the stick! In the meantime, Riker, owner of Riker Electric Motor Company, absorbed in 1900 by Whitney, Widener, Pope and Co., walked away with $2,000,000 in stock.[19] The price of these negotiations to Morris and Salom is that they disappear from the transportation scene in what became the largest business of all time. Riker, subsequently licensing his gasoline powered trucks, departed from electric vehicles.[20] Whitney and Widener had sufficient other interests that they not only survived, but built up large American fortunes. The Editor of *The Horseless Age* chronicles, but is concerned:[21]

> "The Electric Carriage & Wagon Co., which has been operating the electrical cabs in New York, has been merged into the Electrical Vehicle Company of New Jersey, having an authorized capital of $10,000,000, of which $5,000,000 is common and $5,000,000 preferred stock. The incorporators are Gustave Kissel, of Kessler & Co., bankers of Wall Street; Philip Leman and Edward Tuck. The company will put over 100 additional cabs in service."

The above news indicated that Morris and Salom sold The Electric Carriage & Wagon Company to a rather remarkable and astute promoter by the name of Isaac L. Rice. On taking possession of his purchase, Rice reorganized it under the name of the Electric Vehicle Company. Its assets consisted of 13 Morris & Salom taxis, produced in nearby Philadelphia. An opportunist, and ever intrepid, in the Great Blizzard of 1898 with all horse-drawn traffic in New York City unable to operate and off the street, Rice received permission to operate his electric taxis on the then cleared sidewalks. It was an invaluable piece of publicity. By the end of the year he had 200 taxis. With smart growth this company attracted the attention of William C. Whitney and P. A. B. Widener, whose Metropolitan Traction Company was already a substantial shareholder in the Electric Storage Battery Company. These executives bought control of the Electric Vehicle Company from Rice who profited handsomely. Elated with success and visualizing, the new management spoke of 12,000 electric taxis serving the principal American cities. The only producer for that quantity would be the Pope Manufacturing Company in Hartford, Connecticut, operated by Colonel Albert A. Pope. Whitney and Widener gave Pope an initial order for 200 taxis, and later increased the purchase to 1,600. With such heady numbers, and being approached by the above partners, Colonel Pope had the electric

---

[19] Eugene W. Lewis, *Motor Memories*, Alved, Detroit, 1947.
[20] *The Scientific American*, Vol. CXIX, No. 5, August 3, 1918, p. 99.
[21] *The Horseless Age*, Vol. 2, No. 11, September 1897, p. 2.

Figure 4.7. Morris & Salom first commercialized the electric vehicle by establishing a taxi service in New York City in 1896. Under Isaac L. Rice the firm was The Electric Vehicle Company. In 1897 William C. Whitney and P.A.B. Widener incorporated the taxi operation into the Lead Trust along with Pope's vehicle division, and later the Riker Electric Motor Company. The overcapitalized company's bubble began deflating with the liquidation of its subsidiary, the Illinois Lead Cab Company in 1901, and the shares became almost worthless with the subsequent invalidation of the Selden patent. Courtesy: Scientific American.

vehicle division of his company merge with the Electric Vehicle Company through a one step intermediary.[22] Figure 4.7 shows the New York facilities of the Company in 1899.[23]

Before continuing, respect must be accorded entrepreneur Isaac L. Rice. While a flamboyant character, he had vision. He foresaw electric-powered land transportation, and, indeed, electric-powered underwater boats. For Rice was also instrumental in establishing The Electric Boat Company at Groton, Connecticut. This organization, as is known, is now one of the largest submarine building companies in the world, and is a salient factor in the military strength of America. By their similar and general names, The Electric Vehicle Company and The Electric Boat Company, Rice was seen to have surprising perspicacity when viewed from the vantage point of nearly a century.

Notes

The Lead Trust

The Lead Trust was an attempt by New York City financiers to link the following into a single holding corporation: electric street railways franchise holders, lead-acid battery manufactures, electric vehicle companies, taxi companies, and later the Selden patent on the automobile, into a quasi-monopoly. Its purpose was to control rights in order to maximize profit to a small group of inside shareholders. Conceived towards the end of the 19th century the idea was a child of the Trust Era. Oil was largely monopolized by the Rockefeller interest; J. P. Morgan had merged The Carnegie Steel Company, The Frick Coal Company, and the Mesabi Iron Company into the U.S. Steel Corporation. There was also the Sugar Trust, the Beef Trust, the Cement Trust, as well as others. These trusts would be the political windmill against which President Theodore Roosevelt would tilt in his term of office, 1901-1909.

The financial brains of the Lead Trust were P. A. B. Widener and William C. Whitney, both of New York City. Conceivers of trusts were generally far seeing and shrewd personalities. Widener and Whitney, earlier than most, foresaw the importance of electricity to growing cities, the advantages of electric street railway franchises, the electric automobile as taxis, lead-acid battery manufactures, and later, with growth of the gasoline-powered automobile industry, the Selden patent. Using the financial services of the money markets as well as their own fortunes the two formed a corporation which bought the Electric Storage Battery Company in Philadelphia, hence the name: the Lead Trust. Meanwhile, on November 1, 1896, Henry G. Morris and Pedro G. Salom introduced electric taxis on the streets of New York. Writing an optimistic financial report on their New York operation to *The Horseless Age*, the account caught the attention of a promoter by the name of Isaac L. Rice, who bought Morris and Salom's franchise and company.

Accreting city electric railway franchisees, Widener and Whitney witnessed the apparent success of Isaac Rice's in The Electric Vehicle Company taxi company operating in New York City. Buying Rice's New York City franchise, his taxi company, and expanding it (for they

---

[22] *Illinois Lead Company in Liquidation*, The Horseless Age, Vol. 7, No. 24, March 13, 1901, p. 14.

[23] *New York Battery Charging House*, Scientific American, Vol. LXXX, No. 12, March 25, 1899, p. 184.

foresaw electric taxi companies in other major cities), Widener and Whitney placed an order first for 200, then a following order for 1600 taxis on Colonel Albert A. Pope's Pope Manufacturing Company in Hartford, Connecticut. With such a sudden influx of business Pope contracted for vehicle chassis from the Studebaker Company in South Bend, Indiana, the country's largest maker of wagons. Pope's large chassis order awakened the entrepreneurial juices of the five Studebaker brothers, so they, too (but later), started offering electric cars. Influenced by large orders and with blandishments Pope's heretofore conservative and wise management took flight. He merged his company, through an intermediary enterprise, into Widener and Whitney's Lead Trust. With this development Hiram Percy Maxim, Pope's MIT trained chief engineer, not agreeing to the trend of Pope's company, resigned. Maxim was the life blood of Pope's company. So, too, did the Riker Electric Motor Company merge into the Trust, and Andrew L. Riker, the owner, walked away with $2 million in stock of the Lead Trust.

Seeing the emerging growth of the internal combustion engine vehicle manufacture, apparent to many after 1902, the Lead Trust purchased the Selden patents. This sweeping patent on internal combustion engine driven automobiles was granted November 5, 1895. The patent had been owned by George B. Selden, a shrewd patent attorney. Each gasoline-powered car maker to market vehicles was obliged to secure a license under the Selden Patent. Even such an iron individual as Alexander Winton,[24] the man who introduced Rudolph Diesel's high compression heat-engine into America (and subsequent maker of the Winton motorcar, the first automobile to be driven across America) was a licensee.

Apparently Whitney and Widener felt quite satisfied with the Trust they had built. To increase their personal fortunes they now floated a stock offering of $10 million through Kessler & Co., a Wall Street banking firm. With this offering E.P. Ingersoll, Editor and Proprietor of *The Horseless Age*, grew suspicious of Widener and Whitney's motives. His comments appeared in the September 1897 issue.

In 1902 Henry Ford initiated the Ford Motor Company. Ford, offered a Selden patent license, refused to buy. The Lead Trust sued Ford. Fighting a lengthy court battle Ford eventually won, freeing the robust growing automobile industry of this legal shackle. The court held the Selden patent was only valid for automobile engines using the Brayton principle or two-stroke engine, and lacked validity for the Otto principle of four-stroke engine, the engine adopted (and still used) by the automobile industry.

With gasoline-powered car manufacturing growing rapidly, while the electric vehicle building languished, with a stroke of the Judge's pen, the chief asset of the Lead Trust was found almost worthless. As earlier implied by Editor Ingersoll, the shares of the Lead Trust collapsed. Widener and Whitney escaped with their fortune largely intact, but the other shareholders suffered substantial losses. The Lambs had once again been sheared.

---

[24] Alexander Winton was a close friend of the author's father. Frederick William Wakefield became Commodore of the Lakewood Yacht Club (now the Cleveland Yachting Club) in 1905, Winton in 1907.

CHAPTER 5

The Horseless Carriage in America, 1890-1900, Part II

While Morris and Salom were the earliest entrepreneurs in the application of the electric vehicles, other innovators, with a different philosophy, would offer electric carriages both for taxi use and for sale to individuals and to companies. The American Electric Vehicle Company in Chicago and the Riker Electric Motor Company in Brooklyn were two of the leading contenders.

The Woods Electric Vehicles

Inasmuch as Whitney and Widener & Company were negotiating with Colonel Pope, what were other electric vehicle organizations doing both here and abroad? At this time, as can be seen from the wood-spoked wheels, a period identification emblem, the American Electric Vehicle Company was active under the direction of Clinton E. Woods of Chicago.[1] Figures 5.1 and 5.2 show two of Woods' vehicles. His were of one and two motor drive. Woods was one of those rare individuals, a successful entrepreneurial engineer who was sufficiently articulate to lastingly record the operation of electric vehicles of this period.[2] One of Woods' well-designed carriages was the first automobile purchased by the U.S. War Department, in 1899. As the Department stated, "The automobiles were provided for ordinary horse transportation where they serve to furnish electric power in the field for use of telegraphy, telephony, special lights, etc., while, when circumstances permit, the same power is available for transportation itself."[3]

Almost surely electric vehicles of Woods' manufacture would have been in the first American automobile parade held in Newport, Rhode Island on September 7, 1899.[4] Society leaders of Boston, New York, and Philadelphia participated. A prize was awarded Mrs. Herman Oelrichs, whose automobile was overhung with wisteria. Upon the "forward section a flock of pure white doves was seen which appeared to be drawing the carriage."

---

[1] U.S. Patent 590,710 by Clinton E. Woods, Chicago, assignor to the American Electric Vehicle Company, filed May 8, 1896.

[2] C. E. Woods, *The Electric Vehicle: Its Construction, Care and Operation*, New York: H. S. Stone & Co., 1900, 177 pp.

[3] Joseph Nathan Kane, *Famous First Facts*, New York: H. W. Wilson, 1964, p. 54.

[4] *Ibid*, p. 58.

Woods' brougham, landau, and trap were designed to carry 2-4 persons.[5] The former was equipped with 24 batteries each weighing 28 pounds. These energy sources powered two 900-watt motors each weighing 75 pounds. The battery for the landau was more generous, as were the motors. The trap, on the other hand, had 20 cells each weighing 22 pounds, supplying power to one 1500-watt motor. The above gives some indication of the flexibility of electric power.

Woods early gravitated from iron-tired wheels to hard rubber tires, shown on his *hansom* cab, Fig. 5.1, an 1898 model.[6] This vehicle had two motors providing 6 1/2 hp with sufficient battery capacity to yield a range of 30 miles. Electric lights were in the side lanterns, and the interior of the coach also had electric lights and even electric foot warmers.[7] The total weight of the hansom was 2600 pounds. Figure 5.2 shows an admirable two-seated trap with accommodations for four persons. It has wire-spoked wheels and pneumatic tires, again a design of 1898.

Figure 5.1. A Two-motor Victoria Hansom Cab Assembled by The American Electric Vehicle Company. Scientific American.

---

[5] *The Horseless Age*, Vol. 1, No. 3, January 1896, pp. 25-28.
[6] *The Scientific American*, Vol. LXXX, No. 19, May 13, 1899, p. 294.
[7] Presently the heating of an electric vehicle is still a problem. - Author

Figure 5.2. A Two-motor Trap by the same company of later vintage (as noted by the wire-spoked wheels). Scientific American.

Besides the broughams, landaus, hansoms, and traps already cited, The American Electric Vehicle Company built dos-a-dos, victorias, road wagons, and stanhopes, all of which are illustrated in his remarkable volume published in 1900.[8] All bear wagon-style wheels and are equipped with pneumatic tires indicating as a group they are vintage 1897. With Woods' design, pneumatic tires appear on his vehicles only toward the end of 1897. Another dating method for Woods' vehicles is the publication of his book. The date was 1900. His photographs could easily be two years old while the book was in preparation.[9] While Woods was a first rate engineer, he appears never to have been as advanced a vehicle designer as was Riker. Riker's first vehicle was at least four years earlier than was Woods'. In addition, Riker did his design and manufacturing in the East. Detroit, at the time, was known as much as anything for its manufacture of marine engines. The more sophisticated manufacturing appears to have been in the East in the 1890s. That factor may have been telling with Woods.

---

[8] Woods, *The Electric Vehicle*.
[9] The book you are reading was more than fifteen years from inception to publication date. The scientific press was simply not interested in publishing the history of electric vehicles until the major automobile companies indicated they would issue electric cars.

Other electric vehicle makers in the late 1890s were making wood-spoked wheel electric cars. In 1896 Montgomery Ward & Company had two electric carriages, one of which is shown in Fig. 5.3.[10] [11] This brake, considered an elegant specimen of the carriage builders' art, was equipped with two 2 hp, single reduction motors, each with rawhide pinion engaging the axle gear inside the rear wheel. Top speed was given as 14 mph. This *brake* was made by the American Electric Vehicle Company, and the batteries were from the Syracuse Electric Battery Company, Syracuse, New York.

Chas. A. Stevens & Bros. Company, like Wards, a Chicago merchant house, used the Woods vehicles in sales assist programs as shown in Fig. 5.4. As the decade neared its close, Saks and Company Department Stores, Anheuser Busch Brewing Company and others had

Figure 5.3. Montgomery Ward & Co. procured an electric Brake from The American Electric Vehicle Co. in 1896. The large wagon-type wheels bear hard tires. Scientific American.

---

[10] *The Horseless Age*, Vol. 1, No. 10, August 1896, p. 9.

[11] *Ibid.*, Vol. 1, No. 11, September 1896, p. 10.

Figure 5.4. An 1897 Delivery Wagon from The American Electric Vehicle Co. This vehicle has 88 volts of 100 ampere-hour batteries weighing some 572 pounds powering a 3 1/2 hp 4-pole motor. The wheels bear on ball-bearing axles and have three-inch pneumatic tires. "With receipt of two electric vehicles, Stevens & Bros. (of Chicago) have ordered an additional four." The Horseless Age, Vol. 2, No. 10, Aug. 1897, pp. 7-8.

fleets of electric delivery wagons, the latter with as many as fifty for beer transit. For enhancement of range the interchange of batteries was practiced. In 1899 the Woods' company had an authorized capital of $10 million, a figure which gives some indication of the size of his enterprise.[12]

Riker Electric Vehicles

From the record it appears A.L. Riker was the best electric car designer in America in 1897. He early noted the importance of weight in electric automobile design and, as a result, fabricated his own electric motors. He made the fastest electric vehicles for track racing. He early

---

[12] *The Automobile Industry, Scientific American*, Vol. LXXXI, No. 2, July 8, 1899, p. 19.

appreciated the value of the wire-spoked wheel. He built 4-wheeled vehicles which were steered by the front wheels. He applied the pneumatic tire to electric cars as soon as Colonel Pope had made them available, the first in America.[13] Riker's electric vehicles were designed to follow what became the most successful road to progress.

As 1897 was closing, a date which brings to an end this chapter, Riker's Victoria, seen in Fig. 5.5, was one of this engineer's last electric motorcars, for his company would be merged into The Electric Vehicle Company just as had the Pope Manufacturing Company electric car division, the whole a contrivance of the "lead trust." Curb weight of the *Victoria* was 1700 pounds.[14] The frame was of 1 1/2-inch steel-tubing, designating the vehicle's bicycle origin.

Figure 5.5. A Single-motor Riker Electric Victoria. The vehicle is an example of the greater use of wire-spoked wheels and the application of pneumatic tires in the better designs of 1897. The Horseless Age.

---

[13] Kane, *Famous First Facts*. Through his subsidiary of the Pope Manufacturing Company, the Hartford Rubber Works in Hartford, Connecticut, Pope built on the early work of Charles Goodyear who pioneered the vulcanization of rubber in Hartford.

[14] *The Horseless Age*, Vol. 2, No. 11, September 1897, pp. 7-8.

The front wheels had a diameter of 28 inches, the rear wheels stood 32 inches. Tires were Hartford pneumatic. Steering was by pivot. Batteries were forty Willard cells weighing 800 pounds with a capacity of 100 ampere-hours at a 5-hour discharge rate. The controller handle appears between the two passengers. The 1 1/2-kilowatt motor weighed 142 pounds and was geared to the axle in a ratio of 9 to 1. Riker reported his *Victoria* logged 600 miles in New York City at an electric energy cost of $10.35 (1.7 cents a mile) "computed at regular Edison rates."[15] Riker was moving ahead. In September 1897 his company was building four traps, three doctor's buggies, two delivery wagons, and one brougham.[16] The trap and delivery wagon are shown respectively in Figs. 5.6 and 5.7, while Fig. 5.8 illustrates the Riker Demi-Coach of 1899

Figure 5.6. This Riker two-passenger trap of 1897 has economy in design. Steering is by hand. Shown on the floor is the brake pedal. The "emergency brake" is the inside vertical bar. The outer handle on the left achieves voltage switching of the batteries. This control serves to protect the motor from excessive current on start, as well as to control speed and to provide a reverse.

---

[15] If electric energy were fourteen cents a kilowatt-hour, Riker's Victoria was consuming 120 watt-hours per mile in city driving. If ten cents, 170 watt-hours per mile. Present day electric vans in city driving consume 400 to 500 watt-hours per mile.

[16] *The Horseless Age*, Vol. 2, No. 12, October 1897, pp. 5-6.

Figure 5.7. By the wood-spoked wheels and the hard rubber tires, the Riker delivery wagon is more primitive than the trap above. Riker's best and latest designs were always his carriages. Woods' delivery wagon of 1897 is similar to Riker's.

which heralds the coming enclosed touring automobile. The Riker Electric Motor Company was growing. In 1899 its authorized capital was seven million dollars.[17] While Riker was straightforward in electrical design, electricity allows greater versatility in resolving a problem than does a mechanical solution alone. Harry P. Dey and a Mr. Griswold would utilize both techniques and bring forth a unique electric vehicle.

The Dey-Griswold Electric Vehicle

With Dey, a later associate of Dr. Charles P. Steinmetz who became one of America's great theoretical engineers, a new theme was to enter the arena of electric vehicle drive systems, quite

---

[17] *The Automobile Industry.*

Figure 5.8. A Riker Demi-Coach of 1899. With a curb weight of 4200 pounds, powered by two 2-kW motors driving rear wheels, equipped with hard rubber tires on artillery-style wheels, the vehicle presages the coming enclosed touring automobile. Scientific American, Vol. LXXXI, No. 16, 14 October 1899, p. 244.

apart from an electric motor providing torque to the driving wheels of a carriage. Dey of Dey-Griswold Company of New York suggested as a drive system an early example of fluid drive. As explained in the motor magazine of the time.[18]

"A single electric motor is used, the armature and field of which both revolve. On the shaft of each is placed a pump having four cylinders arranged radially (see Fig. 5.9). The pistons are single acting, and all four are attached in the same place to one crank-pin, by adjustable rings AA (Fig. 5.10). This crank pin is adjustable, while in motion, moving 3/4 of an inch either side of the center, giving a maximum stroke of 1 1/2 inches, and a variable pumping capacity from zero to maximum, in either direction, without steps or reversing valves.

---

[18] The Horseless Carriage.

Figure 5.9. Dey Devised the First Fluid-drive Vehicle. The Horseless Age.

"On the rear axle is placed what is known as the gear-type of fluid motors. Two are used, one at each wheel, and piped separately to their respective pumps, allowing each wheel to revolve independent of the other. The pumps, pipes and fluid motors are filled with oil. It is evident that when the pumps are operated they will force the oil through the pipes, to the motors, and pressing against the teeth, will turn the wheels. The greater the stroke, and hence the capacity of the pumps, the faster the speed of the carriage will be. The axle motors will in turn act as pumps, and drive the pumps themselves as fluid motors, and the electric motors as a dynamo, and thus charge the batteries whenever mechanical power is applied to the wheels, as on descending hills, etc. (See Fig. 5.11)."

In his fluid-drive system Dey obviated the concept of voltage switching for speed control, possessing continuous control rather than step control. He also required no differential. In addition, he appears to have been the first to rotate both the armature and the field. Like many complex ideas, the followers of Dey's revolutionary principle were tiny in number. Fluid-drive would be important at a later time and in a different context. Dey had shown the way for a new generation to operate in a different field. The new style motor Dey would retain, as a later section will indicate.

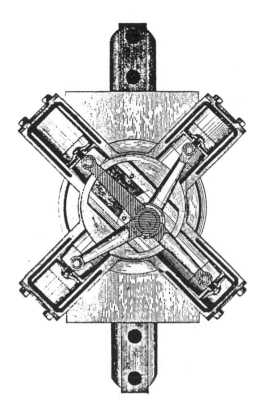

Figure 5.10. The crank-pin of the pump can be continually adjusted, thus allowing continuous speed control. The Horseless Age.

Edison's and Eastman's Three-Wheelers

Before the three-wheeled automobile would 'wink-out' Thomas Edison and H. F. Eastman, the latter in Cleveland, would each construct a three-wheel vehicle, the former as a test-bed for his nickel-alkaline battery. Figure 5.12 shows an older Mr. Edison sitting in his vehicle after it had been acquired by the Henry Ford Museum in Greenfield Village.[19] Note should be made of the rear steering wheel of Edison's three-wheeler. Rear steering is rare on electric vehicles, found only on the first one of Gustave Trouvé, 1881, the second electric vehicle by Professors Ayrton and Perry, both of which were described above, closing with the New York taxis by entrepreneurs Morris and Salom, seen below. Thereafter front-wheel steering becomes universal with the automobile as it advances.

Figure 5.13 illustrates the Eastman Electro-cycle.[20] This vehicle, built in 1899 and coming later than Mr. Barrows', cited above, is more advanced. The rear drive, suitably linked to the rear driving wheels, avoids Barrows' friction contact between the drive pulley of the motor and the rubber tire, a linkage also found on Riker's first three-wheeler. The Electro-cycle was

---

[19] Milo Lindgren, *Electric Car - Hope Springs Eternal, IEEE Spectrum*, April 1967, pp. 48-59.
[20] *The Eastman Electro-cycle, Scientific American*, Vol. LXXXI, No. 4, July 22, 1899, p. 52. See also *Motor Memories*, p. 48.

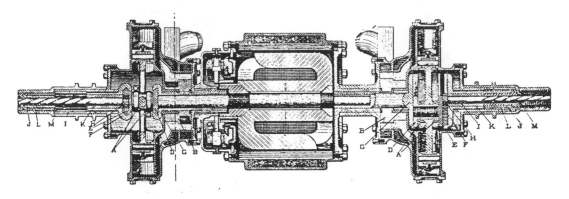

Figure 5.11. Shown is the transverse section of electric motor and pump. The Horseless Age.

Figure 5.12. Circa 1895 Thomas Edison used this three-wheeled vehicle to develop a new type of battery. "From the Collections of Henry Ford Museum and Greenfield Village P.B. 32967" (Mandatory Request).

Figure 5.13. The Eastman Electro-Cycle. Scientific American.

framed with steel tubing bearing side panels of sheet steel. The battery and motor was said to weigh more than three-quarters of the curb weight. A high ratio of battery to vehicle weight is desirable in lead-acid battery vehicle design. Ostensibly speed control of the tricycle was by voltage switching, for there were three forward speeds, and one speed for reverse, a typical combination at this time. The Electro-cycle was a well turned-out vehicle appearing suitable for controlled communities even today, four generations later.

The Electro-cycle, probably built in a shed, is so typical of the entrepreneurial spirit which, as one reads this book, is found so generously in western nations at the end of Queen Victoria's reign.

With 1897 becoming history, this chapter is brought to a close. The motivation for finding an alternate to the horse for personal transportation had been so great that only ten years were to elapse from the perfection of the electric motor to an electrically-powered personal conveyance in 1881.[21] Legislation in England, as cited above, stifled this invention at birth, for immediately on its operation, legal minds reasoned the electric car was subject to the "Red Flag" law.

In a sense electric transportation for the individual had to be re-invented in a freer America, and an electric vehicle appeared in 1890. This first conveyance was crude. It was a three-wheeled approach, just as Trouvé's, Ayrton and Perry's had been three-wheeled cycles. But

---

[21] Zénobe Théophile Gramme's electric motor of 1870 is considered the first of the electric motors capable of delivering over one kilowatt of power.

with the engineering abilities of Morris and Salom, then Riker, the American electric carriage, in 1897, for in-city driving, was considered more acceptable by some than either the gasoline- or steam-powered car. Rivalry of the three aided the rapid progress of each. The lead-acid battery-powered vehicles, in the smaller cities of the era, provided an acceptable, if limited, range. As the first cost of an electric carriage was some two and one-half times the initial cost of a comparable horsedrawn victoria or stanhope, personal transportation at $3,000 for an electric car was only for the affluent, as, indeed, was the horse-drawn conveyance in urban use.

By 1897, however, the influence of the automobile was of sufficient importance that the market price of draft animals was depressed. Horses which formerly were fifty dollars each could be had for two and three dollars a head. One band of 1,100 grazing in Oregon was bought for $2,000 due to the influence of the automobile, the bicycle, and the cable and electric railroads.[22] In short, the beast was having his burden lifted as was man. Mechanical power, whether electric, steam, or petroleum fueled would increasingly relieve the sweating work of man and animal.

As the next chapter will outline, the European scene was little different from the American experience, except for one situation. The presence of many good interurban roads between European cities, and their lack in America, biased the scales toward the longer range internal combustion engine car. But champions of the electric automobile were inventive there as well. As in America scions of wealth provided an impetus for employing the motor car. In personal transportation the gentry was to run interference for the common man until the vehicles were improved and the concept of mass production brought forth the people's car. As is known, it would not be electric.

---

[22] *Illustrated Electrical Review*, Vol. 26, No. 26, June 26, 1895, p. 351.

CHAPTER 6

English Electric Carriages to 1900

In comparing the European and the American development of the electric car, as one retrospects this period of nearly a century ago, there emerges a uniform increase in vehicle sophistication. England and France, considered together, did neither better nor worse than did America alone. The populations of the two countries together were about equal to America itself at the turn of the century.[1] In developed nations new ideas, it appears, are only as numerous as is the total population.[2]

In the United States until 1900, electrically powered vehicles probably had a relative advantage over the internal combustion engine car because of the prevalence of hard surfaced roads in the cities and their lack in the country. Urban areas were small, and range of a vehicle, if 30 miles, was not an overwhelming disadvantage. England and France, on the other hand, with an older culture, had principal cities linked by all-weather roads, some of which dated back to Roman times. There the gasoline-powered car earlier grasped leadership. Such highways promoted the concept of tourism, an activity that required substantial range. France, having a more mature self-propelled vehicle industry than did England, until about 1905, led the world in motorcar exports. At about this time the greater reliance placed on interchangeability of parts by American motor car companies, together with the lower cost offered by these manufacturers, caused America to assume a leadership which it held for many decades.

Germany as a nation was not as advanced as either France or England in exploiting the motorcar. It has been said that the affluent in the land of the Kaiser were more interested in the appreciation of horses. In any event, in the period cited there was a dearth of interest in electric vehicles in Germany. And experimentalists in Italy were feeling their way.

In innovations the standing between the Old World and the New would score as follows: First electric vehicle, France, quickly followed by England. First four-wheel electric vehicle, England. First electric multi-powered car, Italy, in 1894. First conventional differential, America. First, with largest number of electric cars, America, with 33,384 in 1912. First in battery development, Europe. In a series of steps starting with Alessandro Volta's pile in 1800,

---

[1] The 1902 World Almanac gives populations for Great Britain, France, and United States respectfully: 41,400,000; 38,641,000; and 76,295,000.

[2] Nobel Laureate Glen T. Seaborg described this truism during the First International Atomic Energy Conference in Geneva in 1955 when the American and Russian Table of Isotopes were compared for their neutron capture cross-section. The figures for the two countries were virtually the same, and both nations had a population of about 200 million. Private communication.

to the turn of the century, the prime electric battery development applicable to electric cars was European. A chemical and mechanical problem, Europe had a more sophisticated chemical industry than America. In controls of electric motors, all three countries employed voltage switching. In design of electric motors each country was essentially equal.[3]

With the above comparisons, an examination of English electric car development is in order.

In reading the technical reports of the day, The International Exhibition of Electricity held in Paris in August 1881 was seen to have had a telegraphic effect on electrical transportation. Almost surely Professors Ayrton and Perry from London had attended this exhibit. It is also believed Gustave Phillipart made the necessary English Channel crossing, for he and Magnus Volk, as early as September 28, 1882 (one year after the close of the Paris Fair), had an electrically-powered twenty-six foot launch operating, which reportedly cruised at eight knots on the Thames River.[4] While these designers may have known of Jacobi's 1838 experiments with an electrically-powered craft paddle-wheeling on the Neva River in St. Petersburg, Russia, Trouvé's electric powered skiff of 1881, earlier cited, was prominently located and operated in a lake which was a central feature of the Exhibition.

The Ward Electric Omnibus

While Ayrton and Perry's electric tricycle was operating in 1882, and Benz's internal combustion engine-powered tricycle was running in 1885, in 1882 Phillipart, turning his attention to land transportation, had an electric tram-car built in Belgium, shipped to England, to be experimented on in London. There it was in the hands of Radcliffe Ward. These experiments were terminated because of imperfect commercial batteries. In 1887 Ward assembled an electric cab which ran on the streets of Brighton, England, "and it was about this time that Magnus Volk also built his electric Dog Cart...and (this) excited the attention of the Sultan of Turkey for whom Volk had recently constructed a similar vehicle."[5] Ward then built for operation on the London streets an omnibus illustrated in Fig. 6.1.

In this lorry the driver stood in front. Steering was by means of a worm gear, and the brake was foot-operated.[5] Power for the electric motor was from batteries contained in a tray under the seats. On a good macadam road the vehicle had a top speed of seven mph. Ward's omnibus was powered by two Gramme-type electric motors built by Crompton & Company Ltd. These motors were chain-linked to sprocket gears on the wheels of the omnibus. Using Faure accumulators, the lead plates of Planté having been coated with lead-oxide, Ward's omnibus had a striking resemblance to the tram-cars of the day. This electric vehicle appears to have been the first electric bus, operating in 1888. Even at this early date the electric vehicles were recognized as being less destructive of the roadway than were the hooves of horses, and freedom of animal droppings was also seen as a positive feature.[6] Anyone unacquainted with large animals has little appreciation for the magnitude of this earthy problem. "To carry out the

---

[3] The validity of these statements will be exhibited in Chapter 11.

[4] *The Electrician*, Vol. 1, No. 11, November 1882, p. 256.

[5] *Scientific American Supplement*, Vol. XXVII, No. 687, March 2, 1889, pp. 10969-70.

[6] To supply the needs of commerce in New York City in 1900 required an estimated 300,000 horses. While the reader read this page those animals dropped 10,000 pounds of manure in the streets or stables.

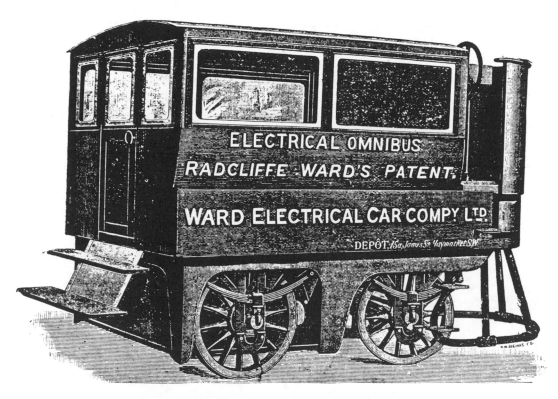

Figure 6.1. Radcliffe Ward's Omnibus in London - 1889. As early as 1882 Ward was experimenting with an electric tram car on tracks, but the red lead applied to the lead plates was so friable that with vibration, would lose its grip, fall to the bottom of the battery container, electrically shorting the positive and negative plates. This fault would be minimized by Swan punching holes in the plates providing a better purchase for the red lead.

commercial development of Mr. Radcliffe Ward," a journal of the day wrote,[7] "the London Electric Omnibus Company was founded with a capital of £250,000 to purchase the Ward Electric Company." It was a case of the inventor receiving a just reward.

From a small pool of innovators, the Channel city of Brighton, due south of London, was for a time England's brightest jewel in personal electric transportation. A popular seaside resort, it had early gained distinction as a mecca for the Prince Regent and his friends. The Prince later became Edward VII.

Volk's Electric Dog Cart for the Sultan

Volk's three-wheeled electric Dog Cart, which titillated the Sultan of Turkey, was tested in the summer of 1887. It is illustrated in Fig. 6.2.[8] Volk had gained experience with electric trams

---

[7] *The Electrical Review*, Vol. 38, No. 967, June 5, 1896, p. 718.

[8] *Scientific American*, Vol. LVIII, No. 6, February 11, 1888, p. 82.

as an employee of the Brighton Electric Railway. Seeking a vehicle for individual use he borrowed the design of an English 3-wheel Dog Cart. In the fox hunting areas of England these vehicles were used to transport fox hounds to the area of interest. This early electric carriage was built by Monsieur Pack, a local coach builder. The 16 batteries were conveniently placed in the dog kennel. The 1/2-hp Immisch motor weighing some 40 pounds was slung beneath the batteries. The motor pinion was linked to a counter shaft with a Renold's steel chain. A gear on the distal end of the counter shaft was chain-connected to the interior of the rear driving wheel, the bearing surface being a series of wooden blocks simulating a gear.

Volk, like Michelin in Paris with his precise traction experiments, discussed later, sought information on road resistance qualities. Asphalt, he found, was a better surface than grooved rail, and a soft macadam road gave less road friction than either, allowing the battery powered dog cart to reach a speed of 4 mph. And testing the vehicle on a grade of 1 to 30 he found, even with two people, the machine would continue to go forward.

Figure 6.2. Magnus Volk's Electric Dog Cart of 1887. Notice the substantial gear reduction always desirable with the high rotational speed of the electric motor. In the dog cart the pinion on the motor links by chain to the intermediate gear. Not shown on the other side of the vehicle, another pinion gear is chain connected to the large circumference of the wheel's rim. For the same horsepower, the size of an electric motor is inversely as the speed of rotation, to a first approximation. The greater the speed, the smaller, and lighter the motor. Courtesy: Scientific American.

While Volk's carriage was underpowered when compared with Professors Ayrton and Perry's earlier electric tricycle, the employment of a balance shaft permitted greater flexibility in speed gearing. The drive gear on the rim of the right rear wheel would be less costly as well. Using the numbers given in the article, the vehicle's batteries would yield about six kilowatt-hours. In 1888 the batteries would have had a weight of some 600 pounds, the total carriage weighing from 1000 to 1200 pounds. Whether the Sultan received one dog cart or several, two conveyances were apparently made for him as the next article indicates, and, as imagined, each vehicle had its own unique design.

An 1888 English electric carriage is carefully illustrated in Fig. 6.3 to show the electric drive system and the steering mechanism. The Sultan having been intrigued with Volk's Dog Cart, the actual delivered vehicle had some modifications:[9] the number of wheels was increased to four, the Immisch motor installed was a more powerful 1 hp supplied with a more intense 48 volts. The pinion of the motor was linked directly to the rear drive-wheel by chain, again riding on wooden blocks bolted to the wheel's inside rim. Steering, too, was modified from a hand tiller to a mechanical wheel whose shaft on the distal end gear linked a quadrant gear that solidly engaged the forward axle. The friction brake, by foot action, braced the rear wheel. Total weight of the Sultan's Dog Cart was given as 1100 pounds, 70 percent of which represented the mass of the batteries. With these modifications the vehicle had a speed of 10 mph.

While the ratio of the pinion gear to the wheel gear is not given, the cut indicates that the ratio is large. The link slack and friction in the long chain and the high ratio would mitigate the need for a current controller. The burned out armature, which unfortunately and frequently occurred on Morrison's American surrey, would less likely occur on this Dog Cart. The vehicle, as described, however, would have only one speed, 10 mph, as given. Ayrton and Perry in 1882 had utilized voltage switching to control speed. If the Sultan's Dog Cart omitted this convenience, the design is retrogressive. The general vehicle, though, did show improvement over earlier design. Interesting is the high ratio of battery weight to curb weight of the vehicle, which is desirable, 7 to 11, or a ratio of 63 percent. From the weight of the battery one might expect it to contain some 7 kilowatt-hours of energy, giving a probable 25-mile range of the vehicle on hard roads, a distance greater than possible with a horse and carriage. So the Sultan's Dog Cart had merit. Conveyances for royalty always had a high priority, and an electric tricycle for the Queen, next discussed, showed improvement in design.

The Cummings Electric Surrey and One for Queen Victoria

Developed somewhat later than the Dog Cart for the Sultan of Turkey, but earlier than the carriage for the Queen of Spain, was the Surrey, developed by George K. Cummings in England. This vehicle, with 200 ampere-hour batteries utilizing a 24-volt system, carried about 4 to 5 kilowatt-hours of energy. The range of the vehicle would be somewhat limited, for it was reported to have used a rheostat to restrict the current to the motor. The motor was rated at 2 hp, and was linked from its pinion gear to a sprocket gear on the rear axle by a link-belt chain.

---

9 *Scientific American*, Vol. LIX, No. 14, October 6, 1888, p. 215.

Figure 6.3. The Sultan's electric Dog Cart of 1888 has the pinion of the motor linked by chain to wheel blocks on the wheel's rim. For cornering the left rear wheel must be independently free of the shaft. Tires are steel. Wheel and axle are greased-friction contact. The steering gear is well illustrated. A feature of nearly all early electric vehicle illustrations is the stress placed on the number of passengers to be carried. With curb weight of 1100 pounds, the 1 hp motor would give a speed of possibly 8-10 mph. As there is no voltage switching, only one speed was possible. The battery weighed 700 pounds and would contain some 7 kwh of energy. Courtesy: Scientific American.

Total weight of the vehicle was given as 1270 pounds, with a nominal speed of 10-12 mph.[10] From the description given, and no picture available, this surrey is not considered innovative, and is included for completeness.

A second vehicle to indicate the growing acceptance electric transportation was designed for Queen Victoria.[11] The Fulmen accumulators used by Charles Jeantaud, later cited, received wide recognition as a superior battery. This information was passed on to Prince Henry of

---

[10] *The Electrical Engineer*, Vol. XVII, No. 316, May 23, 1894, pp. 461-62.
[11] *The Electrical Review*, Vol. 38, No. 955, March 13, 1896, p. 354.

Battenberg, a name subsequently anglicized to Mountbatten at the beginning of World War I (see footnote 15). The Prince proceeded to order an electric chaisse for the Queen. The body of the carriage would be composed of aluminum and be of a tricycle type, each wheel equipped with Michelin tires.[12] It was specified that Fulmen accumulators must be used. As the date was early 1896, this vehicle, one could speculate, would be like the Dog Cart (shown in Fig. 6.2) designed by Magnus Volk.

While no picture for this vehicle is presently available, the Queen, having been born in 1819, was 67 years of age when the vehicle was ordered. From pictures of Her Highness, she became plump as her years increased.[13] It would appear that Prince Henry's tricycle, while ordered for the Queen, would more likely have been employed by more spry grandchildren or others in the household.

Regardless of who used the vehicle, however, the Queen's electric tricycle contained improvements over earlier models. As the body and chassis were to be of aluminum, a relatively new metal in 1896, the vehicle would be light in weight. Jeantaud, the French carriage maker, had already used aluminum in vehicles.[14] The application of Michelin pneumatic tires resulted from the reputation earned by the Michelin brothers using them on their vehicle in the Paris-Bordeaux-Paris race. And the Fulmen accumulator had a grid to allow the lead oxide to better adhere to the metal plate, a design improvement discussed in Chapter 10 on batteries. While not mentioned, as the year was 1896,[15] the vehicle would almost certainly possess speed control by voltage switching. Much more could be imagined, but lacking evidence to cite more would be speculation.

The prime reason for the ascendancy of the electric propelled over the gasoline-engined vehicle for royalty was the former's almost soundless operation. The engined-carriage, in contrast, was extremely noisy. Hiram Percy Maxim's mufflers were yet to be invented.

Two Notable Carriages

For the Queen of Spain, Thrupp & Maberly, 425 Oxford Street, London, built the electric vehicle shown in Fig. 6.4.[16] It was designed by G. Julien, a Spanish engineer. The Queen's victoria-type carriage, stated to be a beautiful example of the coachbuilder's art, had a fixed front axle on the ends of which cylinders of metal were pivoted. The wheel turned on these short pieces, a scheme not greatly unlike on present motorcars. For guidance both elements could be simultaneously positioned at a specific angle to the axle by means of the steering lever. Each rear wheel was linked by a chain from a pulley on a cross shaft, the shaft being provided with a differential.

---

[12] The Michelin pneumatic tire had shown its superiority over the then prevalent hard rubber tire in the Paris-Bordeaux-Paris race of 1895, so the Queen's tricycle was ordered after that race. See Chapter 12.

[13] Joanna Richardson, *Victoria and Albert*, Quadrangle, NYC, 1977.

[14] See the description of Jeantaud's 1896 carriage in Chapter 7.

[15] Prince Battenberg subsequently became the First Sea Lord. With the onset of the 1914 War he was forced to relinquish the post because of his German background. For Lord Mountbatten to become First Sea Lord in post World War II, the Royal Family, it is believed, felt a wrong had been righted.

[16] *The Horseless Age*, Vol. 1, No. 8, June 1896, p. 20.

Figure 6.4. The Queen of Spain's electric carriage of 1896 used a method of steering employed today. The wheel axles themselves pivot from a fixed forward shaft. Speed was given as 10 mph. The vehicle used a primary battery, that is: the plates themselves are chemically consumed in operation. The description implies the driver could replace a consumed plate, add fresh electrolyte, and proceed with a fresh "charge." Courtesy: The Horseless Age.

For power Julien employed a dry-battery stated to weigh only 200 pounds, yet provided sufficient energy to operate the carriage at 10 mph for 60 hours. Lighting had now come to carriages, one on each side of the driver, and one on the front of the dash. Electric filament lamps were used, Edison's and Swan's invention of 1879, with power derived from the traction battery. This victoria for the Queen of Spain was the fifth electric carriage built by the firm of Thrupp & Maberly.

While Engineer Julien appears to exaggerate the time the vehicle would run, it being a primary battery, the negative electrode was annihilated. Typically the consumed plate would be zinc, and the electrolyte might indeed be bichromate of potash as used by the brothers Tissandier in the batteries for their electrically powered balloon which the two brothers flew over Paris in 1883.[17] As the Queen of Spain's vehicle was built in 1896, a 200-pound battery, if of the secondary type,[18] would contain little more than 2 kilowatt-hours of electric energy. This supply would enable her carriage to have a range of 5 or 6 miles, which, within the Palace

---

[17] *Scientific American Supplement*, Vol. XVI, No. 416, Dec. 22, 1883, pp. 6631-34.

[18] An engineer, Edmund Julien, a "Belgian", in 1888 first added the element mercury to the antimony-lead alloy for the battery grid and almost doubled the specific energy of the battery by reducing the resistance of the grid. See Chapter 10.

grounds, or in going to church, might indeed be adequate. Surely with an electric vehicle and with the speed control of the day, the carriage would move silently and the embarrassment of a horse relieving itself would be solved, a perennial concern of wheelmen to royalty.

An early two-seated English electric carriage was one designed by Walter Bersey of 39 Victoria Street, Westminster, S. W., England.[19] Operating in 1896 the Bersey brake carried interchangeable primary dry batteries in a tray under the seats. Voltage switching of the batteries yielded two forward speeds of 4 and 9 mph, as well as a reverse. Range was said to be 35 miles obtained from two motors connected by means of a two-speed tooth-linked wheel-chain connected to each of the rear wheels in a manner similar to the scheme utilized in Volk's first Dog Cart. In this vehicle ball-bearings were used throughout, the first time such bearings were reported. A clutch was used to engage the gearing. The countershaft, bearing pinions, linking the rear wheels by endless chains, were universally jointed to compensate for action of the carriage springs, an indication of sometimes rough roads. Steering was by a worm gear which could be locked into position. Meanwhile a pointer indicated the angle of the front wheels.

In viewing the illustration of the Bersey carriage, Fig. 6.5, it should be compared to both the Holtzer-Cabot Brake, and the Riker Carriage entered in the Providence race. With the former, the Bersey vehicle was quite comparable. The battery interchange feature of the Bersey was surely attractive, a technique extensively practiced by Jeantaud in his remarkable competition in the Paris-Bordeaux-Paris race in 1895, and revived by Robert McKee et al of the USA in the Sundancer in 1972, a feature discussed in Chapter 21. This concept may have sufficient viability to be commonly practiced in modern electric vehicle battery replenishment. The Bersey carriage, however, had neither the sophistication nor the riding comfort of the Riker trap of the same date. For example, Bersey used the brake-block acting on the rim of the rear wheels; Riker employed a brake-band on a flywheel. Riker had uniformly sized wheels with wire spokes and pneumatic tires, the wheels being interchangeable and much lighter than were Bersey's.

The steering, too, of the Riker vehicle would make for a far more nimble carriage. But Riker in 1896 already had six years in designing electric vehicles. At this date he was almost surely America's best electric vehicle designer. Nevertheless, in England Bersey's effort was seen as important, for "The Universal Electric Company was registered with a capital of £5000 in September 1895 to acquire the patents of Mr. Bersey relating to electric carriages, but (the company) has now been purchased by the Great Horseless Carriage Company with capitalization of £750,000."[20]

With Bersey and others, England, after a slow start in electric vehicle design (due to the crippling "Red Flag" legislation [see Chapter 1]), moved rapidly ahead as is illustrated in the Dog Cart next discussed. It demonstrates a remarkable economy of effort.

The Bushburry Electric Dog Cart and London Cabs

In 1897 Magnus Volk, in England, built the Bushburry Electric Dog Cart, shown in Fig. 6.6.[21] Attractive today, it was so appealing to the Sultan of Turkey that he had Volk build one

[19] *The Horseless Age*, Vol. 1, No. 11, September 1896, p. 9-10.
[20] *The Electrical Review*, Vol. 38, No. 967, June 5, 1896, p. 718.
[21] *Scientific American Supplement*, No. 1122, July 3, 1897, p. 17935.

Figure 6.5. This 1896 Bersey-designed English carriage should be compared with the American-built Holtzer-Cabot brake of 1895 shown in Fig. 3-13. Courtesy: The Horseless Age.

for use in his palace grounds at Constantinople. If shipped, this transaction would probably represent the second export sale of an electric vehicle. The Bushburry Electric Dog Cart, designed during the period of the so-called "Red Flag" legislation of Parliament, was built by the Electric Construction Company. As the knowledgeable reader will observe from the quotation appearing at the time, this organization was competent in the electrical engineering design. The Bushburry was a 3-wheeled cart whose wheel-gauge was 4 ft. 6 in., with a wheelbase of 66 inches.[21] The rear driving wheels had a diameter of 39 in., while the steering wheel was of 45 inches. All three wheels bore hard rubber tires, and were ball-bearing equipped. Curb weight was 1350 pounds. In steering, reins were used passing through eyes at the end of handle-bars. A spring-loaded bolt enabled forward motion to continue without hand effort. Batteries were of the Faure-King lead-acid type with a total of 50 cells weighing 500 pounds. Their rated capacity was 40 ampere-hours at a discharge rate of 15 amperes, about 4 kilowatt-hours.

A two-pole, series-wound motor was linked by Renold chain to the sprocket wheel and then to the bevel-wheel differential. For speed control the batteries could be connected: off, two

---

[21] *Scientific American Supplement*, No. 1122, July 3, 1897, p. 17935.

Figure 6.6. Magnus Volk's Bushburry Electric Dog Cart - 1897. This vehicle has the appeal of simplicity and for the time has advanced design, slowing being electrically achieved by "dynamic braking." The dog cart had a top speed of 12 mph and a curb weight of 1350 pounds. A modern day similarly appearing vehicle would weigh in at about one-half as much, possessing similar range. Speed would be established by safety. But the vehicle could not obtain a license for general use. Courtesy: The Scientific American Supplement.

parallels of 20 cells in series, 40 cells in series, and 40 cells in series with a resistance in parallel with the magnets.[22] Braking of the Bushburry is both by a band, foot-operated, applied to a cast-iron drum on the motor axle, and by dynamic braking, wherein the motor is electrically closed on itself and the generated energy is dissipated in a resistance. This concept is called dynamic braking. Top speed of the vehicle was given as 12 mph, with a range of 20 miles. When the Dog Cart had a speed of 10 mph the motor had an efficiency of 80 percent, a current flow of 10 amperes at 80 volts, and was turning at 700 revolutions per minute. With a grade of 1 in 14, the vehicle climbed at a "walking speed." What an excellent vehicle for controlled areas.

Volk's Dog Cart, built a year later than Bersey's carriage, was more advanced. Like Riker, he had the drum brake. In addition, the tricycle could be braked by employing a principle known as "dynamic braking," widely used in fork-lift trucks today all over the world. The cord steering,

---

[22] Each operation would increase the speed.

familiar to horse-lovers as reins, does not match the braking system in sophistication. The wheels, while much lighter than Bersey's, had neither the riding comfort of Riker's, nor did the spokes uniformly stress a large arc of the rim as did the wire-spoked wheel. A reasonable guess as to the range of Volk's Dog Cart would be 20-25 miles on hard roads.

As electric vehicles were constantly being improved in England as in America, the entrepreneurial spirit in Britain asked, as in the United States, how could this alternate means of travel be exploited? Again, as in New York City, the application of the taxi was the answer.

The rescinding of the "Red Flag" Act which had been so restrictive of mechanical powered vehicles enabled the London Electrical Cab Company to be inaugurated. The time was 1897, just the period when Morris & Salom had established their electric taxi company in New York City. The number of these cabs in London was 15, and Gotham found itself with 13 in the summer of the same year. Where the Manhattan cabs were steered by their rear wheels, the London taxis were controlled by the forward wheels. Both fleets, however, used American built motors and controllers.

Figure 6.7 shows one of these yellow painted cabs. The interior had a single, cushioned seat for 2 1/2 persons.[23] The tires were solid rubber, and interior and exterior lights were electric, a plan followed by Morris & Salom in their New York taxis. The English cab had, naturally, right-hand steering operating a worm gear.

A Johnson-Lundell motor was used with unique electrical facilities. The fields had two similar windings, and the armatures also had two similar sets of windings and two commutators. This doubly-wound motor was connected to a series-parallel controller. The first step of the controller connected a small starting resistance, the two field windings and the two armature windings in series. "This is not a running speed, but is only intended to start the motors in motion." On the second step the windings are still in series, but the resistance is removed yielding a cab speed of 3 mph. In the third step the armatures were in parallel, but the field remained in series, giving a speed of 7 mph. In the fourth step the field windings are in parallel providing a speed of 9 mph. The controller was arranged to cut-out when the foot brake was applied. The above system of changing connections within the motor is seen as an alternate of battery voltage switching which nearly all electric vehicles followed until the advent of modern solid state controls.

A pinion on the motor shaft drove a countershaft bearing a differential. Each end of the countershaft was chain-geared to its respective rear wheel. With the lead-acid batteries provided, 80 volts with a capacity of 130 ampere-hours at 30 ampere discharge rate, the cabs were found to give a city range of 50 miles. With batteries of 1400 pounds, and cab weight of 3000 pounds with passengers this range is believable. The taxi batteries were charged at a fixed station by an ac motor driving a dc generator at a conversion efficiency of 86 percent, indicating there was good electrical engineering design.

---

[23] *The Horseless Age*, Vol. 2, No. 9, July 1897, pp. 4-6.

Figure 6.7. A London Electrical Cab Company's Taxi - 1897.[24] Interestingly, the motor and controls were American made, indicating the damage done the English economy by Parliament enacting the so-called "Red Flag" legislation, wherein any vehicle other than horse-drawn must be preceded by a man carrying a red flag. The lesson to be learned is that sometimes government legislation can do far more damage than good.

"The daily receipts of the cabs are said by Mr. W. C. Bersey, the manager, to average 150 percent more than the receipts of the ordinary hansom.[25] The London Cab Trade Council, an organization numbering about 60 and composed of cab owners, has declared itself in opposition to the new vehicles, while the Cab Drivers Union, numbering 10,000, is in favor of the change, and many of its members have applied for positions with the company.

---

[24] *Electric Cab in London, Scientific American Supplement*, Vol. XLIV, No. 1141, November 13, 1897, p. 18243.
[25] *The Horseless Age*, Vol. 2, No. 9, July 1897, p. 6.

"The police authorities of Scotland Yard subject every new motorman to a rigid test, and if he shows himself capable of managing the vehicle he is immediately granted a license. —— In the office of the company may be read these pregnant words:

> "I see the harness flung away,
> I hear the motor's roll,
> Another age dawns clear as day
> On my prophetic soul."

Meanwhile, what were the French, Italian, and the Belgians doing with electric vehicles?

CHAPTER 7

French, Belgian, and German Electric Vehicles Through 1900

While Trouvé's pioneering electric tricycle was the first electrically propelled personal vehicle ever assembled, the country of its builder, France, was slower than England in consistently pursuing the personal electric carriage. In fact, development of the second vehicle in France would await a full decade. Then Monsieur H. De Graffigny brought forth an electric tricycle. Italy's first electric vehicle, the first multi-powered vehicle, was also a tricycle. Thus the first electric vehicles in France, England, America, and Italy were all three-wheeled.

De Graffigny's Electric Tricycle

In France, later than Riker, De Graffigny devised an electric tricycle in 1891. It is illustrated in Fig. 7.1.[1] The vehicle bears a box which contains both the batteries and the motor. The steering wheel is seen to be at the front of the vehicle, with maneuvering achieved by the driver operating the rod and handle. To halt the vehicle one applied a foot brake. Speed, on the other hand, was controlled by battery switching, a technique utilized on nearly all electric vehicles until modern times. De Graffigny's batteries, like those used by the Tissandier brothers in their electric-powered balloons,[2] had an electrolyte of chromic acid, which when used could immerse the plates of the 18 cells. These batteries had a total weight of 44 pounds. Power was transferred from the pinion of the motor to the larger gear at the wheel by an endless chain. As the complete vehicle had a curb weight of 155 pounds, the ratio of battery weight to curb weight was some 28 percent. To ease friction and enhance the range of the vehicle, ball bearings were used with each wheel. In early trials in the city of Albert, Somme, France, the machine was "capable of delivering initially 1/3 hp, then 2/9 hp at the end of four hours of operation." Carrying two normal persons the vehicle had a speed of 10-12 mph. Energy costs at the time were reported to be equivalent of 2¢ per mile.[3]

---

[1] *Scientific American*, Vol. XLVII, No. 2, July 8, 1882, p. 23.

[2] *Scientific American*, Vol. XLVIII, No. 10, March 10, 1883, pp. 143 & 147.

[3] *Scientific American Supplement*, No. 839, January 30, 1892, p. 13410.

Figure 7.1. De Graffigny's electric tricycle of 1891 had a top speed of 10-12 mph while carrying two people. Power was obtained from chromic acid cells driving a 1/3 hp motor. Reference to the section on tricycles indicates that this velocipede is of a later design than the one utilized by Ayrton & Perry. But like Trouvé's original, it was almost surely English-built. Courtesy: Scientific American Supplement.

The range of De Graffigny's vehicle was probably 40 miles as inferred. Surely De Graffigny's tricycle, only a year later than Riker's, was considerably more advanced. De Graffigny, however, slips from sight. While developing an advanced electric tricycle, we do not hear from him again. What claimed him?

French development would rapidly pass to four-wheels, and Paul Pouchain would be the first person in France with a four-wheel electric vehicle.

Pouchain's and Jeantaud's Electric Carriages

In 1894 Monsieur Pouchain of Armentières brought out an electric phaeton, shown in the accompanying Fig. 7.2, with accommodations for six persons and mounted on four wheels.[4] One can detect the mental baggage of the wagon builder in the design of Pouchain, apparent surely to the reader as well. His Dujardin power source was composed of six battery groups with a total of 54 cells. The 2000 watt motor was built by Rechniewski, who would furnish the drive system for Monsieur Charles Jeantaud in the Paris-Bordeaux-Paris race the next year. The steering mechanism acted on the fore carriage with a screw-gear actuated by a hand wheel similar to the Sultan's Dog Cart. Curb weight of Pouchain's phaeton was given as 1350 kilograms. Top speed was 16 km/hr, with lesser speeds of 8, 6, and 3 km/hr. As one Pouchain-impressed reporter of the day opined, "Before the end of the century Paris will have ceased to be the hell of horses in order to become the paradise of electric coaches."

A heavy vehicle, Pouchain's carriage is similar to the Immisch carriage of 1888, built in England, or the electric brake of Holtzer & Cabot constructed in Boston in 1895. For the same period it is primitive compared with the coaches of Riker and of Woods in America. Neither of the latter possessed the percipience of having been a horse coach builder. They had less to unlearn than did Pouchain. Jeantaud, next discussed, appears to have been more mechanically oriented than was Pouchain, and also more daring.

---

[4] *Scientific American*, Vol. LXX, No. 5, February 3, 1894, p. 69.

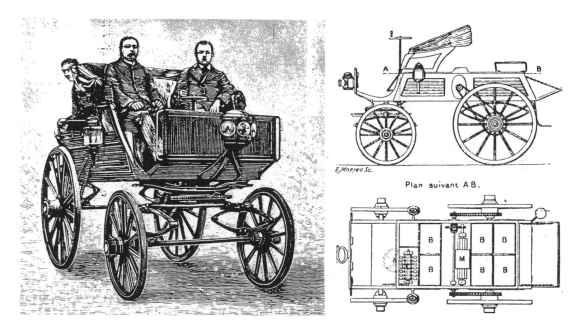

Figure 7.2. Pouchain's electric phaeton of 1894 had a curb weight of some 3000 pounds, and a top speed of 10 mph. Voltage switching permitted three slower speeds, and a provision for reverse.

Monsieur Charles Jeantaud, a celebrated Parisian carriage maker, undoubtedly saw Trouvé's electric tricycle at the Paris Exhibition of Electricity in 1881, for he is reported to have thought of the application to his carriages. By 1895 the "Fulmen" battery had been developed. This battery used honeycombed lead plates filled with lead oxide which were inserted in perforated celluloid envelopes.[5] In Jeantaud's electric carriage of 1895, shown in Fig. 7.3, 21 cells (42 volts) as described could supply 100 amperes. These batteries would stow under the seat. The *Scientific American* continues:[6]

> "The hands are free to steer the carriage and to control the speed; the switch as well as the brake, is controlled by the foot. The foot is placed on the switch and the carriage starts with ease; on removing the foot the carriage stops and the momentum which it has acquired may be checked, if desired, by applying the foot to the brake. The brake is of the ordinary variety, a wooden shoe binding on the rear wheel; a circuit breaker is placed on the brake pedal, so that when the brake is applied the current is cut off at the same time. On a good level road a speed of 20 kilometers

---

[5] The Planté lead acid battery was simply lead plates in an electrolyte of dilute sulfuric acid. Camille Faure improved this battery by applying red lead to the lead surface. But in automobile road vibration this coating would slough off, fall to the bottom of the battery and short the plates. The "Fulmen" technique overcame this limitation by holding the red lead in the perforations of the lead plate. This technology is today's grid plate. See Chapter 10.

[6] *Scientific American*, Vol. LXXII, No. 12, March 23, 1895, p. 177 & 213.

Figure 7.3. The Electric Carriage of M. Jeantaud. Fourteen years after seeing Trouvé's electric tricycle, Charles Jeantaud brought forth his 1895 carriage. A carriage builder by trade he excelled in mechanics. Before proceeding with the electric vehicle, Jeantaud designed and built a carefully arranged differential and gearing system. Courtesy: Scientific American.

(12 miles) per hour has been obtained, while in a hilly country the speed is reduced to 12 kilometers per hour. The weight of the carriage is distributed as follows: Carriage, 490 kilograms; accumulators, 420 kilograms; motor, 110 kilograms; two passengers, 150 to 180 kilograms; total 1200 kilograms — it will be seen that the carriage and contents weighs only about 2645 pounds.

"The electric carriage has a future, and already in London there is a firm which displays a sign saying that they are prepared to charge accumulators of all sizes at any hour of the day or night."

The motor was series-wound, producing 2.4 hp at 1200 rpm, at an efficiency of 74 percent. Figure 7.4 shows the power transmission system in which a differential is used. Pinion gears engaged two internally toothed gears in drums which were fastened to the wheel hub. This vehicle had a range of 18 miles at a speed of 12 mph. For the Paris-Bordeaux-Paris Race M. Jeantaud also was, with the above described vehicle in being, assembling a vehicle with a range of 36 miles.

The first long distance race participated in by an electric vehicle was the Paris-Bordeaux-Paris Race of 1895.[7] Messieurs Jeantaud and Brault initiated the construction of their vehicle only three months before the start of the race, and appeared on the starting line at the Champs du Mars on the 6th of June. For this pioneering event, in order to travel the 705 miles of the race in minimum time, they had battery stations separated by 24 to 42 miles depending on the profile of the route. For this supreme effort Jeantaud, a successful carriage builder, chartered a special train to place these batteries. At these battery stations the race crew would remove the discharged batteries and insert sets freshly charged, an event that on the average consumed some 10 minutes. Jeantaud and Brault, by entering the Paris-Bordeaux race, wished "to prove by an absolute demonstration that electric propulsion was ready to enter the domain of practice." (See footnote 7.) A magnificent achievement. Some 73 years later, in America, there would be a

---

[7] *Scientific American Supplement*, Vol. XL, No. 1030, Sept. 28, 1895, pp. 16458-59.

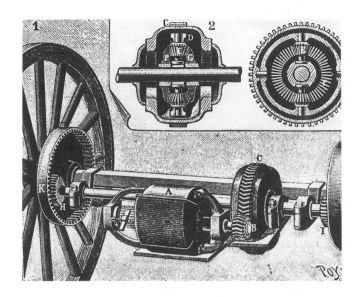

Figure 7.4. Shows Electric Motor, Power Transfer, and Differential.

cross-country race by electrics, reported in Chapter 24. To finish under its own power the first American vehicle required an elapsed time of 9 days, 1 hour and 30 minutes. Where Jeantaud's carriage and motor were built and tested in 3 months and had only a bearing problem, the two modern contestants had thickets of difficulties.[8] Best time in the Paris race was 2 days, 48 minutes for a gasoline car.

Jeantaud's vehicle, Fig. 7.5, had hickory wheels. The rear wheels had a diameter of 55 inches, while those in front, the steering wheels, had a diameter of 39 inches. A high vehicle with a fringed roof, it was of the surrey design with two parallel seats, each for two passengers. A single settee was behind, also seating two passengers. The front of the vehicle had a circular dash supporting three lights. The batteries were stored in the box. The weight on the forward wheels was 1980 pounds, while the rear axle supported 1860 pounds, providing a curb weight for the vehicle of 4840 pounds. The motor was designed and constructed by Rechniewski and was reported to be fault-free over the Paris-Bordeaux segment. At varying horsepower output the motor had an efficiency versus horsepower curve, which, even at this writing would be considered excellent.[9]

POWER	EFFICIENCY
2.4 hp	68.0 percent
4.6	89.0
6.5	92.5
8.0	91.5
9.3	90.0
10.4	89.0

---

[8] *Cambridge or Bust - Pasadena or Bust, Engineering and Science, 7-7*, California Institute of Technology, October 1968, pp. 10-17.

[9] A direct current motor today with a solid state chopper controller would not exceed those efficiencies, despite the improvement in quality of steel for the magnetic field. The increased hysteresis and eddy current losses associated with the pulsating current to the motor, an effect not present in Jeantaud's vehicle, would essentially be balanced out.

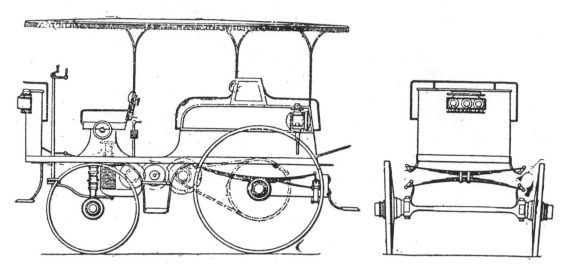

Figure 7.5. Jeantaud's 705 mile race with an electric car, utilizing battery interchange technique, accomplished in 1895, was a phenomenal accomplishment then, as it would be now. Courtesy: Scientific American Supplement.

Aboard the vehicle were 38 batteries each of 33 pounds weight, yielding 300 ampere-hours at a 10-hour discharge rate. At a discharge of 70 amperes the battery had 210 ampere-hours. With a level and good road it was possible to obtain a three hour run at 15 mph. It was reported that in the race, discharge rates as high as 200 amperes were occasioned on hills. Total weight of batteries was 1870 pounds, yielding a ratio of battery to curb weight of 38 percent. The electric vehicles were constantly being improved.

Messieurs Jeantaud and Brault were pleased with the results achieved with their hastily assembled electric vehicle in the Paris-Bordeaux Race. While they had not won, they had shown the reliability of electric propulsion. A new vehicle was initiated for 1896. In a superficial way it would resemble a Paris taxi of that day, as is shown in Figs. 7.6 to 7.8. The vehicle had front wheel drive, and, as a result of the excellent performance of pneumatic tires on the two cars entered by the Michelin brothers, long time pneumatic tire manufacturer for bicycles, Jeantaud's new electric automobile would also bear pneumatic tires. Gone would be the hickory wheels. Metal rims and spokes were beginning to be used both in France and in America.

Jeantaud's 1896 electric carriage van was much lighter than Pouchain's wagon earlier described. The body was of aluminum plate resting on a steel frame which supported the Omega-type batteries.[10][11] This energy source was stated to yield 15 ampere-hours per pound (a high figure). Range of the 2200 pound coupe was a claimed 36 miles. Anticipating in 1896 the current trend to front wheel drive and steering, Jeantaud's mechanical arrangement can best be understood from the accompanying Figs. 7.7 and 7.8. That Jeantaud and Rechniewski, the

---

[10] *Scientific American Supplement*, Vol. XLIII, No. 1100, January 10, 1896, pp. 17588 & 17589.

[11] The first American built aluminum body was placed on a 16 hp Panhard owned by T. A. Griffin, President of the Griffin Car Wheel Company, and imported by Smith & Mabley, of New York City. The body was made by J. M. Quimby & Co., of Newark, New Jersey: *The Horseless Age*, Vol. 10, No. 5, July 20, 1902, p. 130.

Figure 7.6. The Jeantaud Electric Motor. Jeantaud was the best of the French designers of electric vehicles.

Figure 7.7. A Plan View of the Jeantaud Front Axle Drive of 1896. The electric motor is directly connected to the axle through two reduction gears.

Figure 7.8. A front elevation of the Jeantaud front axle drive showing the motor was in the plane of the axle.

Figures 7.6 through 7.8, Courtesy: Scientific American Supplement

motor builder, were quality engineers is indicated by their recognition of the problem associated with interrupting the electric current when driving, for the article quotes, "the breaking of the current and the passage (of the controller) from one point to another are effected at a very slight intensity, say of five or six amperes, owing to a new arrangement, instead of a hundred amperes, a current often approached in the propulsion of a carriage upon the road, and which necessitates heavy, bulky and but slightly resistant apparatus."[12]

---

[12] Induction in electricity corresponds to inertia in mechanics. To interrupt a large current is as difficult as to suddenly stop an automobile. Both insist on continuing.

In the space of two years Messieurs Jeantaud and Brault achieved two brilliant accomplishments: 1) entering into and successfully completing the longest automobile race over hard roads between Paris and Bordeaux. In this contest these French innovators introduced a concept to be followed with electric vehicles in Taiwan today, battery-interchange (see Chapter 23), and 2) devising the first electric four-wheel, front-wheel-drive automobile,[13] innovative in many ways. Despite these outstanding accomplishments, Messieurs Jeantaud and Brault slip away into the shadows of history. Their names apparently do not again appear in electric car development.

Darracq, a Frenchman, seemed to start where Jeantaud left off. Superficially their two vehicles look similar, but whereas Jeantaud utilized front-wheel-drive and steering, Darracq would drive with the rear wheels. And he would be the first to use regenerative braking (see Glossary) in an electric vehicle.

Darracq's Electric Coupe

In the Fourth *Salon du Cycle* in Paris in 1897, M. A. Darracq's electric coupe was displayed as Fig. 7.9.[14] This vehicle should be compared to C. E. Woods' electric taxi of the same date, shown in Fig. 5.1. There is remarkable similarity. Darracq, however, like the Bushburry Dog Cart, used electrical braking. But the Frenchman went further in design. He employed regenerative braking.[15] In regenerative braking, when the vehicle is slowed, the kinetic energy of motion is converted by the motor/generator into electrical energy and replaced in the battery. This action is achieved, by foot pedal action, through allowing more current to pass through the shunt field of the electric motor, thus increasing the magnetic field. With a suddenly increased magnetic field, the rotating armature of what was the motor now generates more voltage then what is present in the battery, and the battery is charged. Probably equally important to the recharging, however, is the redeposition of the sulfide ions back into the electrolyte.

Darracq's coupe had a steel tube chassis on which was a spring-mounted body bearing four wooden wheels with hard rubber tires. Steering was accomplished through a long lever that passed over the roof to act on the front wheels. The wheels pivoted with respect to the axle, a plan similar to that employed by Jeantaud. Three electric lanterns graced the exterior of the vehicle, and a fourth could be actuated to illuminate the interior.

Electric energy was furnished by 40 Fulmen batteries of 100 volts placed in the rear of the coupe to yield 125 ampere-hours at a discharge rate of 25 amperes. The battery weight was given as 800 pounds. The direct current motor was compound-wound controlled by voltage switching. To minimize a jerking start and to reduce starting current to the motor Darracq ingeniously "interposed between the axles of the wheels and the control of the differential a series of springs which, upon being compressed, gives the motor time to get underway before the displacement of the carriage. The resistance couple is null and increases progressively with

---

[13] In 1882 Ayrton and Perry had devised a front-wheel drive three wheeler.

[14] *Scientific American Supplement*, Vol. XLIII, No. 1110, April 10, 1897, p. 17739.

[15] *A Recharging Motor for Electric Vehicles, Scientific American*, Vol. LXXXIII, No. 25, December 22, 1900, p. 389.

Figure 7.9. Darracq's electric coupe of 1897 had a top speed of 6 mph, but he had regenerative braking, a means of transforming energy of motion into recharging of the battery. He also incorporated a set of springs between the drive shaft and the motor, which would allow the motor to gain speed before the vehicle moved, thus protecting the motor from high starting currents. He had a most sophisticated early design. Courtesy: Scientific American Supplement.

the compression of the springs. Owing to this arrangement the accumulators are well under control, and the starting takes place almost insensibly." (See footnote 15.) Darracq's coupe had a top speed of 6 mph, and an effective range of some 30 miles.

To this vehicle Darracq had given much thought. With the Fulmen accumulators (the grid assembly of modern batteries) he had a superior power source, the same as specified in the tricycle for Queen Victoria, and his drive system with regenerative braking was advanced. The spring-tension mounting of the motor was unique. Such an arrangement would remove the jerk start-up and protect the motor from momentary overload current. But Riker's carriage of the same period, with tubular steel construction, uniformly sized pneumatic tires with wire-spoked wheels, the assembly lightweight, was more advanced than was Darracq's carriage. The latter was built by a carriage maker. Riker's wasn't. He had designed it as an electric vehicle directly. A combination of the two vehicles would have been superior.

Of the innovative electric vehicle development earlier cited in England, the bogie from the Continent is worth noting, for, in a sense, Mr. Helman's "bogie" is an early forerunner of the tractor section of the modern highway truck-trailer. This Parisian design is shown in Fig. 7.10.

Appearing in the journal of the day was the statement: "The range is 60 kilometers (38 miles) without charging, and its maximum speed is 25 kilometers per hour (15 mph). A 10 horsepower electric bogie weighs 1,000 kilograms (2,200 pounds). The driver has complete control over the machine. The right hand is practically free, and is only required when changing speed. His left hand guides the vehicle, and the foot controls the brake."[16]

Other French Electric Cars

By 1899 the French electric vehicle, like the American, had departed from the wagon design. Figures 7.11 and 7.12 are models respectively from the George Richard establishment, and of the Compagnie Francaise des Voiture.[17] The former's vehicle was powered with a nominal 88 volt lead-acid battery feeding a d-c motor at a reported 100 watt-hour per mile. The motor is seen to link the rear wheels by a chain drive. Speeds, obtained by voltage switching, were a reported 3 1/2, 6, and 12 mph. As in modern cars there was a foot brake and a hand

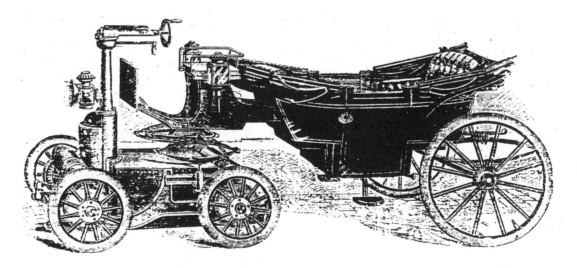

Figure 7.10. "My 'bogie' can be adopted to any kind of a vehicle and replaces horses altogether." M. Heilman of Paris. Courtesy: The Horseless Age, Vol. 5, No. 4, Jan. 3, 1900.

16 *The Horseless Age*, Vol. 5, No. 4, January 3, 1900.
17 *Scientific American Supplement*, Vol. XLVIII, No. 1235, September 2, 1899, p. 19795.

Figure 7.11. The Richard Electric Automobile. Scientific American Supplement.

Figure 7.12. Carriage of the Compagnie des Électromobiles. Scientific American Supplement.

operated brake lever. This model of George Richard was remarkably similar to the models of the same date manufactured by the Pope Manufacturing Company in Hartford, as will be seen in Chapter 8.

The Compagnie Francaise automobile was more innovative. The batteries were beneath the seat and the motor was mounted vertically before the driver, a trend solidified by Walter A. Baker in America, which was followed by nearly all manufacturers for the next eight decades. The motor was capable of developing from 3 1/2 to 20 hp.[18] Speed change and reversal were

---

[18] *Ibid.*, p. 19795.

actuated by the hand wheel controller. The motor revolved a vertical shaft, and through a bronze gear engaged a second vertical shaft. A Cardan (universal) joint absorbed shocks of the roadway. The motion of the balancing shaft was transmitted to the front axle through a beveled pinion. The differential gear and pinions were enclosed and at the center of the axle, making for a front driving and steering carriage.[19] A brake may be seen in the etching for gripping the rear tire tread.

Following the torpedo design (motor forward) above, M. Krieger in 1901, whose deftness will be further seen in Chapter 25, designed and built a diminutive Electrolette with a curb weight of only 1700 pounds, 800 of which were Fulmen lead-acid batteries.[20] The ratio is seen to be an excellent 47 percent. Utilizing two 3 hp motors individually of 110 pounds, some 36 pounds per horsepower, the pinion of each engaged a larger gear linked to a single forward wheel. The Electrolette had a top speed of 21 mph. For different speeds Krieger used the usual voltage switching achieved by a controller with positions: Start, Stop, Slow, Mean, High Speed, Extra Speed, Electric Brake, and Reverse. He used dynamic braking by shorting the motor. Figure 7.13 of the Electrolette is an excellent illustration of an early front wheel drive vehicle.

Figure 7.13. The Krieger Electrical Automobile. Scientific American.

---

[19] An excellent etching of a differential is seen in Chapter 12.
[20] *Electric Automobile - Krieger System, Scientific American*, Vol. LXXXIV, No. 23, June 8, 1901, p. 357.

The two motors are seen as drum-like objects proximal to each front wheel, the shaft pinion engaging the wheel gear.[21] Note the vertical column of the steering wheel and single headlamp which with the side running lights are seen to be electric.

While the French would be the first to exploit the English invented pneumatic tire, Messieurs Michelin initiated an experiment in Paris to determine the coefficient of traction of tires.[22] In this test, shown in Fig. 7.14, the coefficient of traction is defined as the ratio of pulling force in kilograms to the weight of the vehicle in kilograms. The ratio is expressed in thousands to yield whole numbers. In this test the pneumatic tire was found to have a coefficient of traction 20 to 25 percent less than either the iron-tired or hard rubber-tired vehicle. Today we would say the rolling resistance of the then pneumatic tire was least.[23] Similarly the current radial tire has less rolling resistance than does the conventional tire.

The development and accomplishments in electric vehicles achieved by De Graffigny, by Pouchain, by Jeantaud, by Darracq, and by others, together with their silent operation, led to the adoption of electric taxis for the Paris Exposition of 1900. The next section pictures personal transportation on the Exposition grounds.

Electric Vehicle System for the Paris Exposition of 1900

With successful electric vehicles by designers like Jeantaud and Darracq for the Paris Exposition of 1900, some 1000 electric-powered taxis were perceived to be required. [24] At this time internal combustion vehicles were without mufflers, were unbelievably noisy, vibrated substantially on running, and moreover, often had balky engines. Electric vehicles, in contrast, were quiet, readily controlled, and as permitted travel speeds were only 9 1/2 mph, with distances short, conditions were almost ideal for electric-powered hacks. To provide this service a competition was held by the Automobile Club of France. The jury consisted of twelve members: six selected from Club members, and six chosen by the competitors. Twelve competitors supplied 26 vehicles, of which 16 were electric. In performance there was an obligatory run of 36 miles in 16 hours. Classes of carriages were for 2, 4, and 6 passengers, each with 65 pounds of baggage. Moreover, each hack was to bear two brakes: one instantaneous, the second progressive. Figures 7.15 and 7.16 show six of the tested electric vehicles.[25]

As winner of the competition, Compagnie Generale de Voitures built a special electrical system for charging batteries, repairing of vehicles, and for training of drivers.[26] Figure 7.17

---

[21] The 1991 announced General Motors Impact also employs a two motor front wheel drive.

[22] *Scientific American Supplement*, Vol. XLIV, No. 1125, July 24, 1897, p. 17979.

[23] True where all other elements are constant.

[24] *Scientific American Supplement*, Vol. XLVII, No. 1221, May 27, 1899, pp. 19570 and 19571.

[25] *Competition of Automobile Hackney Carriages, Scientific American Supplement*, Vol. XLVI, No. 1174, July 2, 1898, p. 18783.

[26] *Electric Cab System of Paris, Scientific American*, Vol. LXXXII, No. 22, June 2, 1900, pp. 345-346.

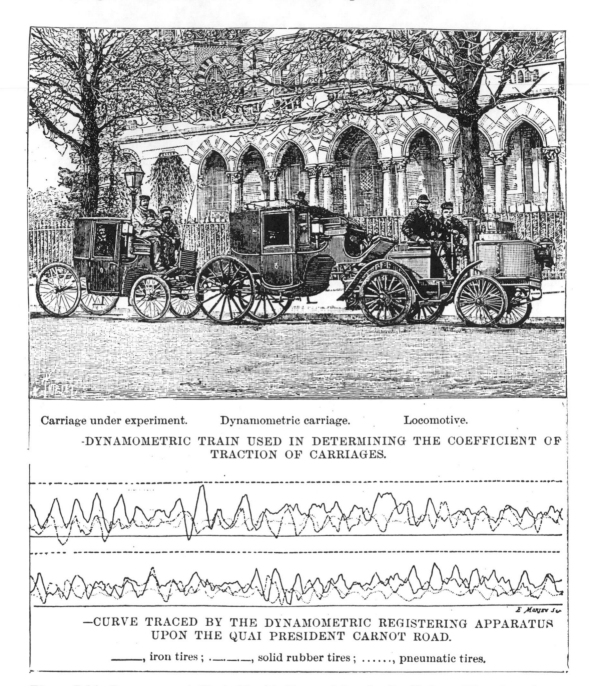

| Carriage under experiment. | Dynamometric carriage. | Locomotive. |

-DYNAMOMETRIC TRAIN USED IN DETERMINING THE COEFFICIENT OF TRACTION OF CARRIAGES.

—CURVE TRACED BY THE DYNAMOMETRIC REGISTERING APPARATUS UPON THE QUAI PRESIDENT CARNOT ROAD.

_____, iron tires ; .__.__., solid rubber tires ; ......, pneumatic tires.

Figure 7.14. Dynamometric Train Used in Determining the Coefficient of Traction of Carriages Courtesy: Scientific American Supplement.

Figure 7.15. 1.) Krieger Electric Coupe, 2.) Coupe of the Automobile Conveyance Company, 3.) Krieger Electric Victoria, and 4.) Dore Electric Coupe. Courtesy: Scientific American Supplement.

shows a phantom view of a French hack. The battery box was spring-mounted and detachable with the chassis. A 3.3 kilowatt, 80 volt d-c motor actuated by suitable gearing and differential, finally provided chain drive to the rear wheels.

For recharging of batteries the vehicle was backed into the station, illustrated in Fig. 7.18, and 1650 pounds of lead-acid batteries were placed on a cart shown under the vehicle and transported to the rear of the station for charging from an a-c motor/d-c generator set shown beyond the vehicle in the foreground. For the American comparison of this operation see Fig. 4.8. The whole facility, including the steam boilers for generating power, is viewed in Fig. 7.19.

Figure 7.16. French Electromobile Carriage Company: 1.) Victoria, 2.) Coupe. Scientific American Supplement.

Figure 7.17. General View of an Electromobile Hack—Details of the Mechanism[27].

---

[27] *Scientific American Supplement*, Vol. XLVII, No. 1221, May 27, 1899, pp. 19570-71.

Figure 7.18. Interior View of the Charging Station on Rue Cardinet[27]

*Figure 7.19.
The Auber-
villiers
Establish-
ment—
Engine
Building,
Charging
Hall,
Carriage
Houses, and
Track*[27]

---

[27] *Scientific American Supplement*, Vol. XLVII, No. 1221, May 27, 1899, pp. 19570-71.

There were provisions for handling 200 hacks at one time. In the foreground is the training grounds for operators with wrought iron figures of men, women, children, nurses, and bicyclists. Figure 7.20 illustrates an instructor's electric car passing an iron bicyclist.

In the meantime, and early, the Belgians had built an electric vehicle for Philippart in England. Now they were to build one for themselves.

The Belgian Electric Carriage

That an organization in Belgium would promptly build an electric carriage could be believed because of its advanced chemical industry. Probably as early as 1883 Phillipart, cited in Chapter 6, had an electric tramcar equipped with Faure type batteries built in Belgium, then shipped to England to be tried on the tracks of the London North Metropolitan Tramway Company.[28] These experiments were abandoned. The tram, operating on uneven roads, the Faure applied red lead, with no grid present, would slough off the lead plates and fall to the bottom of the cell, thus electrically shorting it.

Figure 7.20. Track for Training the Drivers of Automobiles.[27]

---

[27] *Scientific American Supplement*, Vol. XLVII, No. 1221, May 27, 1899, pp. 19570-71.
[28] *Scientific American Supplement*, Vol. XXVII, No. 687, March 2, 1889, p. 10969.

To provide a better battery, and to secure more energy per unit weight, as well as to permit a greater power draw per unit weight, Edmund Julien, a Belgium engineer, completed a lead-acid battery in 1888 with characteristics similar to batteries which are today used in electric vehicles.[29] Planté had conceived and made the first lead-acid battery; Camille Faure had layered the lead plates with lead oxide; E. Volkmann had conceived of perforating the lead plate to better adhere the lead oxide; J. S. Sellons had alloyed antimony with the lead to yield strength; and now Julien added to the antimony-lead alloy, mercury. This additional element, making an amalgam, greatly reduced the internal resistance of the battery, and lengthened its life. Table 10-1 in Chapter 10 designates these improvements. Of the Belgium electric vehicle *The Horseless Age* writes:[30]

> "Besides England and France, L'Electrique (Societe Anonyme), Brussels, Belgium has recently turned out a two-seated electric carriage of very neat appearance. The battery, which is placed under the seats, consists of 48 cells, the plates being of the Planté type. The total weight of the battery is 950 pounds, and it is charged by a current of 25 amperes at 110 volts, the time occupied being about three and one-half hours. The capacity is about 86 ampere-hours at a discharge of 18 amperes. The current actuates a series-wound motor, which runs at 1750 rpm, and weighs 275 pounds. At each end of the armature spindle is a pinion which, by means of a chain, transmits motion to the rear wheels. The ordinary differential gearing is being interposed. The total weight of the carriage is 2420 pounds, and it is claimed that it can be driven, at the rate of 10 miles (mph), a distance of between 40 and 50 miles without recharging."

While an illustration of the Belgian vehicle is unavailable, one can speculate it rather closely resembled the Bersey vehicle in Chapter 6, based on several known factors (it was a two-seated carriage; it weighed 2420 pounds; its time of assembly was 1897; and its location of assembly, the Continent). From the figures given in the article the battery would yield about 8 kilowatt-hours of energy, and the range of the vehicle, as given and at the speed cited, would be reasonable.

German Electric Vehicles

Although Germany was industrially probably the most advanced European nation in the 1890-1900 decade, interest in motorcars was junior to France, said by some because of the Kaiser's admiration for fine horses and his influence on the nation's elite. Nevertheless, Dr. M. Kallman, city electrician for Berlin, wrote a report in *Mitteleuropaischer Motor Wagen Vereins* detailing tests made upon a group of 14 electric vehicles in the spring of 1900,[31] presented in Table 7-1. Both passenger carriages and industrial trucks are included in the list. Kallman, like current electric vehicles designers, knew the higher the ratio of battery weight to curb weight

---

[29] *Ibid*, p. 10968.
[30] *The Horseless Age*, Vol. 2, No. 10, August 1897, p. 6.
[31] *Report on Electric Vehicle Tests, The Horseless Age*, Vol. 7, No. 9., November 18, 1900, pp. 26 & 27.

Table 7-1. Tests on German Manufactured Electric Vehicles in 1900

ITEM	TYPE	CURB WEIGHT (POUNDS)	BATTERY WT. (POUNDS)	RATIO (%) BATTERY/CURB WT.	MANUFACTURE
1.	Vis-a-vis	3570	1620	45	Fahrzenglabrik Eisenach
2.	Delivery wagon	3740	1200	32	Allgemeine Betriesb-Actien Gesfuer Motorfshrzenge, Cologne
3.	Delivery wagon	5200	1870	36	C. Klienst, Berlin
4.	Truck	3900	1105	28	Heinrich Scheele, Cologne
5.	Interchangeable coupe & mylord	3300	1140	35	Heinrich Scheele, Cologne
6.	Delivery wagon	3900	1100	28	Berliner Electromobil & Accumulatoren Werke Fiedler & Co.
7.	Vehicle de luxe	3580	1100	31	do
8.	Coupe, removable top	3830	913	24	Berliner Maschenenfabrik Henschel & Co., Charlottenburg
9.	Phaeton	2040	913	45	do
10.	Truck	6050	1270	21	do
11.	Vehicle de luxe	3830	1250	33	Kruse Bros., Hamburg
12.	Dos-a-dos	—	—	—	Vulkan Automobil-Ges, Berlin
13.	Delivery wagon	4060	1580	38	do
14.	Transfer wagon	9080	2860	29	Saschsische Accumulatoren Werke, Dresden
15.	Sundancer (modern, USA)	1640	720	44	McKee Engineering Corporation, Palatine, Illinois, USA

of the vehicle (with lead-acid batteries), the more acceptable the vehicle (within reason). For comparison purposes the modern Sundancer by Robert McKee et al (USA), item 15 in Table 7-1, is included.

Kallman considered a ratio of 33 percent acceptable for obtaining a "normal range" of 19 miles (30 km). Today a higher ratio is considered more applicable, for a range of 19 miles is simply insufficient. Kallman also considered accessibility of the battery for servicing, and its sometimes odor if placed in the passenger compartment.

In tests the vehicle with the greatest range attained a run of 41 miles, but most would travel from 20-25 miles, and allowing for bad weather the range generally was 20 miles. For economy tests: kilowatts required at speeds of 5 to 6 mph the power consumption varied from 0.97 to 4 kW with a total weight variation of 1.15 and 3.5 metric tons, respectively. These figures for the lighter vehicles gave a power requirement of 0.87 kW per ton for the lighter vehicles, and 1.1 kW per ton for the heavier trucks.

At speeds 6-9 mph the 1.115 ton vehicles required 1.29 kW, and the 1.7 ton vehicles required 1.8 kW. At speeds 9.5-12.5 mph, similar vehicles were 1.8 and 1.9 kW respectively. And for the most economical vehicle the energy consumption was 122 watt-hours per ton mile, at 12 1/2 mph, and 85 watt-hours at 5 mph, a figure probably close to the performance of the Sundancer. Windage power consumption at these modest velocities, a factor which varies as the cube of the speed, is small. Apparent from the above was the usual German thoroughness in understanding electric vehicles. In America the previous year G. C. Severs and R. A. Fliess had written a less thorough but similar report comparing costs per ton mile for horses and for electrics.[32]

A chassis only of the German Siemens-Schuckert electric automobile tricycle is shown in Figs. 7.21 and 7.22. Equipped with wire-spoked wheels, an indication of post 1896 construction, the vehicle was equipped with 24 cells of Tudor storage battery yielding a nominal 48 volts, and weighing 286 pounds. Torque at the wheels was provided by a one hp motor turning at some 800 rpm. The tricycle was equipped with both a foot and an electric brake. "The latter operates so energetically that when going at full speed and carrying two people, the machine can be brought to a full stop in 7 to 10 feet."[33] The quotation is a turn of the century annunciation of the effectiveness of electric dynamic braking, a scheme pioneered in the English Bushberry Dog Cart in 1897. The dotted lines in illustration Fig. 7.20 indicate the position for the single seat on the chassis.

By 1897 France, England, America, Italy, Belgium, and Germany in order cited had developed their indigenous electric means of personal transportation. The electric vehicle industry had been launched. Both in England and in France there was a hiatus of some 5 or 6 years before the pioneering work in electric vehicles by Trouvé, Ayrton, and Perry was amplified and improved upon. By 1896 the British Parliament had rescinded legislation inhibiting the growth of mechanically propelled road vehicles. During this period the rate of advancement in electric carriages was approximately equal for both continents. As the tricycle

---

[32] G. C. Severs and R. A. Fliess, *Cost/Ton Mile for Horses and for Electric Vehicles, Scientific American*, Vol. LXXXI, No. 4, July 22, 1899, p. 50.

[33] *Scientific American Supplement*

Figures 7.21 & 7.22. The Siemens-Schuckert Electric Automobile Tricycle. Courtesy: Scientific American Supplement.

heralded the electric vehicle innovation in both countries, to better bear the increasingly greater load of batteries, the four-wheeled wagon soon came to dominate electric carriage advancement in each of these rivals.

While there was a standoff in the rate of development of electric carriages between England and France, the American advancement, while starting some 8 or 9 years later, soon outpaced both the Channel-bound countries. The American emphasis on lighter weight bodies pioneered by Riker; the early use of steel tubing by Morris & Salom, Pope Manufacturing Company, and Riker; the emphasis on wire-spoked wheels, invented by C. S. Mott; and the pneumatic tire, had earned American leadership in electric carriages by 1898. However, with internal combustion engine-powered vehicles, in 1890 France was clearly the leading country in the world. The presence of superior inter-city roads, and particularly the interest with which the affluent participated in the motor car, led to the rapid exploitation of the gasoline-powered carriages. Carli in Italy was the first to attempt the multi-powered electric vehicle, a task that would be repeated again and again almost every decade through the 20th Century. As the next chapter will portray, America would become the preeminent country in electric cars, while England, France, and Germany would direct their principal effort in personal transportation to the gasoline-powered motorcar. The strong electric interest in France after about 1900 would direct itself to multi-powered electric vehicles.

For whetting the public's interest in the motorcar, the widely reported Paris-Bordeaux and return race of 1895, a distance of some 705 miles, was the key event, more than anything else. As E.P. Ingersoll, publisher of *The Horseless Age*, would comment in his columns after the race, "Where before there were several dozen inventors in their workshops working on mechanical vehicles, there would be hundreds after the race." And as the next chapter indicates, these innovators would obtain results.

CHAPTER 8

Transitional Electric Cars

A transitional electric car is characterized by its carriage derivation. In the early history of electric vehicles Colonel Albert A. Pope and his cousin, Colonel George N. Pope, were key figures. In the Civil War, Albert, the moving force of the two, had been a cavalryman and had saved some $3,000 of his army pay. On discharge he had established an enterprise to manufacture small patented items in Boston. By 1877 he was attracted to the possibilities of bicycles, which, as is well known to the reader, would reach their apogee as a means of personal transportation in the 1890's. Not completely satisfied with the bicycle as prototyped by his own company, he soon began to import English makes.

The Pope Manufacturing Company

In a June 1882 advertisement Pope was offering to the public the ordinary bicycle.[1] Shortly he would shrewdly retail the so-called safety models invented by H. J. Lawson in England in 1873-74,[2] as opposed to the then popular ordinary bicycle with the gargantuan diameter front and lilliputian rear wheel, seen in Fig. 8.1, then so popular and known for its speed. A 100-mile trip had been made in 7 hours, 7 minutes, and 10 seconds on an English road. The safety bicycle imported by Pope was probably the Lawson safety bicyclette with more comparable diameter wheels. Such a model is shown in Fig. 8.2. Pope's choice of the safety bicycle was wise, for although the ordinary bicycle was the more numerous at the time of his decision, its demise was patent as illustrated in Table 8-1.[3] This ability for timing may have most importantly led to the success of the Pope Manufacturing Company. Other bicycles of the time are shown in Fig. 8.3.[4]

Within the year, witnessing the surge in popularity of the bicycle, Pope decided to manufacture cycles under his name with the actual assembly accomplished by the Weed Sewing Machine Company of Hartford. In England the Coventry Sewing Machine Company had

---

[1] *Scientific American*, Vol. XLVI, No. 24, June 17, 1882, p. 390.

[2] C. F. Caunter, *The History & Development of Cycles*. Part I, Her Majesty's Stationery Office, London, 1955, pp. 26-27.

[3] *Encyclopaedia Britannica*, Vol. 3, Encyclopaedia Britannica, Chicago, 1956, p. 544.

[4] The first true bicycle with crank, pedals, driving rods, a seat, and handlebars was assembled by Kirkpatrick Macmillan of Scotland in 1839. - C. F. Caunter.

Figure 8.1. At the time of Colonel Pope's entry into the field of bicycles, the style most popular was the ordinary bicycle. Courtesy: Her Majesty's Stationery Office.

Figure 8.2. A popular safety bicycle at the time of Pope's decision to import English bicycles. Courtesy: Her Majesty's Stationery Office.

similarly fabricated the French Michaux bicycle as earlier described. Weed's sewing machine business was in decline, possibly due to the supreme promotional ability of Isaac Merritt Singer of the company which bore his name. With inherent advantages of the bicycle over the horse and buggy for many tasks, Pope's cycle venture was an immediate success. Soon, therefore, all of Weed's manufacturing facilities were being devoted to the former's manufacture. As is often the case in similar situations, Pope acquired Weed's business.[5]

By 1890 the Pope Manufacturing Company was the largest bicycle manufacturer in America. Pope had entered the industry at the appropriate time. He had selected excellent associates, as is noted below, and his army experiences had given him a broad background as well as one disciplined for command. Observing the importance of pneumatic tires as proved by the Michelin brothers in the Paris-Bordeaux-Paris car race of 1895, Pope established the Hartford Rubber Works, drawing on the skilled pool of workers in that area resulting from the earlier operations of Goodyear.[6] With his tire manufactory Pope was the first to offer pneumatic

---

[5] The 1890's was the decade of the bicycle. In 1899 there were 350 bicycle factories in America, manufacturing 1,113,000 bicycles valued at $23,000,000. George B. Catlin, *The Story of Detroit*, The Detroit News, Detroit, 1923.

[6] Bradford K. Pierce, *Trials of an Inventor*, Phillip & Hunt, NYC, 1866.

Table 8-1. Market Penetration of Wheeled Vehicles in England in Percent				
Type	1873	1889	1891	1893
Ordinary	important	11.5	3.3	—
Rear-driven safety	invented	53.6	86.7	84.6
Single tricycle	important	22.1	7.7	5.3

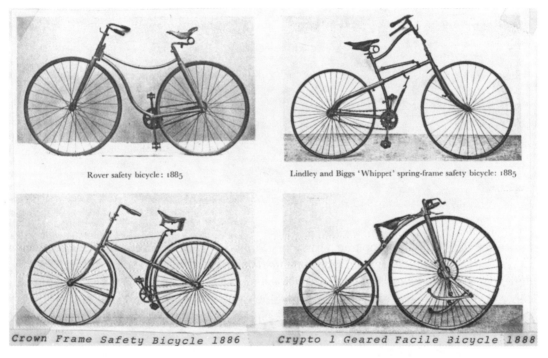

Rover safety bicycle: 1885

Lindley and Biggs 'Whippet' spring-frame safety bicycle: 1885

Crown Frame Safety Bicycle 1886

Crypto 1 Geared Facile Bicycle 1888

Figure 8.3. English style bicycles at the time of Pope's manufacture of bicycles in America. The Pope Manufacturing Company became the largest bicycle manufacturer in America. The company then went on to become the first to mass produce automobiles, electric cars in 1899. Courtesy: Her Majesty's Stationery Office.

tires in America.[7] Sales of bicycles, peaking in 1894, had indeed placed in short supply steel tubing for frames. A believer in what is now known as vertical integration, Pope initiated the production of this tubing for bicycle frames. By 1894 Colonel Pope, pictured in Fig. 8.4, had the most modern mill in the country for the manufacture of cold-drawn tubing.

Recognizing the importance of maintaining quality, a trait based on his army experience, Pope instituted a Research Department for improving materials and bicycle designs. This

---

[7] Joseph Nathan Kane, *Famous First Facts*, H. W. Wilson Co., NYC. 1964.

Figure 8.4. Colonel Albert A. Pope[8]

engineering department was operated by Henry Souther, a Massachusetts Institute of Technology graduate. Managing the steel tube department was Lieutenant Hayden Eames, USN Ret., an ordinance inspector for the Navy, shown in Fig. 8.5.[9] A person experienced in business, George H. Day, from the Weed Sewing Machine Company, was Vice President and General Manager, while Cousin George Pope was Treasurer. Joining the organization in 1896 as an engineer in the new motor carriage department was Hiram Percy Maxim, who, after graduating from MIT, had gone to the American Projectile Company, then aided Morris & Salom in their assembly of the first Electrobat, a vehicle shown in the Chicago-Evanston-Chicago race of 1895, and reported on in Chapter 15. Joining Pope's enterprise with Maxim was Herbert W. Alden who subsequently became President of the Timken-Detroit Axle Company. Like Maxim, Alden was already schooled in vehicles, for together they had assembled a tricycle gasoline-powered vehicle. From the above roster the Pope Manufacturing Company was seen to be a formidable and competently manned enterprise. Fate, however, would exact a toll.

It was Maxim, with Alden, who developed the electric vehicle for Colonel Pope; the latter had been encouraged by Whitney and by Widener, the would-be electric taxi magnates. The decision changed the Pope Manufacturing Company, so able in bicycle fabrication, into the

---

8 Robert A. Smith, *The Social History of the Bicycle: Its Early Life and Times in America*, New York: Am. Heritage Press, p.45. (796.6 s658s.)

9 Hiram Percy Maxim, *Horseless-Carriage Days*, Harper & Bros., NYC, 1936.

Figure 8.5. Lieutenant Hayden Eames (ret.), an ordinance inspector for the Navy, joined the Pope Company and was placed in charge of the steel tube department. Early electric cars were constructed from tubing in their frames, just as were bicycles.[10] Courtesy: Harper & Bros.

largest maker of electric vehicles. Hardly a mean feat. And finally, it was Pope who made the prediction to Maxim, with a vision in his eyes that the latter would long remember[11], "Maxim, I believe this horseless carriage business will be one of the big businesses of the future." How true. It became the biggest. Having introduced the electric vehicle to Pope, Maxim later presented the gasoline-powered vehicle to him. Pope and Maxim were an effective combination. Maxim's first electric vehicle had been a three-wheeled velocipede, a form adopted both from Trouvé, and from Professors Ayrton and Perry. Subsequently, Maxim, sensing the greater stability accorded by four wheels, gravitated toward the centuries-old concept of the conventional wagon. The first vehicle Maxim made for Pope was the Columbia in 1897 shown in Fig. 8.6.[12] Figure 8.7 is another view showing positioning of passengers, while Figs. 8.8 and 8.9 are later models.[13] The tires have become uniform in size, and the side riding lamp has been modified. Model changes at this time were probably based on improvement gained from experience rather than from planned obsolescence.

---

[10] Hiram Percy Maxim, *Horseless Carriage Days,* Harper Bros., NYC, 1936.

[11] Hiram Percy Maxim, *Horseless Carriage Days,* p. 175. He is best known for inventing the Maxim silencer whose principles are used for silencing exhaust by the use of mufflers, a device which permits the gases to escape, but traps the sound.

[12] *Scientific American*, Vol. LXXVI, No. 21, May 22, 1897, p. 331.

[13] *The Horseless Age*, Vol. 2, No. 6, April 1897, pp. 4-6.

Figure 8.6. The first Columbia horseless carriage was electric and assembled by Hiram Percy Maxim for the Pope Manufacturing Company in 1897. Scientific American.

The Electric Vehicle Company

As strategy for combining his electric automobile division with Whitney and Widener's taxi company, Pope formed the Columbia Automobile Company, and two weeks later this indepen-dent division and The Electric Vehicle Company jointly owned the Columbia and Electric Vehicle Company. The new entity proceeded to manufacture some 2000 electric taxis, the first large scale electric vehicle assembly in America, or indeed, anywhere in the world. In an era of mergers when J. P. Morgan had formed the Northern Securities Company, a railroad trust, and had brought together independents to form the integrated United States Steel Corporation, and while John D. Rockefeller had assembled the Standard Oil Company, it was natural that merging was active in the growing electric vehicle industry. Therefore, it was not surprising that The Electric Vehicle Company absorbed the Columbia and Electric Vehicle Company. The merged companies were touted to have soon an expected capital structure of $200,000,000.

Another important asset of The Electric Vehicle Company of the time, this paper colossus held the rights to license the Selden Patent. This patent, Fig. 8.10, described the gasoline

Figure 8.7. Rear view showing the drive system, the ventilated battery box. The vehicle would be rear heavy. Courtesy: Scientific American.

automobile, an important invention, which patent-wise was held by George B. Selden, a Rochester lawyer. Shrewdly guessing that the internal combustion powered vehicle would become important, Selden had obtained from the U.S. Patent Office rights to the gasoline powered car. Testing the power of the patent in court, The Electric Vehicle Company filed suit on the Winton Motor Carriage Company of Cleveland, a then-emerging gasoline-powered automobile manufacturer. After three long, contentious years, Winton acquiesced and agreed to pay royalties to the Electric Vehicle Company. Recognizing the force of this patent and desiring there be an equal starting point, Winton and nine other companies established the Association of Licensed Automobile Manufactures. This organization, acting for its members, agreed to pay royalties regularly to The Electric Vehicle Company which held the patent for Selden. But Henry Ford, an independent, self-reliant entrepreneur who had formed the Ford Motor Company, chose not to make this tribute. Subsequently Ford was sued in 1903. Finally, after eight years of litigation, the Court of Appeals decided the case in Ford's favor, a most momentous decision in a dynamic industry. With this yoke removed from the companies, the industry could move ahead unhampered by threat of entanglement.

Figure 8.8. A later 1897 Columbia "Dos-A-Dos" now equipped with wire-spoked wheels and forward riding lamp. Scientific American. (See Footnote 15)

The legal chink in the Selden patent exploited by Ford was: the Selden patent called for a two-cycle Brayton engine, while already the automobile makers were utilizing the four-cycle Otto type, developed by Nicholas Otto in Germany in 1867. What was thought to be a major asset held by the Electric Vehicle Company, was, with a stroke of a pen, reduced to almost zero value. With this decision the worth of the Company's share fell appropriately. The Corporation, woefully overcapitalized, never recovered from this legal ruling. Furthermore, Maxim, the key engineer in the electric vehicle development, had little interest in the merger of his division of the Pope Manufacturing Company into the Electric Vehicle Company. It is here he leaves the electric vehicle story, for his next effort would be the gasoline-powered car, for another company. Subsequently Maxim, a professional inventor like his father, would innovate the Maxim gun silencer; he would develop mufflers for the noisy gasoline engines. He became an accomplished inventor. His first try had been electric cars.

The Pope Manufacturing Division of the Electric Vehicle Company, making its own tubing for the chassis, fabricating its own tires, being well-known, had gained much momentum, for the growth of electric vehicles was rapid in the marketplace. In 1900 a total of 1575 electric cars

Figure 8.9. Columbia Two-Seated Surrey Motor Carriage. Scientific American.[15]

were assembled in America, with motors averaging 2.6 hp, bearing an average cost of $63.00.[14] Pope's 1899 vehicles are both described and pictured in the *Scientific American* of the day.[15]

Of these early electric vehicles manufactured by The Pope Manufacturing Company, Hiram Percy Maxim has given us an eyewitness description of the event, the operation of their first electric carriage.[16] The story may be compared with the firsthand account by Abbé Moigne, who described the operation of Gustave Trouvé's electric tricycle, the first electric vehicle ever, in 1881, and, the account by the author of the initial extensive trip of an early alternating-current electric powered car in 1969, described in a later chapter.

The Quickening Pace

This introduction to the local people of the Pope Manufacturing Company's first electric car, recounted in 1936 by Maxim a year before he died, enables the reader to almost taste the

---

[14] Census Reports, Vol. X, *Manufactures*, Part IV, Washington D.C.: United States Census Office, 1902, p. 165.
[15] *Scientific American*, Vol. LXXX, No. 19, May 13, 1899, pp. 304-305.
[16] Hiram Percy Maxim, *Horseless Carriage Days*, New York: Harper Bros., 1936.

Broad Claims on a Hydro-Carbon Road Engine.

———

Since the possibilities of horseless road locomotion have become apparent to the popular mind and capital has turned its attention to it as a field for investment, there has been much speculation in regard to the value of patents in this line of invention.

Many have contended and still contend that no basic patents can be held in the application of a hydro-carbon engine to the propulsion of road vehicles. Others, however, are more confident in this respect, hoping as the industry develops to realize from some old claim, now almost forgotten or at least overlooked by the average investigator, that generous reward which Uncle Sam occasionally gives to pioneer inventors in great industrial lines.

For the searcher among the files of the Patent Office under the class of road engines, or vehicle motors as they would now be properly called, one patent is of preëminent interest because of the early date of the application and the broad and generous nature of the claims. It is patent No. 549,160, dated Nov. 5, 1895, and granted to George B. Selden, a patent attorney of Rochester, N. Y. Although this patent was granted only last year the application was filed on May 8, 1879.

The title of the patent is "Road Engine," and in the preface to his description the inventor calls attention to the difficulties that have been encountered in the attempt to apply steam to this purpose, and claims by the use of a hydro-carbon engine to so reduce the weight and fuel supplies as to render his engine a practical "road engine."

The body of this vehicle is of any conventional shape, accommodating few or many people. The driving is done with the front wheels, and the steering with the hind wheels. A fifth wheel is employed, and a foot brake, operating upon the hind wheels.

The "road engine" may be any one of the compression type, and the inventor prefers to attach it to the front axle, placing the cylinders transversely to the driving shaft, and connecting them with a compressed air tank, carried on the axle below the engine and filled by an air pump of usual construction.

The engine illustrated here is supposed to have three cylinders, and as the principles involved are now well known to our readers no further elucidation is necessary.

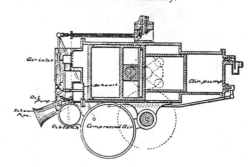

Several different methods of transmitting the power to the wheels are suggested, and clutches are provided on the axle to enable the wheels to rotate independently in turning corners. In order to operate the clutches and valves of the engine flexible connections are employed, passing into a journal on the engine. Above this journal each connection is provided with a universal joint which permits the oscillation of the driving shaft with reference to the body of the carriage.

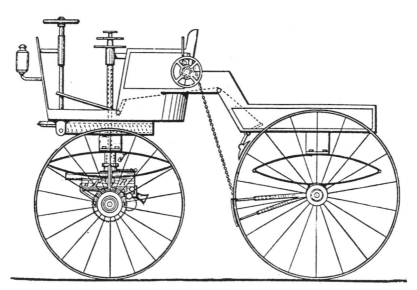

"ROAD ENGINE."—GEO. B. SELDEN, ROCHESTER, N. Y.

Figure 8.10. The importance of the Selden Patent to the automobile industry was forewarned by the editor of The Horseless Age, Vol. II, No. 2, December 2, 1896. Through litigation Henry Ford rendered the patent valueless in 1911.

excitement and the anticipation of introducing a revolutionary product in 1896. Maxim had earlier introduced a gasoline-powered tricycle, but only with Herculean effort. Every part had first to be designed, then seen through manufacture, assembly, and operation. It was with such painstaking background that Maxim arrived at the Pope plant in Hartford to be in charge of electric vehicle research under Lieutenant Hayden Eames.

For Maxim to design and fabricate the first electric car proved to be a far more tractable task. And the timing of Pope's first electric car, the Columbia, proved most propitious. The Paris-Bordeaux-Paris automobile race of 1895 had quickened the pulse of all in the Western world to the possibilities of personal travel. The Chicago-Evanston-Chicago race of the same year had brought auto racing to America. And the race soon to be held at Narragansett Park already had many people discussing the merits of motoring. Personal travel in 1896 was heady, dynamic, and in flux. Change was everywhere. Colonel Pope, Hiram Percy Maxim, Andrew Riker, Morris & Salom, Walter Baker, C. A. Woods and their associates in America were causing to dawn the Golden Age of Electric Vehicles which, sparkling towards the very end of Queen Victoria's reign, would begin, at first unobservant, its slow, relative decline with her death. The next chapter touches upon this apogee of interest in electric vehicles in America.

CHAPTER 9

The Golden Age of Electric Vehicles

The golden age of early electric vehicles was from 1895 to 1905. America was in an expansive mood. The West had been won. The U.S. Navy and the Army had recently given a splendid account of themselves in the Spanish-American War. The seas of the Western Hemisphere were an American lake. An exuberant president, Teddy Roosevelt, was soon to enter the White House. The country was prosperous. And America had a new calling which, starting in 1902, would grow as fast as the nation could build a new industry, an activity that would expand continuously for two decades. But that growth of the internal combustion vehicle industry was to be in the future. In personal transportation in America the year 1900 belonged to the electric carriage.

The electric vehicles of the era represented high style and pride of the carriage building art. The graceful surreys, dos-a-dos, traps, hansoms, and road wagons would start instantly, gain speed, and run with almost complete absence of sound. Bearing wire-spoked wheels, pneumatic tires, comfortable springs, and rich upholsteries, they could buzz along the city streets up to 25 miles per hour. Vehicles by Riker, Woods, Pope, Baker, all were well designed. The steam car, on the other hand, was vulnerable in cold weather; it was slow in raising steam, and its range before water became necessary was less than the electric car. And the gasoline-powered car still had limitations. The engine could be balky, particularly in low temperatures, when the water would need to be drained from the radiator; and as exhaust mufflers were unknown, the vehicles were so noisy as to scare horses. So, in 1900 the electric car was at the pinnacle of success. Not until 1902, when all automobiles—electric, steam, and gasoline-powered—adopted the Torpedo body, the same as employed today, would the electric car lose favor. In that short period of dominance Hiram Percy Maxim writes lovingly of touring in an America that saw the end of the Victorian period.[1] Figure 9.1 shows an electric touring car.

The Philadelphia Electric Company in 1902 had a vehicle fleet consisting of 56 electrics, 62 internal combustion vehicles, 22 motorcycles, and 56 horse drawn wagons with 63 horses.

---

[1] Hiram Percy Maxim, *The Radius of Action of Electric Motor Carriages, The Horseless Age*, Vol. II, No. 9, July 1897, pp. 2-4.

Figure 9.1. The golden age of the early electric vehicles was at the end of the 19th and the beginning of the 20th Century—the close of the Victorian Age.[2]

A sampling of commercial electric vehicle fleets (1/3 to 5 ton capacity) in the Philadelphia area in the year 1914 revealed the following:[3]

Adams Express	146	Philadelphia Electric Co.	31
American Gas Co.	8	F. A. Poth & Son (brewers)	34
Berdoll Brewing Co.	16	C. Schmidt Brewing Co.	25
Curtis Publishing Co.	11	Adam Scheidt Brewing Co.	8
T. Finkenauer Brewing Co.	8	United Gas Improvement Co.	15
Horn & Hardart Baking Co.	11		

For the use of these electric trucks and passenger vehicles The American Automobile Association issued road maps indicating by circles where electric charging stations were located, as illustrated in Fig. 9.2. But the impact of the internal combustion engine as a superior motive source was being felt, and the Pope Company, despite its early lead, would eventually succumb.

---

[2] *Scientific American*, Vol. LXXX, No. 19, May 13, 1899, p. 291.
[3] *Electric Vehicle News*, November 1977, pp. 28-29.

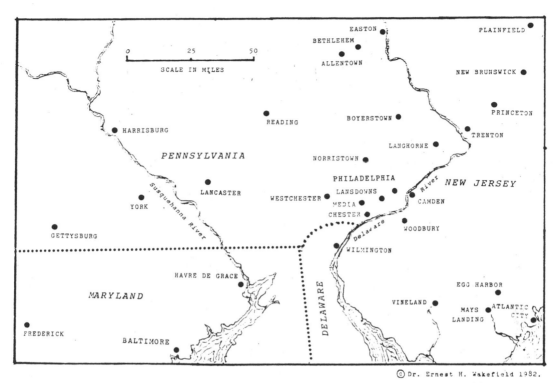

© Dr. Ernest H. Wakefield 1982.

Figure 9.2. Charging stations in the first decade of the 1900's in the environs of Philadelphia and Baltimore. Ernest H. Wakefield.

Decline of the Pope Manufacturing Company

Ten years after merging with Pope's division, The Electric Vehicle Company became the Columbia Motor Company. Having little engineering distinctiveness, it joined the United States Motor Company which shortly failed. This company, together with a host of others, were part of the Lead Trust organized by Widener and Whitney. The ruling on the Selden patent caused the bubble to burst.[4]

Quite apart from the above case of over-capitalization and manipulation, there was electric car competition and rivalry from the dynamic internal combustion automobile industry. Yet growth was all around. From July 1911 to July 1912 the number of electric cars in New York City increased by 45 percent. The letter below from J. A. Kingman,[5] with the author's identification as to type of drive system and the calculations, show the strong position of steam, and the growing popularity of gasoline powered vehicles. As a percent of total registered cars, those equipped with electric power, while increasing numerically for a decade or more, would, as the years passed, approach the vanishing point. The ascendancy of the internal combustion powered automobile had begun, though, at the time, few seers knew how dominant would become this marvelous engine for transforming chemical energy into mechanical energy.

---

[4] *Illinois Lead Cab Company in Liquidation, The Horseless Age*, Vol. 7, No. 24, March 13, 1901, p. 14.

[5] *Ibid.*, Vol. 9, No. 21, 1903. p. 612.

Some Automobile Registration Figures in New York State New York, May 16, 1903	
Editor *Horseless Age*:	
We have just been looking over a list of automobiles registered in New York State from the beginning of the new law up to April 1. Following is a list of the first fifteen machines registered:	
Locomobile 345	steam
Mobile 138	steam
Winton 104	gasoline
De Dion 48	gasoline
Columbia...45	electric*
Gasmobile 39	electric*
Oldsmobile 32	gasoline
Panhard 32	gasoline
Woods Electric 22	electric*
Baker 20	electric*
Haynes-Apperson 20	gasoline
Autocar 18	electric*
Riker 17	electric*
Foster 13	electric*
United States Long Distance 13	gasoline
We, as a company, have turned out 4,000 machines. We believe this is a very large proportion of all the automobiles actually running in the United States to-day.	53 percent steam-powered 27 percent gasoline-powered 20 percent electric-powered* — 100 %
The Locomobile Company of America, per J. A. Klingman.	column added by author

As can be seen from this list of automobile makes in the year 1903, steam-powered cars were dominant, while of the electrics, Pope's Columbia was most numerous, followed by Woods Electric, made in Chicago; the Baker, assembled in Cleveland; and the Riker, a New York City product.

Colonel Albert A. Pope died in 1909.[6] While he had made honest mistakes, his achievements were rather remarkable. His company, a large bicycle manufacture, suffering a recession, with an able engineering staff sparked by Hiram Percy Maxim, became the first to manufacture motor vehicles in quantity, both electric and gasoline powered. He was also a pioneer in making

---

[6] John B. Rae, *American Automobile Manufactures*, Chilton Co., NYC, 1959.

technological research a part of industry, and finally he was the organizer of the Good Roads Movement, a step that led America from a nation of dirt highways, almost impassable in wet weather and in winter, to a country with an incomparable highway net.

The Condition of Roads in America

For those with a memory that reaches back no further than 1930, the average condition of roads between cities can scarcely be appreciated. For an example of the highways of those days we owe a description to Edward W. Staebler. In America Staebler was an early enthusiastic automobile dealer in the Michigan city of Ann Arbor, where the family still resides. Describing roads in 1901 in driving a car from Toledo to Ann Arbor, he wrote to the American Bicycle Company in Toledo after driving a steam carriage:[7]

> "We encountered some very rough roads. We left your place at 11:45 (A.M.) and reached home at 7:30 (P.M.). We did not lose more than 45 minutes altogether, oiling, filling with water, and lunch. That makes the actual running time 6 3/4 hours, for the distance covered, 58 miles. The roads from Toledo to Sylvania were fair. From Sylvania through Ottawa Lake to Blissfield they were horrible. All clay and the rainy weather of the week before left them in bad shape. The clay baked hard and as passing teams had worn practically no path you may imagine how rough the road was. Over that road we travelled at the rate of five miles an hour. Faster than that would have been severe on the carriage as well as ourselves. Out of Blissfield the roads were sandy, but certainly more desirable than the rough clay road. After a few miles this again changed to another rough road until within a few miles of Ridgeway where the roads were fine and continued so for about ten miles, when again we found them bad until near Salina. From Salina to Ann Arbor they were fine, in fact there is no nicer road in the State. We consumed 11 gallons of gasoline on the trip and a quart of cylinder and lubricating oil."

The steamer had travelled five miles per gallon of gasoline, and had driven through quagmires. It was an achievement. Such roads are illustrated in Figs. 9.3,[8] and 9.4,[9] respectively, country and city.

The Studebaker Electric

While Pope Manufacturing had been a bicycle maker that had gone into motor vehicles, another class of manufacture gravitated toward this newly emerging industry. The wagon builders. Below is related how electric automobiles came to be made by The Studebaker Company.

---

[7] F. Clever Bald, *Horseless Carriages in Ann Arbor*, Michigan Historical Collection, Bulletin #6, December 1953.

[8] *The Horseless Age*, Vol. 18, No. 4, September 1912, p. 343.

[9] Hiram Percy Maxim, *Horseless-Carriage Days*, Harper & Bro., NYC, 1937.

Figure 9.3. Wet red clay roads made the going heavy near Crest View, Tenn. Courtesy: The Horseless Age.

The American War with Spain, and the British Boer War in South Africa, had created a substantial demand for horse-drawn vehicles. Those examples of imperial adventure had begun in 1898 and 1899 respectively. As a measure of importance in 1899 America produced 1575 electric cars, and 936 gasoline powered vehicles.[10] Who at that time was so sanguine as to dream that a single year would see over ten million motorcars produced! With war orders on their books few wagon makers saw fit to exploit the motorization of wagons. One of the few was the Studebaker Brothers Manufacturing Company of Fort Wayne, Indiana. Initiated by five brothers in 1852 the company had become the largest wagon maker in the United States. John M. was the most influential brother of this remarkable family. Joining the company was an avid motor enthusiast, Frederick S. Fish, a lawyer, who entered the organization in 1891 as general counsel. With the interest of Fish, the company began to experiment with electric cars and drive systems as early as 1895.[11]

The media of the day, always interested in giving their readers news from a company so well known in the personal transportation field as the Studebaker Company, queried the organization for its plans, if any, in the newly emerging horseless wagon field. A letter came forward, signed

---

[10] Andrew Jamison, *The Steam Powered Automobile*, Indiana University, Bloomington, 1970, p. 166.

[11] *The Horseless Age*, Vol. 2, No. 1, November 1896, p. 20.

Figure 9.4. The streets of Hartford in 1897 after a heavy rain. Finding hard going is one of the first electric vehicles of the Pope Manufacturing Company. Courtesy: Harper & Bros.

by Fish, dated October 19, 1896, which read in part: "We are not yet prepared to give to the public what we have accomplished. However, we anticipate within a very short time to be able to present what we consider, from the standpoint of utility, a practical motor wagon."[12]

The cat was out of the bag. Studebaker would have a mechanically powered automobile. Whether electric, steam, or gasoline, Fish wasn't saying. But the management recognized, as Colonel Pope had, a new age was dawning in personal transportation.

Studebaker's first horseless carriage, which was anxiously awaited by the knowing, was electric. To a company steeped in wagon building such a choice would be logical. In 1896 when their experimentation was proceeding in earnest, easily the best developed drive system was the electric. It was quiet, easily manipulated, and had sufficient power. The Studebaker electric was available in 1902. Undoubtedly an incentive for the pursuit of this new form of transportation had been the order for 100 bodies from the Electric Vehicle Company of New York, whose fortune we had earlier seen rise. While the Studebaker electric was long in gestation, the brothers watched with growing interest the advance in the drive system of the gasoline-powered automobile. Their electric cars assembly lasted only two years when they switched their allegiance to vehicles powered by this liquid fuel.

---

[12] *Ibid*, p. 20.

While the Studebaker development of horseless carriages had been in Fort Wayne, an effort also in automobiles and one to gain lasting fame was emerging in Lansing, Michigan with the genesis of Oldsmobile.

The Olds Electric Car

In 1898 Ransom E. Olds, a Michigan resident, was producing two electric models of the horseless carriage, early Oldsmobiles, the Stanhope, and the Phaeton.[13] In a fire at his Lansing, Michigan works all that was rescued was a new model electric car, Fig. 9.5.,[14] pushed out by a faithful employee. But R.E. Olds was a persistent man. In 1892 he had built a steam carriage. A four wheeler,[15] with larger wheels forward than at the rear, the former had a shorter axle than that used to couple the rear wheels. At the rear the vehicle had an upright steam boiler.

Not content with the then-popular steam propulsion, Olds devised the model electric cars cited above and, finally, in 1897 he completed his first gasoline powered car. At one and the same time he advertised "15 years experience" and was offering vehicles powered by steam, electricity, and gasoline, probably the only manufacturer to offer all competing types of personal transportation. It was apparent that Olds, like many others, could not clearly distinguish which of these drive systems would survive. Olds, however, unlike the other pioneers, left no bases uncovered. In the surviving names in automobiles R.E. Olds must be considered a giant, but his final laurel would be the gasoline-powered car. A measure of his versatility is his wheel and tire invention of 1899, shown in the Notes at the conclusion of this chapter. Alert he had to be in view of the Tillinghast patent on pneumatic tires, also seen in the Notes, even though the basic work on pneumatic tires had been done by Dunlop cited in the Prologue. Olds, like his peer Henry Ford, was noted for simplicity in design.

Figure 9.5. A 1902 Electric Oldsmobile. Courtesy: The Horseless Age.

---

[13] Fitzroy Stanhope was a British clergyman, 1787-1864 who was the first to have built a lightweight, four wheeled buggy with a high seat, closed back, and characterized by a heavy erect piece on each side. This type buggy is pictured in American Western movies. Phaeton was the son of Helios, the sun god. He borrowed his father's sun chariot and, through careless driving, would have set the world on fire had not Zeus struck him down with a thunderbolt.

[14] *The Horseless Age*, Vol. 9, No. 21, May 21, 1902, p. 111.

[15] *Scientific American*, Vol. LXVI, No. 21, May 21, 1892, p. 329.

Just as Olds could not foresee the direction the personal transportation industry would proceed in its drive system, neither, of course, could the journalist. The account below encounters all worlds. In 1899 *McClure's Magazine* carried an article which read in part:

"It is not hard to imagine what a country touring station will be like on a summer afternoon some five or ten years hence. Long rows of vehicles will stand backed up comfortably to the charging bars each with its electric plug filling the battery with power. The owners will be lolling at the tables on the verandas of the nearby road house. Men with repair kits will bustle about tightening up a nut here, oiling this bearing and regulating that gear. From a long rubber tube compressed air will be hissing into pneumatic tires. There will be many gasoline carts and road wagons and tricycles, and they too, will need repairs and pumping, and their owners will employ themselves busily filling their little tin cans with gasoline, recharging their tanks, refilling the water jackets, and looking to the working of their sparking devices. And then there will be boys selling peanuts, arnica, and court-plasters, and undoubtedly a cynical old farmer or two with a pair of ambling mares to carry home such of these new-fangled vehicles as may become hopelessly indisposed. Add to the bustling assembly of amateur self-propellers a host of bicycle riders—for there will doubtless be as many bicycles in those days as ever and it will be a sight to awaken every serious-minded horse to an uneasy consideration of his future.

"The new electric cabs are unquestionable immensely popular as fashionable conveyances. A number of the wealthy people of New York, including Mr. Frank Gould, Mr. Cornelius Vanderbilt, Mr. O. H. Belmont, and Mr. Richard McCurdy have a cab or brougham and driver constantly on call at the home station of the company, for which they pay at the rate of $180 a month. Several prominent physicians are similarly provided, motor vehicles being especially adapted to the varied necessities of a physician's practice."

The McClure story indicated the electric vehicle had a good press. When compared with a horse and buggy, an electric car was really a substantial advance. Its rate of travel on city streets was from 3-4 times faster. It required no groom. It was instantly available in fair weather and in foul. It was sanitary.[16] It was almost noiseless. And it was of the technological advance that seemed to be thrusting America forward. It had charisma and it had appeal. As a consequence, horseless carriages were not long in reaching the public. Therefore, at the first automobile show at Madison Square Garden in November 1900 were 34 makes of cars. Nineteen were internal combustion powered, seven were steam, and six were electric. Of the latter there were representatives of the following organizations: the Pope-Waverly Company, Baker Motor

---

[16] Barton Peck of Detroit developed a gasoline-powered vehicle in 1897, and a second car in Feb. 1900. In a newspaper interview in August 1899 he gave up, for the reason which must surely be the first complaint on automobile air pollution. George S. May, *A Most Unique Machine*, W. B. Erdman Publishing Co., 1975. Peck (p. 85) says regarding gasoline cars, "There is one great obstacle that must be overcome and that is the offensive odor from gasoline that has been burned and that is discharged into the air. It is a sickening odor and I can readily see that should there be any number of them running on the street, there would be an ordinance passed forbidding them."

Vehicle Company, Buffalo Carriage Company, Electric Vehicle Company, Woods Motor Vehicle Company, and National Automobile and Electric Company. The Electric Vehicle Company was cited earlier; the Baker Motor Vehicle Company will be discussed for its innovativeness; and the Woods Motor Vehicle Company deserves special mention not only because its product was the first to be used by the U.S. Army, but because C. A. Woods, its President, was the most articulate, leaving a book, published in 1900, wholly devoted to the explanation and care of electric cars. This volume referred to in Chapter 4 serves to link early and modern electric vehicles.

The development of the automobile was so profound an invention as to change with time the mores of the Western world, for the concept of touring was perceived. Probably the earliest practitioner and writer on this subject was Hiram Percy Maxim, who, first building an electric car for the Pope Manufacturing Company, then, while testing his handiwork, discovered touring. It would place wings on the feet of the family, and the Western world would be forever changed.

The Origin of Touring and the Impetus for Better Roads

In the short golden years of electric vehicles, when interurban roads were only half travelled with here and there a lonely buggy, or possibly a trotting horseman, only natural sounds greeted the ear. Hiram Percy Maxim, a true Renaissance man, like Henry David Thoreau in his appreciation of the grandeur of nature, probably earliest caught the sense of what would become "touring," a phenomenon that would transform America. It would cause a transcontinental network of roads to be established, transform the petroleum companies, and cause the West to drill for oil in the Middle East. Maxim was the first to experience touring while making neighborhood visitations from Hartford, the headquarters of the Pope Manufacturing Company, when Maxim was in charge of electric vehicle development. On one such sojourn he writes:[17]

> "The batteries were completely filled at Thompsonville. The return trip over the road to Windsor Locks was a very rapid and most enjoyable one, and owing to the daylight and the publicity of the occasion, considerable excitement was caused along the road. Although carriages equipped with other kinds of power have passed along this road in the past, the fact that this was the first motor *voiture de luxe* prevented any diminution in the interest shown. Windsor Locks was passed at a good twelve-mile gait and Windsor reached without a stop from the time we left the electric light station at Thompsonville. The distance between the two places is between twelve and fourteen miles and the time occupied in making it was one hour and five minutes...."

Touring would prove a poison for electric vehicles, and a tonic for gasoline-powered automobiles. For the first time the range of a vehicle became significant. A fully charged battery

---

[17] Hiram Percy Maxim, *The Radius of Action of Electric Motor Carriages, The Horseless Age*, Vol. 11, No. 9, July 1897, pp. 2-4.

would propel Hiram Maxim's electric 25 miles; a full tank of gasoline would move Alexander Winton's gasoline motorcar 200 miles! The tank could be refilled in five minutes; a battery recharge required five hours. What was true in 1900 is, unfortunately, valid at the close of the 20th century.[18]

As the reader can observe, electric vehicles were more highly developed in America than in Europe. Conversely, the gasoline automobile was more advanced in the Old Country. Let us now turn to the new year of 1900. The first Automobile Show was held in this year. The first journal, *The Horseless Age*, chronicling this new industry was already five years old, as Fig. 2.1 attests, and steam, electric, and gasoline drive systems were highly competitive. Before continuing the romantic history of the development of the electric automobile, the next chapter details the evolution of the elements which made the electric car possible: the charger for batteries, the motive power battery, the controller, and the electric motor. Each is a classic story in its own right; an interrelated tale that has probably never been told.

Notes

A Semi-Pneumatic Tire

"R.E. Olds, of the Olds Motor Works, Detroit, Mich., has recently invented a semi-pneumatic tire illustrated herewith, consisting of a series of open rubber pockets with round corners, fitting on to an ordinary tire by means of screws passing through steel washers in the bottoms of the pockets, and then into the steel tire. These washers are vulcanized on to the rubber pockets. The pressure comes between two flat surfaces, and there is no cutting edge. When the pockets presses against the pavement the air is compressed in the pockets and its walls thickens, forming a cushion. In passing over an obstruction the rubber expands, it is claimed, and distributes the strain. When one pocket is injured it can be replaced with ease and at small expense."[19] As this section shows, R.E. Olds was an inventor, production man, salesman, entrepreneur, and financier, an early giant of the automobile business. Illustrations are from *The Horseless Age* and shown in Fig. 9.6 and 9.7.

Illustrations from *The Horseless Age*, Vol. 5, No. 10, December 6, 1899, p. 59.

Costs of Electric Cars

In 1913 popular electric cars had costs as shown in Fig. 9.8 at the time when like gasoline-engined automobiles could be had for $1000.00 less. The apogee of electric vehicle production was 1912.

Illustrations from *Scientific American*, CVIII 2, Jan. 11, 1913, p. 46.

---

[18] Ernest H. Wakefield, *The Consumer's Electric Car*, Ann Arbor: The Ann Arbor Science Publishers Inc., 1977.
[19] *The Horseless Age*, Vol. 5, No. 17, Jan. 24, 1889.

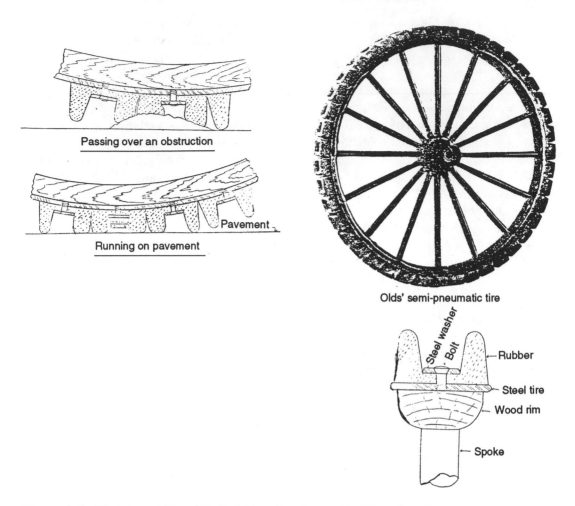

Passing over an obstruction

Running on pavement

Pavement

Olds' semi-pneumatic tire

Steel washer
Bolt
Rubber
Steel tire
Wood rim
Spoke

Figure 9.6. The Versatility of R. E. Olds. Courtesy: The Horseless Age.

CAUTION.

Pneumatic Tires for Automobiles or Vehicles.

All persons are notified that I am the owner of the

TILLINGHAST PATENT,

(Number 497,971, of May 23, 1893, for Improvements in Pneumatic Tires.)

which, after four years of litigation, has been sustained by the United States Court, in a decision by Judge Colt, on November 14, 1899.

This Patent covers all single-tube tires used for any purpose whatsoever, including the great majority of automobile or vehicle tires; and no person can make, sell or use any such tires without a license from me.

No license on automobile or vehicle tires has as yet been granted, and

ALL PERSONS ARE WARNED

that any infringement of the Tillinghast Patent by the manufacture, SALE or USE of such tires will be prosecuted to the full extent of the law.

Upon all Single-Tube Tires for automobiles or vehicles MADE, SOLD OR USED in the past, a royalty must at once be paid to me.

☞ **The undersigned believes it wiser to rely on the opinion and decree of a Judge of the United States Court, after nearly a year's mature consideration of evidence, briefs and arguments, than on the opinion of any firm of lawyers whatsoever, and notifies the trade that he shall claim full damages for future infringements.**

THEODORE A. DODGE,

ROOM 1238, N. Y. LIFE BUILDING NEW YORK CITY.

Figure 9.7. The Tillinghast patent, like the Selden patent, was among the thicket of thorns with which any successful manufacturer had to contend.

What Electric Pleasure Car Can I Buy?

A Table Which Gives the Name, Manufacturer and Price of the Principal American Electric Pleasure Cars

Name of Car.	Name and Address of Manufacturer.	Under $2,500.	$2,500 to $3,000.	Over $3,000.
Argo	Argo Electric Vehicle Company, Saginaw, Mich		4p Rd., $2,500, 4p Bro., $2,800.	Fore-Drive 5p $3,100
Bailey	S. R. Bailey & Co., Amesbury, Mass	2p Roadster, $2,250-$2,500	Phaeton, $2,600	4p Roadster, $3,200
Baker	Baker Motor Vehicle Company, Cleveland, Ohio	2p Victoria, $2,000	4p Coupé, $2,800	Brougham, $3,100
Borland	Borland-Grannis Company, Chicago, Ill	5p Brougham $2,500	3p Rd., $2,500, 5p Coupé, $2,900	7p Limousine, $5,500
Broc	Broc Electric Vehicle Company, Cleveland, Ohio	2p Stanhope $2,000, Vic. 2p 2,050	5p Brougham, $3,000	6p Brougham, $3,200
Buffalo	Buffalo Electric Vehicle Company, Buffalo, N. Y.		2p Roadster, $2,600	2p Coupé, $3,200
Century	Century Electric Car Company, Detroit, Mich		5p Brougham, $2,550	
Chicago	Chicago Electric Motor Car Company, Chicago, Ill		"131" Coupé, $2,800	"132" Coupé, $3,100
Church-Field	Church-Field Motor Company, Detroit, Mich	2p Roadster, $2,300	Brougham, $2,800	
Colonial	Colonial Electric Car Company, Detroit, Mich.		5p Brougham, $2,700	
Columbus	Columbus Buggy Company, Columbus, Ohio			
Dayton	Dayton Electric Car Company, Dayton, Ohio	2p Victoria, $2,100	4p Coupé, $2,700	
Detroit Electric	Anderson Electric Car Company, Detroit, Mich	2p Roadster, $2,350, Vic., $2,300	4-5p Brougham, $3,000	5p. C.V. Brougham, $3,600
Flanders	Flanders Manufacturing Company, Pontiac, Mich	4p Victoria, $2,250	4p Coupé $2,500	
Fritchle	Fritchle Auto and Battery Company, Denver, Colo	2p Roadster, $2,100	4p Touring, $2,500	4p Coupé, $3,600
Grinnell	Grinnell Electric Car Company, Detroit, Mich		5p Coupé, $2,950 Broug'm $3,000.	
Kimball	C. P. Kimball & Co., Chicago, Ill.		2p Phaeton, $3,000	
Ohio	Ohio Electric Car Company, Toledo, Ohio	3p Victoria, $2,300	5p Coupé, $2,900	5p Brougham, $3,200 and $3,500
Hupp-Yeats	R-C-H Corporation, Detroit, Mich.	4p Regent, $1,750		
Rauch & Lang	Rauch & Lang Carriage Company, Cleveland, Ohio	4p Victoria, $2,500	4p Coupé, $2,900, 5p Bro. $3,000	
Standard Electrique	Standard Electric Carriage Company, Jackson, Mich.	4p Coupé, $1,885	5p Coupé, $2,250	
Studebaker	Studebaker Corporation, South Bend, Ind	"17" Stanhope, $850		
Van Wagoner	Clark Motor Carriage Company, Buffalo, N. Y.	2p Roadster, $1,800	Coupé, $2,200	5p Coupé, $3,000
Waverley	The Waverley Company, Indianapolis, Ind.	2p Roadster, $2,250		5p Limousine, $3,500
Woods	Woods Motor Vehicle Company, Chicago, Ill.	2p. Rd., $2,400, 4p Vic. $2,500.	5p Brougham, $2,700	4p Lim., $3,100, 5p Lim. $3,600

Figure 9.8. Cost of electric cars in 1913.

CHAPTER 10

The Evolution of the Battery Charger and the Battery

In detailing the history of transportation it is conventional to present only the vehicle itself, the chassis and the body. It is, however, the drive system which makes the electric car unique. Therefore, for completeness, in this account, the development of the electric power elements is an integral part. Surely the early electrical engineers who were so influential in electric vehicle design such as Walter C. Baker of the Baker Motor Vehicle Company, and C.E. Woods of the Woods Electric Vehicle Company, were cognizant of improving the drive system. That idea was central. In discussing the origins of the power train of an electric automobile, the order which is followed is of the electric current as it flows from the electric utility receptacle into and through the drive system elements of the car. In an electric vehicle the electric drive system in entirety may be listed as: the charger for the battery, the battery for motive power, the controller for the motor, and the electric motor. The antecedents for the charger and the controller are no older than the electric car itself. The battery, however, has a richer background, as does the motor.

Development of Battery Chargers

On all but the modern, high performance vehicles, the source of d-c power was almost always off-board: the vehicle was not internally equipped with a charger. Today, the practice is to place a charger aboard the vehicle. Figures 10.1 and 10.2 show a battery charger of the 1890's[1] The voltage of the mains is 110 volts, direct-current, d-c. Following the circuit from the mains in the illustration, there is a safety fuse, a switch, a voltmeter on the left to read the voltage of the mains, an ammeter to read the current flow to the battery, a rheostat or resistance box which can be adjusted to determine the amount of current permitted to flow into the car batteries. To replenish the batteries, the vehicle was driven to the charging station. With the switch open, the vehicle plug was inserted into the electrical receptacle. With the rheostat adjusted for minimum voltage, the switch was closed. The rheostat was then varied to permit the recommended initial charging current to flow, which might be twenty amperes. As the

---

[1] C. E. Woods, *The Electric Automobile, Its Construction, Care and Operation*, H. E. Stone & Co., Chicago, 1900, pp. 177.

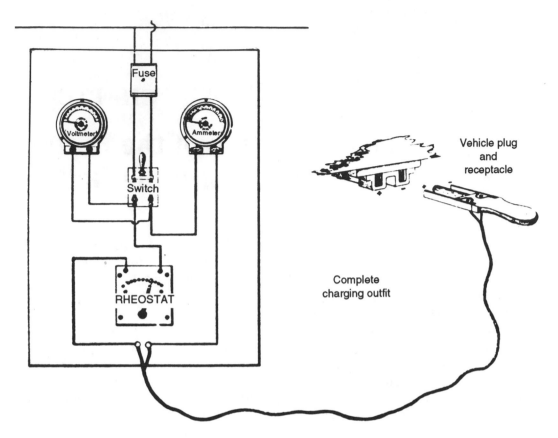

Figure 10.1. To charge the electric car's battery, from the direct-current mains current passes through a safety fuse, the switch, to the rheostat, then to the automobile's receptacle. From the receptacle the current entered the battery, out the receptacle, through the ammeter, and finally to the other side of the mains. The meter on the left read the voltage of the mains.

battery reached full charge, as determined by testing the density of the battery electrolyte with a hydrometer, the rheostat was adjusted to allow a minimum "finishing" current. The charger was simple, but required an attendant. And, of course, such a simple charger was possible because, at the turn of the century, d-c mains were readily available in the cities, the result of Thomas Alva Edison's early belief in the advantages of d-c service, rather than the alternating-current, a-c, method of electricity generation now almost universally used.

In actual practice a garage wherein electric vehicles were brought to have their batteries charged was presented with problems. For not only might each vehicle have a different battery complement than the other, and, in addition, one have lead-acid batteries, another Edison iron-nickel batteries, but the batteries might be of different discharge. J. F. Lincoln of the Lincoln Electric Company, now a major manufacturer of electric welding equipment, gave his solution for this dilemma in the March 27, 1912 issue of *The Horseless Age*.

Figure 10.2. A rare picture of a 1912 class electric vehicle and a charger. The snake-like cable on the floor provides a-c power to the transformer. The upper section bears a circuit for rectifying the a-c to d-c power. And a rheostat is seen for adjusting the d-c voltage to that value required for charging the battery aboard the vehicle. Such a charging system would post-date the system in Fig. 10.1. Courtesy: Commonwealth Edison Company.

Modern Methods for Charging Batteries

With a-c power now being almost universal, and electric utility furnished d-c power a rarity, battery chargers, if of the isolated type, require a transformer to adjust the line voltage to the potential required by the battery. This a-c voltage is fed to a full-wave rectifier, the output of which is d-c power. As illustrated in Fig. 10.3, a smoothing capacitor finished the "tailoring" of the voltage for acceptance by the battery.[2] Figure 10.4 provides traces of the voltage wave forms as the current traverses the charger.[3] The d-c current enters the battery at a rate commensurate with the recommended charging cycle of the battery.[4]

---

[2] Ernest H. Wakefield, *The Consumers' Electric Car*, Ann Arbor Science Publishers Inc., Ann Arbor, 1977, p. 71.

[3] Ibid, p. 72.

[4] Wally E. Rippel, *Charge Acceptance Characteristics of the Lead-Acid Cell*, California Institute of Technology, Pasadena, California.

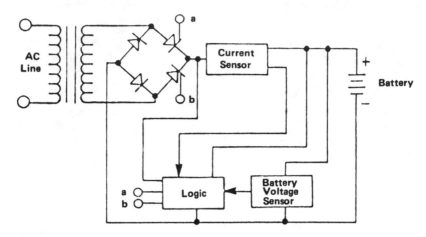

Figure 10.3. A circuit diagram of a battery charging circuit with constant current and a voltage-sensing cutoff. From left to right are the isolating transformer, a full-wave rectifier, and circuits which control current and voltage supplied to the battery being charged. Courtesy: Gould Inc. [5]

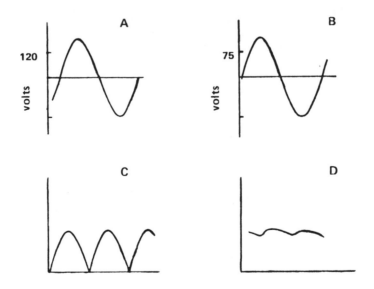

Figure 10.4. Diagram of wave forms (a) out of receptacle into transformer, (b) out of transformer into rectifier, (c) output from full-wave rectifier, and (d) the wave-form smoothed at the output of the capacitor. This final tailored dc voltage is applied to the battery, but only after it has been regulated by the current sensor and the battery voltage sensor. [6]

---

[5] Ernest H. Wakefield, *The Consumer's Electric Car*, Ann Arbor: The Ann Arbor Science Publishers Inc., 1977, p. 71.

[6] Ibid, p. 72.

Many modern battery chargers bear a battery voltage sensor. With the battery approaching full charge, or 2.35 volts per cell, a circuit senses this ever increasing cell voltage and feeds to the battery current regulator a signal which informs a control circuit to limit the current flow to the battery. Many modern chargers also contain a timer. With such a device, after a time period selected by the attendant, the charging current is automatically terminated. Modern chargers, being composed largely of solid state elements, have a high reliability. For the recent state of battery charging technique Don P. Wilson has made a significant contribution,[7] and on the care of batteries a group of Italian scientists, following in the steps of their 1800 compatriot pioneer, Volta, have made important comments.[8]

Let us now investigate the motive power battery of the vehicle which, in the example above, was being charged with electricity.

The Development of Motive Power Batteries

An electric battery, providing a steady source of electric current, is one of the all time great inventions.[9] A battery is capable of supplying instantly large quantities of electric power, with little attention, no noise, few fumes, and with great reliability.

Before reviewing the history of batteries, at the outset one should be aware there are two basic types of cells or batteries—designated primary and secondary. A primary battery converts chemical energy irreversibly into electric energy. Dry cells, cells for hand-held calculators, are primary batteries. A primary battery cannot be conveniently recharged. A replacement of the constituents of the battery is required to restore it to the original condition. Once primary cells or batteries are used to their limit they are usually discarded. A secondary cell or battery, on the other hand, is a device which stores electric energy by means of a reversible chemical reaction. When the energy is depleted, the battery is recharged, restoring it to a facsimile of its original self. The batteries used in gasoline-powered motor cars, in propelling electric vehicles, and in telephone exchanges are examples of secondary batteries.

Any battery is defined as having two or more cells. A cell is an assembly of two dissimilar metals called electrodes separated by an ion conducting solution called an electrolyte which contains a chemical which allows a reversible change in the metals. In the primary cell the negative electrode or anode consists of a readily oxidizable material such as zinc.[10] It acts as a source of electrons. The positive electrode, or cathode, in contrast, is an oxidizing substance such as carbon or copper and is the receiver of electrons. In the external circuit of a primary cell the electrons leave the anode and travel to the cathode. This flow of electrons is balanced by the flow of ions through the electrolyte.

---

[7] Don P. Wilson, *Battery Chargers Since EVS-5*, Eighth International Electric Vehicle Symposium, Washington, D.C., 1986.

[8] A. Buonarota, P. Menya, and V. Scarioni, *Setting Up Effective Procedures for Battery Management As Regards to Charging and State of Charge Evaluation*, do.

[9] W. E. Ayrton, *Storage of Power, Scientific American Supplement*, Vol. XIII, No. 338, June 24, 1882, pp. 5388-5389.

[10] For a discussion of some 35 other electric couples suitable for batteries, see: Sidney Gross, *Review of Candidate Batteries for Electrical Vehicles, Energy Conversion*, Vol. 15, No. (3/4), 1976, pp. 95-112.

   While dissecting a frog, Luigi Galvani, Professor of Medicine at Bologna, Italy, found the frog's leg twitched when he touched a muscle with a copper probe and the connecting nerve with a zinc probe.[11] While Galvani incorrectly guessed the effect to be animal electricity, Alessandro Volta, learning of this experience, assembled plates of copper and zinc, separated by pasteboard soaked in salt water. With this assembly Volta discovered he could withdraw a continuous electric current. He had the first electric battery.[12] (See Fig. 10.5.)

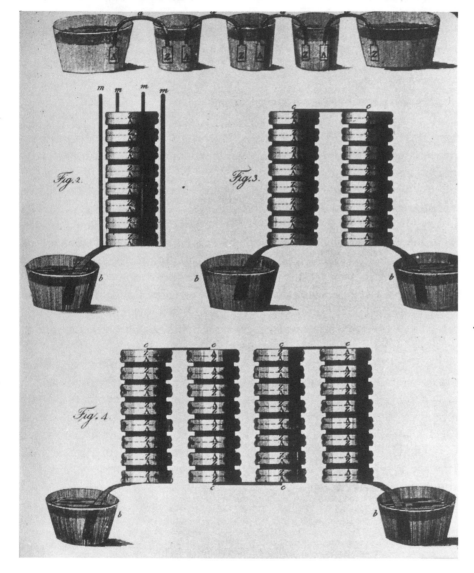

Figure 10.5. The first electric battery was described in Volta's letter to Sir Joseph Banks sent from Como, Italy on March 20, 1800, and was read before the Royal Society on June 28, 1800. The important science of electrolysis awaited only until April 30, 1800.[12]

[11] Luigi Galvani. *De Veribus Electricitis in Motu Musculari Commentarius.* Bologna, 1791. Tr. by Margaret Foley, Norwalk, Conn.: Burndy Library Publication, No. 10, 1953.

[12] *Philosophical Transactions of the Royal Society of London*, 1800, Vol. 90, p. 430.

Secondary batteries used in electric vehicles may be of the lead-acid type and consist of a container filler with dilute sulphuric acid. The effectiveness of this electric couple was discovered in 1859 by the distinguished French chemist Gaston Planté only after sedulous effort.[13] Today the negative plate is incorporated with pure sponge lead, while the positive plate grid is filled with lead dioxide. With battery discharge both the sponge lead and the lead dioxide are converted to lead sulfate. The sulfate ions in the above reaction originate from the sulfuric acid of the electrolyte and hence the density of the acid is decreased. Thus, the state of charge of a battery can most conveniently be determined by measuring the degree of acidity of the electrolyte. As sulfuric acid is more dense than water, the amount of acid present is measured by the use of a hydrometer. On charging, the chemical change which occurred is reversed. The lead sulfate formed in discharge reacts with water and again becomes sponge lead and lead dioxide, while the sulfuric acid content of the electrolyte is increased. In relating the history of the battery for electric vehicles only the lead-acid battery is discussed, because few other electric couples at this writing have been commercially used in electric cars. But the reader should realize that in developing an effective means of storing electric energy many different cell-types were and are being investigated. For the history of the electric battery two books are recommended.[14] [15] For present lead-acid batteries the reader may consult another text.[16] And for a review of forthcoming batteries there is an excellent review issue.[17] Included here is only sufficient information to enhance the reader's appreciation of a battery and its operation.

Figure 10.6 indicates how mechanical energy, in this case by a crank, is supplied to a generator, a device for converting mechanical energy into electric energy, which in turn charges a battery. Figure 10.7 is a bank of early lead-acid battery cells. When fully charged each is capable of supplying 2.3 volts. If an electric car requires 100 volts for operation, nominally 50 cells would be in series (50 cells x 2.3 volts). Now, because this same car when driven would require 25-200 amperes of current, the lead electrode area in each cell would need to be much larger than the example illustrated. Returning again to Fig. 10.6, if the battery shown were in a charged state, and if one's hand were released from the crank, the battery itself, by means of the generator/motor, would turn the crank in a direction opposite to that when charging. This double-action phenomenon was first observed by the Belgian scientist Zénobe Théophile Gramme.

---

[13] Gaston Planté, *The Storage of Energy*, P. B. Elwell, Tr., Whittaker & Co., London, 1887.

[14] Birn Dibner, *Galvanti-Volta*, Burndy Library, Norwalk, Conn.: 1952, pp. 11-26.

[15] W. James King, *The Development of Technology in the 19th Century*, U. S. National Museum, Bulletin 228, Smithsonian Institute, Washington, D. C., 1963.

[16] George Wood Vinal, *Storage Batteries*, New York: John Wiley & Sons, 1951.

[17] Sidney Gross, *Review of Candidate Batteries for Electrical Vehicles, Energy Conversion*, Vol 15, No. (3/4), 1976, pp. 95-112.

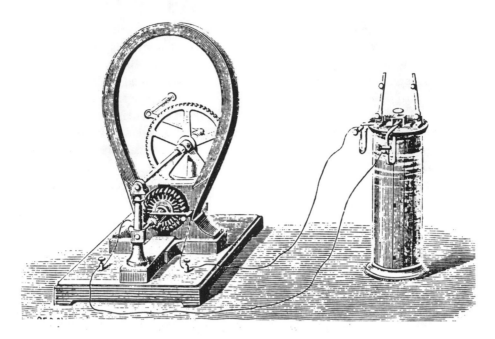

Figure 10.6. Charging a Planté cell with a Gramme magneto generator. From Gaston Planté, Recherches sur l'Electricité, Paris, 1883, p.80.[18]

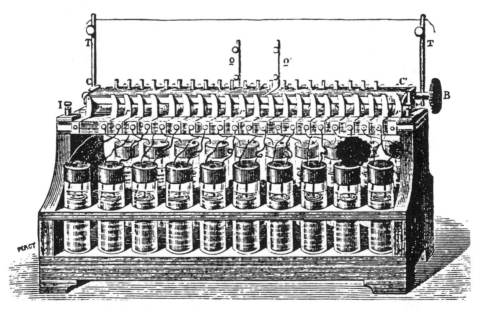

Figure 10.7. Battery of Planté cells arranged for high-voltage experiments. From Gaston Planté, Recherches sur l'Electricité, 1883, p. 97.[19]

---

[18] Planté, *Recherches sur l'Electricité*, p. 80.
[19] Ibid, p. 97.

All illustrations courtesy: Whittaker & Co.

Pacinotti in Italy earlier had also observed this electrical proceeding, but his call to military duty prevented its pursuit.[20] Planté in charging the battery used his muscle to operate Gramme's generator. He showed mechanical power was transformed by the generator into electric power. Conversely, when electric power was furnished the assembly, it gave forth mechanical power. Soon the human muscle used to operate Gramme's generator was replaced by a steam engine. The cycle of energy transformation was now complete. The date was 1873. At this time, therefore, all of the elements for the drive system of a self-propelled electric vehicle were present. Humankind, however, would need to wait until 1881 and the pioneering work of Gustave Trouvé before an electric vehicle would be operated.

Incremental Improvements to Lead-Acid Batteries

Planté having discovered the importance of chemical changes on the surface of lead electrodes when a lead-acid battery was charged and discharged, a Frenchman, Camille Faure,[21] recognized the importance of the build-up of peroxide of lead during this so-called formation process, and patented a means for pasting onto the surface of lead plates a compound of lead. (See Fig. 10.8.) The reactions, therefore, occurred on the chemically active surface and the lead plate itself was less exposed to the corrosion. Faure used red-lead on the smooth surface of the plates, then rolled the sheets together with a flannel separator. While superior in electrical capacity to the Planté battery because of the porosity of the red-lead, the adherence of the active material was poor, particularly when the batteries were exposed to the vibrations of street driving. It was this proclivity for the red-lead to slough-off the plates which caused Phillipart and Ward to terminate their 1882 experiments on an electric tram car, as cited in Chapter 6. Despite this shortcoming the Faure battery, issuing one horsepower-hour weighed but 75 pounds, and had an efficiency of 80 percent. In energy per unit weight, known as specific energy, this battery was probably one-half as effective as batteries which are placed in modern electric vehicles.[22]

While Planté and Faure were perfecting the lead-acid cell in Europe, Charles F. Brush, an American who contributed so much to arc-lighting, about the same time as Faure, also

---

[20] Antonio Pacinotti, *Descrizione di una Machinetta Electomagnetica, Il Nuovo Cimonto*, Vol. 99, 1863, pp. 378-384.

[21] *The Electrician*, Vol. 1, No. 9, March 1882, p. 256.

[22] Thirty Faure cells and 7 Edison lamps were used in lighting a Pennsylvania Railroad Car in 1882. *Scientific American*, Vol. 4, November 1882, p. 286.

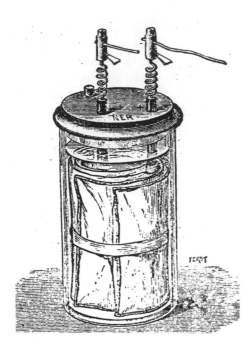

Figure 10.8. Camille Faure improved Planté's lead-acid cell by placing an application of red lead to the lead plate surfaces.[23] Essentially this action increased the chemical surface on which the sulfuric acid could induce a chemical reaction.

discovered the importance of placing a porous coating on the lead plates of batteries.[24] Progress now accelerated, for in 1881 E. Volkmann, J. S. Sellon, and Joseph W. Swan patented the use of lead plates bearing holes.[25] These holes were filled with pulverized lead mixed with sulfuric acid. This secondary cell generated one horsepower-hour for 60 pounds of metal. Swan, who, shortly after Edison, perfected the incandescent lamp in England, established a lead cellular structure, shown in Fig. 10.9.[26] These efforts served to better bind the active material to the grids. Then Sellon in 1881 modified the grid to better hold the active material, and to add strength to the lead grid, he followed the practice of typesetters and alloyed the lead with antimony, an element presently used in the grid of modern batteries for the same reason. To reduce the electrical resistance of the grid assembly, Edmund Julien, a Belgian chemist, added, in 1888, to the already alloyed grid a third element, mercury.[27] This liquid metal increased the electrical conductivity of the grid which significantly increased its life, as well as lowered the power loss in the battery. How these successive improvements effected the specific energy of the lead-acid battery is presented in Table 10-1.

---

[23] Gaston Planté, *The Storage of Energy*, P.B. Ewell, Tr. London: Whittaker and Co., 1887.

[24] *Scientific American*, Vol. XLVII, No. 27, Dec. 30, 1882, p. 423.

[25] *Scientific American Supplement*, Vol. XII, No. 332, May 13, 1882, p. 5299.

[26] *Scientific American*, Vol. XLVI, No. 20, May 20, 1882, p. 309.

[27] Ibid., Vol. LXI, No. 9, Aug. 31, 1889, p. 135.

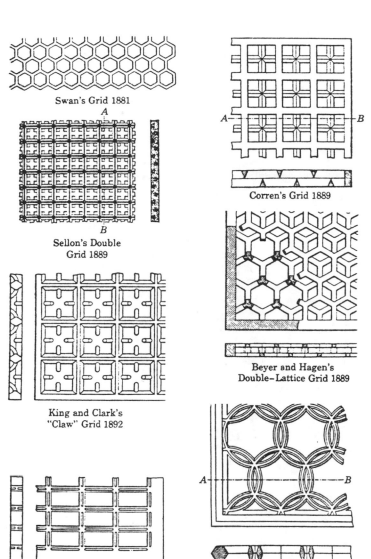

Swan's Grid 1881

Sellon's Double Grid 1889

Corren's Grid 1889

King and Clark's "Claw" Grid 1892

Beyer and Hagen's Double–Lattice Grid 1889

Heyl's Grid 1889

Farbarky and Scheneck's Grid 1886

Figure 10.9. To promote the adherence of friable lead-oxide to the lead-alloy grid in batteries the grid was serrated in numerous ways as illustrated. Such design minimized the effect of vibrations experienced by lead-acid batteries in electric vehicles joggling on rough roads and contributed to longer battery life.[28] Courtesy: John Wiley & Sons.

Table 10-1. Battery Improvement with Grid Change[29]			
DATE	INVENTORY	CONTRIBUTION	SPECIFIC ENERGY
1859	Planté	lead	8.1 Watt-hours per kilogram
1881	Faure	lead + red lead	12.6 Watt-hours per kilogram
1888	Julien	lead, red lead, alloy	23.8 Watt-hours per kilogram

[28] George Wood Vinal, *Storage Batteries*, John Wiley & Sons, NYC, 1951, p. 5.
[29] *Scientific American Supplement*, Vol. XXVII, No. 687, Mar. 2, 1889, P. 10968.

An illustration of the batteries as used in electric vehicles in 1898 is shown in Fig. 10.10.[30]

As one reads the genesis literature on electric vehicles, this emphasis for holding the active material to the grid is repeatedly commented on, for its sloughing off contributed to the shortened life of the battery, particularly where vibration was severe due to the road structure.

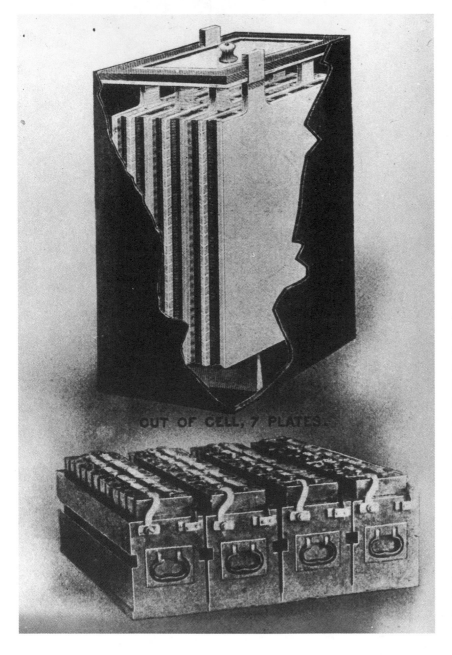

OUT OF CELL, 7 PLATES.

Figure 10.10. An electric vehicle battery complement of 1899. Above is a 7 plate cell of the lead-acid type, while below are 40 cells in four trays of ten each. With such a configuration using voltage switching, as discussed below, the voltage applied to the motor could be 20 volts, 40 volts, and 80 volts, giving three speeds.[31] Courtesy: H. E. Stone & Company.

---

[30] C. E. Woods, *The Electric Automobile*, H. E. Stone & Co., Chicago, 1900.
[31] Woods, *The Electric Automobile*.

The active material, flaking off, would ultimately deposit itself in the lower recesses of the battery. This detritus would mound-up and serve to short-circuit the positive and negative plates of the cell, making an inutile battery.

With incremental improvements cited above, and with new needs, the requirements for batteries of substantially higher specific power and specific energy increase. The next chapter focuses on improvements in lead-acid as well as the more exotic batteries.

Notes to Chapter 10

Luigi Galvani, Professor of Medicine at Bologna, while dissecting a frog found the leg would twitch when he simultaneously touched a muscle with a copper probe and the connecting nerve with a zinc probe. It will be noticed the probes were of different metals. Galvani called this effect "animal electricity."[32] Taking this raw information, but correctly interpreting it, Count Alessandro Volta, Professor of Natural Philosophy in the University of Pavia in Italy, assembled the first electric battery, which he called a pile.[33] He wrote Rt. Honorable Sir Joseph Banks, President of the Royal Society of London, the following letter on March 20, 1800. Banks, scion of a wealthy family, had more than two decades earlier accompanied Captain James Cook on board the *Endeavour* as a botanist on the latter's voyage to Tahiti to observe the transit of the planet Venus across the sun on June 3, 1769.[34] Because England and France were at war during this period of Napoleon Bonaparte's ascendancy, Volta wisely dispatched two copies, only one of which reached Banks. The letter, in part, follows:[35]

"I shall now give a more particular description of this apparatus and others analogous to it, as well as of the most remarkable experiments made with them.

"I provide a few dozen of small round plates or disks of copper, brass, or rather silver, an inch in diameter more or less (pieces of coin for example), and an equal number of plates of tin, or, what is better, of zinc nearly of the same size and figure (again different metals). I make use of the term *nearly*, because great precision is not necessary, and the size in general, as well as the figure of the metallic pieces, is merely arbitrary: care only must be taken that they may be capable of being conveniently arranged one above the other, in the form of a column. I prepare also a pretty large number of circular pieces of pasteboard, or any other spongy matter capable of imbibing and retaining a great deal of water or moisture, with which they must be well impregnated in order to ensure success to the experiments. These

---

[32] Luigi Galvani. *De Viribus Electricitis in Motu Musculari Commentarius*, Bologna, 1791, Translated by Margaret Foley, Norwalk, Connecticut: Burndy Library Publication, No. 10, 1953.

[33] Another Italian, Enrico Fermi, experimenting 142 years later alternately spaced uranium cylinders and graphite blocks and found the assembly yielded a continuous flow of neutrons (and heat). He also, after Volta, called his assemblage a *pile*. It was the first human-built self-sustaining nuclear reactor. The date was December 2, 1942. (Author)

[34] *Journals of Captain James Cook on His Voyages of Discovery*, Edited by J. C. Beaglehole, Cambridge University Press, 1955-74.

[35] *Philos. Trans. R. Soc. London*, Part 2, Vol. 90, 1800, p. 430.

circular pieces of pasteboard, which I shall call moistened disks, I make a little smaller than the plates of metal, in order that, when interposed between them, as I shall hereafter describe, they may not project beyond them.

"Having all these pieces ready in a good state, that is to say, the metallic disks very clean and dry, and the non-metallic ones well moistened with common water, or, what is much better, salt water, and slightly wiped that the moisture may not drop off, I have nothing to do but to arrange them, a matter exceedingly simple and easy.

"I place them horizontally, on a table or any other stand, one of the metallic pieces, for example one of silver, and over the first I adapt one of zinc; on the second I place one of the moistened disks, then another plate of silver followed immediately by another of zinc; over which I place another of the moistened disks. In this manner I continue coupling a plate of silver with one of zinc, and always in the same order, that is to say, the silver below and the zinc above it; or vice versa; according as I have begun, and interpose between each of these couples a moistened disk. I continue to form, of several of these stories, a column as high as possible without any danger of its falling.

"But if it contains about twenty of these stories or couples of metal, it will be capable not only of emitting signs of electricity by Cavallo's electrometer, assisted by a condenser, beyond ten or fifteen degrees, and of charging this condenser, by mere contact so as to make it emit a spark, etc., but of giving to the fingers with which its extremities (the bottom and top of the column) have been touched several small shocks, more or less frequent, according as the touching has been repeated. Each of these shocks has a perfect resemblance to that slight shock experience from a Leyden flask weakly charged, or a battery still more weakly charged, or a torpedo (fish) in an exceedingly languishing state, which imitates still better the effects of my apparatus by the series of repeated shocks which it can continually communicate."

Figure 10.5 illustrates Volta's batteries. Within ten days of Banks' reception of Volta's letter electrochemistry was born. William Nicholson and Anthony Carlisle assembled a column as outlined by Volta using 17 silver half-crown coins alternated by an equal number of zinc discs with brine-soaked pasteboard separating the couple. To insure an electrical connection the two experimenters had placed a drop of water at a wired electrical junction. From this drop they noticed the evolution of bubbles, which they subsequently determined were respectively composed of hydrogen and oxygen gases. This observation was the first known useful work of the Volta battery. Later Sir Humphry Davy would remark: "The true origin of all that has been done in electrochemical science was the accidental discovery of Messrs. Nicholson and Carlisle of the decomposition of water by the pile of Volta, on 30 April 1800."[36] Davy would shortly present the scientific world with two new pure chemical elements, sodium and potassium, through electrochemical separation.

Volta's battery was designated a primary battery. Its metallic couple is consumed as electric current is delivered. In 1802 N. Gutherot performed an experiment which was the genesis of the secondary battery, which today we commonly call the storage battery. With a pair of test

---

[36] Dibner, Bern. *Galvanti-Volta*, Norwalk, Connecticut: Burndy Library Publications, 1971.

tubes he sealed a platinum wire into the closed end of each. Inverting the tubes into water, and with a primary cell passing a current through the wire, he succeeded in decomposing the water into hydrogen and oxygen in the respective test tubes. Disconnecting the battery and placing in its stead a galvanometer he observed a feeble current flow in the opposite direction. Gutherot had made the first secondary cell, the genesis of the storage battery.[37] An electric cell, it should be mentioned, is two electrode plates separated by an electrolyte, while a battery is an assembly of cells.

Carrying this concept further Gaston Planté, a Belgian chemist, after many experiments, assembled two layers of lead sheet, separated, it is said, by swaths from his wife's petticoat. The assembly was wound into a spiral and inserted into a container of dilute sulfuric acid. This cell yielded a flow of electric current, the sulfur from the acid forming a layer of lead sulfate on the positive plate.[38] Planté had a rechargeable source of electrical energy, an assembly which became known as a secondary battery. The date was 1859. As the density of the sulfuric acid electrolyte from a fully charged battery is measurably more than the electrolyte when the battery is discharged, a simple hydrometer can be used to find the charge of the battery. This simple method is still used in battery shops to determine the remaining electrical charge in a battery.

Planté's battery, with improvements, has had a surprisingly long life. In 1990, 130 years after Planté's discovery, it is still the preferred battery for many electric vehicles, *viz.*, the 1990 announced General Motors *Impact*. Figure 10.6 shows a Planté cell being charged; and Fig. 10.7, an assembly of a Planté cell. To close this chapter Fig. 10.11 illustrates Professor Planté.

[37] Vincent, Colin A. *Modern batteries: An Introduction to Electrochemical Sources*, London: Edward Arnold, 1984.
[38] Planté, Gaston. *Recherches sur l' électricité*, Paris, 1883.

Figure 10.11. Gaston Planté. Professor Planté first assembled a lead-acid battery in 1859. This electric couple was still one of the best batteries for electric cars in the 1990s. Courtesy: Scientific American.

CHAPTER 11

The Newer Batteries and Fuel Cells

The casual reader of this volume may wish to only scan Chapters 11 and 12 because batteries are discussed in some detail.

The potential for using batteries has been ever rising. New uses could be for electric vehicles, and for electric utilities as a possible solution of system load unbalance. After World War II the polypropolene case served to lighten the non-active parts of the lead-acid battery. The development of and the substitution of permeable plastic for separators of membranous material made from Port Oriford cedar, a tree which grows and is harvested only in moist areas of the American West Coast, all contributed to improving the specific energy and the life of the modern lead-acid storage battery. Such a series of cells as used in the popular golf-cart battery is seen in Fig. 11.1. In actual practice these low-cost batteries, made in large quantities, are found to be more acceptable than more expensive industrial batteries, partly due to the better quality control in manufacturing processes.[1]

A. All new container material: Container and one piece cover are made of polypropylene—a super-tough, space-age plastic unaffected by acid, gasoline, motor oil, anti-freeze, hydraulic fluids, solvents, and temperatures to 250°F. Walls, only 1/4 as thick as hard rubber, yet have 20 times the impact strength at 0°F. Container and cover are fused together under heat and pressure, become one solid, inseparable piece of plastic.

B. More plates: Stronger, thin walls allow 12% more inside space for additional plates, bigger plates, and up to a pint more acid. Results in faster cranking, more total cranking power, and greater reserve capacity than in same size hard rubber batteries.

C. Hi-torque construction: All cell connections are made straight through the partition walls. Shortens the power path—reduces internal resistance. Results in greater power efficiency and higher terminal voltage.

While many other types of electrical couples for batteries have since been devised, the lead-acid battery, first constructed by a Planté in 1859, it is more and more realized, will long be used for electric cars. While lower in specific energy than more exotic batteries which are constantly

---

1 John MacDougall, *Electric Vehicles in Bell System Use*, 28th IEEE Vehiclular Technology Conference, Denver, Colorado, March 1978.

Figure 11.1. A Lead-acid Cell. Gould Inc.[2]

discussed,[3] but which, at least until 1992, fail to appear commercially, the lead-acid battery has high specific power so useful in acceleration.[4] In addition, it has a relatively low cost per kilowatt-hour installed and a short but acceptable life. In the careful study by Sidney Gross on competitive batteries for electric cars, his Table 11-1 provides the criteria, and Table 11.2 demonstrates that the lead-acid battery has an "excellent" near term prospect through 1981, and a "good" prospect 5-15 years beyond 1976.[5] Later studies concur in the conclusions of Gross.[6]

To the reader batteries are seen to have improved through the years by incremental gains. The following section outlines current battery development given impetus by two needs: 1) electric vehicle requirements, and 2) the economic desirability for achieving a more uniform

---

[2] Ernest H. Wakefield, *The Consumer's Electric Car*, The Ann Arbor Science Publishers Inc., 1977, p. 80.

[3] The specific energy of a battery is the deliverable energy per unit weight, expressed in watt-hours per kg.

[4] The specific power of a battery is the deliverable power per unit weight, expressed in watts per kg.

[5] Sidney Gross, *Review of Candidate Batteries*, p. 109.

[6] L. G. O'Connell, et al, *Energy Storage Systems for Automobile Propulsion: Final Report*, V.1, *Overview and Findings*, Lawrence Livermore National Laboratory, December 15, 1980, p.4.

Table 11-1. Requirements for Electrical Vehicle Batteries[7][8]
• High energy density (at least 20 W hr/lb at 2-hr rate)
• Capable of low manufacturing cost
• Long life with low maintenance
• Long activated stand capability with low self discharge or degradation
• Good high rate capability for acceleration and hill climbing
• Efficiently and quickly recharged with little or no special equipment
• Small size
• Safe during accidents or charge control failure
• Easily replaced
• Little or no special handling equipment

load-level for electric utilities, so capital in this capital intensive industry is more efficiently employed.[9][10]

While Gross in Table 11-2 assesses batteries in 1976, Gary L. Henriksen *et al*[11] present a comparable study in 1989 for batteries to be used in a van of moderate power, writing:

"Figure 11.2 illustrates one method of graphically displaying the results of the assessment. Battery suitability values—as defined by the cumulative scores of the five technical and economic criteria—are plotted along the ordinate, while Technical Risk Values—as defined by a value of ten less the score for the Likelihood of Success criterion arc plotted along the abscissa. The graph is partitioned equally along both axes to illustrate that the twelve technologies are located in the "More Acceptable" regions of the graph and that they span the three risk segments of the graph. The "Low Risk" technologies are relatively mature batteries, which have a strong commitment on the part of a manufacturer to commercialize them for EV applications: Eagle-Picher, Inc. (and Westinghouse) for the nickel/iron technology; Electrosource, Inc. and Concorde for the sealed lead/acid; and BBC/Powerplex Technologies, Inc. and Chloride Silent Power Limited for the sodium/sulfur technology.

"The "Medium Risk" technologies are somewhat less mature in their development status, but possess firm support from an industrial developer. Westinghouse and Electrofuel Manufacturing Co. are pursuing lithium/iron sulfide; Johnson

---

[7] Sidney Gross, *Review of Candidate Batteries*, p. 109.

[8] William T. Reid, *Energy Sources for Electrically Powered Automobiles*, *Battelle Technical Review*, Vol. 14, No. 4, April 1965, pp. 9-15.

[9] William J. Walsh, *Advanced Batteries for Electric Vehicles*, *Physics Today*, June 1980.

[10] J. Gray, *New Developments in Battery Technology,"* *Endeavor*, Vol. 6, No. 2, 1982, pp. 78-82.

[11] Gary L. Henriksen, Pandit G. Patil, Elliot Ratner, & Charles J. Ward, *Assessment of EV batteries and Application to R&D Planning*, SAE 890781.

Table 11-2. Evaluation of Selected Candidate Secondary Batteries (1976)

Battery	Major factors affecting possible use	Near-term prospects 0-5 yr	Long-term prospects 5-15 yr
Lead-acid	Low cost; better energy density and life needed	Excellent	Good
Nickel-zinc	Need improved cycle life, better oxygen transport	Fair	Good
Zinc-bromine	Need separator for long activated stand	Poor	Fair
Nickel-iron	Uncertain cost	Good	Good
Nickel-cadmium	High cost, limited cadmium supply	Poor	Very poor
Nickel-hydrogen	Cost and hydrogen tank weight	Good	Good
Zinc-chlorine hydrate	Weight, cost and reliability	Poor	Fair
Zinc-air	Weight, cost and life	Poor	Poor
Aluminum-air	Rechargeable aluminum electrode	Poor	Fair
Iron-air	System complexity, cost, life	Fair	Good
Lead-air	Weight and life	Very poor	Very poor
Sodium-sulfur	Solid separator, life, cost	Fair	Good
Sodium-phosphorous/sulfur	Solid separator, life, cost	Poor	Fair
Sodium-selenium	Limited selenium supply, cost, improved energy density	Very poor	Poor
Lithium-sulfur	Improved sulfur electrode life	Poor	Good
Lithium-chlorine	Improved energy density	Poor	Good
Lithium-tellurium tetrachloride	Improved energy density	Poor	Good
Lithium-selenium	Limited selenium supply, cost, improved energy density	Poor	Fair
Aluminum-chlorine	Improved aluminum electrode	Poor	Good
Lithium-phosphorous/sulfur	Improved sulfur electrode, life	Poor	Good
Magnesium-chlorine	Requires more basic research	Very poor	Poor
Calcium/barium-chlorine	Requires more basic research	Very poor	Poor
Calcium-nickel fluoride	Improved solid electrolyte doping, better electrode geometry	Very poor	Fair
Lithium-sulfur dioxide	Cost, high rate capability	Poor	Poor
Lithium-lamellar structure	Cost, high rate capability	Poor	Poor
Antimony redox	Requires more research and development	Poor	Fair
Potassium-sulfur	Solid separator, life, cost	Fair	Good
Lithium-bromine	Requires more research and development	Poor	Good

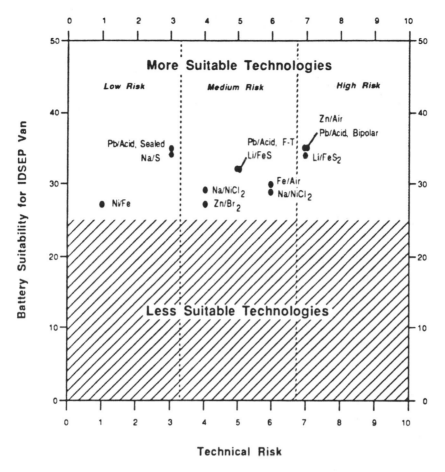

Figure 11.2 Risk/Suitability Relationship for EV Battery Technologies Qualifying for IDSEP Van

Controls, Inc. is developing zinc/bromine and flow-through lead/acid; Westinghouse Electric Corporation is also pursuing iron/air; and Beta R&D Ltd. is working jointly with Harwell Laboratories on the development of the sodium/metal chloride systems.

"In the case of the "High Risk" batteries, they are the least mature and are being pursued primarily at universities and/or the national laboratories. The Argonne National Laboratory is studying lithium/iron disulfide, the Lawrence Berkeley Laboratory is investigating zinc/air options, and the Jet Propulsion Laboratory is pursuing bipolar lead/acid. Some R&D activities are being conducted on these systems in industry, but at relatively low levels of effort."

Recent Battery Improvements

The lead-acid battery has been sufficient for most tasks requiring rechargeable batteries and, thus, efforts to improve this energy source or to develop new batteries has proceeded at only a moderate pace during much of the twentieth century. During this time, the rechargeable nickel/cadmium battery was developed in Europe and in the United States for small appliances, such as calculators, and recently for electric vehicles.[12] The late Dr. Samuel Ruben holds some of the early patents for development of this battery in the United States.[13] Dr. Ruben also patented the zirconium nitride grid to enhance the specific energy of industrial lead-acid batteries.[14] Also during this time, zinc-air primary batteries for vehicle propulsion were developed by Lockheed Corporation,[15] and later Westinghouse Electric Corporation began a program to improve Edison's nickel-iron battery. Then, for the most recent battery developments Dr. Paul A. Nelson, Director, Electrochemical Technology Program Argonne National Laboratory wrote in 1983[15a]:

"Work on secondary batteries was accelerated with the establishment of the Energy Research and Development Administration (which later became a part of the Department of Energy, DOE) in 1974. The Energy Storage Division of that agency began development of advanced battery systems that showed promise of achieving an increase in specific energy of several fold over that of the existing lead-acid battery. Batteries that would be useful in the near-term were given an additional boost by the passage of the Electric and Hybrid Vehicle Research, Development and Demonstration Act, Public Law 94-413 in September 1976, which was amended by Public Law 95-238 in February 1978. Under these laws, the DOE initiated a program in 1977 to develop electric vehicles and the necessary batteries. The batteries selected for development were those that showed promise for the near-term and were already under development in small projects in private industry: improved lead-acid, nickel/iron, and nickel/zinc. The firms given contracts were the major companies in the industry and in 1980 included: Exide Management and Technology Company, Globe Battery Division of Johnson Controls, and C&D Battery Division of Eltra Corporation, for improved lead-acid batteries; Westinghouse and Eagle-Picher Industries for nickel/iron batteries; and Exide Energy Research Corporation and Gould, Inc. for nickel/zinc batteries.

"For the near-term batteries, the results obtained by 1981 are shown in Table 11-3.[16] Because of cycle life problems with the nickel/zinc batteries, this effort has been cut back drastically since 1980. The nickel/iron battery probably has the best overall performance, but is considerably more expensive than the lead-acid battery because of the cost of the nickel electrode. The marginal improvement in performance would warrant the higher cost only if very long life (>1000 cycles) can be achieved for nickel-iron batteries."

[12] D. Glenn, Sivaswamy Viswanathan, *Ni-Cd Battery for Electric Vehicles*, Eighth International Electric Vehicle Symposium, Washington, D.C., 1986.

[13] Personal communication.

[14] Personal communication.

[15] *Lockheed Develops Compact Electric Power Source,"* Electric Vehicle News*, Vol. 1, No. 2, May 1972, p. 9.

[15a] Personal communication 1983.

[16] *Electric and Hybrid Vehicle Program*, 5th Annual Report to Congress for Fiscal Year 1981, U.S. Department of Energy, DOC/CE-0028, March 1982.

Table 11-3. Typical Best Performance of Near Term Electric Batteries[17]

TYPE	SPECIFIC ENERGY Wh/kg.[18]	SPECIFIC POWER W/kg.[19]	CYCLE LIFE 80% discharge[20]
lead-acid[21]	42	104	>450[22]
nickel/iron	48	103	>700[22]
nickel/zinc	68	131	179

It is interesting to note that after a century of effort, the most commercially suitable battery in 1990 for electric vehicle propulsion is a derivative of Planté's lead-acid battery of 1859. Also, the modern version is less than twice the delivered energy per unit weight of Julien's 1888 lead-acid battery. Nelson continues:

"The above lead-acid batteries have given the General Electric/Chrysler type electric car with regenerative braking, discussed in Chapter 21, an urban cycle driving range of 74-77 miles.[23]

"During the development of these near-term batteries, work has continued on the advanced batteries. These advanced batteries have included three main types: (1) zinc-electrode flow batteries, (2) high temperature batteries, and (3) air electrode batteries.

"Zinc-electrode flow batteries are distinguished from other batteries proposed for vehicle propulsion in that the cathode material, either chlorine or bromine, is stored in a separate container apart from the electrode stack.[24] These systems use a continuously flowing electrolyte with pumps, valves, and flow control devices. They promise moderately high specific energy, very long life, and moderate cost.

---

[17] DOE/CE-0028, *ibid*.

[18] Watt-hours per kilogram. Energy per unit weight at 3-hour discharge rate.

[19] Watts per kilogram. Power per unit weight sustained for 30 sec.

[20] The useful life of a battery is highly dependent on depth of discharge.

[21] Comparison should be made with Table 10-1. Discharge rate is important.

[22] Tests still in progress in 1981.

[23] *Development of Near Term Batteries for Electric Vehicles*, Summary Report, Argonne National Laboratory, ANL/OEPM-80-5, June 1980.

[24] Jeff Zodronik, *JCI Testing of Exxon's 30 kWh Zinc-Bromine Battery Z30-A*, Eighth International Electric Vehicle Symposium, Washington, D.C. 1986.

"There are two main types of high-temperature batteries, Beta batteries and molten salt batteries. Beta batteries, which operate at about 320°C, have molten sodium and sulfur electrodes and a solid electrolyte of beta-alumina (hence, the name).[25] [26] [27] Molten salt batteries, such as the lithium-iron sulfide battery,[28] operate at about 450°C and have solid electrodes, such as lithium-aluminum negatives and iron sulfide positives. Both of these high-temperature batteries show promise of very high specific energies of greater than 100 W-hr/kg, more than two and one-half times the best present lead-acid batteries. Many problems remain to be solved, however, in achieving simultaneously long life, high performance, and low cost when operating at high temperature.

"The most prominent air-electrode battery in the DOE program is the aluminum-air battery which differs from the others in that it would be recharged mechanically by replacing the aluminum electrodes.[29] [30] Aluminum hydroxide precipitated from the electrolyte in a storage tank associated with the battery would be recycled to an aluminum production plant. The advantages of the aluminum-air battery are very high specific energy (300 Wh/kg) and, therefore, a long vehicle range; additions of water and removal of aluminum hydroxide reaction products would be required at intervals of 250 miles and the aluminum and alloy plates would be replaced at about 500 to 1000-mile intervals. The replacement of the plates would be a rapid, but perhaps expensive, refueling process.

"Although these advanced batteries show exciting promise, the problems of solving the associated research problems and of producing a practical battery at low cost is a great challenge. These advanced batteries may hold out the best hope for a substantial replacement of gasoline cars with electric cars."

Below are Tables and illustrations of some of these batteries.

[25] William L. Auer, *A Sodium-Sulfur Battery for an Electric Vehicle Application*, Eighth International Electric Vehicle Symposium, Washington, D.C. 1986.

[26] Herman Bimbreier, *Sodium-Sulfur Batteries for Electric Vehicles - Status Report for Canada & German*, do.

[27] H. Haskin and G. A. Reitz, *Sodium-Sulfur Battery Development for an Advance Electric Powertrain*, do.

[28] A. A. Chilenskas, R. L. Biwer, and W. H. DeLuca, *Lithium-Metal Sulfide Battery Development and Sub-Module Demonstrations*, do.

[29] L. G. O'Connell, *A comparison of Future Battery Systems for Application to General-Purpose Electric Vehicles*, Livermore, California: Lawrence Livermore National Laboratory, August 1980, p.11.

[30] *Aluminum-Air Battery Looks Good, Technology Forecasts*, April 1983, pp. 6-7.

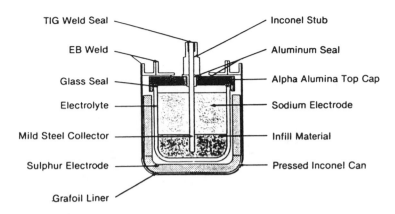

Figure 11.3. One Type of Sodium-sulfur Battery Design (1986).[31] Courtesy: Chloride Silent Power, Ltd., Wayne, Pennsylvania, U.S.A.

	LEAD ACID	SODIUM SULFUR		
Table 11-4. Sodium-Sulfur Electric Vehicle Predicted Performance (1986).* **Comparison Between Lead-Acid and Sodium-Sulfur Batteries**				
BATTERY ENERGY	40 kWh	40 kWh	60 kWh	85 kWh
RANGE-URBAN CYCLE*	52 MILES	70 MILES	105 MILES	150 MILES
MAXIMUM PAYLOAD TONS	1.0	1.9	1.8	1.7
BATTERY WEIGHT	1250 kg	330 kg	424 kg	580 kg
POWER AVAILABLE (2h RATE)	19 kW	19 kW	27 kW	39 kW
*1 TON PAYLOAD	Chloride Silent Power, Ltd., Wayne, Pennsylvania, USA (1986).			

[31] William L. Auxer, *A Sodium-Sulfur Battery for an Electric Vehicle Application*, Eighth International Electric Vehicle Symposium, Washington, D. C. 1986.

Table 11-5. Electric Vehicle Battery Technology Status (1989).[32]

Battery	Developer	Designation	Status*	Specific Energy (Wh/kg)	Specific Peak Power at 50% DoD (W/kg)	Projected OEM Cost (1989 $/kWh)	Cycle Life (Cycles to 80% DoD)**	Cost/Cycle/kWh (1989 $)
Flow-By Lead-Acid (Pb/A)	JCI	C472	M	53	104		130***	0.16
			BG	56	79	72	450	
Zinc/Bromine (Zn/Br$_2$)	JCI	J-1	M	55	88		142***	0.12
			BG	75	79	75	600	
Lithium Aluminum/ Iron Sulfide (Li Al/FeS)	ANL/ Westinghouse	36V	M	90	86		130***	
			BG	100	106	91	600	0.15
Sodium/Sulfur (Na/S)	CSPL	PB	M	96	130		261***	0.15
			BG	100	106	91	600	0.15
				65[a]	70[a]			
Iron/Air (Fe/Air)	Westinghouse	W-3	C	70	50		200-300[a]***	0.15
			BG	100	106	91	600	

* Status: C, Cells; M, Modules; B, Battery
** Depth of Discharge
*** Current R&D Core Program is Aimed at Improving Cycle Life While Maintaining Specific Energy & Power.
BG: Mission Directed Goals for EV Battery R&D Based on IDSEP Van and Tested Under Simplified Federal Urban Schedule (SFUDS).

Note: a - Projected from 40 cm^2 cells operating at 25 mA/cm^2 to full-size cells operating on SFUDS.

32 Paul J. Brown, *Overview of the U. S. Government's Electric Vehicle Program*, 1989.

The Aluminum/Air Battery

Of this interesting energy source William A. Adams and John H. Morgan write:[33]

"Work on Al/air batteries began in 1981 with a project to design an alkaline electrolyte battery that would enable the hydroxide product to be precipitated from NaOH solution. Alloys have been developed that do not corrode and are capable of 4.2 kWh/kg in pure NaOH. In 1984, a jointly funded project by Transport Canada and Alcan, lead to the production of a saline electrolyte Al/air battery to provide power for a golf cart in a hybrid battery system. They have studied the fundamental corrosion processes in aluminum in both alkaline and saline electrolytes and used this information to optimize the design of the aluminum/air battery. Alcan has successfully developed a standby Al/air battery for British Telecom which can replace 60 lead-acid batteries having 32 kWh of stored energy as shown in Figure 11.4. Alcan is working on battery/battery hybrid concepts and has an active commercial interest in advanced electric vehicle designs and propulsion systems."

For fleet vehicles and many urban personal cars the vehicles cited above with range of 70-120 miles show promise. But the ordinary driver with one car may choose a longer range and one which can be "recharged" in less than 20 minutes. Here the combination Aluminum-air fuel cell in combination with more prosaic batteries such as the lead-acid shows promise as D.W. Parish, et al, write in 1989.[34]

Figure 11.4. A wall of 24 lead/acid batteries storing 32 kWh of electrical energy can be replaced by a single Al/air battery which has demonstrated over 36 kWh. (See Footnote 33)

---

[33] William A. Adams and John H. Morgan, *Canadian Electrochemical Power Sources Research and Development for Traction Applications*, The 9th International Electric Vehicle Symposium, Toronto, 1988.

[34] D. W. Parish, N. P. Fitzpatrick, W. B. O'Callaghan, and W. M. Anderson, *Demonstration of Aluminum-Air Fuel Cells in a Road Vehicle*, SAE 891690.

"The test to compare the aluminum-air/lead-acid powered hybrid vehicle with the lead-acid-only powered vehicle consisted of running the same vehicle on the same track under similar conditions for as long as each would maintain the performance baseline, and logging the relevant data to allow quantitative analysis at a later time. The first tests were conducted in October 1988 and the second tests in March 1989 on a 0.9-mile closed-loop road track in Mead, Colorado.

The Altrek Vehicle

"The Altrek vehicle is pictured in Figure 11.5. It is a specially modified Electrek with a compartmentalized rear hatch area for the aluminum-air batteries, a DC-DC converter for boosting the aluminum-air battery voltage to the 96-volt lead-acid battery system bus, and a PC based data acquisition computer for data logging and controlling the batteries.

"The aluminum-air batteries are shown in Figure 11.6, and a typical performance curve for a stationary discharge of a single battery in Figure 11.7. These batteries were designed and built

Figure 11.5. The Altrek Vehicle (See Footnote 34)

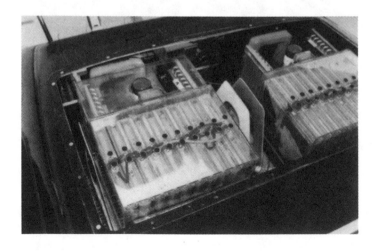

Figure 11.6. The Aluminum Air Battery (See Footnote 34)

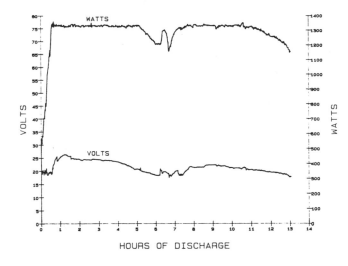

HOURS OF DISCHARGE

Figure 11.7. Aluminum Air Battery Performance Curve (See Footnote 34)

at Alcan's Research Centre in Kingston, Ontario, and are modified versions of the award-winning standby reserve battery. The modifications included a 50% reduction in electrolyte storage space, up-graded wiring, extra heat-exchange capability and improved seals. Each battery has a reservoir of caustic electrolyte which is pumped through the cell-stack between the aluminum anodes and air cathodes to generate electrical power. The battery by-product of aluminum hydroxide is gradually precipitated out and collected in the sump area. This non-hazardous by-product can be recycled, thereby allowing clean, replenishable power. A stream of air is blown through the cell-stack to supply oxygen to the cathodes in order to maintain the electrochemical power-generating reaction."

Table 11-6. Characteristics of the Altrek Vehicle				
Altrek Specifications		Base Line System	AluPower Hybrid	
General:	Batteries	Lead Acid	Al Air	Lead-Acid
Wheelbase: 95.5 in. (2.42 m)	Quantity	16	2	8
Length: 171.5 in. (4.35 m)	Weight Each	24.1 kg	71 kg	24.1 kg
Propulsion Motor: 32 HP (23.87 kW)	Total Battery Weight	386 kg	335 kg	
Shunt wound	Battery Capacity	14.2 kWh	41.1 kWh	
Controller: Hybrid Armature Field	Gross Vehicle Weight	1,510 kg	1459 kg	
Transistor	Estimated Range at	75 mi.	200+ mi.	
Body: Glass and Carbonate	30 MPH			
			(See Footnote 34)	

Worldwide Nickel/Iron Battery Development for Electric Vehicles

While the above studies show five batteries programs for electric vehicles being carried on in the United States, other countries, for the near period application of electric cars, have testing systems with nickel/iron batteries. Useful parameters for these batteries collected in 1986 are shown in Table 11-7 below:[35]

In any review of batteries for electric vehicles the carefully performed test by the Tennessee Valley Authority should be studied.[36]

	Country (Developer)					
EV Battery Parameter	United States (EPI)	Germany (DAUG)	France (SAFT)	Sweden (SABNIFE)	Japan (Matsushita)	USSR (Istochnik)*
Experimental Cells						
Capacity (Ah)	320	*	150	*	165	*
Specific Energy[a]	53	*	*	*	60 (C/5)	*
(Wh/kg)	*	*	*	*	1120	*
Cycle Life[b] (cycles)						
EV Batteries	270	140	230	270	160	200
Capacity (Ah)	45	45 (C/5)	60	44	56 (C/5)	36
Specific Energy[a]	1100	*	*	1500	*	1000-2000
(Wh/kg)						
Cycle Life[b] (cycles)						
Goals						
Capacity (Ah)	*	*	150	*	*	*
Specific Energy[a]	56	*	70	60	*	45-50
(Wh/kg)	1200	*	2000	2000	*	*
Cycle Life[b] (cycles)						
OEM Price ($/kWh)	125	*	125	*	90	*

Table 11-7. World Wide Nickel-Iron Battery Technology Development Status (1986).

* Information is not available
** Leningrad Industrial Amalgamation Istochnik.
[a] At the three-hour discharge rate.
[b] Under cycling at 80% DOD; end of life defined at 25% loss of initial capacity.   (See Footnote 35)

[35] P. G. Patil, W. J. Walsh, and J. F. Miller, *Worldwide Nickel/Iron Battery Development for Electric Vehicle Applications*, Eight International Electric Vehicle Symposium, Washington, D. C. 1986.
[36] J. H. Barnett, W. A. Thomas, T. W. Blickwedel, *Battery In-Vehicle Life Testing At TVA*, do.

Nickel-Cadmium Battery Progress

Also in Sidney Gross's list of candidate secondary batteries was the nickel-cadmium couple. The Department of Energy provided a contract to Energy Research Corporation of Danbury, Connecticut for an improved nickel cadmium battery. Illustrations below indicate how these cells have been improved.[37] While 1988 water consumption per cell equalled 139

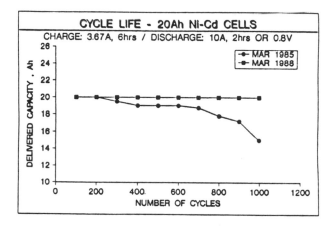

Figure 11.8. Life Cycle Performance of 20 Ah Ni-Cd Cells (See Footnote 37)

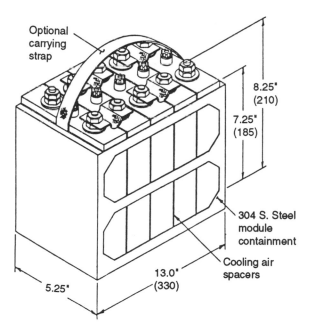

Figure 11.9. 6 V Nickel-Cadmium Module (See Footnote 37)

---

[37] Siva Viswanathan, *Nickel-Cadmium Battery for EV Propulsion*. The 9th International Electric Vehicle Symposium. Toronto, 1988.

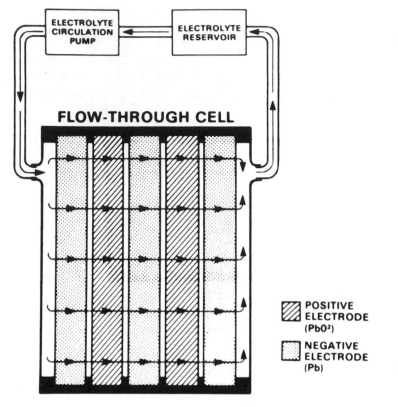

Figure 11.10. Flow-Through Lead-Acid Electric Vehicle Cell. (1987). 10th Annual Report to Congress for Fiscal Year 1986, U. S. Dept. of Energy, p. 11.

cc for 1000 miles of driving, work is underway to develop a maintenance free cell. Battery life has been shown to be more than 30,000 miles, which for an electric vehicle could be translated to four years or more.

Zinc-Bromine Batteries

One of the candidate secondary batteries also listed by Sidney Gross in 1976 was the zinc-bromine battery. The Department of Energy recognized the potential of this energy source and

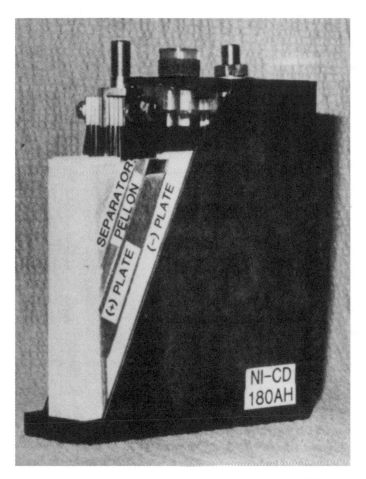

Figure 11.11. Improved Nickel-Cadmium Electric Vehicle Cell (1987). 10th Annual Report, p. 12.

Figure 11.12. Improved Nickel-Iron Battery Module.[38]

offered to Johnson Controls, Inc. a contract for its development.[39] Parallel with this creation has been the work of Toyota Motor Corporation of Japan.[40] Implicit has been the battery's specific energy of 72 Wh/kg. Illustrated are a zinc-bromine battery by Johnson Controls, and a golf cart (Chapter 23) sized vehicle developed for this battery. Progress is quoted from the 13th Annual Report to Congress for Fiscal Year 1989.[41]

"Sandia placed a three-year, $2.3M, 18% cost-shared contract with Johnson Controls, Inc. (JCI), in December 1986, to design, fabricate, and evaluate an improved zinc-bromine battery system suitable for EV propulsion. The new "V" design, which utilizes vibration-welded flow frames, has undergone extensive review and design modifications. The "V" battery stack is a welded polymer unit which will eliminate any nuisance bromine leaks or odors (see Fig. 11.13). Through a core technology improvement program directed at extending battery life and

---

[38] F. Tonnerieux, *Initial Testing of a SAFT Nickel - Iron Battery on a Renault Master (3.5 T) Proving Vehicle Has Resulted in Accumulator Overheating, Reducing Vehicle Availability*, Eighth International Electric Vehicle Symposium, Washington, D. C., 1986.

[39] J. P. Zagrodnick and M. D. Eskra, *Zinc Bromine EV Battery Development at Johnson Controls*, The 9th International Electric Vehicle Symposium, Toronto, 1988.

[40] Hathuo Nakao, Yoshihiro Suzuki, and Mashiro Okawa, *Zinc-Bromine Battery Development*, do.

[41] *Electric and Hybrid Vehicle Program*, 13th Annual Report to Congress, for Fiscal Year 1989, April 1990, pp. 11 & 12.

increasing energy efficiency, JCI has addressed flow frame and electrode material composition, separator development, cathode activation layer improvement, supporting electrolyte composition, and zinc bromide concentration. In addition to hermetically sealing the battery stack and addressing safety concerns, such as electrolyte containment, JCI has demonstrated that the battery stack and its auxiliaries can be packaged into a simple, compact design. For an 8-cell battery, total battery volume and weight have been reduced 70% and 23%, respectively, as compared to the previous battery generation ("Z" design).

Lithium Based Batteries

A high specific energy battery, now in small size, but possibly capable of being scaled up is the Li/MoS_2 battery. William A. Adams and John H. Morgan write:[42]

<u>Moli Energy Ltd.</u>

Moli Energy has been working on rechargeable lithium batteries for twelve years. They have built the world's first commercial plant to produce lithium rechargeable "AA" cells in British Columbia capable of production of more than 1 million cells per month. This Li/MoS_2 technology was developed in Canada from

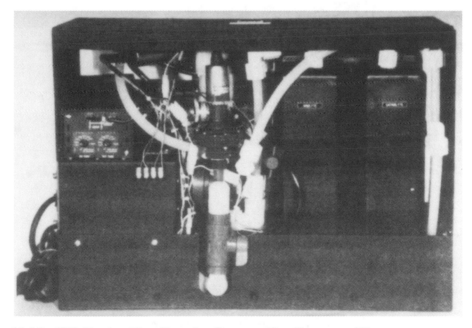

Figure 11.13. "V" Design Zinc-Bromine Battery (See Footnote 41)

---

[42] William A. Adams and John H. Morgan, Ibid.

a research base at the University of British Columbia. Although the company is currently aiming at the electronics consumer market, research at Moli has indicated that "AA" cells scale-up to at least 50 Ah size cells which have a specific energy of over 100 Wh/kg. Figure 11.14 is a diagram of such a cell. There are no plans to enter the traction battery market in the near future with current Moli technology. This is a rapidly advancing field."

The reader can see from the above that batteries and fuel cells are receiving a great amount of research and development. In retrospect how simple was Alessandro Volta's experiment on the first battery! An electric energy source for electric vehicles must have high specific energy, high specific power, be of low cost, have safety in handling, be compact and light weight. Quite an order. Below are described more energy sources.

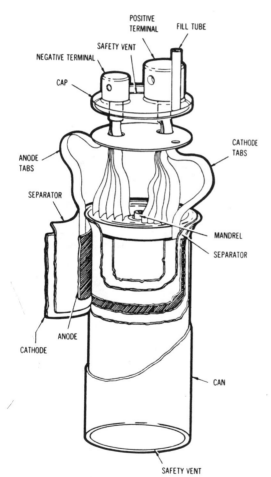

Figure 11.14. Exploded View of Cell Used in the 50-ampere-hour Battery (See Footnote 42)

Li-Alloy/FeS Batteries

A promising battery with a specific energy of some 100 wh/kg has been developed by G. Barlow of Westinghouse Electric Corporation and by A. A. Chilenskas of Argonne National Laboratory and associates. For this energy source the authors write:[43]

"The present electric vehicle Li-alloy/FeS cell is a 7-plate, monopolar, prismatic design with a nominal capacity of 200Ah at the three hour discharge rate, Fig. 11.15. The cell stack comprises three iron monosulfide, positive electrodes, which are electronically separated from each other by magnesium oxide separators. The electrolyte is a ternary salt mixture of LiBr:LiCl:LiF, which has a melting point of 445°C. All the electrolyte necessary for the lifetime operation of the cell is incorporated into the electrodes and separator during their fabrication. The electrodes are made by compacting powder blends of the respective active materials and electrolyte. Similarly, the separator is a compacted powder blend of magnesia and electrolyte. Each electrode package consists of a central current collector/bus bar assembly sandwiched between two electrode plaques of the same polarity. These components are encased in two photoetched particle retainer baskets which are welded around their periphery. The cell stack is housed in a stainless steel can and cover which are at the negative electrode potential. The positive terminal of the cell is electrically isolated from the cell cover by a ceramic compression feedthrough seal.

Figure 11.15. 7-Plate Lithium Alloy/Metal Sulfide Cell (See Footnote 43)

---

[43] G. Barlow and A. A. Chilenskas, *Fabrication and Testing of Li-Alloy/FeS Batteries*, The 9th International Electric Vehicle Symposium, Toronto, 1988.

"The cell is typically operated between 450°C and 500°C which is above the electrolyte melting point but well below the melting point of the lithium-alloys in the negative electrode.

"The performance of the state-of-the-art cell at various constant current discharge rates is shown in Figure 11.16. These cells typically operate at coulombic efficiencies >95% and energy efficiencies of approximately 85%. The power obtained from a cell is a function of the depth of discharge, current, and the duration of the current pulse. For electric vehicles the acceleration currents are typically in the 300-500 ampere range for between 15-30 secs. Cells of the present design are capable of delivering between 100 to 120 W/kg at 80% depth of discharge when pulsed at these currents for 15 secs. Further improvements in power are possible by tailoring the cell design, however, increases in power are at the expense of a small decrease in the specific energy. It will be necessary therefore, to optimize the cell energy and power for each particular vehicle design.

"The life of the present cell is approximately 350 cycles when operated continuously to 100% depth of discharge between voltage limits of 1.5 and 0.9 volts on a C/6 charge and a C/3 discharge at a constant current. The primary mode of cell failure is due to shorting which results from the deposition of metallic iron in the separators. It is believed that this iron is deposited progressively as the result of the cell being overcharged to some degree on each cycle, whereupon iron halides are formed at the positive electrodes. These compounds are subsequently reduced by lithium to form metallic iron and lithium halides."

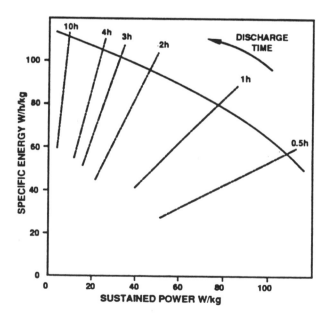

Figure 11.16. Performance of 7-Plate Lithium Alloy/Iron Monosulfide Cell at Various Discharge Rates. (See Footnote 43)

Advantages and Disadvantages of Several Batteries

Some of the advanced batteries cited above have been succinctly described by M. DeLuchi et al in their excellent 1989 report on the status and comparison of electric vehicles with IC means of transportation as cited in Table 11-8.[44]

Fuel Cells as an Energy Source for Electric Vehicles

A fuel cell, like a battery, is defined as a two-electrode system separated by an electrolyte. For the system to produce electricity a gas or liquid fuel is supplied to one electrode with oxygen or air applied to the other, the electrolyte, meanwhile, being unchanged. In the process electrons are freed when atoms combine to form molecules.

In November of 1968 the author and a representative of Union Carbide, who had done extensive work with fuel cells, proceeded on invitation to the Manhattan headquarters of AT&T to discuss powering electric vehicles, there to meet with battery personnel from Bell Laboratories. The conclusion of the meeting was fuel cells were presently prohibitively expensive for automobile use, but iron-nickel batteries had possibilities.

	Table 11-8. Advantages and Disadvantages of Batteries	
Battery	Advantages	Disadvantages/R&D issues
Pb/acid	Proven, commercially available technology	Low specific energy and power due to great weight of lead, decrease in voltage and performance as battery discharges
Ni/Fe	Durable, high cycle-life, good energy density	High initial cost of nickel, excessive hydrogen gassing, high water consumption, low efficiency
Zn/Br	High power, inexpensive	Bulky, complex, short life, corrosion, difficulty of containing bromine
Li-me/Fe-S	High specific energy and power, compact	High temperature, high cost and weight of insulation, high cost of current collectors, unstable cell components?
Na/S	High specific energy and power, inexpensive, widely available materials	High temperature, high cost and weight of insulation, corrosion of seals and casing, safety concerns
Zn/air	High specific energy and power, mechanically rechargeable	Complex, low cell efficiency, CO_2 scrubber needed, problems with air electrode and management of electrolyte
Al/air	Very high specific energy, high power, mechanically rechargeable	Complex and bulky, short life of air electrode, CO_2 scrubber needed, high cost of aluminum, low cell efficiency
Sources: Quinn et al. (1985), Walsh and Rajan (1985), DOE (1988), Sen et al. (1988).		

[44] Mark DeLuchi, Quanlu Wang, and Daniel Sperling, *Electric Vehicles: Performance, Life-Cycle Costs, Emissions, and Recharging Requirements, Transportation* (Res. A, Vol. 23A, No. 3, 1989).

In 1983 two papers appeared outlining a simulated experience of a fuel cell applied to the General Electric/Chrysler ETV-1 vehicle, shown in Chapter 21, and to a General Motors X-type car.[45][46] In operation the methanol fuel is vaporized by waste heat from the system in the form of steam. The vaporized methanol is disassociated by a catalytic cracker (platinum) into hydrogen and carbon monoxide. A shift reactor converts the latter into carbon dioxide and additional hydrogen. In the fuel cell the hydrogen produces electric power for vehicle propulsion as illustrated in Fig. 11.17. The placement of the active elements in the motorcar is shown in Fig. 11.18. A flow diagram of the vehicle consists of a fuel processor, fuel cell, motor controller, and electric motor. The system could start at zero degrees Centigrade and had a peak power of 66 kilowatts. The X-car was designed to cruise at 96 Km/hr with a 15 kw direct-current motor. Top speed was 113 km/hr. For the ETV-1 vehicle a top speed of 129 km/hr was achieved on simulation. Acceleration was from 0-80 km/hr (50 mph) in 10.2 seconds. In highway driving the energy efficiency was equivalent to 66 miles per gallon of gasoline.

While the above is only simulation, in the real world in 1984 fuel cell development was being directed to large systems capable of supplying a multiple number of city blocks with both electric and with heat energy.

Research work on fuel cells continues, driven as well by the increased need for electrical energy in space. One of the fruitful developments is the application of knowledge in ceramics to monolithic design fuel cells. In this approach a thin ceramic component is repetitively employed in a strong, lightweight honeycomb structure of small cells, thus achieving high power per unit of mass or volume. As is claimed "the light weight and low volume, as well as the efficiency and reliability of electrical systems, are advantageous in space systems." Figures

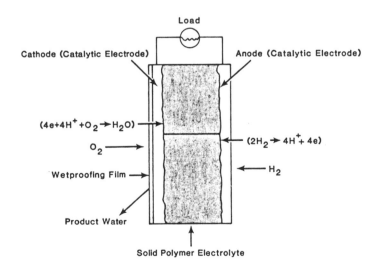

Figure 11.17. A solid polymer electrolyte fuel cell shown with chemical reactions. (Figures 11.17 and 11.18, Courtesy: Automotive Engineering, Vol. 91, No. 5, May 1983, pp. 39-41.)

[45] L. J. Nuttal and J. F. McElroy, *Technical and Economic Feasibility of Solid Plymer Electrolyte Fuel Cell Powerplant for Automotive Applications*, SAE Paper: 830348, Aircraft Equipment Division, General Electric Co.
[46] David K. Lynn, Hugh S. Murray, J. Byron McCormick, and James R. Huff, *Simulated Performance of Solid Polymer Electrolyte Fuel-Cell-Powered Vehicles*, SAE Paper: 830351, Los Alamos National Laboratory.

11.19, 11.20, 11.21, and 11.22 illustrate hydrogen-oxygens fuel cell systems.[47] As a possible power source for electric road vehicles, the subject of this book, this development appears as a 21st century possibility.

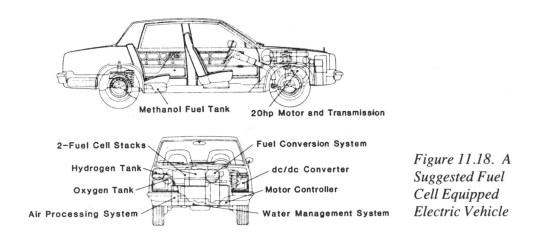

Figure 11.18. A Suggested Fuel Cell Equipped Electric Vehicle

MONOLITHIC FUEL CELL

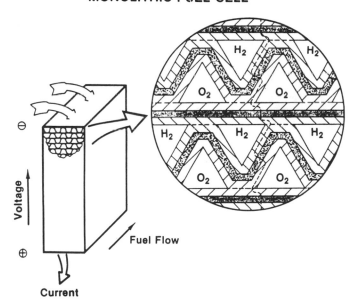

Figure 11.19. Monolithic Fuel Cell. (See Footnote 47)

[47] D. C. Dee, et al, *Monolithic Fuel Cells*, 22nd Intersociety Energy Conversion Engineering Conference, Philadelphia, Paper 789202, August 1-14, 1987.

Figure 11.20. Monolithic Fuel Cell Stack. (See Footnote 47)

Figure 11.21. Expanded View of Monolithic Solid Oxide Fuel Cell Assembly. The electrodes are shown before and after corrugation. (See Footnote 47)

Fuel Cell/Battery Powered Bus System Development

In 1987 the U.S. Department of Energy initiated a research, development, and demonstration of such a transportation bus. As the 13th Annual Report to Congress for the Fiscal Year 1989 states:

"The objective of this program is to develop a methanol-fueled, phosphoric acid fuel cell/battery propulsion system for a 30-ft urban bus. Fuel cells, operating on non-petroleum fuels, can potentially provide a propulsion system alternative with nearly twice the fuel economy and greatly reduced emissions compared with the internal combustion engine.

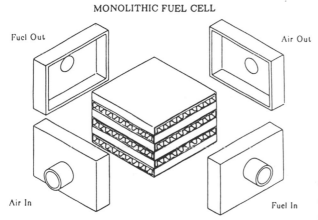

MONOLITHIC FUEL CELL

Fuel Out

Air Out

Air In

Fuel In

Figure 11.22. Cross-Flow of Monolithic Fuel Cell Design. (See Footnote 47)

"During FY 1989, work was continued on Phase I of this four-phased program. Phase I is a two-year effort directed at demonstrating proof-of feasibility of a phosphoric acid fuel cell/battery system as the prime source of power for an urban bus. Phase I is a system design and integration effort that includes system trade-off analyses, cost projections, and culminates with the fabrication and laboratory evaluation of a half-size fuel cell/battery brassboard power source. Phase II will encompass the integration of a full-size fuel cell/battery propulsion system into a testbed bus to demonstrate proof-of-concept. Track testing and field evaluation of this testbed bus will be accomplished in Phase III. Phases I through III will provide the technology development and demonstration needed to proceed to Phase IV, which encompasses field testing of a small fleet of prototype buses. The results of Phase IV will provide the data and experience needed by industry to make commercialization decisions.

"During FY 1989, the team of Booz-Allen & Hamilton, Chrysler Pentastar Electronics, and Fuji Electric completed the design of a liquid-cooled phosphoric acid fuel cell/battery propulsion system for an urban bus. A fuel cell/battery hybrid power source and electric drive system that is one-half the size planned for the bus was fabricated to demonstrate proof-of-feasibility for the concept. Laboratory evaluation of this 68-kW brassboard system (25-kW fuel cell and 43-kW lead-acid battery) was initiated in late FY 1989 and will be completed during early FY 1990.

"The team of Energy Research Corporation (ERC), Los Alamos National Laboratory, and Bus Manufacturing, Inc., completed the design of an air-cooled phosphoric acid fuel cell/battery propulsion system for an urban bus. ERC constructed a fuel cell/battery hybrid power source system that is one-half the size planned for the bus. Laboratory evaluation of this 62-kW brassboard system (32-kW fuel cell and 30-kW nickel/cadmium battery) was initiated in late FY 1989 and will be completed during early FY 1990."

There are other fuel cell systems. In a fuel cell invented by Alan H. Gelb of Physical Sciences, Inc. of Andover, Massachusetts Edmund L. Andrews writes,[48] "The fuel cell has an electrolyte solution, which conducts electrical current between a positive and negative electrode. Hydrogen and chlorine are pumped through the cell, forming hydrogen chloride, which yields one electron for every two molecules of hydrogen chloride. These electrons constitute the usable electrical current." Because the hydrogen and chlorine are easily linked the system has high efficiency. Moreover, he continues, the resulting product, hydrogen chloride, has commercial value. Gelb contends this fuel cell could capture up to 60 percent of the electrons from the chemical reaction, a ratio which compares favorably with the 30-35 percent efficiency of large internal combustion engines. In addition, emissions are tiny.

The output of the fuel cell, when combined with the high specific power of more conventional batteries as described in the above bus power system, might indeed supply electric power to a motor of an electric car.

Advanced-Battery Powered Vehicles

Anticipating the application of lithium-sulfur batteries as a power source for electric vehicles, Argonne National Laboratory, now a part of the U.S. Energy and Development Agency, ERDA, contracted in 1974 for the design of an electric drive system to be placed in a Detroit vehicle. This computer design study performed by Linear Alpha, Inc. of Evanston, Illinois led to a vehicle the size of a Ford Mustang shown in Fig. 11.23. Using the Figure's legend, under the front hood are 1) the lithium-sulfur battery; 2) the controller is near the right front tire; 3) the electric motor is rear mounted; 4) is a 2-speed automatic transmission; 5) a battery charger is behind the front seat; 6) a radiator to cool the lithium-sulfur battery is behind the front bumper; and 7) the heat-exchanger rides under the battery and serves to heat the car, when desired.

The energy stored in the 806 pound battery of 128 cells is 42 kilowatt-hours at 150 volts nominal. The vehicle is designed to accelerate from 0-60 mph in 23 seconds, with a speed of 50 mph obtained in 15 seconds. The range of the vehicle at a constant speed of 50 mph was calculated to be 110 miles, with an estimated range in urban driving of 80-110 miles. Before 75 percent utilization of the battery is achieved, the battery is unable to sustain a cruising speed of 60 mph.

---

[48] Edmund L. Andrews, *The New York Times*, October 5, 1991, p. 16.

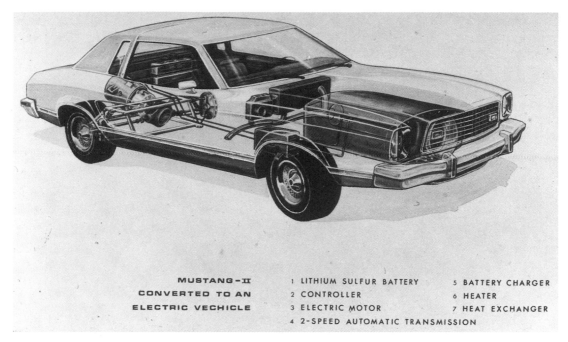

Figure 11.23. A computer-designed vehicle study employing a lithium-sulfur battery. Linear Alpha, Inc.

The car illustrated has batteries which may be commercially available in the 1990s, and may still be utilized in electric vehicles in the year 2000. In this design, in order to achieve the desired range for the car, a substantial mass of batteries were employed to provide an energy of 42 kwh. Such a car would need be charged from a 230 volt receptacle, simply to have a reasonably short charging time of 10-12 hours with a reasonable current. Supplementing these competitive designs would be the impact on the industry of the Electric Vehicle Act of 1976, discussed in Appendix G. Figures 11.24 through 11.28 show a number of vehicles and their power supplies using sodium sulfur batteries.

Figure 11.24 specifically shows a British demonstration van operated with an experimental sodium-sulfur battery. It bears the legend: First in the World. Ernest Marples, a previous Minister of Transport, arrives at the House of Commons after a run through Central London in the test vehicle. A British Bedford 18 cwt. van equipped with an experimental sodium-sulfur battery.[49] Range is 65 miles in urban driving; top speed is 40 mph; and acceleration is 0-30 mph in 20 seconds. Future sodium-sulfur batteries of 570 pounds are expected to yield 33.8 kWh. (See Fig. 11.30 for a phantom sodium-sulfur battery powered vehicle). (Courtesy: Electric Vehicles.)

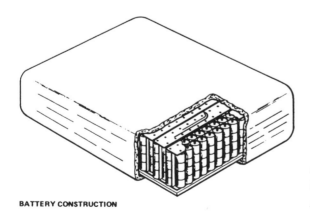

BATTERY CONSTRUCTION

Figure 11.25. A 70 Kwh Sodium Sulfur Battery Integrated into the Bedford CF Electric Van 1986.

[49] *Advanced Traction Battery Programme, Electric Vehicles*, March 1973, pp. 1 & 3.

178

The Battery[50]

The current battery design used at Powerplex Technologies, Inc. is shown in Fig. 11.27. Its characteristics are shown in Fig. 11.28. Called the B11, it consists of 360 cells, weighs 277 kg and is rated at 24 kWh. Glass fibre packed vacuum insulation keeps the heat energy loss to less than 200 watts in standby mode. Dozens of these batteries have been built and operated mostly for internal life and performance evaluation.

Other sodium-sulfur battery equipped vehicles are shown in Figs. 11.29 to 11.32, all of which are referred to by Angelis and Sedgwick.[51]

Figure 11.26. Two Examples of EV Test Vehicles. (See Footnote 50)

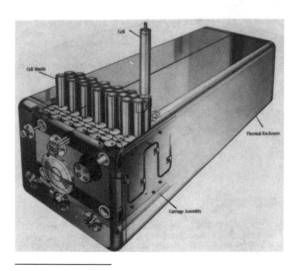

Figure 11.27. The Current Battery Generation. (See Footnote 50)

---

[50] M. Altmejd and E. Spek, *Capabilities of Na/S Batteries for Vehicle Propulsion.* SAE 89078, 1989.

[51] J. Angelis and D. Sedgwick. *Drive Characteristrics of Sodium Sulphur Battery Operated Vehicles.* The 9th International Electric Vehicle Symposium, Toronto, 1988.

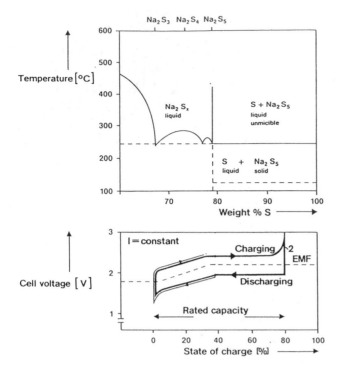

Figure 11.28. The Sodium Sulphur Charge-Discharge Behaviour and Phase Diagram. (See Footnote 50)

Figure 11.29. High-energy NaS Battery Type B11. (See Footnote 51)

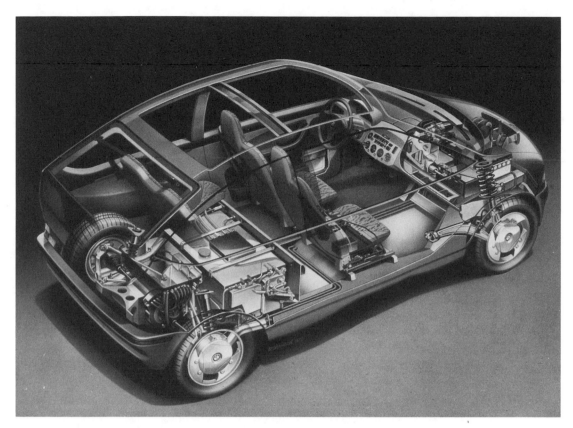

Figure 11.30. NaS Equipped BMW. (See Footnote 51) Amy L. Quarmby (BMC)

Figure 11.31. NaS Equipped Volkswagon Caddy. (See Footnote 51)

Figure 11.32. NaS Equipped Daimler Benz 190 E. (See Footnote 51)

The G & W Zinc-Chlorine Hydrate Battery

Another type battery being developed for electric vehicles has as its electric couple, zinc-chlorine hydrate, listed in Table 11-2. The principle of this energy source has been described:[52]

> "In the new battery a mixture of chlorine and water is cooled slightly to a slushy state, forming what is called a hydrate. This is stored in an insulated tank. When water is pumped into the chamber containing the hydrate, it melts the slurry and carries it to another chamber containing graphite electrodes coated with zinc, forming zinc chloride and providing an electric current."

In recharging a 220 volt receptacle feeds a portable converter which permits 110 volt d-c power to be furnished the vehicle. The power flow reverses the chemical process described above. Simultaneously a portable chiller is connected to the system to form chlorine hydrate.

A 1972 model of the "engine" was said to have powered a Chevrolet Vega at track speeds between 50 and 67 mph while yielding a range of 150 miles on a single charge. A 45 kWh G&W electric "engine," referred to by the developers, weighed some 1,200 pounds. Specific power was unavailable. A cut-away version of the "engine" is shown in Fig. 11.33. Figure 11.34 shows a van equipped with this battery.

One of the substantial costs of an electric vehicle is intimately associated with the cycle-life of a battery. Samples of this "engine" have accumulated 1400 cycles, said to be the equivalent

---

[52] *G & W (now Paramount Communications Inc.) Announce Electric Car Battery, The New York Times,* June 6, 1980, pp. 1 & D3.

Figure 11.33. Gulf & Western's President, David Judelson (center), and Technology Vice-president Dr. Milton Hollander discuss the new electric engine unit with John Rowan, (left), President of Energy Development Associates, the subsidiary responsible for the system's development. (Source: Electric Vehicles.[53])

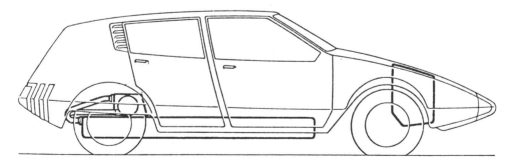

Figure 11.34. Battery/Motor Position. (Source: Electric Vehicle News)

---

[53] *Gulf & Western Optimistic Over New Energy Storage System, Electric Vehicles.* Vol. 66, No. 3, September 1980, pp. 23-25.

of 200,000 miles of driving.[54] Specific energy of the "engine" is given as 80 watt-hours/kg. For a comparison with other batteries reference should be made to Table 11-2. Commenting on the report of the new battery, Dr. Ping Yao, Field Project Manager of a Department of Energy Electric Vehicle Battery Program warned, "Gulf & Western can make all the noise they want, but there is still much more work to be done."[55]

Contributing to the G & W battery funding has been the Energy Department and the Electric Power Research Institute of the electric utilities. Together they have provided $16 million, and G&W have committed $11 million more. With the battery described a Volkswagon Rabbit has a top speed of 65 mph and an acceleration from 0-30 mph in 9.8 seconds. Mr. David N. Judelson is President of G & W Industries, Inc.[56] Later information sustains the above.[57]

Dual-Shaft Electric Propulsion (DSEP) System Program

In the 13th Annual Report to Congress for Fiscal Year 1989, issued in April 1990, the DSEP project was completed 30 September 1989. Responsible for carrying forth the program was the Eaton Corporation, Eagle-Picher Industries, and ASC, Inc. The task was to advance "electric propulsion technology through integrated development of a nickel-iron battery, and AC motor and controls, and an automatic, two-speed transaxle within a light-weight van suited for use in an urban/suburban environment." Additional details about these cars are in Chapters 19 and 20.

While the goal was for a battery cycle life of 1200, the two test vehicles were terminated at 650 and 900 cycles, respectively. As the result of the test the life cycle cost estimate of the entire DSEP vehicle/powertrain system indicated a disadvantage relative to a gasoline-powered vehicle. Below in Table 11-9 are results and illustrations of the cars. These vehicles are shown in Fig. 11.35.

Second Generation Single-Shaft EV Vehicle, The ETX-II[58]

Building on the experience gained with the ETX-I vehicle Ford/General Electric assembled a van-type vehicle bearing a sodium/sulfur battery, a 3-phase, permanent magnet, synchronous motor. The motor is provided power from a variable frequency, variable amplitude inverter supplied from the 200 volt battery. Below in Fig. 11.36 is the ETX-II, its preliminary specifications, and the temporary mounting of the sodium/sulfur batteries. The motor is detailed in Chapter 12, and the propulsion system goals are in Table 11-10 while Table 11-11 are preliminary specifications.

---

[54] *Gulf & Western Gets Publicity Mileage By Recharging News of Electric Car," The Wall Street Journal*, June 9, 1980, 12:2.

[55] *Batteries Are Still Far From Acid Test That Will Spark Electric Car Industry, Ibid*, June 10, 1980, 34:2.

[56] *G & W Announces Electric-Car Battery, The New York Times*, June 6, 1980, pp. 1 & D3.

[57] *Tests on G & W System Are Looking Good, Electric Vehicle News*, Vol. 11, No. 2, May 1982, p. 11.

[58] *Electric and Hybrid Vehicle Program, 13th Annual Report to Congress for Fiscal Year 1989*, U. S. Department of Energy, April 1990.

Table 11-9. Characteristics of DSEP Vehicles			
		Actual Results	
	Goals	DSEP-1 Vehicle	DSEP-2 Vehicle
Acceleration			
0-80.4 km/h (50 mph)	20 sec.	20.5 sec.	18.6 sec.
0-48.3 km/h (30 mph)	10 sec.	8 sec.	7 sec.
Top Speed	90.6 km/h (60 mph)	112 km/h (70 mph)	117 km/h (73 mph)
Gradeability from rest maintain 88.5 km/h (55 mph)	greater than 20% on 3% grade	28% 4%	32% 4%
Range at 72.4 km/h (45 mph)	104.7 km (65 mi)	109.4 km** (68 mi)	117.6 km** (73.5 mi)

**with the battery capacity at its nominal 170 ampere-hour rating
Source: 13th Annual Report to Congress, U.S. Energy and Development Agency.

Figure 11.35. Three Final DSEP Vehicles. (Source: 13 Annual Report to Congress, U. S. Energy and Development Agency.)

Figure 11.36. ETX-II Test Vehicle. (See Footnote 58)

Table 11-10. ETX-II Propulsion System Goals	
Energy Consumption (FUDS)	0.25 kWh/km
Maximum Speed	96 km/h
0 - 80 km/h acceleration	< 20 s
Gradeability	30%
Automotive Industry Acceptable Driveability	
	(See Footnote 58)

Table 11-11. ETX-II Preliminary System Specifications	
Vehicle	Aerostar
Test Weight	2050 kg
GVW	2310 kg
Rolling resistance	0.009
Drag Coefficient (C_d)	0.37
Frontal area	2.9 m^2
Battery	
Energy	50 kWh
Power	65 kW
Weight	500 kg
Inverter	Variable Voltage & variable frequency
Motor	70 hp
	Interior permanent magnet ac
Transaxle	Automatic, Two-Speed, Integral with rear axle
System Controller	Common bus multi-processor, Inverter/ Motor controls, Vehicle controls
	(See Footnote 58)

It is in such competitions as described below that batteries and motors may be tested, and, probably most importantly, youth is provided a healthy outlet for their originality.

Note

How Far Can You Travel Competition

In road testing of batteries and as a marketing concept a novel promotion was arranged in Britain in the waning years of the 1970s, using lead-acid batteries.[59] While electric car racing contests are now indeed sparse in number, the Lucas sponsored Battery Vehicle contention has attracted much interest in the United Kingdom. Backed by the Institute of Mechanical Engineers, in the competition each machine was required to be powered with two Lucas 12-volt

---

[59] *'Flying Coffin' Wins Battery Vehicle Trials, Electric Vehicles*, Vol. 65, No. 3, September 1979, pp. 10-12.

(CA9 type) batteries. Recharging was limited only to regenerative braking. The game is to determine which vehicle has the greatest range in the time allotted for the contest. A moment's reflection indicates speed is also included in the winning formula.

The 1979 confrontation attracted 97 entrants. The winner was William Yates who completed 89 laps (41.61 miles) at an average speed of 20.81 mph in his prone position, ground-hugging racer. Figures 11.37 and 11.38 show an awkward spill and the winning car, No. 45,

Figure 11.37. An Awkward Spill. (Courtesy: Electric Vehicles)

Figure 11.38. The winning car, No. 45, passes to victory. (Courtesy: Electric Vehicles)

passing rivals to overall victory. Prizes totalled £1925, including a first prize of £1000. The awards were presented by Sir Francis Tombs, Chairman of the Electricity Council.

It was stated the onset of the Depression terminated the event.

As the development of the battery was elucidated the reader understands the electric car, as a viable means of personal transportation, is no better than the motive power battery it contains. Let us now proceed to the electrical drive system, the controller, the motor itself, whose origin began only a few decades after the genesis of the battery. To develop an electric motor, a battery was essential. The researches of Volta, therefore, were a prerequisite for the major discoveries of Faraday, who discerned the physical laws enabling later innovators to develop the electric motors.

CHAPTER 12

The Development of Current Controllers and Electric Motors

All large electric motors on start-up require current limitation. This restriction prevents excessive current from flowing in the motor windings. As the motor accelerates while overcoming the inertia of its rotating elements and that of its load, i.e., a car, an internal current-limiting phenomenon becomes evident.[1] When the motor reaches rated speed an external and internal voltage balance is achieved, then the initial current control may be removed.

Motor Protection by Voltage Switching

The above words may be illustrated with numbers. On a motor for a vehicle the armature resistance may be as little as 1/20th of an ohm. If the motive power battery is 108 volts and it is directly impressed upon the terminals of the motor, the resulting current would approach 2000 amperes. Such a flow of current would dissipate in the motor some 200 kilowatts of power and would soon burn-out its electrical elements. If, on the other hand, at start-up a means is found such that, let us say, a voltage of 12 volts is impressed on the motor, power dissipation in the motor is less than three kilowatts for a moment. Moreover, the electric vehicle begins to roll with an adequate and pleasant sensation. As the vehicle gains speed, an ever greater voltage is provided the motor, thus maintaining the acceleration to the point desired by the driver. Such a voltage control in the early days of electric cars was achieved by a technique known as voltage switching. Figure 12.1 is an illustration drawn in 1899 representing a battery with 40 cells.[2] On start-up the cells are connected with four rows of 10 cells. Some 20 volts are impressed on the motor. As the vehicle gains speed, two rows of 20 cells are applied yielding 40 volts. Top speed is obtained when all 40 cells are placed in series giving a nominal 80 volts. This vehicle is seen to have three speeds forward. In the 1895 electric cars these speeds were 3, 6, and 12 mph, as noted for the victoria shown in Fig. 5.5. Typically there was one speed for reverse; in this case

---

[1] As the moment of inertia of a motor is large, time is required for any motor to gain speed. Current limitation is essential during this period. The current self-limiting phenomenon results from the rotating armature conductors traversing the magnetic flux of the motor field. This action generates a *back electromotive force*, a voltage which counteracts the impressed battery voltage. The resulting small voltage limits the armature current to values of balance.

[2] Wood, *The Electric Automobile*.

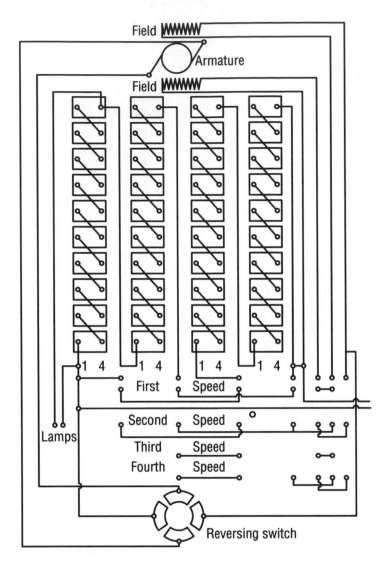

Figure 12.1. The above illustration represents 40 electric cells forming a battery for an early electric vehicle. In speed control the concept of voltage switching was utilized in which the 40 cells could be in 4 rows of 10, 2 rows of 20, or placing in series all 40 cells. Respectively the voltage applied to the motor would be 20, 40, and 80 volts, providing 3 speeds forward: 3, 6, and 12 mph. Typically there would be one speed for reverse.[3] Courtesy: H. E. Stone & Co.

3 mph. The multi-switching device that would enable the driver to make this manipulation is shown in Fig. 9.1 and is illustrated on the left side of the driver's seat in Fig. 5.6. A symbolic representation of voltage switching is given in Fig. 12.2, showing the step voltage, in this case seven steps. In some slight variation, all early vehicles had such a controller.

Electric trolley cars of this period utilized resistance insert achieved by utilizing a rheostat to control the voltage applied to the motor. Such an energy wasteful method of speed control, however, could not be tolerated on energy-limited-battery powered automobiles.

Inexperienced vehicle builders of any period have sometimes used a motor too large for the application. Figure 12.3 shows how the efficiency of any motor decreases as its load is reduced from full load.

---

[3] Ibid.

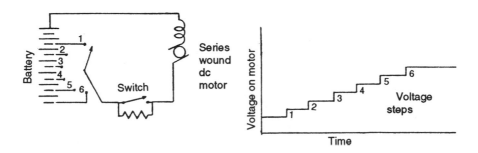

Figure 12.2. Voltage switching of batteries is symbolically shown as a voltage step-function. On acceleration an ever higher voltage is applied to the motor; on deceleration a lower voltage is applied.[4]

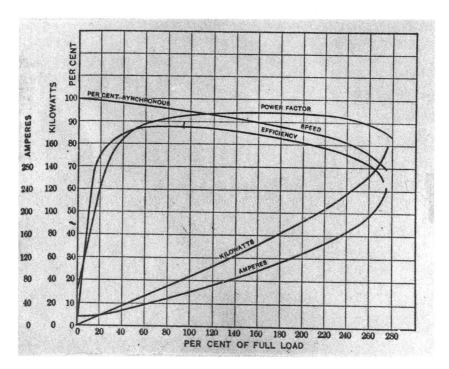

Figure 12.3. Note the low in efficiency of any motor as its load is decreased from full load. Dugal E. and John Price Dugal. Alternating Current and Alternating Current Machinery, New York: MacMillan, 1913, p. 857

---

[4] Wakefield, *The Consumer's Electric Car*, p. 86.

Solid State Controllers

Until the emergence of the silicon control rectifier, an SCR,[5] a solid state element, voltage switching was probably the best means of controlling the speed of an electric vehicle. With an SCR and its associated circuitry between the battery and the motor, the SCR is used as a switch. On motor start-up the full battery voltage is across the motor for a succession of short intervals. As the motor gains speed these time intervals become longer, as illustrated in Fig. 12.4. At full speed, or full acceleration, the intervals of current-flow join and become continuous. Because the action of the SCR, as a switch, is seen as chopping of the current entering the motor, this type of controller is known as a chopper. Figure 12.5 demonstrates a chopper installed under the hood of a modern, high-performance electric vehicle. As a chopper is constructed of all solid state elements with no moving parts, its reliability is excellent, its efficiency is 97-98 percent, and when used, it provides the car a smooth acceleration. The disadvantages of chopper control are its relatively high cost, its considerable size and weight, and its substantial reduction of motor efficiency at partial loads.[6] Nearly all choppers are controlled by simple accelerator action. The function of SCR controllers can be had in more detail from the manufacturer's literature. Small, direct-current motors, on the other hand, require no such elaboration for current limitation on start-up. They possess a higher armature resistance, and most importantly, the inertia of their rotating parts is small. Still, if speed adjustment is desired utilizing voltage variation, some control of armature current is required.

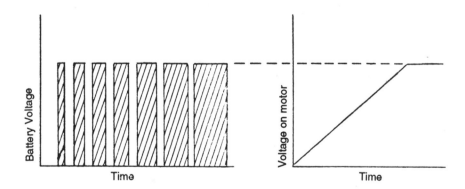

Figure 12.4. ,With chopper control, the armature current is voltage limited by the "average" voltage available. The average is increasing in amplitude as one proceeds from left to right in both diagrams.[7]

---

5 The SCR was invented by Dr. Nick Holonyak, now Professor of Electrical Engineering, University of Illinois, Urbana.

6 Paul D. Agrawal, Private communication.

7 Wakefield, *The Consumer's Electric Car*, p. 86.

Figure 12.5. A view under the front hood of a modern high-performance electric car. To the left is the battery charger, then the motor, the alternator, and the controller. This vehicle, the Thunderbolt 240, seats four, has a speed of 60 mph.[8] Courtesy: Linear Alpha, Inc.

Controls and Inverter for AC Electric Motors

While understanding the controls for a DC motor is rather straightforward, modern controls for an AC motor are sufficiently complex to relegate to Appendix B an article prepared by Dr. Gordon J. Murphy, Professor of Electrical Engineering and Computer Sciences, Northwestern University. Dr. Murphy has hands-on experience with AC drives in vehicles. See also the reference cited below.[9] In actual practice one of the great advantages of AC drive control is its accomplishment of using tiny currents.

---

[8] Ibid, p. 5.

[9] R. D. King, E. Delgado, P. M. Szczesny and F. G. Turnbull. *High-performance ETX-II 70 hp Permanent Magnet Motor Electric Drive System*, The 9th International Electric Vehicle Symposium, Toronto, 1988.

But first the electric motor had to be invented. As in the section on the history of batteries, Chapter 10, the author has chosen to give references on the history of the electric motor as well.[10]

The Development of Electric Motors

To move a wheeled vehicle requires the application of torque to the driving wheels. Torque is a twisting motion, a rotation. How can one obtain rotation from electricity, itself unseeable, only its manifestations being visible? With the first practical source of electric power available from the primary battery of Volta, experimentation with electricity could be more effectively carried forward. In 1820 a Copenhagen professor, Hans Christian Oersted (1777-1851), first observed that an electric current, arising from Volta's battery, would deflect a compass needle. A major event, for only two weeks after learning this news at the French Academy, André Ampère (1775-1836) found that a coil of wire acted as a magnet if a current were flowing in the wire. And that two such coils repel or attract each other just as like or unlike poles of a magnet. By these experiments Oested and Ampère had shown a relationship between electricity and magnetism. And by 1825 Ampère had collected his results into a system of mathematical laws.[11]

Michael Faraday,[12] an English chemist, being familiar with Ampère's work, in 1821 demonstrated that a suspended wire, having one end free to move and touching the surface of mercury contained in a beaker, the wire would revolve continuously around an upright permanent magnet as long as the wire and mercury were connected to opposite ends of a voltaic battery supplying current to the wire. This concomitance of electricity, magnetism, and motion was fundamental to the electric motor. In 1831 Faraday also showed that if a copper disc were rotated between magnetic poles a direct current was generated. This discovery led to the homopolar generator, and, indeed to all generators. His third pregnant observation, that an interrupted current in one circuit induces a voltage in a neighboring circuit, led to the principle of induction, to the transformer, and to the alternating-current induction motor (the true work-horse of mankind, but until the early 1980s used in only a few electric automobiles).[13]

Because of the importance of Faraday's discovery of electricity and motion which is the essence of the electric motor, a section of his *Diary* is given in Fig. 12.6. As shown on September 3, 1821, he recorded the interrelation of an electric current, magnetism, and motion of the current carrying wire.[14] It would be more than fifty years before an electric motor larger than one kilowatt would be commercially available.

---

[10] Aug Gueront, *The History of Magneto & Dynamo Electric Machines, Scientific American Supplement*, Vol. XIV, No. 357, November 4, 1882, pp. 5694-5697.

[11] For Ampère's Laws, see: *Encyclopaedia Britannica*, Vol. 8, 1959, p. 158.

[12] For a warm story of Faraday the man read: John Meurig Thomas, *Michael Faraday and the Royal Institution: The Genius and the Man*, London: Adam Hilger, 1991.

[13] Ernest H. Wakefield, *An a-c Drive Electric Vehicle*, IEEE Trans. on Industry Applications, Vol. 1A-10, No. 5, Sept/Oct 1974.

[14] Michael Faraday, *Faraday's Diary*, Vol. I, Sept. 1820 - June 11, 1821, G. Bell & Sons, Ltd, London, 1932, pp. 50-51.

SEPT. 3RD, 1821.

11. The effort of the wire is always to pass off at a right angle from the pole, indeed to go in a circle around it; so when either pole was brought up to the wire perpendicular to it and to the radius of the circle it described, there was neither attraction nor repulsion, but the moment the pole varied in the slightest manner either in or out the wire moved one way or the other.

12. The poles of the magnet act on the bent wire in all positions and not in the direction *only* of any axis of the magnet, so that the current can hardly by cylindrical or arranged round the axis of a cylinder?

13. From the motion above a single magnet pole in the centre of one of the circles should make the wire continually turn round. Arranged a magnet needle in a glass tube with mercury about it and by a cork, water, etc. supported by a connecting wire so that the upper end should go into the silver cup and its mercury and the lower move in the channel of mercury round the pole of the needle. The battery arranged with the wire as before. In this way got the revolution of the wire round the pole of the magnet. The direction was as follows, looking from above down [see diagram].

Very Satisfactory, but make more sensible apparatus.

TUESDAY, SEPT. 4.

14, 15 †. Apparatus for revolution of wire and magnet. A deep basin with bit of wax at bottom and then filled with mercury, a Magnet stuck upright in wax so that pole just above the surface of mercury, then piece of wire floated by cork, at lower end dipping

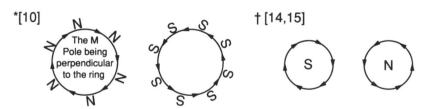

into mercury and above into silver cup as before, and confined by wire or capillary attraction from leaving the M. Pole.

16*. Now Magnet round wire. The magnet had one pole so far sunk by platinum as to be low under the surface, leaving the other just above the surface whilst the whole floated; then the wire of connection was made to dip into the mercury near the pole.

Figure 12.6. Section of Faraday's Diary recording the interrelation of an electric current, magnetism, and motion of the current carrying wire.

A more careful drawing from Faraday's later book,[15] illustrated a Fig. 12.7, shows the motion of the wire rod around the upright magnet, and the motion of the upright magnet around the current carrying wire rod on the left.

Michael Faraday is so important to the emergence of the electric vehicle that a short biography is in order. Faraday was born at Newington in Surrey, south of London, 22 September 1791. His father, a blacksmith, apprenticed the son to a bookbinder at the age of 14. While

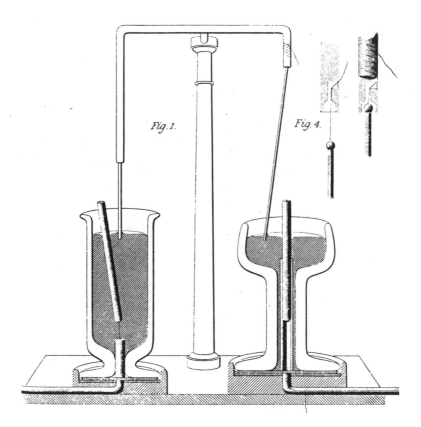

Figure 12.7. Faraday demonstrated that a wire rod carrying an electric current would rotate around a vertical magnet. If the polarity of the magnet were interchanged, the direction of rotation would reverse. In the experiment on the left, if a magnet were floated in mercury as shown, and a current passed through the wire rod, the magnet would rotate around the current-carrying rod. A change in the direction of the current would cause a reversal in the direction of rotation.[16] Bernard Quaritch.

---

[15] Michael Faraday, *Experimental Researches in Electricity*, Vol. II, Bernard Quaritch, London 1844, p. 130.
[16] Faraday, *Experimental Researches*, Appendix.

working as a journeyman bookbinder, Faraday attended a chemistry lecture given by Sir Humphry Davy. Faraday carefully wrote up the notes on this lecture, illustrating the principles by means of drawings, and carefully bound the whole, presenting it to Davy with a request he be given a post of assistant in the Royal Institution of Great Britain. Receiving the assignment, Faraday soon accompanied Davy on a tour through France, Italy, and Switzerland from October 1813 to April 1815, a period when Napoleon was notorious. In 1833 Faraday was appointed Fullerian Professor of Chemistry for life, as one of the world's most seminal scientific experimentalists.

Faraday in his genius, like Nikolai Tesla, subsequently discussed, would demonstrate principles knowing others would develop the hardware as illustrated by the following possible apocryphal story.[17]

> "When the Earl of Liverpool, the then British Prime Minister, was shown the wire with a cork at its end, floating in mercury, rotating around the vertical magnet, he asked, 'And Mr. Faraday, of what use is it?' To which the savant replied, 'Sir, its principle will someday form a useful commodity, and then you can be sure that the House of Commons will tax it.'"

Before studying specific electric motors the reader should appreciate there are many types. Figure 12.8 is a breakdown of the several types. The first discussed is the direct current motor, the earliest devised.

The Direct Current Motor

In 1832 Hippolyte Pixii demonstrated an operating electric motor before the Académie des Sciences in Paris.[17a] It was not until 1835, however, that the principle of the electric motor was fully demonstrated. Frances Watkins of London assembled a model system. This operating model had stationary coils of wire through which current flowed. These field coils surrounded a shaft on which was mounted a bar magnet. A set of contact makers (today's commutator) was on the shaft which allowed current to be sent through successive coils. This time in current flow induced the shaft to spin. The very next year, Thomas Davenport, an American blacksmith, was the first to build an electric motor and apply it to useful tasks in 1836.[18] He used the electric motor with a drill to pierce iron and steel, and to operate a wood-turning lathe. The initial motor of Davenport had magnetic fields established by permanent magnets, a concept presently used in small motors. This motor, operating in his Philadelphia shop, Davenport showed to Joseph Henry, the first head of the Smithsonian Institution, who, at the same time as Faraday, had discovered the principle of induced voltage. The motor is shown in Fig. 12.9.

---

[17] Anonymous.

[17a] Ann. Chimig. Phy., Vol. 50 (1832), p. 322; and Vol. 51 (1832), p. 76.

[18] Thomas Davenport, *Specification of a Patent for the Application of Electro Magnetism to the Propelling of Machinery*, Journal of the Franklin Institute, 1837, Vol. 20, pp. 340-343. U.S. Patent 132, February 25, 1837. Also, *Notice of the Electro-Magnetic Machine of Mr. Thomas Davenport of Brandon, Near Rutland, Vermont*, American Journal of Science, 1837, Vol. 32, appendix, pp. 1-8.

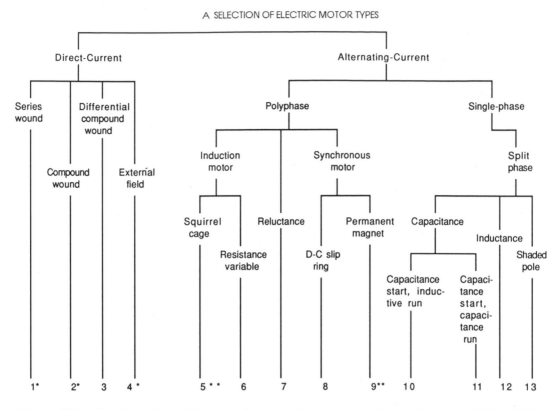

Figure 12.8. Single and double starred motors have been used for electric vehicles. The trend in recent vehicles is to the double starred motors. Both have modulated frequency and pulse-width controls. Ernest H. Wakefield.

From the above diverse investigations d-c motors/generators were being constantly improved with better understanding of electricity and magnetism. Central station generation was nearly everywhere becoming more common. The industrial nations of the world were entering an electric age. Conditions were ready for Andrew L. Riker of Brooklyn to assemble the first American electric vehicle in 1890. An engineer, he could manufacture a creditable electric motor, assemble electric batteries, possess means for charging them, and he had available the wheeled tricycle on which to mount all the elements. Figure 12.10 illustrates an assembled electric vehicle motor of vintage 1899, while Fig. 12.11 shows the same motor unassembled. The armature and commutator rest on the motor housing. In the upper picture the shaft on the right connects with the differential, shown in Figs. 12.12 and 12.13.[19] The

---

[19] C. E. Woods, *The Electric Automobile.*

Figure 12.9. The first motor to perform useful work operated in 1836. Visible are the four pole windings, the iron ring to carry the flux, the vertical rotating armature, which by means of a spindle gear, gave rotation to the horizontal shaft. (Source: Smithsonian Inst. photo 44978.)

braking wheel with friction applied would slow and finally halt the car, as the motor was gear-connected to the wheels. Figure 12.13 illustrates the differential of the period in more detail. Most early electric vehicles had curb weights from 550 to 2300 pounds.

Direct Current Motor Improvement

Motor improvements since 1900 are: 1) the use of laminations in both the field poles as well as the armature; 2) the introduction of silicon steel in laminations (both factors serve to lessen iron loss); 3) the introduction of superior insulation to enable the motor to operate at higher temperatures; 4) the greater economy of metal; and 5) the application of the computer in design calculations. All these techniques provide more horsepower per unit weight. While the material of construction and the means of calculation have changed, the assembly of d-c motors of the size used in electric vehicles have been modified relatively little in the 40 years the author has

Figure 12.10. An electric vehicle motor of 1899. The shaft on the right engages the differential, while the wheel on the left is the brake, actuated by reducing the diameter of the friction band.[20] Courtesy: H. E. Stone & Co.

observed the making of d-c electric motors. They are heavy, labor intensive in their manufacture. Figure 12.14 is a cut-away model of a direct-current motor such as has been used in electric vehicles of the 1970s and '80s.

With the electric motors well developed in 1900 and the batteries readily available, what would be the prognosis for the electric vehicle industry in the new Century?

Apparent from the above illustrations was the recognition that with electricity many tasks could be done more easily, or better, or even made possible, and the inventors were anxiously seeking out these new paths. Only by experimenting could physical truths be learned, and they led to our present motors and generators—designs which have not greatly changed in more than six decades.

[20] Ibid.

Figure 12.11. The above motor is disassembled. The armature rests upon the housing for the field poles, and is properly oriented with the housing. End bells containing the shaft bearings are seen both to the left and to the right of the housing.[21] Courtesy: H. E. Stone & Co.

Development Three-Phase Alternating Current Motor

Whilst the above illustrations show the evolution of transforming mechanical power into electric power, a generator, and contrariwise, a motor, the principle employed direct-current, a system favored by Edison. Meanwhile, in the early 1880s, at the time the Menlo Park inventor was perfecting the direct-current total system for lighting, Nikola Tesla, born in what is now

---

[21] Ibid.

Figure 12.12. Rear axle view of an 1899 electric car showing rear of driver's seat, mounting of motor, and differential. Cutaway wood-spoked wheels are at the extremities.[22] Courtesy: H. E. Stone & Co.

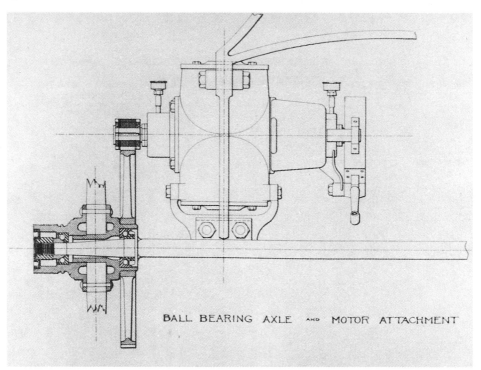

Figure 12.13. The differential gears from an 1899 electric car. That a differential would be required for cornering was early realized.[23] The differential was a French invention. Courtesy: H. E. Stone & Co.

[22] Ibid.
[23] C. E. Woods, *The Electric Automobile.*

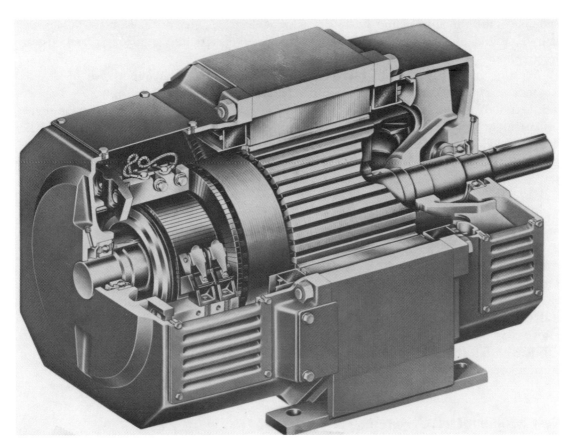

Figure 12.14. A modern dc electric motor such as is used in today's electric vehicles. A section is cut out to show its internal construction. Courtesy: Reliance Electric Company.

Croatia was cogitating the measure presently designated as polyphase alternating current.[24] Tesla was educated at the Technical University of Graz in Austria and at the University of Prague. In the former school he first saw a dynamo built by Gramme, and, like the Belgian inventor, observed it could be either a motor or a generator, depending whether the input was electrical or mechanical power. At this time he conceived of polyphase electricity and the concept of the rotating magnetic field. On graduation Tesla proceeded to Paris where he worked in the shops of the Continental Edison Company. Like many other Europeans of the time, he was drawn to America. In 1884 he arrived in New York with four cents and his drawings, and, with introductions, began working with the inventor of the electric lamp. The two, both geniuses, were dissonant.

Edison, a largely self-taught individual, failed to grasp the implications of Tesla's theoretical reasoning based partially on the elegant mathematical treatment of electromagnetism elucidated by James Clerk Maxwell.[25] Tesla's concept of the rotating magnetic field, the

---

[24] Nikola Tesla, *Lectures, Patents, Articles*, ed. by Vojiu Popovic, Radoslav Horvat, and Nikola Nikolic, Beograd: Nikola Tesla Museum, 1956.

[25] James Clerk Maxwell, *A Treatise on Electricity and Magnetism*, 2nd ed., Oxford: The Clarendon Press, 1881.

principle of the transformer, and the transmission of electric power, not Edison's, would be the pathway to today's electric economy. Tesla, a conceiver, required an actuator, and George Westinghouse would be that compliment.

Westinghouse, a successful inventor-manufacturer, sensed the importance of Tesla's sketches, and bought the patents for $1 million plus a royalty of $1 per horsepower.[26] The two and their staff placed in hardware form: a 3-phase generator, a 3-phase transformer, and a 3-phase induction motor forming an alternating current system, just as Edison had collated the elements of a d-c system. While Edison continued to oppose the installation of the a-c system, its greater flexibility eventually led to its almost universal use. The electric vehicles described in Chapter 19 are based on the principles enunciated by Tesla, while all other electric cars go back to Faraday.

For the reader who desires a greater understanding of Tesla's polyphase system, reference may be had to the authors and books cited in Chapter 19, where the 3-phase motor drive is discussed for vehicles produced both by General Motors and by Linear Alpha, Inc. Also useful in evaluating motors for electric vehicle drives is the monograph issued by the Scientific Research Staff of the Ford Motor Company.[27]

The above is a truncated presentation of the 120 year evolution of electric motors, so useful in all of yesterday's battery-powered carriages and in many of today's electric cars. The second point exposed was that, despite Edison's dominance in electricity over a 60 year span, a quiet, diffident youth, Nikola Tesla, would develop a largely competing system which, with Westinghouse's ability for pragmatism, would truly usher in the electric economy.[28]

New Modern Drive Systems

While the d-c motor drive system pictured in Fig. 12.10 had been earlier almost universally used in electric car drives, Britain's Chloride Technical, the R & D arm of the Chloride Battery Group, together with England's Department of Industry, is sponsoring the development of a new control and drive motor for battery powered vehicles. The work is being done at Nottingham and at Leeds Universities. Their motor is a 12.5 kW variable reluctance drive system, said to be simpler and less expensive, capable of reducing manufacturing costs by 25 percent.[29]

After the above studies, a 60-kW variable reluctance motor to operate with a low cost inverter would be studied in detail by David A. Torrey and Jeffrey H. Lang of the Massachusetts Institute of Technology (MIT) for electric vehicle use indicating that,[30] with the above, this

---

[26] Nikola Tesla, *Experiments with Alternate Currents of High Potential and High Frequency*, with biographic data, New York: W. J. Johnson Co., 1892.

[27] L. R. Foote *et al, Electric Vehicle Systems Study*, Scientific Research Staff, The Ford Motor Company, Dearborn, Michigan, Technical Report SR-73-132, October 25, 1973.

[28] The development of the single-phase alternating-current motor (and generator), an outgrowth of Tesla's work, a device so useful in household appliances, forms a second story. One of the author's professors, Dr. Benjamin F. Bailey, invented the capacitor split-phase alternating-current motor, now exceedingly widely employed.

[29] *1/4- M Research Contract for New Motor and Control System, Electric Vehicles*, Vol. 65, No. 4, December 1979, pp. 1-2.

[30] David A. Torrey and Jeffrey H. Lang, *An Inverter for a 60-kW Variable Reluctance Motor Drive for Electric Vehicle Propulsion*, Eighth International Electric Vehicle Symposium, Washington, D. C. 1986.

principle of motor operation offered promise. Also to be watched as a possible drive system for electric cars is the disc type motor developed for the MIT entry in the first university transcontinental race of 1968, pictured and referenced in Chapter 24. See in Figs. 12.15 and 12.16 the elegant 5-kW 3-phase, 12 pound (5kg) synchronous motor developed by General Motors for their Sunraycer, a solarmobile, in 1987.

Advanced AC Powertrains for Electric Vehicles

As the U.S. Department of Energy program progressed, interest by this body in AC drives enhanced, with government funding. Two contracts, in general, with different approaches, were awarded. One to the Chrysler/Eaton group, or to Eaton alone, and the other to the Ford/General Electric doublet. The former was based on the induction motor principal, the latter on the permanent magnet synchronous motor concept. One of the advantages of the former is low cost. For the latter, a few percentage points in higher efficiency because of lower copper and iron heat-losses.

Figure 12.15. A frequency and pulse-width modulated controller capable of changing d-c power to 3-phase variable frequency a-c power designed and built by Cocconi Engineering for the GM Sunraycer. (Source: Bruce McCristal, GM-Hughes.)

Figure 12.16. A 3-phase, 6-pole, 5 kW. 11 lb (5 kg), permanent magnet, synchronous motor made by GM Research Labs for Sunraycer in 1987. (Source: Bruce McCristal. GM-Hughes.)

The induction motor solution developed into a 3-phase induction motor with transistorized pulse-width and frequency-modulated inverter/battery charger, microprocessor-based controller, and two speed automatic transaxle.[31][32] As Sliker and Kalns write:

"The 3-phase AC induction traction motor and transaxle are mounted together in a 2-axis configuration. The motor is cooled by circulated transaxle oil.

"The induction motor has an 18.6-kW, one-hour thermal rating and base speed of 5640 RPM operating on a 192-volt battery pack. The transaxle hydraulic system is derived from a DC motor driving a gear pump which saves substantial pumping power at high speeds compared to a transmission input-driven pump.

"The pulse-width-modulated inverter employs two-paralleled, 100-amp, 450-volt transistors per switch in a conventional 3-phase bridge configuration for driving

[31] James M. Slicker and Ilmar Kalns. *Advanced AC Powertrain for Electric Vehicles*, SAE, 850200.

[32] Susan R. Citanek, Ahmad Sereshteh, and James M. Slicker. *Driveline Torsional Vibration Control Method in an Electric Propulsion System*, The 9th International Electric Vehicle Symposium, Toronto, 1988.

the motor...A 4-kW on-board battery charger has been integrated into the inverter circuit...This converter operates at either 220 or 110-volt AC lines...

"The microprocessor-based controller performs real-time closed loop control of motor currents. Included in the controller is a digital slip control scheme which is derived from a 120-toothed pickup on the motor. The controller also coordinates the gearshift sequence, monitors critical drive system parameters and provides the operator/vehicle interface...."

The Single-Shaft Electric Motor System

The second contract cited above, Ford/General Electric, has as its core

"a 70-hp interior permanent magnet synchronous motor.[33][34] This high power factor motor uses Neodymium-Iron-Boron (NdFeB) magnets to supply rotor flux, which almost eliminates rotor losses and results in a highly compact, efficient design. The variable speed control strategy operates the motor from 9 to 11,000 RPM, with a torque accuracy of plus or minus 5 percent range. The four quadrant control scheme employs a closed-loop torque control system. The constant torque region of the controls, 0 to 3400 RPM, is based on vector control. A flux-weakening strategy is used to control the motor in the constant power region, 3400 to 11,000 RPM.

"...The system controller has two major sections, one for the vehicle controls and one for the inverter/motor controls. The two sections communicate by using a shared memory for common data and status messages. Each section is microprocessor-based and a significant improvement for ETX-II is that most of the inverter/motor controls are digitally implemented.

"...The inverter/motor controls...are responsible for the feedback control of motor torque and provide the switching signals to the power modules to deliver the torque commanded by the vehicle controller...

"A pulse-width-modulated (PWM)...vector control mode is employed from zero speed to motor base speed. At the motor base speed the controls enter a quasi-PWM region in which overlay current loops maintain smooth operation during the transition into the square-wave mode. Above base speed, a delta angle (torque or power angle) scheme, operating in a six-step-square-wave mode, is used to control the motor up to its maximum operating speed of 11,000."

[33] B. Bates, C. P. Stokes and M. F. Ciccarelli. *ETX-II - A Second Generation Advanced AC Propulsion System*, The 9th International Electric Vehicle Symposium, Toronto, 1988.

[34] R. D. King, E. Delgado, P. M. Szczesny and F. G. Turnbull. *High-Performance ETX-II 70-hp Permanent Magnet Motor Electric Drive System*, The 9th International Electric Vehicle Symposium, Toronto, 1988.

Figure 12.17. Motor and Transaxle (Courtesy: Cikanid et al.)

CHAPTER 13

Electric Cars 1900-1935

The users and manufacturers of electric vehicles were optimistic in the new year of 1900. While some producers who initiated their vehicle production with electrics early in the century changed to gasoline motorcars, there were persons with substance and knowledge who backed the electric cars against the growing competition from this quarter. In addition, the production of electrics was increasing, and their reliability was proven. Some electric cars had a cruising speed of 20 mph, and on November 1, 1901, A.L. Riker startled the transportation industry by driving his Riker electric over a one-mile course in one minute three seconds, for a speed of 57.1 mph. For a short time that was an American automobile speed record. Only a steam train on specially cleared tracks had gone faster. The decade would see a series of races between electric, gasoline-powered, and steam-driven automobiles, events which will be described in Chapter 15. Each drive system had its champions.

The Form of the Modern Automobile

The 1900s would also see the emergence of the present configuration of the automobile. The horseless character, so evident in the pictures earlier seen, and in Figs. 13.1 and 13.2, would with surprising rapidity yield to cars designed as electric from the first. The motor would be forward with the battery in the rear, giving a satisfactory weight distribution; the heaviest mass aft for improved traction, the light weight forward for ease in steering. The first third of the century would witness continuous improvement in the mechanical features of the electric vehicles: wheels, bearings, gears, tires, body, and fastenings. With the efficiency of the electric motor an already surprising 80-90 percent and voltage switching likewise, there was little room for improvement in the electric drive components with the small power requirements of the early electric cars. The battery, the electro-chemical element, would be made more rugged for better acceptance of driving vibrations.

In 1900, on the Paris-Dijon road, where grades were reported to be as much as 11-12 percent, an electric car travelled 164 miles at an average speed of 10 mph on a single charge. The car curb weight was 5,060 pounds. The battery was 2,770 pounds giving a battery-to-curb weight

Figure 13.1. American electric vehicles of the turn of the Century were characterized by their low curb weight, ranging from 550 to 2,300 pounds and a scope of operation of some 30 miles. This range met the need of the smaller city of that day. (Courtesy: The Horseless Age, Vol. 15, No. 1, October 4, 1899.)

ratio of 55 percent. The battery had a nominal voltage of 88 volts, was of 320 ampere-hour capacity. At a speed of 13 mph the motor required 36 amperes at 90 volts. At this relatively low current draw the energy aboard the vehicle would be about 30 kilowatt-hours of electric energy—some 90 pounds per kWh. As the Paris-Dijon road was probably hard-surfaced at the time, and the car was almost surely equipped with solid rubber tires, a calculation indicates the vehicle used about 0.3 kWh per mile. This figure coincides remarkably well with the computer derived curves of Dr. Gordon J. Murphy for a vehicle of comparable weight moving at the same

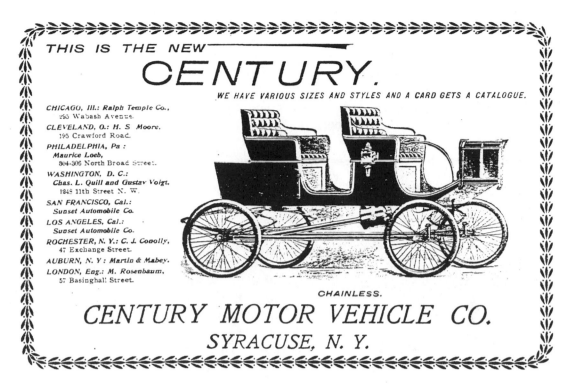

THIS IS THE NEW
CENTURY.
.WE HAVE VARIOUS SIZES AND STYLES AND A CARD GETS A CATALOGUE.

CHICAGO, Ill.: **Ralph Temple Co.**,
    265 Wabash Avenue.
CLEVELAND, O.: **H. S Moore.**
    195 Crawford Road.
PHILADELPHIA, Pa :
  Maurice Loeb,
    804-306 North Broad Street.
WASHINGTON, D. C.:
  Chas. L. Quill and Gustav Voigt.
    1248 11th Street N. W.
SAN FRANCISCO, Cal.:
  Sunset Automobile Co.
LOS ANGELES, Cal.:
  Sunset Automobile Co.
ROCHESTER, N. Y.: **C. J. Cooolly,**
    47 Exchange Street.
AUBURN, N. Y : **Martin & Mabey.**
LONDON, Eng.: **M. Rosenbaum,**
    57 Basinghall Street.

CHAINLESS.

CENTURY MOTOR VEHICLE CO.
SYRACUSE, N. Y.

Figure 13.2. In the Century Electric one can see the extremely simple chassis. The controller to the motor would be to the left of the driver on the side of the seat.[1]

speed.[2] In energy equivalence, this electric car travelled 183 miles per gallon. At the time, steam vehicles were achieving six miles per gallon, over atrocious roads,[3] and gasoline powered cars 12 miles per gallon.[4] Fuel costs, as is shown in Table 13-1, have had little impact on the choice of the motive power of cars, indicating there have been other subjective and objective reasons.

Meanwhile the internal combustion (IC) engine cars were continually being improved, and as highways became all weather and extended, the nation's families, obtaining their first car, and having but one, used it for both commuting and taking outings. And this travel, described as touring in Chapter 9, required range, a characteristic for which the electric car suffered in comparison. The magazine of motoring, too, *The Horseless Age*, demonstrated the growing dominance of IC vehicles. The six month issues from July 1 to December 31, 1902 had five articles listing new electric cars, 67 announcing gasoline-powered cars and 19 introducing steam cars. And at the same time Fig. 13.3 illustrates how one manufacturer straddled the issue by offering a Runabout for either drive.

---

[1] *The Horseless Age*, January 23, 1901.

[2] Gordon J. Murphy, *Considerations in the Design of Drive Systems for On-the-Road Electric Vehicles, Proc. IEEE* (December 1972), pp. 1519-1533.

[3] F. Clever Bald, *Horseless Carriages In Ann Arbor*, Michigan Historical Collection, Bulletin No. 6, December 1953.

[4] George F. Jessup, *Lessons Of The Road, The Horseless Age*, Vol. 10, No. 15, October 1902.

Figures 13.3A and 13.3B illustrate another light weight vehicle, the Ajax Runabout. With a curb weight of 1,000 pounds and equipped with a 24 volt-motor geared to an idling shaft, the Ajax was less a foreshadowing of what was to come than were the differential equipped Baker diminutive cars. General use minikin 4-wheel electric cars are prohibited by modern safety requirements.

The style of all motor cars, regardless of their motive power, was changing as illustrated in Fig. 13.4 of the Baker Electric Runabout.

Special Light Weight

RUNABOUT.

Intended for Gasoline or Electric Motors.

We Manufacture six other styles of Gears.

Send for Catalogue.

$175.00.

B. V. COVERT & CO.,
Lockport. N. Y.

Figure 13.3. This manufacturer chose to offer only a chassis and a body. The drive system would be furnished by others. Note the low curb weight such a vehicle would offer. At the time of the advertisement the style of the horseless carriage was fading, the torpedo body, introduced by Walter Baker, would be on the ascendancy. Here was an early do-it-yourself kit.[5]

Figures 13.3A and 13.3B. An Ajax Runabout, built by the Ajax Motor Vehicle Company of New York City. (Courtesy: Scientific American.)

---

[5] *The Horseless Age*, January 8, 1902.

Figure 13.4. Baker 1910 Phaeton. Walter C. Baker, a graduate electrical engineer, was one of the most gifted early manufacturers of electric vehicles. His turn-of-the-century Torpedo Electric racer established a one kilometer record in 1902, and initiated the present design for automobiles, representing the break-away from the horseless carriage. Baker was one of the largest of the electric car manufacturers. An early Stanhope had a curb weight of only 550 pounds while bearing 180 pounds of batteries, yielding a battery-curb weight ratio of 34 percent, and giving a range of 20 miles in urban driving. Baker's vehicles were well designed and attractively finished. He early used nickel-steel for durability, and wire wheels all of uniform size. Baker Electric Runabout, Scientific American CII 3 Jan. 15, 1910, p. 61.

The year 1912 would be the high point in the manufacture of electric cars. From that date the annual production of electric cars would decline, reaching zero for commercial electric vehicles in the United States. America had begun its love affair with the gasoline-powered vehicle, a special arrangement that was only jarred in the early 1970s by an enhancing realization of problems in pollution and the growing recognition that America was increasingly living on imported oil.

In 1900 C. E. Woods wrote an excellent book, *The Electric Automobile, Its Construction, Care, and Operation*.[6] He had university degrees both in mechanical and electrical engineering. From reading the text one can conclude he was a guileless man, writing information just as he understood it. The book is in a language that the literate can comprehend, and it was sufficient to enable the driver of the day to have a rudimentary appreciation of motive power batteries, the method of limiting current to the motor, the operation of the motor itself, and the means of

---

[6] C. E. Woods, *The Electric Automobile*, Herbert Stone & Co., NYC, 1900, p. 177.

transferring mechanical power to the wheels through the differential. He also instructs the reader in the care of these items, plus means of keeping gears clean. For comparison purposes he makes cost studies for operating a horse and buggy taxi and an electric vehicle taxi. A person learned in electric vehicles today can appreciate the excellent grasp Woods had of the electric vehicle field.

The reason these vehicles of 1900 obtained the relatively high mileage per battery-charge was that they had a low curb-weight, varying from 550 pounds to 2,800 pounds, some of the Baker Electric being of the lower figures. Their ratio of battery weight to curb weight was 40 percent or more. Their rolling resistance was low because they used small cross-section, highly pressurized tires. Their speed was low, 10-20 mph. And there was little stop and start driving as the streets were relatively free of traffic.

Today's batteries have a somewhat higher energy density. The then series-parallel switching for the motor controller was efficient, yielding pronounced acceleration. Both the present and the 1900 motors would be of comparable efficiency, some 90 percent. Present day motors, however, have less weight per horsepower. This decrease has resulted from employment of silicon steel for the armature and stator as a path for the magnetic flux, and much superior types of insulations for the copper conductors allowing the motor to operate at an elevated temperature. In addition, there is superior material used in the brushes. Also improved today in modern electric cars are the mechanical parts, and in high-performance electric vehicles, creature comfort. Nearly everywhere in the Western world the desirability for the automobile was recognized, for this contrivance was seen as a modern magic carpet for personal transportation.

The Insatiable Demand for Motorcars

Shortly after the turn of the Century, advertisements for automobiles began appearing in quantity. As sufficient vehicles of all powered types had been assembled, a secondhand car market developed, the first ever. Reference to Fig. 13.5, clipped from the January 1, 1902 issue of *The Horseless Age* indicates that steam, electric, and gasoline-powered cars could be had, previously used, for immediate delivery, a phenomenon that existed in richness of variation in a particularly dynamic period of personal transportation. The advertisement in the lower right hand corner of the Figure by S. Goff & Co. of London reflects the pent-up demand for motorcars. In 1902, the time of the ad, essentially all well-informed people knew that the automobile was most advantageous over the horse as a source of power. From the galvanic market of 1902, the time of this advertisement, essentially until the post World War I depression of 1921, the demand for motorcars in America, in England, and on the Continent, was insatiable.

America, with its early genius for mass production and consequent reduction in prices for automobiles, was soon to lead the world in their rate of production. In short, the motor car industry during this period grew as fast as was possible. That the market was insatiable, many manufactures recognized, as exemplified by the electric vehicle offered by the White Sewing Machine Company in Fig. 13.6. Sewing machine manufactures seemed to have a proclivity for transportation: the first bicycles in England were made in the Coventry Sewing Machine Company, and Colonel Pope, it will be recalled, subcontracted his first American made bicycles to the Weed Sewing Machine Company. The manufacture of the motorcar would lead to probably the most rapid reassignment of capital the world had ever seen.

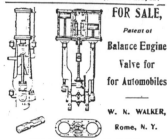
Figure 13.5. The second-hand market for motor cars was evident in 1902.[7]

---

[7] *The Horseless Age*, January 1, 1902.

Figure 13.6. This White Electric was on the streets in 1901. It is still a horseless carriage. Wire-spoked wheels have replaced the wagon style wheels. They are also of the same diameter enhancing interchangeability. Steering is yet by tiller. With small diameter, high pressure tires and the battery compartment shown, this car probably had a city range of some 25 miles; in urban areas of 1902, a respectable distance.[8]

The late Claud R. Erickson was a child of this era, and was also a history buff.[9] Erickson continues:

"By 1911 the Electric Vehicle Association of America, a trade association group of electric car manufactures, electric utilities, and battery manufactures, was formed. From a charter membership of 29, by 1913 there were 335 members. At this time seeing competition from gasoline-powered cars, the group wished to secure reduction of electric rates. As fuel costs were largely constant at this time, and consumption of electricity was rapidly rising, rate reductions could be made. In 1903 the average cost of a kilowatt-hour of electric energy was 23 cents. By 1913 its cost had declined to seven cents in New York City. The price of gasoline, meanwhile, was 10 cents per gallon, and by 1913 was 24 cents."

As the production of gasoline powered cars in 1913 were orders of magnitude greater than electric vehicles, it can be seen that the relative price of the two fuels really was unimportant.

---

[8] *The Horseless Age*, January 15, 1902.

[9] Private communication.

Electricity prices decreased by a factor of three, and gasoline increased by a factor of 2.4. Table 13.1 tabulates the IC automobile registration, the average cost of electric energy, and the price per gallon of gasoline for selected years.

Innovative All-Electric Drives

Erickson then tells of Edison and Steinmetz, who were his older peers.

"In this period of new personal transportation means, Thomas Alva Edison and Dr. Charles P. Steinmetz, both of whom were electrical research leaders of their day, had an immense faith in the electric car, believing it would displace the then-emerging internal combustion car. Edison himself, possibly apocryphally, told Walter Baker,[10] who at that time was making the Baker electric car:

'If you continue to make your present caliber of automobile, and I my present quality of battery, the gasoline buggies will be out of existence in no time.'

Table 13-1. USA Passenger Electric Vehicle Production Halted in the 1930s. The table shows that fuel costs had little or no importance.			
Date	IC automobile[1] registration	Avg. kWh[2] price cents	Avg. gasoline[3] price cents
1900	8,000	18.0*	
1906	105,900	11.2	
1910	458,377	9.62	
1916	3,367,889	7.6	25.1 - 1918
1920	8,131,522	7.45	29.8
1926	19,220,885	7.00	23.4
1930	22,972,745	6.03	20.0
1936	24,108,467	4.67	19.4

*1897 was 19.8; 1902 was 16.2
[1] *Facts and Figures,* Automobile Manufactures Association, NYC, 1950.
[2] *Historical Statistics of the Electric Utility Industry,* Edison Electric Institute, NYC, 1974, p. 165
[3] *Petroleum Facts & Figures,* American Petroleum Inst., Washington DC, 1971, p. 604. Also, Amoco, personal communication, 18 December 1987.

---

[10] Walter C. Baker was a graduate of Case School of Applied Science. In 1921 Baker Electric ceased production of electric cars and began to specialize in the manufacture of electric industrial trucks.

"Later, Steinmetz's group produced the most advanced electric vehicle yet. The auto had a revolutionary concept, so it was said. The inventor was Harry E. Dey, an associate of Dr. Steinmetz. The new car was to have had, instead of the ordinary differential gearing, a motor designed to allow both the armature and field to revolve in opposite directions with one element connected to one-half the axle, and the other element connected to the other half, thus dividing the power between the two halves of the axle so that in taking a turn, one could move faster than the other in proportion to its load. A gearing system was introduced which would allow both halves of the axle to travel in the same direction but at different speeds. The entire weight of the two-horsepower motor and axle was under 100 pounds which was less than the weight of the common rear axle with its differential. The motor was designed to act as a generator when certain speeds were exceeded in going down a hill, the principle of regenerative braking. This latter action would help recharge the battery. In a full page article in *The New York Times*, Steinmetz extolled the virtues and potentials of this vehicle and predicted that these electrics would dethrone the gasoline car." (Such type motor is shown in Fig. 13.7.)

"Steinmetz also believed that for short hauls the electric truck would prove superior to the gasoline truck. So he designed and built one. In February 1922 he demonstrated the ability of the truck as a hill climber. The truck of 1500 pound capacity, negotiated a two-block long hill of 14 1/2 percent grade in 51 seconds. He further had the truck stop and start on the hill." A hill of this grade is comparable to one of the steeper streets in San Francisco.

"Later that year the first model of an electric car designed by Steinmetz was completed. K. E. Turner, Assistant General Manager of the Steinmetz Motor Car Corporation which was to manufacture the machine, claimed the car would travel 200 miles on a charge, would attain speeds from 15-40 miles per hour, weighed 2,000 pounds and would sell for less than $1000." Like some claimants in the 1980s and 1990s this manager was optimistic on the range for the electric car.

"The Steinmetz Corporation was formed by a group of business promoters who gave Dr. Steinmetz an office in the company which was strictly honorary. The business organization was by no means as efficient as the vehicles themselves. There was an evident lack of good management and the venture did not prove an enduring success. And Steinmetz was wholly without business ability himself; his genius lay in quite a different direction. Consequently, the Steinmetz truck was never produced in any quantity nor did it become popular among business concerns up to the time of the inventor's death in October 1923.

"Dr. Steinmetz remained convinced of the superiority of the electric truck over the gasoline truck. His views on short hauls by electric trucks as compared with short hauls by gasoline trucks were summarized by him at the time he brought out his own electric truck:

'Reductions in the cost of delivering merchandise would be distinctly a service to the public, for the merchant who effects such savings is usually able and eager to pass them on to his customers. One of the

---

MOTOR VEHICLE PATENTS
∴ ∴ OF THE WORLD ∴ ∴

UNITED STATES PATENTS.

667,275. Electric Motor.—G. E. Weisenburger, of Sharon, Pa., February 5, 1901. Application filed February 21, 1900.

An electric motor for automobiles, in which both the armature and field revolve in opposite directions, each driving one

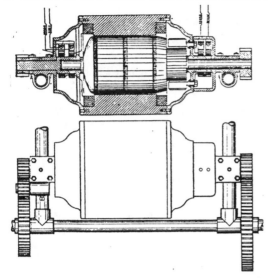

of the wheels of an automobile, thus avoiding the use of a differential gear with a single motor.

The field magnet of the motor is provided at each end with a bearing plate, each of which is formed with a centrally located bearing for the two journals of the armature shaft. One of these bearings is extended axially with reference to the bearing plate to form a trunnion, which is journaled in and extends beyond a bearing fixed on the frame of the vehicle. The portion of the armature shaft supported by the motor frame at the opposite side is extended and is mounted in and projects beyond another bearing fixed on the vehicle frame. On each of the motor frame bearings are mounted a pair of insulated collector rings. Those on the commutator end of motor serve to convey the current to and from the commutator brushes, while those on the opposite end serve to convey current to the revolving field coils. The brush holders for the commutator brushes are bolted to the end plate casting and are insulated therefrom. They thus always retain the same relation with regard to the field poles. The two sets of sliding rings and their brushes are protected by metal casings, as shown, which, with the exception of the joint between the stationary and movable parts of the casing, are practically closed. As the two parts revolve in opposite directions, the direction of transmission from them to the wheels has to be different. This is effected by gearing the armature direct and the field through an intermediate gear.

Figure 13.7. An electric motor for vehicles in which the armature and the field revolve in opposite directions, each driving one of the wheels of an automobile, thus avoiding the use of a differential gear with a single motor.[11]

---

[11] *The Horseless Age*, February 20, 1901.

greatest evils of our economic system today is the high cost of distribution, and I am convinced that a greater use of the electric truck will mean a considerable decrease in the cost of distribution especially of food commodities.

'It has always seemed a surprising thing to me that electricity—the greatest driving power known—has not yet been given its full position in the transportation world. I do not think I exaggerate when I say that the use of electric motor trucks for short hauls will mean a saving of millions of dollars to the people of the country.'"

At this time Steinmetz was not alone in his optimism; Walter Baker, a most capable electrical engineer, was also a strong believer in the merits of the electric car. Erickson continues:

"In the fall of 1905 a French electric car made a run from Paris to Frouville, about 130 miles, on one charge of the batteries. Even more worthy of notice was a trip in this country from Cleveland to Erie, 100 miles, over ordinary country roads some of which were sandy and which included many steep hills. One vehicle on the market had a guaranteed range of 85 miles. But this type of performance was the exception and not the rule among early electrics and their limited range more than anything else led to their gradual loss of popularity. Many of the early electrics could not be depended on for a trip of over thirty-five miles on a charge.

"In June 1917, an electric car drove from Atlantic City to New York, a distance of 123 miles at an average speed of 20.5 miles an hour. In this run 283 ampere-hours were used, an average of 2.29 ampere-hours per mile. Assuming an 84 volt motor and 80 percent efficiency, the cost, at the then 5-cent kilowatt-hour rate of New York City, would have been $1.55."

Using the above numbers the driver withdrew from the battery some 30 kWh. His energy usage was about 1/4 kWh per mile. One could believe this vehicle weighed 3,500 pounds, and possessed a high ratio of battery to curb-weight. Reference to the test on German vehicles in Chapter 7 can be valuable for comparison. Another long run, London to Brighton, was made by a victoria built by Joel Electric Vehicle Co.[12]

The Milde Electric Coupe

Just as Dey of the Dey-Griswold Company in America had conceived a new style electric motor, so did engineers of the Milde Company in France. In the 1904 Paris Automobile Show this French company demonstrated the car shown in Fig. 13.8. Unique was the motor and the transmission as was reported at the time:[13]

"The motor is mounted in the rear, in front of the axle. There are two motors in one. It has two independent armatures running with a single field. The armatures are mechanically separated, and each drives one of the rear wheels. The field of the

---

[12] *The Horseless Age*, Vol. 7, No. 11, December 12, 1900, p. 22.
[13] *Scientific American Supplement*, Vol. 15, No. 14, January 7, 1905, p. 24260.

Figure 13.8. The Milde Electric Coupe was equipped with a drive system with twin armatures running in a common magnetic field. From such a configuration Milde had eight forward speeds, two positions of dynamic braking, two positions of regenerative braking, and three reverse speeds.[14]

motor is excited by lathe-wound coils which are placed on one side, and the magnetic circuit is completed through the other half. This arrangement allowed a good balance on the two armatures, even when the fields were shunt operated. Each motor shaft has a pinion on the outer end which gears with a large wheel in the ratio of 5 to 1. The latter gear is mounted on a countershaft. At the end of the latter is a sprocket from which a chain passes to the rear wheels of the car. The motors are built to receive 35-50 amperes in the two armatures when coupled in parallel, and can operate with 180 amperes without overheating. The controls give eight speeds, two positions of regenerative braking, and three reverse speeds."

As the introspective reader will observe as he scans the above, both Dey and Milde were attempting to solve the d-c motor control problem and the question of the differential, both of which are real challenges for the engineers on today's electric vehicles. Seventy years later, as recounted in Chapter 18, Agarwal, Duff, Dewan, Murphy, the author and their teams would, by more sophisticated methods, use electrical functions to achieve what had heretofore been done by mechanical means. The invention of solid state electronics had been the intervening key, and the above group would apply it to cars. The number of man-hours devoted to the subject of speed control of d-c motor in the last century one can believe has been substantial. That is why the invention of the silicon control rectifier, the SCR, by Holonyak, as earlier described, and the transistor has been such an important factor in enhancing current interest in electric vehicles. From the ingenuity of the inventors described above, which of the many manufacturers showed survivance in the competitive market place?

---

[14] *Scientific American Supplement*, Vol. 15, No. 13, January 7, 1905, p. 24260

CHAPTER 14

Two Long-Lived Electric Vehicle Companies

In observing the roster of companies which assembled electric vehicles listed in Appendix C, their short life is apparent. One to three years is typical. Two companies which enjoyed a longer span were the Baker Electric Company and the Detroit Electric. The former is still in existence as a division of Otis Company, which in turn is a unit of United Technologies, Inc. The Baker Electric Company imaged its founder.

The Baker Electric Company

A giant in the early electric car manufacture was Walter C. Baker,[1] cited above. He, with Hiram Percy Maxim, the latter afterwards joining with Colonel Pope, was first employed by the Morris & Salom Company in Philadelphia. Both Baker and Maxim had helped build the Electrobat for the Chicago Exhibition of 1893. The Electrobat was an electric road wagon,[2] built of tubular steel, the construction followed by bicycle makers. It was an advanced vehicle. The wheels, equipped with anti-friction bearings, were those of a bicycle with pneumatic tires. The vehicle weight with batteries, the so-called curb-weight, was 1,180 pounds. The top speed was 20 mph. With this industrial experience behind him, and equipped with an electrical engineering degree from Cleveland's Case School of Applied Science, in 1897 Baker founded the Baker Motor Vehicle Co. In this task he had the cooperation of Edison who furnished batteries. On the first Baker Electric the drive system shaft was equipped with beveled gears. This train supplanted the chain-drive which had been introduced by the Panhard-Lavassor firm of France, whose notabilities were with gasoline-powered cars. From the above we might conclude the vehicle was equipped with a differential.

As Baker was a college-trained engineer, like Woods, earlier cited, he was the first to seriously consider wind resistance, a retarding force which, while less important at the fast buggy trot of electric cars in the 19th Century, became significant as electric car speeds advanced. This restraining potential (force) indeed increases as the square of the velocity.

---

[1] William Ganson Rose, *Cleveland, The Making of a City*, The World Publishing Co., Cleveland, 1950, pp. 564.

[2] *Scientific American*, Vol. LXXIII, No. 20, November 16, 1895, p. 315.

Remembering his physics, Baker gained world recognition for car building with his electric-powered Torpedo notwithstanding Jeantaud had constructed a similar shape in 1899. Significantly the date of Baker's Torpedo was 1902, the same year the Wright brothers were determining in their home-made wind tunnel the optimum wing curvature for the first plane destined to fly.[3] Not content with vehicle streamlining, and observing the rapid growth in the adoption of the gasoline-powered car, Baker in 1912 assembled an early American multi-powered vehicle, gasoline-electric-powered following in the footsteps of Count Felix Carli of Italy, who made the first multi-powered vehicle. The Count alternately drove his car both by batteries operating an electric motor, and by a wound spring. The date was 1894. The ingenious contraption, discussed in more detail in the second volume of this work, was discarded then as too cumbersome and expensive, a judgement still maintained by many almost a century later. Figure 14.1 is an advertisement for a Baker Electric, while Fig. 14.2 illustrates a patent issued to Baker.

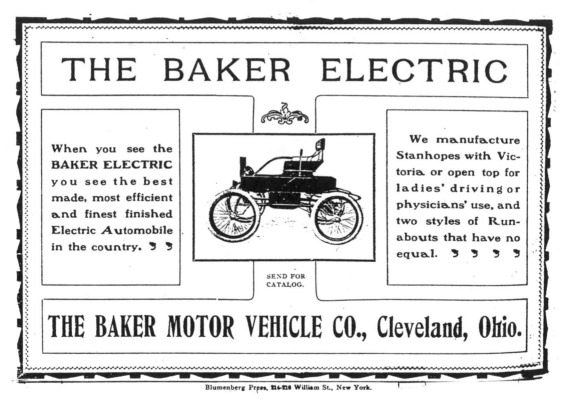

Figure 14.1. An advertisement for a Baker Electric appearing in a 1901 issue of The Horseless Age. As the IC vehicles of the day were unequipped with mufflers, they were exceedingly noisy, hence Baker appeals to the ladies. And for the physicians, the electrics always started immediately.

---

[3] Malcome L. Ritchie, *The Research & Development Methods of Wilbur & Orville Wright, Astronautics & Aeronautics*, Vol. 16, No. 7/8, July/August 1978, pp. 56-67.

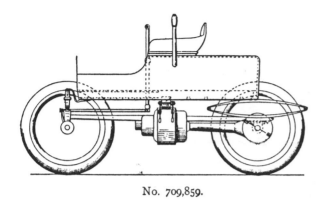

No. 709,859.

Figure 14.2. Baker's patent is used in the car advertised in Fig. 14.1.[4]

Probably his most popular design, reached at the apogee of production, was the two-passenger electric phaeton shown in Fig. 13.4. Walter C. Baker, a graduate electrical engineer, was one of the most gifted early manufacturers of electric vehicles. His turn-of-the-century Torpedo Electric racer established a one kilometer record in 1902 and initiated the present design for automobiles, representing the break-away from the horseless carriage. Baker was one of the largest of the electric car manufacturers. An early Stanhope had a curb weight of only 550 pounds while bearing 180 pounds of batteries, yielding a battery-curb weight ratio of 34 percent, and yielding a range of 20 miles in urban driving. Baker's vehicles were well designed and attractively finished. He early used nickel-steel for durability, and wire wheels all of uniform size. Like C. E. Woods of Woods Motor Vehicle Co., Baker constructed an electric-gasoline powered vehicle which he discarded as too cumbersome. A later Baker Electric, shown here, had steel tubular spokes and steel rim. The Baker Electric Vehicle Company absorbed the R.E. Owen Company, a maker of magnetos, in 1915, and Rausch & Lang, an electric vehicle maker a little later. Today, Baker Electric, a subsidiary of United Technologies Company, makes fork-lift trucks, both electric and propane powered.

Despite Baker's competitiveness he was receptive to a merger with another electric vehicle manufacturer as seen below for already, in the middle of the second decade, his company was feeling competition from the gasoline-powered car.

Paralleling Baker's progress in making a large number of electric cars was the firm of Rausch & Lang in Chicopee Falls, Massachusetts. In 1905 this company was the first to equip an automobile with a closed body. Until that time the drivers and passengers were exposed to the vagaries of the weather. The company had made this move primarily as a means to furnish a market for bodies. With the growth in demand for the internal-combustion engine automobile, the market for electric cars declined. As sales continued to contract, manufacturers of personal electric vehicles were phased out. With World War I, the newly merged company began making the electric fork-lift truck, widely used in material handling. An integrated company making electric motors, the Baker Electric Company, as it later became known, is today one of the largest makers of material handling equipment. Walter Baker's company survived against the

---

[4] *The Horseless Age*, Vol. 10, No. 15, October 8, 1902, p. 398.

See 1910 Baker in Fig. 13.4.

Figure 14.3. 1911 Bailey Two-passenger Electric Phaeton. (see page 231.) Robert S. McKee.

onslaught of the gasoline-powered vehicles, but only by applying his electric vehicles to a specialized field. In 1988 L. R. Leembrugen of Australia (see Chapter 22) used the phrase "purpose-built electric vehicles" to describe designing for niches.

The Detroit Electric Company

Another longer lived electric car organization was the Detroit Electric Company. These vehicles were such a favorite with Henry Ford that he owned four.[5] The company was the last American concern to commercially manufacture the early electric car. Peak production of the company was achieved between 1912 and 1920. The 1912 model, Fig. 10.2, is yet remembered by the author while a student in Ann Arbor in the 1930s. Silent, clean, reliable, the success of the *Detroit Electric* was the demand by ladies for a simple urban car. Immediately before World War I, sales reached 1,000 per year, with production gradually tapering off as the 1920s progressed. To more closely ape the design of the gasoline powered cars, the management of the company in 1920 made the vehicle available with a false front hood, an act in itself of questionable value. Yet what does one do when a competitive system is so overwhelmingly successful as was the gasoline-powered car? Fig. 14.4 shows a look-alike 1908 Standard Electrique.

In 1930, with the coming of the Great Depression, production was cut to individual orders. For these modest requests bodies were obtained from the Willys-Overland Automobile Company, but the original and well-known design, illustrated in Fig. 10.2, with round front and rear battery covers, was yet available. Less well known, the *Detroit Electric* was also offered as a commercial delivery cab as shown in Fig. 14.5, a design reminiscent of the earlier Riker and Woods vans.

---

5 James Wren, Motor Vehicle Manufactures Association, Detroit.

Figure 14.4. The 1908 Standard Electrique is still fondly recalled by many Americans. In the 1970s it was the popular image of the electric car. The Horseless Age, Vol. 30, No. 10, p. 22.

During its corporate existence the firm had three names, an oft-time symptom of changing times. The corporation began as the Anderson Carriage Company and remained so from 1907 through 1910, when it became the Anderson Electric Car Company, a name which better reflected its main product. This nomenclature was retained from 1911 through 1918. The business then was given the name for which it is best remembered, The Detroit Electric Car Company, with its home in Detroit for the period of 1919 to 1938. In 1913-1914 a few Detroit Electrics were made in Scotland by Arrol-Johnson under license. Joining the best known electric car companies one would list besides the Detroit Electric, The Baker Electric, The Waverley Electric, The Pope-Waverley, The Woods Motor Vehicle Company, and the Century Electric. All vehicles bearing the names of these makers had become commonly known in the earliest decades of the 20th Century.

WRITE for this book before purchasing any commercial vehicles. It contains 48 pages illustrating DETROIT ELECTRIC COMMERCIAL VEHICLES together with detailed information. Whether you intend to buy a fleet or a single self-propelled vehicle, it will pay you to get in touch with us.

Remember—that to electrify is to simplify. This book will give you information on the following subjects:

Life of the Vehicle	Fire Hazards—Insurance
Reliability of the Vehicle	Speed
Simplicity of Operation and Care	Yearly Operating Cost

DETROIT Electric Delivery Service will save you money and extend your territory of delivery operation.

Commercial  Vehicles

Our Service Department will be glad to help you solve your delivery problems and methods, both inside and out; and will recommend the proper types and sizes best suited for the work to be accomplished.

Kindly give us all the [information you can in your first letter.

To those writing on their business stationery, indicating their position, no charge will be made for the book. Otherwise please enclose 8c. in stamps.

Anderson Electric Car Company, 453 Clay Avenue DETROIT, MICHIGAN

BRANCHES:—NEW YORK, Broadway at 80th Street   CHICAGO, 2416 Michigan Avenue (Also branch at Evanston, Ill.)
Brooklyn   Buffalo   Cleveland   Kansas City   Minneapolis   St. Louis

Selling Representatives in all Leading Cities

In writing to advertisers please mention THE HORSELESS AGE.

Figure 14.5. The commercial application of electric vehicles paralleled the acceptance of personal cars, and, indeed, were used for a much longer time. The author was invited to inspect daily-used electric trucks in Manhattan operated by United Parcel Service Company as recently as the early 1970s. Shown are Detroit Electric vans.[6]

---

6 *The Horseless Age*, Vol. 29, No. 4, p. 60.

From 1890 to 1915 the electric vehicle was in competition with both the internal combustion vehicle and the steam car.[7] The high tide of the electric car was 1912 with an estimated thirty thousand on American roads, some twenty thousand being passenger vehicles. In that year a total of 356,000 passenger cars of all types were produced in the country and the registration was 901,596 cars.[8] In a period of increasing eclipse the electric vehicles had a reputation of being easily operated, of possessing great reliability thus being popular with the physician, and of having little danger of freezing, a relevant problem with water-cooled gasoline engines.

At this time also the electrics were popular with the elite due to their quiet, gliding operation; one was a Bailey Electric. The Bailey Electric was made in Amesbury, Massachusetts from 1907 to 1915. If the era of early electric vehicles extended from 1890 to 1935, the Bailey was in the middle. In 1911 the Bailey could be obtained as a Victoria phaeton with wheel steering. Unlike the Baker Electric, the Bailey as late as 1913 had a chain-linked drive system. The Bailey illustrated above in Fig. 14.3 with tubular steel spokes and rims, pneumatic tires, electric head lamps, and general styling, is recognizable as a middle era electric car.[9]

The Detroit Electric was the last electric car which could be commercially bought of this early period. They were still made on special order in the 1930s. Today, even though the main stream of thought is the electric car, the idea and the possibility of other electric-powered vehicles has not been ignored by innovative people who envision applying this potential to boats, to railroads, to agriculture vehicles, and the motor itself, as the power source for a myriad number of tasks. The electric economy, indeed, to some, is the only direction the Third World countries can proceed. Already heavily in debt their road to the future is in generating their own electric power using indigenous fuels such as wind electric generators, biomass electric generators, hydroelectric generators, and, in the future, sun-powered photovoltaic-cell generators. For the emerging nations with yet little petroleum-based infrastructure and with cities of small area, the electric vehicles, using indigenous fuels, built from the ground-up as an electric, offers many advantages, inducements which are absent in the economy of industrial nations.

When the horseless carriage was new what names were applied? Quite naturally the nomenclature previously used. The next section illuminates name-classes of early electric vehicles.

Name Classes of Early Electric Vehicles

Many names given present vehicles had their origin in the past and they in turn had built on designations of earlier times. The early horseless carriages were exactly that, applying existing carriage styles for motorized vehicles. Carriage body styles and names bridged with immediacy

---

[7] According to Professor Joseph Keenan of MIT the steam car faded as a power source because: the large size and weight of the engine system necessitated by poor methods of heat transfer, problems with lubricating oils that contaminated the water and led to corrosion of the system, and the failure of the system to recirculate the water completely. There were probably subjective reasons as well.

[8] *Facts and Figures*, Automobile Manufactures Association, New York, 1950.

[9] Robert S. McKee refurbished a 1911 Bailey in 1992 and kindly furnished the author a colored slide of it, Fig. 14.3.

to the automobile. Sedan, Coupe, Brougham, and Limousine are familiar today. Stanhope, Phaeton, Victoria, Runabout, Roadster, Torpedo, and Hansom[10] are less well-known yet were applied to the early body styles of electric cars.

The phrase horseless carriage was coined and first used in print by E. P. Ingersoll in his publication *The Horseless Age* November 1895, and illustrated in Chapter 3. He was both editor and proprietor.

The name automobile was first applied by the *Pall Mall Gazette* of London in October 1/3, 1895 — *Three miles an hour gives the automobile....*[11]

Sedan is derived from the Latin word "seder," meaning "to sit," and was first used by Sir Sanders Duncome in 1634 to describe a personal enclosure in which the occupant was hand-carried.[12]

Coupe is derived from the French word "couper," meaning "to cut," and was used to class a light-weight, closed carriage seating two passengers, with a seat outside for the driver.

The Brougham, named after Lord Brougham, was a closed four-wheeled carriage with the driver's seat outside and before the cab.

The Limousine, from the central French province of Limousin, means hood, the dress of that area, and came to represent a carriage with a closed compartment seating three or more passengers. The top is extended forward over the driver's seat, which is open at the sides.

The Stanhope was a light, open, one-horse English carriage with high seats and a closed back, named after the original user Fitzroy Stanhope, an English clergyman.

Phaeton is from Greek mythology, and designated a light, four-wheeled carriage, drawn by one or two horses, with front and back seats, and usually a folding top; a fast driving, sporting style.

A Victoria was a low, open, four-wheeled carriage for two passengers, with a folding top, and a high seat in front for the coachman. The carriage was designed to allow easy mounting by the ladies wearing the hoop-type dresses of the period.

A Runabout was a light, one-seated, open carriage.

A Roadster was formerly a bicycle or tricycle for road use.[13]

A Torpedo was the name given to the early in-line vehicles, the first of which was a racing car developed by Walter A. Baker in 1902, a style universally followed today.

Other vehicle names, each with a descriptive style to categorize the many vehicles for advertising and conversation purposes were:

Berline	Droshky	Surrey
Breail	Landaulet	Talleyho
Cabriolet	Mylord	Touring car
Drag	Spider	Trap

---

[10] After John A. Hansom (1803-1882), an English inventor.

[11] *A supplement to the Oxford English Dictionary*, Ed., R. W. Burchfield, v. 1, A-G, Oxford, At the Clarendon Press, 1972, p. 159.

[12] *Ibid.* v. IX, p. 371.

[13] *Webster's New World Dictionary of the American Language*, David B. Guralnik and Joseph H. Friend, Eds., 1, The World Publishing Company, NYC, 1962, pp. 1318, 338, 186, 851, 1142, 1625, 1276, 1259, 658.

What were the names of these American electric car manufacturing companies which introduced personal transportation into the economy? We are fortunate for the detailed records maintained by Claud Erickson, for he provided an initial list of electric car builders.[14]

His records have been supplemented, with permission from Temple Press Ltd,[15] and E.P. Dutton & Co.[16] The author and others have contributed names of the more recent companies as well as others. This roster of American producers of electric cars should, therefore, be reasonably complete at this writing. But a moment's perusal will indicate omissions. The silent winds of time have swept away the embers of burning hopes, and have served to dry the rivers of honest sweat—the self-rectifying changes of a marketplace economy. A list of names of electric vehicle manufactures, their products, the city of production, and the dates is found in Appendix C.

---

[14] Claud Erickson, Private communication.

[15] G. R. Doyle, *The World's Automobiles, 1880-1955*, Temple Press Ltd, London, 1957.

[16] G. N. Georgano, *Encyclopedia of American Automobiles*, E. P. Dutton & Co., NYC, 1968, and 1976.

CHAPTER 15

Electric Vehicles in Early Racing

Speed has always been a fascination. The chariot competition of Rome is today matched with the harness races of America. Every age has its Hippodrome; each period has its competitors. Until first mechanical, then electrical power, speed of land travel was limited to fleetness of foot of man or of animals. Trains fail to lend themselves to racing. Neither are they accessible to a grandstand. Yet engine #999 established a speed of 102.8 mph between Syracuse and Buffalo in 1893.[1] But few witnessed the event.

With the application of steam, electricity, and gasoline to vehicles, automobile racing became a possibility for innovators and for the sporting set before the turn of the century. Auto racing was highly visible and appreciatively competitive for newspapers to exploit. And they did with shrillness. In 1891 the Smithsonian Institution recognized electric transportation allotting one sentence in an article on the evolution of commerce:[2] "A few cars and small vessels are moved by electricity, the forerunner of greater things," was prophetically predicted. By 1900 C.E. Woods, a university trained electrical and mechanical engineer and an electric vehicle manufacturer, had published his earlier mentioned book on electric vehicles.[3]

Recognizing this fascinating sport the Smithsonian related one day at the races as a scientific event.[4] As France was the initial center for automobile development, racing began there. The challenge involved speed, reliability, and distance. Hence, Continental contests were matched to power other than electric. The first automobile race was Paris to Rouen, a 75-mile reliability run, on July 22, 1894.[5] Thirteen steam and eight gasoline-powered vehicles participated.[6] Of the finishers, a steam and a "petroleum" fueled, each finished in 5 hours and 40 minutes for an average speed of 12.36 mph.

The watershed race, however, was the no-rest-stop Paris-Bordeaux-Paris Race of June 11, 1895.[7] While the electric entry was not the winner, Charles Jeantaud drove his battery-powered

---

[1] John Marshall, *The Guiness Book of Rail Facts and Feats*, Business Superlatives Ltd, Enfield, Middlesex, England, p. 253.

[2] Gardiner C. Hubbard, *The Evolution of Commerce*, Smithsonian Institute Proceedings, 1891, pp. 647-660.

[3] C.E. Woods, *The Electric Automobile, Its Construction, Care, and Operation*, H. E. Stone & Co., Chicago, 1900, pp. 177.

[4] Harrison Fournier, *The Automobile, Smithsonian Institute Proc.*, 1901, pp. 593-609.

[5] *Paris to Rouen Race, Scientific American Supplement*, Vol. XXXVIII, No. 979, October 6, 1894, pp. 15648-50.

[6] *Paris to Rouen Race, Engineer*, London: July 20 and 27, 1894.

[7] *Paris to Bordeaux, Le Velo*, Paris: June 11 and 17, 1895.

carriage, with Brault as an assistant, to the Atlantic port of Bordeaux, a truly remarkable performance. Jeantaud's faithful machine, and his preparation for the contest, is reported in Chapter 7. Ripples from this race pitting gasoline, steam, and "accumulator" powered vehicles would travel far. It was in this contest the pneumatic tire proved superior. Monsieur Michelin's vehicle alone was without "wheel trouble."[8] [9]

The Chicago-Evanston-Chicago Race of 1895

News of the Paris-Bordeaux Race having reached America, the first competition was promoted by Publisher H.H. Kohlsaat of *The Chicago Times-Herald*. After several postponements which allowed the hastily built vehicles to assemble, the 53-mile event was run on Thanksgiving Day, November 18. A worse day, because of the weather, could scarcely have been chosen. As reported at the time and related in Appendix I,[10] a 53-mile race with six to eight inches of snow on the road was too long a trip for the Electrobat and the Sturges electric vehicles. Each reached Lincoln Park and each on return to the starting point at Midway Plaissance depleted their batteries. They had travelled about 20 miles. No infrastructure for enroute charging was in existence, nor was the battery interchange practiced by Jeantaud employed. Charles Duryea with his gasoline-powered vehicle was the winner, but the tables would be turned in track-racing where speed rather than range was the determining factor.

Test Equipment for America's First Automobile Race

For America's first automobile race described above, the judges specified more than a speed contest. To learn more about the vehicles a test apparatus was constructed. Before any vehicle could compete its performance must be certified. Because of the variety of prizes each contestant received a reward. A picture of the equipment appears in the Appendix I taken from *The Horseless Age*.[11]

With *The Chicago Times-Herald* extolling automobile racing, other alert promoters saw possibilities. In the Fall of 1896 another American competition would be held, but on a closed track. In a new setting, and with man/machine competitors the Hippodrome of ancient Rome was being staged. How much do people change?

The Narragansett Park Race[12] [13]

This contest featuring both electric and gasoline-powered cars would start September 7, 1896. The Rhode Island State Fair Association offered the successful contestants $50,000 in

---

[8] *Race for Carriages, Scientific American Supplement*, Vol XL, No. 1023, August 10, 1885, pp. 16343-4.

[9] *L'Illustration*, No. 2730, June 22, 1885, p. 529.

[10] *The Horseless Age*, Vol. 1, No. 2, December 1895, pp. 29-30.

[11] *Ibid*, Vol. 1, No. 1, November 1895, p. 13.

[12] *The Horseless Age*, Vol. 1, No. 11, September 1896, pp. 6-7.

[13] *Providence Horseless Carriage Race, Scientific American*, Vol. LXXXV, No. 13, September 26, 1896, p. 253.

prizes, the automobile entrants to receive their share. The track was one mile in length and 72 feet in width. There were five races of five miles—a five-lap race. The grandstand was 1/8 mile long and had a seating capacity of 10,000. Of the first three finishers each has been discussed above: Riker Electric Motor Co., the Electric Carriage and Wagon Company (Morris & Salom using the name of their New York City taxi company), and the Duryea Motor Wagon Company, the firm which participated in the Chicago race. Riker had not entered *The Chicago Times-Herald* race. For the Narragansett Park Race contestants were six gasoline-powered cars and two electrics. For this race Riker was the required passenger while A. H. Whiting drove. While the race was originally for five heats, inclement weather reduced it to three. One heat was to be raced each afternoon of the Fair. The prize was $1,000 for each day. Figure 15.1 shows the line-up. The vehicle on the far right is a Morris & Salom Electrobat with steerable rear wheels as shown in Fig. 4.1. Figure 15.1A is an advertisement for this race.

Stated as witnessed by some 40,000 spectators, the races were won by Riker with an average speed of 24 mph. This rivalry had a noticeably higher speed than the Chicago contest 10 months

Figure 15.1. The Narragansett Park Race of 1896 is believed to be the first track automobile race in the world. Entered were six gasoline-powered cars and two electrics: Morris & Salom's Electrobat, shown in Fig. 4-1, and Riker's electric trap, illustrated in Fig. 3.8. The Electrobat, seen on the far right, can be identified by the small, steerable rear wheels. The Riker vehicle won with two firsts and one second. The Electrobat placed second with a first, a second, and a third. Winning time was an average speed of 24 mph. The prize was $900. The Horseless Age.

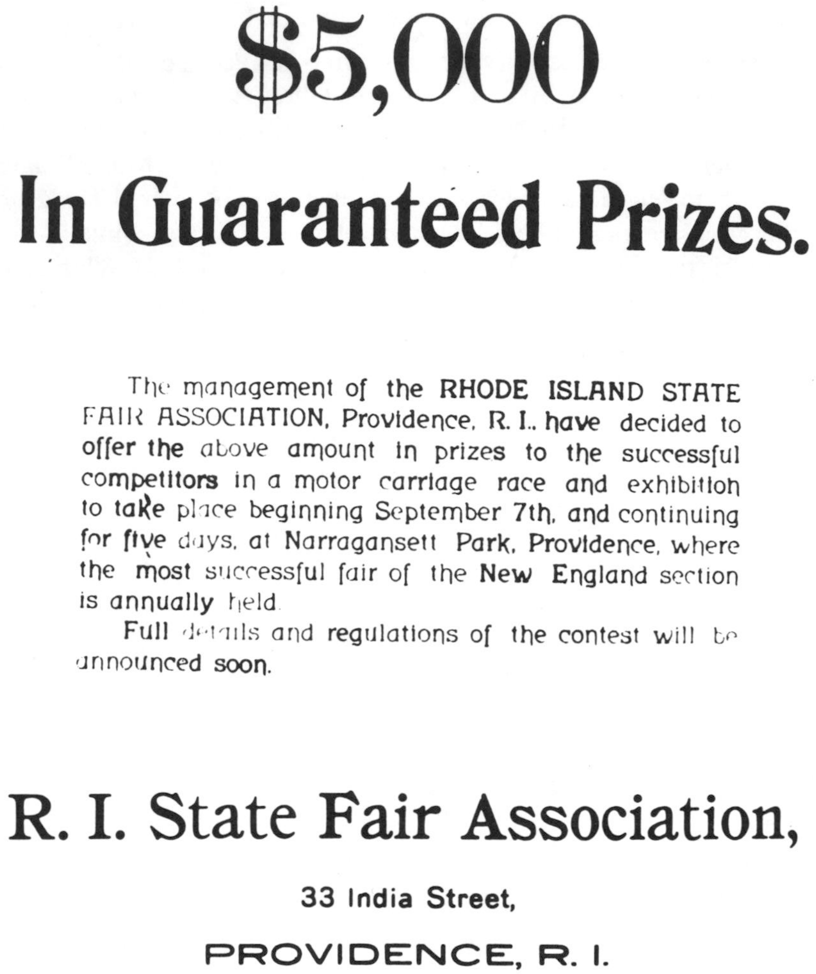

$5,000

In Guaranteed Prizes.

The management of the RHODE ISLAND STATE
FAIR ASSOCIATION, Providence, R. I., have decided to
offer the above amount in prizes to the successful
competitors in a motor carriage race and exhibition
to take place beginning September 7th, and continuing
for five days, at Narragansett Park, Providence, where
the most successful fair of the New England section
is annually held.

Full details and regulations of the contest will be
announced soon.

R. I. State Fair Association,

33 India Street,

PROVIDENCE, R. I.

Figure 15.1A. An Advertisement for the Narragansett Park Race. The Horseless Age.

earlier. Riker's vehicle is shown in Fig. 15.2 together with himself in Fig. 15.3. The other vehicles were Duryea's. As can be seen they are tiller-steered and bear a Cyclops headlamp. As this competition was the first automobile track race anywhere it, together with comments by Professor W. H. Pickering of Harvard University, is reported in some detail in Appendix I.[14]

The vehicle which Riker used for the Providence Race was described as follows:[15]

"The throng of visitors at the watering-places on the Jersey coast about Long
Branch and Seabright was recently treated to the sight of a very nobby trap spinning

---

[14] W. H. Pickering, the Chairman of the Judges, was probably the leading astronomer in America at the time of this race. He had a career of distinction establishing observatories on Mt. Wilson in California, in Peru for Harvard, in Flagstaff, Arizona for Dr. Percival Lowell (of canals on Mars fame), and in Jamaica. Three years after this Providence Race Pickering discovered the ninth satellite of Saturn, Phoebe, and explained its contrary revolution. *The Horseless Age*, E. P. Ingersoll, Vol. 1, No. 11, September 1896, p. 5.

[15] *The Horseless Age*, Vol. 1, No. 10, August 1896, p. 18-19.

Figure 15.2. The Riker Special Electric Trap of 1896. This vehicle won the Providence Race of the same year at an average speed of 24 mph against a field of six Duryea gasoline-powered cars and one Morris & Salom electric. Courtesy: The Horseless Age.

along the ocean boulevards without the aid of the customary horse. This trap, here illustrated, is the vehicle built by the Riker Electric Motor Company, 45 and 47 York Street, Brooklyn, N. Y. for entry into the Providence race.

"The vehicle weighs 1,500 pounds and carries four passengers. The gear is built throughout of tubular steel, and the wire wheels, thirty inches in diameter, are the product of the Crawford Wheel & Gear Company, Hagerstown, Md.

"The current is derived from 800 pounds of special chloride cells of 100 ampere-hours capacity at a discharge rate of 25 amperes. There are 32 of these cells, which furnish sufficient power for a four-hours' run at 10 miles an hour, over ordinary level roads. Two Riker motors of normal three horse-power each weighing 180 pounds, and completely enclosed so that no dust or mud can reach them, are geared to the rear wheels by pinion and gear at a ratio of 5 to 1.

"On the opposite end of the motor shaft from the pinion is a band wheel, around which a powerful strap brake is applied, thus avoiding all braking of the wheels of the vehicle.

"Speeds of 5, 10, 18 and more miles an hour are obtained by turning a hand wheel at the side of the seat. Four speeds each way are given, the wheel being turned

Figure 15.3. Andrew L. Riker Courtesy: Motor Memories.

forward for forward motion of the vehicle and backward for reversing. The vehicle is steered by a tiller in front of the seat, the wheels being pivoted at the hub as is the custom in motor vehicles. So sensitive is this mechanism that two fingers only are required to guide the vehicle. By pressing down on the tiller the wheels are locked firmly in position until a change in course is desired. Inasmuch as the steering gear is carried by the body of the vehicle, and has a flexible connection with the wheels, no shock is communicated to the hand of the operator.

"The Riker Electric Motor Company will soon be prepared to furnish electric running gears complete to carriage builders or private parties wishing to follow their own fancy in the design of the vehicle body."[16]

This vehicle was photographed probably in the month of July 1896. In comparison with other electric vehicles, Riker's was well advanced. In short, Riker's designs were sound. Morris & Salom cars, shown in Chapter 4, proved the competition.

Racing was now on both sides of the Atlantic, and the next significant and recorded speed race involving electric cars would be in Paris.

The Racing Car *La Jamais Contente*

In 1899 the Frenchman, Camille Jenatzy, using a new alloy of aluminum and tungsten, constructed a racing machine powered with batteries. The alloy was called partinium after its inventor, Henry Partin. When rolled this metal had a density of only 3.0 grams per cubic centimeter,[17] and had high ductility, splendid characteristics for high speed travel while pure aluminum has a density of 2.7.

Jenatzy's vehicle, La Jamais Contente, was bullet-shaped, as indicated in Fig. 15.4. The body was filled with batteries, allowing only room for the driver's legs. The racer was equipped

---

[16] Possibly the first example of an electric vehicle "kit."

[17] *Scientific American Supplement*, Vol. XLVIII, No. 1251, December 23, 1899, pp. 20050 & 20051.

Figure 15.4. The Jenatzy Carriage, with Partinium Body. Courtesy: Scientific American Supplement.

with pneumatic tires, proved so superior in the Paris-Bordeaux race a scant four years earlier. To minimize windage, pressed-steel wheels were adopted. The finished vehicle weighed almost 4,000 pounds.

Before a sun-drenched crowd of Parisians Jenatzy established a world speed record of 61 mph—a mark that would stand for two years. The man of the hour is seen in Fig. 15.5.

With such an accomplishment quite naturally the structure of La Jamais Contente would be discussed. Aluminum had been employed by Jenatzy and had been used in the construction of Queen Victoria's electric vehicle, as earlier recited. This new metal, first separated from the earth's crust in 1824 by the Danish electro-magnetist Hans Christian Oersted (following the discovery of Volta's battery), would later be used in the highly innovative Sundancer in 1972 by Robert McKee. In reviewing Jenatzy's La Jamais Contente, the reader is referred to A. L. Riker's four-wheeled racing machine in Fig. 15.6,[18] and Walter C. Baker's Torpedo design of 1902 in Fig. 15.7. The basic shape of these three vehicles were destined to be the genesis of the modern automobile, for essentially all cars built since 1902 have been of the modified torpedo form.

As Pickering wrote of the Providence Race "before long much higher speeds will be obtained upon the track, as soon as it becomes an object to construct vehicles for that purpose...." This prediction would be proven in the Coney Island Race of 1901 discussed below.

---

[18] A. L. Riker would also win the Guttenburg, New Jersey race of 1900; *The Guttenburg Races, The Horseless Age*, Vol. 6, No. 26, September 16, 1900, p. 10.

Figure 15.5. Jenatzy, the garlanded hero, after establishing a world speed record in 1899. Courtesy: Forbes, October 15, 1976, p. 71.

The Coney Island Race of 1901[19]

On November 16, an automobile race was held on a specially prepared dirt strip on Old Coney Island Boulevard in New York. This area is a geological spit into the ocean, and the land is naturally flat with only a slight downgrade. The straight-away was finished to acceptable smoothness. The drivers were permitted a quarter-mile flying run before crossing the starting line. The course was one mile. In the race, which was against the clock, were successive automobiles powered by gasoline, by steam, and by electricity. It was a period of desperate jockeying for the best means of propulsion. Each type had its champions. And each surrogate might be equally learned.

A. C. Bostwick drove his formidable 40 hp. gasoline-powered vehicles, its exhausts roaring, over the mile in 56 2/3 seconds. S. T. Davis piloted his silent steam automobile, leaving a vaporous trail, in 1 minute 39 seconds. The surprise was A. L. Riker's electric entry. Towing his car to the beginning of the quarter-mile acceleration strip so as not to discharge his batteries,

---

[19] *Scientific American*, Vol. LXXXV, No. 22, November 20, 1901, p. 347.

this four-wheeled carriage with an electric drive system, and two seats behind in tandem, scorched the mile in 1 minute 3 seconds. His machine is shown in Fig. 15.6. On that day both Riker and Bostwick bested the previous record speed for automobiles.

Riker's electric vehicle had a curb-weight of 1,850 pounds, and a battery complement of 900 pounds, yielding a ratio of 48 percent, a proportion remarkably similar to the best modern vehicles such as the Sundancer, shown in Chapter 21, with a ratio of 47 percent. Riker's racer had a lead-zinc battery with 60 cells providing a potential of some 130 volts dischargeable at a 100-ampere rate. Using the product of voltage and current to equal power,[20] and a motor efficiency of 75 percent, Riker applied some 13 to 15 hp to the drive shaft. His motor armature turned at 3,300 rpm. Dwelling on the illustration of his vehicle, one can see Riker mounting his

Figure 15.6. Riker's electric racing automobile which made the record of 1 mile in 63 seconds on Saturday, November 16, 1901.[21]

---

[20] Ernest H. Wakefield, *The Consumer's Electric Car*, Ann Arbor: Ann Arbor Science Publishers, describes such calculations and much more about electric vehicles.

[21] *Scientific American*, Vol. LXXXV, No. 22, Nov. 30, 1901, p. 347.

machine, adjusting his goggles, then, with both hands grasping the T-shaped steering wheel, an assistant places the switch on START. With the batteries in parallel configuration he accelerates, gaining speed quietly. He now switches to a higher potential, and finally he shunts all batteries in series, providing a maximum voltage. He has reached peak speed on crossing the starting line. At the end of slightly more than a minute he had established a land speed record for electric automobiles in America.

The year 1901 was a time when electric cars were produced at the rate of a few thousand a year, a quantity somewhat more than were gasoline vehicles. Each automobile was equipped with typically a 3-hp electric motor to yield a speed up to 20 mph. Riker's one-mile average speed was 57.1 mph, which broke the American record gained by Alexander Winton in his gasoline-powered car (for the mile it was one minute 6 2/5 seconds, 54.1 mph).[22]

In a time when city dwellers were accustomed to viewing carriages travelling a sedate five to six mph, and saw wagons moving at half that speed, these records of nearly a mile per minute made an impact seen by many.[23] In contrast Wilbur and Orville Wright's pioneering aircraft flight, witnessed by less than a handful,[24][25] was four years in the future. With media reporters covering the races,[26] with avid artists etching the spirit of the competitors and relayed to the readers by newspapers, the collective mind of citizens was being interested and prepared for the coming revolution in personal transportation. It was a heady age. At no other period before or since has there been this dramatic competitiveness of different types of motive power in personal land travel. And it was in a context the man in the street could witness and comprehend. Which system became dominant for almost the whole 20th Century is known.

Baker's *Torpedo* Racing Car

The trend in Europe was toward long distance automobile racing, a sport encouraged by the historically excellent, existing hard surface routes between cities. These contests led to Le Grand Prix of today. In mournful contrast with the above were the unimproved, mud roads linking American urban areas. Such racing gave an unmatched premium to the gasoline-powered car, despite Jeantaud's remarkable dash in the Paris-Bordeaux-Paris Race with an electric vehicle in 1895, an achievement described above. Not so in America, however. In the sprints on a track, a surface both attuned to the impossible roads and the demand of promoters of fairs and carnivals to attract crowds, the electric car could give a good account. This capability was based on characteristics of a battery to give power instantly, and the quality of a series-wound direct-current motor to yield high starting torque, a necessity for rapid acceleration.

---

[22] *Scientific American*, Vol. LXXXV, No. 22, November 30, 1901, p. 347. Winton, a pioneer with the gasoline-powered automobile, introduced the diesel engine into America. His Winton Engine Works in Cleveland, Ohio was the genesis of the General Motors Electromotive Division. He was a close friend of the author's father.

[23] There were 12,000 spectators, *Scientific American*, Vol. LXXXV, No. 22, November 30, 1901, p. 347.

[24] Witnessing the first heavier-than-air flight, beside the Wright Brothers, were Lifeguardsman John T. Daniels, who recorded the event on film, two other guardsmen, and a boy from Nog Hill. The Associated Press, *The Instant It Happened*, H. N. Abrams, NYC 1976.

[25] Malcolm L. Ritchie, *The Research & Development Methods of Wilbur & Orville Wright, Astronautics & Aeronautics*, Vol. 16, No. 7/8, July/August 1978, pp. 56-67.

[26] *Ibid*, p. 347.

The expectation of racing being in the very air of the time, W. C. Baker, the graduate electrical engineer and electric car manufacturer, decided to build his electric Torpedo[27]—one of the streamlined cars whose revolutionary shape was to keynote and to influence all subsequently built automobiles. It marked the departure from expediency based on the horseless carriage. Economically, this radical design change shook out a host of wagon builders from the ranks of early automobile assemblers. Those manufacturers who misunderstood this almost non-Darwinian mutation failed to survive. Baker may have been influenced by Jenatzy's bullet-shaped racing car of 1899 and Riker's electric racer of 1901, for in order to reduce the drag of windage Baker covered his racer with a light, torpedo-shaped super-structure of wood and black canvas, which completely hid the occupants of the car. The driver viewed the track through a small isinglass window. Further, to minimize air resistance even the wheel webs were enclosed with similar canvas on oil-cloth shown in Fig. 15.7.

To establish the setting the mile trial for the gasoline and steam machines had all been run, and the latter were aligned for the kilometer speed tests when the electric racer was started. The Torpedo swept the kilometer, or six-tenths of a mile, in 36 seconds (60 mph) and was rapidly accelerating. After making one slight turn in the road just beyond the kilometer point the Torpedo was seen to swerve inside. It then crossed the road again, reaching the opposite side near the providently supplied hospital tent, after which it careened toward the infield and struck the trolley tracks. These prominences caused the vehicle to bounce. Apparently all four wheels left the ground. When they again touched, the powerful band brakes had been applied, one of them probably tighter than the other, for the machine skidded and whirled sharply, smashing broadside into the spectators, killing two and seriously injuring half a dozen others. The racer finally rested in the position shown in Fig. 15.8 with its nose pointing in the direction from which

Figure 15.7. For racing purposes W. C. Baker, Cleveland graduate electrical engineer and manufacturer of electric cars, constructed the streamlined Baker Torpedo. Still accelerating the car had completed one kilometer at an average speed of 60 mph. Baker's vehicle was the first departure from the design known as the horseless carriage.

---

[27] *Scientific American*, Vol. LXXXVI, No. 24, June 14, 1902, p. 419.

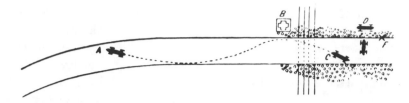

Figure 15.8. An insecure steering gear caused the driver to over-correct. Striking the irregular trolley tracks all four wheels left the road. The car spun around crashing into and killing two spectators, stopping at point D.

it had come. The body was knocked off, but the two operators stepped out unhurt. The two outer wheels were demolished, but the inner, as will be seen in the photograph Fig. 15.9 were not damaged. This havoc indicated the momentum had thrown the vehicle upon its two outer wheels as it whirled around in a 180 degree spin.

A contemporary analysis cited two causes for the accident: the roadbed was insufficiently smooth for the speeds attempted, and second, the steering gear of the racer was less than positive.[28] Commenting on this unfortunate incident the authorizing agent wrote:

> "The Automobile Club of America has decided to hold no more road speed tests
> of automobiles in the future, and it is to be hoped that the energies of its members will
> be devoted to the development of pleasure and commercial automobilism with the
> same zest that they have shown in developing and patronizing the racing vehicles."

Truly, the organized automobile group halted racing for a time, but there were great pressures to continue this accelerated and intensive means of testing components. Racing from this time forward would be limited to gasoline-powered cars.[29] To more and more people they were seen as the preferred means of personal transportation, a position they still occupy nearly a century later. How Baker would affect subsequently designed electric vehicles will be seen in the next chapter.

Figure 15.9. After the wreck. The electric motor, seen tangent to the irrelevant bicycle wheel, is observed to have had four poles with balancing commutator poles.

---

[28] *Scientific American*, Vol. LXXXVI, No. 24, June 14, 1902, p. 419.

[29] In 1968 the *Autolite Lead Wedge* set an electric vehicle record for the flying mile of 128.862 mph as certified by the United States Auto Club. *Electric Vehicle News*, Vol. 1, No. 2, March 1969.

CHAPTER 16

Advancing Electric Vehicle Design

The automobile was everywhere changing America. The clippings from the 1902 *The Horseless Age* relate street urchins advancing the throttle on a steam carriage and having it run away. Speeding of cars posed a problem which called for solutions both in America and on the Continent. Traffic and its control would become a major occupation for the police and for the courts. In the 1912 magazine account, charging stations had been established to enable the electric car owner to travel between New York and Buffalo, and from Philadelphia to New York, and thus "tour." This development was an infrastructure that enhanced the value of an electric car, an omission which today limits the value of a modern electric automobile. The gasoline service station, in contrast, is everywhere present. The reporter who wrote the article on charging stations earlier cited in Chapter 9 was on the mark. He was writing 12 years in the future. *McClure's Magazine* was on target. Other period clippings appear in the Appendix.

The Century and the Argo

A review of the following advertisements for electric vehicles reveals an increasing sophistication of design. The stories the advertisements tell, however, are strangely silent on speed and on range. The year 1912, for which these ads reflect, would represent peak production for the electric vehicle industry. When the attractive Century Electric Roadster was selling at $1,750, the Ford two-seater gasoline car was offered at $550. Economy of manufacturing scale was being achieved. As a consequence the sales of electric automobiles would thereafter dwindle. The energy contained in gasoline was speaking, and the American public was listening.

In these 1912 electric vehicles the Century particularly appears well-designed. The motor couples directly to the differential. The car has acceptable weight distribution. Speed control has been attractively arranged. The different, integral speeds available from the voltage switching system has been further refined, at a sacrifice in range, by resistance control, and electric field winding adjustment.[1] Figures 16.1 through 16.3 illustrate electric cars at their first apogee. On the chassis of the Century, the elements numbered 16 and 18 are known as the

---

[1] See any electric motor textbook.

Figure 16.1. One Century electric car of 1912, the apogee of this mode of propulsion. Ford gasoline cars were being offered at $550. Courtesy: The Horseless Age, Vol. 29, No. 2, January 10, 1912.

controller, adjustment of which gives speed change. Today, the manufacture also has a controller, more sophisticated to be sure, but for the exact same reason. Many, even today, might like such an electric roadster to drive, for the body has appeal.

The Waverley, the Buffalo, and the Automatic Electric Roadsters

The torpedo design originated by Baker in 1902 became universal. Among the electric car makers to follow Baker were the Waverley Co., of Indianapolis, Indiana,[2] and the Buffalo Electric Vehicle Co., of Buffalo, New York.[3] The former's 1912 Model 90 is shown in Fig. 16.4. It was a sheltered roadster type with a low hung body, upholstered double seat, and a sliding seat for a third passenger. The car bore a folding landau top with plate-glass windshield, sliding glass panels, and buttoned curtains. The Waverley completed a 1,400 mile endurance run over unimproved country roads with a running time of 124 hours.

The market for the Buffalo roadster was for the more "sporty" driver. Its speed capability was greater. The Model 29 shown in Fig. 16.5 had a top speed of 35 mph. The roadster could be had with either artillery or with wire wheels. Both the Waverley and the Buffalo, vehicles of 1912, were at the apogee of electric vehicle production. Annual quantities would decrease each year, and with great rapidity. The sun was setting on electric vehicles. Only the alert, well-managed companies would survive, and they by making another product. Both the Waverley and the Buffalo companies would perish from natural market forces which constantly glean the economy.

Probably the last new-model electric car to be offered by a manufacturer in the first flowering of battery-powered personal transportation was the Automatic. The two-seater was

---

2 *Waverley Electric of New Design, The Horseless Age*, Vol. 30, No. 6, August 7, 1912.

3 *Buffalo Electrics Reveal New Features, The Horseless Age*, Vol. 30, No. 19, November 6, 1912, p. 712.

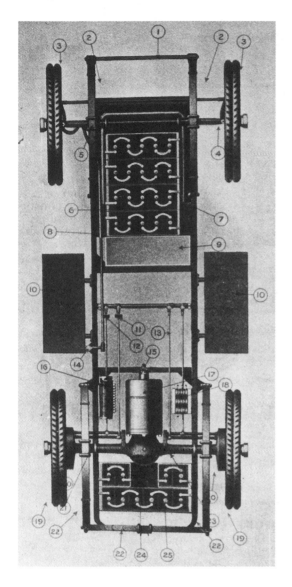

Figure 16.2. Plan view of Century chassis from the ground with identifiable elements. Courtesy: The Horseless Age, Vol. 29, No. 2, January 10, 1912.

assembled by the Automatic Transmission Company of Buffalo, New York in 1921. This vehicle had a wheelbase of 65 inches, a top speed of 25 mph, and a claimed range of a respectable 60 miles.[4] It sold for $1,200 when the Ford Model T had a list price of less than $300, a figure which would drop to $260 in 1925. Residents of industrial nations were being placed on wheels, and these wheels were being given their torque by petroleum-based engines. To those modern day aficionados familiar with today's electric cars the present relatively high price for battery-powered automobiles was true then as now. And the market place in its efficient and unmerciful operation made the last flower of the 1881 to 1921 era, a four decade period, only a memory. Despite the best efforts of the Trouvés, the Ayrtons, the Perrys, the Rikers, the Bakers, the

---

[4] G. N. Georgano, *The Complete Encyclopedia of Motorcars, 1885-1973*, New York: Dutton & Co., 1973.

Figure 16.3. An advertisement for the Argo sedan and wagon at the apogee of electric vehicles. Courtesy: The Horseless Age, January 17, 1912, p. 13.

Wards, the Maxims, the Woods, the Olds, and the Edisons, an opulence of talent, the electric vehicle simply could not satisfy the consumer, so the industry would die a lingering death.

The electric car manufacturers of 1912, for the most part, failed to foresee their industry would die, and, with a few exceptions, so would their enterprises. The next significant work with electric vehicles would take place only in the active years of their grandsons and of their granddaughters. But the innovators had shown the way. The next chapter explains in some detail why these events transpired, doleful to some, inevitable to others.

Figure 16.4. Waverley Electric Model 90, Sheltered Roadster. Courtesy: The Horseless Age.

Figure 16.5. Model 29, Buffalo Electric Two Passenger Roadster. Courtesy: The Horseless Age.

The moving finger writes,
And having writ, moves on;
Neither all your piety nor wit
Can lure it back to cancel half a line;
Nor all your tears wash out a word of it.

—Omar Khayyam

CHAPTER 17

The Dead Years for Electric
Vehicles 1935-1955

Of the long list of manufacturers of electric vehicles, the ones who would survive the onslaught of the internal-combustion engine and its energy-rich fuel, gasoline, would be electric car manufacturers who had the agility to move into a different endeavor. A few entered allied fields. Walter Baker successfully led his company into the industrial fork-lift truck industry. Today the former Baker Company is a division of United Technologies, Inc. Clark, too, moved into the fork-lift manufacture. The electric truck's freedom from fumes, a use where range was less important, led to an ever-increasing share of material handling vehicles being electric. And the air health standards of later years encouraged the use of these vehicles. Elwell-Parker, a Cleveland manufacturer of electric cars, also entered the fork-lift truck field, and today makes electric-powered equipment which will tote 30-ton loads of copper and steel. Studebaker, as earlier outlined, by 1902 had jumped to making the gasoline-powered vehicle, being at the time the largest maker of wagons in the world. R. E. Olds, in what would become Oldsmobile, quickly perceived the inevitable, the growing dominance of the personal transportation market by the gasoline-powered cars, even though his early automobiles, the Stanhope and Phaeton, were electric.

Reasons for the Decline of the Electrics

Yet, half hidden from the human eye, and more than a half-century in the future, was a rebirth of the electric car. In the intervening era monarchies would fall. Tens of millions would die in two world wars, and two historic revolutions, the Russian and the Chinese, would transpire. Man's mind and his body would be unprecedentedly assaulted for an ideology. The concept of terror would rape the grace of love. Through it all technology was unabashed. Its morality is to serve any master. Despite storms of destruction, whirlwinds of change, knowledge continues to pass to the next generation. But seldom in human experience is there the resurrection of a principle which formerly existed in physical form. For example, can we foresee the rebirth of giant passenger liners again plying the Atlantic, or steam trains racing across the plains, or the sky commonly dotted with dirigibles, or the revitalization of the horse and buggy. One believes these developments occupied their center of life's stage, to forever disappear like the North Atlantic Great Auk, or the Mauritian Dodo. Yet almost surely we are now slowly witnessing the rebirth of the electric automobile. True, it is appearing in somewhat different superficial garb, but not basically changed. Under such conditions, it is perhaps fitting that a search of writings be made of that earlier period if anything may be learned. If scholarship is needed for the pursuit, George Santayana's phrase is apt: "Those who cannot remember the past are condemned to repeat it."[1]

C.E. Woods, author of *The Electric Vehicle, Its Construction, Care and Operation*, was particularly well equipped for writing what is probably the most complete, the most articulate, and the most scientifically correct presentation on the electric vehicle at the turn of the century.[2] Woods had a sound technical education, possessed a degree in both electrical and mechanical engineering at a time when a college education was a rarity. In addition, he was president of the Woods Motor Vehicle Company, an organization he had inaugurated. He was a working president in a technical field, not unlike today's entrepreneurial souls who have initiated some of the more advanced microelectronic companies, or, like the Fords, the Firestones, the Edisons, and the Westinghouses of their own day. All four were innovators of the time.

Few realized at the time their names would become titans of their age. Each or their successors successively navigated and nurtured a corporate entity from a barn or a basement operation to a multi-national corporation. Surely it takes what Napoleon called, "Three AM courage," balancing adequately a host of conflicting forces, wisely choosing associates, treating them fairly, and selecting with wisdom that main chance which becomes an important ubiquitous piece of hardware. Destiny, too, undoubtedly was important: being at the right place at the right time. Ford chose the internal-combustion engine-powered automobile. Firestone chose the rubber tire for that car. Westinghouse and Edison chose the electric power industry. Today we are engulfed with the IC automobile riding on rubber tires. And the electric power industry is the single largest aggregation of capital now extant in America, or in any industrial country.

At about the same time Ford was developing his IC-powered car, Woods was improving the electric automobile, for the first one was driven in America in 1890.[3] The electric vehicle industry peaked in 1912 and completely died in America in 1935. And with it the hopes of the Woods and many other innovators of the turn of the century. Still in 1936 the IC vehicle registration was 13,108,467 vehicles.[4] Why did the inefficient (some fifteen percent) internal combustion engine, spawned somewhat later[5] than the highly efficient (90 percent) electric motor, so handsomely win near-universal acceptance for both personal and truck transportation world-wide when both the electrically-powered vehicle and the gasoline-powered automobile were being experimented on at almost the same time? Both vehicles were superior to the horse and buggy. Both were faster. Both had longer range. And, at the same time, both were cheaper.[6]

---

[1] George Santayana, *Life of Reason I, "Reason in Common Sense"*, *Dictionary of Quotations*, Berger Evans, Delacorte Press, 1968, p. 511.

[2] For a modern treatment, read Ernest H. Wakefield, *The Consumer's Electric Car*, Ann Arbor: Ann Arbor Science Press, 1977.

[3] See Chapter 2, footnote 13.

[4] *Facts and Figures*, American Petroleum Inst., Washington, DC, 1971, p. 604.

[5] Michael Faraday discovered the principles of the dc electric motor in 1831. While the internal combustion engine cannot be credited to a single inventor, N. A. Otto in 1867 brought forth a four-cycle engine which operated on illuminating gas. Gasoline was soon substituted as a fuel.

[6] C. E. Woods, his book, pp. 11-12.

In a sentence, the dominance of the internal combustion engine is associated with the energy in gasoline, and fuel's relatively low cost. One gallon of gasoline weighs 6.15 pounds, and contains in energy the equivalent of 37.4 kilowatt-hours. To store that amount of energy in chemical form would have required a battery weighing some 2,200 pounds. Even though the electric drive system is four times more efficient than is the internal combustion system, there is still a beneficial factor of 80 for the gas-fueled vehicle.[7] With the exotic batteries of the late 1990s, this factor will still be possibly 15 to 20. One might conclude IC-powered cars, or their equivalent, will be around for many years.

The second factor in the dominance of the IC vehicle is the cost of energy. Energy, both as gasoline or as electricity, were early so inexpensive the relative efficiencies of the two modes of locomotion had little bearing on their competition or their acceptance.[8] If energy in the form of electricity could have been stored as compactly as energy in the form of gasoline, or if gasoline had been very much more expensive such that relative efficiencies would have been important, today the streets might be crowded with electric vehicles. And there would be fewer gasoline automobiles. But this is the real world, and the IC motor industry (and its affiliates) is the largest employer in America.

There was another subtle, but nevertheless important, factor spelling dominance for the gasoline-powered vehicle. The designs of the latter appeared more relevant. The product was perceived as more dashing, more dynamic, and more earthy. Moreover the advertising was directed to the American male. In addition, the IC car makers earlier and better appreciated urban Americans wanted to "tour." And they invented the "touring car." Meanwhile, the manufacturers of electric vehicles were making quaint "glass houses" which failed in their appeal to rampant, ambitious male chauvinism. And in automobile buying, decisions were made by the male head of the household. In 1912, cigar-chewing, hard-driving Barney Oldfield was their hero. He had won many automobile races. What satisfied Barney satisfied the American buyer. And that was power and speed. The basic dichotomy of the two schools of design, electric and gasoline, appear in the same January 3, 1912 advertisement in *The Horseless Age*, Fig. 17.1. It was a psychological factor in the decline of the electric car.

Modern electric cars, it is believed, will enter the American market through a combination of enhancement of electrical energy storage, government action, the increasing price of gasoline relative to electric energy, the application of modern solid state electronics, the increasing cost of gasoline vehicle repair, the low maintenance needs of electric vehicles, the effort of a number of automobile companies, and finally by the increasing demand for cleaner air. The electric vehicle, then, is like the ancient phoenix bird of legend, having died some four decades after birth, it has again risen from the crematory pyre.

---

[7] One gallon is 6.15 lbs. One kWh of stored electric energy is in a battery weighing 60 lbs. An automobile secures about 24 miles per gallon in urban driving, or about 4 miles per lb of gasoline. The best of the electrics travel about 3 miles per kwh in urban driving or about 0.05 mile per lb of battery. Beneficial factor is 4.0/0.05 = 80 by weight.

[8] In 1920, the first date that both numbers become available, the average cost of electric energy in the United States was 7.45 cents per kWh for electricity, and 19.8 cents per gallon, including tax, for gasoline. In 1936 the figures were respectfully, 4.67 cents, and 19.4 cents. Both had decreased.

Figure 17.1. Psychology was a factor in the death of the electric car industry, as this advertisement implies. Courtesy: The Horseless Age.

Some Impacts of the Automobile

In the growth of the gasoline-powered automobile, few realized the scope of its ultimate impact.[9] The news stories from several issues of the 1902 volume of *The Horseless Age*, (Appendix D), indicates how improved personal transportation affected railroads, horsebreeding, accidents, and the law. Only a sampling. When Henry Ford introduced his Model T he said, "I shall make it for the multitude." Yet even a person so productive as Thomas Alva Edison incorrectly guessed the future of personal transportation. In 1910 the Wizard of Menlo Park related, "In fifteen years more, more electricity will be sold for electric vehicles, than for light."

---

[9] *The Social Impact of the Automobile*, Museum Exhibit, Greenfield Village, Detroit, 1988.

In fact, in 1925, the year of his prediction, electric vehicle production had come very nearly to a standstill, and the production of IC automobiles was 3,735,171. In that intervening decade and one-half, the nation had been lighted, and relighted. Edison had guessed wrong with the motor car industry. He also guessed wrong in the mode of generation and transmission of electrical power. Edison backed the direct-current principle of generation and transmission of energy, while George Westinghouse developed the alternating-current principle. Today, except for tiny, but important exceptions, alternating-current electric energy runs our factories, heats our homes, and lights our highways. It is indeed a credit of Edison, despite two major errors, his competency was sufficient to still be considered the father of the electric industry. While all except the Divine make catastrophic mistakes, the truly epic persons use them merely as a foundation for future greatness.[10]

While the men above became household words because of the nature of the star they followed, the name of C. E. Woods did not, for he founded a company to manufacture electric vehicles, and, at the time, the turn of the century, his company and that of Walter C. Baker's probably made the best electric vehicles in America. But the industry was destined to die. Fortunately, Woods was one of those few entrepreneurs of the electric vehicle industry who had literary talent and motivation to record his knowledge in book form. His thoughtfulness illuminated his time and the electric vehicles of that period.

In referring to the electric vehicles which are described and illustrated in Woods' book a few observations, based on modern thinking, may be illuminating. First, of course, the basic vehicle is different only in degree from its modern cousins both mechanically and electrically. Both vehicles have a floor and a seat on which passengers sit. Both vehicles have four wheels. In both vehicles the front wheels establish steering. Both vehicles had a differential gear system at the rear axle.[11] Electrically, both vehicles utilize a lead-acid motive power battery. To control current flow to the motor both vehicles had a current-limit device: Woods' car, relying on voltage switching of the batteries. Modern full-sized vehicles generally use solid state controls but small electric vehicles may very well use voltage switching. The motor used in Woods' vehicle was series-wound d-c in principle. A share of modern vehicles are of the same concept. The range of Woods' automobiles was surprisingly good. This positive feature resulted from the lightness of the total vehicle, the high ratio of battery/curb weight, the vehicle's low speed which reduced windage, and the presence of high pressure tires with low rolling resistance. Safety in automobiles is today, and should be, a fetish, a factor which restricts design freedom.

In reviewing the above description of Woods' vehicle of 1900 the basic difference with modern cars is found in voltage control of the motor, in the motor itself, in the tires, and in the battery. While voltage switching can be used in modern vehicles, and is in electric golf carts, a solid state chopper control,[12] in which the battery voltage is switched on and off, providing pulses of voltage and current and thus a controllable average voltage to the motor, provides the driver with the precise speed variation to which he is accustomed. Though somewhat more expensive than voltage switching, the solid state control, having no moving parts, is extremely

---

[10] Victor J. Danilove, *America's Greatest Discoveries, Inventors, and Innovations, Industrial Research*, November 15, 1976. Edison with 1093 patents has generally been considered as the greatest of America's scientists, engineers, inventors, and innovators.

[11] Invented by a Frenchman, Onesphores Pecquer in 1827.

[12] See Ernest H. Wakefield, *The Consumer's Electric Car*.

reliable. Woods, in using a series-wound d-c motor, anticipated the use of the same principle today. The motor is simple. It yields high starting torque and provides adequate speed range. It may be said, however, some present designers utilize the compound-wound d-c motors wherein they can use the shunt winding for additional speed control, but such increased complexity adds cost, and its desirability can be argued by experienced engineers. Today's electric motors yield far greater horsepower per pound of motor weight. This improvement results from better quality steel for the magnetic flux. And insulation for the current carrying copper wire in the motor has been much improved. It more readily withstands the heat from motor operation. Further, weight from the motor has been removed by more efficient design. While the principle of the motive power batteries remain the same, the electrical couple of lead and sulfuric acid, with better and more rugged plates, is now employed. The net results: modern batteries are considerably improved yielding greater energy densities and longer life, but still too short.

While Woods' cars illustrated in his book of 1900 differ surprisingly little from today's electric vehicles, his automobiles are actually of design vintage of probably 1898. The same observation could be made of gasoline cars of the same time. Now if Woods had published a few years later and shown automobiles of 1902, there would be even less variation in appearance. For just after the turn of the century, both electric and gasoline-powered vehicles adopted a physical layout of drive system, shape of chassis, and arrangement of body which has lasted to this day, more than three-quarters of a century. At that time it was designated the "torpedo design" discussed above.

Why do we now observe an industry, personal electric transportation now rising, which had peaked in 1912 and died in 1936? It is phoenix-like. The reasons? Surely the persistence of a few brave souls has been important;[13] the recognition of air pollution has been a factor; the steady and resolute inching increase of energy to weight ratio in storage of electric energy should be included; the commercial availability of highly efficient solid state controls of electric energy has contributed; the short distance of urban travel has been a positive force; the Arab oil embargo and the action of the OPEC nations in increasing the price of petroleum has been a consideration; the development of vehicle design which happily combines aluminum and fiberglass has been a forward step; and, important, too, has been the subtle change of tone in American life, away from the flashy, the bombastic, and the grand, toward the simple and the nature-like.[14] All these developments in thought, events, and in hardware contributed to the re-emergence of electric automobiles. And currently, a government action has encouraged electric vehicle use, amplifying the efforts of the hardy souls listed.

While the electric vehicle industry is increasingly making news, a perspective should be borne in mind, barring unforeseen circumstances, petroleum-based personal transportation will be dominant until well into the 21st century. For long distance over-the-road trucking no electric energy storage source has yet been conceived, except the interchange of high energy density batteries at division points, similar to the earlier practice of locomotive changes on a long run with steam trains. But the reader will observe that starting in the 1990s, nearly a century after Woods wrote his charming and informative book, electric personal transportation may assume,

---

[13] Some are listed in the Preface.

[14] Mores of an ever growing number of citizens.

in a gradual fashion, an ever-larger share of personal travel. And much of what Woods described at the turn of the century is still relevant, and still true to those readers who are considering the purchase of an electric vehicle.

The electric automobile industry, having been in slumber for two decades, wiggled a little in 1955, then again slept soundly. What about Europe?

The Electric Vehicle Abroad

Conditions abroad were somewhat different than in America. In England the electric vehicle, elsewhere touted, found a niche in the delivery of dairy products. Figure 17.2 illustrates the original W & E electric vehicle, number one, restored and now on display at the Kenning Motor Group's Chesterfield head office. The 1951 rear wheel drive model had a carrying capacity of 25 cwt., a range of some 20 miles, allowing for 200 stops. Since the original, the company has built, it is reported, some 16,000 electric vehicles and "a large percentage of these are still in use."[15]

The next chapter chronicles the reawakening interest in electric vehicles in America. The driving organizations would be the electric utilities, and the impelling force would be their perennial problem of imbalance between their daytime and their nighttime electrical load, and the consequent inefficient utilization of equipment in a capital intensive industry. The instrument of execution would be the entrepreneurial founded company.

Figure 17.2. The restored original electric vehicle ready for delivery to the Group's headquarters at Chesterfield. Courtesy: Electric Vehicles.

---

[15] *W & E's Number One, Electric Vehicles*, Vol. 67, No. 2, June 1981, p. 3.

Reawakening Interest in Electric Vehicles 1955-1965

With the cessation of made-to-order electric vehicles by the Detroit Electric Company in 1935, America, while spawning the internal combustion automobile and webbing a network of highways,[1] produced almost no commercial electric, over-the-road vehicles for more than two decades. Coincident with the abandonment of electric vehicles was the scrapping of the interurban and the electric city trolleys. For personal travel on land the petroleum-powered vehicle swept all alternate sources of propulsion into discard. The remarkable fount of 37.4 kilowatt-hours in each gallon of gasoline—6 kWh in each pound of gasoline—was a factor some 500-600 times greater in 1888 and about 300 times greater in 1981 than could be in one pound of a lead-acid battery. So even with the five-fold increase in efficiency of the electric drive over the IC powered vehicle, the factor would still be 50 to 100 times greater—insurmountable odds. America, and to a lesser extent the rest of the world, was experiencing from 1920-1970 a half-century of low-cost energy as a percent of per capita income. Figure 18.1 demonstrates how much faster was per capita dollar income rising than was the cost of fuel. As a result the IC vehicle was king of the road and enjoying a love life with its American owner. The same was true in other industrial nations.

The Paley Report,[2] given to President Dwight Eisenhower in 1957, indicated the coming shortage of certain raw materials, but like many earlier clouds in the sky "no larger than a man's hand," the predictions made were accorded scant heed. In research on electric batteries, for example, it has been estimated that if as much as five million dollars were invested per year starting in 1950 in seeking a battery of high specific energy, high specific power, low cost, and commercial reproduction, America in 1990 would have had electric vehicles able to travel 150 miles at 50 miles per hour on a single charge. But the lead-acid battery for automobile engine cranking, the so-called starting-ignition-lighting (SIL) battery, was "good enough," and use in the IC automobile was its principal application.

---

[1] Little could Colonel A. A. Pope, an electric vehicle pioneer earlier cited, dream that his work for better highways would yield such handsome dividends as the National Interstate Highway System.

[2] *Resources For Freedom: A Report To The President*, Paley Commission, Washington, U.S. Government Printing Office, 1952.

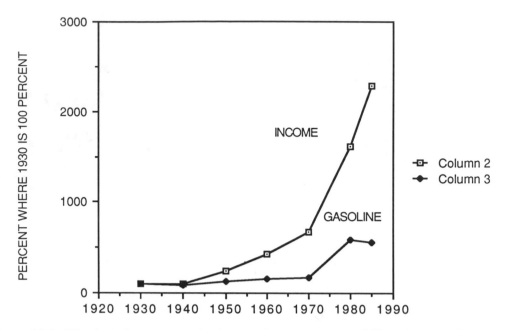

Figure 18.1. The American per capita income in non-constant dollars increased more rapidly than did the pump price of gasoline plus tax between the years 1930 and 1985. Prepared from: Bureau of Census, Dept. of Commerce data, American Petroleum Institute: Petroleum Facts & Figures, 1971, Basic Petroleum Data Book, 1987. Original data courtesy: Dr. R. L. Promboin, Senior Economist, Amoco. Ernest H. Wakefield.

The First of the New Electric Vehicles

As the early 1930s was the end of the original electric vehicle assembly in America, the 1940s saw no organized effort to produce over-the-road electric automobiles. In 1960, however, some 150 Henny Kilowatt electric cars were assembled by the Eureka Williams Corporation of Freeport, Illinois under the direction of the company's founder, Russell Feldmann.[3] The vehicle was an electrical conversion of a 4-door Renault Dauphine. A number of electric utilities purchased these vehicles. Roger Suffin in Glen Ellyn, Illinois was driving one of these cars in the 1990s according to William H. Shafer, Commonwealth Edison Company (ret.).

The Dauphine was a 4-passenger sedan with a vehicle weight of 2,260 pounds bearing 72 volt, 115 ampere-hour (Ah) of lead-acid batteries. Motor current control was by series-parallel battery switching. The motor was a 7.1 hp General Electric. Top speed was a reported 30-40 mph, and the advertised range was given as 40 miles, but under what conditions of driving?[4] The author rode in one of these vehicles on a Connecticut estate in 1969, some time after he was well

---

[3] Victor Wouk, *Two Decades of 'High Performance' EV Fleet Experience.* Eighth International Electrical Vehicle Symposium, Washington, D. C. 1986.

[4] *The Electric Car - A Design Challenge, Electro Technology*, 1968, p. 58.

engaged in three-phase power drive-train for electric vehicles. The car rode pleasantly. Silent, only the sound of relays closing was heard as the driver varied the pressure of his foot on the accelerator. Of the 150 assembled, only half had been sold.

Reportedly, a little earlier than the Henny Kilowatt, Stinson in San Diego initiated a few electric vehicles.[5] Possibly this effort was related to the Scottish Aviation Ltd. Scamp, a small electric vehicle built before 1966, and discussed in Chapter 22. Was not aviation business in the doldrums worldwide? To go forward with electrics when gasoline was 25¢ per gallon, and the words "air pollution" and "ecology" on the tongues of only a few biologists, required courage.

With the modest effort above some thought a new day in alternate personal transportation had been born. The way would be hard for those who tried, frustrating, debilitating, but satisfying. The little trickles of interest would someday be seen as a mighty stream, for transportation in the world would be electric. There was a new group of innovators, and they would not be denied. And their electric vehicles would be innovative as well. Had a new age dawned? The alert media sensed the coming of the electric vehicles.[6] Rather symbolic of this increasingly heady atmosphere, W. J. Clapp, President of the Edison Electric Institute, would help initiate an associated organization, the Electric Vehicle Council March 16, 1968 with Edward Campbell as Executive Secretary.[7]

The New Electric Vehicle Publications

A measure of alertness and of enterprising spirit in journalism is how quickly a magazine arises to satisfy a new need and to fill an apparent vacuum. In the nations of the West this time delay is short. Only five years elapsed from the first electric vehicle in America and the issuance of *The Horseless Age*. The front page of its No. 1 issue is reproduced in Chapter 2. Its publisher, E. P. Ingersoll, was a critical connoisseur of electric vehicle development, and of the personages of the new industry.

February 1972 saw Vol. 1 No. 1 of the slick paper journal *Electric Vehicle News* with color, a commercial sequel to an Electric Vehicle Council multilith publication of the same name. The first issue of *Electric Vehicles News* is illustrated in Fig. 18.2. Possessing an editorial policy encouraging the electric vehicle industry, the publication has offered useful, if at times insufficiently discriminative, reporting. A scalpel as wielded by an Ingersoll can mute the excess. Admittedly, the present electric car constituencies are scattered in area, ill-defined in technology, slow in growth, and difficult to serve. And ever-ready to invade the electric vehicle turf are richer, longer established, petro-engine designated periodicals. Likewise informative is the British journal *Electric Vehicles,* whose non-critical editorial policies differ little from its American cousin of like name.

---

[5] W. H. Shafer, Commonwealth Edison Company, communication April 16, 1982.

[6] Elliot Carlson, *Rowan Controller to Show Electric Cars in U.S., The Wall Street Journal*, December 8, 1967, p. 3.

[7] W. J. Clapp, *On the Move - Electrically, Edison Electric Institute Bulletin*, June/July 1969, pp. 232-238.

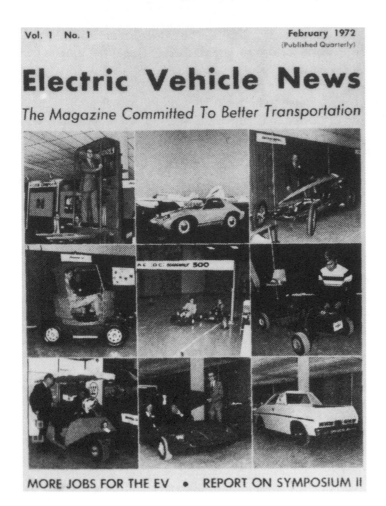

Vol. 1 No. 1   February 1972
(Published Quarterly)

Electric Vehicle News
The Magazine Committed To Better Transportation

MORE JOBS FOR THE EV   •   REPORT ON SYMPOSIUM II

Figure 18.2. Front cover of the first issue of Electric Vehicle News.

Satisfying the need for the more technical articles in the United States is the journal of the *Society for Automotive Engineering*, and in England, the recently established *Electro Technology*. Without the enquiry exampled by the contributors and these publications, the world would be less informed and less free, and the path for alternate personal transport would be more obscure.

There were other public recognitions for electric vehicles: Postage stamps.

Illustrations of Electric Vehicles on U.S. Stamps

Electric vehicles have been of sufficient importance to be featured on several U.S. stamp issues. Mary Longbrake of Chicago, a philatelist, has informed the author the manufacturer of the automobile represented on the Pan-American 4 cent stamp of 1901 is in debate.[8] The vehicle is a dual-motor electric brougham made by the Pope Manufacturing Company of Hartford,

---

[8] *What is the Car?, Topical Times*, Vol. 33, No. 5, Sept./Oct. 1982, p. 61.

Connecticut in 1899. Figure 18.3 is an illustration of the 4 cent stamp.[9] Figure 18.4 shows a brougham constructed by the Riker Electric Motor Company of Brooklyn, New York in the same year as was the Pope carriage.[10] That the vehicle adorning the stamp is electric is attested by the electric motor visible inside the left rear wheel. The same would be inside the right rear wheel. A similar structure is seen in both the Pope and Riker vehicles, and was a common design on vehicles at the turn of the century.[11] As to delineating which one of the two carriages, look to the configuration of the two dashboards. The angled section of Riker's is unlike the representation on the stamp. The shape of the dash, however, is similar to Pope's. While the 1899 period was one of bicycle-type wire-wheels and growing use of pneumatic tires, both the Pope and Riker broughams bore artillery-style wheels and hard rubber tires, a reflection of the personal desires of the buyers in a time of strong personal choice.

Figure 18.3. Pan-American Stamps of 1901. Courtesy: U.S. Postal Service.

---

[9] *United States Postage Stamps: 1847-1967*, Washington: United States Government Printing Office, 1968, p. 28.
[10] *An Electric Brougham, Ibid.*, Vol. LXXXI, No. 7, August 12, 1899, p. 101.
[11] C. E. Woods, *The Electric Vehicle: Its Construction, Care and Operation*, New York: H. S. Stone & Co., 1900.

Figure 18.4a. Automobile Brougham for a City Physician – Pope. Courtesy: Scientific American.

Figure 18.4b. The Riker Electric Brougham. Courtesy: Scientific American.

The Pope brougham was the apogee of the coachmaker's art and was finished in a dark green polished lacquer. Satin, broadcloth, and leather lined the interior bearing pockets for documents. A clock, a reading lamp, a bell for communication with the driver, and external running lights completed the electrical equipment.

Another reason for the artist to choose the Pope carriage for the stamp engraving was the well-known leadership of his company in the 1890s for producing the finest electric vehicles. In this decade Pope had already become America's largest maker of bicycles, the Columbia venerated to this day.[12] Further, the company was excellently staffed and equipped. This reputation for quality was established by the company's founder, Colonel Albert A. Pope, a Civil War cavalry officer, and was continued into the production of electric vehicles under Lieutenant Hayden Eames, a former naval ordinance inspector, and Hiram Percy Maxim, a Massachusetts Institute of Technology graduate. The Pope Company was one of the first industrial organizations with a standards testing laboratory to assure quality control, and his corporation was the first to mass-produce horseless carriages. Further, Colonel Pope's firm had in 1899 joined forces with New York financiers William C. Whitney and P. A. B. Widener.[13] With the above does it not appear likely an artist would choose the Pope brougham for a stamp illustration? The cited is not to be construed to belittle Andrew L. Riker, an excellent engineer and winner of automobile races par excellence as described in Chapter 15. Riker, likewise, made well-designed carriages, but his organization was newer, smaller, and less well-connected. In conclusion, one can almost categorically state the Pope brougham is represented on the 4 cent stamp of 1901.

One of the most innovative drive systems for electric cars is the application of a 3-phase induction motor and 3-phase permanent magnet synchronous motor. Both are discussed at the end of Chapter 12. Also related are solid-state controls to convert d-c power from the battery into 3-phase a-c power. To the electrical engineering reader this task is seen to be an elegant accomplishment, and the next chapter relates this electronic "alchemy." The obtaining of 3-phase power from a battery and the ability to shape the torque-speed curve of a polyphase induction motor to yield high initial starting torque is believed by some experts to be the single most significant technical contribution to electric cars since their invention by Gustave Trouvé more than 100 years earlier. Solid state electronics, particularly the elements known as the silicon control rectifier, the transistor, and the microprocessor, made this tour de force possible.

---

[12] John B. Sadler, personal communication, October 27, 1982.
[13] To join The Electric Vehicle Company of New York City.

CHAPTER 19

Alternating-Current Electric Drive Vehicles 1966-1992

The mid-1960s saw the initiation of work on battery-powered electric vehicles with innovative drive systems at two centers. Each was an independent investigation: one by the giant of motordom, the General Motors Company, the other by an independent, Linear Alpha, Inc. The GM Program, with corporate blessing, was an effort expending an estimated $15 million. Two vehicles initially resulted: The Electrovair and the Electrovan shown in Figs. 19.1 and 19.2.[1][2] This program was under the general direction of Dr. Paul D. Agarwal. The second effort but congruent in time was initiated in 1965 in Evanston, Illinois. Key personnel were Gary F. Comiskey, David L. Duff, Robert E. Kaney, Richard A. Karlin, John I. Murphy, and the author, with Dr. S.B. Dewan from the University of Toronto as a consultant.[3] Subsequently, acting as a consultant, Professor Gordon J. Murphy of Northwestern University had direct technical responsibility,[4][5] working with Andrew M. Wohlert, Robert E. Kaney, and the author.[6]

Photos courtesy General Motors Corporation.

Acting incommensurably both groups in their research had conceived of a modern drive system for electric vehicles. Alternating-current rather than direct-current, previously employed, would be the means for converting battery power into mechanical power. The reason for this a-c approach was two-fold: 1) Commercial thyristors had become available of sufficient power to be used in an electric vehicle, and 2) There were simple, low cost squirrel-cage induction motors. Those readers familiar with electric drives know that rotational equipment in factories of the world are largely run by a-c induction motors of the Tesla design—a motor introduced in Chapter 12.

---

[1] J. T. Salihi, P. D. Agarwal, and G. J. Spix, *Induction Motor Control Scheme for Battery Powered Electric Car - GM Electrovair I, IEEE Trans. Ind. Gen. Appl.*, IGA-3, pp. 463-469, Sept./Oct. 1967.

[2] P. D. Agarwal, *The GM High-Performance Induction Motor Drive System*, IEEE Trans Power App. Syst., Vol. PAS-88, pp. 86-93, February 1969.

[3] S. B. Dewan and David L. Duff, *Optimum Design of an Input-Commutated Inverter for AC Motor Control, IEEE Trans. on Industry and Gen. Applications*, V. IGA-5, Nov./Dec. 1969. pp. 699-705.

[4] G. J. Murphy, *The Design and Development of a Van with A-C Electric Drive, Proc. of the Second Int. Elec. Vehicle Symposium*, Atlantic City, N. J., Nov. 7-9, 1971, New York, Elec. Vehicle Council, 1971.

[5] G. J. Murphy, *Considerations in the Design of Drive Systems for On-the-Road Electric Vehicles*, IEEE Proc. Vol. 60, No. 12, Dec. 1972, pp. 1519-1533.

[6] Ernest H. Wakefield, *A High-Performance A-C Electric Drive for Vehicles, Proc. 1st Int. Electric Vehicle Symposium*, Phoenix, Arizona, Nov. 5-7, 1969. New York: Electric Vehicle Council, 1969.

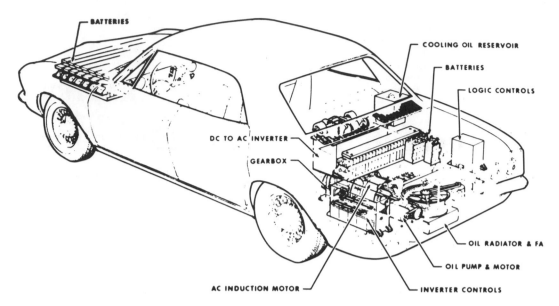

Figure 19.1. The General Motors a-c drive Electrovair. General Motors.

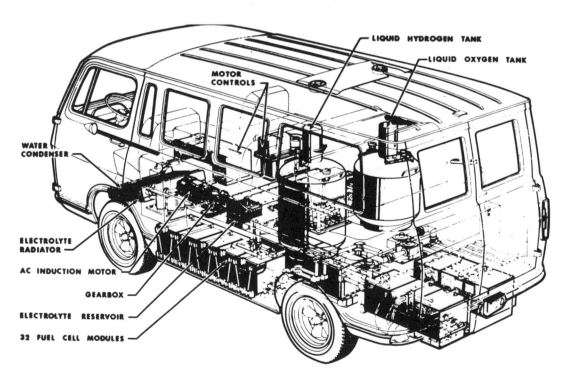

Figure 19.2. Cutaway View of General Motors Electrovan. General Motors.

In a practical way, before this motor could be used in a vehicle solid-state electronics had to be invented. In an automobile only solid-state elements are sufficiently rugged to perform the electronic switching to change d-c power from a battery to 3-phase power to operate Tesla's induction motor. The development of the transistor, leading to a Nobel Prize for each of the three scientists,[7] premised the invention of the silicon control rectifier (SCR) by Dr. Nick Holonyak. A properly connected SCR in an alternating current circuit can be used as a valve. The dimming of lights in a theater is accomplished by SCRs. With direct current circuits associated with batteries an SCR may also be used as a switch. With a properly wired control system, a microprocessor, a group of SCRs correctly connected can change d-c power from a battery to a reasonable facsimile of 3-phase power, and hence Tesla's 3-phase induction motor may be operated. As described below, that intricate task was achieved.

While both General Motors and Linear Alpha conceived of electric to mechanical power conversion and use of the three-phase induction motor, the method of providing three-phase electrical power from the d-c power available from the battery utilized different principles. GM's original approach was to chop the d-c power from the battery into time-displaced multiple blocks of power of equal time flow, varying the number of these blocks per half cycle. The Linear Alpha principle was to introduce one additional variable: to vary the number as well as the time-length of each block. The latter feature aided in suppressing the higher harmonics which resulted in reducing the motor noise level considerably. Figures 19.3 and 19.4 illustrate, for simplicity, the two principles in single phase. If drawn a three-phase power flow diagram would appear too complex. As both the GM and Linear Alpha approaches were indeed novel in employing the induction motor to drive the vehicle this work received great interest from the electrical fraternity. Subsequent investigators would obtain excellent sine waves to supply 3-phase motors as illustrated in Chapter 12. Furthermore, both projects were dedicated to executing high performance vehicles which could challenge the IC cars in all characteristics except range. For the reader to understand the operation of a three-phase induction motor he

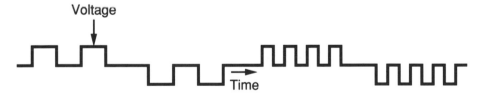

Figure 19.3. In developing an a-c motor drive system the General Motors approach was to switch the battery current off and on, then reverse the polarity, and repeat, varying the number of pulses per half-cycle, depending on power demand.

---

[7] The 1956 Nobel Prize is physics was awarded to John Bardeen, Walter Brattain, and William Shockley.

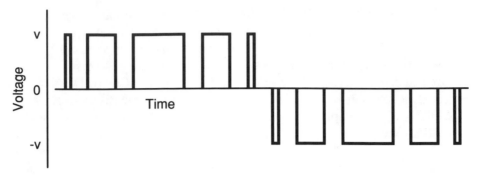

Figure 19.4. In developing the a-c drive electric vehicle, Linear Alpha varied the number of pulses per half cycle while varying the time-width of the pulse as well. In both approaches cited in the text the frequency was a variable and determined the speed of the vehicle. Courtesy: Gordon J. Murphy.

is referred to an appropriate electrical engineering text.[8] [9] [10] [11] [12] [13] Speaking electromechanically, the induction motor is probably the simplest motor which man knows how to build, hence their almost universal use, except in electric vehicles.

Both GM and Linear Alpha companies attempted and were successful in exploiting the induction motor in driving electric vehicles. Figure 19.5 shows the van, the d-c to a-c inverter, and Dr. Gordon J. Murphy holding the controller. Figure 19.6 illustrates the motor, the d-c to a-c inverter with the author pointing to the tachometer. With inductance due to the iron in the circuit, a scalloped wave-form roughly similar to a sine wave was impressed on the stator of the induction motor to produce a rotating field. To control the speed of the vehicle, the frequency supplied the motor varied from essentially zero to 80 cycles per second. Table 19.1 presents the characteristics of the Linear Alpha a-c drive electric vehicle, and the team which brought it forth is shown in Fig. 19.7. The basic idea of frequency and pulse-width modulation had come to the author in an inspired burst in great detail in 1965 while walking on Sherman Avenue where it crosses Clark Street in Evanston, Illinois in company with Richard A. Karlin and Gary F. Comiskey. Subsequently frequency and pulse width modulation of a-c motors would also be considered for powering the San Francisco Metropolitan Transit System, BART.[14]

The speed of the vehicle, independent of the transmission, is seen to have a great range with continuous control, all achieved electronically. As alluded to above, Dr. Murphy had added to the concept of three-phase power generation the additional feature of variation of pulse width.

---

[8] A. E. Fitzgerald and Charles Kingley, Jr., *Electric Machinery*, 2nd Ed., New York: McGraw-Hill, 1961.

[9] M. E. Valkenburg, *Network Analysis*, 3rd Ed., Englewood Cliffs, N.J.: Prentice-Hall, 1974.

[10] W. H. Hayt, Jr., and Jack E. Kemmerly, *Engineering Circuit Analysis*, 2nd Ed., New York: McGaw-Hill.

[11] M. G. Say, *The Performance and Design of Alternating Current Machines*, London: Sir Isaac Pitman & Son, Ltd., 1948.

[12] William H. Timbie, *Elements of Electricity*, 4th Ed., London: Chapman Hall, 1953.

[13] Michael Liwschite-Garik, Clyde C. Whipple, *Electric Machinery*, New York: D. Van Nostrand Company, Inc., 1946.

[14] Private communication from Westinghouse Electric Corporation.

Figure 19.5. The inverter is below the steering wheel. Professor Gordon J. Murphy holds the controller. Courtesy: Commonwealth Edison Company.

This added fillip allowed the torque-speed curve to be modified at will. A higher starting torque could now be obtained from an induction motor, a particularly desirable feature in an automobile. As remarked by E.F. Yahnke of Illinois Bell Company, the Linear Alpha development, electronic torque control, achieved by a mass produced, low price electronic chip, represented the first throw-away transmission.[15] Figure 19.8 has historical interest for it is a copy of what is believed to be the first purchase order for an a-c drive electric car. The Illinois Bell Telephone Company placed the order on Linear Alpha Inc. Two vehicles were subsequently built and operated, accruing finally to Northwestern University, Evanston, Illinois. Table 19.1 presents the characteristics of the vehicle and Figs. 19.9 and 19.10 the vehicle and the switching system.

Because of the relatively high costs of thyristor controls as compared to the use of d-c drive systems, these two developments of using a-c power, by GM and Linear Alpha, were ahead of

---

[15] Ernest H. Wakefield, *An a-c Drive Electric Vehicle, IEEE Trans. on Industry Applications*, Vol. IA-10, No. 5, September/October 1974.

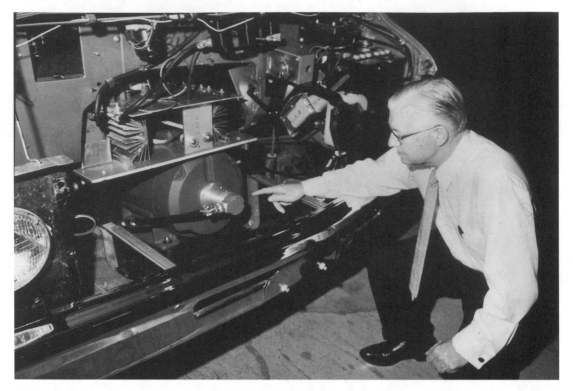

Figure 19.6. Mounting details of 27 kW, 3-phase induction motor. Author is pointing to tachometer which feeds into the microprocessor. Photos: Courtesy of Commonwealth Edison Company.

their time. They were to the electric vehicle what the Great Eastern was to passenger liners and what the Concorde was to commercial aviation,[16] a remarkable development, but not at the time economically feasible at the relatively small horsepower required.

The two a-c powered GM vehicles, besides having an innovative electric drive system also had electric energy storage means which were unconventional. As the Corporation directive was to provide two high performance vehicles, this request was interpreted by the engineers that the vehicles should have acceleration, speed, and range which approached the gasoline-powered vehicle of a similar configuration. To obtain the acceleration and speed requires an electrical energy source of high specific power—able to supply energy at a high rate. And to obtain the necessary range there must be storage facilities for a substantial number of kilowatt-hours, inasmuch as a large vehicle, in urban driving, needs some 0.4-0.6 kWh per mile. To meet this

---

[16] *The Great Eastern*, designed by the remarkable Isambard Brunel, dwarfed the ships of her day and was unique in many ways. The *Concorde*, supersonic in speed, is so current as to need no introduction.

Table 19-1. Design Specifications for an Alternating-Current Drive Vehicle - 1968 Linear Alpha, Inc., Evanston, Illinois

1. DRIVE MOTOR SPECIFICATIONS

Horsepower	40
Voltage	100 volts, three phase
No. of Poles	4
Nominal Frequency	60 Hertz
Maximum Frequency	80 Hertz
Nominal Speed	1725 RPM
Maximum Speed	2375 RPM
Output Torque	@60 Hz: 116 foot pounds
Maximum Output Torque	350 foot pounds
Constant Torque Range	0 to 520 RPM
Constant Horsepower Range	520 to 2375 RPM
Type	Squirrel-cage, induction
Weight	Approx. 275 pounds

2. BATTERY SPECIFICATION

Nominal voltage	144 volts
End-of-Discharge voltage	134 volts
Kilowatt-hour rating	24 KWH
Recharging cycles	700
Type	Lead-acid (17 WH/# at 3 hr. discharge rate)
Weight	1316#

3. INVERTER SPECIFICATIONS

Input voltage	144 volts nom., 124 volts min.
Output voltage	0 to 100 volts
Output phases	3
Output Frequency	0 to 80 Hertz
Control Mode	Controlled torque, adjustable slip-speed, current limited
Output power	40 HP Max.
Efficiency	90%
Weight	Approximately 290 pounds

4. BATTERY CHARGING USING ON-BOARD INVERTER

Input voltage	220 volts
Input frequency	60 Hertz
No. of Phases	1 phase
Input current	Selector switch: 50, 25, 15 amp. gas pressure regulated

5. VEHICLE PERFORMANCE SPECIFICATIONS

Maximum Speed:	50-60 MPH for a 7600# vehicle
Range:	30-35 miles. On-board charger

Figure 19.7. One of two Linear Alpha Inc. a-c drive electric vehicles developed by, from left to right: Dr. Gordon J. Murphy, consultant, Dr. Ernest H. Wakefield, Robert E. Kaney, and Andrew M. Wohlert. Courtesy: Commonwealth Edison Company.

request called for fresh thinking and the presence of a large purse indeed. For the Electrovair, Dr. Agarwal and his team chose as an energy source a silver-zinc battery.[17]

For the Electrovan, on the other hand, the GM team obtained the services of Union Carbide Company to supply a hydrogen-oxygen fuel cell. A fuel cell is an electric cell that converts the chemical energy of a fuel, in this case hydrogen, into electric energy in a continuous process. The liquid oxygen and liquid hydrogen tanks, with interiors at -183°C and -252°C, respectively, are shown in Fig. 19.2. Such a fuel cell produces electricity and water. The cost of a fuel cell was about $2,000 per kilowatt of power generated. In a van type vehicle cruising at 50 mph, some 40 hp is required. If all the power were to come from the fuel cell, a sixty thousand dollar source of power would be required in addition to the many peripheral items as seen in the illustration.[17a] In short, the energy storage of both GM vehicles represented what could be done if cost were no object. If there were two camps in General Motors whether the Corporation should offer electric vehicles, both parties could have been satisfied. The first: "Yes, an electric

---

[17] The first battery ever assembled used the copper-zinc electric couple. Count Alessandro Volta in 1800. See Chapter 10.

[17a] $\dfrac{40 \times 746}{1000} \times \$2000 = \$59680.$

FORM 1295 (9-65)

ILLINOIS BELL TELEPHONE COMPANY

PURCHASE ORDER

DATE October 8, 1968

ORDER NUMBER

A 12577

THIS ORDER NUMBER MUST BE SHOWN ON INVOICE.

TO: Linear Alpha Company

823 Emerson Street

Evanston, Illinois

Mail Invoice to: **IN DUPLICATE**

ILLINOIS BELL TELEPHONE COMPANY

c/o **Mr. E. F. Yahnke, Gen. Operations Supv.**
(NAME) (TITLE)

HQ 23C - 225 W. Randolph St.
(ROOM NO.) (STREET ADDRESS)

Chicago, Illinois 60606
(CITY) (STATE) (ZIP CODE)

Ship to:

ILLINOIS BELL TELEPHONE COMPANY

c/o **Contact Mr. E. F. Yahnke for delivery**
(NAME) (TITLE)

instructions on 727-6325.
(ROOM NO.) (STREET ADDRESS)

(CITY) (STATE) (ZIP CODE)

QUANTITY	DESCRIPTION OF ARTICLE	AMOUNT
1	1969 - Ford Econoline Display Van Model E-364 to be converted to a complete Linear Alpha Electric Drive Installation Van in accordance with the attached specifications, See Exhibit A, B & C. New Outfit No: 1693014 It is agreed that Dr. Ernest H. Wakefield and Linear Alpha Corporation deliver the above vehicle on or before June 30, 1969, and in the event that such delivery is not made by October 31, 1969, this agreement shall be null and void.	

Total Cost: $15,000.00

WHERE TRANSPORTATION CHARGES ARE INVOLVED. ATTACH RECEIPT OR BILL OF LADING TO YOUR INVOICE NOTING THEREON THE ABOVE ORDER NUMBER.

ILLINOIS BELL TELEPHONE COMPANY

BY:

TITLE: **General Operations Supervisor**

Figure 19.8. First purchase order for an a-c drive battery-powered vehicle, a tour de force made possible by solid state electronics. Ernest H. Wakefield.

Figure 19.9. The First a-c Drive Electric Vehicle Sold in Commerce Being Driven by Charles L. Brown, President of Illinois Bell, Inc. Courtesy: John T. Trutter.

vehicle can really perform." And "No, but at what cost?" With their pioneering work both General Motors and Linear Alpha had shown that a-c drive of electric vehicles was possible.[18]

About a decade later, with newly developed power transistors, a transistorized inverter would be shown to be more efficient than a SCR type inverter because the former "withdraws energy from the tractor battery in a smooth fashion whereas the [SCR inverter] withdraws it in millisecond pulses."[19] George Prans and Henry J. Chaya Jr. of Manhattan College in Riverdale, New York report the transistorized controller in a sedan saves 21 and 12 percent respectively over the thyristor controller for city driving and for highway driving. In addition, the authors give the savings and the reasons in the several elements of the drive system.[19]

The Eaton AC Propulsion System for an Electric Vehicle

Among other significant studies on a-c propelled electric vehicles was the work carried forward by the Eaton Company of Cleveland for the U.S. Department of Energy. Their base vehicle was a 1981 Mercury-Lynx Ford chassis and body which when electrified had a curb weight of 1,364 kg (3,000 pounds). The 25 hp (18.6 kw), 3-phase traction induction motor

---

[18] At about the same time there were a-c drive off-the-road vehicles using an alternate principle, but they were ac-ac based.

[19] George Prans and Henry J. Chaya, Jr., *Comparative Performance of an SCR—and a Transitor-Controlled Electric Vehicle*, Eighth International Electric Vehicle Symposium, Washington, D.C. 1986.

Figure 19.10. The d-c to a-c Converter for the Illinois Bell Vehicle. Left to Right, John T. Trutter, Dr. Ernest H. Wakefield, Professor Gordon J. Murphy, and Charles L. Brown. Courtesy: John T. Trutter.

system had a total weight of 139 kg (motor 55 kg. inverter 43 kg, transaxle 37 kg, and the controller 3 kg). Battery voltage was 192 volts nominal from 6 volt lead-acid batteries.

Instead of using silicon control rectifiers for current switching in the inverter as in the much earlier Linear Alpha Inc. a-c drive vehicle, Eaton engineers, led by J. M. Slicker, employed transistors. The vehicle, a front wheel drive type, had a top motor speed of 12,500 RPM. The vehicle's acceleration for 9 to 48 km/h was 8.5 sec; for 40-88 km/h was 27 sec. Top speed was 104 km (65 mph). Creep speed gradibility was 16 percent as derived from acceleration data. A measured peak d-c to mechanical system efficiency of 82 percent was reached. Energy consumption at the battery terminals was:

0.214 kwh/mile at 25 mph
0.225   do   35 do
0.266   do   45 do

Energy consumption of the vehicle was 0.320 kWh/mile as measured at the battery terminals over the SAE J2277a - D driving schedule.[20]

Other Alternating-Current Drive Developments

Later, other countries would investigate the a-c drive for personal electric vehicles both in England,[21] and in the USSR.[22] The main stream of activity in the 1970s, however, would be with d-c motors placed in converted IC automobiles, a subject developed in the next Chapter. Later, in the 1980s and 1990s the thrust of motor drive development, based on experience gained above, and particularly the genesis of new electronic components, was accelerated with a-c system encouragement under the jurisdiction of the U.S. Department of Energy. With contracts valued in the low two-digit millions the Eaton Corporation of Cleveland, and the Ford Motor Company with the General Electric Company as subcontractor, developed some most promising a-c electric vehicle drive systems and placed them in vehicles.[23] [24] Even academe worked with a-c drives, Professors D. W. Novotny and T. A. Lipo at the University of Wisconsin, Madison being an example,[25] as well as a system developed by Wally E. Rippel of Jet Propulsion Laboratory,[26] an innovator who earned his spurs in being a moving force in the first transcontinental electric car race, an event described in Chapter 24. The a-c drive system, because of its rapidly decreasing weight and price, was also pursued and shown in Tokyo in 1983 and in Versailles in 1984 by Nissan using the 3-phase induction motor approach.[27] Later, a conglomerate of companies in Finland built an a-c drive system employing a 228 volt lead-acid series of batteries, transistorized controller, a 20 kw motor placed on a 1,450 kg Talbot Horizon chassis. Range was 62 km at 60 km/hr. Finland being subject to cold weather the batteries bore temperature controls.[28]

---

[20] J. M. Slicker, *AC Propulsion System for an Electric Vehicle: Phase 2 Interim Report*, Cleveland, OH: U.S. Department of Energy, Office of Transportation Program, 1983.

[21] D. J. Byers, *A-C Motor Control for Advanced Electric Vehicles, Electric Vehicle Development*, November 4, 1979, pp. 4 & 5.

[22] *A-C Motored Vehicles in Moscow, Electric Vehicles*, Vol. 64, No. 4, December 1978, p. 21.

[23] Ilmar Kalns, *Two Speed Transaxle for AC-Powered Light Truck Drive-Trains*, Eighth International Electric Vehicle Symposium, Washington, D.C. 1986.

[24] B. Bates, P. B. Patil, and M. F. Ciccarelli, ETX-II, *A Second Generation Advance AC Propulsion System*, do.

[25] D. S. Kirschen, *Optimum Efficiency Control of Induction Motor Machines*, Ph.D. Thesis in Electrical Engineering, University of Wisconsin, Madison, 1984.

[26] Wally E. Rippel, *A High Performance, Low Cost AC Traction Drive*, Eighth International Electric Vehicle Symposium, Washington, D.C., 1986.

[27] Tornio Jindo, *Development of AC Induction Motor Control Systems for EVs*, Eighth International Electric Vehicle Symposium, Washington, D.C., 1986.

[28] Heikki Tikkenen, *On-Road Performance of an AC-Drive Passenger EV*, do.

Ford/GE ETX-I AC Propulsion System

Continuing the development of electric vehicles was the Ford/GE ETX-I. Of this vehicle R. D. MacDowell and R. L. Crumley wrote:[29]

"The ETX-I advanced AC electric vehicle powertrain was designed and built by Ford Motor Company and General Electric Research and Development Center under U.S. Department of Energy sponsorship. The objective of this research and development program was to advance the state-of-the-art in AC powertrain technology.

"Ford was the prime contractor with overall system design responsibility for the transaxle and vehicle. General Electric was the subcontractor responsible for development of the electric drive subsystem, consisting of the AC induction motor, inverter, and inverter/motor controller.

"Ultimately the ETX-I test bed vehicle was developed with the Lucas Chloride EV System's (LCEVS) tubular lead-acid batteries. Tubular lead-acid batteries are recognized for their longer life expectancy as compared to flat-plate technology. However, life is gained at the expense of energy and power. The LCEVS program included the development of a microprocessor based battery management system to control charging, provide overdischarge protection and provide state-of-charge indication (fuel gauge).

"The ETX-I program focused on the design, build, test, and refinement of the experimental advanced electric vehicle powertrain packaged in a front wheel drive, two-seat Mercury LN7 (Fig. 19.11). The motor and transmission are concentric with the drive wheel axis. The powertrain includes the two-speed automatic transaxle and three-phase AC motor with common lubricating and cooling fluid; a 250 A, 400 V Darlington transistor-based water-cooled inverter which operates up to 300 A from a 200 V battery pack; an inverter/motor controller that generates the necessary motor drive signals; and an EEC IV-based vehicle controller that interfaces with the driver and vehicle subsystems to control motor torque, regenerative braking, and transmission shifting.

"The traction motor is an oil-cooled 37 kW (50 hp, 2-pole AC induction motor. Motor stall torque is 104 N-m (76.5 ft-lb). The corner point speed (transition between constant torque and constant power operation) is 3,800 rpm. The motor was designed to operate up to 9,000 rpm. The maximum motor output power (at the minimum battery voltage of 153 V) is 39.5 kW (53 hp) at 6,000 rpm, at 244.5 A. The DC current from the traction batteries goes through the main contactors to the inverter where it is converted to three-phase AC and then delivered to the induction motor.

"The primary function of the inverter/motor controller is to control the inverter in a manner that provides control of the motor torque for both motoring and braking in response to the torque command from the vehicle controller. The inverter/motor

---

[29] R. D. MacDowell and R. L. Crumley, *Comparative Performance Evaluation of Advanced AC and DC EV Propulsion Systems*, The 9th International Electric Vehicle Symposium, Toronto, 1988.

Figure 19.11. Ford/GE ETX-I. R.D. MacDowell and R.L. Crumley

controller provides the sequenced signals to turn on and off the six power Darlington transistor modules to produce the correct fundamental frequency and AC current/voltage in the motor.

"The inverter/motor controller operates the inverter in a manner which provides closed-loop control of the induction motor torque for both motoring and regeneration. The inverter operates in two modes: pulse width modulation (PWM) and six-step square wave (SSSW). At low vehicle speeds and power settings, the inverter operates in a pulse width modulation mode. During high vehicle speed and power demand the inverter operates in the six-step square wave mode.

"The inverter and induction motor control strategy primarily operates in three distinguishable modes: constant torque, constant power, and slip limited. Constant torque mode operation occurs from zero speed up to the corner point (3,800 rpm) which is obtained by controlling the inverter in a PWM mode to maintain a constant flux density while the fundamental frequency and voltage increase linearly with speed. Slip frequency and AC current are constant in this mode. Constant torque operation at less than the maximum envelope is obtained by decreasing the flux, slip frequency and AC current."

In America in 1988 there appeared the first truly viable commercial electric vehicle, meeting all U.S. safety requirements. It was a small fleet-style van, the Ford Aerostar, energized with sodium-sulfur batteries discussed next.

A Second Generation Advanced A-C Propelled Vehicle - The ETX-II

Some score of years after the two a-c drive systems first described above, the Ford Motor Company with the General Electric Company as a major subcontractor (the Department of Energy provided some subsidy) were in the process of completing by July 1988 what appeared to be a most attractive electric vehicle based on the a-c drive train developed for a previous a-c powered vehicle, the ETX-I. The designated vehicle is a small commercial van, a type vehicle adapted for commercial fleet use, a class believed most exploitable for electric vehicles. As described by the program leaders:[30] "Major technological advances that will result from the research program include: a.) a new interior permanent magnet motor in the transaxle assembly, which would in turn be integrated into the rear axle of the van, b.) development of the control algorithms required for control of the interior permanent magnet motor, c.) further development of the unique power modules, d.) improvements to the inverter to bring it a step closer to production, and e.) integration of the vehicle controller and the electric subsystem controller to provide a system controller that is in command of the entire propulsion system. In addition, specification and integration of an advanced sodium-sulfur battery is included in the program to assure that this important portion of the propulsion system is included in all of the system design trade-offs."

In following through the flow of propulsion power: The d-c power from the traction battery is converted into three-phase, variable frequency, variable amplitude, a-c power by the transistor-type inverter and delivered to the interior permanent magnet motor. The motor is a synchronous a-c type machine, that is, the rear-axle-integrated-rotor turns at a speed proportional to the frequency emitted by the inverter. Or, stating the principle in other words, the speed of the vehicle is a function of the frequency of the power supplied the motor. The latter drives the rear wheels of the vehicle through a concentrically mounted and automatically shifted transmission. The use of neodymium-iron-boron magnets, stated to be eight-times stronger than iron ferrite magnets previously used, allows an energy dense, small motor, and since it has speeds up to 11,000 rpm, can be small yet deliver substantial power. The van promises to have a range of over 100 miles, and because sodium-sulfur batteries, its power plant, have been cycled several thousands of times with little depreciation, the industrial community may indeed find this vehicle has commercial viability. Table 19.2 and Figs. 19.12 and 19.13 summarize the characteristics of this electric automobile.

Two AC-drive ETX-II electric vehicles were delivered to the Department of Energy by Ford/General Electric in December 1988. With their special batteries they had a range of over 100 miles and speeds greater than 60 mph. These vans are possibly the first truly viable electric vehicles for general purpose use.

---

[30] B. Bates, P. B. Patil, M. F. Cicarelli, *ETX-II: A Second Generation Advanced A-C Propulsion System*, Eighth International Electric Vehicle Symposium, Washington, D.C., 1986.

Table 19-2. ETX-II Preliminary System Specifications	
Vehicle	Aerostar
Test weight	2050 kg
GVW	2275 kg
Rolling resistance	0.01
Drag Coefficient (C_d)	0.37
Frontal area	2.9 m^2
Battery	
Energy	40 kWh
Power	65 kW
Weight	500 kg
Inverter	Variable Voltage & variable frequency
Motor	70 hp
	Internal permanent magnet ac
Transaxle	Automatic, Two-Speed, Integral with rear axle
System Controller	Common bus multi-processor,
	Inverter/Motor controls, Vehicle controls
Courtesy: Ford Motor Company	

The Ford *Ecostar* and the Modular Electric Vehicle Program (MEVP)

With the delivery of the Ford/General Electric ETX-II van equipped with sodium-sulfur batteries and a permanent magnet, synchronous motor to the Department of Energy (DOE) as reported in the 14th Annual Report to Congress, a subsequent contract with the same contractors was signed on September 18, 1990 for the next phase. This phase was known as the Modular Electric Vehicle Program (MEVP). The four-year research and development effort provided the cost be shared between Ford and DOE. "Under the project, Ford will design and develop three modular propulsion systems (50, 75, and 100 hp.) that will be suitable for a variety of vehicles ranging from a small passenger car to a full size van. The project's goal is to make the production of electric propulsion systems more commercially viable, allowing electric vehicles to enter the marketplace sooner than through traditional design programs[31]. Phase I and Phase II of this program were subsequently spelled out in the 15th Annual Report to Congress[32].

---

[31] *Electric and Hybrid Vehicle Program,* 14th Annual Report to Congress for Fiscal Year 1990, April 1991, p. 17.
[32] *Electric and Hybrid Vehicle Program,* 15th Annual Report to Congress for Fiscal Year 1991, May 1992, p. 29.

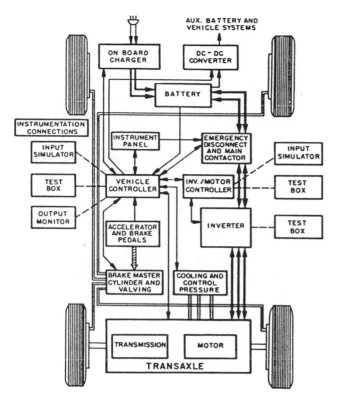

Figure 19.12. ETX Powertrain Block Diagram. Courtesy: B. Bates et al.

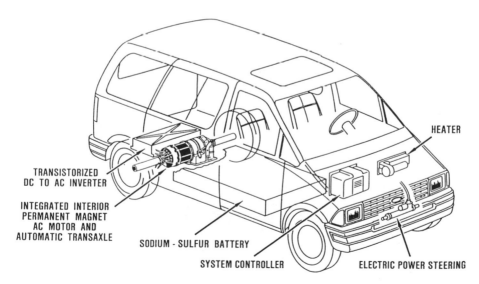

Figure 19.13. Diagram of the ETX-II Electric Vehicle (1988). B. Bates et al.

Figures 19-14a, 19-14b, 19-14c, and 19-14d show some of the results of this contract. While both vehicle approaches were ac-powered, two of the most significant departures from the ETX-II vehicles to the resulting Ford Ecostar is front-wheel drive and the employment of a 3-phase induction motor rather than the use of the 3-phase permanent magnet, synchronous motor as used in the ETX-II. The latter motor is slightly more efficient (1-2 percent) than is the induction motor, but the induction motor is less expensive to manufacture. And with both motors properly maintained their life will exceed that of the automobile by several times. Induction motors have been known to give yeoman service for more than 50 years, and the permanent magnet, synchronous motor would be expected to yield an equivalent life. With the Ecostar equipped with an induction motor, this vehicle has reverted to a more modern but similar power system as provided in the Linearvan sold to Illinois Bell Telephone Company by Linear Alpha Inc. in 1968, specified in Table 19.1 with the full-sized van illustrated in Fig. 19.9.

The Ecostar has a curb weight of 3100 pounds with a carrying capacity of 800 pounds, and is equipped with a 30 kwh sodium sulfur battery. It employs a 75-horsepower, 3-phase induction motor with provision for regenerative braking. The van has a top speed of 70-75 miles per hour, can accelerate from 0 to 50 mph in 12 seconds, and has "an urban driving range (Federal Urban Driving Schedule) of 100 miles and up to 200 miles at 25 miles per hour steady-state driving." The van comes equipped with an air-conditioner. There is provision for a engine-generator for continuously charging the battery, making the van multi-powered[33].

Another potentially attractive a-c drive system is an Eaton Corporation development, again, like the system developed above, partially subsidized by the U.S. Department of Energy. This

Figure 19.14a. Ford Ecostar. Ford Motor Company

---

[33] Release April 10, 1991, *Ford Announces Electric Vehicle Pilot Production,* Ford Motor Company, Chicago office, February 25, 1993.

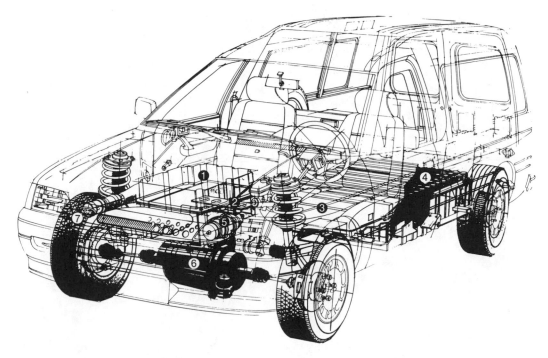

Figure 19.14b. Phantom View of Ecostar. Ford.

vehicle, shown below, is a front-axle drive minivan developed by Chrysler. The vehicle is powered with nickel-iron batteries. The transistor-type inverter provides variable frequency alternating-current to an induction motor, whose speed from 4,000 to 15,000 rpm is reduced to wheel speed by a novel arrangement of gearing.[34] The layout of the vehicle is shown in Fig. 19.15.

In Fig. 19.16 President Bush is shown driving the Eaton-Chrysler vehicle. At the New York Auto Show, April 15, 1992, on NBC *Today Show*, the president of Chrysler announced limited numbers of these vehicles would be made available to electric utility fleet owners in 1993. Further linking Chrysler to an electric car is *The Wall Street Journal's* March 4, 1992 report that Chrysler and Westinghouse Electric Corporation have signed a "multimillion-dollar" agreement to develop an alternating-current motor-powered car to accelerate "from zero to 60 miles per hour in 15 seconds and will have a maximum range of 200 miles while driving at 'normal highway speeds.'"

---

[34] W. Kelledes, *Optimization of An Integrated A-C Propulsion System*, Eighth International Electric Vehicle Symposium, Washington, D.C., 1986.

Figure 19.14c. 75-hp prototype motor/transaxle cutaway. 15th Annual Report to Congress, May 1992, p. 32.

General Motors' 1990 *Impact* [35] [36] [37]

Where the previously described ac-drive electric vans have but a single motor, the General Motors 1990 Impact, a two-passenger subcompact coupe, has one motor for each front wheel. This vehicle is shown in Figs. 19.17 and 19.18. This approach was first used by M. Krieger of France in 1901 as shown in Chapter 7. Responsible for the design of Impact was GM's Advanced Engineering Staff, AeroVironment, Inc., Delco Remy for batteries, the GM Advanced Concepts Center in California, the Tech Center Wind Tunnel, and GM Research, with Dr. Alec N. Brooks of AeroVironment as Project Manager.

---

[35] David E. Sloan, General Motors, January 4, 1990.

[36] GM *Impact* Electric Vehicle, personal communication, Alec N. Brooks, January 20, 1990.

[37] Richard W. Stevenson, *GM Displays the Impact, An Advanced Electric Car, The New York Times*, January 4, 1990, pp. C2 & C33.

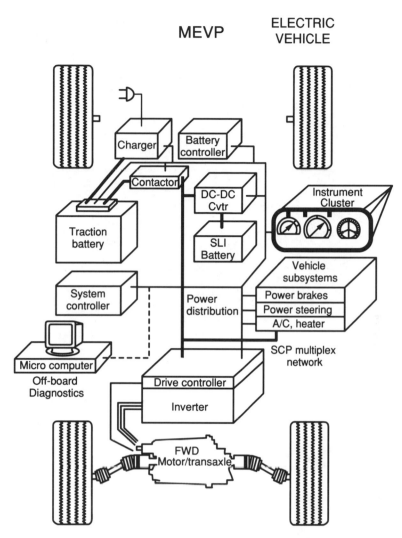

Figure 19.14d. MEVP propulsion system schematic. 15th Annual Report to Congress, May 1992, p. 31.

The unit-constructed body is designed in molded fiberglass. All driveline equipment is under the hood. The 32 10-volt lead-acid batteries, operated in series, are contained in a backbone tunnel design as introduced in the Robert S. McKee's 1972 Sundancer illustrated in Chapter 21. Of the coupe's 2,200 pounds curb weight, the batteries comprise 870 pounds yielding a battery-to-curb-weight ratio of some 40 percent. This energy source occupies 6.5 cubic feet of volume and has an energy capacity of 13.5 kWh at a two-hour discharge rate. The pack has a 100-kilowatt power capability. The lead-acid couple was chosen, for similar batteries have long been manufactured in high volume at low cost. The vehicle has a remarkably low drag coefficient of 0.19, a feature which contributes to the Impact's stated cruising range of 120 miles at 55 mph. Such specifications yield an energy consumption of 113 watt-hours per mile, the equivalent of 370 miles per gallon of gasoline.

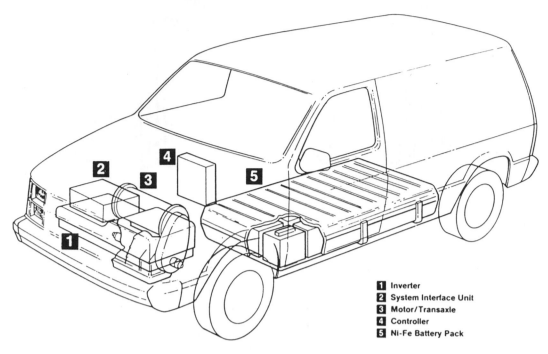

1 Inverter
2 System Interface Unit
3 Motor/Transaxle
4 Controller
5 Ni-Fe Battery Pack

Figure 19.15. Components in the Eaton-Chrysler Vehicle (1988).

Figure 19.16. President Bush Driving the Chrysler a-c Drive Electric Van. Chicago Tribune, Oct.26, 1991.

Figure 19.17. The General Motors Impact. David Sloan, Public Relations, General Motors Technical Center.

Figure 19.18. Installation of Impact's batteries. David Sloan.

The motor drive electronics consist of two inverters, one for each motor, which deliver near sinusoidal frequencies ranging from zero to 400 hertz. The use of two inverters and two motors serve to reduce any problems associated with high current. Within the inverters are 144 MOSFET (metal-oxide-silicon field-effect transistors) switching devices enclosed in three compact aluminum heat sink/heat exchangers. A separate electric system provides 12-volt power for the Impact's accessories. The electronic package weighs but 61 pounds.

The two 3-phase induction motors have efficiencies ranging from 90 to 95 percent depending on load. Normal operating speeds are up to 12,000 rpm. Each of the 57-horsepower motors weigh 50 pounds. The two motors in the forward section of the car drive the front wheels through a 10.5:1 planetary gear-reduction unit and conventional drive shafts. As the single-stage reduction gear is built integrally with the motor housing, little length is added to the package. Through careful design the gear-train has an efficiency of 94 percent. For heat-relief the motors and reduction units are equipped with a forced-air cooling system. Additional motor characteristics appear in the Table 19.3 below.

For the suspension each Impact wheel is joined to the fiberglass chassis by means of two wishbone-type control arms. Coil springs and gas-charged shock-absorbers further control ride motions. In addition to conventional disc-type brakes on the front wheels, and kevlar-compound brake-shoes bearing directly against cast-aluminum brake-drums for the rear wheels, the Impact comes equipped with regenerative electric braking.

As for heating and cooling "the Impact includes an electrically driven heat pump system to provide heated or cooled air to the occupants. The small rotary compressor is driven by a 1-hp magnequench motor....The system is capable of operating when the vehicle is unattended, allowing the car to be cooled or heated at a pre-determined time."

To secure low rolling resistance the Goodyear Tire and Rubber Company developed special high-pressure tires for Impact. Inflated to 65 psi, the tires weigh 12.5 pounds each yielding some one-half the rolling resistance of conventional tires. To ease the load on the air conditioner Sungate glass is used. GM has said the car will be built in Lansing, Michigan.[38]

The first public showing of the GM Impact was at the February 10-18, 1990 Chicago Automobile Show. The Impact's motor is shown in Fig. 19.19, and the Impact's inverter is shown in Fig. 19.20. Roger Smith, then General Motors Chairman, was quoted, "Customer reaction around the world has been, to my mind, nothing short of astounding. We have calls from prospective customers from Perth to Paris."[39] The article continued stating the Impact would have an annual operating cost probably twice greater than a similar gasoline-powered vehicle.

General Motors could consider offering three classes of Impacts: 1) basic model equipped as shown in Table 19.3; 2) the Impact equipped with some three square-meters of silicon-based solar cells, offering some 20-30 miles additional range per day on a single initial battery charge; and 3) the Impact equipped with an equal area of gallium-arsenide cells adding some 40-70 additional miles per day over the basic model. With the latter accessory the Impact would have a daily range approaching 200 miles which, while an expensive vehicle would almost surely rapidly reduce in price as costs of gallium-arsenide cells (like the history of other solid state elements) lower in price. With such an extended range few drivers would be concerned with running out of "gas" even in a city as extended as Los Angeles.

---

[38] *The New York Times*, March 5, 1991, pp. C1 & C5.
[39] *The New York Times*, February 10, 1990, p. 19.

Table 19-3

Impact Specifications

General

Curb weight, lb.	2,200
Gross weight, lb.	2,550
Weight distribution (w/driver) f/r	53/47
Wheelbase, in.	95.0
Track, f/r	57.9/48.4
Length, in.	163.0
Width, in.	68.2
Height, in.	47.5
Ground clearance, in.	6.0
Drag coefficient	0.19

Drivetrain

Type	front-wheel drive one motor for each wheel
Transmission	single-ratio planetary
Final drive ratio	10.5:1
Lubrication	oil spray
Efficiency, typical	94 to 98%

Motors

Type	AC induction
Bhp @ rpm	57 @ 6600 rpm × 2, 114 total
Torque, lb/ft	47 @ 9 to 6000 rpm × 2, 94 total
Efficiency, typical	90-95%

Electronics

Type	dual MOSFET inverters
Max current, A (to each motor)	159 A rms
Max System voltage	400V
Frequency range	0 to 500 hz
Battery charger	integral part of dual inverter package, computer-controlled
Max charge rate	50 Amps, 400V

Table 19-3 (Cont)

Impact Specifications

Batteries

Type	Delco Remy recombinant lead-acid
Pack configuration	32 10V batteries in series packaged in central tunnel
Capacity	42.5 Amp-hours, 13.6 kWh
Pack weight	870 lb.

Chassis and Body

Type	glass-fiber unit body simulating aluminum
Brake system	front: 10.7-inch solid discs with 4-piston aluminum calipers
	rear: 7.1-inch aluminum drums regenerative braking through drive motors
Tires	low rolling resistance Goodyear radials P-165/65 R 14,65 psi
Wheels	forged aluminum, 14 × 4
Steering	rack and pinion
Suspension f/r	double wishbone, coil springs
Glazing	PPG "Sungate"

Calculated data

lb/hp (gross weight)	22
Motor rpm at 65 mph	9500

Performance

0-60 mph, sec	8.0
Standing 1/4 mile, sec	16.7
Range at 55 mph, mi	120
Urban driving range, mi	124

*   *   *

Figure 19.19. The Induction Motor from GM's Impact. David Sloan, GM.

Figure 19.20. Impact's Inverter (under hood). David Sloan, GM.

In 1969, more than two decades before the writing of this book was completed, an early AC drive van had its tryout as written by the author at that time. With this background there can be an appreciation of the historical paragraphs below. Where Hiram Percy Maxim discovered the concept of "touring" as related in Chapter 9, the author felt a similar exhilaration in the next section. It was a fulfillment of the 1965 sudden burst of inspiration as cited above.

Note

An Early AC-Drive Electric Vehicle Trip

At long last the day had come to demonstrate our alternating current drive electric vehicle. It was believed to be the first ever sold, and would be an outgrowth of the sudden inspiration I had received of using voltage pulses from a battery to operate an alternating current induction motor.

The method of achieving this transformation of direct current power to alternating current power had come to me as a sudden flash while in Evanston walking along Sherman Avenue, in the company of Richard Karlin and Gary Comiskey. They were speaking of power silicon control rectifiers, while I was listening. The concept that flashed through my mind was given in considerable detail. From this revelation to driving a vehicle, however, would entail far greater travail than I ever expected, for the effort was surely the state of the art, and it would cost me what had remained of my fortune, and much more.

The first very considerable effort, where we had an excellent operating stationary a-c motor, I had largely funded myself, with ancillary money from a fork-lift truck company. However, the project required still more money. It was then that Thomas Ayers, President of Commonwealth Edison Company, with good heart, had written a letter to the several presidents of electric utilities bordering his own, in which he concluded "kindly receive Dr. Wakefield as you would me." In this letter he had outlined the a-c drive electric vehicle, as presented to him.

With Ayers' recognition and my persistence I visited what ultimately became 63 presidents of electric utilities from Florida to Washington State, from Southern California to Connecticut, and telephoned possibly 30 more whom I was not able to visit. With this effort I raised some $110,000 as outright grants, a tiny sum compared to the amount subsequently spent by General Motors Corporation on what would be a similar project, but of much greater scope. By letter I also contacted a large number of companies which could conceivably contribute product to such a vehicle. Twenty-five responded with the product I asked them to furnish. Again a grant for the a-c drive electric vehicle utilizing the principle of frequency and pulse width modulation. These gifts were: fuses, insulators, resistors, cable, instruments, batteries, capacitors, insulating tape, stand-off insulators, etc. The squirrel-cage motor, specially designed, and the silicon control rectifiers, the SCRs, we had to buy. The Chrysler Corporation was gracious enough to supply the Dodge van.

At long last, under the technical supervision of Dr. Gordon J. Murphy, Professor of Electrical Engineering at Northwestern University, Andrew M. Wohlert, a good basic electrical engineer with experience with SCRs, and Robert Kearney, who had worked with me in my previous nuclear instrument company, our electric a-c drive vehicle was ready to try. For this attempt the left rear wheel was jacked-up. Would it turn? That was the question.

The transmission was placed in low gear, the ignition switch of the Dodge van was closed, the accelerator pedal depressed, which closed the contactor placing power on the inverter from the battery. Sure enough the wheel did turn, but like a movie picture of a wheel which jerked ahead and then stopped, etc. Apparent to all, the three phases of the inverter were not properly functioning. Hardly an impressive performance, but wonderful to those of us who were the sole witnesses, after the many months of trial.

With more adjustments of the inverter control, by watching the oscilloscope screen, Dr. Murphy, Wohlert, and Kaney had the wheel turning uniformly, and, as the pedal was depressed, or let up, the speed of rotation was controlled. The car was then lowered, the jack removed. With proper manipulation of normal vehicle controls the van, we found, would go forward and backward, as the gear-shift was varied. I suggested we try driving the vehicle around the outside of the building. This task was done, but only at the cost of three inverter fuses, which, in our earlier experiments, we surely must have consumed at least 1,000, and at $3.75 each, one could appreciate the supply given us by the Shawmut Company, the fusemaker.

As the circuit now appeared to operate properly, on the subsequent day I drove our a-c electric car a number of times around the block to accumulate 11 miles. All worked well. As Illinois Bell had advanced us some $15,000, the time came at last for calling in the TV cameras. With both audio and camera both Dr. Murphy and I were interviewed. Then with the cameraman stationed at a corner for pictures, the interviewer aboard, along with Wohlert driving, Dr. Murphy in the passenger seat, and myself behind, we departed the shop, turned right on Emerson Street, proceeded under the two viaducts with their respective slopes and slight hills, north on Green Bay Road, going between 30-35 mph, the speed of the other traffic, up a small rise, onto the bridge which here crossed the canal, right on Lincoln Street, right again on Sherman Avenue, right again on Emerson, returning to the shop, a distance of probably two miles. All had gone well. The audio interviewer had been impressed, but those of us who had done the travail were even more awed. The TV men had obtained some good footage and gained a story. This trip, in the vehicle shown in Fig. 19.9, I believed, was the first public demonstration of an a-c drive electric car that was sold.

CHAPTER 20

Electric Vehicles from Conversions—
Early 1970s

After the tour de force a-c drive systems of both General Motors and Linear Alpha, Inc., a few other American companies initiated work on electric vehicles. For the most part they were vehicles which assembled the current best in electric elements which had been developing over the preceding ten years, a period of great progress in solid state components. In either conversion of the Detroit vehicles or in modification of chassis and body, both the Ford Motor Company, under Lewis E. Unnewehr, and Linear Alpha applied computer design to electric cars. In this technique a computer program is written linking the many characteristics of a vehicle such as its mass, acceleration desired, top speed requested, battery characteristics, gear ratios, windage factors, rolling resistance, and other parameters. The computer then prints out the torque-speed requirements for the motor to yield the desired vehicle performance. The motor must be designed to meet these needs.

This elegant, time-saving, and successful computer approach to electric car design enables one to predict with reasonable accuracy a vehicle's performance based on a paper study. One then has a true electrical-mechanical-chemical vehicle system yielding superior value to the consumer. The unsuccessful electric cars of the 1970s which marred the development of electric personal transportation failed to pass through this sophisticated design sieve.

American Conversions

Late 1960 American IC vehicles converted to battery power were privately shown by both the Ford Motor Company and by General Motors. Figure 20.1 illustrates an experimental Ford E-car described by Dr. W.H. Koch at the Electric Vehicle Symposium of 1969. Curb weight was 3,086 pounds. Power was supplied by nickel-cadmium batteries to a conventional 52-hp d-c motor.

In addition to the two a-c drive cars cited in Chapter 19, General Motors also constructed a sophisticated d-c electric drive system in an Opel Kadette,[1] shown in Figs. 20.2 and 20.3. This

---

[1] The General Motors *XEP* electric vehicle.
   See Also: M.A. Hind, *An Appraisal of Battery-Electric Vehicles*, Part II, *Electric Vehicles*, September 1973, p. 11.

Figure 20.1. The Ford experimental E-car described by Dr. W.H. Koch at the Electric Vehicle 1969 Symposium. A 108 volt nickel-cadmium battery powers a 52 hp d-c motor. General Motors Corp.

car, powered with both lead-acid and zinc-air batteries with mechanical recharge features, used two d-c drive motors, with current and speed control regulated by a d-c chopper. This car, like other GM efforts, is a research design vehicle. The GM XEP had a reported range of 90 miles at 55 mph. The principle of zinc-air batteries utilized in the GM XEP received considerable investment in their original development from the electric utilities through funding from the Edison Electric Institute. The work was done by the General Atomics Corporation. The prime interest of the electric utilities was an attempt to develop a battery that could be charged at night, and used to supply energy to their distribution system during the day. It was an attempt to achieve "peak shaving," a subject discussed in the section Edison Electric Institute Electric Truck Purchase, Chapter 24.

Examples of the computer-designed vehicles were the Thunderbolt 240, and the Linearvan 240, where the digits represent the voltage to the on-board charger. With "polishing," which one can achieve with computer manipulation, these vehicles can reach a high standard of excellence. This method obsoletes more primitive approaches while reducing the cost of development. In addition, the consumer is assured a superior product. These two vehicles were produced by Linear Alpha, Inc. of Evanston, Illinois in the early 1970s. The electric-powered Linearvan 240 was based on the Dodge van, and, like the gasoline version, was available in its many styles and options. The 108-inch wheelbase models had a top speed of 55 miles per hour. Acceleration from 0 to 30 mph was 10 seconds. The urban driving range was from 25 to 30 miles. An on-board 240-volt charger supplied power to the 144-volt motive power battery system. The battery complement weighed some 1,600 pounds. Curb weight of the smaller van was about

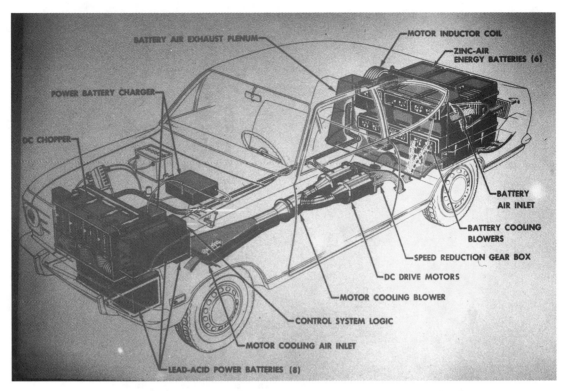

Figure 20.2. The General Motors XEP electric car had lead-acid batteries for acceleration, and zinc-air batteries for energy to enhance range. The vehicle was a tour de force where cost is no object. General Motors.

4,880 pounds. Figure 20.4, right to left, shows both the Linearvan 240 and the Thunderbolt 240 in Washington, D.C., June 3, 1975, during the Congressional hearings before the Electric Vehicle Research, Development, and Demonstration Act of 1976. Figure 12.5 is under the hood of the Thunderbolt 240 showing five major components. The balance of the drive system is similar to the description below, except each element is designed for the van with its greater curb weight. Figure 20.5 shows qualitative energy losses at various speeds for a van.

The Thunderbolt 240 was a converted Ford Pinto. Harry Schmerler, then Chicago's largest Ford dealer, exclaimed after driving with a Ford executive, "One can't fault this vehicle." The Thunderbolt had a top speed of 60 mph, an acceleration of 0-30 mph in 8 seconds, a range in urban driving of 35 miles. Bearing an on-board 240-volt charger, the vehicle employed a 108-volt motive-power battery system. Both vehicles had chopper-controlled current flow to the series-wound motor. These vehicles were offered until 1979 when the absence of market led to discontinuance of manufacture.

A persevering developer of electric vehicles in the middle 1960s and beyond was Robert R. Aronson, President of Electric Fuel Propulsion Company of Detroit. Figure 20.6 illustrates one of his high performance automobiles, the 1977 Transformer I, unveiled in Dusseldorf in August 1976. Aronson used a battery of his own manufacture containing three internal connectors (Tripolar) and a cobalt additive which, he claimed, permitted a more rapid charge

Figure 20.3. General Motors engineer Harold A. Schulte inserts zinc anodes into one of the six zinc-air batteries which give the experimental XEP car its long range. Developed at GM Research Laboratories, the electric car can travel about 150 miles at 30 miles per hour. GMResearch Photo 6-11-70.

Figure 20.4. Linear Alpha, Inc. Thunderbolt 240 and Linear Van 240 driven respectively by Howard C. Collins and Professor Gordon J. Murphy to the U.S. Congress June 3, 1975. Courtesy: Potomac Electric Power Company.

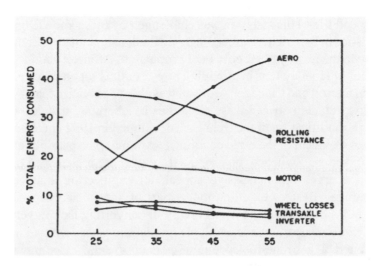

Figure 20.5. Qualitative energy loss distribution at various speeds (for an electric van ETX-1). J. E. Fenton & P. B. Patil.

Figure 20.6. Transformer I, an electric-powered car by Electric Fuel Propulsion Corp., Detroit. Courtesy: Electric Fuel Propulsion.

while prolonging cell life. This assertion was challenged by those knowledgeable in the field, but the characteristics of batteries are exceedingly difficult to quantify under dynamic operating conditions. Early in the history of Electric Fuel Propulsion, Aronson obtained the cooperation of the management of Holiday Inns in providing power outlets for electric vehicles in a stretch of motels between Detroit and Chicago. Aronson was able to publicize that it was now possible to drive an electric vehicle between these two cities by charging at successive hotels. This achievement was a modification of the technique developed in 1902 and discussed in Chapter 9. Aronson was an exponent of the rapid charging technique. The batteries used in propulsion were connected in series. Switched, on CHARGE, they were replenished in parallel strings. While the "rapid charge" has persuasive appeal, an engineering analysis illuminates its unattractive features.[2] Besides extolling the virtues of specialized batteries, Electric Fuel Propulsion design has been directed toward luxury in converting Detroit vehicles.

Subsequently, the company made available an electric sedan with an attached trailer in which was mounted a gasoline-fueled engine-generator set.[3] Continually charging the batteries, the vehicle was able to travel substantial distances, making, indeed, in 1976 the passage from Detroit to Washington, with time out only for the driver to rest.

Government Subsidized Electric Vans

The specific vehicle known simply as a van in America was developed in the United States by designers from General Motors, Ford, and Chrysler in close association with the automotive staff of American Telephone & Telegraph Company (AT&T) and transportation engineers from other utilities. This vehicle undoubtedly had a bearing on the British Bedford AC van.[4] Capable of adequate speed, the closed-in van protects both the driver as well as the contained equipment from the weather, and the latter from vandals. This van, designed for industrial needs, soon became a favorite of the general public as a recreational vehicle as well. All the above is generally well known. Perhaps more obscure is that historically this commercial vehicle was one of the earliest of the modern transportation types to be converted to electric power, as observed in Chapter 19. It was natural therefore in implementing the Electric & Hybrid Vehicle Act of 1976, the U.S. Department of Energy (DOE) would choose a group of vans for fleet-trial operation. The Culver City, California section of AT&T was chosen by the DOE for a test of 20 vans.

Developed by GMC Truck & Coach Division of General Motors for AT&T, this van had a top speed of 50 mph. The conversion is said to have a range in excess of 40 miles, an acceleration from 0-30 mph in 12 seconds with a 50 hp d-c motor transversely mounted.[5] The controller is a silicon-control rectifier providing pulse-width modulated d-c current to the motor for speed control. The useful pay load is 1,500 pounds. The van contains 36 Delco-Remy

---

[2] A *demand charge* is levied by a utility to defray the cost of providing distribution to an outlet that has highly irregular use.

[3] Ernest H. Wakefield, *The Consumer's Electric Car*, Ann Arbor: The Ann Arbor Science Press, Inc., 1977, presents 26 additional ideas for increasing the range of an electric vehicle.

[4] See Chapter 22.

[5] Paul O. Larson, *Commercial Electric Vehicle Program at General Motors, Electric Vehicle News*, Vol. 8, No. 2, May 1979, pp. 4-7.

maintenance-free lead-acid batteries each of 12 volt rating, connected to series-parallel to yield a 216 volt system. The contained energy is 32 kWh. A fan exhausts and cools the battery box. Equipped with regenerative braking, the range of the vehicle is expected to be increased by some 10 percent. The fleet of vans were placed in service the end of 1979 for a test expected to last three years.

Further American Conversions

In 1975 Electric Vehicle Associates (EVA) of Cleveland, Ohio commercially offered the electrically converted Lancia. It had a claimed speed of 60 mph, an acceleration from 9-30 mph in 9 seconds. Its claimed range was 60 miles.[6] The vehicle carried an 108 volt battery system and a 120 volt on-board charger. Figure 20.7 illustrates this model. Earlier EVA had shown an electric-powered Ford Pinto, and later, as shown in the next chapter, the company was to offer the Otis Elevator developed electric van, as well as the Electrobus produced by Boris Borisoff who will again appear as a co-designer of the Sundancer. To more fully participate in the American battery market, and to be a part in the development of electric vehicles in America, Chloride Battery Company of Great Britain assumed a financial stake in Electric Vehicle Associates, Inc., allowing an enhanced participation in the emerging field. The key person in EVA has been President Warren C. Harhay.

Similar to the above electric car is the 1982 offering by EVA as shown in Fig. 20.8 together with the performance characteristics of the EVsport. The strict U.S. government safety regulations for public road travel, in practical terms, limits smaller manufacturers to converted

Figure 20.7. The Electric Vehicle Associates Lancia, converted from the Italian automobile of the same name. Courtesy: EVA, Cleveland.

---

[6] High, but dependent on characteristics of test.

Figure 20.8. The 1982 EVsport by Electric Vehicle Associates, Inc. Courtesy: EVA Inc.

vehicles, whose safety standards have been already met by the major IC car assemblers. The two-passenger EVsport had a wheelbase of 94.2 inches, a curb weight of 3,100 pounds, a given top speed of 70 mph, and a claimed range of 50 miles.

From 1974 to the beginning of 1982—seven years—EVA has placed 185 cars.[7] In the second revival of electric cars, this is one of the best records. Contrast that number with the 1902 figures in Chapter 9 when the growth of the automobile industry was limited only by what the nation could produce. Present electrics are even encouraged by a subsidy. One would conclude, therefore, that the niche then available in the economy was small. Electric Vehicle Associates, a well conceived firm, would cease operation in 1982 because of the anemic demand for electric cars.

In the second coming of electric cars, one of the larger manufactures converting standard IC automobiles to electrics was Jet Industries. This new Austin, Texas company developed a commercial d-c powered van which was shown at the 1975 Electric Vehicle Exposition in Chicago. The Electra Van, illustrated in Fig. 20.9, had been driven under its own power from its home city to Chicago. Batteries were charged enroute and on-board from an engine-generator mounted on a separately powered nurse-vehicle. Periodic stops were thus required. This practice is both a variation of battery interchange first practiced by Camille Jeantaud, the Frenchman, in the 705 mile Paris-Bordeaux and return race, described in Chapter 15, and the Aronson trailer bearing a battery charger. With this auspicious beginning the company has produced a few electric vehicles. The Electra Van had a reported curb weight of 2,350 pounds, a top speed of 55 mph, an acceleration from 0-30 mph in 20 seconds, and a range of 60 miles. Providing the energy were 960 pounds of batteries providing a nominal 96 volts.[8]

---

7 *Electrical Vehicle News*, Vol. 11, No. 1, February 1982, p. 14.

8 *Electric Light & Power*, October 1981, p. 10.

Figure 20.9. The Jet Industries, Inc., Electra Van of 1975. Courtesy: Commonwealth Edison Company.

An outgrowth of the subsidized electric fleet vehicle based on the Electric & Hybrid Vehicle Act of 1975 led Jet Industries Inc. to offer a pick-up truck to the successful winner of this competition, one of which was GTE. The vehicle's characteristics are similar to that of the van, while the vehicle is illustrated in Fig. 20.10. Of the 1,523 electric vehicles produced in the fiscal year ending July 1981, Jet Industries was reported as the second largest maker.[9]

By June 1982, the new Chairman of the Company, Mr. Frederix P. DeVeau, had been charged by the Security and Exchange Commission: "In April 1982 Mr. DeVeau acquired control of Jet Industries," the (SEC) complaint charges, "and once again did so by fraudulently arranging for his shares to be paid for from the corporation assets of the company he acquired."[10] The *Times* continued, "The Commission complaint also charged (the Chairman).....diverted more than $2 million in company assets for his own use. Mr. DeVeau, a convicted felon, was also accused of hiding his criminal record from the stockholders and officials of the company."

Several days later a financial journal wrote, "Jet Industries Inc. directors fired Frederix P. DeVeau, its Chairman and Chief Executive Officer, who was recently charged by the Securities and Exchange Commission with 'looting' the company....John W. Tillus, a Dallas businessman familiar with Jet, will assume the post of Chairman and Chief Executive on an interim basis."[11]

---

[9] *Electric Vehicle News*, Vol. 8, No. 4, November 1979.
[10] *The New York Times*, June 2, 1982, p. 10.
[11] *Jet Industries Fires Chairman Who Faces SEC Looting Charge, The Wall Street Journal*, June 4, 1982, p. 10.

Figure 20.10. The Jet Industries pick-up truck. Courtesy:[9] Electric Vehicle News.

Finally, the company's losses[12] increased from $268,376 on sales of $1.9 million in 2nd quarter of 1981, to $471,544 on sales of $110,877 in 2nd quarter of 1982. Such a precipitous drop in sales almost surely reflects a greater stringency of federal subsidies to the Electric Vehicle Program. And finally for Mr. DeVeau the media reported he was serving a twenty-year sentence for fraud.[13]

Shortly before the above financial development President Fred Klamach had introduced a battery-powered Ford Fiesta, and subsequently the Ford Escort, renamed on being battery-powered to Electrica. The re-emerged Fiesta bore an 84 volt lead-acid battery component. Its reported top speed was 60 mph, with a stated range of 60 miles at 35 mph. In the Electrica additional batteries were added to yield 96 volts. This added charge gave a reported top speed of 70 mph, and a range of 65 miles at an average speed of 35 mph. Ten Electricas at this writing are being tested by the Austin Texas Northeast Post Office. Over a three-month period the average energy used had been 0.88 kWh per mile with average route miles of 1,522 per month.[14]

---

[12] David Stipp, *SEC Investigation of Jet Industries Centers on Where the Money Went, The Wall Street Journal*, July 12, 1982, p. 15.

[13] Stanley Penn, *Con Artist's Fraud Case Reveals Flaws in Witness Protection Plan, The Wall Street Journal*, May 22, 1984, p. 22.

[14] *Electric Vehicle News*, Vol. 11, No. 1, February 1982, p. 9.

The reader will recall the 1917 Atlantic City to New York City electric car trip consumed 0.25 kWh per mile.[15] In one sense the modern design was advancing backwards. The Electrica should be compared with the British Firefly, a converted Fiesta, reported in Chapter 22. Figure 20.11 is the Jet Industries Electrica.

The G Van

Arriving late in the 1980s was the G Van. The vehicle was based on the GMC Vandura, a production line IC vehicle. Modification to an electric was by Cars & Concepts of Brighton, Michigan. The battery pack is 36 six-volt lead-acid batteries with a central watering hole. The vehicle has an on-board 200/250 volt charger. "The G Van propulsion system is a separately excited 216 volt, 42 kW d-c motor mated to a single-ratio, chain-driven primary reduction unit. The propulsion unit is located under the cargo floor to the right rear of the vehicle. A short drive shaft connects the chain drive to the rear axle. The controller has transistor armature and field choppers. Regenerative braking is provided with a dash-mounted switch for disabling purposes."[16]

Figure 20.11. The Jet Industries battery-powered Electrica.

---

[15] *Ibid*, pp. 14-15.
[16] R. L. Driggans and G. D. Whitehead. *Performance Characterization Testing of the GM Griffon and G Van.* The 9th International Electric Vehicle Symposium, Toronto, 1988.

Below, in Table 20-1, are the measured characteristics of both the G van and the Griffon electric van. The latter, a forerunner of the G Van, was assembled by the General Motors Luton, England works. The G Van, shown in Fig. 20.12, was tested along with the Griffon at the Tennessee Valley Authority test facilities. It may be produced.

The Soleq Evcort

The Evcort is equipped with an air-conditioner and heater/defroster which are powered from the main traction battery pack. The effect of operating the air-conditioner on vehicle energy consumption and range was determined from dynamometer test data, and the effectiveness of the air-conditioner and heater/defroster were assessed by performing field tests of the Evcort under both summer and winter conditions. The performance of the air-conditioner and heater/defroster in the Evcort was compared to that of the factory packages in the ICE Escort by performing side-by-side tests of the two vehicles.

From dynamometer tests, it was found that the average power from the battery to operate the air-conditioner in the Evcort was about 1.5 kW and that its effect was to increase the energy consumption by 25% at 48 km/h, 11% at 88 km/h, and 27% on the FUDS driving cycle. The corresponding reductions in range were 22%, 10%, and 17% respectively.

Table 20-1. Griffon and G Van Test Results		
	Griffon	G Van
Test Weight (kg)	3,076	3,530
Maximum Speed (km/h)	85	83
Constant speed 56 km/h dc Energy Consumption (Wh/km)	204	223
Acceleration Time 9 to 48 km/h (s)	11.4	12.9
Braking Distance from 48 km/h (m)	15.6	16.3
Range on 10-Percent Grade (km)	17.4	3.7
Battery Capacity at 75 A Discharge		
Rated (Ah)	144.2	175.5
Measured (Ah)	139	161
MEASURED DATA		
Constant Speed 56 km/h Range (km)	154.8	163.0
SAE J227a C Cycle Range (km)	114.3	111.0
Urban Route Range (km)	95.8	73.3
TEMPERATURE COMPENSATED DATA		
Constant Speed 56 km/h Range (km)	150.2	153.6
SAE J227a C Cycle Range (km)	104.4	95.9
Urban Route Range (km)	88.2	64.5

Figure 20.12. GM G Van. R. L. Driggane and G. D. Whitehead.

In field tests of the air conditioner in Phoenix, Arizona at an ambient temperature of 34°C (94°F), relative humidity of approximately 25%, the cool-down time to 26°C (80°F) from an initial temperature of 48°C (118°F) inside the vehicle was 24 minutes with the Evcort stationary and 20 minutes when the vehicle was moving at 56 km/h. The corresponding values for the ICE Escort were 17 minutes and 14 minutes respectively. The 2 kW heater/defroster in the Evcort was evaluated in an outdoor test in Idaho Falls, Idaho during the winter with an ambient temperature of -12°C (15°F). The heat-up time to 0°C (32°F) with the heater operating was 10-12 minutes in the Evcort and 5-6 minutes in the ICE Escort. The time required (starting with a thick layer of ice) to defrost 50% of the windshield was 27 minutes in the Evcort and 18 minutes in the ICE Escort.[17]

Tables 20-2, 20-3, and 20-4 show Evcort vehicle and powertrain characteristics and a summary of test results while Fig. 20.13 shows the vehicle.

While the prose and pictures of Chapter 20 have related the conversion of IC vehicles to electric drive in a manner earlier followed in modifying wagons to electric vehicles at the close of the 19th century, the next chapter discusses the more seminal development, the assembly of compleat electric vehicles, here defined as a type of personal and truck transportation conceived and built solely for electric power propulsion. The analogy with the pioneer period is the evolution to the Torpedo design in both electric and in IC vehicles of 1902,[18] a form still followed today.

---

[17] R.L. Crumley, R.D. MacDowell, J.E. Hardin, and A.F. Burke, *Performance Testing and System Evaluation of the Soleq Evcort Vehicle,* Idaho National Engineering Laboratory, U.S. Dept. of Energy, DOE/ID-10232, March 1989.
[18] See Chapter 15, the Jenatzy and Baker racing cars.

Table 20-2. Evcort Vehicle Characteristics	
Test weight (kg)	1968
Tire Rolling Radius (m)	0.289 @ 35 psi
Aerodynamic Drag Coefficient	0.42
Frontal Area (m^2)	1.90
Rolling resistance (@ 80.5 km/h) CO	0.011
Battery System Weight (kg)	672
Peak Motor Power (kW)	32

Table 20-3. Evcort Vehicle Characteristics	
Motor	
Type	Separately Excited dc
Peak Power (kW)	32 @ 98V, 400A, 1600 RPM
Maximum Speed (rpm)	6000
Maximum torque (N-M)	191
Corner Speed	1600
Manufacturer	General Electric Company
Controller	
Manufacturer	Soleq (U.S. Patent 4322667)
Maximum Current (A)	400
Transmission	
Type	5-speed manual
Manufacturer	Production Ford unit
Battery	
Type	Sealed lead-acid
Weight (kg)	
Individual module (6 V)	37.3
System	672
Voltage (nominal system)	108
Capacity (new)	
AH at C/3	168
kWh at C/3	18
Capacity (after 34 cycles)	
Ah at C/3	119
kWh at C/3	13
Manufacturer	Concorde

Table 20-4. Evcort Summary Test Results

	Energy Consumption (wh/km) (without air conditioning)					Energy Consumption (Wh/km) (with air conditioning)				
Test Type	Range (km)	Wall AC	System DC	Gross DC	Net DC	Range (km)	Wall AC	System DC	Gross DC	Net DC
48k m/h (constant speed)	154.3	172	154	119	119	119.7	208	186	149	149
88 km/h (constant speed)	76.6	299[a]	269[a]	160	160	70.5	255	243	179	179
C-cycle	74.8	341[a]	306[a]	214	201	60.9	440	393	283	272
FUDS	67.6	313	278	226	212	60.2	408	364	281	270

Acceleration (seconds)

Battery State-of Charge	100% SOC	55% SOC	37% SOC	17% SOC
Speed				
0-48 km/h	8.3	8.7	9.2	12.5
0-80 km/h	25.6	26.1	28.1	48.5
0-88 km/h	32.5	32.8	36.0	--

<u>Note</u>: Test with the air conditioner on, indicated acceleration performance of the Evcort was not affected by use of the air contitioner.

<u>Energy Consumption Definitions</u>

$$AC = \frac{\text{AC Energy to Charger for Recharge}}{\text{Distance Traveled}}$$

$$\text{System DC} = \frac{\text{DC Energy From Charger for Recharge}}{\text{Distance Traveled}}$$

$$\text{Veh. DC Gross} = \frac{\text{DC Energy From Battery While Driving (not including Regen Benefit)}}{\text{Distance Traveled}}$$

$$\text{Veh. DC Net} = \frac{\text{DC Energy From Battery While Driving (including Regen Benefit)}}{\text{Distance Traveled}}$$

a These values are due to significant battery overcharge caused by an inappropriate charger cutoff criteria.

Figure 20.13. The Evcort Electric. S. Ohba (1993).

CHAPTER 21

The Compleat Electric Vehicle

The year 1977 would be the important year for electric cars just as 1902 had been the critical time for all types of automobiles. The innovative a-c drive systems were perceived at the time as too complex and too expensive. The d-c conversions of standard Detroit models, on the other hand, gave insufficient range for the vehicles to be viable in the marketplace, and the low performance electric cars with their premium prices offered insufficient quality of transportation to succeed. In part, vehicles designed after the oil crisis of 1973 would be influenced by the impact of events discussed in a subsequent chapter, and by the pacesetting vehicle Sundancer.[1]

One of the early companies to design a high performance compleat[1a] electric vehicle was the McKee Engineering Corporation of Palatine, Illinois. Cooperatively designed and developed by Robert S. McKee and personnel from the Exide Battery Company in 1970 the Sundancer was one of the first third-generation electric vehicles—one designed wholly as battery propelled. The two-seated Sundancer had a curb weight of 1,640 pounds, a speed of 60 mph, an acceleration from 0 to 30 mph in 8 seconds, and a single-charge range in urban driving of some 60-70 miles. The vehicle possessed a 120-volt on-board charger. Energy consumption of the vehicle was 0.3 kWh per mile, an equivalence for gasoline of 123 miles per gallon. This car is shown in Fig. 21.1. In Fig. 21.2 McKee demonstrates access to the batteries, while the belt-linked motor drive and subsequent gear-reduction to the wheels is shown in Fig.21.3.

Innovative also was the concept of battery interchange, first practiced by Jeantaud in the Paris-Bordeaux Race of 1895. In this principle, not unlike that followed by the New York Central Railroad for the *20th Century Limited* with locomotive interchanges at division points, the discharged batteries are exchanged for freshly energized ones so the trip may continue, a practice similar to the change of horses on the London-Brighton coach *Old Times*. With all its fine features the Sundancer as built fails to meet present standards for road safety. Builders today, unlike in the period of Riker, Wood, Baker, and designers discussed in earlier chapters, are far more restricted by government regulations.

Shortly after the revolutionary concepts of electric drive developed both by GM and by Linear Alpha, the Ford Motor Company, under the general direction of Dr. Louis Unnewehr,

---

[1] Robert S. McKee, Boris Borisoff, Frank Lawn, and James F. Norberg, *Sundancer: A Test Bed Electric Vehicle*, *Soc. of Auto. Engineers*, Detroit, January 10-14, 1972, Paper 720188.

[1a] A compleat electric vehicle is one originally built as an electric vehicle, as differentiated from a conversion.

Figure 21.1. The Sundancer greatly influenced the revival of electric cars. Courtesy: McKee Engineering Corporation. Photos by Su Kemper.

Figure 21.2. Sundancer body with batteries withdrawn. Courtesy: McKee Engineering Corporation. Photo by Su Kemper.

Figure 21.3. In the Sundancer the motor was belt-linked to the countershaft which in turn was geared to the wheels. The box-chassis contains the battery for interchange. Courtesy: McKee Engineering Corporation. Photo by Su Kemper.

conceived and brought forth the technically attractive disc type d-c motor.[2] One version, built by students at MIT for the cross-country race of 1968, is illustrated in Chapter 24. In 1967 the Ford Company demonstrated a compleat electric car, the d-c powered Comuta City illustrated in Figs. 21.4 and 21.5.[3] This vehicle had a curb weight of 1,550 pounds, had space for two adults and two children, was powered with 380 pounds of lead-acid batteries with characteristics of 48 volts and 120 Ah. Power to the wheels was furnished by two 3 3/4 hp, 24 volt motors each weighing 39 pounds. The controller was by time-ratio. Top speed was 40 mph, and the range at 25 mph was some 37 miles. Another Ford electric was seen earlier, but like the work at GM, effort was referentially directed to the more specific task of enhancement of energy storage in batteries.[4]

Earlier than the Sundancer cited above, but less influential, in 1968 the General Electric Company, with a team headed by Dr. Peter J. Stewart, designed and built the Delta,[5] shown in

---

[2] *Electric Vehicle Systems Study*, Ford Motor Company, Technical Report SR-73-132, October 25, 1973.

[3] L. Martland, A. E. Lynes, L. R. Foote, *The Ford Comuta - An Electric Car for Use in City and Suburb*, SAE 680428.

[4] *The Electric Car: A Design Challenge, Electro Technology*, May 1968, p. 58.

[5] B. R. Laumeister, *The GE Electric Vehicle*, Soc. of Automotive Engs., Inc., Two Pennsylvania Plaza, New York, N.Y. 10001. #680430, pp. 20-24, May 1968.

Figure 21.4. Comuta City Car. Courtesy: Ford Motor Company.

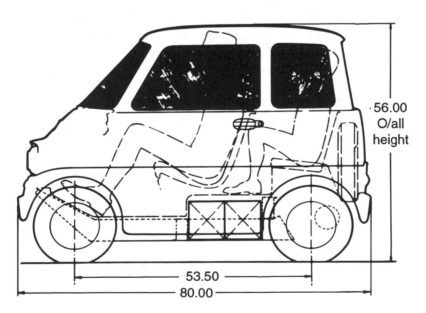

Figure 21.5. Comuta package, side view. Courtesy: Ford Motor Company.

Figure 21.6. The General Electric Delta was built to show the status of electric vehicles in 1968. It contained both iron-nickel and lead-acid batteries, the former for acceleration, the latter for cruising. Courtesy: General Electric Company.

Fig. 21.6. This car was the result of a research program. It had a curb weight of 2,300 pounds, a top speed of 55 mph, an acceleration of 0-30 mph in 6 seconds, and an urban driving range of 40 miles. An attractively designed automobile, unique to the Delta, besides it being a truly high performance vehicle, was its energy storage system. For the high specific power required for acceleration, iron-nickel batteries supplied a significant share of the total energy;[6] while for cruising the lead-acid batteries provided power for the d-c motor. The motor of cumulative-wound compound design obtained continuous speed control both by employment of a chopper in the armature circuit and by field control. With the Delta, GE demonstrated the validity of their computer program. Its development, during a refreshing engineering period in personal transportation, represents an excursion into public relations. The Delta, because it was well done, was a positive force in making more people electric vehicle conscious. Ten years after the Delta General Electric would produce the Centennial, shown a few pages beyond.

In 1969 Wayne E. Goldman was instrumental in organizing the "Electro-motion" Transportation System Laboratory of Anderson Power Products, Inc. The latter company had been in existence as a producer, among other electrical items, of heavy current junction connectors used in the well-established electric fork-lift truck industry. Goldman's group brought out a vehicle designed from the ground up as an electric. Offered for sale at the 1973 Third Annual Electric

---

[6] Ray Hudson, *The Nickel-Iron Battery for Electric Vehicle Propulsion, Electric Vehicle News*, November 1981, pp. 12-16.

Vehicle Exposition in Washington for $5,995, this open, two-seated runabout received some sales to island resorts. Production ended in 1974.

Electromotion also developed a test van for the Post Office contract, designated the T-3. It had a top speed of 40 mph, an urban range of 30 miles, accelerated 0-30 mph in 15.6 seconds. The 84 volt battery system, through a solid state chopper control, operated a nominal 20 hp motor with capacity for a peak of 35 hp. The vehicle had a curb weight of 3,000 pounds, with a payload capability of 700 pounds. Only a few of these test vehicles were made. Finding little market, Anderson Power Products disposed of this electric vehicle division to the division employees. A financial transfusion was given by the Exxon Corporation, but the company became defunct in 1974. The Electromotion test van is illustrated in Fig. 21.7.

In 1973 the Otis Elevator Company, purchasing an operating company making small electric vehicles, announced their P-500 van, ostensibly as a service vehicle, and for a pending Post Office order. The vehicle had a top speed of 43 mph, an urban driving range of 40 miles, a battery system of 96 volts, utilizing McCullough batteries. The vehicle had an acceleration of 0-15 mph in 3.6 seconds and 0-30 mph in 10.2 seconds. In curb weight the vehicle was 3,150 pounds, and in gross vehicle weight 4,200 pounds. Feeding through a solid-state chopper the power flowed to a nominal 30 hp motor. In 1975 the price of the P-500 was $9,078 less batteries and charger. Batteries were $2,450, while the charger was $750. The vehicle had been accorded an elaborate introduction with flowers and with female models. About 15 were sold at full price before senior management closed the facility.[7] The equipment was subsequently auctioned. Electric Vehicle Associates (EVA), in conjunction with Chloride of Great Britain, obtained the completed vehicles and inventory, which had been transported from Davis, California (some construction continued at the new site of Bedford, Ohio). It was a dismal demise from the flashbulb popping ceremony when the vehicle was first offered to the public at the Third International Electric Vehicle Conference. The van, bearing the subsequent purchaser's logo, is shown in Fig. 21.8.

Figure 21.7. Electromotion Test Van. Wayne E. Goldman.

---

[7] *The Wall Street Journal*, July 1975.

Figure 21.8. The Otis Elevator Van was designed as a compleat electric vehicle. The vehicle was subsequently available from Electric Vehicle Associates, Bedford, Ohio. Courtesy: EVA

Active in the second half of the 1960s, and later as exhibited in Chapter 19, Electric Fuel Propulsion Inc. of Ferndale, Michigan brought forth the complete 1/4 ton electric van illustrated in Fig. 21.9. The van with wheelbase of 88 1/2 inches, a capacity of 80 cu ft, a curb weight of 3,250 pounds, and a gross weight of 4,100 pounds was powered by a 20 hp series-wound d-c motor.[8] Speed control was achieved by chopper action. The motive power batteries could receive rapid charge from a 3-phase, 240 volt, 150 ampere rate, or at a more conventional 240 volt, 30 ampere circuit. The vehicle came equipped with hydraulic 4-wheel brakes, and had pressed steel wheels.

All the complete electric cars seen earlier were one of a kind or of limited production; the Citicar, however, in its two models seen below, was made in quantities of a few thousand.

---

[8]*Electrical World*, April 6, 1970, p. 53.

Figure 21.9. Compleat electric van by Electric Fuel Propulsion Inc., 1970. Courtesy: ASARCO.[9]

Tapping the Low Cost Market

In 1972 Robert G. Beaumont organized the Sebring-Vanguard Company.[10] The object of the corporation was to introduce to the public a low cost, two-seat vehicle of modest speed for local city driving. The vehicle was aptly named the Citicar. The first model was constructed on a then existing golf cart chassis, whose shocks and springs had been strengthened to assume the increased weight for the heavier load of batteries. Its length was 95 inches, width 55 inches. The body, of distinctive shape, as featured in Fig. 21.10, was vacuum heat-formed from acrylic. The chassis carried six 6-volt nominally 220 ampere-hour batteries. The vehicle was powered by a 3 1/2 hp series-wound d-c motor, had a curb weight of 1,305 pounds, a top speed of 30 mph, and accelerated from 0-30 mph in 18 seconds. In urban driving the Citicar had a range of 25 miles. Citicar was designed to sell originally at a price less than the lowest priced gasoline car which was being produced in far greater volume, about $3,000. *Consumer Reports'* agents paid $2,946 for a Citicar in 1975. When in production the vehicle was distributed through conventional automobile dealers, recreation vehicle dealers, and some were sold at Marinas.

Introduced at the 2nd International Conference on Electric Vehicles in Washington in 1973, the Citicar received much comment. The vehicle was excused for one year of provisions of the Federal Motor Vehicle Safety Standard in the following regards: defrosting and defogging, turn-signal cancellation, load bearing capabilities of latches and hinges, and omission of Type 2 seat belts. In use the modest speed of the car allowed only special licensing limiting the

---

9 ASARCO advertisement of June 18, 1970.
10 *Electric Vehicle News*, Vol. 1, No. 4, November 1972.

Figure 21.10. The first Citicar, Courtesy: Sebring Vanguard Co., Kingston, New York.

vehicle's use to secondary roads. A *Consumer Reports* article was very severe on reporting this vehicle.[11] While, indeed, there was much to be critical about the Citicar, the evaluator, in writing of his experiences, revealed enough about himself to indicate he thought that an electric car is a one-to-one replacement of a gasoline-powered car. Unfortunately, it is not.

In the second year of production, a modified model, employing a slightly changed body and chassis, was offered, including some 29 improvements, as stated by the company. *Consumer Reports* gave a tested speed of about 32 mph achieved by employment of a 6 hp motor. Acceleration from 0-30 mph was 19 seconds, 1.3 seconds longer than last year's model. Curb weight was now 1,405 pounds. Again a *Consumer Reports* article was extremely severe on the performance of this vehicle.[12] CR had paid the dealer $3,396 for a Citicar, which they tested. By the time of this second devastating article some 2,175 of both Citicar models had been manufactured before cessation of production as reported in the *Chicago Tribune*.[13] The Citicar failed to make the competitive grade despite an immense amount of publicity freely given by the media. On analysis one would need to conclude that the first two models of Citicar were insufficiently engineered, and profit margins were inadequate to provide sufficient cash flow to sustain manufacture. Figure 21.11 is an example of the last model.

In yet another attempt to find an electric car market the Yare was designed and built. As a 4-wheeled vehicle is far more restricted by government regulations, a 3-wheeler can possess more original designs. Unique about the Yare experimental electric vehicle, produced in 1975

---

[11] *Consumer Reports*, October 1975.

[12] *Consumer Reports*, October 1976.

[13] *The Chicago Tribune*, October 18, 1976.

Figure 21.11. The Citicar is inspected by a young lady under the steely gaze of Picasso's sculpture in Chicago City Hall's Plaza. Courtesy: Commonwealth Edison Company.

by T. P. Laboratories of LaPorte, Indiana, was the 3-wheel suspension. The number of wheels on a vehicle has always been of interest. There is, of course, the unicycle. Two-wheel bullock carts move a large share of commerce in India, and the 2-wheel bicycle is one of the most efficient machines ever invented, and the only one capable of carrying 10-times its own weight, as discussed in Chapter 8. The first electric vehicle by Gustave Trouvè was a 3-wheel velocipede; and Thomas Edison used a 3-wheel vehicle as a test-bed for his evolving nickel-alkaline battery.[14] The 4-wheel cart has an early lineage, and electric vehicles since the 1890s have been 4-wheeled. The modern Yare, therefore, is unique for its three wheels. It is believed only one Yare was assembled, Fig. 21.12.

The Yare, the manufacturer states, is a nautical term meaning: ready, complete, eager, lively, etc. The vehicle was designed by Dr. H. D. Kesling; motor and controls were by Robert Borisoff, whom we recognize from the Sundancer shown earlier; electrical installation was by Edward Arnold; fiberglass application by Albert Bates; customizing seating and upholstery by Jerry Landgraff; the design and machining of special parts was by Dennis Henderlong.

The Yare has a length of 168 inches, a height of 52 inches, a width of 72 inches, a wheel base of 144 inches, a turning radius of 17 feet, and a curb weight of 2,300 pounds. Seventy-two volts of lead-acid batteries (probably 720 pounds to yield a battery/curb weight ratio of 31 percent) powers a 12 hp, 2-speed motor to provide a top speed of 55 mph. Acceleration from 0-55 mph

---

[14] Milo Lindgren, *Electric Cars - Hope Springs Eternal, IEEE Spectrum*, April 1967, pp. 48-59.

Figure 21.12. The Yare, an experimental 3-wheel electric car, made by T. P. Laboratories, LaPorte, Indiana. Courtesy: Commonwealth Edison Company.

is in 12 seconds. The range is said to be 50 miles.[15] The Yare is an example of physical design change which is more likely to occur with an entrepreneur who combines an alternate drive system with the flexibility of plastics and an appreciation of aerodynamics, a freedom still possible to exercise under government regulations as long as three wheels are employed.

One of the better electric sedans constructed at the end of the 1970s was the one-of-a-kind Endura, owned by Globe-Union Battery Company, and shown in Fig. 21.13. Built by McKee Engineering Corporation the Endura was a complete electric vehicle featuring a fiberglass body of low windage, late-style, high specific energy and power lead-acid batteries. The latter could be readily interchanged by the method illustrated in Fig. 21.2, an outgrowth of the Sundancer system pictured earlier.

Specifications for the Endura included a wheel base of 108 inches, with a rear wheel drive powered by a 20 hp, 120 volt, series-wound, 0-5000 rpm motor. Energy was supplied from 1,300 pounds of lead-acid batteries. Top speed was reported 60 mph with an acceleration from

---

[15] Dr. H. D. Kesling, Westerville, Indiana

Figure 21.13. The Globe-Union Endura of 1977. Twenty lead-acid propulsion batteries in Globe-Union's latest electric car are mounted in center line roll-out rack.[16]   Courtesy: Globe-Union.

0-30 mph in 8.7 seconds. Range on a track at 35 mph was found to be 115 miles.[17] A prime reason for the Endura was a battery test-bed reminiscent of Thomas Edison's 3-wheel electric vehicle shown in Chapter 5.

Ten years after building the Delta, the General Electric Company, in celebration of the 100th anniversary of the firm's founding,[18] brought forth the Centennial in 1978,[19] shown in Fig. 21.14. The company's intention was to determine how competitive a battery-powered car could be when compared to a conventional IC vehicle.

To achieve this quest the Centennial was equipped with 18 six-volt, deep discharge, lead-acid batteries especially produced by the Globe-Union Company of Milwaukee, Wisconsin which could be charged in 6 hours from a 220 volt source. Initial tests on the vehicle gave a top speed of 60 mph, a cruising speed of 55 mph, a range of 75 miles at a constant speed of 40 mph. Acceleration from 0-30 mph was nine seconds. Curb weight of the vehicle was 2,150 pounds; length was 160 inches; height was 53.5 inches; wheelbase was 92 inches; while ground

---

[16] *Midwest Engineer*, March 1977, p.3.

[17] *Electric Vehicle News*, Vol. 6, No. 3, August 1977, pp. 10-11.

[18] The General Electric Company had as its genesis the patents of Thomas Edison. His electric lamp was invented in 1879.

[19] *The General Electric Company's Centennial Electric, An Experimental Electric Vehicle*, General Electric Company 79PR002, 1978.

Figure 21.14. The General Electric Centennial Electric of 1978. Courtesy: Commonwealth Edison Company.

clearance was six inches. Radio, windshield wiper, defroster, fans, headlights, etc. were connected to a standard 12-volt battery which was linked to the on-board charger. This 1978 vehicle was perceived as being non-competitive with a comparable IC vehicle, and probably represented the apogee of <u>public</u> interest in battery-powered cars. From this time inquisitiveness waned in all industrial countries. By 1982 the large U.S. federal bureaucracy to promote the electric vehicle was gradually being disbanded.[20] The race to provide an early alternate to the heat-engine-powered automobile had been lost. The pronouncement of Henry Ford II, "The Ford Motor Company will not offer an electric car in my lifetime" had proven true. He died in 1987.

The 1978 Centennial was perceived by the more mature in the electric vehicle industry as an insufficient match in the marketplace for the moving target of the constantly improving petroleum-powered vehicle. Yet no electric automobile was in near-term sight which would be a significant improvement over the Centennial. Because the Department of Energy was mandated by Congress to pursue the development of electric/hybrid vehicles, and because any government has little flexibility, some have postulated as much as $100 million of taxpayers' money could have been saved if the Electric and Hybrid Vehicle Research, Development and Demonstration Act had been terminated after the Centennial had been evaluated.[21] President Gerald Ford had vetoed the Bill in 1976, but Congress would not be denied in obligating the taxpayers, so the effort would continue, largely in funding government national laboratories until the regime of President Ronald Reagan, who, with Budget Director David A. Stockman, would gradually slow the hemorrhaging.

---

[20] See comments of Dr. Paul A. Nelson of Argonne National Laboratory in Chapter 11.
[21] Personal communication April 20, 1982.

The Department of Energy Compleat Electric Vehicle of 1979

As a continuing example of the public sector involvement was the Department of Energy ETV-1 delivered in 1979 and seen in Fig. 21.15. The prime contractor was the General Electric Company which developed the car's complete electrical drive system. One subcontractor was the Chrysler Corporation which was responsible for styling, body design and fabrication, suspension, brakes, and vehicle testing. The Globe Battery Division of Johnson Controls, Inc. designed and constructed the advanced lead-acid power batteries.

Charged from a household outlet the car contains 18 6-volt batteries with an energy density of 38 watt-hours per kg. The batteries are housed in a tunnel similar to the technique pioneered in the Sundancer illustrated in Fig. 21.1. Battery life is some 500 cycles estimated to yield a service life of about 50,000 km.[22] The wind tunnel tested vehicle has a reported drag of some 40 percent less than a conventional sub-compact vehicle. A microcomputer manages energy flow throughout the system, including power demands to minimize driving abuse, while enhancing range. Top speed is 60 mph; acceleration is 0-30 mph in 9 seconds. The computer projected range is a reported 70 miles in stop-and-go urban driving. The car is designed to climb a 5 percent, one-mile gradient at 50 mph. The vehicle is designed to meet American Federal Safety Standards in protecting the occupants from battery acid and structure intrusions, battery leakage, electrical shorts while crash driving into a wall at 30 mph.[23]

Figure 21.15. The ETV-1 developed in 1979 for the U.S. Department of Energy by the General Electric Company of the U.S.A.'s Research and Development Center and Chrysler Corporation. Courtesy: U.S.A. Department of Energy.

---

[22] *Discourse on an Advanced Passenger Car, Electric Vehicles*, Vol. 67, No. 2, June 1981, pp. 12-14.
[23] *Advanced Test Car Delivered, Electric Vehicles*, Vol. 65, No. 3, September 1979. p. 4.

The Unique Mobility Inc. Elektrek

With the encouragement of the Electric & Hybrid Vehicle Act of 1976 the Unique Mobility Company of Denver, Colorado brought forth the only compleat electric vehicle wholly financed by the private sector as a result of the Act. The motorcar features a plastic-bonded fiberglass body, an over-excited shunt (direct-current) motor with transistorized controls. Using the battery mounting exchange developed for McKee's Sundancer, illustrated in Fig. 21.2, the battery tray runs the length of the vehicle, and, like the Sundancer, may be withdrawn for servicing. It may be observed that with two trays of batteries and a central operating base the vehicle, operating first with one tray and then the other, could be operated almost continuously with lead-acid batteries, a very attractive feature as well as illustrating a conservation of capital. Wouk stated in 1986 that this strictly electric vehicle company was the only one in production in the U.S.A.[24]

The vehicle is powered by 16 6-volt lead acid batteries through a transistorized controller to a 32-hp motor. It has a 4-speed manual transmission and disc-brakes in front with drum type in the rear. The vehicle is equipped with regenerative braking.[25]

After the U.S. government money began flowing in the 1977-1978 organizing period of the Department of Energy, a growing number of vehicles, either conversions or compleat vehicles, were government subsidized in one way or another. And essentially all bore the 1859 Plantè derived lead-acid battery. In the early 1980s the battery was a logical area for intensified government/industry research for here indeed was the bottle-neck to effective, affordable, personal electric transportation. In the meantime, what were conditions abroad where there was little government generosity? The next chapter considers modern foreign electric vehicle development, just as earlier overseas electric carriage advancements were pictured and discussed. Now, however, instead of only a few European nations, other economies would investigate as well. The countries are taken in alphabetical order.

---

[24] Victor Wouk, *Two Decades of 'High Performance' EV Fleet Experience.* EV-9.

[25] E. J. Dowgiallo, Jr. and R. D. Chapman. *Baseline and Verification Tests of the Unique Mobility, Inc. Elektrek 2 x 2 Final test report.* Fort Belvoir, Virginia: Army Mobility Equipment Research & Development Center, March 1982. 127 pp., NTIS, PCAO&/MFAO1.

CHAPTER 22

Modern Foreign Electric Vehicle Development — Part I

In the first half of the 1970s foreign interest in electric cars, like in America, was also found in Britain, France, West Germany, Japan, and, to a lesser degree, in Italy. These nations, except for Nippon, were the same as had developed electrics at the beginning of the century as discussed in Chapters 6 and 7. The vehicles, like their American counterpart, would also be unable to compete in the market place with their gasoline and with their diesel-powered cousins. It would be a repeat of the 1902-1912 story. There would be, however, a difference in this second round of electric vehicle development. In Britain, as in America, the entrepreneur would play a dominant role. Elsewhere the established automobile manufacturers would represent almost the entire innovative thrust.

All who manufactured electric vehicles would find the IC car a moving target both in improved quality and in enhanced efficiency. The 8-20 mpg car of the 1970s would become the 25-50 mpg vehicle in the 1980s. And, as the price of gasoline rose, so did electric rates. Japan was the first nation to mute the statements on electric cars. They withdrew from showing them almost as quietly as they entered the field.

As the 1970 decade ended companies in other nations were offering electric cars or vans: Australia, Belgium, Brazil, Bulgaria, Canada, Denmark, Holland, Hong Kong, India, Mexico, the former Soviet Union, Sweden, Switzerland, and Taiwan. The ever-increasing price of oil at the beginning of the decade, and the announcement by such a knowledgeable person, for example, as the late Dr. Armand Hammer, Chairman of Occidental Oil Company, that the price might reach one-hundred dollars a barrel, provided encouragement for an alternate energy source. With few exceptions these vehicles bore lead-acid batteries with d-c motor drive. Probably most important, the electric vehicle concept encouraged middle-level nations to pursue their own indigenous transportation industry independent of transnational corporations. Their own governments need only provide the local entrepreneurs an attractive economy and free political environment.

Where the latter half of the 1960s and all of the 1970s would be fruitful in developing electric vehicles, there was understanding in the 1980s that the emphasis on electric vehicles should center on battery and drivetrain improvement. Below demonstrates some of the international vehicles in alphabetical order from the 1960s through the 1980s.

Australian Electric Vehicles

An industry/university relationship can hold promise as is illustrated by the work at Flinders University in Adelaide, Australia. There, a group headed by Professor Daryl Ross Whitford, an electronics engineer, has developed a 4-wheeled battery-powered car. Particularly unique is the use of a printed-circuit shunt-motor running at a constant speed when the vehicle is in use. Between the motor and the drive wheels is a transmission that is a positive displacement hydraulic system "variable from infinity to l:l."[1] The vehicle is identified as Investigator Mk I, shown in Fig. 22.1.

A second vehicle, a later development, is known as Investigator Mk II, Fig. 22.2. The latter assembly is based on a Fiat 127 body. The car is said to have a top speed of 75 km/h, a range of some 60 to 80 km. Twelve 12-volt batteries power the 10 kW motor.[2][3] In contemplation of the fluid-drive transmission above, the reader may wish to refer to Chapter 5 and review the Dey-Griswald fluid-drive electric vehicle of 1895.

Figure 22.1. An Australian electric car. Electric Vehicles.

---

[1] *Australian Electric Car Passes Road Test, Electric Vehicles*, Vol. 61, No. 1, March 1975, p. 24.
[2] Jonathon Stone, *Australian Electric Car Offered for Production, Electric Vehicles*, Vol. 63, No. 4, December 1977, pp. 28-29.
[3] *Australian Made Delivery Vans, Electric Vehicles*, Vol. 67, No. 1, March 1981, p. 4.

Figure 22.2. Darryl Whitford checks the batteries of the Flinders electric vehicle. A second bank of batteries is housed at the rear. Electric Vehicles.

The Townobile B5 and B10

Another entry from Australia responding to the perceived need for electric postal vehicles is the Townobile. Designed and built by Elroy Engineering Pty. Ltd, of Pennant Hills, the Townobile B5 commuter car/van has a capacity for five adults, bears lead-acid batteries, and includes a solid state controller for a d-c drive motor.

In a "stretched" model, known as the B10 Townobile, the payload is increased to 10 persons with a usable volume of 6 cubic meters. The Managing Director of the firm is L. Roy Leembrugen.[4]

---

[4] *Letter from Australia, Electric News*, Vol. 66, No. 4, 1980, p. 18.
  Also: *EVE-80 Marks Beginning of Australian EV Era, Electric Vehicle Development*, November 4, 1979, p. 7.

Phase II Electric Vehicles

At the October 1981 Baltimore Exposition an Australian entry was Phase II, powered with probably the first commercially offered disc-type d-c motor of 10 kW capacity. Such a motor type is illustrated in Chapter 24 for the MIT race entry of 1968. Phase II is also reported to be equipped with a stepless variable automatic transmission. The electric vehicles in Australia are proving to be wholly indigenous in capital needs, design, construction, and sales, and is an indication how research creates local jobs.

Purpose-Built Electric Vehicles

Rather than develop general purpose electric vehicles useful for many tasks such as the van class or the pick-up truck, L. Roy Leembruggen of Pennant Hills, New South Wales, Australia believes the purpose-built electric cars will have greater acceptance. While he fails to cite the example, electric-powered fork-lift trucks, introduced by Baker Electric when they observed their electric cars were no longer selling in 1916, introduced these purpose-built vehicles. The company was not only saved, but, indeed, prospered and in 1990s is an important division of a larger enterprise as discussed in Chapter 14.

Below are illustrated two views of the Townobile B10 car/van purpose-built prototype.[5]

Figure 22.3a. Townobile B10
Commuter Car/Van Prototype.
L.R. Leembruggen.

Figure 22.3b. Townobile B10
Rear Ramp and Hatch Open.
L.R. Leembruggen.Belgium
Electric Vehicle Progress

---

5 L. R. Leembruggen, *The Sure Way Forward - Purpose-Built Electric Vehicles*. The 9th International Electric Vehicle Symposium, Toronto, 1988.

Belgian Vehicles

Historically Belgium was the site of early battery development, and origin of the 1883 tramcar built by Phillipart as cited in Chapter 7. In the 1980s and early 1990s Belgian engineering effort appears limited to the testing of electric cars.[6] As an example:

The Universities of Brussels secured nine electric vehicles from PGE (Italy). Two different models are available.

> PGE 3P: 3 person + 50 kg capacity;
> 60 km/h max speed; 50 km range;
> 72 volt battery.
> PGE 5P: 5 person + 50 kg or 2 person + 350 kg capacity;
> 60 km/h max speed; 50 km range;
> 96 volt battery.

Presently the vehicles are equipped with lead-acid batteries and on-board charging units. All PGE vehicles acquired in 1980 were in use as of 1988. "The vehicles are nowadays available to any member of the university community, consisting of 7,500 students and 1,800 academic and technical staff, against a small fee." Since 1980 the nine vehicles have covered over 100,000 km. Below are data on these vehicles.

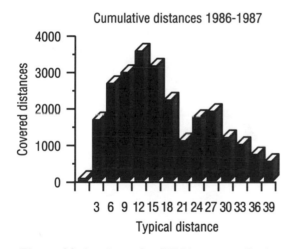
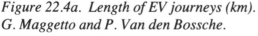

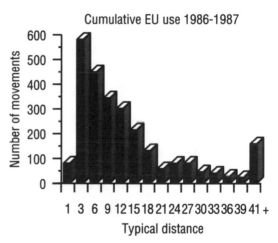

Figure 22.4a. Length of EV journeys (km).
G. Maggetto and P. Van den Bossche.

Figure 22.4b. Cumulative distances (km).
G. Maggetto and P. Van den Bossche.

---

6 G. Maggetto and P. Van den Bossche, *The Twelve Electric Hours of Brussels*, The 9th International Electric Vehicle Symposium, Toronto, 1988.

Electric Vehicles in Brazil

In Brazil's rapid industrialization, in the nation's drive for exports, in the country's paucity of indigenously produced oil, the entrepreneurs of this dynamic state have built electric vehicles, an example of which is shown in Fig. 22.5. The Gurgel E-400, named after the company founder, Joao Augusto Conrado do Amaral Gurgel, is produced in three versions: pick-up, van, and 5-passenger double-cab pick-up. Range of the E-400 is given as some 80 km, with a top speed of 60 km/hr. The lead-acid batteries are stated to be 2-40 volt traction type. Curb weight is given as 1,450 kg, with a pay load capability of 400 kg.[7]

A later version is the Gurgel ITAIPU E-40.[8] Battery voltage was increased to 96 volts to drive a 10 kW motor. In the pick-up model, load capacity is cited as 400 kg., a range of 100 km, with a vehicle speed of 35-40 km/hr. Note the later version has a greater battery load. Nearly all manufacturers in their second model enhance the energy in the battery complement, and always to mitigate that problem of range limitation. The key question in Brazil as in other nations: is there a maintained market for electric vehicles when there is no subsidy? For more than 80 years in Britain the answer has been yes.

British Electric Vehicle Development

Unlike all other countries British manufacturers never ceased building electric lorries. A small clutch of English companies, a remnant from early in the century, continued to assemble

Figure 22.5. A Brazilian designed and built electric van. Courtesy: Electric Vehicle News.

---

7 *Electric Vehicle News*, Vol. 10, No. 3, August 1981, p. 23.

8 *Ibid*, Vol. 11, No. 1, February 1982, p. 15.

a few thousand 'milk floats' a year, and, as many had a life of from 20-40 years, an estimated 33,000 electric-powered milk trucks were in use in 1982.[9] The author visited two electric milk-float vehicle assembly plants in England. Contributing to the vehicles' economic success is the method of milk delivery in England. A particular dairy producer will have a continuous block of flats to serve, each one in series, taking the bottled milk. With this multi-stop need, a slow moving, battery-powered milk float was, and is, serviceable. The U.S. Post Office original electric vehicle experiment in Cupertino, California, discussed later, was indeed based on an English Harbilt Electric 'milk float,'[10] one of which is shown in Fig. 17.2.

Inasmuch as England continued making electric vehicles, as seen above, and the Americans indeed halted their assembly of electrics, this procedural contrast contributed a quite different approach with the resurrection of interest in electric cars: The first new British designs, i.e., the Scamp, were compleat electric vehicles—designed originally as electric. They then evolved to conversions of IC vehicles. In contrast, the American initial designs were conversions, i.e., the Renault Dauphine, and some time later reached compleat electric vehicle designs, namely, the Sundancer.

Three Pre-1966 British Designed Electric Vehicles

Three pre-1966 British electric vehicles of the resurrection period were the BMC Minitraveller I, assembled by AEI Ltd,[11] and the BMC Minitraveller II, developed by Telearchics Ltd,[12] both for the Electricity Council of London. The former vehicle weighed 2,599 pounds, had 96 volt, 66 ampere-hour (Ah) batteries storing 6.3 kWh of energy. A 7.5 kW motor had speed control from a time ratio controller. Top speed was 40 mph, with a range of 36 miles. Minitraveller II, in contrast, weighed 2,380 pounds and had 64 volt, 105 Ah batteries storing 6.7 kWh, and two 64 volt, 2.25 kW motors in parallel, with a carbon-pile controller, to yield a maximum speed of 40 mph with a reported range of 28 miles. A carbon controller is effective, low in cost, but wasteful of energy.

Scamp, built by Scottish Aviation Ltd, also before 1966,[13] weighed in at 1,000 pounds, had a 48 volt, 105 Ah lead-acid battery of 344 pounds, two motors in series, with a carbon-pile

[9] *Europe's Electric Commercial Vans Lead the World, Electric Vehicles*, Vol. 68, No. 1, March 1982, p. 12.
[10] *British Battery Company Beat U.S. Competitors, Electric Vehicles*, Vol. 66, No. 4, December 1980, pp. 2-3.
[11] *The Electric Car - A Design Challenge, Electro Technology*, May 1968, p. 68.
[12] *Ibid*, p. 58.
[13] *U.S. News & World Reports*, March 20, 1967.

controller. Range was a stated 15-20 miles. Top speed was 35 mph.[14] The three vehicles did no better in the market place than the later designed Enfield. Figures 22.6 and 22.7 illustrate the British designed Scamp and the Minitraveller.[15]

Sir John Samuel also demonstrated and entered into production an electric car, the Enfield. Sixty-one were tested by the Electricity Council. One model is shown in Fig. 22.8. The Enfield 8000 had a curb weight of 1,800 pounds, was powered by eight 12 volt 92 Ah capacity batteries connected in parallel to yield 48 volts which supplied power to a 6 kw, 4-pole, d-c series motor. Control was by voltage switching. The Enfield 8000 is a 2-seater with an aluminum body. Top speed was a reported 40 mph, with an acceleration of 0-30 mph in 13 seconds.[16] Range has been reported as much as 50 miles. Before production stopped 112 Enfield 8000s were produced in shipowner John Goulandris' Greek yards from British parts. Shipped back to Britain, they were checked out on the Isle of Wight.[17] [18] [19]

Compleat English Vehicles (Continued)

Possibly the most innovative group to exploit electric vehicles in Britain was Electraction Ltd of Heybridge Basin, Malden, Essex. This company demonstrated a series of four electric

Figures 22.6 and 22.7. The British designed Scamp and Minicar. Source: U.S. News & World Reports.[14]

[14] *The Electric Car - A Design Challenge, Electro Technology*, May 1968, p. 58.

[15] *Electric Vehicle News*, Vol. 3, No. 3, August 1971, pp. 17 & 48.

[16] *Electricity Council Starts to Assess the Enfield 8000, Electric Vehicles*, Vol. 61, No. 3, Sept. 1975, pp. 8-11.

[17] *The Story Behind the Enfield Car, Electric Vehicles*, Vol. 61, No. 3, Sept. 1975, pp. 16-17.

[18] *Electricity Council Reports on Enfield Car, Electric Vehicles*, Vol. 65, No. 3, Sept. 1979, pp. 2-3.

[19] *Enfield Closes, Electric Vehicles*, Vol. 66, No. 2, June 1976, p.4.

Figure 22.8. The Enfield 465.[20] Electrical World.

vehicles: The Precinct, a two-door sedan; the Tropicana, a roadster;[21] a Beach Buggy; and the Electric Box Van. Each body was of fiberglass, with styling by Haynes Automotive International. Common to each vehicle was the chassis with length overall of 126", width 65", wheelbase 76", and a turning circle of 25 feet. Gross vehicle weight of the Precinct was a reported 3,200 pounds. Power for all vehicles was provided from 72 volt lead-acid batteries flowing through a chopper controller to a 7.5 hp d-c motor. A top speed of 35 mph was claimed with a range of 50 miles.[22] The author drove the Beach Buggy in an enclosed room. Figures 22.9 through 22.12 show these vehicles and the accompanying common chassis. While some vehicles were reportedly sold in England, Iran, Korea, Nigeria, and the USA, 1979 saw the company's cessation of production.

Why the market failed to accept these attractively designed and enthusiastically promoted vehicles is not easily discernible, a subject mused upon by the editor of *Electrical Vehicle News* recently.[23] But somewhere in England are unused molds, leftover parts, and a bag full of dreams of what might have been. Directors of the company were given as: Roy D. Haynes, Michael R. Heerey, and Leslie A. Steere, F.C.A.

As if to defy prediction, at the same time Electraction Ltd had announced and were operating a fleet of original electric vehicles, Lucas Electric Vehicle Systems of Birmingham, England, long an assembler of compleat electrics, built a number of conversion vehicles, seen below.

---

[20] *Enfield 465, Electrical World*, November 24, 1969, p. 48.

[21] *Tropicana Marks "The Parting of the Ways", Electric Vehicles*, Vol. 63, No. 2, June 1977, pp. 8 & 10.

[22] *Electric Vehicle News*, Vol. 6, No. 2, May 1977, p. 23.

[23] *£500,000 Could have saved Electraction, Electric Vehicles*, Vol. 65, No. 3, September 1979, p. 7.

Figure 22.9. The Precinct was a two-door sedan offered by the Electraction Ltd with fiberglass body. Courtesy: Electraction, Ltd.

British Conversions

An old line British electric vehicle manufacturer and one long in the 'milk float' field was Lucas. One of their first conversions was a Bedford CA van,[24] similar to vans converted by General Motors and by Linear Alpha Inc., and subsequently by GMAC. The Lucas electric lorry is available in two sizes of which only the larger is cited:[25] curb weight is 5,818 pounds; ratio of battery weight to GVW, 24.5 percent; acceleration from 0-30 mph, 10 seconds; maximum speed 50 mph; and range, 40 miles. These figures are rather comparable to American style electric vans.

Significantly Lucas management concluded in 1977: 1) the lead-acid battery is the only practical power system for at least seven years; 2) a competitive electric private car for British markets in the above period is not possible; 3) the electric vehicle niche is fleet operation; 4) electric vehicles will sell in quantity only when cheaper to own and to operate than IC vehicles. The same conclusion as cited in Item 3 was propounded by Morris & Salom for the New York City taxis in November 1896, as written in Chapter 4. As Scamp did no better in the marketplace than did the Enfield, or the system of cars by Electraction, there is experience adding credence to the Lucas conclusions cited above. Each country, however, is different and each entrepreneurial group must above all satisfy itself.

---

[24] *Electric Vehicle News*, Vol. 7, No. 1, February 1978, p. 8.
[25] *A Design Capable of Mass Production, Electric Vehicles*, Vol. 63, No. 3, September 1977, pp. 7-10.

Figure 22.10. Tropicana, a leisure electric car offered by Electraction Ltd with its fiberglass body. Courtesy: Commonwealth Edison Company.

Seeking the same market as the Bedford CA van above, in 1982 Karrier Motors Ltd began a production line converting vans with an offer from the British government of a 4,500 British pound sterling subsidy each to the buyer.[26] Their initial order based on a sample was for 20 electric vans from the Southern Electricity Board. Fig. 22.13 shows the Karrier production line. Plans of this company, 50 percent of which is owned by Renault Vehicles Industriels, are to produce 20 vehicles per month. The Dodge 50 have a top speed in excess of 40 mph, a 0-30 mph acceleration of 19 seconds, and a range of some 45 miles. Another British conversion is the Firefly, shown next.

---

[26] *Karrier Motors Building 20 Units a Month, Electric Vehicles*, Vol. 68, No. 1, March 1982, p. 3.

Figure 22.10A. Beach Buggy. Courtesy: Electraction.

Firefly Automotive Ltd of Bletchley, in converting the Ford Fiesta (a conversion also chosen by Jet Industries Inc., of Texas), provided an energy storage source of 48 volts of lead-acid batteries with chopper control to the 6 kW d-c motor. The ancillary 12-volt battery uses a dc/dc converter from the drive batteries. A cut-away drawing of the Firefly is shown in Fig. 22.14. "The 6-volt batteries (1) are housed in two locations: five in a force ventilated pack at the rear seat area and three in the motor compartment. The motor (2) picks up the drive through the gear box differential and drive shafts to the front wheels. The controller (3) has been specially designed to give a positive control by steps. The heater (4) is a paraffin operated hot air type linked to the existing ventilation box. The charger (5) is an on-board type suitable for plugging into any 13-amp standard house ring main socket. Because of its policy of continuous improvement, Firefly Automotive Ltd. reserves the right to make alterations to and departures from the current specification, design and equipment."[27]

The Sinclair C-10, described by P. J. Milner of Coventry, England, is a minimum type town car which in 1986 was only in design form, but like the Hong Kong vehicle described below, his paper furnishes a small car designer with a useful template of performance curves.[28] This vehicle, if built, could only be used on restricted-use roads in America.

---

[27] *Firefly Automotive Converts the Fiesta, Electric Vehicles*, Vol. 64, No. 4, December 1981, pp. 12 & 13.

[28] P. J. Milner, *Suitability of Lead/Acid Batteries for Powering a Town Car.* Eighth International Electric Vehicle Symposium, Washington, D.C., 1986.

Figure 22.11. An Electric Box Van offered by Electraction Ltd. Cab of fiberglass, box of aluminum. Payload: 700 lbs; range: 50-60 miles at 30 mph. Courtesy: Electraction Ltd.

The Griffon Electric Van

The 1988 Griffon Electric van varied from the earlier 1978 Bedford van primarily in body style. The drive train was a choppered d-c motor powered by lead-acid batteries. Little was new; the whole resembled the GM G Van described in Chapter 20 and assembled in America. Illustrated below is the GM Griffon Van. Its characteristics appear in Chapter 20 with the G Van and in Table 22-1 below.

As will be seen in the next section, other Commonwealth nations were also active.

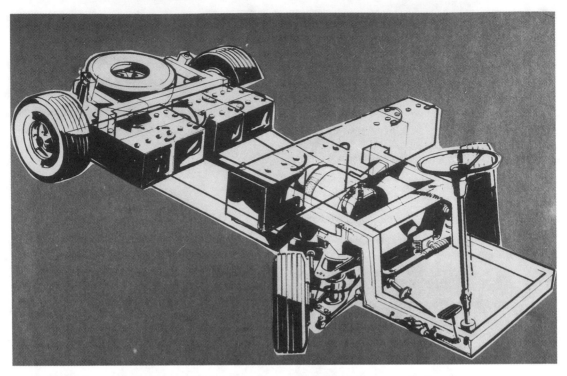

Figure 22.12. The chassis on which all Electraction vehicles were built. Courtesy: Electraction Ltd.

Table 22-1. Griffon Physical Specifications	
Gross Vehicle Weight:	3,500 kg
Curb Weight:	2,640 kg
Maximum Payload Weight:	860 kg
Length:	4.4 m
Width:	1.9 m
Height:	2.0 m
Wheelbase:	2.7 m
Cargo Volume:	5.9 m^3

Figure 22.13. Production line for British Dodge 50 electric vans. Thought to be the first electric commercial vehicle to go into assembly line production, the first 20 units are being built for the Southern Electricity Board. Courtesy: Electric Vehicles.

Canadian Electric Vehicles

The Marathon Electric Car Ltd, located in St. Leonard, Quebec, had, by 1978, made more than 600 battery-powered vehicles of various types. The C-300 vehicle, shown in Fig. 22.16, has a fiberglass body and top, or possesses a canvas hood. Of an overall length of 153 inches with a wheelbase of 92 inches, the curb weight is reported to be 2,100-2,600 pounds. Payload is said to be 500 pounds. There are 12 6-volt batteries supplying 72 volts to an 8-hp d-c motor. The type controller is not given. An on-board charger may be plugged into a 30 ampere, 110-volt outlet. The vehicle has a variable speed transmission.[29]

Other Commonwealth countries: Australia, New Zealand, and South Africa had active groups: Australia early developing an elegant computer study on electric vehicles; South Africa assembled a few entrepreneurial samples; New Zealand with little indigenous oil, but with abundant natural gas, gave serious consideration to the assembly of electric cars, linking with Linear Alpha Inc. in America.[30]

---

[29] *Electric Vehicle News*, Vol. 7, No. 1, February 1978, p. 25.
[30] Personal communication.

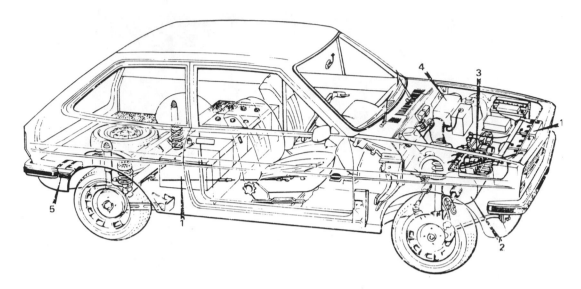

Figure 22.14. Firefly Automotive's Batford Saloon, a Ford Fiesta Conversion. Courtesy: Electric Vehicles.

In the 1980s the Canadian effort in electric vehicles was largely limited to emphasis placed on batteries as reported in Chapter 11. Canadian advanced electrochemical power sources research is summarized in Table 22-2.[31]

Chinese Electric Vehicle Progress

As reported at the 9th International Electric Vehicle Symposium Beijing, thinking on electric vehicles is to emphasize effort on batteries, a program similar to plans in the West.[32]

A Danish Electric Vehicle

As an example of smaller nations forging an automobile industry, cited earlier, innovators in Denmark have introduced a commuter type electric vehicle in the face of repeated failures in America and in England. During the years 1982 and '83 the Energy Research Laboratory of Denmark participated in the electric vehicle project U-36. The work was under the responsibility of Dronningborg Maskinfabrik.[33] In characteristics the vehicle would have three wheels

---

[31] William A. Adams and John H. Morgan, *Canadian Electrochemical Power Sources Research and Development for Traction Applications*, The 9th International Electric Vehicle Symposium, Toronto, 1988.

[32] Du Hua-min and Wu Xiachua, *The Status and Function of Electric Vehicles for Communication and Transportation in Beijing*, The 9th International Electric Vehicle Symposium, Toronto, 1988.

[33] Steen V. Jensen and Ole S. Nissen, *Mini-el, A New Danish Commuter Vehicle Concept*, Eighth International Electric Vehicle Symposium, Washington, D.C., 1986.

Figure 22.15. GM Griffon Van

and one seat, be of light weight with a monocoque chassis/body construction. Specifications are set forth in Table 22.3. It would be designed to serve as the second car for a family in many instances.

Finnish Electric Vehicles

Arto Haakana was kind enough to furnish a summary of recent progress on electric vehicles in this northern country writing:[34]

"A prototype electric delivery van for inner-city operations has been designed and constructed by a group of Finnish companies: Neste Oy, Imatran Voima Oy and Lokari companies and supported by the Finnish technology development centre.

"The aim of the project was to design and build a lightweight delivery van with suitable solutions for easy operation.

"The chassis of the vehicle was built from the ground-up to fit the light corrosion-free polyethylene body. The electrical system is based on DC and lead-acid technology since only these have presently both technical and economical feasibility. To make the operation of the vehicles possible also in the local harsh winter conditions, the battery box was thermally insulated and equipped with electrical heating synchronized with the off-board charger of the batteries.

"The design of the vehicle is based on the idea that when doing deliveries one has to have easy access to the driver seat as well as to the cargo area. Also the turning

[34] Arto Haakana, *A Half-Ton Electric Van for Urban Operation*, The 9th International Electric Vehicle Symposium, Toronto, 1988.

Figure 22.16. The Marathon C-300 electric vehicle of 1978.

radius is of importance when speaking of easy handling of the vehicle, a good visibility from the drivers seat is also essential from the safety point of view.

"A pre-series of 10 vehicles with DC series motors and lead-acid batteries will be built during 1987 and tested in everyday use by the Finnish post office and newspaper companies. Also new technical solutions like combined chopper/charger and new types of batteries will be tested in the near future."

Later French Electric Cars

The effort by the French government for the nation to be ever more energy self-sufficient through the increasing use of nuclear power went hand-in-hand with encouragement for the development of a French produced electric car. As in Germany well-known IC vehicle manufacturers made electric conversions of standard sedans. Again there was the largely conventional approach of using d-c motors for the power system. After a few years of interest and tests this work was quietly muted.

In 1973 Electricité de France converted 80 standard model automobiles to battery power. Pierre Volf, utility research director at Dijon was quoted, "We have enough faith in the project

	Table 22-2. Summary of Advanced Electrochemical Power Sources Research in Canada	
System	Developer (location)	Status for Traction Applications
Al/Air	Alcan (Kingston)	Prototype EV batteries on test
SPe fuel cell	Ballard (Vancouver)	Prototype fuel cell stacks on test
Zn/MnO_2	BTI (Toronto)	Small cells only
Li - Al/FeS	Electrofuel (Toronto)	200 Ah traction cells and battery modules available
Li Polymer	IREQ (Varennes - near Montreal)	Small cells only
Li/MoS_2	MOLI (Vancouver)	50 Ah prototype cell in 12V module
Na/S	Powerplex (Toronto)	Full size EV battery prototypes in Vehicles
Li/TiX_2	NBRPC (Fredericton)	Small cells only
Alkaline fuel cell	University of Toronto on test (Toronto)	Small cell stacks

to have planned building 250 for our own use by 1975." Some 800 pounds of lead-acid batteries furnish power to an electric motor linked to each axle. Range is a reported 40 miles, with a top speed of 40 mph. Recharge requires 10 hours.[35] [36]

In March 1973 the French Compagne Generale d'Electricité and the Fulmen Battery Company offered the Gregoire electric mini-van. This van bears 400 kg of batteries with a rating of 96 volts said to have a specific energy of 41 watt-hours/kg. The 14 kW motor may be separately excited, or the field may be placed in series configuration. There is also provision

---

[35] Claude Muller, *EV Progress in France, Electric Vehicle News*, Vol. 7, No. 3, August 1978, pp. 36-37.
[36] *The French Policy for the Development of Electric Vehicles, Electric Vehicles*, Vol. 64, No. 4, December 1978, pp. 23 & 24.

Table 22-3. Specifications of the U-36 Vehicle		

Batteries
- Type: flat plate
- Number: 2
- Voltage: 24 V
- Capacity C5: 105 Ah
- Weight: 75 kg
- Lifetime: 1.5-2 years
  500 cycles

Charger: on board

Controller: Power transistors with by-pass

Transmission: electronic/mechanical

Braking: mechanical-hydraulic

Steering: not power assisted

Suspension: mechanical

Coachwork: plastic

Motor source: American Bosch P.M.
- rating 1 hr: 0.88 kW
- rating peak: 2.8 kW

Ancillaries:
- heating: electrical
- ventilation:
- converter: DC/DC
- battery topping-up: manual

Weight:
- kerb weight (incl. batteries): 230 kg
- gross weight: 365 kg

Speed:
- cruising: 40 km/h
- max.: 40 km/h

Acceleration at 80% D.O.D.

	0.30 km/h	0.50 km/h
unladen	sec	sec
laden	8.5 sec	sec

for regenerative braking. Motor control is effected by a chopper in the armature circuit, with a provision for a maximum draw of 220 amperes. Characteristics of the Grigoire are given below in Table 22-4.

In 1988 C. Bassac described the electrical vehicle systems in France.[37]

The Situation in France in 1988

"The total fleet strength of electric vehicles in France is approximately 500, but this figure is insignificant when compared to the 25,000,000 vehicles on French roads.

"These 500 electric vehicles form two subgroups:
- approximately 50 units, manufactured by leading carmakers, that are currently in experimental use;

---

[37] C. Bassac, *Experimental Uses of Electric Vehicles in France*, The 9th International Electric Vehicle Symposium, Toronto, 1988.

- between 400 and 450 vehicles, manufactured by craftsmen or small-scale manufacturers, that have been in full-time service for over 15 years.

"The PSA Group (Peugeot and Citroën) has produced a series of test vehicles based on the Peugeot 205 and the Citroën C15 van (see Figs. 22.17 and 22.18 and Table 22-5) that are currently in experimental use in a number of industrial vehicle fleets (e.g., EDF and the City of La Rochelle operate five 205s and 2 C15s).

"Further, ten Peugeot J5 and J9 goods vehicles (see Figs. 22.19 and 22.20 and Tables 22-6 and 22-7) have been used for transporting staff inside EDF's nuclear facilities for a number of years.

"PSA joined forces with the coachbuilder Heuliez to produce 5 minibuses, based on the Citroën C35 diesel and equipped with an electric booster module. The vehicles have been in service since 1973 with the City of Tours, and the municipal authorities recently authorized the purchase of 5 all-electric vehicles equipped with nickel-cadmium batteries.

"Régie Renault has produced a first series of 10 electric vehicles—designated Master[38]—for the City of Chatellerault. Nine of the vehicles are powered by nickel-iron batteries while the 10th is equipped with a lead cell.

"Since the vehicles went into service with the city's technical departments they have covered over 150,000 miles, and malfunctions have been limited to standard prototype development faults. The 10 electric vehicles operate under exactly the same conditions as their thermally powered equivalents.

Table 22-4. General Characteristic for the CGE Gregoire

Body .... :	Mini-van (driver + 125 kg of useful load)
Length .... :	3.30 m (3.29 for Fiat 600)
Height .... :	1.41 m
Width .... :	1.34 m
Weight empty .... :	600 kg
Maximum speed on the flat .... :	Economical version 60 km/h
	Fast version 75 km/h
Maximum slope which may be climbed ..... :	15%
Acceleration .... :	0 to 30 km/h in 6 seconds
Range .... :	variable as a function of the traffic density:
	- up to 120 km in easy traffic
	- up to 50 km in dense city traffic

---

[38] *The New York Times*, January 22, 1990.

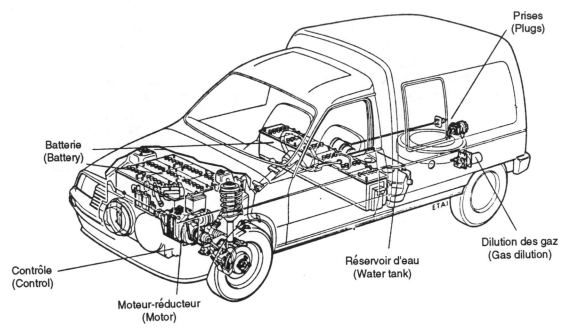

Figure 22.17. Schéma de la Citroën C15 électrique[39]

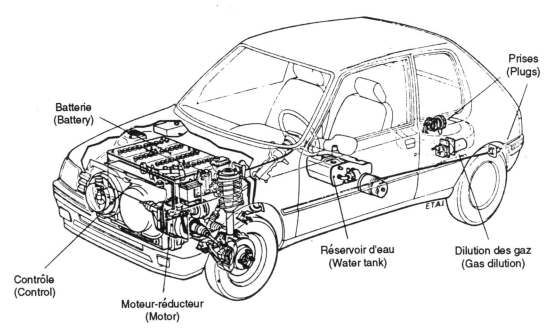

Figure 22.18. Schéma de la Peugeot 205 électrique—3 portes[40]

[39] C. P. Peyriere, *PSA's Electric Vehicles Fitted With Batteries*, The 9th International Electric Vehicle Symposium, Toronto, 1988.
[40] Ibid.

Table 22-5. Characteristics of Citroën C15

The drive unit operating at 90 V gives the following characteristics:

Nominal voltage	90 V
Maximum current	300 A
Maximum rotational speed	5500 rpm
Maximum power	23 kw at 1800 rpm
Maximum continuous power	16 kw
Maximum starting torque	125 mN

The battery comprises 15 monoblocks; nine are located at the front and six at the central area of the vehicle (Figure 22.17). It is cooled by liquid and has an automatic electrolyte top-up system.

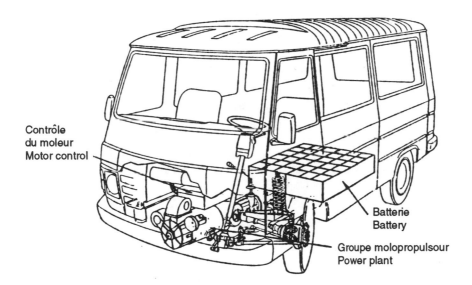

Contrôle
du moleur
Motor control

Batterie
Battery

Groupe molopropulsour
Power plant

Figure 22.19. Peugeot J9 Goods Vehicle.[41]

---

[41] *Ibid.*

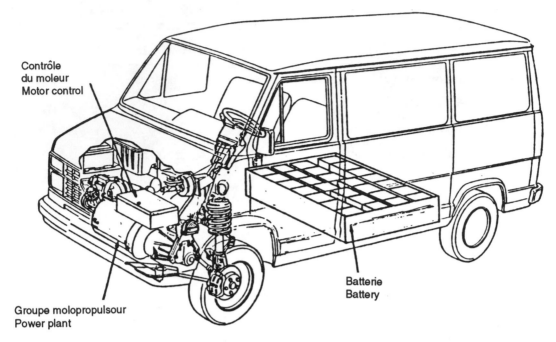

Contrôle
du moteur
Motor control

Groupe motopropulseur
Power plant

Batterie
Battery

Figure 22.20. Peugeot J5 Goods Vehicle[42]

Table 22-6. Characteristics of Peugeot J9		Lead (Ceac)	NiCd (Saft)
Battery 204 V			
Curb weight	kg.	2643	2507
Payload	kg	1307	1443
Load volume	m^3	8	8
Maximum speed	km/h	90	90
Acceleration 0-50	km/h	12	12
Urban range	km	90	130

---

[42] *Ibid.*

Table 22-7. Characteristics of Peugeot J5			
Battery 168 V		Lead (Ceac)	NiCd (Saft)
Kerb weight	kg	2277	2165
Payload	kg	623	735
Load volume	m³	6	6
Maximum speed	km/h	90	90
Acceleration 0-50	km/h	12s	12s
Urban range	km	80	115

"It should also be pointed out that independent carmakers have made remarkable progress in developing new vehicles, as the following examples illustrate:

"Elestra-Electricité de Strasbourg and the West German firm Alko have developed a three-wheeled light delivery van. Two hundred of the vehicles are in use with municipal technical departments and in Electricité de France's nuclear powerplants.

"Although the vehicles are ideal for short journeys involving frequent stops they are difficult to incorporate into the normal traffic flow, especially because of poor acceleration.

"There are further potential applications for the new vehicle, particularly in the pedestrian precincts of large cities.

"Rocaboy is a multipurpose goods vehicle, manufactured since 1976 by a small-scale nonindustrial producer, Mr. Rocaboy.

"To date, the 150 vehicles currently in operation have clocked up over 1,000,000 km.

"In recent months, the newly formed Société d'Exploitation des Electromobiles Rochelaises (SEER) company has taken over production of the Rocaboy, and is capitalizing on the opportunities offered by the creation of an industrial production facility in La Rochelle.

"Twenty Rocaboys are currently in service with Electricité de France, between 60 and 70 with the CEA and some 30 more in towns and cities throughout France. Twenty of the vehicles are in the hands of private owners.

"The Rocaboy goods vehicle is highly reliable and needs only to gain greater market share in order to be a complete success. One particularly strategic market for the Rocaboy is the large number of craftsmen who could use such a vehicle for travelling around town.

"Company fleets form another niche area, and efforts will be stepped up to increase sales to major enterprises.

"Teilhol is a three-wheeled vehicle produced by a French manufacturer for use as an airport liaison vehicle.

"The French airline Air France participated in the development of the Teilhol, and a total of 100 vehicles are in service in the airports of Paris and Nice.

"The vehicle is not being developed for applications other than airport use and distribution will thus remain very limited.

"In the field of conventional vehicles, the following development should be noted for electric refuse collection vehicles:

"At the request of a number of municipal authorities, the vehicle manufacturers SITA and SEMAT are developing an electric refuse collection vehicle with a collection capacity of 7 cm^3.

"The City of Paris operates a fleet of 500 refuse collection vehicles, 100 of which are electrically powered. Unfortunately, the number of electric vehicles is declining since the capacity of the on-board batteries is insufficient to allow for two successive collection rounds.

"Studies into the use of more efficient batteries have been inconclusive in view of the sluggish French market for this type of vehicle.

"Despite this drawback, it would appear that ecological considerations—and especially problems of noise and environmental pollution—will stimulate development of electrically propelled refuse collection vehicles in the medium term.

"Because of the difficulties of traffic flow caused by overcrowding in a number of French cities, the collection capacity of the new collection vehicles will have to be significantly reduced (maximum 5 cm^3). This is already the case in countries such as Japan.

Development Outlook for Electric Vehicles

"This rapid overview has illustrated the difficulties encountered in attempting to gain a larger share of an automotive market that is generally hostile to electric vehicles.

"Out of a total of 25,000,000 vehicles currently on French roads, between 1m and 2m goods vehicles are likely candidates for electrical propulsion, primarily because this category of vehicle is designed for urban use and is returned to a parking garage at the end of a day's service.

"The results obtained by vehicle users in ongoing experiments point to a promising outlook for electric vehicles in the coming years. However, this buoyant prospect is subject to one vital condition: significant gains must be made in the reliability of materials and in acquisition costs."

While interest in electric vehicles had been keen in France in the 1890s, in Germany at the same time interest lagged, as it did indeed with the entrepreneurial class, as compared with America and with England in the 1970 revival. In this later period, the large German companies would assert a leadership.

CHAPTER 23

Modern Foreign Electric Vehicle Development — Part II

Vehicles of German Manufacture

The German corporation which carried the development of the electric vehicle furthest in the 1980s was Volkswagen *et al.* They applied a largely conventional d-c motor drive to their well-known vans. Figure 23.1 shows a series of German electric vehicles, *circa* 1977, assembled by a cooperative effort of Robert Bosch GmbH, Daimler-Benz AG, M.A.N. AG, Siemens AG, VARTA batterie AG, J.M. Voith GmbH, and Volkswagenwerk AG.[1] By the end of the 1970s this very considerable emphasis on electric vehicles had been largely spent.[2] Methods of storing energy were simply not compatible with the perceived needs of the driver. But there had been some ingenious approaches in battery interchange, as shown in Figs. 23.2 and 23.3, not greatly unlike the scheme pioneered by Robert McKee in the Sundancer, pictured earlier in Fig. 21.1.

Figure 23.1. A series of German manufactured electric vehicles and trucks. Courtesy: Electric Vehicle New, February 1977, p. 31.

---

1 *Electric Vehicle News*, February 1977, p. 31.
2 *Ten Years of German Development, Electric Vehicles*, Vol. 67, No. 3, September 1981, p. 13.

Figures 23.2 and 23.3. Fast battery-changing technique developed by a West German firm, which extends operating range of Mercedes-Benz's and Volkswagen's electric vehicles, takes no longer than normal "fill-up" at a gas station—about three to four minutes at most. Courtesy: Electrical World.

The Volkswagen electric Commercial, stated to be in production in 1977,[3] had a top speed of 70 km/h, an acceleration from 0-50 km/h in 12 seconds, a range from 50-80 km using 55 kWh per 100 km. Batteries are lead-acid weighing 860 kg and operate at 144 v, with a capacity of 180 Ah. The d-c motor has a continuous rating of 14 kW, and a peak output of 33 kW. Development on the van began in 1969. Over the period from 1974-85 seventy electric vehicles were built by Volkswagen, and 60 by Daimler-Benz. The program is on-going.[4]

In the design for the Volkswagen, shown in Fig. 23.4, care of the battery is through the forward hatch, with attention to the motor obtained through the boot.

Battery Interchange

One need almost make a battery interchange to realize what a heavy, dirty, acid job this task is unless a developed system is employed. Figures 23.2 and 23.3, above cited, show a scheme evolved by Gesellschaft Fur Electrischen Strassenverkehr of Dusseldorf, West Germany, demonstrated at the Brussels Symposium of 1972.[5]

For changing the battery, the battery compartment being between the axles of the vehicle, a low-level fork-lift platform is first raised to the height of the compartment. As the operator cranks a lever the freshly charged battery contacts and forces out the initial energy source onto a similar fork-lift platform. The time taken, it is said, is equivalent to fuel an IC vehicle. In

Figure 23.4. A Volkswagen sedan bearing a rear-mounted d-c motor drive. Courtesy: Commonwealth Edison Company.

[3] *Electric Vehicle News*, Vol. 6, No. 4, November 1977, pp. 16-17.

[4] Victor Wouk, *Two Decades of 'High Performance' EV Fleet Experience*, Eighth International Electric Vehicle Symposium, Washington, D.C., 1986.

[5] *Electrical World*, April 15, 1972, p. 78.

studying this illustration an interesting comparison may be made by referring to an etching, Fig. 7-18, showing a similar operation at the Paris Exposition of 1900. Range limitation and battery care are the twin *"bête noire"* of electric vehicles.

While battery interchange may have interest for long range electric vehicles, it has little value for dash racing by battery-powered cars, as the next section investigates.

A Compleat Electric Racing Vehicle

In every age there is a special niche for instruments designed for speed. It might be a dog, a horse, a boat, an aircraft, a bullet, or an electric vehicle. The HAGEN-Elobil (German) is such an instrument, along with the Autolite Lead Wedge (USA), both of which were constructed for dash racing. The record created by Jens Knoblock in a HAGEN-Elobil on July 6, 1981 was 161.3 km/hr (100.2 mph) for 1 kilometer, and 158.9 km/h (98.7 mph) for one mile. The acceleration was 0-99.7 km/hr (62.0 mph) for one kilometer. The race track was the Hockenheim-Ring. Figure 23.5 shows the HAGEN-Elobil with hood aside.[6] The Autolite Lead Wedge flying mile 1968 record was 138.862 mph, as certified by the United States Auto Club.[7] The place: Utah salt flats.

Figure 23.5. The electric-powered HAGEN-Elobil raced 161.3 km/hr for one km, and 98.7 mph for one mile in 1981 from a standstill. Courtesy: Electric Vehicle News.

---

[6] *World Record in the Elobil, Electric Vehicle News*, Vol. 10, No. 4, November 1981, p. 19.

[7] *Ibid*, Vol. 1, No. 2, March 1969.

These speeds may be compared with Riker's electric car 1901 record of 57.1 mph for a flying mile on a sand track, as related in Chapter 16. While dash speed is good sport, the commercial niche for electric vehicles is city driving. Below is a German approach to the problem.

The GES CitySTROMer

As reported by R. L. Driggans and G. D. Whitehead:[8]

"The CitySTROMer is an electric passenger car produced by Gesellschaft fuer elektrischen Stassenverkehr (GES) in the Federal Republic of Germany (FRG) based on the production VW Golf CL. In creating the CitySTROMer, internal combustion engine (ICE) components are removed and replaced by electric propulsion components. In addition, the floorpan beneath the rear seat and the cargo area is cut away, and a fiberglass-reinforced plastic battery compartment is installed. The CitySTROMer, shown in Fig. 23.6, features an all-steel unitized body/chassis

Figure 23.6. CitySTROMer

---

[8] R. L. Driggans and G. D. Whitehead, *Performance Characterization Testing of the GES CitySTROMer*, The 9th International Electric Vehicle Symposium, Toronto, 1988.

with a protected passenger compartment. Basic vehicle physical specifications are included in Table 23-1. The front-wheel drive CitySTROMer retains the standard VW Golf fully-independent front suspension system, but the rear axle and shock absorbers were replaced with production components from a VW Dasher station wagon. The rear coil springs are nonstandard parts sized for the higher maximum rear-axle load of the CitySTROMer. Steering is rack-and-pinion, and the mechanical brake system is the standard Golf power-assisted front-disc, rear-drum arrangement. An electrically-powered pump and vacuum tank were added to provide the required vacuum assist.

"The CitySTROMer was designed to meet European safety standards. Compliance with U.S. Federal Motor Vehicle Safety Standards would require modifications such as door reinforcement and replacement of components such as bumpers, signal lights, and headlights.

"A block diagram of the CitySTROMer propulsion system is shown in Fig. 23.7. The vehicle is powered by a BBC separately-excited, 90 V, 12 kW dc motor mated to a standard Golf

Table 23-1. CitySTROMer Physical Specifications	
Gross Vehicle Weight:	1,665 kg
Curb Weight:	1,352 kg
Maximum Payload Weight:	313 kg
Length:	4.0 m
Width:	1.7 m
Height:	1.4 m
Wheelbase:	2.5 m
Cargo Volume:	0.4 m^3

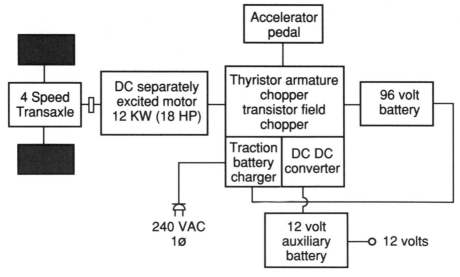

Figure 23.7. CitySTROMer Propulsion System

4-speed manual transaxle. A BBC all-electronic, microprocessor-based controller is mounted on top of the motor/transaxle assembly beneath the hood. The controller has a thyristor chopper which regulates motor armature current by means of a 10-position, discrete-step control circuit and a transistor chopper which regulates field current. Regenerative braking is provided in both armature- and field-chopping modes and can be set to a maximum current of either 30 A (weak braking force) or 100 A (strong braking force) via a dash-mounted switch.

"Constant speed 56 km/h driving range was 92.2 km when the CitySTROMer was driven in its normal operating mode. When the RT feature was activated, the vehicle could be driven an additional 4.5 km, an increase of 5 percent. The range tests were ended when battery voltage dropped to the manufacturer's recommended cutoff level. AC energy required to recharge the vehicle's traction battery following the 56 km/h range tests was 0.2 kWh/km.

"Vehicle driving range on the SAE J227a C Cycle was 43.6 km in the normal operating mode. When the RT feature was activated the CitySTROMer could be driven an additional 2.3 km, a 5 percent increase. The range tests were ended when the vehicle could no longer maintain the prescribed speed profile (Fig. 23.8). AC energy consumption was 0.3 kWh/km.

"In the Urban Route range test, the vehicle was driven on level streets in downtown Chattanooga in a manner compatible with traffic conditions (the average speed was 18 km/h). Driving range was 39.4 km in the normal operating mode and 44.4 km with the RT feature activated (a 13 percent increase). The tests were ended due to low battery voltage.

"Maximum acceleration test results with the "Speed" limit feature activated are available. Acceleration time from 0 to 48 km/h was 14.5 seconds at full charge."

The results of the CitySTROMer are shown in Table 23.2.

As innovative thinking had established a daring speed and acceleration for a vehicle in Germany, a Netherlands citizen filled a niche for an electric personnel carrier in Amsterdam.

The Electric Vehicle in Holland

Lund Schimmelpennink of Holland is an example of the European entrepreneur. A member of the Amsterdam city council, Lund believed urban travel could be made more convenient by

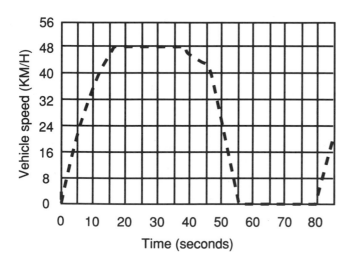

Figure 23.8. SAE J227a C Cycle

Table 23-2. CitySTROMer Test Results		
Test Weight (kg)	1,665	
Maximum Speed (km/h)		
Speed Limit on	78.9	
Speed Limit off	95.6	
Constant Speed 56 km/h dc Energy		
Consumption (Wh/km)	105	
Acceleration Time 0 to 48 km/h (s)	14.5	
Braking Distance from 48 km/h (m)	14.6	
Range on 10-Percent Grade (km)	11.8	
Battery Capacity at 72.5 A Discharge		
Rated (Ah)	110	
Measured (Ah)	110	
	Reserve Tank Off	Reserve Tank On
MEASURED DATA		
Constant Speed 56 km/h Range (km)	107.9	113.1
SAE J227a C Cycle Range (km)	51.7	54.3
Urban Route Range (km)	48.2	54.2
TEMPERATURE COMPENSATED DATA		
Constant Speed 56 km/h Range (km)	92.2	96.7
SAE J227a C cycle Range (km)	43.6	45.9
Urban Route Range (km)	39.9	44.9

employing readily accessible electric-powered taxis from stations, the whole linked by computer assist. His vehicles, which he designed, are designated the Witkar, of which two are shown in city traffic in Fig. 23.9.

In the Witkar system for improving the quality of life while facilitating pedestrian mobility in cities, citizens buy a lifetime membership in a Witkar Association.[9]

"As the vehicles are registered with the Department of Transportation a driver's license is required for use. On joining the group a member is assigned an account number in the banking system and receives a metal key magnetically coded. Each Witkar station is terminal linked to a central computer. In renting a Witkar the key is inserted into a station terminal, the destination is dialed and checked for parking-recharge space. If no space is available, a signal indicates a new destination must be determined. With the computer check fulfilled passage is registered, and the personal key is used to unlock the initial car in the charging line. As the lead car departs

---

[9] W. M. Senger, *Silent Car in Amsterdam, Environment*, Vol. 16, No. 8, October 1974, pp. 14-17.

Figure 23.9. The Witkar driver-operated electric taxis in Amsterdam. Photo by David Halperin.

the computer causes all local Witkars to advance one station. The departing renter may stop enroute, his key locking the car with the 'meter running.' Arriving at his final destination the car is parked at the tail of the charging queue, the key is removed signaling the computer the final destination has been reached. The elapsed time is calculated and the charges subtracted from the user's bank account.

"The Witkar stands 86 inches high on a 55-inch wheelbase and occupies one-half the space of a compact car. The vehicle is powered by a quick-charging nickel-cadmium battery which is claimed to have a life of 30,000 charges as compared to a vehicle battery life of some 300-500 for conventional lead-acid energy sources. The battery powers a 2-kW, 24 volt Bosch motor belt connected to the single rear wheel. In actual practice only 5 1/2 minutes charging time was required for a 1 1/2 mile ride. Both the handbrake and the footbrake bear microswitches to disconnect the motor when the brake is applied. As these Witkars have an energy use of 0.2-0.3 kWh per mile, they are limited to downtown use."

The market place, that remorseless and honest testing ground, allowed the Witkar organization to seek bankruptcy some eighteen months after initiation,[10] a time span indicating the

---

[10] Scott D. Schuh, *Car-Sharing Experiment in San Francisco Promises to Trim Auto Use & Expenses, The Wall Street Journal*, August 1, 1984, p. 21.

program was too modestly capitalized. Meanwhile, vehicle building was proceeding in other national areas.

A Hong Kong Alternating-Current Electric Vehicle

Observing the need to conserve petroleum fuel and taking advantage of the developing a-c drive principle as applied to electric vehicles, a subject introduced in Chapter 19, C.C. Chan *et al* of the Department of Electrical Engineering, University of Hong Kong, designed and constructed a pulse-width-modulated (PWM) transistorized three-phase inverter and solid-state controller for an induction motor drive system. This system was placed in a conventional two-door sedan. As introduced as a technique in Chapter 19, the Hong Kong motor was built by computer-aided design for optimization. Of especial interest in this vehicle, besides the care in the design of all elements, is a "microprocessor-based Battery Prediction Device incorporated in the battery system. This device provides the driver a real-time estimation of the remaining battery capacity as well as residual range" remaining for the vehicle. For anyone who has driven an electric vehicle, and the need to park on the shoulder of a road waiting for the battery to depolarize before resuming travel, this feature is too often an overlooked convenience. The paper outlining the Hong Kong vehicle is an excellent reference for any designer of an electric automobile.[11] Table 23-3 gives specifications for this vehicle.

For comparison purposes the interested reader might refer to Chapter 19 and the earlier Linear Alpha designed a-c drive electric vehicle, where values for many like parameters are given.

Table 23-3. Specifications for the Hong Kong Alternating-Current Powered Sedan

Vehicle gross weight:	1120 kg
Climbing capability:	20 degrees or 36 percent grade
Acceleration:	Ten seconds from 0 to 40 km/h (24 mph)
Range per charge:	100 km (60 miles) at 40 km/hr
Top speed:	80 km/h (48 mph)
Battery system:	12 12-volt lead-acid batteries
Inverter type:	Transistorized, sinusoidal pulse-width-modulated
Output voltage:	15V to 100 V
Output frequency:	4 Hertz to 100 Hertz
Output current:	Up to 150 amperes peak
Motor:	3-phase, 2-pole induction, 11kW, 100 Volts

---

[11] C. C. Chan, W. L. Lang, and W. C. Lo, *An Electric Vehicle with High Performance Inverter, Controller and Battery Prediction*, Eighth International Electrical Vehicle Symposium, Washington, C. C. 1986.

Professor C.C. Chan and his associates have continued to refine their AC powertrain drive, writing:[12]

Electric Van Propulsion System

"The proposed ac propulsion system is applied to a 1.8 tonne electric van. Table 23-4 gives the design specifications of the electric van. The electric van is designed for use in urban areas with many steep roads, hence the climbing capability and start-stop performance are the prime concerns, while the top speed is of less importance. Figure 23.10 shows the functional block diagram of the electric van. A 216 V battery pack provides main power source to a high power transistorized inverter where it is inverted to variable frequency three phase ac and delivered to the drive motor. The ac induction motor then drives the rear wheels through a clutch and variable ratio gear box assembly. The power flow is reversed in the case of regeneration, i.e., the motor becomes an induction generator and hence the inverter becomes a rectifier to convert ac power into dc and charges the batteries.

(A) Motor and Inverter

"The motor used was designed by a computer-aided optimization program to maximize the performance of the electric van. The motor frame size is 160L, which is one class smaller as compared with standard motor.

Table 23-4. Hong Kong Vehicle	
Gross vehicle weight (battery included)	1800 Kg
Maximum speed	75 Km/h
Climbing capability	20°
Battery	Lead acid, 216V, 105Ah
Range per charge	100 Km @ 40 Km/hr
Motor	20 Kw continuous, 135 V, 3-phase induction motor, 4 pole
Inverter	PWM transistorized, 2Hz-100Hz, 400 A peak

---

[12] C. C. Chan and C. W. Ng, *Adaptive AC Propulsion System for Electric Vehicles*, The 9th International Electrical Vehicle Symposium, Toronto, 1988.

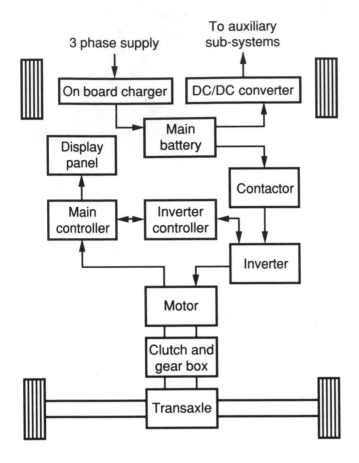

Figure 23.10. Functional block diagram of the electric van. (See Footnote 12)

"The inverter used is a full bridge transistorized inverter, it has the advantages over its thyristorized counterpart in the aspects of commutation, size, weight, cost and efficiency. In addition, higher switching frequency may be used to produce a better sinusoidal ac output. The most advanced power transistors available in the market of 400A, 450V are employed. The inverter output frequency range is from 2Hz to 100Hz.

(B) Controller

"The controller of the electric van is composed of a main controller and an inverter controller. The two controllers form a 8086 based multiprocessor system with each processor allocated different task. Information interflow between processors is done by means of the 16K global memory through the global bus. The inverter controller fetches the 3-phase current commands from the global memory and generates the gating signal to the transistorized inverter based on the current Band

Band Control. This current Band Band Control enables the adoption of a voltage source inverter in a current command oriented type of control method. Furthermore, it minimizes the transistor switching spike current, providing an inherent output current limit, and resulting in an approximate sinusoidal current for lower motor harmonic losses. An example of the current Band Band Control is shown in Fig. 23.11.

Conclusion

"A new control scheme for induction motor drives was developed. It is shown in Fig. 23.12. The control scheme adopted the modern control theory, namely the decoupling control and adaptive control. With the integration of decoupling control and adaptive control, the dynamic performance and robustness of the induction motor drive was significantly enhanced. The special features of the new control scheme lie in its high dynamic performance, simple control configuration which can be easily implemented by microprocessors with modest cost. Experimental results are satisfactory. The proposed control scheme is suitable for high performance robust speed control and position control, particularly those in hazardous environment."

From electric vehicle development in Hong Kong we pass to India.

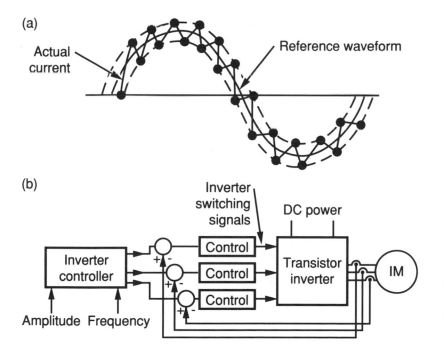

*Figure 23.11.
Current band band
control scheme.
(See Footnote 12).
(a) Motor current,
(b) Block diagram*

Figure 23.12. The electric drive system on test. (See Footnote 12)

Indian Electric Car and Vans

The Indian Government College of Technology personnel, like scientific personnel in Western countries and in Japan, have interested themselves in electric-powered personal transportation. To meet their perceived needs a vehicle capable of seating four adults was developed. A 2-hp series-wound d-c motor was employed, powered from lead-acid batteries. Control is by a solid-state chopper. Top speed is a reported 25 km/hr. Range is given as 80 km.[13] The large number of personnel and animals observed on Indian roads by the author mitigates the need for high speed travel.

Observing the above work, in 1984-85 Bharat Electrical Limited (BHEL) designed and built seven 16-passenger Electravan class electric vehicles for commuter service between Delhi and New Delhi, a number subsequently increased to 30. A comparison cost system for both the diesel equivalent and the electric-powered vans was maintained by the Delhi Energy Development Agency much like the comparison cost between horse carriages and electric taxis evolved by C.E. Woods in moving passengers in New York City in 1900, as described in Chapter 4. In

---

[13] *Electric Vehicle News*, Vol. 7, No. 3, August 1977, pp. 10-11.

addition the Delhi Agency recorded problems encountered. The end result of the experiment, like all others that have been made, was that until the cycle life of the battery was substantially increased, its energy density greatly enhanced, and cost of the vehicle greatly decreased, the electric commuting vehicles were not economically viable. Table 23-5 and Fig. 23.13 both characterize and illustrate the Electravan.

Indian Purpose-Built Electric Vehicles

American and European electric vehicle designers, particularly, have sought van and saloon-sized electric vehicles comparable in acceleration, speed, and comfort of the well-established IC type. A different approach has been voiced by L. Roy Leembruggen of Australia as given in Chapter 22. He has argued for purpose-built electric vehicles. Anil Ananthakrisna of Bangalore, India also has this belief. He has placed into production 2- and 3-wheeled electric cycles which may very well fulfill the needs of Third World nations—a vehicle a step above a

Table 23-5. Characteristics of the Commuter Electravan			
Unladen Weight	- 2800 Kgs	Traction Motor	- 15 KW, Separately Excited DC Motor
Pay load	- 15 Persons		
GVW	- 3800 Kgs	Controller	- Transistorized Chopper Controller, 96 volts, 200 amps
Wheelbase	- 3000 mm		
Maximumum Speed	- 50 Kms per hour	Battery	- 96 volts, 300 AH (C5), Lead Acid Battery
Range per Charge	- More than 75 Kms		
		Battery Formation	- 16 Nos., 6-volt units
Energy Consumption	- 0.5 Kwh/km	Battery Charger	- Off Board Type

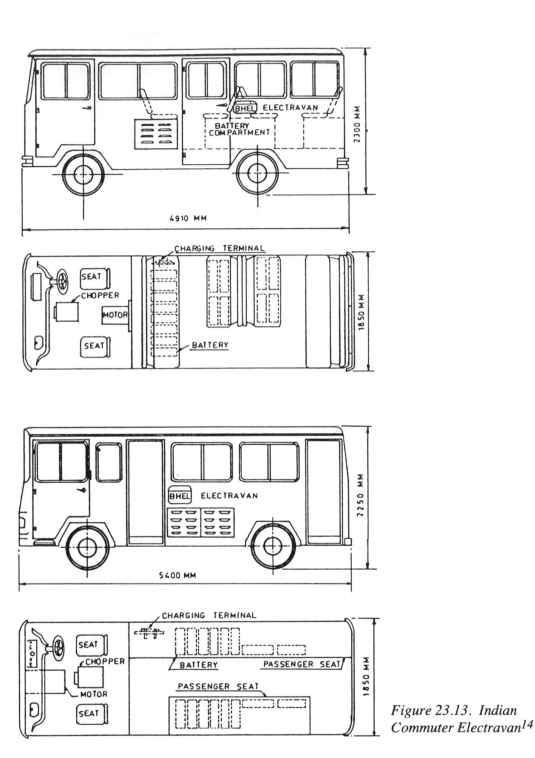

Figure 23.13. Indian Commuter Electravan[14]

[14] D. P. Dodeja and B. H. Agarwal, *Development of Electric Vehicles in India By BHEL*, Eighth International Electric Vehicle Symposium, Washington, D.C. 1986.

bicycle. Characteristics of these vehicles are in Table 23-6,[15] and a comparison with the General Motors Sunraycer is given. Figures 23.14 and 23.15 illustrate these modes of transportation.

Italian Electric Cars

Probably the earliest modern, made-in-Italy electrical motorcar following Count Felix Carli's unique electric multi-powered vehicle of 1894, recounted in *Multi-Powered Electric Cars* by the author,[16] was the American Rowan Controller Company's Ghia SpA De Tomaso electric automobile. It was demonstrated November 1967. This vehicle had a curb weight of

Table 23-6. Details of Product Developments and Improvements Achieved as per Table B				
a) Electric Two Wheelers			b) Electric Three Wheeler Autorickshaw	
Period:	Table A 1982-86	Table B 1987-88	Period:	1985-87
Vehicle Weight	115 Kg	85 Kg	Vehicle Weight	430 Kgs
Pay Load	70 Kg	70 Kg	Pay Load	200 Kgs
Battery Weight	56 Kg	32 Kg	Battery Weight	180 Kgs
Range/Charge	59/60 Kms	50/60 Kms	Range/Charge	80 Kms
Battery Cost	Rs. 2300	Rs. 1100 ($60.70)	Battery Cost	Rs. 6000 ($327.60)
Battery Life	300 Cycles	300 Cycles	Battery Life	300 Cycles
Operational Cost	14 Ps/Km	7.7 Ps/Km (0.4¢ American/km)	Operational Cost	30 Ps/Km (1.6¢ American/km)
Based on a foreign exchange of January 14, 1991: 100 paise = one Rupee = 0.0546 American dollars				
(For comparison purposes the General Motors Sunraycer, a solar-powered vehicle with a coefficient of drag of 0.12, consumed 1500 watts when travelling 80 kilometers per hour. With electric energy at 10¢/kwh, the energy cost is 0.19¢/km.)				

---

[15] Anil Ananthakrishna, *Electric Two and Three Wheelers for Personal Transport*, The 9th International Electric Vehicle Symposium, Toronto, 1988.

[16] Ernest H. Wakefield, *History of the Electric Automobile: Multi-Powered Electric Cars*, To be published.

Figure 23.14. Electric Two Wheeler (Vidyut - 24). Anil Ananthakrisna.

Figure 23.15. Electric Three Wheeler Autorickshaw. Anil Ananthakrisna.

only 1340 pounds, bore 550 pounds of lead-acid batteries (a ratio of 41 percent) with a rating of 48 volts at 150 Ah, furnishing power to two 11,000 rpm, 2.25 kW compound-wound motors. The controller was a contactor type. Top speed was a reported 45 mph. The vehicle was equipped with regenerative braking,[17] and with 7.2 kWh of stored energy, had a probable urban range of 25 miles. The high rotational speed of this motor should be noted. As horsepower is directly related to speed of the motor, the latter can be very light in weight. The compensatory problem introduced, however, is the increased difficulty of linking high speeds to the much slower turning wheels.

Modern Italian electric cars, like the pioneer British models, were modest in size and were propelled with small motors. For example, at the 1970 Turin Auto show Urbanina SpA offered a car powered by a one kW, 24 volt, 1300 rpm Bosch motor. Subsequently another early Italian entry in electric vehicle development was the ELCAR 2000. After a few dozen had arrived in the United States, its manufacture also ceased. This vehicle is shown in Fig. 23.16.

The Elcar was an Italian import offered by the Elcar Corporation of Elkhart, Indiana. Powering the Elcar were eight 12-volt batteries which serve to drive a 2.7 hp d-c motor. Current control to the motor was achieved by voltage switching, being 24, 36, and 48 volts with resistance buffering, yielding six speeds. Top speed was about 30 mph. Urban driving range was some 30 miles. When viewed by the author the suspension was very lightweight. Acceleration from 0-29 mph was about 27 seconds. *Consumer Reports* was severely critical of the model they tested.[18] Production was short-lived.

Far better designed than the Elcar was the Fiat Xl/23B experimental vehicle shown in Chicago at the 1975 Electric Vehicle Show and illustrated in Fig. 23.17.[19] Basically a

Figure 23.16. An Italian manufactured Elcar. Courtesy: The Elcar Company.

[17] *The Electric Car: A Design Challenge, Electro Technology*, May 1968, p. 58.

[18] *Consumer Reports*, October 1976.

[19] Sergio Taranto, *EV Status in Italy, Electric Vehicle News*, Vol. 7, No. 4, November 1978, p. 34.

2-passenger sedan, the designers recognized the need for modest curb weight so becoming to the performance of an electric car. As is seen in the charts, the electric Fiat is powered by a chopper controlled, separately excited d-c motor. Giving scale to the vehicle is Mr. William H. Shafer who, at the time, was spokesman for Commonwealth Edison Company for electric cars, and a member of the Electric Vehicle Council of America.

Progetti Gestioni Ecologiche SpA delivered two electric vehicles to British Rail and Godfrey Davis Europcar Ltd. to determine if rail and car rental at terminals might join in a common effort. These vehicles, designated PGE3P, are of welded steel with integral body. Fiat components are used. Power is supplied by 12 lead-acid batteries forming a 72 volt, 195 Ah system. A 12-volt ancillary battery serves auxiliary circuits. Driving power to the forward wheels is from a 7.5 kW d-c motor with separate field, and series windings. The vehicle has solid-state control and regenerative braking. Top speed is a reported 37 mph. Range is some 30 miles. Figure 23.18 illustrates one of these vehicles. If the two sample cars meet the travelling public needs, additional vehicles may be placed at the Euston Station, it was stated.[20]

Figure 23.17. The Fiat Xl/23B 2-door sedan electric vehicle. Courtesy: Commonwealth Edison Company.

---

[20] *Assessing Cars for Rail Drive Service, Electric Vehicles*, Vol. 67, No. 4, December 1981, pp. 6 & 7.

Figure 23.18. One of the two PGE3P cars bought for evaluation by British Rail and Godfrey Davis Europcar. Courtesy: Electric Vehicles.

In the 1980s the Italian program in electric vehicles has been directed to cars, minibuses, multi-powered vehicles, and the improvement of components, particularly batteries.[21] [22]

The Fiat *Panda Eletta*

As announced in Italy, "Fiat SpA will begin selling an electric car next June. The introduction of the *Panda Eletta* ends the experimentation phase for the electric car and marks the beginning of its mass distribution." The two passenger vehicle can travel between 45 and 65 miles before it needs to recharge its battery. Its speed is reported as much as 65 mph. The vehicle is expected to sell for approximately $20,000.[23]

While the British, French, and Italians had assembled electric vehicles before the turn of the century, the nation of Japan would bow-in for the revival with great strength as is related below.

---

[21] G. Brugsaglino, *Electric and Hybrid Vehicles Status and Development in Europe*, Eighth International Electric Vehicle Symposium, Washington, D.C. 1986.

[22] L. Mazzon, P. G. Milasni, G. Brocchetti, E. Marelli, G. Brusaglino, and A. Roggero, *The C.N.R. - Fiat IVECO 471 BM Trolleybus*, Eighth International Electric Vehicle Symposium, Washington, C.C. 1986.

[23] William Mathewsen, *The Wall Street Journal*, February 8, 1990, p. 12.

Japanese Electric Vehicles

The entry of Japan into electric vehicles was, indeed, impressive. In the early 1960s Japanese automobile makers formed five well coordinated groups to develop battery-powered cars.[24] By standards of the 1960s all but one had battery and power systems not greatly unlike the vehicles discussed above, as seen in Table 23-7 below. The Toyota Publica Van, however, had an advanced power plant: a brushless type (d-c motor with electronic commutation) with SCR commutation, and of substantial power—20 kW, yielding a top speed for the 2000 pound van of 62 mph.

As the principal energy for electricity generation in Japan has been oil, and as petroleum was a few dollars a barrel, electric energy in Japan, like in all Western nations, was relatively cheap. The philosophy for control of air pollution gaining in Japan, the battery-powered vehicle was perceived as a means for reducing air defilement in Japanese cities. As is seen later, the sharp rise in petroleum prices reduced interest in Japanese electric vehicle development. Instead the IC automobile manufacturers opted for more miles per gallon and found a waiting world market. There have been many explanations for the vacuum the Japanese found and filled.

One school of economists has maintained U.S. car makers were damaged by the government regulated low-priced petroleum in America.[25] When Japanese oil prices were mounting, market forces allowed Japan to anticipate preferred design. Moreover, artificially low-priced gasoline discouraged electric vehicle development. U.S. Government regulations, these savants argue, damaged the citizenry in two ways: American IC automobile manufacturers lost leadership, and electric vehicle development was dissuaded. Here again over-regulation was seen as a "Red Flag" Act as discussed in Chapter 2, when in 1882 Professors Ayrton and Perry found their frail electric tricycle, to operate within the law, required three people to be aboard, and another, 300 feet ahead, to bear a red flag. In a dynamic society government regulation can be interpreted to be almost always wanting. Should members of Congress be historians rather than lawyers?

In the 1970s Japan continued to evolve electric vehicles.[26] The four companies experimenting were: Daihatsu, Toyota Motor Co., Toyo, and Nissan Motor Co. The Japanese government had funded this work with a $20 million 5-year program starting in 1971. Whether the companies would proceed with mass production was to be left to their management.[27]

Daihatsu chose to develop a plastic bodied, 2006 pound curb weight sedan with a d-c motor powered by four 24-volt lead-acid batteries. Control was by a silicon-control-chopper system. The range claimed was 80 miles at 50 mph, with an acceleration of 0-18 mph in 4 seconds. In 1973 the company also produced 20 electric vans. Both vehicles are shown in Figs. 23.19 and 23.20.

---

[24] *The Electric Car: A Design Challenge, Electro Technology*, May 1968, p. 58.

[25] A Japanese spokesman intimated America's quality of management and concept of work ethics had both fallen. Scott Hall, Northwestern University, May 21, 1982.

[26] Gordon W. Jones, *Japanese Electric Vehicle Development Status*, Dana Corporation Technical Center, Ottawa Lake, Michigan, June 6, 1974.

[27] Eugene F. Gorzelnik, *Electric Vehicles Meet Test in Japan, Electrical World*, April 19, 1979, pp. 101-102.

Table 23-7. Characteristics of Japanese Electric Vehicles Demonstrated in 1966 - 1967

Model and developer	Demonstrated	No. of passengers	Vehicle weight, A, lb	Battery	Motor	Controller	Max energy stored, b, kWh	B/A Wh/lb	Speed, mph Top	Speed, mph Optimum	Range, miles	Hill climbing	Regenerative Braking
Daihatsu Compagno Kansai Elec Power Co Japan Storage Batt Co Daihatsu Kogyo Co Nippon Yusoki Co	Nov. 1966	2	2180	Lead acid: 84 V, 120 Ah	5 kW, 80 V, 80 A, 2900 rpm	Time ratio	10.1	4.62	43.5	31.1	49.7	6.2 mph for 1/4, 28.1 mph for 1/20	Yes
Corona Van 1200 Chubu Elec Power Co Yuasa Batt Co Shinko Denki Co.	Dec. 1966	4	3870	Ni-Cd: 96 V, 120 Ah	6 kW, 80V, 89 A, 2300 rpm	Time ratio	11.5	2.97	49.7	29.9	55.8	13.7 mph for 1/6, 31.3 mph for 1/20	Yes
Mitsubishi 360 Van Tokyo Elec Power Co Japan Storage Batt Co Mitsubishi Jyokogyo Co Mitsubishi Elec Mach Co	Dec. 1966	2	1650	Lead-acid: 96 V, 70 Ah	5.5 kW, 90 V. 80 A, 5550 rpm	Time ratio	6.7	4.06	46.6	37.2	59	7.5 mph for 1/4, 12.5 mph for 1/8	Yes
1962 Cabail Light Van Yuasa Batt Co	Dec. 1966	2	4890	Lead-acid: 80 V, 400 Ah	7.9 kW, 63 V, 2400 rpm	Time ratio	32.0	6.53	40.4	24.8	101	12.5 mph for 1/7, 28.1 mph for 1/20	Yes
Toyota Publica Van Tokyo Shibaura Elec Co	1967	2	2000	Lead-acid: 500 lb	Brushless SCR commutator: 20 kW, 2000 rpm	Time ratio	7.5 at 15 Wh/lb	3.75	62	NR	50	1/5 negotiable	Yes

Courtesy: *Electro Technology.*

Figure 23.19. Daihatsu Sedan. Gordon W. Jones.

Toyota in 1974 had developed a 5-passenger sedan with a curb weight of 3047 pounds. Power was furnished by a d-c motor with external excitation. Control, like Daihatsu, was a solid state chopper. Figure 23.21 illustrates this vehicle.

Toyo was working on a lightweight flat-bed electric truck prototyped by Mazda. This vehicle had a curb weight of only 1718 pounds. Power was from a d-c motor with chopper control. Range was given as 80 miles at 45 mph, with an acceleration of 0-18 mph in 5 seconds.

Figure 23.20. Daihatsu Electric Van. Gordon W. Jones

Figure 23.21. Toyota Sedan. Gordon W. Jones.

Nissan completed the planned program by producing a fiberglass bodied pick-up truck with a curb weight of 5388 pounds powered by a d-c shunt motor, chopper controlled. Batteries were lead-acid, 20 6-volt type. Range was reported 100 miles at 45 mph, with an acceleration equal to the Toyo vehicle.

With the sharp increase in the price of petroleum in the second third of the 1970s, these vehicles, suddenly thrust upon the world, were as quickly withdrawn. With a limited range, and with electric rates linked in Japan with the price of oil, the Japanese car producers switched their effort to more efficient IC vehicles. But before the above happened, in the 1979 Tokyo Motor Show, eleven types of electric vehicles were exhibited to the public as Table 23-8 illustrates.[28] The manufacturer's names are familiar to most Americans in the 1980s because of the competitive inroads of their IC vehicles.

---

[28] *Update EVs in Japan, Electrical Vehicle News*, Vol. 9, No. 1, February 1980, p. 8.

		Maximum Loading Capacity (kg)	Maximum Speed (km/hr)	Running Distance per Charging (km) (at 40 km/hr.)
Model Name	Passenger Capacity			
1. Coure Van EV (Daihatsu Kogyo Co., Ltd.)	2	---	80	80
2. Electric Guide Car (Daihatsu)	4	---	16	40
3. Familia EV (Toyo Kogyo Co., Ltd.)	4	---	70	65
4. ALT EV (Suzuki Motor Co., Ltd.)	2	---	75	90
5. Carry Van EV (Suzuki)	2	250	70	70
6. Module Type Electric Mobile Chair (Suzuki)	1	---	6	20 (40)*
7. Delica Star Wagon EV (Mitsubishi Motor Co., Ltd.)	6 adults + 2 children	---	70	100
8. Toyota Sports 800 Gas Turbine Hybrid Car (Toyota Motor Co., Ltd.)	2	---	160	---
9. Electric Bicycle (Matsushita Electric Industrial Co., Ltd.)	1	6	18	18
10. Delta Wide Van EV (Japan Electric Vehicle Assn.)	5	---	80	45
11. Coure Van (remodeled) (JEVA)	2	---	80	50

Table 23-8. Eleven Types of Electric Vehicles at the 1979 Tokyo Motor Show

* Carries two batteries

The Daihatsu Kogyo Co., item 1 in the Table above, also developed a rental system, mini-sized electric car called PREET. The sociological-economic thought behind this system is the same as conceived by Holland's Witcar prospectus described above: Public rental cars would reduce traffic congestion and demand for parking space.[29] Members receive an identity card. This identification would be inserted into a terminal station recorder, the operation then follows the Witcar pattern. The plan appeared muted by accelerating energy costs.

What is impressive in the Japanese performance, especially to American and European auto makers, was Nippon manufacturers were prepared to invade the North American and northern European markets with well developed electric cars if, indeed, there were a demand. It appears

---

[29] *Ibid.*

to the author that their product was 2-4 years in advance of Western world automobiles. The possibility of invasion was mitigated by the high cost of oil-generated electricity in Japan, and a consequent small domestic market for electric cars, and recognition by the Asian builder that they could enhance miles per gallon while lowering the cost of gasoline-powered cars. This latter choice satisfied the home island's needs, and at the same time enabled the perceived American gap for compact autos to be filled. Their potential power of providing electric automobiles is substantial. With such management alertness small wonder Japan had captured by 1992 a substantial share of the U.S. domestic automobile market, and a high percentage of the home electronics field. Catch-up is a difficult game to play. An example of Japan's present import leader, an electric, is seen in Fig. 23.22 at the Chicago Electric Vehicle Exposition. Table 23.8 above lists other Japanese electric vehicles. Future plans of electric vehicles for Japan through the 1990s are available.[30]

Figure 23.22. The Toyota 2-door sedan, d-c powered. Courtesy: Commonwealth Edison Company.

---

[30] Yutaka Akikawa, *State of the Art and Overview on R & D and Demonstration for EHVs in Japan*, Eighth Electric Vehicle Symposium, Washington, D.D., 1986.

The Nissan AC Drive Vehicle

The Nissan Motor Company Ltd. Central Research Laboratory has reported an electric vehicle bearing nickel-iron batteries and a permanent magnet, synchronous motor drive-train. It is shown in Fig. 23.23. Interesting is the comparison of drive-train efficiency when compared with Nissan-designed DC and AC induction motor drive systems. Tables below characterize the vehicle which is shown in the illustration. Battery capacity is given as 20.8 kWh, range of 186 km on a driving range at a constant speed of 40 km/hr. This value is 16 percent better than with the former AC motor drive. Maximum speed is 70 km/hr, and an acceleration from 0-40 km/hr in nine seconds. Climbing performance was tangent of the angle of 9.3 (17 degrees).[31] Tables 23-9, 23-10, and 23-11 give this vehicle's characteristics.

Figure 23.23. Nissan AC Drive Vehicle. Gordon W. Jones.

Table 23-9. Comparison with Other Systems			
System	DC drive	AC induction drive	AC p.m.* drive
Maximum efficiency of system (motor and controller	75%	82%	89%
*Permanent magnet, synchronous motor			

---

[31] Tadashi Imaseki and Masahiko Tahara, *Development of AC Permanent Magnet Motor Drive System for Electric Vehicles*, The 9th International Electric Vehicle Symposium, Toronto, 1988.

Table 23-10. Specifications of This System

Power transistor:	Mitsubishi QM150 x 9 (150A x 9)
Inverter input voltage:	80 ~ 180V
Switching frequency:	PWM 3 kHz
Inverter frequency range:	0 ~ 200 Hz
Rotor phase angle sensor:	Resolver (Db = 0.3°)
Computer:	6809B (8 MHz) x 2
Control cycle:	5 msec

Table 23-11. Test Vehicle Specifications

Vehicle	Length		3,785 mm
	Width		1,560 mm
	Height		1,395 mm
	Wheelbase		2,300 mm
	Track	Front	1,345 mm
		Rear	1,330 mm
	Passenger Capacity		2
	Curb Weight		1,070 kg
	Tire		155 SR 12
Transmission (2 speed A/T)	1st		2.6
	2nd		1.3
	Final		4.5
Battery	Type		Ni-Fe
	Capacity		160 Ah
	Rated Voltage		130 V
	Weight		370 kg

The Toyota AC Drive Vehicle — EV-30

This miniature off-road, four-wheel vehicle is an example of purpose-built electric vehicles and typifies much of the current effort in Japan for electric vehicles. Go after the niche markets, and gain experience while batteries and drive-trains are being gained for the more general purpose area. Tables 23-12, 23-13, 23-14, 23-15, and 23-16 and Figures 23.24 and 23.25 characterize the EV-30. Energy consumption if 63 Wh/km at 40 km/h.[32]

Table 23-12. Vehicle Specifications		
Overall Length		2100 mm
Overall Width		1320 mm
Overall Height	Closed	1525 mm
	Open	1140 mm
Kerb Weight (incl. battery)	Closed	490 kg
	Open	470 kg
Seating Capacity		2
Gross Vehicle Weight	Closed	600 kg
	Open	580 kg
Minimum Turning Radius		2.7 m

Table 23-13. Motor Specifications	
Type	AC Induction Motor
Output Power	4.1/5.5 kW
Maximum Speed	5500 rpm
Rated Voltage	60 V
Weight	32 kg

[32] Masayuki Furutani, Masato Yokota and Masahiro Okawa, *Development of Toyota EV-30*, The 9th International Electric Vehicle Symposium, Toronto, 1988.

Table 23-14. Inverter Specification	
Switching Frequency	10 kHz
Input Voltage	106 V
Maximum Current	100 A
Efficiency	95%
Cooling	Natural Air Cooling

Table 23-15. Battery Specifications	
Voltage	106 V
Energy Capacity	0.7 kWh
Energy Efficiency	69%
Dimension (L x W x H)	650 x 540 x 300 mm
Total Weight	120 kg

Table 23-16. Driving Performance		
Top Speed		43 km/h
Hill Climbing Ability		Tan θ = 0.15 (9 degrees)
Acceleration (0-30 km/h)		9.4 sec
Range per Charge	Constant Speed 30 km/h	165 km
	Constant Speed 40 km/h	140 km
	J227a B mode	80 km

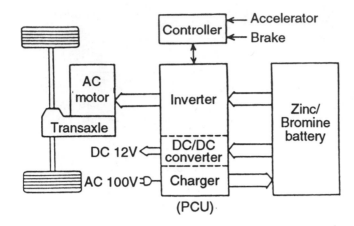

Figure 23.24. Electric Drive System. (See Footnote 32)

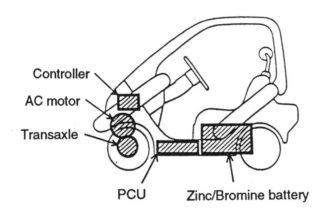

Figure 23.25. Components in Vehicle. (See Footnote 32)

Other Japanese Electric Cars[33]

The Japan Electric Vehicle Association sponsors an active development program on electric vehicles.[34] 1) Nissan Motors has developed an electric vehicle with an a-c permanent-magnet disc motor. The battery is of an iron-nickel type. They also have a d-c series-motor vehicle with thyristor chopper and lead-acid batteries. 2) Electric Vehicles Engineering Research Association has a d-c shunt-motor powered vehicle with nickel-zinc batteries. 3) Toyota Motor Corporation has an electric vehicle powered by an a-c induction-motor with a transistor inverter-control equipped with zinc-bromide batteries. 4) Suzuki Motor Co., Ltd. offers a d-c series powered electric vehicle with transistor chopper control and lead-acid batteries. 5) Mitsubishi shows a d-c motor electric vehicle with a transistor-chopper control and

---

[33] F. A. Wyczalek, *Electric Vehicle Propulsion and Magnetic Levitation*, The 9th International Electric Vehicle Symposium, Toronto, 1988.

[34] *EV Techno City*, Japan Electric Vehicle Association, Tokyo, Japan, p. 12.

Figure 23.26A. Toyota EV20 with Pb-acid battery pack and 15 KW AC induction motor. Specific Range is 8.9 km/kWh. (See Footnote 34)

Figure 23.26B. Toyota EV30 two passenger 580 kg electric vehicle is powered by a Zn/Br battery and 4.1 kW AC induction motor giving a range of 165 km at 30 km/h. Specific range is 19.4 km/kWh at 30 km/h. (See Footnote 34)

Figure 23.26C. Suzuki Alto CA71V two passenger electric vehicle with Pb-acid battery pack. This public utility service vehicle has a specific range of 7.6 km/kWh. (See Footnote 34)

Figure 23.26D. EVERA E32 prototype-2 electric vehicle in the Daihatsu Charmant with a Ni/Zn battery pack and specific range of 8.5 km/kWh. (See Footnote 34)

Fig. 23.26E. EVERA E42 prototype-2 high performance electric vehicle in Mazda Familia with a Ni/Zn battery pack and specific range of 9.5 km/kWh. (See Footnote 34)

lead-acid batteries. 6) Daihatsu Motors, Ltd. offers a d-c series-motor vehicle with transistor chopper controls and lead-acid batteries. 7) Tokyo Research & Development Co., Ltd. offers a synchronous-motor with permanent-magnets bearing a pulse-width modulation control with lead-acid batteries. 8) Mazda Motor Corporation offers a d-c shunt-motor electric vehicle with transistor-chopper and lead-acid batteries. 9) Honda is building a $13.5 million factory for the production of gallium-arsenide solar cells. Do they foresee the use of solar cells in automobiles?[35]

From the information above the Japanese automobile companies, with a national absence of a domestic source of petroleum and a constantly expanding base of nuclear electric power, may be expected to be a most competitive player in the electric vehicle field. Already Honda has announced "it was working on a highly energy-efficient compact model...(and) will also begin public testing of what it says is the world's first electric motorcycle this year in Japan."[36]

While the above was transpiring in Japan, in Mexico the leisure use for electric cars was being explored in manner strikingly similar to the British Beach Buggy shown in Fig. 22.10A.

---

[35] *Ibid*, pp. 1-12.
[36] *The New York Times*, January 10, 1991, p. C2.

Mexican Electric Recreation Vehicles

Viniegra Vehiculos Electricos S.A., recognizing the importance of tourism, announced two classic, turn-of-the-century type electric vehicles for a purpose also seized upon by Electraction Ltd of England, cited above. Viniegra brought forth the Cinderella, a two-passenger model, and the Calesa, shown in Fig. 23.27, a four-passenger carriage.[37] Both vehicles are reported to be powered with lead-acid batteries yielding 72 volts at 70 ampere-hour, providing a nominal energy of some five kWh, for a speed of 20 mph. At this velocity range is said to extend to some 40 miles. As readily observed the carriages are designed for resorts, leisure villages, clubs, and large estates.

Note should be taken that Viniegra's vehicles most closely resemble in weight and in speed the early 1900 electric carriages of Riker, and of Pope, shown in Chapters 5 and 8 respectively. With modest and ample speeds for their environment of use, and with batteries weighing no more than 300 pounds, the Viniegra modern Victorias are designed to fill a special and possibly viable economic crevice, not, to be sure, found by the British company Electraction Ltd. with a similar design.

Supplementing the above, the Mexican Electric Sports Car Association would sponsor the most recent electric car race, held on an oval track.[38]

Figure 23.27. The Viniegra Company's Cinderella, for resorts and estates.[37]

---

[37] *Electric Vehicle News*, Vol. 6, No. 3, August 1977, p. 28.
[38] *Automotive News*, 1977.

As is seen below, the concept of electric personal transport penetrates borders more readily than do ideologies.

Soviet Union (Former) Electric Automobiles

While the Soviet Union is no more, electric vehicle progress was made when that land mass was so constituted. The movement for electric vehicles also reached into the Soviet Union where K.A. Termkrtchyan, E.M. Dilanyan, and G.L. Arasheyan of the Karl Marx Polytechnic Institute in Yerevan initiated work on the Electromobile in 1968, called YERPL-1.[39] The vehicle's carrying capacity is reported to be 800 kg, with a maximum speed of 75 km/hr, and a range of 60 km. Lead-acid batteries are the source of energy. The vehicle was a sedan type.

"The Institute group will next build a hybrid electric vehicle." The hybrid will have a low power internal-combustion engine driving an electric generator which charges the batteries which in turn provide power for the traction motor. "A buffer battery supplies the extra power needed for the heavier loads, or it stores energy from the generator when there is plenty of power." Interestingly, the Pieper Company in Belgium used this technique in 1899.

Personnel at the Karl Marx Institute plan to apply computer design to electric vehicles, a subject discussed in Chapter 21. Apparent from the reading is the parallelism in vehicle design in the former USSR and in the Western countries cited above.

The former USSR had also developed an a-c drive system, designated UAZ-451-M1.[40] These vehicles, similarly powered to those American a-c transports described in Chapter 19, have a curb weight of 2200 kg, a range of 45 km, a speed of 60 km/hr, and have an energy consumption of 0.5 kWh/km, a requirement similar to Western practice. The van has a built-in charger for the lead-acid batteries. The vehicles are said to be used as delivery vans by the Moscow trading centers and school cafeterias. A 0.5-ton load carrying lorry of this type is shown center, top row in Fig. 23.28. The Soviets are also said to have experimented with nickel-zinc cells, but find them too expensive for broad scale application.

While these developments were transpiring in the former USSR, what was the impact of events on the nations of Spain, Sweden, Taiwan, and others?

Electric Vehicles in Spain

Spain is a nation which has great need for electric vehicles since its domestic sources of both coal and petroleum are modest. To overcome these energy shortfalls the nation has executed an active nuclear energy program, and has highly utilized its hydro resources. The companies most closely allied with electric vehicles formed an amalgamation of interests, The Electric Development Association of Spain (A.D.V.E.). The Association has embarked on the following projects: an urban car, a delivery Van, and a city bus.

---

[39] G. Arakelyan, *When Will the Electromobile Start, Pravda*, September 22, 1972, p. 6.

The Current Digest of the Soviet Press, Columbus: Ohio State University, Am. Assoc. for the Advancement of Slavic Studies, Vol. XXII, No. 43, 1972, pp. 24 & 32. *Electric Vehicle News*.

[40] *The USSR Releases Data on Its EVs*, Yuri Domatovsky, *Electric Vehicle News*, Vol. 11, No. 2, May 1982, p. 14.

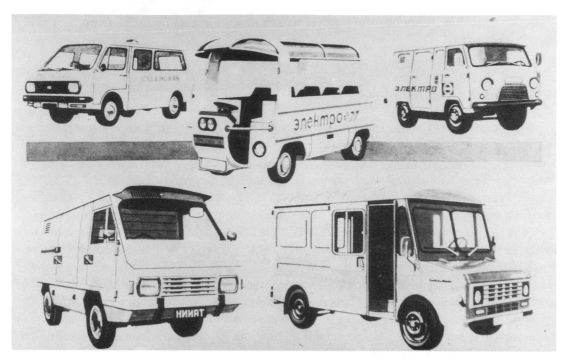

Figure 23.28. EVs designed in the former USSR: Top Row, from left to right: RAF-2210—referee's van used during the 1980 Moscow Olympics; the specimen of the All-Union Electric Transport Research Institute model which served the world Electro-77 exhibition; UA-Z451-M1 with 0.5 ton load-carrying capacity (this model used to carry breakfasts to Moscow schools). Bottom Row, left to right: the electric motor car of the Automobile Transport Research Institute; the EV produced by Yerevan Motor Works. Courtesy: Electric Vehicle News.

One of the most successful projects is ARCO IRIS, a microbus, which, since 1983, has been in routine service in several Spanish cities. Moreover, 20 were exported to Casablanca in Morroco. This vehicle has a length of 6.9 meters (23 feet), a curb weight of 6230 kg, and contains 2750 kg (44 kWh) of lead-acid batteries. The motor is a series-wound, 200 volt, 45 kW direct-current motor with a nominal speed of 1500 rpm controlled by a chopper designed to yield a maximum speed of 85 km/hr (50 mph), and a maximum range of 100 km (60 miles). An outline of the vehicle is shown in Fig. 23.29.[41]

Another interesting Spanish development is a larger bus which carries a load of motive power batteries in an easily disconnected trailer which, at a pre-arranged infrastructure stop, is exchanged for a trailer with freshly charged batteries. This practice has also been experimented with in Germany, and is a modification of an earlier approach pioneered by Robert R. Aronson, U.S.A., described in Chapter 20.

[41] Jose Ignacio Pastor, Ignacio Egea, and Jose Felix Gonzalez De La Cruz, *Recent Spanish Development of Electric Buses*, Eighth International Electric Vehicle Symposium, Washington, D.C., 1986.

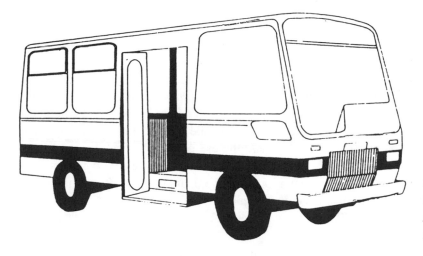

Figure 23.29. The Spanish Microbus, Arco Iris. (See Footnote 41)

Swedish Electric Vehicles

Supplementing the work carried forth by the Volvo Company on electric vehicles in 1977, two additional experiments in Sweden should be mentioned: the field test on five battery vans, and experience gained on electric vehicles with a hydraulic buffer, both performed and reported by Hans Ristborg of the Swedish Power Board in 1986.[42]

Apparent in reading the report on the five battery vans both the manufacturer of Mercedes Benz 307 van conversion, and the operating group of the Swedish Power Board had to learn, like everyone else, the distinct operating peculiarities of electric vehicles. When the vans were received, there were almost no end of problems in making them serviceable. Then, as all users of lead-acid batteried electric vehicles soon learn, there are distinct limitations not suffered by the highly developed gasoline-powered vehicles. As Hans Ristborg concludes:

"The technical performance and utility were fully acceptable during the latter part of the project. However, this was only achieved after our own major design modifications and after having established a certain amount of our own service capacity. The use of electric vehicles thus will involve a number of difficulties on different planes. However, there is nothing to suggest that the present problems give a representative picture of the long-term technical and economic opportunities offered by electric vehicles. Our assessment is therefore that current problems can be surmounted by continued utilization of electric vehicles to a growing but limited extent and in carefully selected applications."

---

[42] Hans Ristborg, *Field Test With Five Battery Vans*, eight International Electric Vehicle Symposium, Washington, D.C., 1986.

The Taiwan THEV IV

Sparked by Dr. Ru-yih Sun, a Purdue University Ph.D. graduate, Tsing Hua University, with the Taiwan government offering encouragement, is engaged in a local electric vehicle industry. The design now being concentrated upon is THEV IV (<u>T</u>sing <u>H</u>ua <u>E</u>lectric <u>V</u>ehicle). An all-purpose van/car, the THEV IV is 3m long, 1.8m high, with a 2m wheelbase. The gross vehicle weight is a reported 1287 kg. Earlier vehicles reportedly had eight 12-volt lead-acid batteries. As is indicated from the number designation attached to the vehicle, the University team has experimented with several designs. To encourage the use of electric vehicles in Taiwan the government is "building a network of battery-exchange stations for users who prefer exchange to the delays of recharging,"[43] a concept pioneered by Jeantaud and Brault in the Paris-Bordeaux-Paris Race of 1885, discussed in Chapter 7, and widely practiced at the Paris Exposition of 1900, and illustrated in the same Chapter. The Taiwan government decision was motivated by the 1973 oil embargo.

Apparent from the above sections the industrial nations in the 1970s had seized upon electric vehicles as an alternate type for personal travel. Table 23.17 demonstrates characteristics of other vehicles.

Each nation, in executing its program, had impact events. The following chapter relates impact events on American electric cars since 1965.

---

[43] *Taiwan To Produce 20,000 EVS by 1983, Electric Vehicle News*, Vol. 10, No. 4, November 1981, p. 26.

Table 23-17. Electric Vehicles from Some Other Countries

COUNTRY	REPORTED	PASSENGERS	CURB WT.	BATTERY	MOTOR	CONTROLLER	ENERGY	SPEED	RANGE	ACCELERATION
Australia[1]	1978	4	X	12 12-v.	X	X	X	75 km/hr	60 km	X
Bulgaria[2]	1977	van	X	X	X	X	X	40 km/hr	100 km	X
India[3] (College of Technology)	1977	4	X	lead-acid	series wound 2 hp	chopper	X	25 km/hr	80 km	X
Spain[4]	1978	Avia	X	210 Ah 133 v.	15 kw at 4500 rpm	X	28 kWh	50 km/hr	110 km	1.2 m/sec^2
Sweden[5] (Volvo)	1977	2	X	60 v.	10 kW	X	X	70 km/hr	100 km	X
	1977	4	X	lead-acid 72 v.	8 kW	X	X	70 km/hr	100 km	X
Switzerland[6] (Pfander AG)	1977	6	X	48 v.	2-4 kW	X	X	25 km/hr	60 km	X
	1977	4	X	X		X	X	90 km/hr	90 km	X
Taiwan[7]	1981			96 v.						

[1]*Electric Vehicle News*, Vol. 7, No. 1, February 1978, p. 25.
[2] *Ibid*, Vol. 6, No. 2, May 1977, p. 25.
[3] *Ibid*, Vol. 6, No. 3, August 1977.
[4] *Ibid*, Vol. 7, No. 4, November 1978, p. 30.
[5] *Ibid*, Vol. 6, No. 2, May 1977, p. 26.
[6] *Ibid*, Vol. 6, No. 2, May 1977, p. 25.
[7] *Ibid*, Vol. 10, No. 1, February 1981, p. 44.

397

CHAPTER 24

Impact Events on American Electric Cars Since 1965

Events which had an impact on resurgent interest in American electric vehicles were: 1) the development of solid-state electronics which made for more compact and rugged the control of power flow; 2) the Massachusetts Institute of Technology vs. California Institute of Technology cross-country electric car race, which mustered interest in electric vehicles and mobilized electric utilities; 3) the Sundancer electric vehicle whose design and performance opened new vistas; 4) the oil embargo, which stimulated the need for alternate energy sources for transportation; 5) the Edison Electric truck purchase program, which focused the electric utility personnel on electric vehicles; 6) the Postal Service electric truck test program, which funded a substantial number of electric trucks; 7) the Electric & Hybrid Vehicle Act of 1976, which stimulated development of batteries and accrued some fleet purchases; 8) The California Clean Air Act, which requires two percent of the vehicles sold in that state in 1998 to have essentially zero emission; and 9) the Zeitgeist (spirit of the time) which encouraged experimenters in many nations to build one or more electric vehicles.

That the long and passionate love affair between the American male and his gasoline-powered motorcar was cooling became evident in the middle 1960s. The citizens sought to have a choice in means of personal transportation. The word 'ecology' was in the air, and thereafter America and the world would never be the same. The quality of life insisted on having an effect on the bottom line of profit.

Of the impact events, cited above, solid-state electronics application to motor control was related in Chapter 19. An omen of interest in alternate types of travel surfaced in the friendly challenge issued by students from the California Institute of Technology to their peers at the Massachusetts Institute of Technology, dubbed by the students the Great Transcontinental Electric Auto Race. The electric utilities also would sense a change and make a group purchase of electric trucks. Lansing, Michigan would opt for electric buses. The Post Office would have a design competition to provide electric-powered vans to deliver mail. ERDA, Energy Research & Development Administration (superseded by the Department of Energy in 1977), would fund a design for a vehicle system for molten salt batteries, and later would issue design awards for new style electric cars. There would be the frivolous claims, but the excellence of the two-fold combination of gasoline and the internal-combustion engine would be more widely appreciated. It would not be easily replaced for decades to come.

University Cross-Country Electric Car Races

There would be two intercollegiate electric car races across America. The first, in 1968, would be the more appropriate. In the second, two years later, too many agencies and companies became involved. The purity of the electric car cross-country race would be impugned by many forces. The end result was that there was not a third intercollegiate race of battery-only powered electric cars. A fine, spontaneous series of challenges had been aborted. And the nation suffered. An all-pervasive government, hoping to do its best, was a factor in causing this amateur collegiate sport to die, for the heavy hand of government in its insensitivity had done its worst.

While a long-distance electric automobile race on the surface appears preposterous, for range of the vehicle is the electric car's Achilles' heel, there can be other benefits. Reliability of design components peculiar to the electric drive system can be one. The involvement of young minds in a national challenge can be another. The dragooning of the electric utilities along the race course to provide permanent electrical outlets can be a third. And probably most important, by offering an alternate method of personal transportation, the mental processes of individuals are stimulated. "There is always another way." Originality, that tireless and noble fighter of any nemesis, is preserved. How much is it worth for a nation to challenge its original thinkers?

While all who are informed know that electric vehicles are currently meant for intra-city travel, no history of electric vehicles would be complete if omitted were the outpouring of university talent in two electric vehicle cross-country races. Just as youth was ahead of their elders in viewing the fruitlessness of the Vietnam War, so were they among the earliest harbingers of calling for an alternate means of personal transportation—in a sense a Children's Crusade.[1] The action of the university students undoubtedly was and remained a positive force in initiating a revival of interest in electric vehicles. The media[2] was to give the whole program an assist.

In 1968 students in the electrical engineering department at California Institute of Technology in Pasadena issued an invitation to their counterpart in the Massachusetts Institute of Technology in Cambridge for a cross-country race of electric cars.[3] The challenge was accepted. Leon S. Loeb captained the MIT team, while Wally E. Rippel was the central figure for Cal Tech.[4] With late hours on the part of the professors, shop technicians, enthusiasm and work by the participants, and much aid from industry, the two vehicles, shown in Figs. 24.1 and 24.2, were ready to embark on the odyssey to the other's campus, the starting times coordinated by the starter shown in Fig. 24.3. With each team departing from their respective sites, the first

---

[1] To the imaginative, like the Children's Crusade against the Mohammedan leader Saladin in 1222, this stirring and lamentable event led Pope Innocent III to write, "the very children put us to shame, while we sleep they go forth gladly to conquer the Holy Land." Alas, the children, on arriving in Italy, travelling to reach Saladin, were kidnapped and sold into slavery in Egypt, leaving posterity the legend of *The Pied Piper of Hamlin*. See D. C. Munro, *The Children's Crusade, American Historical Review*, Vol. 19, pp. 516-524, 1914.

[2] *The New York Times Index*, Ag 27, 1968, 43:8.

[3] *Great Electric Car Race, Technology Review*, October/November 1968, pp. 83-85.

[4] *Cal Tech News*, October 1968.

Figure 24.1. The Cal-Tech electric car and winner of the first electric car race across the United States. Cal Tech News, October 1968.

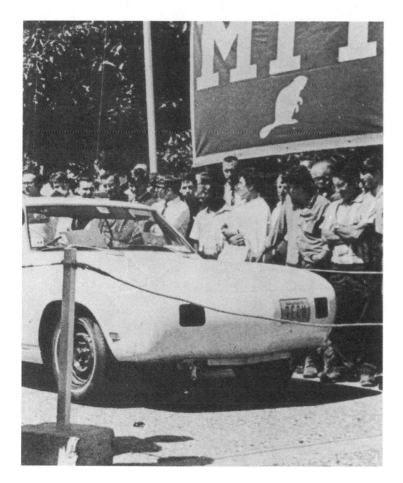

Figure 24.2. The M.I.T. electric car, which was towed across the finish line. It Takes a Little Pull to Get Ahead, Technology Review (M.I.T.) October/ November 1968, pp. 83-84.

Figure 24.3. The Great Race started on August 26 at M.I.T. under bright sunshine, before a sizable crowd, and to the tone of a cross-country countdown by Leon Loeb, '70, M.I.T. student coordinator.

to reach the other's would be the winner. Penalties would be inflicted for towing. Table 1 in Appendix F traces the 2900 mile trek, gives the highway routes, preferred charging locations, and the names of the electric utilities responsible for the proper operation of the charging stations.

After an elapsed time of 7 1/2 days, an endless series of problems (over-heated batteries, blown fuses, a burned-out motor suffered by each participant), and a thoroughly delightful but exhausting ordeal, the MIT vehicle crossed the finish line towed the last 100 miles. While 37 hours and 20 minutes later the Cal Tech entry reached Cambridge under its own power. In an off-hand remark, Wally Rippel, Captain of the Cal-Tech entry was quoted, "our electricity cost was about $25.00."[5]

Table 24-1 gives the characteristics of the two participating cars.

Not widely known in this first cross-country race was the innovative disc-type motor of the proposed MIT entry, which, sadly, was not ready in time for the competition. The Eastern entry,

---

[5] *Electrical World*, February 17, 1969, p. 51.

Table 24-1. First Cross-Country Electric Car Race[6]		
Vehicle Characteristics		
	CAL TECH	MIT
Car	Volkswagon van	GM Corvair
Batteries	Aronson's lead-cobalt	Gulton Nickel-cadmium
Motor	Series wound d-c, 77 hp peak	Baker electric d-c[7]

therefore, like the Cal Tech vehicle, used a well-tested conventional d-c motor. The hoped-for MIT drive system is illustrated in Fig. 24.4. To the technical reader the motor is similar to a 12-phase, high frequency, d-c motor with electronic commutation.[7]

Long distance car racing is not easy. See the section, The Conditions of Roads in America, Fig. 9.3 in Chapter 9.

Not content with the tour de force race of 1968, MIT, not to be outdone by a victorious Cal Tech, issued the following year a challenge for a second race to be held in 1970. Instead of two universities, several dozen were to enter vehicles. And the propulsion plants would be more varied.

The Second American Cross-Country Race

The first electric vehicle cross-country race emitted ripples of interest not only in other universities, but in the councils of the National Air Pollution Control Administration of the federal government. So, when two years later, in 1970, Massachusetts Institute of Technology issued an invitation to California Institute of Technology for a second cross-country race, the scope of the program had changed.

The race was called the Clean Air Race of 1970. With the complex computer rating system of measurement, vehicles with a variety of power drive systems would be permitted to participate. The winners in each category of drive system would be determined on a point base system computed by a formula assessing performance, fuel economy, actual race time, and

---

[6] Ronald L. Bern, *News:* Commonwealth Public Relations, 300 Park Av., NYC 10022, August 8, 1968.
[7] W. S. Brown, *A Light Weight Motor for an Electric Car, Norem Record*, 1968, pp. 126-127.

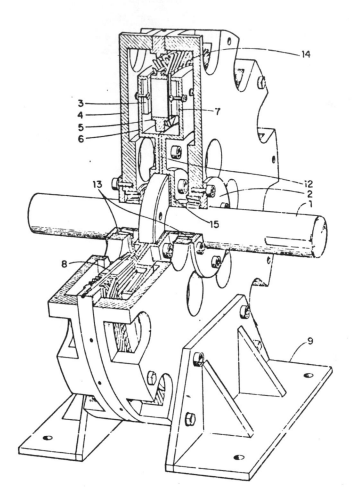

Figure 24.4. The proposed lightweight, electronically commutated, d-c motor for the MIT entry. For comparison of the motor used by both entries, see Fig. 12.14 in Chapter 12.

pollution emission[8] In addition to the class winners an overall winner would be picked by a panel of experts.[9] In this second cross-country race the cars would all start from the same campus. For this epic 42 cars were entered in six classifications: internal-combustion-fuel in gaseous form, internal-combustion-fuel in liquid form, multi-power electric, electric, turbine, and steam. Thirty-two of the participants were internal-combustion, two were multi-power

---

[8] The formula used to determine class winners was: $S = E(P + R + TE)$, where S is total score, E is emission factor, R is race score, TE is thermal efficiency. P is the sum of four separate tests: braking (B), acceleration (A), urban driving cycle (UDC), and noise (N). The emission factor is determined from cold start data on hydrocarbons (HC), carbon monoxide (CO), and nitrogen oxide (NO), as well as the ratio of hot-start data (HC_p/HC_b, CO_p/CO_b, NO_p/NO_b) and particulate emission (PART). R consists of seven leg scores ($L_i - L_t$), while TE is judged in miles per million BTU (m/mBtu).

[9] Dr. David Ragone, Dean of Engineering, Dartmouth College; John Brogan, National Air Pollution Control Administration; Harry Barr, President of the Society of Automotive Engineers; Dr. S. W. Grouse, Office of Science & Technology; and John Maga, Executive Secretary of the California Air Resources Board.

electric, five were electric, one was turbine, and two were steam. Again the route of the race was the same as the first challenge. Again the electric utilities would serve as shepherds to the participants.

As each of the 42 entrants had at least one service car, there were nearly 100 automobiles in this caravan of novel-powered vehicles. Figures 24.5 and 24.6 show the Georgia Institute of Technology entry and some of the other entrants.

This second competition would be more fully covered by the media, reflecting in part the growth of interest in pollution control, and also because more areas had this time an entrant. *The New York Times* followed the race, and editorialized:[10]

"The Clean Air Car Race for all the suggestions of a stunt about it, is neither a campus caper, nor a far-out demonstration. The contest, featuring 42 vehicles driven by college students and supposedly innocent in varying degree of polluting the atmosphere, is sponsored by the Massachusetts Institute of Technology and the California Institute of Technology. Representatives of electric power, natural gas,

Figure 24.5. Drivers of Georgia Tech's entry in the Clean Air Car Race, among the first to cross the finish line at Cal Tech, get a warm welcome from Harold Gordon, western coordinator of the race. Courtesy: Caltech News, Vol. 4, No. 7, October 1970, p. 1.

---

[10] *The New York Times Index:* Ag 23, 1970, 74:1, Ag 25, 1970, 74:2, Ag 28, 1970, 30:1, Ag 30, IV, 10:1, Mr 1, 1970, 59:1.

Also *Clean Air Car Race Winners Announced, Air Pollution Control Association Journal*, 20: 764-5, N 1970.

Also Michael Feirtag, *65 Cars in Search of the Future, Technology Review*, October/November 1972, pp. 43-54.

Figure 24.6. Clean Air cars cluster in Pasadena's City Hall Plaza.

and oil industries have been working closely with the drivers, who left Cambridge Monday...The more such activity and awareness spreads, the less the automakers can expect to put-off that change at their pleasure."

Beside the media support, the National Air Pollution Control Administration provided $220,000 to document the engineering data, and each winner in a category would receive $5000 for a two-month lease of their vehicle. On starting, the two steam cars were early forced out because of malfunctions. Most other cars finished after travelling the 3000 miles from Cambridge, Massachusetts to Pasadena, California. The winners in the categories cited above respectively were: Worcester Polytechnic Institute in a Chevrolet Nova, Stanford University in an American Motors Gremlin, Worcester Polytechnic Institute and University of Toronto, Cornell University, and MIT, the only entry in the turbine class.

There would be no more battery-only car races. Solar-powered cars, yes. The comment of many was that the diversity of power drive systems had sapped interest from the competitiveness of the race.[11] The involvement of the government in an innocent college contest was also considered a negative factor. In any case, the simple, all-electric car race which had made the first event so appealing had been lost in the indistinctness of the second run. Race goals, to attract interest, must be clearly etched.

As race shepherds, in providing technically manned battery charging stations, clearly the electric utilities had had their latent interest in electric vehicles sharpened. The sales

---

[11] *Detroit Dominates Clean Air Car Race, Electrical World*, October 1, 1972, pp. 76-77.

departments of this largest capital intensive industry have succeeded in lighting American homes, and promoted home appliances of American industry. Why not follow this path <u>and</u> improve the electric load factor, a need, which for the most part, appliances failed to satisfy. An electric vehicle could also be considered an appliance—only a mobile one. The trade association for these companies would take, as it turned out, a lugubrious step. It was an action in the minds of some which cast the die for all subsequent development in electric vehicles, and was the most important non-technical single event in the revival of electric automobiles. At the time the decisions were made few foresaw their consequences, least of all personnel of the electric utilities involved. A reading of electric vehicle history would almost surely have mitigated the disaster which was to ensue. A disaster which created a vacuum, a space in which a vigorous government is sure to intrude upon, just as in the second college electric car race above.

Edison Electric Institute Electric Truck Purchase

President of both the Edison Electric Institute (EEI) and Florida Power Corporation in 1969 was William J. Clapp, a delightful, far-seeing man. In addition, he was on the Electric Vehicle Council. As head of an electric energy company he had given thought and was concerned with the coming anticipated increase in the cost of gasoline. For his company and like utilities, he wished to develop an electric load to use night-generated power. Such a task has occupied utility operators for more than three generations, and in the intervening time little progress has been made. Figure 24.7 indicates the instant power demand on the lines of Green Mountain Power Corporation of Burlington, Vermont versus time of day. From the graph, peak demand is about noon. Minimum demand, on the other hand, is about 3:00 AM. The swing is considerable, the minimum being but 46 percent of the maximum. With such a variation in power demand, during night hours the capital intensive utility system, designed to generate and distribute peak-power demand, has a capacity only partially utilized. In general, the larger the utility system the more uniform the load.

Good management requires the base load, the night minimum, be supplied by the most economical generating equipment in the system currently available, for there is a 24-hour requirement for such load. As successive increments of power are needed, progressively more costly energy is provided the customer. This difference in energy cost may result from a number of factors: an already amortized plant, a newer, more efficient generating system, or differing fuel needs. In modern electric utility companies sources of energy may be: nuclear, hydro, gas-fired, oil-fired, coal-fired, peat-fired, wood chip-fired boilers, gas, earth thermal, kerosene-fired turbine, sun thermal turbines, wind generators, and diesel heat engines. All produce electric energy at different costs. The wise application of company electric generating resources is the responsibility of the System Operation Manager, now aided in many subtle calculations by a computer assist.

Clapp was very much aware of this daily variation in power requirements. The phenomenon represents one of the unsolved problems of electric power generation resulting from our daytime

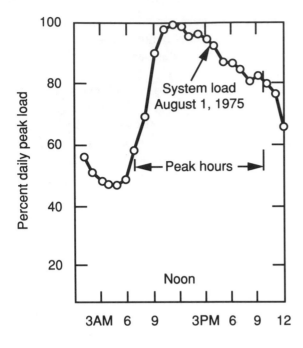

Figure 24.7. Daily system load demand plotted over 24 hours. The curve represents the instant power the cited utility company must supply, where the peak demand is 100 percent. Ideally electric cars would be charged from midnight to 6:00 AM. Courtesy: Electrical World, November 1, 1976.

activity as a people,[12][13] and the unavailability of an economical means of storing huge amounts of electric energy throughout America. To help resolve this knotty and persistent problem, what better than to encourage an electric car industry? The vehicle batteries could be charged at night, a time of low power demand. Such a period provides relatively inexpensive off-peak energy and yields a better utilization of capital.

As President of EEI, Clapp presented this always latent suggestion to the Board of Governors. A resolution was passed to purchase electric vehicles. According to H.J. Young,[14] then Executive Secretary of the Electric Vehicle Council, "the primary purpose of the electric vehicle purchase program is to develop load research data which will assist electric utilities in planning for the significant number of electric road vehicles expected in the 1980s. By 1990, according to the Federal Power Commission's National Power Survey, there will be 38 million electric road vehicles." From this statement a reader can understand how far from facts a prediction can be, for there were probably no more than 10-20 thousand.

A committee was authorized. This group would select a likely truck vehicle from the several companies who were then developing electric vehicles. Subsequently the members of EEI, some 220 in number, would be asked to purchase one or more electric trucks so a bulk order of probably 400 vehicles might materialize. That scenario was the intent. Funding for the bulk purchase was to be from individual electric companies, with about $150,000 allowed the winning vehicle builder to assist in development.[14] The utter modestness of this development

---

[12] *Two Innovative Rates Get High Marks, Electrical World* Vol. 186, No. 9, 1 Nov. 1976 has an informative discussion on useful incentives to smooth the daily system load demand of a utility company.

[13] Charlie F. Jack, *Peak Shaving - A way to Fight Rising Costs, IEEE Trans. on Industry Applications*, Vol. 1A-12, No. 5, Sept./Oct., 1976.

[14] *Electric Vehicle Council Awards Contract for 100 Electric Work Vehicles, Electric Vehicle News*, Vol. 1, No. 4, November 1972.

money indicated how little these well-meaning men understood the problem even though their companies dealt in hundreds of millions of dollars. Possibly if this committee had had on its roster automotive engineers who had hands-on experience with electric vehicles the end results would have been happier.

The Electric Vehicle Council appointed a committee whose names are omitted. In addition to this committee, the following organizations were invited to have their representatives in attendance:

> American Public Power Association
> U.S. Department of Transportation
> Consolidated Edison Co. of New York
> Detroit Edison Company
> Florida Power Corporation
> Iowa Power & Light Company
> Pacific Power & Light Company
> Public Service Co. of New Hampshire

Unknown to the above committee members and, indeed, to the award winner, this program would become a disaster—an event which for all practical purposes would remove the electric utility industry from sponsorship for electric vehicles. It was a watershed case. It might be safely argued that before this award the electric utility industry was the most important force in the development of electric vehicles in America, while after the award they were a minor factor because their representatives were insufficiently versed in history. Here was an example where private enterprise could have provided impetus for an electric vehicle industry, which, not fulfilling the need, the Federal government in turn entered. Such means of government entry into the heretofore private sector is repeatedly found. In the American society as now composed, an aggressive government nearly always moves on a reluctant investor-exploited segment of the economy.

At the time of this EEI award, admittedly knowledge in America on electric vehicle design was modest, exceedingly so when compared with the IC car understanding encompassed by the major automobile manufacturers. But the real ambush awaiting the EEI procurement was that collectively the committee, as is true to almost everyone except those living with electric vans, failed to realize successful personal transportation is more complex than generally realized. But is that observation not true of any technical field? This committee visited the following facilities and found work proceeding on the electric drive shown:

Company[15]	Drive System	Location
Allis Chalmers	d-c	Matteson, Illinois
Anderson Power Products	d-c	Boston, Massachusetts
Battronics, Inc.	d-c	Boyertown, Pennsylvania
Electric Fuel Propulsion	d-c	Detroit, Michigan
Linear Alpha, Inc.	a-c	Skokie, Illinois
Tork-link, Inc.	d-c	Studio City, California
Westinghouse Electric Corp.	d-c	Pittsburgh, Pennsylvania

---

[15] So designated at the time of the competition.

The award was given to Battronics Inc., which, as a division of the Boyertown Body Works Inc. was already producing in small quantities an electric truck designed for the Lead Industries Association (LID), a project strongly encouraged and substantially financed by LID at the urging of Connell Baker, the Association's Executive Director. Surely lead-acid battery-powered vehicles could be a new and large application for lead. In due time the prototype truck was shown to representatives of the utility industry. This multi-purpose work vehicle was the fully enclosed, walk-in truck shown in Fig. 24.8. The wheelbase was 91 inches. There was an interior height of 63 inches. The overall length was 145 inches, with a width of 78 inches, and total height of 92 inches. Range was to be 68 miles at 20 mph, 42 miles at 30 mph, and 30 miles at 40 mph.[16] The committee recognized the decrease in range due principally to increasing windage with speed, and the lessened availability of energy with power demand due to internal polarization of the battery.[17]

With this demonstration, the number of orders, instead of the anticipated 400 (for there are over 200 members in the EEI), totalled only 107, and many of those purchases were allegedly obtained by strong persuasion by EEI on recalcitrant utility officers. Such a decrease in orders has an obvious bearing on unit cost. On analysis the three basic weaknesses in design of the procured vehicles were the control circuit, the brake-acceleration system, and, as subsequently

Figure 24.8. The Edison Electric Institute, acting for a number of members, authorized the purchase of some 107 Battronic electric trucks. A Lead Industries Association vehicle of similar design was aggressively shown in many American regions.[18] [19]

[16] *EEI Electric Truck Program Specification, Electric Vehicle News*, November 1972, p. 10.

[17] Ernest H. Wakefield, *The Consumer's Electric Car*, Ann Arbor: Ann Arbor Science Publishers, Inc., 1977, pp. 74-83.

[18] *"Goliath" Demonstration in Washington, Electric Vehicles*, Vol. 63, No. 1, March 1977, p. 24.

[19] *Van's 10,000 Mile American Tour, Electric Vehicles*, Vol. 61, No. 1, March 1975, p. 6.

was found, the employment of an insufficiently strong axle. The control system was relay voltage switching, a surprisingly primitive choice in an era when the solid-state chopper was already highly developed and routinely being employed on fork-lift trucks.

These 107 vehicles were eventually deployed to their new owners, the utility companies. While it was natural to assign these trucks to the transportation department, whose members were proud of their knowledge of IC vehicles, the electric vehicles were a minority and not a well understood truck. It was an environment in which, possibly, even the best designed electric van might have failed. Many of the trucks soon developed shaft failures that were not hastily replaced. In others the awkward and complex appearing controls failed to function.[20] Very quickly numerous trucks were immobilized, and, in hardly a sympathetic environment, many of the vehicles were parked in a corner to be forgotten.[21] In some cases, however, the Marketing Department of the utility routinely used the truck. With so many field problems this program was nearly disastrous to the award winner. It had turned out to be a trap. No one had profited. But possibly some humility had been learned. What was the fallout? In a survey of electric utility executives authorized by the research arm of the utilities, Electric Power Research Institute, the negative aspect of electric vehicles was still extant in 1982.[22]

This obtrusion, which deserved to be forgotten, encouraged the government mandarins to move in on a potential industry, and they did, as is related in Appendixes G and H. The cost to taxpayers—over $180 million and counting.[23]

Demonstration City - An Alternate Program

Shortly after the EEI Award cited above, an alternate plan was inaugurated. More modest, and with far better control, as outlined by William H. Shafer, spokesman for Commonwealth Edison Company of Chicago on electric vehicles, related: a better plan would have been "Demonstration City" wherein a fleet of electric vehicles, maintained by the highly motivated builder, would have travelled from utility to utility. While at a site the vehicles would have been operated by utility personnel under the watchful eye of the builder's representative. After a month's visit the caravan would then move on.

The Demonstration City program was launched May 17, 1971 with a Mayor's Committee,[24] and a letter from Thomas G. Ayers, Chairman of Commonwealth Edison Company, Chicago, addressed to presidents of surrounding utility companies, introducing the author, President of Linear Alpha, Inc. which would assemble the electric-powered vans with an a-c drive system. In Table 24-2 below are listed the companies who contributed in cash or appropriate material for a prototype Dodge van converted to electrical operation.

With 48 grants from the above organizations, the company, with additional funding, produced the a-c powered van, Fig. 19.9 in Chapter 19, and for Demonstration City, delivered

---

[20] *EEI Electric Truck Program Failure, Electrical World*, February 15, 1978, pp. 62-63.

[21] Eugene F. Gorzelnik, *Electric-Vehicle Test Program Appraised, Electrical World*, February 15, 1978, pp. 62-63.

[22] *Electric Light & Power*, February 1982.

[23] General Accounting Office in a report to Richard Ottinger, Chairman, April 1982.

[24] Ernest H. Wakefield, *A Series of Demonstration Cities for Electric Vehicles*, Evanston, Illinois: Mayor's Committee, March 25, 1971.

Table 24-2. Companies Making Grants to the Demonstration City Program	
Manufacturing Companies	Utilities
Allen-Bradley Company	Atlantic City Electric Company
AMP Incorporated	Central Illinois Light Company
Anderson Power Products, Inc.	Central Illinois Public Service Co.
Anixter Bros. Inc.	Columbus & Southern Ohio Electric Co.
Augat, Inc.	Commonwealth Edison Company
Automatic Switch Co.	Delmarva Power & Light Co.
Belden Corporation	Florida Power Corporation
Chase-Shawmut Company	Georgia Power Company
Chrysler Corporation	Illinois Bell Telephone Company
Cornell Dubilier Electronics	Illinois Power Company
Dana Corporation	Interstate Power Company
Engler Instrument Co.	Iowa-Illinois Gas & Electric Co.
Glastic Corporation	Iowa Southern Utilities Company
Gould, Inc.	Kansas Gas & Electric Company
Grainger Co., W. W.	Long Island Lighting Company
International Rectifier Co.	Madison Gas & Electric Company
3M Company	Ohio Edison Company
Mallory, P. R., Co.	Pacific Power & Light Company
Potter Brumfield Company	Portland General Electric Company
Reliance Electric Company	Potomac Electric Power Company
Skil Corporation	Public Service Company of Indiana, Inc.
Wakefield Engineering Co.	Sierra Pacific Power Company
WGN Continental Broadcasting	Tucson Gas & Electric Company
	Union Electric Company
	Washington Water Power Company

the d-c powered van. In the meantime the above mentioned EEI Program had so disappointed the electric utility industry that the Demonstration City Project was a casualty. The test vehicle was acquired by the Madison (Wisconsin) Gas & Electric Company for messenger service. It is illustrated in Fig. 24.9. Characteristics were: Top speed of 55 mph, range in urban driving 25 miles, acceleration 0-30 mph in 8 seconds. Power was supplied from 24 6-volt batteries for a series-wound, 24 hp d-c motor of nominal 144 volts. The vehicle had chopper control. Nominal energy in the batteries was 24 kWh, from an on-board charger with an input of 240 volts. Donor cost—less than $150,000.

The philosophy behind Demonstration City, fleet operation, had been recognized by Morris & Salom in their New York taxi company, and, indeed, related by Charles E. Woods in 1900. Then, as now, it was a prudent plan to follow. Because history was not studied, mistakes, obviated in the 1890s, were unfortunately made in the 1970s.

Figure 24.9. Linear Alpha Inc. d-c drive electric van. Professor Gordon J. Murphy's hand is on the 220-volt charger. Courtesy: Commonwealth Edison Company.

Electric Vehicles for Lansing, Michigan

Lansing, Michigan has a municipally-owned electric utility system. If there is anyone in America who had the distinction of bearing the title "Mr. Electric Vehicle," it was the long-time chairman of the municipal utility board, the late Claud R. Erickson, who is extensively quoted in this book.

Like many older cities, downtown Lansing had lost customers to outlying shopping districts. But uniquely this city on the winding Cedar River is also the capital of the state. The heart-city merchants wished their area economically more attractive. With such impetus and the presence of an early believer in electric vehicles, the city applied to the Department of Transportation for a grant to establish a small scale inner-city bus line which would employ electric coaches. The basic thrust of the proposal was: with improved local loop transportation more people would be attracted to the inner city. For this experiment a grant of $144,000 was awarded for six 15-22 passenger electric buses on October 2, 1971.[25]

---

[25] *Electric Vehicle News*, Vol. 3, No. 2, November 1971, p. 4.

There were to be two travel loops: one with a two-mile round trip; the second had a 2 1/2 mile route. With proper scheduling both are distances which can well be adapted to electric vehicles. Three buses were purchased. Any two could be used at a particular time, while the third vehicle would be charging. Public monies being spent, bids were issued. The winner was the same make of vehicle as purchased by the Edison Electric Institute. And like the disaster of that purchase, so ended the Lansing experience.

Still another unfortunate experience loomed.

The Postal Service Competition for Electric Vans

"Electric mail delivery was inaugurated in Minneapolis last week," related a new item in the January 1902 issue of *The Horseless Age*.[26]

In 1969, through the efforts of Mr. Donn P. Crane of the U.S. Postal Service, two electric vehicles were obtained and tested for postal use in Cupertino, California.[27] One, from Westcoaster Inc., a subsidiary of Otis Elevator Co., had a 72-volt lead-acid battery with a 2-speed transmission and an 8 hp, 72-volt d-c motor. This combination gave a speed of 25 mph. The second vehicle was a van built by Harbilt Electric Vehicle Company of Leicester, England. The latter had no transmission, a series-wound 10.5 hp d-c motor of nominal 72 volts, yielding a top speed of 30 mph.[28] The van is shown with a U.S. Post Office symbol in Fig. 24.10. In this test the Post Office was assisted by Pacific Gas & Electric Company, the utility for that area of California. The results of the trial were deemed promising, so the Postal Service held a competition.[29] Responding with vehicles were AMC-Gould, Automation, Inc., and Westinghouse Electric Corporation. All entries met the technical specifications. AMC-Gould won the bid, and 352 postal trucks would be ordered subsequent to 1971.

AMC-Gould offered the Postal Service a small van based on the Jeep. An electric van may be viable for postal use because of the limited range of routes, and because of the multiple stops. The mini-truck was designated the AM General DJ-5E. The electric drive system for this vehicle was developed under the general supervision of Mark J. Obert. The on-board charger for this truck, the body being a closed type with two side-sliding doors, and a full-opening rear door, can be either a 120 volt 20 amp, or alternately, a 240/480 volt 20/10 amps. The former weighs 90 pounds, the latter 250 pounds. For propulsion the battery was a 27 cell, semi-industrial of 330 Ah at a 6-hour rating, weighing 1300 pounds including the tray. The auxiliary battery was 93 Ah at 20 hours. In curb weight the vehicle was 3625 pounds, and the Gross Vehicle Weight was 4300 pounds. The cruising speed of the van was 33-40 mph, with an acceleration 0-30 mph in 20 seconds. Gradeability was 10 percent at 16 mph. The range of the vehicle with 300 stop/starts, a postal cycle, was 29 miles. At this writing a substantial number of these vehicles have been delivered to the U.S. Post Office and are operated on routes in Cupertino, California. Figure 24.11 shows one.

---

[26] *The Horseless Age*, Vol. 9, No. 5, January 1902.

[27] *Electric Vehicle News*, Vol. 4, No. 1, March 1972, pp. 5 & 6.

[28] Personal communication: William H. Shafer, April 23, 1982.

[29] *American Postal Service Makes a Promising Start, Electric Vehicles*, Vol. 62, No. 4, pp. 24-26.

Figure 24.10. The English constructed the Harbilt Electric Vehicle. (Source: Unknown)

Figure 24.11. The U.S. Post Office currently designed electric vehicles of 1978. Courtesy: AM General Corporation.

In 1978 Donn P. Crane reported on the test results of these 352 Post Office vehicles:[30]
" 'Down time' of the electric vans was 1.2 percent, a figure 55 percent of the equivalent down-time for the IC vehicles. Fuel consumption, based on thermal units of fuel delivered to the electric utility for production of electricity, was 75-80 percent of the fuel units delivered to the refineries to provide gasoline for the IC vehicles. At Cupertino the cost of energy was $143 for electric vehicles, versus $521 for IC vehicles (not including battery cost)."[31]

In accounting the battery cost can be considered a fuel cost, for lead-acid batteries have a cycle life. Donald K. Miner, writing in 1981, reported a battery cost of 29¢ per mile over a six year period, at an annual travel of 6000 miles.[32] William H. Shafer, Commonwealth Edison Company (ret.), writing on February 29, 1992, based on seventeen years of accumulated record keeping, reports a battery cost for his sedan of ten cents per mile (cost based on lead-acid batteries, five-year life, and purchase cost of $55).[33]

A second group of electric vehicles are reported to have been purchased by the U.S. Postal Service.[34] These Comuta-Vans are assembled by Commuter Vehicles, Inc., of Sebring, Florida, who purchased the assets of the Sebring-Vanguard Company, builders of the Citi-Car, discussed in Chapter 21. Commuter Vehicles is a division of General Engines, Inc. of Thorofare, New Jersey. The Comuta-Vans are described as having an aluminum frame, a plastic body, possessing a curb weight of 2400 pounds, and powered by a 12-hp d-c motor. The vehicle has a top speed of 50 mph, a maximum range of 30 miles, while making the Postal Service required 350 stops and starts with a reported load of 500 pounds.

If the Postal Service had pursued its option a total of 375 vans would have been purchased, including the 15 already accepted. Figure 24.12 illustrates the Comuta-Van in Postal Service colors. Mr. F. W. Flowers, Sr., is President of Commuter Vehicles, Inc. As it developed this program was canceled after 150 Comuta-Vans had been delivered. Again a failure.[35]

Apparent to the reader from the above are the developing penances of an industry, and one of the seminal limitations of an electric vehicle has been its range. What attempts have been made to extend its reach besides stored chemical energy (electricity)? The story begins in 1894 in Italy.

---

[30] Donn P. Crane, personal communication to W. H. Shafer, April 23, 1982.

[31] *Postal Vans Get Good Report, Electric Vehicle News*, Vol. 8, No. 4, Nov. 1979. p. 11.

[32] *Donald K. Miner,* A Six Year Service Test Comparison of Electric vs Gasoline Power for Utility Vans, Electric Vehicle News, Vol. 20, No. 4, November 1981, pp. 4-7.

[33] Personal Communication. See Appendix J.

[34] *Delivery Vans by Commuter Vehicles Accepted by U.S. Postal Service, Electric Vehicle News*, Vol. 10, No. 3, August 1981, pp. 18-19.

[35] Victor Wouk, *Two Decades of 'High Performance' EV Fleet Experience*, Eighth Electric Vehicle Symposium, Washington, D.C., 1986.

Figure 24.12. Commuta-Vans procured by the U.S. Postal Service on their second advertisement. Courtesy: Electric Vehicle News.

At Last the Moment is Seized

Having witnessed much failure in introducing electric vehicles by a piecemeal approach the electric utilities established the Electric Vehicle Development Corporation in 1984. Soon joining this body were major automotive and component manufacturers: General Motors Corporation, Chrysler Corporation, Ford Motor Company, Chloride EV Systems, and Powerplex Technologies. This development holds so much promise for the future development of electric vehicles that Appendex A is wholly devoted to its description.

Also of great import was the establishment in 1991 by the Big Three United States automakers of a venture to share the cost of developing suitable batteries. Initially pledged to the effort was $35 million.[36] Called the United States Advanced Battery Consortium, they wish to raise $100 million annually by 1993 from the government and the electric utilities. The consortium will contract with battery manufacturers and other organizations for advanced battery development. Finally, the Chicago Tribune reported,[37] "President Bush endorsed a $260 million public-private venture Friday to develop batteries for electric cars, saying the project would save more energy than proposed tougher fuel-economy standards.

" 'The development of a competitive electric auto industry will do more to reduce oil imports than rigid fuel-efficiency standards that risk jobs and public safety,' Bush said."

---

[36] *The New York Times*, February 1, 1991.
[37] The *Chicago Tribune*, October 26, 1991, Sec. 2, p. 1.

Figure 24.13. Cal Tech race team 1968. Courtesy: Richard Rubinstein, Wellesley Hills, MA (1993).

CHAPTER 25

Worked-On But Unsolved Problems

As an industry matures the central idea, an electric vehicle, both resolves and accumulates problems. If resolved, the car's performance or afforded comfort is increased. Presently an efficient and appropriate a-c transaxle drive system has been developed for electric vehicles as described in Chapter 12. So has a reasonably high specific energy battery been tested—the sodium sulfur couple—and others appear to be in the wings. Such attributes can offer a minimal electric vehicle, but one hardly approaching the comfort of the IC-powered automobile for the seasonal temperature variations in, for example, the American Midwest. Here temperatures can be below zero in the winter and over one hundred degrees in the summer.

Among the desirable attributes for the electric vehicle yet to be fully implemented besides range are: 1) remanent battery charge indicator, 2) heating and air conditioning of the vehicle's cabin, and 3) electric power steering, particularly on heavier vehicles.

For the first, while the experienced operator soon gains a "feel" for when the battery is near discharge, the author has witnessed numerous examples of a neophyte electric car driver being trapped with insufficient battery energy to return "home." Despite considerable effort directed toward an indicator, A.F. Burke of the Idaho National Laboratory writes:[1]

"Methods for accurately including the effects of changes in battery temperature and age must be developed and demonstrated before any battery state-of-charge unit can be used with confidence in a vehicle. None of the battery management systems tested exhibited sufficiently accurate and reliable operation in both the charge and discharge modes that they could be used in the test programs to control the cycling of the batteries. (While) considerable progress has been made in battery management systems for electric vehicles in recent years...the available systems are...insufficiently dependable...for unattended use."

---

[1] A. F. Burke, *Evaluation of State-of-Charge Indicator Approaches for EVs*. SAE 8990816, 1989.

Development of an EV Air Conditioner and Controls for Electric Steering

Already some observers have indicated air conditioning would be highly desirable in an electric vehicle, writing:[2]

"Request for a cooler equipment is a recent problem. The widespread use of a cooler in office, internal combustion engine car, and home calls for its installation in EVs. (A) cooler consumes comparatively large electric power. If cooler power is obtained from the battery, it is natural that the range per charge be significantly affected. To solve this problem in the future, it is essential to develop a new high-performance battery and an energy-conserving cooler."

To answer the above S. Ohba of Soleq Corporation in Chicago developed an air conditioning system for an electric Ford Escort.[3] Realizing the energy requirements for air conditioning might reduce the already modest range of an electric car by some 10 percent, he allowed the air conditioner to operate while the battery of the vehicle was being charged. Thus the vehicle started its trip pre-cooled with energy being supplied from the electric utility. In his paper, pre-cooling the car's skin and cabin temperature with time is recorded for the actual system. In addition, the article contains a block electrical diagram showing how air conditioning was obtained. Table 20-4 gives air conditioning consumption of energy.

In driving an electric station wagon in Chicago's winter, the author has come to know the importance of cabin heating. Ohba, in addition to considering air conditioning, has designed a system using a heat-pump for both heating and cooling electric vehicles, a trend also observed in American homes. And because large electric vans may be equipped with electric steering as well Ohba has given in his paper some consideration to that feature as well.

If, indeed, designers of electric vehicles continue to copy what is or may become standard on IC automobiles: automatic window, clock, radio, dashboard position locator, internal lighting, trunk opener, etc., all of which require electric energy, continual effort will need be directed toward enhancing the energy source. For the personal use vehicle Mark De Luchi, Quanlu Wang, and Daniel Sperling state a battery charge requiring more than 20 minutes will make the electric vehicle unattractive and minimize personal electric car use.[4] If, indeed, the concept advanced by these contributors has validity some such quick-change energy source such as possessed by the combination aluminum-air battery plus a high specific power battery may appear even more attractive for the personal use vehicles.[5] [6] [7]

---

[2] Yutaka Akikawa, Takeshi Matsuo and Tsuyoshi Sakamoto. *Status of Electric Vehicles in Japan*, The 9th International Electric Vehicle Symposium, Toronto, 1988.

[3] S. Ohba. *The Development of an EV Air Conditioner and Controls*, The 9th International Electric Vehicle Symposium, Toronto, 1988.

[4] *Transportation* (Res. A, Vol. 23A, No. 3, 1989).

[5] Nigel P. Fitzpatrick and David S. Strong. *Aluminum-Air, a Battery/Battery Hybrid for an Off-Road Vehicle*, The 9th International Electric Vehicle Symposium, Toronto, 1988.

[6] E. J. Rudd. *The Development of Aluminum-Air Batteries for Electric Vehicles*, do.

[7] William A. Adams and John H. Morgan, *Canadian Electrochemical Power Sources Research and Development for Traction Applications*, do.

What then does the future hold for electric vehicles? Up to this point the reader has been brought through a litany of successes and failures for more than one hundred years. Reported has been the work of experimenters of many nations. In addition, there has been a maze of technology for the components of electric vehicles. To sum up, possibly De Luchi et al states most clearly what may be the future for electric vehicles, writing:[8]

"If progress continues as expected, electric passenger vehicles with lightweight, efficient ac motors and high-performance batteries will have a city range of at least 150 miles, a cruising speed of at least 70 mph, and be able to accelerate as quickly as some comparable ICEVs. If all low-cost projections are fulfilled, EVs will have considerably lower life-cycle costs than comparable ICEVs, at most likely interest rates and electricity prices, even allowing for high vehicle taxes and occasional recharging away from home. Thus, by the turn of the century, EVs could be viable second cars in multicar households. Electric vans are expected to be attractive in fleet applications sooner. And although the successful commercialization of such EVs is far from guaranteed, no longer does it depend on breakthroughs—successful market penetration probably would result if incremental progress typical of the last 10 years continues, and if the lower-bound cost estimates are realized. This success would be very beneficial environmentally, because EVs would practically eliminate HC, CO, and NO, air pollution attributable to highway travel, assuming stringent control of power plants emissions, and also could reduce emissions of greenhouse gases. These substantial environmental benefits, and the improving prospects for EV marketability, warrant policies and incentives promoting EV development and use.

"The availability of an economical means of quickly recharging EVs, or the successful development of mechanically rechargeable batteries, may be the most critical factor in the future of EVs and could mean the difference between a minor and major role for EVs in transportation. Therefore, as R&D on powertrains and batteries continues, and the commercialization of advanced EVs draws near, R&D work on charging systems, and the cost and performance of batteries designed to accept very fast (20-minute) recharges, should commence. The development of a suitable infrastructure and the successful completion of advanced EV development programs will bring the electric vehicle dream much closer to reality."

A product having been developed, to be significant, must be marketed. Appendix A relates how.

---

[8] Mark De Luchi, Quanlu Wang and Daniel Sperling, *Transportation*, (Res. A, Vol. 23A, No. 3, 1989.)

CHAPTER 26

Latent Thoughts

The author has written this book over a period of more than a decade. During this long gestation he has wondered if there is a parallelism in the historical entry of electricity into the home and the mode by which it may enter personal transportation. If so we might gain a better understanding of a more proper allocation of resources in the pursuit of developing electric vehicles.

Parallelism on Electricity into the Home and into Transportation

Electricity first came into buildings through lighting. In fact, the author's father installed the first electric lights in Cleveland in 1882 for The Society for Savings Bank, three years after Edison's invention. We know electricity first entered the home with lighting. Lights could be turned on and off more easily with a switch than a like operation with a gas jet. In addition, the hazard from fire was reduced. As one whose family has been closely associated with the electrification of America,[1] the author observed that the early role of electric utilities in electrifying the home was essential. Of great importance in the 1920s, utility promotion of electricity use gradually waned in the late 1930s as home appliances became available from other outlets. Starting with a few items which used electricity, now many homes have dozens of electrical devices. So too, but to a lesser degree, an electric automobile.

Let us presently view the application of electricity to personal transportation. For the road vehicle electricity was first applied in 1881. Trouvé in France used electric power to propel a vehicle as described in Chapter 1. The second electric vehicle, by Aryton and Perry in England and described in the same chapter, bore two lights to read the experimenter's mounted ammeter and voltmeter. The increased strength and rigidity of tungsten filaments compared to carbon filaments, besides increasing the lumens per watt resulting from higher filament operating temperatures, enabled the filaments to withstand vibrations of road operation. Soon electric car

---

[1] According to the late Willard F. Brown, Chief, Commercial Lighting, General Electric Lamp Works, Nela Park, Cleveland, the author was the first to design and sell a commercial fluorescent lighting installation in America, August 1937, McGarvey's Restaurant, Vermilion, Ohio. The equipment was manufactured by his father's F. W. Wakefield Brass Company, Vermilion, Ohio. The lamps were made by General Electric Company, at Nela Park.

manufacturers added electric headlamps. Woods in Chicago, described in Chapter 5, installed electric heating to the electric taxis.

All these energy sinks increased the load on the battery whose specific energy during this period was enhanced but little. The range of Walter A. Baker's simple, 550-pound curb-weight electric vehicle, cited in Chapter 5, was acceptable for the small cities with improved cobblestone streets of the 1900s. But, to both increase range and to provide power to the above appliances, EVs gained in weight. Soon American, British, and French electric vehicles weighed more than a ton. Further, the IC vehicle, at the comparable period, was rather crude, and surely noisy before the advent of mufflers on exhausts. But then, suddenly, the sun shone on IC cars, and clouds engulfed the EVs. Hiram Percy Maxim, with the Columbia electric vehicle he designed, discovered touring in 1895. For touring, increased range was essential. With the impetus for touring and the constant improvements in IC automobiles, the golden age of electric vehicles waned. It had lasted about a decade, 1895-1905. Gasoline, with a specific energy from 400 to 600 times greater than offered by a lead-acid battery, would carry the day in horseless carriages bearing IC engines. Alexander Winton's turn of the century IC vehicle, for example, had a range of more than 200 miles. And his car's gasoline tank could be filled in five minutes, as opposed to an eight-hour charge!

Purpose-Built Electric Vehicles

But just as electricity entered the home first with electric lights and then expanded, so did electricity find new uses in transportation: the fork-lift truck, introduced as a World War I measure, saved the Baker Electric Company from extinction when other electric vehicle manufacturers closed. Electricity also made possible vertical transportation and, with steel skeleton frames, permitted the skyscraper. Street-use personal transportation with electricity, however, was stuck for some 40 years. The prime problem was lack of range. The philosophy of keeping alive the personal electric vehicle has been expressed by L. Roy Leembruggen of Australia. He applied the niche method to use electricity in personal transportation, coining the term "the Purpose-Built electric vehicle," cited in Chapter 22. Thomas Bandl and Joachim Bernt of Germany and others have described other purpose-built electric vehicles—the electric wheelchair and special vehicles for the handicapped, now a substantial industry.[2][3][4] And all readers know how entrepreneurs developed the shop personal transport, the electric airport vehicle, the resort vehicle as demonstrated by the British, the Mexicans, and the Japanese in Chapters 22 and 23. The electric golf-cart, too, became ubiquitous. And Anil Ananthakrisna of India demonstrated the electric motorcycle as shown in Chapter 23. Now Honda of Japan is publicly showing their electric motorcycle, with high specific energy batteries, capable of limited touring. It also is described in Chapter 23. These vehicles are all purpose-built as, indeed, are the electric vans extensively treated above.

---

2 Thomas Bandl and Joachim Bernt. *Electric Vehicles for the Physically Challenged People*, The 9th International Electric Vehicle Symposium, Toronto, 1988.
3 Roland Borer and Peter Mackert. *Special Technology in Electric Vehicles for the Physically Challenged*, do.
4 N. D. Durie, O. Z. Roy and R. L. Farley. *A New Electric Vehicle for Indoor Use by Disabled Persons*, do.

New Impelling Forces for Electric Vehicles

Presently a newly recognized driving force has appeared encouraging electric vehicles, more important even than the increasing price of gasoline—environmental concerns. Already the teeth of this movement are biting, particularly in atmospheric regulations in California. What will almost surely become of greater importance in the promotion of electric cars and light trucks is the wisely fashioned Electric Vehicle Development Corporation established in 1984 and described in Appendix A. And more convenient and high specific energy batteries and more efficient drive trains go without saying. Another new force for electric vehicles is the increasingly high efficiency for transforming sunlight into electricity. The General Motors Sunraycer, a lightweight racing car bearing gallium arsenide cells and a small, high energy density battery, is one of the best of this international breed. In the World Challenge Solar Car Race in Australia in 1987 this vehicle, generating 1500 watts from its solar array with a vertical sun, averaged 42+ mph over a 1950 mile race course.[5] Several thousand solar-powered electric cars have been built through 1992. They are proving an admirable means of promoting electricity in personal transportation to the general public.

One might argue from the above recitation, therefore, that electricity will come into personal transportation much as electricity entered the home through purpose-built appliances, by creating purpose-built electric vehicles. And this gradual approach will provide time for both the public to be educated, the equipment to be perfected, and an infrastructure to be formed thus easing the economic pain of introducing electric cars and light trucks into the transportation landscape.

As we approach the close of this work on battery-only powered electric automobiles, summarizing a period which began in 1881, the reader has seen the ascension, the decline, and once again the growing interest in electric vehicles. Nearing center stage, as this book is completed, are electric cars and light trucks bearing efficient AC motors and high energy density batteries capable of yielding a range of some 150 miles with a possible lower cycle-life cost than IC vehicles. The great force impelling this latter day resurgence, interestingly, is not the high cost of gasoline, but the desire for a cleaner environment. In 1897 Barton Peck of Detroit developed a gasoline-powered vehicle saying, "There is one great obstacle that must be overcome and this is the offensive odor from gasoline that has been burned and that is discharged into the air. It is a sickening odor and I can readily see that should there be any number of them running on the street, there would be an ordinance passed forbidding them."[6]

Peck in 1897 had probably unknowingly found the Achilles' heel of the gasoline-powered motor car. In its enormous success as a means of transportation a niche is being opened for the non-polluting electric vehicle. How successful the latter will be in supplementing the former, only the future knows.

---

[5] Howard G. Wilson, Paul B. MacReady and Chester R. Kyle. *Lessons of Sunraycer, Scientific American*, March 1987, pp. 90-97.

[6] George S. May. *A Most Unique Machine*, W. B. Erdman Publishing Co., p. 85, 1975.

A Century of Electric Vehicle Trends

As one reviews the more than ten decades of electric vehicle progress, what is evident? Apparent to the readers of this volume is that the first electric vehicles were based on the tricycle. Later they were indeed the horseless carriage of various types. The early innovators mated the then four-wheel wagon or carriage with batteries, an electric motor, and a method for readily transferring this rotating mechanical power to the rear wheels. Steering would be with the front wheels by means of a tiller. And the first brakes were identical to those employed to halt a wagon—a friction block applied to the wheel's rim. The motive power batteries were re-energized from an off-board charger where the vehicle was maintained.

Chassis, Body, Wheels, and Tires

To execute the above the innovators who developed vehicles in barns and sheds had centuries of talent and experiments upon which to draw, an opportunity not always realized and seldom stated, for any machine of the present exists only because of the past. The first chapter, indeed, indicates how rich were early sources in providing the knowledge and the tools for these vehicles. While the discoveries which led to the electric and mechanical drive system were largely based on the work of the 19th century, the spoked-wheel and axle had an ancestry reaching back to Grecian times. Wood was in the wheels, and Fig. 27.1 advertises to use sap gum wood in early electric vehicle bodies.

From the first electric car in America in 1890 to those in 1902, only 12 years elapsed for the designers to change from the tricycle, wagon, and carriage of the house to the chassis and body of today's vehicle configuration. The early builders, moreover, were quick to apply applicable material and devices to enhance the value of the electric vehicle. Ball-bearing for wheel and axle came before the turn of the century—a distinct departure from the horse and wagon cart which used, largely, a tallowed friction bearing surface. The greater speed of the electric vehicles, 12-25 mph, called first for smaller wheels, and, with the invention of the wire-spoked wheels, based on an A-frame figure, in which the axle was suspended from an arc of the rim, wheel collapse on cornering was resolved. This major invention in wheel design, a concept which allowed high speed travel was due to C.S. Mott and his patent of November 1896. Detachable wheels, a great help to the motorist, were introduced in 1910. Welded steel wheels and rims were commonly used in 1912 as shown on vehicles seen in Chapter 16.

Figure 27.1. Wood, a magnificent creation of nature, was long used in the automobile industry. Courtesy: The Horseless Age.

In early motoring the driver and passengers were exposed to the vagaries of the weather. Dust, rain, cold, and wind could make travel an ordeal. Great coats of fur or leather were worn, as well as visored caps, dust jackets, and goggles. Indeed, the driver resembled almost a later day astronaut. Advertisements for ladies pictured mask veils to protect the coiffure, to prevent discolored cheeks and watery eyes. The discomforts of such exposure led to the enclosed body, which came onto the scene about 1910. This new, more commodious method of enclosure is owed to the innovations of Rauch & Lang Electric Inc., of Chicopee Falls, Massachusetts. The importance of power loss to windage was first recognized about the same time as the enclosed body. Walter A. Baker, himself a graduate of Case School of Applied Science, early identified the importance of streamlining, although A.J. Riker's racer of 1896 had only a modicum of obstructions for air flow. Bodies became somewhat lower, but chassis and axle clearance from the road remained substantial because of the potential irregular street surface.

At the higher travelling speeds exemplified by the electric vehicles, as compared to the horse-drawn carts and carriages, brakes became ever more important. The friction brake applied to the rim gave way to a foot brake which acted by contracting onto the transmission shaft behind the gear-box. The hand brake could be actuated on the rear wheels. In 1914, the application of the more modern internal expanding brake began, located on a brake-drum concentric to the wheel, but proximate to the differential. Soon came disc brakes. The greater stress on the chassis reflected from the higher speeds, the weight of the iron motor, the concentrated load of the lead-acid batteries, caused the early wood constructed wagon chassis to utilize metal members for added strength. Some steel tube construction for chassis came into being, an outgrowth of electric vehicle manufacturers earlier being bicycle builders. And the chassis was reslung, lowering the center of gravity. This change, together with increasing the length of the wheel base, also resulted in better car handling, particularly in cornering. The chassis illustrations appearing at the close of Chapter 16 demonstrate improved engineering.

In parallel with electrical and bicycle experiments Charles Goodyear was investigating the exudations of a tropical plant, given the name "rubber," for its ability to rub-out pencil marks on paper.[1] Accidentally and only after painstaking experiments he learned in 1843 that if rubber were combined with sulfur and lead oxide in the presence of heat, the act of vulcanization, useful articles of commerce could be fashioned.[2] Goodyear was an example of the biblical quotation, "One soweth, and the other reapeth," for all his years were spent in poverty.

In 1845 Robert W. Thomson invented and tested the pneumatic tire, but because of inadequate marketing knowledge, manufacturing ceased. A Scotsman, practicing veterinary medicine in Ireland, James Boyd Dunlop, used inflated rubber tubing on his son's tricycle, shown in Fig. 27.2, and reinvented the pneumatic tire in 1888 in time for the explosive increase in bicycle use.[3] Two brothers, André and Edouard Michelin in France, who had a firm manufacturing bicycle tires in Paris, learned the technique of bolting pneumatic tires onto the

---

[1] *Oxford English Dictionary*, Clarendon Press, Oxford, England, 1970, p. 855.
[2] Bradford K. Pierce, *Trials of an Inventor, Life and Discoveries of Charles Goodyear*, Phillip & Hunt, NYC, 1866.
[3] Arthur du Cos, *Wheels of Fortune*, Chapman Hall Ltd, London, 1938, p. 56.

Figure 27.2. Johnny Dunlop and the first pneumatic tires for light vehicles developed in the year 1888. In 1845 Robert W. Thomson had thoroughly and scientifically tested pneumatic tires on road wagons, but for lack of promotion, were forgotten until reinvented by James Boyd Dunlop. Their advantage on bicycles was quickly recognized, and their almost uniform adoption rapidly followed their introduction. Note that Johnny Dunlop's tricycle is a later model than the one used by Professors Ayrton and Perry in their 1882 electric tricycle. Courtesy: Chapman Hall Ltd.

rim of an automobile wheel. It was used in the 1895 Paris-Bordeaux-Paris race.[4] Early Michelin pneumatics are shown in Fig. 27.3. Other tires from the Rubber Tire Company are shown in Fig. 27.4.

Running Lights and Horns

On turn-of-the-century horse-drawn vehicles, enclosed candles or oil lamps were fixed. Kerosene burning from a wick generally was available for a light source. By 1906 lighting by acetylene became popular. The light was concentrated and directed forward by suitably placed

---

[4] *Scientific American Supplement*, Vol. XL, No. 1023, Aug. 10, 1895, p. 16343.

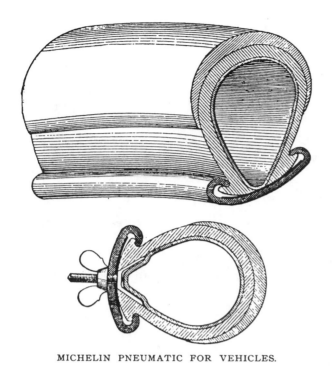

MICHELIN PNEUMATIC FOR VEHICLES.

Figure 27.3. The Michelin Brothers were the first to apply pneumatic tires to automobiles in 1895. They found that if the power required to draw a pneumatic-tired car be represented as 100, the power to draw the same vehicle equipped with steel tires was represented by 139 to 156. In addition, the vibration was greatly reduced. These tests were made in Paris. The Horseless Age, Vol. 1, No. 6, April 1896, p. 18.

and shaped mirrors. These headlamps, often made of brass, were carefully maintained, the result of the owner's pride. The acetylene gas was obtained by the controlled dripping of water onto carbide. Somewhat later a cylinder containing dissolved acetylene was provided. At about the same time automobile bodies were enclosed, electric lighting was used. Such application of the incandescent lamp could arise only after the fragile carbon fibril of the early light source was replaced by the more rugged, jar-resistant, tungsten filament. Tungsten proved a particularly refractory element to purify, to work, to sinter, and to draw into the required fine wire of a filament. Later, for headlamps, the high-pressure gaseous discharge source has been preferred. Such improvements in technology as exemplified by the above, originating and being perfected in other parts of the economy, contributed to the constantly improving electric vehicle. The addition of electric light, Fig. 27.5, is one of the first examples of how weight was being added to the elegant, lightly designed vehicles of earlier time. For, with lighting, an auxiliary battery was borne by the vehicle.

In the earliest electric vehicles, power from the motor was transferred to the wheels by means of gears. In 1891, the French company, Panhard-Levassor, introduced the cross shaft, mounted on the chassis frame. From a sprocket mounted on this shaft, power to the rear wheels could be transferred by chain. While chain drives long lasted on big, fast, gasoline-powered racing cars, the electrics by 1905 were adopting the propeller shaft passing into a differential, the latter element an invention of Onisephore Pecquer. Earlier, a motor driving each wheel had also been employed as seen in Chapter 5 and later. Figure 27.6 demonstrates the rear axle, the transmission, and brakes of 1912. The steering of early electric vehicles was by tiller, based on

Figure 27.4. Some of the tires offered by the Rubber Tire Company. The Horseless Age.

the English Ackermann patents of 1818.[5] The wheel as a steering mechanism soon came into use. Originally the shaft was vertical, then, in later years, it was established at an angle, like the wheels of today, providing more convenience to the driver.

Kimball's early American electric vehicle almost surely had the metal tires so expertly heat-sweated onto wooden rims, a practice elegantly mastered by countless blacksmiths. The electric vehicles shown in the first chapter had hard rubber tires, even though Dunlop had re-invented the pneumatic tire in 1888. Seizing on this invention, the brothers Michelin, André and Edouard, for two years tried to solicit automobile owners to employ air-cushioned tires, with little success. As their superiority was recognized, pneumatic tires were applied to the electric vehicles in the first decade of the 1900s. Punctures of these early tubes were a real problem, a fact which present automobile drivers are almost unaware, and for which today's older drivers bear a nostalgia they would wish to forget.

For pedestrian safety, the foot-actuated bells on early electric vehicles were subsequently replaced by the rubber squeeze "honk-honk" horn to be in turn superseded by the electric "ah-uga" horn. This warning device was energized by the newly installed auxiliary electric system.

---

5 John B. Rae, *A History of the Motor Car*, Pergamon Press, Oxford, 1966.

Figure 27.5. While the incandescent lamp was developed in 1879, electric lamps for the automobile had to await introduction of the more rugged tungsten filament. Courtesy: The Horseless Age.

433

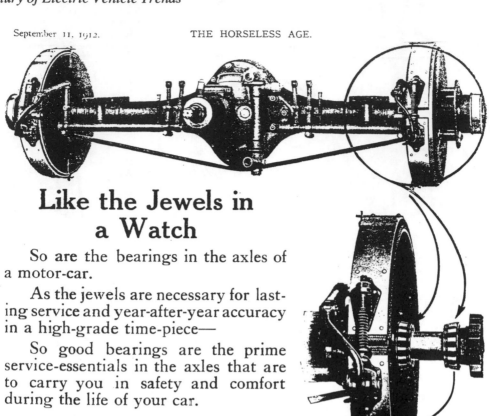

Figure 27.6. An advertisement of 1912 indicates the status of the rear axle, the transmission, the brakes, and the bearings at the apogee of the electric vehicle. Much of this mechanical advance arose from the growth of the gasoline-powered car some of which the electrics could borrow. Courtesy: The Horseless Age, September 11, 1912, p. 55.

Trends in Modern Electric Cars

The genetic difference between early electric cars and modern electric vehicles is the employment of solid state electronics in the latter. The invention of the transistor by John Bardeen, Walter Brattain, and William B. Schokley at Bell Laboratories in 1948, won for the three a Nobel Prize. The proliferation of this invention into many useful electrical components is one of the ingredients contributing to the increasing attractiveness of the electric automobile. All of the electrically innovative vehicles discussed in Chapter 20 have used solid state electronics, the outgrowth of the transistor discovery.

With today's insistence on high performance automobiles, the presence of good roads, and a quicker tempo of life, electric cars are now designed with far higher horsepower motors than used in earlier vehicles. The electric current delivered to a motor of a modern vehicle is perhaps ten times greater than the current supplied in accelerating, for instance, an early Baker Electric. The increased armature current and the higher applied voltage of modern vehicles give substantial power which is required for rapid acceleration. This higher power can, in the 1990s, best be controlled by transistors, earlier cited.

Considering the modern electric vehicle systematically, starting from the a-c electric receptacle, the point at which power is available from the electric utility, what have been the newer trends?

In the present reawakening of interest in electric vehicles, conversion of the Detroit product was the natural first direction to proceed. While in some circles it is popular to deride the Detroit passenger cars, these vehicles are superbly built, provide great value,[6] are readily maintained, are safe, and are amply accoutred. But, they are indeed heavy. A result partially related to the many demands asked of the motor car. For, as shown above, the application of electric lights required the addition of a 50-pound battery, a 12-pound alternator, and about 50-100 pounds of cabling, reflectors, and prismatic surfaces, etc. A total of over 100 pounds associated with lighting.

The curb weight of electric cars in 1900 was 550 to 1800 pounds. The curb weight of the Thunderbolt 240, earlier shown in Fig. 20.4, is 3900 pounds. The early electric cars were neither as comfortable nor as fast, but had comparable range with modern Detroit conversions. The design in 1972 of the Sundancer, described in Chapter 21, recognized the importance of light weight and streamlining.[7] While the body and chassis of the Sundancer were innovative, the electric drive system was prosaic, and eschewed solid-state controls, using instead voltage switching.

Slowly rippling out from the application of fiberglass for body and aluminum for the chassis, the late 1970s were beginning to show an increasing use of this combination. The end of the 1970s, it would appear, would introduce the fiberglass body electric vehicle with a modern drive system employing solid state controls as exemplified by the Endura. It is believed this

---

[6] The Detroit car reaches the customer, in all its complexity, at about $3 - $10 per pound in the 1990s, just a bit more expensive, at the lower end, than butter.

[7] R. S. McKee *et al, Sundancer, a Test Bed Electric Vehicle*, Automotive Engineering Congress, Detroit, Michigan, January 1972, Paper 720188.

juncture of design change will be just as sharp and as clearly marked as was the change in configuration of the automobile that occurred in 1902, when the horseless carriage design was obsoleted by the torpedo configuration of present motor cars.

The great majority of high performance electric vehicles seen or planned for the 1990s were equipped, or will be, with on-board chargers. This module, usually requiring a 120-volt supply, enables a useful electrical charge to be gained from the increasing availability of the electric vehicle charging station.[8] As the electric personal cars of the late 1970s and early 1980s, employing lead-acid batteries, would carry almost surely less than 18 kWh of energy in their batteries, a 120-volt charging system with 1.5 kW demand[9] will require some 12 hours of charging. For many users such a rate of on-board power flow was found to be adequate. With electric vehicles equipped with the higher energy density batteries of the future, where double the energy may be placed aboard the electric vehicle, both an off-board (to save weight and where the run is reproducible) and an on-board 240-volt charger may be found desirable, providing 4 to 8 kW demand. It was in looking to the future that electrical receptacles of both 120 and 240 volts have been specified as standard.[10]

Power flows from the battery charger to the batteries. In the 1970s vehicle batteries were of the 6-volt 160 ampere-hour type placed in series or series-parallel. For higher performance vehicles, the trend is to higher total voltage. Values of 72 to 320 volts are commonplace.[11] Safety limits the voltage used. Cold weather has relatively small import on batteries. Batteries are heated on charging; they are also producing heat on discharge. In both cases, heating is due primarily to the internal resistance of the battery to current flow, the so-called I^2R (I squared R) loss.[12] At times other than charging or discharging, the large mass of the batteries, together with the high heat capacity of the electrolyte (principally water) provides a relatively constant temperature for the battery. The above reasoning fails if the electric vehicle has multi-days "soaking" without charging in extremely cold weather. Such negative treatment adversely affects the car's range. Conversely, for operation in a high ambient temperature, the best vehicle designs allow an adequate air flow over the battery. Watering of the battery in normal electric car usage was found to be once every 6-8 weeks in the northern section of America. More frequent watering might be expected in the southern states. Recent sealed batteries can eliminate this problem.

In the 1970s power control for the high performance vehicles was usually with solid state electronics. These "chopper" controllers, so named because a solid state switch is repetitively turning off and on the d-c voltage, allow complete variation of current flow to the motor.[13] Later, with the advent of higher power transistors, controls using these solid state devices replaced SCR elements because of the higher efficiency of the total system. While many vehicles of this period had armature current speed control, some cars, such as those requested

---

[8] Several hundred are listed in *Electric Vehicle News*, Vol. 15, No. 4, November 1976, pp. 25-28.

[9] Ernest H. Wakefield, *The Consumer's Electric Car*, Ann Arbor: The Ann Arbor Science Publishers, 1977.

[10] Ibid.

[11] General Motors release on *Impact*, Jan. 4, 1990.

[12] Watt's law indicates the power is the product of voltage and current. P = E x I, where P is power, E is voltage, and I is current. Ohm's law postulates that voltage is the product of current and resistance. E = I x R, where R is resistance. By substitution, $P = I^2R$.

[13] General Motors release on *Impact*, Jan. 4, 1990.

by the U.S. Post Office had, in addition, shunt-field speed-control as well. Cars were found both with and without regenerative braking.[14] And in the later 1980s and early 1990s nearly all electric cars were being designed with a-c drive systems.

Nearly all electric vehicles in the 1970s had an auxiliary 12-volt power system. By using this voltage configuration, advantage can be taken of the high volume accessory production which results from IC vehicles. This auxiliary battery was charged by either an alternator with power pick-off from the electric motor shaft, or had power secured from the motive power batteries.

In the 1970s, mechanical power from the motor was generally passed through a transmission and thence to the differential. The user's demand for rapid acceleration required this torque conversion. In converting Detroit cars the electric motor was placed on the same engine block as formerly occupied by the IC engine. Later vehicles such as the ETX-II, described in Chapter 19, had planetary or novel gearing to reduce the motor speed to wheel speed.

Heating of the fiberglass vehicles has been accomplished by the application of electric blowers securing their energy from the motive power batteries. Larger vans used gasoline heaters. A few of the smaller electric vehicles have been known to have their seats electrically heated. Headlamps for road illumination were of the sealed-beam variety and were operated from the auxiliary 12-volt battery, as were dash, safety, and turn-indicator lights. Mr. George M. Hartley, President of Copper Development Association (CDA), Inc. in New York City, together with his assistant, Mr. Donald Miner, were the moving force behind this program. As in the case of the Lead Industries Association and the application of lead to transportation, the interest of Copper Developments was similarly to increase the use of copper in transit. In a vehicle, with the exception of the battery whose active elements are alloys of lead, all current carrying components are of pure copper. In this vehicle, the third developed by CDA, curb weight is 3800 pounds, top speed is 60 mph, range is 100 miles at 45 mph, or 63 miles in urban driving.[15] [16]

In 1890, the time of introducing personal electric vehicles in America, there were two other competing power sources: steam and the gasoline-powered internal-combustion engine. By 1902 the most perceptive innovators had determined that the IC engine would be supreme on the highway. How supreme and important it would eventually become, few offered sufficiently optimistic predictions. The automobile changed America in a way possibly equalled by no other single invention. Domestically it affects our lives; internationally it influences our foreign policy. The combination of energy contained in gasoline, the relatively low cost of this remarkable fuel, and the reliability of the IC engine served to extinguish all companies which continued to manufacture electric over-the-road vehicles in America.

It has only been in the 1960s that a few brave souls did dare to take action to revive the alternate of electric power for personal transportation. What had died in America in 1935 with the early electric vehicle would be reborn—similar in principle, but with a much newer and more glistening armor. In the late 1970s the modern, high performance electric vehicle was being

---

[14] In regenerative braking, the vehicle's kinetic energy of motion is transformed by the motor turned generator into electrical energy to recharge the battery. In dynamic braking, the generated electric energy is dissipated as heat.

[15] *New 'From Ground Up' Electric Van Exhibited, Electrical World*, January 10, 1972, pp. 75-76.

[16] *CDA Unveils Electric Van, Electric Vehicle News*, Vol. 1, No. 2, May 1972, p. 35.

observed to enter the economy. But it would have to earn its way. And its most likely habitat for successful competition would be found in the urban areas, as a second or as a third car in a family, and in fleet use.

The year 1977, it appeared, would be the most important period for electric cars, just as 1902 had been the critical year for all types of automobiles. The innovative drive systems of General Motors and Linear Alpha, described above, were in their time too complex. The Detroit conversions, on the other hand, provided insufficient range to sell the car easily. And the low performance electric cars were thought too poorly designed to survive. In 1976 the Federal government entered the domain of electric vehicle development under the guise of an alternate energy source, a fallout of the steep increase in the price of petroleum product instituted by the Persian Gulf nations. Partly as the result of government subsidy for vehicle development and partly because of enhanced technology, the year 1988 saw introduced a possibly economically viable, high performance electric van suitable for certain fleet operations. The total overall design of the electric vehicle, including new techniques in batteries, in electronics, and in permanent magnets, had reached a higher standard, in the best cases, than the citizens in general realized.

While the above discussion was of vehicles in the main stream of development, emerging in the late 1980s, and gaining currency particularly in Europe, were lightweight, solar-powered electric vehicles. Some 123 such solarmobiles competed in the Tour de Sol Race in Switzerland, and 24 started in the Darwin to Adelaide race across Australia. Both contests were held in 1987. Many more of these competitions may occur in the future much like sail-yacht regattas, and over time these vehicles will be improved much as has happened with IC race cars. There appears to be a possible minute market in high-daily-sun-hour regions of the world for entrepreneur- or company-built solarmobiles which in 1988 bear a cost, depending on sophistication, of between $50,000 to $1,000,000, figures in the same class as gasoline-powered race cars.

Further Readings

In writing about battery-powered or multi-powered electric vehicles accessibility to large technical libraries is essential. The basic sources were the Northwestern University Libraries at Evanston, Illinois USA together with its inter-library loan system, and the University of Illinois Libraries at Urbana-Champaign, Illinois. Supplementing the above institutions were the collections of the Commonwealth Edison Company in Chicago, and specialized papers furnished by my many peers in the electrical vehicle industry.

For specific information on the very earliest electric cars the *Scientific American*, and its counterpart, the *Scientific American Supplement* are most helpful. These two journals also detail the then-current batteries, electric motors, and accessories. *The Horseless Age*, initiated in 1895 in New York, is the single best journal on early electric vehicles. In about 1903 the editor became enthralled with gasoline-powered motorcars and his interest in electrics waned. There are scattered articles on electric cars in *McClure Magazine*, likewise for the English and Continental scene *The Electrical Review* and *Nature* have interest. Also in *The Electrical Engineer, The Telegraphic Journal & Electrical Review, L'Electricité, Les Mondes, La Nature, La Petite Republique Francais*, there are occasional relevant articles.

For the genesis of the electric battery Bernd Dibner's *Galvanti - Volta* (1952) is choice as is Gaston Planté's *Récherches sur l'Electricité* (1887). W. James King's *The Development of Technology in the 19th Century*, Bulletin 228 (1962), contains excellent drawings on early batteries and photos on venerable motors. A recent well-illustrated book on the history of electric energy storage is Richard H. Schallenberg's *Bottled Energy, Electrical Engineering and the Evolution of Chemical Energy Storage* (1982). George Wood Vinal's *Storage Batteries* (1951) contains much that is useful as does *Batteries*, Ed., Karl Kordesch, New York: M. Dekker, (1974).

For the newer batteries, reports issued by the U.S. Department of Energy are informative, particularly L.G. O'Connell *et al*, *Energy Storage Systems for Automobile Propulsion: Final Report*, Vol. 1 (1980). A most useful document for new batteries and innovative drive systems, *The Eighth International Electric Vehicle Symposium*, Washington, D.C., (1986), as well as *The Ninth International Electric Vehicle Symposium*, Toronto, (1988) are excellent. They offer some hope for the future of electric vehicles and bulwark the 1982 statement of the U.S. General Accounting Office cited in Appendix H. The books are also generous with chapter bibliographies. Also of this nature are publications of the Society of Automotive Engineers.

For proprietary batteries specific issues of *The Wall Street Journal*, and *The New York Times* are helpful. Probably the best summary article on high specific energy batteries easily available is Sidney Gross' *Review of Candidate Batteries for Electrical Vehicles, Energy Conversion* (1976). Available in book form is Colin A. Vincent, *Modern Batteries: An Introduction to Electrochemical Sources* (1984).

For early treatises on motor action Michael Faraday's *Faraday's Diary*, Vol. 1 (1832), and *Experimental Researches in Electricity*, Vol. II (1844), of course, are the original sources. Bernd Dibner's *Faraday* (1952) is well done. One of the best reviews on the development of d-c motors is by Aug Gueront, *The History of Magneto and Dynamo Electric Machines, Scientific American Supplement*, November 4, (1882). Also of this vintage is Professor Elihu Thomson, *Electricity During the Nineteenth Century, Smithsonian Institute Annual Report*, 1 (1900), p. 333. Then, for understanding general motor theory there are a host of university type textbooks. Two of several dozen are: W.W. McCullough, *Electric Motor Maintenance*, New York: John Wiley & Sons, Inc. (1947), and Eugene C. Lister, *Electric Circuits and Machines*, London: McGraw-Hill Book Co., (1945). For frequency and pulse width control of a-c motors the footnotes in appropriate chapters of this volume, Ernest Henry Wakefield's *History of the Electric Automobile,* are probably most authoritative. As this subject is complex I have enclosed in Appendix B an article by Dr. Gordon J. Murphy, Professor of Electrical Engineering and Computer Science at Northwestern University, Evanston, Illinois. Dr. Murphy has hands-on experience in designing, building, and installing this new drive system in a vehicle.

For a description of the life and works of Gustave Trouvé, the inventor of the electric vehicle, together with a description and tests of this tricycle, Georges Barral, *Histoire d'un Inventeur: Gustave Trouvé* (1891) is seminal. For understanding electric automobiles both early and late, probably the earliest book in English is J.H. Knight, *Notes on Motor Carriages with Hints for Purchasers and Users (1896)*. Clinton Edgar Woods' rather uncommon *The Electric Automobile, Its Construction, Care & Operation* (1900) is a classic. Rare is G.D. Hiscox, *Horseless Vehicles, Automobiles, and Motorcycles Operated by Steam, Hydro-Carbon, Electric and Pneumatic Motors*, New York: Munn & Co., (1900). In German, the report by M. Kallman, *Mitteleuropaischer Motor Wagen Vereins* summarizes tests made on 14 German built electric vehicles of 1900. In French, *Le Véhicle Electrique Utilitare á Accumulateurs, Conference Données á la Societé des Inginieurs de l'Automobile, par L. Krieger et al*, Paris: Dunod, (1947).

The author's *The Consumer's Electric Car* (1977) is modern. An informal 'how to' book is Michael A. Heckleman's *Electric Vehicles: Design and Build Your Own* (1977). Sheldon Shacket's *The Complete Book of Electric Vehicles*, 2nd ed., (1982), while having little theory is primarily a picture book of current electric vehicles. Barbara Whitener has written *The Electric Car Book* (1981). Present journals and reports are: the *American Electric Vehicle News*, the British *Electric Vehicles*, and *The U.S. Department of Energy 5th Annual Report to Congress for Fiscal Year 1981, Electric & Hybrid Vehicle Programs*. Cited in each chapter are other references.

For a treatment on solarmobiles, the German language bulletin *Tour de Sol 1987, Schweizer Illustrierte*, Dufourstrasse 23, 8008 Zurich, Switzerland is authoritative as the official race publication. With the Pentax World Solar Challenge Race both the *Darwin (Australia) Northern Territorial* and the *Adelaide (Australia) Advertiser* Editors (no street address required) were most gracious in sending me photocopies of appropriately dated issues of their newspapers. Helpful in the design of solarmobiles and electric vehicles in general is Barnes W. McCormack's *Aerodynamics, Aeronautics, and Flight Mechanics*, New York: Wiley, (1979). McCormack himself is a pilot. Available from the Society of Automotive Engineers is Dr. Paul B. MacCready's *Notes*. They have been published by *The Society of Automotive Engineers* (1990). An excellent story-picture of the 1987 Trans-Australian Race has been written by Bill Stuckey entitled *Sunraycer's Solar Saga* and privately published by Berghouse Floyd Tuckey Publishing Group, P.O. Box 303, NSW, 2072 Australia (1987). The March 1989 *Scientific American* bears an article by Howard G. Wilson, Paul B. MacCready, and Chester R. Kyle on the *Sunraycer*, and the booklet *GM Sunraycer USA - 1990* is available from the General Motors Corporation. The Society of Automotive Engineers offers *GM Sunraycer Case History* (1992).

For the design of race car chassis Michael Costins and David Phipps *Racing and Sports Car Chassis Design*, B.T. Batsford Limited (1961) is most helpful.

Making Peace With the Planet (1990) by Barry Commoner will serve as an introduction for pollution and its control.

For background material on rubber making, Bradford K. Pierce's *Trials of an Inventor* (1866) is authoritative about Charles Goodyear. C.F. Caunter's *The History & Development of Cycles* (1955) is most helpful in orienting the forerunner of the automobile, and illustrates tricycle frames used by the earliest electric vehicle builders. More general books on the automobile industry are: Hiram Percy Maxim's *Horseless-Carriage Days* (1937), for steam-powered cars Andrew Jamison's *The Steam Powered Automobile* (1970), John B. Rae's *The American Automobile* (1965), Allan Nevin's *Ford* (1954), George S. May's *A Most Unique Machine* (1975). Alfred A. Chandler's *The Visible Hand: The Managerial Revolution in American Business* (1977), Eugene William Lewis' *Motor Memories* (1947), and others.

The newest elements on a solar-assist electric vehicle are the solar cells. Important texts are *Photoelectricity and Its Applications* by V.K. Zworykin and E.G. Ramberg (1947); *Semiconductor Opto-Electronics* by T.S. Moss, G.S. Burrell, and B. Ellis (1973); *Solid State Devices 1986*, D.F. Moore, Editor; and for clear presentation there is *The Solarex Guide to Solar Electricity*, edited by Edward Robertson and by the Technical Staff of Solarex Corporation (1983). There is also important information which appears in the popular media.

Of informative books on electric- and gasoline-powered cars there are: Joseph Floyd Clyman, *The Wonderful Old Automobile* (1953); Joseph Floyd Clymer, *Treasury of Foreign Cars Old & New* (1957); Ralph Stern's *Sport Cars of the World* (1952); G.N. Georgano, *The Complete Encyclopedia of Motorcars, 1885 - 1968*, (1968); and for steam vehicles, Joseph Floyd Clymer, *Album of Historical Steam Traction Engines* (1949), and many others. Finally, a useful codex on electric automobiles is Rose Weaver, *Electric Vehicles in Transportation: A Brief Bibliography* (1980).

Other books, mostly devoted to gasoline-powered vehicles, include: John Grand-Carteret, *La Voiture de Demaine: Histoire de L'automobile*, Paris: Libraire Charpentier et Fasquelle (1898); *Automobiles of America*, Detroit: Wayne State University Press, (1974); Anthony Rhodes, *Louis Renault, A Biography*, London: Cassell, (1969); Ralph D. Gray, *Alloys & Automobiles: The Life of Elwood Haynes*, Indianapolis: Indiana Historical Society, (1979); James J. Flink, *America Adopts the Automobile, 1895 - 1910*, Cambridge: MIT Press, (1970).

Even though the first electric vehicle had been assembled in 1881 and the intervening years had seen much experimentation, an additional decade of learning was required, after Congressional passage of the Electric and Hybrid Vehicle Act of 1976, before America found what promises to be a wise path leading to significant use of electric vehicles. A knowledge of vehicle history would have possibly reduced the time. A well thought out route, however, is outlined below:[1]

Electric Vehicle Commercialization

Jerry Mader, Jim Brewer, and Oreste Bevliacqua

Introduction

In the last two years, the Electric Power Research Institute (EPRI) and automobile manufacturers have developed an electric van that can compete with petroleum-powered vans in the service-fleet market. The successful introduction of this van—and future electric vehicles (EVs)—depends on the careful development of EV markets and the EV service infrastructure. Through its work to build these markets and the EV infrastructure, the Electric Vehicle Development Corporation (EVDC) will ensure that today's EVs become a permanent part of the national transportation picture. National interest in EVs is increasing as transportation-related air-quality problems continue and dependence on foreign oil rises. This paper reviews the coordinated activities of EPRI, EVDC, the government, individual electric utilities, and automobile manufacturers working together to commercialize EVs.

Background

Electric vehicle commercialization requires the parallel development and evolution of technology, market, and infrastructure. Since the mid-1970s, significant effort and resources have been committed to EV technology research and development. Until 1984, however, little

---

[1] Jerry Mader, Jim Brewer and Oreste Bevilacqua, *Electric Vehicle Commercialization*, The 9th International Electric Vehicle Symposium, Toronto, 1988.

attention was directed to defining and building an initial market for EVs and establishing the support systems required to keep EVs operating and productive in the field.

Recognizing this, and the long-term potential for EVs, a group of electric utility companies formed this Electric Vehicle Development Corporation in 1984. EVDC's sole purpose is to successfully commercialize EVs in North America by consolidating the interest and activities as key stakeholders. EVDC is supported by its membership, which includes electric utility companies that collectively account for some 40% of U.S. electricity generation, as well as major automotive and component manufacturers such as General Motors Corporation (GMC), Chrysler Corporation, Ford Motor Company, Chloride EV Systems (CEVS), and Powerplex Technologies, Inc.

EV technology development is currently being performed by the U.S. Department of Energy (DOE), the Electric Power Research Institute, and private industry. EVDC works in partnership with these organizations to review market needs and technology R&D priorities. It also plays a significant role in organizing and monitoring joint development programs. Much of EVDC's success can be traced to building good working relationships with DOE, EPRI, manufacturers, user groups, and EVDC member organizations. These relationships are essential to achieving steady and progressive commercialization.

Because the EV represents a substitute for the petroleum-powered vehicle, the automotive industry is not motivated to take the lead in EV commercialization. This situation gave rise to the need for an organization such as EVDC to shepherd EV technology. EVDC's efforts to bring together the various elements necessary for EV introduction represent a model for commercializing a new technology. This paper provides an overview of EVDC's ongoing programs and plans for ensuring the timely development and introduction of market-compatible EVs.

EVDC's EV Commercialization Strategy

EVDC has designed and adopted a near-term EV commercialization strategy to advance the market debut of cost-effective electric vans for commercial fleet applications. On the basis of personal-use-vehicle and fleet-vehicle market assessments, vans were selected as the most suitable near-term vehicle technology. These assessments also targeted the fleet market as an ideal starting point for EV introduction for several reasons:
- The performance capabilities of near-term EVs are more compatible with the requirements of fleet vehicles than those of personal-use vehicles.
- Fleet vehicles in general, and vans in particular, are garaged at central locations during the night, which facilitates overnight battery recharging.
- Most larger fleets perform their own vehicle maintenance, which simplifies providing EV service and support.
- Fleet buyers are more likely to evaluate alternative vehicles based on total life-cycle cost rather than initial cost, an important factor when comparing the economics of EVs to conventional vehicles.
- Fleet managers have flexibility to assign EVs to missions that are compatible with their performance capability.

As the technology and infrastructure systems mature, this market for EVs will broaden. Whereas the first electric vans will be marketed as replacements for conventional vans in fleet use, the next generation of electric vans, with enhanced performance capabilities, will be suitable substitutes for conventional passenger fleet-vehicles. As the vehicles prove themselves and are accepted into the market, these improved vans could begin to penetrate the personal-use market. However, the large-scale use of EVs as personal vehicles is tied to the availability of advanced batteries and drivetrains that will make long-range, high-performance EVs practical. Fig. A.1 illustrates EVDC's commercialization strategy.

To implement this strategy, EVDC is focusing its efforts in four areas:
- Vehicle demonstrations
- Infrastructure development
- Market development
- Industry/government relations

The following sections briefly describe these activities.

Griffon Demonstrations

In 1985, EVDC launched a major project to introduce the Griffon—an electric van manufactured by GM in England—into North American service fleets. The Griffon was the first

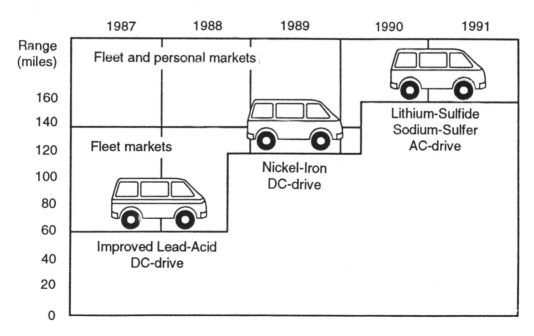

Figure A.1. Introduction of Prototype Electric Vans.

modern-day van to be produced on an assembly line; the same line was used to produce gasoline- and diesel-powered vans as well.

The Griffon uses a propulsion system made by CEVS that has accumulated more than six million miles in field operations worldwide. EVDC chose Griffon for the first commercial demonstration of EVs because of its performance capability, its proven reliability as a fleet vehicle in the United Kingdom, and the fact that it was backed by GM.

Over a period of almost three years, the 32 Griffons employed in the demonstration have logged over 400,000 miles service at 11 electric utilities across the United States and Canada. The vans have been used in applications ranging from mail delivery, employee shuttles, van pools, and plant maintenance to security and public relations. This project has provided a real-life laboratory for:

- Demonstrating the suitability of electric vans in fleet applications
- Identifying and evaluating van improvements
- Creating the critical vehicle service and parts support systems
- Developing marketing methods and incentives

The Griffon demonstration has successfully broadened interest and confidence in the feasibility of EVs. The key elements of the demonstration are described below.

User Feedback

User reactions to the Griffon have been very positive. EVDC has initiated a reporting system to monitor van operations, soliciting user feedback on the suitability and acceptability of the van and its support systems. The EVDC-implemented data system collects, analyzes, and reports on the vans' service requirements and operations. In addition, a Users' Group serves as a direct communication link between EVDC and Griffon operators.

The Demonstration Program has helped identify product and support system improvements that will increase EV fleet integration and market acceptance. Recommended vehicle design changes include modification of heating and ventilation controls, addition of a parking pawl, improvement of the suspension system and of handling, and the availability of air conditioning as an option. Many of these features are now being incorporated into the design of new electric vans. For example, interest in improved handling prompted investigations into 'electric' power steering for future electric vans.

Infrastructure

The establishment of a service and support system—an initial EV infrastructure—was one of the most important factors in conducting the Griffon demonstration. The system put in place for the demonstration consisted of:

- Manuals and Training: Vehicle operations, maintenance, and parts manuals were provided to all van operators. Comprehensive maintenance and repair training programs were also available.

- Service Assistance: GM and CEVS service technicians provided remote and on-site vehicle service assistance. A maintenance program option was also offered through which a trained CEVS technician would conduct all regularly scheduled service on the vans' electric propulsion systems.
- Spare Parts: Standard procedures and arrangements were established for ordering, distributing and billing spare parts. A Griffon parts center was set up in Detroit, Michigan, to handle the stocking and shipping of mechanical, electric/electronic and frame parts.
- Warranties: The Griffon was sold with a standard 12-month warranty guaranteeing all vehicle components except for the propulsion battery, which was covered by a 48-month warranty. Warranty claim and labor reimbursement procedures were also established.

This service and support system will be the foundation for the comprehensive EV infrastructure required to establish EVs as a viable transportation option.

Marketing

Demonstration marketing activities have focused on increasing fleet operator awareness of and exposure to electric vans. Through the Griffon promotional activities, EVDC and utilities have identified potential new electric van users. They have also obtained valuable insights into how to design an effective EV marketing program.

The "Ride and Drive" has been a particularly effective marketing approach. Ride and Drives have given utility and non-utility fleet operators with the opportunity to get a first-hand look at the Griffon and to experience the drive and feel of a state-of-the-art EV. Perhaps most importantly, Ride and Drive participants have left with a better perception of EVs. Utilities continue to use Ride and Drive programs to educate fleet operators and identify potential customers for new electric vans. For example, more than 100 fleet operators attended a Ride and Drive event sponsored by Detroit Edison conducted at GM's Milford Proving Grounds near Detroit.

In addition, individual utilities are experimenting with other approaches for introducing electric vans to fleet operators and providing incentives for their use. For example, Florida Power Corporation has exhibited a specially modified demonstrator van at several car shows and technology fairs. Detroit Edison Company set up a program through which Griffons were loaned out to work in selected fleets, including an auto parts distributor, a university, a florist, and a telephone service company. These loans, which lasted from four to six weeks each, were made in order to interest the fleet owners in a subsidized Griffon lease program. And Public Service Company of New Mexico is developing a special off-peak electricity rate as an incentive for EV operators.

G-Van Demonstration

The current phase of EVDC's EV commercialization strategy involves the introduction of the G-Van, the first modern EV to be produced in North America (see Fig. A.2). The product of a cooperative program between GMC Truck and CEVS, this full-size van will look and handle very much like its gasoline-powered counterparts, the GMC Vandura and Rally. The main difference lies in the electric propulsion system, which is based on the technology used in the Griffon. However, an improved battery and upgraded controller and motor allow the G-Van to provide driving performance comparable to that of the Griffon while offering a substantially larger cargo space and many new features.

Based on recommendations from Griffon users, the G-Van is equipped with features and options that should broaden the marketability of the vehicle. For example, the G-Van will be available as a cargo van or 8-passenger wagon. It will come equipped with all the standard features found in conventional GM vans plus electrically driven power steering and power brakes. Air conditioning and battery heating (for use in cold climates) will also be offered as options. All these additions help make the highly functional G-Van suitable for a wide range of fleet applications.

This year, the G-Van development project is maintaining steady progress. The initial proof-of-concept van is being road-tested at the Tennessee Valley Authority's Electric Vehicle Test Facility, and EVDC is working with the manufacturer and EPRI to construct additional prototype vehicles. Once completed, these vans will be field-tested to evaluate the G-Van's design and performance, and to assess driver reactions to the vehicle's capabilities and features.

Figure A.2. The Electric G-Van. Electric Power Research Institute.

Following this evaluation, EVDC is planning to direct large-scale G-Van market demonstrations in two or three regions in the United States. Approximately 100 G-Vans will be used in each region. The demonstrations should begin in late 1989. Like the Griffon demonstration, the G-Van demonstrations will:

- Evaluate and exhibit the G-Van's market suitability and acceptability
- Refine the systems and procedures for EV service and support
- Test alternative marketing programs and user incentives
- Verify the G-Van's cost-effectiveness and reliability
- Establish the air quality effects of EVs

As part of the demonstration, regional infrastructure systems and facilities for EV distribution and service will be examined and established.

EVDC is also beginning plans for the introduction of the Chrysler TEVan, an electric van based on the popular Chrysler Voyager and Caravan minivans. This van incorporates a high-performance propulsion system that will substantially expand the market for EVs (see Table A-1 for a comparison of Griffon, G-Van, and TEVan capabilities). TEVan prototypes (seen in Fig. A.3) will be available for demonstration in 1990.

Table A-1: Griffon, G-Van, and TEVan			
	Griffon	**G-Van**	**Chrysler TEVan***
Top Speed	53 mph	53 mph	65 mph
Range	60 mi	60 mi	110+ mi
Acceleration (0-30 mph)	11 sec	12 sec	7 sec
Payload Capacity	1900 lb	1800 lb	1200 lb
Cargo Space	208 cu ft	256 cu ft	120 cu ft

*projected

Near-term EVs will be suitable for a variety of applications. With its large payload capacity, the electric G-Van will be a service fleet "work horse", perfect for hauling cargo and for local shuttles. The smaller Chrysler TEVan, offering increased range and higher top speed, will blend well with highway traffic and help EVs enter the passenger fleet-vehicle market.

Figure A.3a. Chrysler TEVan Electric Minivan. Chrysler.

Figure A.3b. Chrysler TEVan Battery Pack with Integrated Support System. Chrysler.

Figure A.3c. Chrysler TEVan DC Motor, Solid State Controller. Chrysler.

Infrastructure Development

The establishment of a comprehensive and accessible infrastructure is a prerequisite for achieving EV commercialization. Recognizing this, EVDC, EPRI, and several member utilities are working together to develop an EV distribution operation dedicated to selling and supporting EV products. This operation will establish the infrastructure that EVs will need to compete in the nationwide automotive marketplace.

A national office will be set up to direct the new EV distribution operation. This office will be responsible for marketing EVs on a national scale, establishing policies and procedures for regional operations, coordination national fleet sales, and training EV sales and service staff. In addition, the national office will establish and direct a series of franchised regional offices responsible for setting up local EV dealerships and service centers. The regional offices will also manage vehicle warranties and financing packages, monitor inventories of vehicles and parts, and provide customer service. Electric utilities are expected to play a direct role in creating these regional distribution operations.

Although the national office will provide guidelines and standards for the regional and local operations, the regional offices will have the discretion to decide how they will actually provide the prescribed EV sales, service, warranty, and support functions. For example, a regional office may choose whether to establish its own exclusive EV sales and service dealerships or to use existing GMC truck dealerships to provide these functions. Offices may also choose whether to offer special incentives, such as battery leasing, or pursue other related business opportunities.

According to plans, the initial capitalization required to launch this operation will be raised through direct investment by electric utilities and through the sale of charter franchise agreements. Operating revenues and a return on the initial investment will be generated by further franchise sales and through charging a nominal distribution service fee for each vehicle processed.

The national EV distribution office and the initial regional operations will be inaugurated by mid-1989—in preparation for the G-Van market demonstrations. The national office's initial efforts will focus on developing operational guidelines and coordinating the regional roll-out of the G-Van. The first regional offices will be established in those areas where the G-Van demonstrations will be conducted. The G-Van demonstrations will provide a valuable testing ground for the regional EV distribution operations.

A similar distribution strategy will be adopted for products now under development at Chrysler and Ford and for vehicles that other organizations develop and introduce. As with the G-Van, the national EV distribution operation will coordinate both automotive/truck dealers and utilities in the distribution process. It will also provide policies and procedures, national advertising, and an entire range of management services.

Market Development

EVDC market development activities are pursued at two levels. The first, discussed previously, encompasses the work of EVDC and individual utility companies to identify and test alternative marketing approaches. Ride and Drives, loan-lease programs, demonstrator vans, preferential electricity rates, and special promotions are some of the techniques that have stimulated interest in and awareness of modern-day EVs. Gaining user feedback on the capabilities, performance, and design of prototype electric vans is also a critical part of these marketing activities.

The second level of market development pertains to EVDC's work to define and character-ize the market potential for near-term EVs. This information is gathered through comprehensive market-survey efforts.

In 1987, EVDC prepared for the introduction of the G-Van and TEVan by conducting an extensive survey of commercial fleets in 30 of the largest urban markets in the United States. As the most comprehensive study to date of EV sales potential, the survey provides a clear picture of the future demand for electric vans.

The results indicate that the 60-mile-range G-Van could replace 161,000 vans within these 30 metropolitan areas. Analyses show that current-technology G-Vans will have the greatest sales potential in large van fleets (those with more than 11 vans). The survey points up the advantages of targeting this fleet market segment, showing:

- Over 60% of commercial vans are operated in only 3% of fleets; this 3% is made of fleets with more than ten vans.
- Large fleets have indicated a significantly higher willingness to buy EVs than smaller fleets.

- Large fleets, which have a higher public profile, are in a better position to realize the EVs' indirect benefits such as improved urban air quality and fuel substitution.
- Larger fleets have more flexibility to blend limited-range electric vans into their operations.
- Managers of large fleets use life-cycle costs in making purchasing decisions and recognize the benefits of lower operations and maintenance costs.
- The in-house service capabilities of large fleets will minimize the need for establishing extensive electric van service and training systems.
- Selling to large fleets will be more cost-effective because of the higher sales potential per customer and per marketing dollar.

The introduction of electric vans with extended range capability will significantly increase market potential (see Fig. A.4). For example, an electric van with 90-mile range (50% more than the current G-Van) will increase the potential demand for EVs by more than 100% to 283,000 vans—nearly 80% of the vans in large fleets.

To help launch the G-Van in 1989, EVDC is developing a G-Van Promotion Program to be targeted both at large-fleet operators in the primary G-Van markets and at the general public. The program will include media events, test drives, and other activities designed to draw attention to this new vehicle.

These results indicate that achieving an annual sales volume of 20,000-25,000 electric vans within the top 30 markets is a practical objective. By expanding the market reach of electric vans to include all vehicle market areas as well as small and public-sector fleets, this sales potential could nearly triple.

Although modest by traditional automotive-industry standards, this market size is sufficient to obtain an acceptable return on investment for manufacturers, distributors, and providers of sales and service.

As noted previously, EV markets will be developed on a regional basis to ensure a responsiveness to local transportation needs. In addition, regionally centered marketing will maximize the interest and involvement of local utility companies. It will also allow the national EV distribution operation to use cost-effective marketing approaches in targeting and pursuing large-fleet customers. The regional surveys conducted as part of the national fleet survey effort support this market strategy by providing region-specific information including:

- Definitions of the fleet van market according to fleet size, industry type, driving requirements, and van configurations
- A profile of attitudes among van users toward the benefits and limitations of current-technology EVs
- Projections of the effect that improved EV performance will have on potential market share

The recent market surveys substantiate the large potential for electric vans. As advanced technologies mature, EVs could meet the demands of the vast personal-vehicle market and thereby dramatically expand the sale potential of EVs.

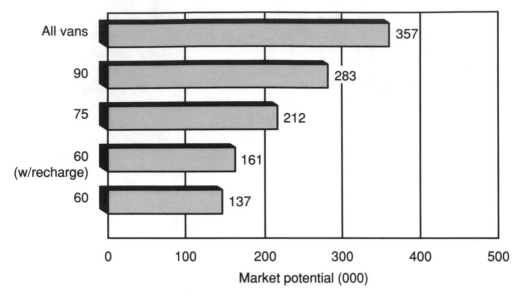

Figure A.4. EV Market Survey Results

Industry/Government Relations

Industry/government relations activities are another important part of EVDC's commercialization efforts. Because the development of the EV market is tied to continued progress in EV technology, it is important for EVDC to monitor the status of the extensive R&D being sponsored by DOE and EPRI. To facilitate the exchange of information, EVDC, DOE, and EPRI have established the National EV R&D Steering Committee. This committee gives the three organizations a forum in which to define R&D priorities and cooperative programs on the basis of market requirements.

By participating in the activities of this steering committee and an EPRI advisory committee called the Electric Transportation Working Group, EVDC obtains information and insight with which to form long-range market and business plans.

To stimulate the market for early EVs, EVDC has recently instituted a Government Relations Program. Through this program, the utility industry will interact with federal, state, and local agencies to develop incentives and regulatory mechanisms to help promote the use of EVs. Justification of government support for such incentives lies in the fact that EVs offer societal benefits not directly valued by individual users: fuel diversity and reduced vehicle emissions.

The implementation of government economic incentives, such as air quality credits and vehicle tax and registration waivers, could have a significant effect on getting EVs into the market and making them cost-competitive with conventional vehicles. Present economic analyses show that electric vans produced in large quantities would be roughly equivalent to conventional vans on a total life-cycle cost basis. Produced in small quantities, EVs could be more costly to own and operate than conventional vans. Government programs to encourage the acquisition and use of EVs in commercial fleets, even for an interim period, would help build an initial demand for EVs. This demand would reduce EV cost, because components and vehicles produced in larger volumes would allow production economies.

In the coming months, EVDC's Government Relations Committee will:

- Monitor legislation and public-sector initiatives that would have an impact on the EV industry. Emphasis will be placed on ensuring that EVs are included in any clean air or alternative fuel legislation.
- Publish a government relations newsletter that highlights these initiatives and promotes additional action at the federal, state, and local levels.
- Publicize the beneficial effects of EVs on air quality and the role EV technology can play in providing transportation that uses alternate fuel sources.

In addition, EVDC participates in the California EV Task Force. This group includes representatives from several state and regional government agencies. It recommends R&D funding, demonstration programs, and legislative and regulatory actions that will facilitate EV commercialization.

Success in building public sector support for and involvement in EV commercialization is critical to achieving EVDC's near- and long-term market objectives.

Closing

EVDC is putting in place all of the elements needed to foster the timely and systematic commercialization of EVs—demonstrations, infrastructure, marketing, and industry and government support. At the same time, EVDC has worked to involve all key EV stakeholders—the utility industry, the automotive industry, component manufacturers, users, and the government—in its efforts to introduce the first modern-day production EV and build a new industry.

New technical, organizational, and institutional challenges lie ahead. But EVDC is well-positioned and prepared to deal with these uncertainties and looks forward to the successful commercialization of this promising new technology—electric vehicles."

APPENDIX B

Three-Phase Induction Motors and Controls for Electric Cars

G.J.Murphy
Department of Electrical Engineering
Northwestern University

The purpose of the author in writing this chapter is to present a broad view of a-c motors and electronic controls for such motors appropriate for use in electric vehicles. Because this book is directed to the reader who wishes to gain a reasonable familiarity with many aspects of electric vehicles, rather than to the experienced designer of electric motors and/or electronic control systems, the depth of the technical treatment has been limited.

It is assumed, however, that the reader is familiar with the fundamental concepts of electric-circuit theory. In particular, steady-state relationships between voltage and current in various circuit elements are assumed to be understood. It is desirable also that the reader be familiar with the difference between single-phase circuits and polyphase circuits, but it is possible that an appreciation of that difference can be gained through the reading of this chapter.

Single-phase a-c motors are not treated here, because they do not appear to offer sufficient advantages over d-c motors for use in on-the-road electric vehicles. Polyphase a-c motors are of interest because they offer several advantages. First, they operate without a commutator; therefore, they require virtually no maintenance. Second, they are relatively small and light in weight, for a given voltage, power, and speed rating. And third, they are far less expensive (in some cases between one-fifth and one-third as expensive) than comparable d-c machines.

As is true of d-c motors, polyphase a-c motors have a stator, or stationary member, and a rotor, or rotating member.

Although the nature of the stator winding is basically the same for all polyphase a-c motors, there are significant differences in rotor windings. These differences serve as a basis for classification and are treated in detail later in this appendix. In the interest of simplicity, the treatment in this section has been limited to three-phase machines, which appear to be by far the most appropriate of polyphase machines for vehicular propulsion. The basic concept can readily be generalized by the reader.

The stator of a three-phase motor has wound on it a set of three windings, with their magnetic axes displaced from one another by 120 degrees around the circumference of the stator, as illustrated in Fig. B.1. Half of each winding is wound on one pole, and the other half on a second pole diametrically opposite the first, if the machine has one pair of poles per phase. The three windings are connected together in a wye connection, as in Fig. B.1(a), or in a delta connection, as in Fig. B.1(b). In addition, a fourth connection is sometimes made to the neutral, N, in the wye connection. For the remainder of this appendix, it will be assumed that a wye-connected stator with no neutral connection is used.

In normal use, the stator windings are connected to a balanced three-phase supply of sinusoidal voltages. The line-to-line voltages applied to the terminals 1, 2, and 3 of the stator windings then may be represented by three phasors 120 degrees out of phase with one another (in time), as illustrated in Fig. B.2.

The applied voltages cause the induction of magnetic flux in the iron on which the stator coils are wound. In the steady state, neglecting nonlinearity in the magnetic circuit, each of the three windings thus produces a sinusoidally varying magnetic flux, and the three components of flux (one due to each of the three windings) are 120 degrees out of time-phase with one another. The net effect is then that of a magnetic flux vector of constant magnitude, rotating with a constant angular velocity about the center of the interior of the stator.

The speed at which the flux vector rotates is determined by the number of stator poles per phase and the frequency of the voltages applied to the stator windings. That is, if the machine

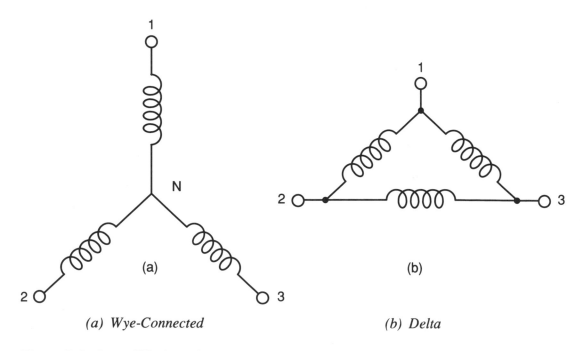

(a) Wye-Connected   *(b) Delta*

Figure B.1. Stator Windings for a Three-Phase Motor. Connected.

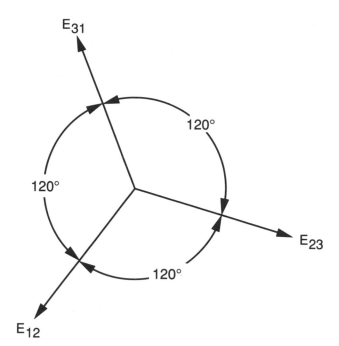

Figure B.2. Line-to-Line Voltages of a Normally Excited Three-Phase Stator.

has $\underline{p}$ pairs of poles per phase, the magnetic vector appears to advance $360/\underline{p}$ degrees in space around the periphery of the stator during one cycle of the applied voltage. If the frequency of the applied voltage is $\underline{f}$ Hertz (i.e., $\underline{f}$ cycles per second), then the magnetic vector appears to complete one revolution every $\underline{p/f}$ seconds. The speed of this rotating magnetic field, in revolutions per minute, is known as the synchronous speed and denoted by $\underline{N_s}$. It follows that

$$N_s = 60 \ f/p \tag{1}$$

revolutions per minute.

The magnetic field established by the currents in the stator windings, rotating at the synchronous speed, acts on the rotor of the machine. The nature of the action depends on the type of winding carried by the rotor. Regardless of the kind of rotor winding, however, the force exerted on the rotor produces a torque that causes the rotor to tend to turn. If the mechanical load attached to the rotor is not too great, the rotor does in fact turn continuously, or rotate, in the same direction as the stator field.

In many synchronous motors the rotor has the shape illustrated in Fig. B.3. The winding is wound around the iron rotor between the two salient poles. The ends of the rotor winding are connected, through slip rings, to a d-c supply. The current in the rotor winding produces a magnetic field of magnitude proportional to the rotor current and to the number of turns in the rotor winding, assuming linearity of operation. One of the salient poles is a north magnetic pole; the other, a south pole. In other synchronous motors the same result is achieved by use of a permanent magnet for the rotor.

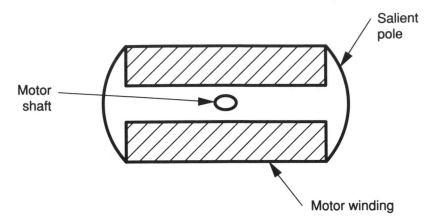

Figure B.3. Cross-Section of a Rotor for a Synchronous Motor.

If the rotor of a synchronous motor is stationary, its north pole is alternately attracted by the south pole of the rotating field due to the stator and repelled by the north pole of the stator field, as that field rotates with respect to the rotor. The south pole of the rotor is similarly alternately attracted and repelled by the poles of the stator field. The average torque exerted on the rotor by the stator field is zero. Therefore, a synchronous motor cannot start itself.

If the rotor is caused to turn in the same direction and at the same speed as the rotating field produced by the stator, however, the net torque is no longer zero. The rotor then tends to be "locked to" the rotating field. If the mechanical load on the motor changes, the position of the rotor relative to the rotating stator poles must change to maintain torque equilibrium, but the rotor must continue to run, on the average, at the synchronous speed.

Therefore, the only means by which the average speed of a synchronous motor can be varied is to vary the frequency of the excitation to the stator windings. The maximum torque developed by the motor, can, however, be varied by varying the amplitude of the stator excitation.

The most common type of rotor winding for a three-phase induction motor is the squirrel cage winding. The rotor conductors are bars that run through slots in the iron core of the rotor. The bars are connected at the ends to form a closed circuit. When the rotor is stationary, the rotating flux established by the stator field passes through these conductors and induces in them voltages similar to the voltages induced in the stator windings.

The voltages induced in the rotor winding cause a motion of electric charge, which constitutes a rotor current. This current produces magnetic poles on the periphery of the rotor. The number of these poles is equal to the number of stator poles.

The frequency of the voltage induced in a stationary rotor is the same as the frequency of the stator voltages. If the rotor is rotated at synchronous speed, in the same direction as the stator field, the voltage induced in the rotor has zero amplitude and zero frequency, because the stator flux then does not cut the rotor bars at all.

Between zero speed and synchronous speed, the rotor frequency varies linearly with motor speed, as shown in Fig. B.4.

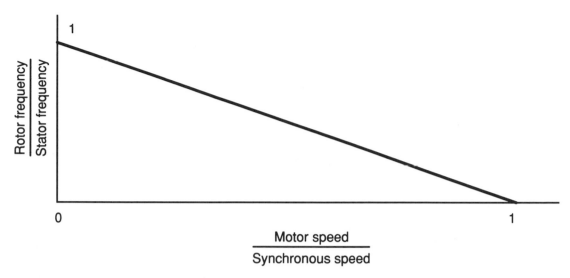

Figure B.4. Normalized Rotor Frequency Versus Normalized Motor Speed.

Some induction motors have a wound rotor, instead of a squirrel cage rotor. As its name implies, a wound rotor contains a conventional winding, similar to the stator winding, in slots in the iron core of the rotor. The ends of the various phases of the rotor winding can be connected together directly on the rotor, or they can be brought out through slip rings to be connected together through external resistances.

The operation of a wound-rotor induction motor is basically the same as the operation of a squirrel-cage induction motor. Variations in the external resistance connected in series with each phase of a wound-rotor winding cause variation in starting current, starting torque, power factor, and efficiency.

Regardless of whether the induction motor contains a wound rotor or a squirrel-cage, the motor must run at a speed less than the synchronous speed in order to develop a positive load torque. For a given magnitude of stator voltage, the motor speed must decrease, in normal operation, to produce a larger load torque. Therefore, the induction motor is not a constant-speed machine as the synchronous motor is. The speed of the induction motor can also be controlled by varying the frequency of the stator excitation, and the magnitude of the torque developed by the induction motor can be varied by varying the amplitude of the stator excitation.

In normal operation, the stator of a three-phase induction motor is connected to a balanced three-phase supply of sinusoidal voltages at a frequency of $\underline{f}$ Hertz. The rotor rotates in the electrical steady state at a speed of $\underline{N}$ revolutions per minute (rpm). The difference between the synchronous speed and the rotor speed is known as the slip speed. That is,

$$N_{slip} = N_{syn} - N \tag{2}$$

The normalized slip speed is denoted by $\underline{S}$ and is known as the slip.

461

Since

$$S = N_{slip}/N_{syn} = (N_{syn} - N)/N_{syn} = 1 - N/N_{syn} \quad , \tag{3}$$

the slip is seen to be a linear function of motor speed that is equal to unity when the motor is stalled and to zero when the motor is running at its synchronous speed.

The frequency of the current and voltage in the stator windings is the synchronous frequency $\underline{f}$. In the rotor, however, as has been mentioned previously, the frequency of current and voltage is a linear function of rotor speed and has a value of $\underline{f}$ Hertz when the motor is stalled and a value of 0 when the motor is running at its synchronous speed. Therefore, the rotor frequency is

$$f_r = S \, f \text{ Hertz} \quad . \tag{4}$$

It is common practice to use a per-phase equivalent circuit[1] in the analysis of an induction motor operating in this manner. A diagram of such an equivalent circuit is shown in Fig. B.5. In this diagram, $\underline{L_m}$ denotes the magnetizing inductance, in henrys, and $\underline{R_c}$, the equivalent core-loss resistance, in ohms. $\underline{L_1}$ and $\underline{R_1}$, denote the leakage inductance in henrys and the resistance in ohms, respectively, of the stator winding. $\underline{L_2}$ and $\underline{R_2}$ denote the leakage inductance in henrys and the resistance in ohms, respectively, of the rotor, referred to the stator winding. The rms (root-mean-square) value of rotor-induced voltage, in volts referred to the stator winding, is denoted by $\underline{E_m}$, and $\underline{V}$ denotes the rms value of the voltage applied to each phase of the stator windings.

The quantity $\underline{R_2} ((I-\underline{S})/\underline{S})$ is a resistance, in ohms, that represents the mechanical power output of the motor. That is, the mechanical power output of the motor is equal to the electrical power dissipated in $\underline{R_2} ((1-\underline{S})/\underline{S})$ multiplied by the number of phases in the stator winding.

It is evident in Fig. B.5 that the net series resistance of the rotor per phase, referred to the stator, is

$$R_2 + R_2 ((I - S)/S) = R_2/S \tag{5}$$

The rms value of rotor current per phase, referred to the stator, is therefore

$$I_r = \frac{E_m}{\sqrt{\left(\dfrac{R_2}{S}\right)^2 + \omega^2 \, L_2^2}} \text{ amperes} \quad , \tag{6}$$

where

$$\omega = 2 \, \pi \, f \tag{7}$$

is the stator frequency in radians per second. It follows that, for a three-phase motor, the average mechanical power output, in watts, is

$$P_o = 3 \, I_r^2 \, R_2 \left(\frac{1-S}{S}\right) = \frac{3 \, R_2 \, E_m^2}{\dfrac{R_2^2}{S^2} + \omega^2 \, L_2^2} \, \frac{1-S}{S} \tag{8}$$

---

[1] Fitzgerald, A. E., and Charles Kingsley, Jr., *Electric Machinery, Second Edition*, McGraw-Hill Book Company., New York. 1961.

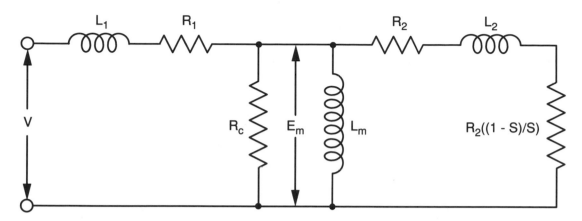

Figure B.5. Diagram of a Per-Phase Equivalent Circuit for an Induction Motor, Referred to the Stator.

The average torque in pound-feet at the shaft of the three-phase motor, neglecting windage and friction, is, therefore,

$$T = \frac{2.21\,pR_2}{S\,\omega}\;\frac{E_m^2}{\dfrac{R_2^2}{S^2} + \omega^2\,L_2^2} \tag{9}$$

Under normal conditions, $|\underline{S}|$ is small (typically, 0.05), and $|R_2/S|$ can be much larger than $\omega\,\underline{L}2$. In that event,

$$T \cong \frac{2.21\,p\,S\,E_m^2}{\omega\,R_2} \tag{10}$$

If the magnetizing current and the equivalent core-loss current are negligible, the general expression for torque as a function of $\underline{S}$ can be rewritten in terms of the applied voltage $\underline{V}$. Thus, (9) can be replaced by

$$T = \frac{2.21\,p\,R_2}{S\,\omega}\;\frac{V^2}{\left(R_1 + \dfrac{R_2}{S}\right)^2 + \omega^2\left(L_1 + L_2\right)^2} \tag{11}$$

The expression given in (11) for the torque developed by the motor indicates that there is a maximum value of torque for a given value of $\underline{V}$. This maximum value can be found by differentiating the right-hand side of (11) with respect to $\underline{S}$ and equating the result to 0, to determine the value of $\underline{S}$ at which the maximum torque occurs. Thus, it can be shown that the value of slip corresponding to maximum torque is

$$S_{mt} = \frac{R_2}{\sqrt{R_1^2 + \omega^2 (L_1 + L_2)^2}} \tag{12}$$

Substituting this value for $\underline{S}$ in (11) yields the maximum torque

$$T_m = \frac{1.1\, p\, V^2}{\omega \left[R_1 + \sqrt{R_1^2 + \omega^2 (L_1 + L_2)^2} \right]} \tag{13}$$

A curve of motor torque versus motor speed for a typical three-phase induction motor in steady-state operation on a balanced three-phase sinusoidal supply of voltage at constant amplitude and constant frequency is shown in Fig. B.6. In normal operation, the speed $\underline{N}$ is less than the synchronous speed $\underline{N}_{syn}$ and greater than the speed at which the maximum torque $\underline{T}_m$ occurs. As the torque demanded by the load varies, the speed varies, with the operating point of the motor moving along the portion of the curve just described to maintain a balance between the load torque and the torque developed by the motor.

By properly varying the amplitude of the voltage and the frequency, it is possible to generate a family of torque-speed curves as shown in Fig. B.7. At any given time, the steady-state operation of the motor is represented by a single point on one such curve. The operating point can be caused to move from one curve to another, however. Thus, it is possible, by controlling

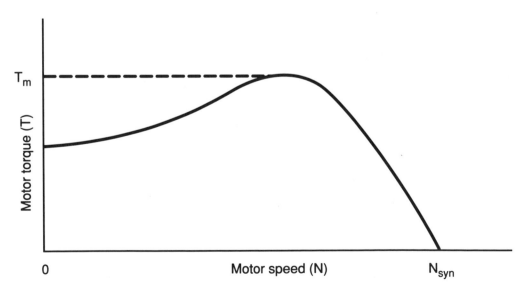

Figure B.6. A Torque-Speed Curve for a Typical Three-Phase Induction Motor.

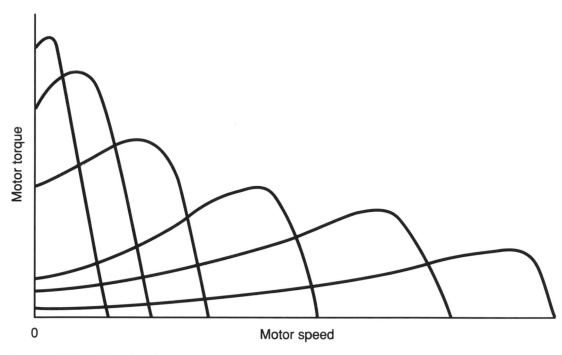

Figure B.7. A Family of Torque-Speed Curves.

the amplitude and the frequency of the supply voltage, to generate any desired torque-speed curve that falls within a large region of the torque-speed plane illustrated in Fig. B.7.

Care must be taken to ensure that the current demanded by the motor is not excessive, as it might otherwise be at low speeds. For this reason, it is customary to monitor the current and to include, in the controller, electronic circuitry that will automatically limit the current at some predetermined value.

In a vehicle intended for on-the-road use, it is not practical to provide a balanced three-phase source of sinusoidal voltages with controllable amplitude and frequency. The source of power is usually a battery, which ideally provides a single constant voltage between two terminals. An inverter is used to obtain from such a source a set of three voltages that is in some sense equivalent to the balanced, controllable three-phase supply described previously. To minimize power losses and circuit complexity, the inverter is usually built of some kind of switching elements, as shown in Fig. B.8.

With switches 1, 2, and 6 closed and switches 3, 4, and 5 open, as indicated in Fig. B.8, output terminals A and C are connected to the positive side of the battery, and terminal B is connected to the negative side. Consequently the voltage drop from A to B is $\underline{V}$ volts, the voltage drop from B to C is $-\underline{V}$ volts, and the voltage drop from C to A is 0 volts. By opening certain switches and closing others, the voltages between A and B, B and C, and C and A can be changed. If the switches are opened and closed cyclically in the proper pattern, a voltage waveform such as that shown in Fig. B.9 can be applied between each pair of output terminals, and these three voltage

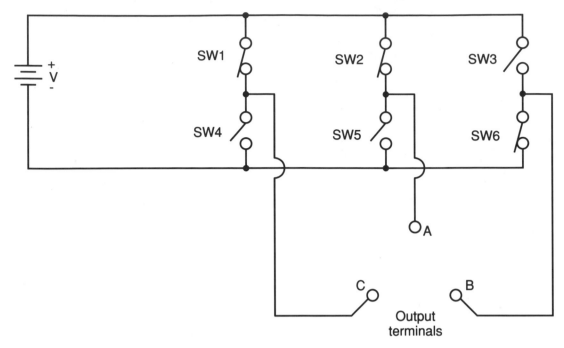

Figure B.8. A Basic Diagram of a Switching Inverter.

waveforms can be made to be 120 degrees "out of phase" with one another in the sense that each of the three leads one of the other two by one third of a cycle and lags the other by one third of a cycle.

For a given periodic pattern of such voltage pulses applied to the motor terminals, it is possible to determine a fundamental sinusoidal component and various harmonics of the three voltages ($\underline{V}_{AB}$, $\underline{V}_{BC}$, and $\underline{V}_{CA}$).[2] If the motor operates approximately in a linear manner, the superposition theorem[3] can be applied to determine the response of the motor to the voltages it receives from the inverter.

The switching of the inverter elements is designed so that the fundamental components of the three output voltages produce the desired motor response. Since the higher harmonics of the voltages cause undesired heating and torque variations, and since the analysis of the operation of the motor is significantly complicated, if the higher harmonics must be taken into account, it is desirable that the amplitudes of all of the higher harmonics be kept small relative to the amplitude of the fundamental component. If that is done, the rms value of the fundamental component of the voltage obtained from a pair of inverter output terminals (Fig. B.9, for example) may be substituted for the value $\underline{V}$ in Fig. B.5, and the previously described analysis based on Fig. B.5 may be used.

---

[2] Van Valkenburg, M. E., *Network Analysis, Third Edition*, Prentice Hall, Inc., Englewood Cliffs, N. J., 1974.

[3] Hayt, William H., Jr., and Jack E. Kemmerly, *Engineering Analysis, Second Edition*, McGraw-Hill Book Company, Inc., New York, 1971.

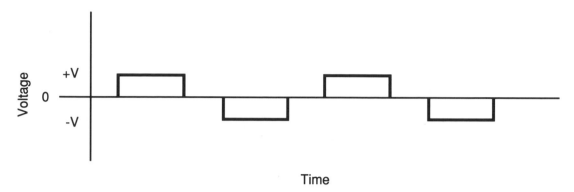

Figure B.9. Two Cycles of Periodic Output Voltage Waveform for the Inverter Illustrated in Fig. B.8.

Control of the amplitudes of the harmonic components of the output voltages obtained from the inverter can be achieved by modifying the switching pattern appropriately. Instead of generating a single wide pulse during each half cycle, as shown in Fig. B.9, one might generate a train of narrower pulses, as shown in Fig. B.10. The number of pulses, their width, and their locations should then be chosen so as to maintain the desired value of the fundamental, while decreasing the values of the higher harmonics. Another form of output voltage waveform that has been suggested for harmonic reduction is shown in Fig. B.11. Here, the widths of the individual pulses are modulated sinusoidally at the fundamental frequency.

In a practical system, the switches indicated in Fig. B.8 are replaced by solid-state electronic devices (transistor or silicon controlled rectifiers - SCRs). In addition, a diode is connected around each of these devices, to provide a path for the motor currents in a free-wheeling mode of operation following the opening of a normal current path when a solid-state switch is turned off.

One approach that can be used to adjust the magnitude of the voltage applied to the input to the inverter is to connect the inverter to and disconnect it from the battery alternately at a fairly

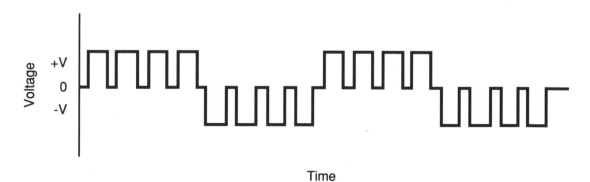

Figure B.10. An Alternative Output Waveform for the Inverter Shown in Fig. B.8.

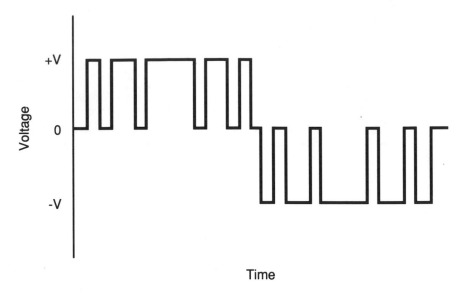

Figure B.11. Pulse-Width Modulation for Suppression of Harmonics.

high frequency. The frequency of the voltage applied to the stator windings must then still be varied separately by controlling the frequency at which one set of three conducting SCR's in the inverter is replaced by another set of three conducting SCR's. The two frequencies must be coordinated to maintain an appropriate level of motor current. A practical means of varying the input voltage to the inverter in such a system is to connect a chopper and an associated filter between the battery and the inverter input. The average value of inverter input voltage can then be varied by pulse-width modulation of the chopping waveform. The chopping frequency should be kept high enough to keep the size of the filter components required within practical limits. The losses in the filter inductor and the motor increase with frequency, however, and the chopping frequency must therefore be kept low enough to prevent those losses from becoming excessive.

A different method of controlling the amplitude of the voltage applied to the motor is to use pulse-width modulation within the inverter itself. When this method is used, the input terminals to the inverter are connected directly to the battery, without an intervening chopper. To obtain a low amplitude of motor voltage, the duration of each interval in which charge Is allowed to flow from the battery through inverter SCR's and the motor windings is kept small relative to the time from the beginning of one such interval to the beginning of the next. A large amplitude of motor voltage is obtained by making the width of each such conduction interval equal to a large fraction of the repetition period.

Again it is necessary to coordinate the synchronous frequency with the relative pulse width, to ensure that motor current remains within acceptable bounds.

Although the adjustable voltage approach using a chopper, as described previously, results in a simpler control system and a smaller number of low-power electronic circuit components, it requires more high-power electronic devices and a heavy, bulky filter. Such a system is therefore significantly more expensive than a comparable pulse-width-modulated inverter. The increased cost, size, and weight must be carefully weighed against the complexity of control and the increased harmonic content present in a pulse-width-modulated inverter before a final decision is made on which approach to use.

In an alternative approach, the inverter is connected to a "constant-current source" instead of to a "constant-voltage source". The conversion of the latter to the former is accomplished by connecting a large inductance in series between the voltage source and the inverter. Since this inductance tends to oppose any change in current, the current tends to remain fairly constant over short intervals of time, if closed circuit paths are always provided for current in the inductor.

Thus, if the inverter control system is designed so that as one SCR is turned off, another is simultaneously turned on, the current in the inductor can switch from one path through the stator windings of the motor to another, with constant magnitude. In such a system, a constant current is supplied to the stator, and hence control of the torque developed by the motor must be achieved entirely by variations in the slip. If the maximum rated stator current is provided at all times, the speed of the motor can be varied by varying the frequency of stator excitation, and the motor will then adjust its slip to meet the torque demands of the load, within the power capability of the machine.

A different method of torque control is to utilize pulse-width modulation, as in the case in which the inverter is supplied with energy by a constant-voltage source. In this method, there are time intervals during which it is desired that the stator winding of the motor be disconnected from the source. In order to maintain the constant current in the series inductance during such intervals, it is necessary to provide some other path for this current during those intervals only. This can be done, for example, by use of a free-wheeling diode connected across the series inductance in such a way that it is reverse-biased while the source is supplying current to the motor.

The use of a constant-current source instead of a constant-voltage source offers certain advantages in control and reliability; but, for a given vehicle and a given range of driving conditions, a higher efficiency is obtained with a constant-voltage drive than with a constant-current drive.

An a-c propulsion system using a three-phase motor has several important advantages over a d-c system. The relatively low cost of the induction motor has already been mentioned. Because there are neither slip rings nor a commutator on a squirrel-cage motor, the maintenance requirement of such a motor is negligible. The same can be said of a permanent-magnet synchronous motor. The commutator and brushes of a d-c propulsion motor, by contrast, should be examined several times a year, if the vehicle is driven daily. In addition, the brushes in the d-c motor must be replaced in time as a result of wear, and the commutator bars and separators might require servicing from time to time.

The lack of starting torque in a synchronous motor can be overcome by adding circuitry to cause the excitation of the stator windings to advance in step with the rotor, instead of independently of the rotor position, as in a true synchronous motor. A combination of such circuitry and a synchronous motor is sometimes referred to as an electronically commutated motor.

If the direction of travel of the vehicle is to be reversed electrically instead of by use of a mechanical transmission, the a-c system has another advantage. Reversing the direction of rotation of a d-c motor requires the reversing of the direction of current in either the armature winding or the field winding. In either case, a relatively bulky and costly device is needed to provide the switching. To reverse the direction of rotation of a three-phase a-c motor, however, it is necessary only to reverse the phase sequence of the stator excitation. This can be done, very simply, in an integrated circuit, at virtually no cost and negligible increase in size and weight. Moreover, the contacts needed to perform the switching required for reversal of a d-c motor present an additional maintenance problem that has no counterpart in the integrated circuit used to reverse the phase sequence in the a-c system.

Similarly, if regenerative braking is to be used, electrical contacts are required to provide the necessary switching in the d-c system. In the a-c system, regenerative braking is achieved by operating with a negative slip. This is accomplished electronically, without the use of electrical contacts, simply by controlling the frequency of the excitation applied to the a-c motor so that the magnetic field in the motor rotates a little less rapidly than the rotor.

The major disadvantage of the a-c system is the complexity of the electronics. The inverter is substantially larger, heavier, and more expensive than a d-c chopper, for a given power output. Moreover, the logic required for control of an a-c system is far more complex than that required for control of a d-c system.

A more detailed description of the operation of one kind of a-c propulsion system and an extensive bibliography on electric drive systems can be found in Reference 4.

---

[4] Murphy, G. J., "Considerations in the Design of Drive Systems for On-the-Road Electric Vehicles", IEEE Proc., Vol. 60, No. 12, Dec., 1972, pp. 1519-1533.

APPENDIX C

Many organizations have manufactured electric cars. Unlike the relatively few IC engined cars which have survived: GM, Ford, Chrysler and those foreign automobiles known to the reader, few have lasted making electric cars. Below are listed those makers who tried.

Table 1. Name Table of American Electric Cars

Name	Company of Manufacture	Location	Period
	A		
Ajax	Ajax Motor Vehicle Co.	New York NY	1901-1903
Altha	Altha Auto & Power Co.	Dover DL	1901-1905
American Electric	American Electric Vehicle Co.	Chicago IL	1899-1902
American Electric	American Motor Car Co.	Cleveland OH	1902-1910
Andover Motor	Andover Electric Truck Co.	Andover MA	1915-1917
Anthony	Earle C. Anthony	Los Angeles CA	1897
		Colorado Springs CO	1899-1900
Argo	Argo Electric Vehicle Co.	Saginaw MI	1912-1915
Argo-Borland	Merger, Borland-Grannis	Chicago IL	1912
Arnold Electric	B. J. Arnold	Chicago IL	1895
Atlantic	Atlantic Electric Vehicle Co.	Newark NJ	1912-1914
Auto-Car	Pittsburgh Motor Vehicle Co.	Pittsburgh PA	1899
AutoCar	AutoCar Equipment Co.	Buffalo NY	1904
Autodynamics	The Autodynamics Co.	New York NY	1901
Autoette	Autoette Electric Car Co.	Long Beach CA	1965-1968
Automatic	Automatic Transmission Co.	Buffalo NY	1921
	American Bicycle Co.		1900

471

Name	Company of Manufacture	Location	Period

B

Name	Company of Manufacture	Location	Period
Babcock	Babcock Electric Carriage Co.	Buffalo NY	1906-1912
Bachelles	Otto Bachelles	Chicago IL	1901-1902
Bailey	S. R. Bailey & Co.	Amesbury MA	1907-1915
Baker	Baker Motor Vehicle Co.	Cleveland OH	1899-1915
	Baker-Rauch & Lang	Cleveland OH	1894
Baker & Elberg	Baker & Elberg	Kansas City KS	1896-1905
	Sold to Stone, altered J. A. Barrent	New York NY	1894-1895
Banker	Banker Bros. Co.	Pittsburgh PA	1905
Barrow	Barrow Vehicle Co.	Willimatic CN	1897-1898
Battronics	Battronic Truck Corp.	Boyertown PA	1964-1980
Beardsley	Beardsley Electric Car Co.	San Francisco CA	1915-1917
Belmont	Belmont Electric Car Co.	Wyandotte MI	1916
Berwick	Berwick Auto Car Co.	Grand Rapids MI	1904
Binney-Bernham	Binney & Burnham	Boston MA	1899-1902
Blakeslee	Blakeslee Co.	Cleveland OH	1906-1907
Borbein	H. F. Borbein Co.	St. Louis MO	1903
Borland	Borland-Grannis Co.	Detroit MI	1903-1913
Borland Electric	Borland-Grannis Co.	Chicago IL	1912-1914
Bowman Electric	Sidney B. Bowman Cycle Co.		1900
Brecht	Brecht Automobile Co.	St. Louis MO	1901-1903
Broc	Broc Carriage & Wagon Co.	Cleveland OH	1909-1915
Buffalo	Buffalo Electric Car Co.	Buffalo NY	1900-1913
Byrider	Byrider Electric Automobile Co.	Cleveland OH	1908-1911

C

Name	Company of Manufacture	Location	Period
California	California Automobile Co.	San Francisco CA	1901
Cantono	Cantono Electric Tractor Co.	Canton OH	1904-1905
Capitol	Washington Motor Vehicle Co.	Washington DC	1911-1912
Carpenter	H. H. Carpenter	Denver CO	1895
Century	Century Motor Vehicle Co.	Syracuse NY	1900-1903
Century	Century Electric Motor Car Co.	Detroit MI	1911-1915
Centennial	General Electric Co.	Schenectady NY	1978
Chapman	W. H. Chapman, Belknap Motors	Portland ME	1899-1902
Chicago	Chicago Auto Mfg. Co.	Chicago IL	1905-1907
Chicago Electric	Chicago Electric Motor Car Co.	Chicago IL	1912
Church-Field	Church-Field Electric Co.	Sibley MI	1911-1913
Citicar	Sebring-Vanguard Co.	Kingston NY	1972-1976
Clear & Dunham	Clear & Dunham	Cleveland OH	1900-1905
Cleveland	Cleveland Machine Screw Co.	Cleveland OH	1900

Name	Company of Manufacture	Location	Period
Collins	Collins Electric Vehicle Co.	Scranton PA	1901-
	Collins Motor Co.	Huntington NY	1920
Colonial	Colonial Electric Car Co.	Detroit MI	1912-1921
	Colonial Motor Co.	Boston MA	1922
Columbia	Pope Manufacturing Co.	Hartford CN	1895-1898
	Electric Vehicle Co.	Hartford CN	1898-
	Columbia & Electric Vehicle Co.	Hartford CN	1921
Columbia	Columbia Perambulator Co.	Chicago IL	1895
Columbus	Columbus Buggy Co.	Columbus OH	1902-1912
Comuta City Car	Ford Motor Co.	Detroit MI	1973
Conklin			
Crowdus	Crowdus Automobile Co.	Chicago IL	1901-1903
Covert Motorette	B. V. Covert & Co.	Lockport NY	1902

D

Name	Company of Manufacture	Location	Period
Darling	Beardsley & Hubbs Mfg. Co.	Shelby OH	1901-1902
Daulong Electric			
Coach	Baker-Rauch & Lang Co.	Cleveland OH	1915
Dayton	Dayton Electric Car Co.	Dayton OH	1911-
		London, England	1922
Delta	General Electric Co.	Schenectady NY	1968
De Mars	Electric Vehicle Co.	Cleveland Oh	1905-1906
Detroit Electric	Detroit Electric Co.	Detroit	1907-
	Anderson Electric Car Co.		
	Detroit Electric Car Co.		1935
Dey	Dey Electric Corp.	New York NY	1895-
	Dey-Griswold & Co.		1898

E

Name	Company of Manufacture	Location	Period
Eagle	Eagle Electric Automobile Co.	Detroit MI	1915-1917
Eastman	H. E. Eastman	Cleveland OH	1899-1902
Eaton	Eaton Electric Mfg. Carriage Co.	Boston MA	1898
Eaton/Chrysler			
I & II	Eaton/Chrysler	Detroit MI	1988-
Eddy	Eddy Electric Mfg. Co.	Windsor CN	1902
Electra	Electra Storage Battery Power Co.	Chicago IL	1901
ElectraKing	B & Z Electric Co.	Long Beach CA	1972
Electra-Van	Jet Industries Inc.	Austin TX	1975-
Electric Brake	Holtzer-Cabot Electric Co.	Boston MA	1896

Name	Company of Manufacture	Location	Period
Electric Leopard	Electric Car Corp.	Athol MA	1980-
	SunWind Ltd.	Sebastopol CA	1983
Electric Trap	National Automobile & Electric Co.	Indianapolis IN	1900-1902
Electric Vehicle	Electric Vehicle Co.	New York NY	1897-1910
Electric Wagon	Morris & Salom	Philadelphia PA	1895-1897
Electrobat	Morris & Salom	Philadelphia PA	1895-1897
Electrocar (taxi)	Designed by Jos. Anglada	New Brunswick NJ	1922
Electromobile	Belknap Company	Portland ME	
Electromotion	Anderson Electric Products Co.		1972-1973
Elektrek	Unique Mobility Co.	Englewood CO	1978-Present
Ellis	Triumph Motor Vehicle Co.	Chicago IL	1901
Elmore	Elmore Mfg. Co.	Clyde OH	1900-1903
Elwell-Parker	Elwell-Parker Electric Co.	Cleveland OH	1909-Present
Endura	McKee/Globe Union Battery Co.	Milwaukee WI	1977
Erie	Erie & Sturgis	Los Angeles CA	1897
ETX-I & II	Ford/General Electric Co.	Detroit MI	1988-

F

Name	Company of Manufacture	Location	Period
Fanning	F. J. Fanning Mfg. Co.	Chicago IL	1902-1903
Flanders	Flanders Motor Co.	Pontiac MI	1909-1914
Foster	Foster Automobile Mfg. Co.	Rochester NY	1896-1905
Fritchie	Fritchie Auto & Battery Co.	Denver CO	1907-1920

G

Name	Company of Manufacture	Location	Period
G-Van	General Motors Corp.	Detroit MI	1988-Present
General Electric	General Electric Automobile Co.	Philadelphia PA	1898-1899
Gibbs Truck	Gibbs Eng. & Mfg. Co.		1904
Grinnell	Grinnell Electric Car Co.	Detroit MI	1910-1915

H

Name	Company of Manufacture	Location	Period
Healey	Healey & Co.	New York NY	1905-1916
Hellectric 120	Hellectric Co.	Milwaukee WI	1971
Henney Kilowatt	Henney Motor Car Co.	Freeport IL	1960
Hercules	James MacNaughton Co.	Buffalo NY	1907
Hupp-Yeats	Hupp-Yeats Electric Car Co.	Detroit MI	1911-1916

Name	Company of Manufacture	Location	Period

I

Ideal	Ideal Motor Car Co.	Cleveland OH	1905-1906
	Ideal Electric Co.	Chicago IL	1909-
		Buffalo NY	1914
Illinois	Illinois Electric Vehicle Co.	Chicago IL	1897-1901
	Illinois Automobile Co.	Chicago IL	1899
Impact	General Motors Corp.	Detroit MI	1990-
Imperial	Imperial Automobile Co.	Detroit MI	1903-1904

J

None

K

Kennedy	Kennedy Electric Carriage Co.	Philadelphia PA	1898-1903
Kensington	Kensington Automobile Mfg. Co.	Buffalo NY	1899-1903
Kimball	C. P. Kimball & Co.	Chicago IL	1922

L

Lennox	The Maxim Goodridge Co.	Hartford CN	1908-1909
LinearVan	Linear Alpha Inc.	Evanston IL	1962-1978
Lindsley	J. V. Lindsley	Seymour IN	
		Dowagiac MI	1908

M

Mark II	Electrodyne Inc.	Seal Beach CA	1972
Marketeer	Westinghouse Electric Corp.	Redlands CA	1968
Mars	Electric Fuel Propulsion Co.	Detroit MI	1966-1980
Metro	Electric Vehicle Associates, Inc.	Cleveland OH	1973-1982
Milburn	Milburn Wagon Co.	Toledo OH	1914-1922
Morrison	Wm. Morrison	Des Moines IA	1891-
	Sturgis Electric Motocycle Co.	Chicago IL	1892
		England	1905
M & P Electric	M & P Electric Vehicle Co.	Detroit MI	1912

Name	Company of Manufacture	Location	Period

N

Name	Company of Manufacture	Location	Period
National	National Vehicle Co.	Indianapolis IN	1900-1924
New England	New England Electric Vehicle Co.	Boston MA	1900-1901

O

Name	Company of Manufacture	Location	Period
Ohio	Ohio Motor Car Co.	Cincinnati OH	1909-1915
	Ohio Electric Car Co.	Toledo OH	1917-1921
Oldsmobile Electric	Olds Motor Works	Lansing MI	1899-1904

P

Name	Company of Manufacture	Location	Period
Parsons	Parsons Electric Motor Carriage Co.	Cleveland OH	1905-1906
Phipps	Phipps-Grinnel Auto Co.	Detroit MI	1911-1913
Pittsburgh Electric	Pittsburgh Motor Vehicle Co.	Pittsburgh PA	1896-1899
Pope-Waverly	Pope Motor Car Co.	Indianapolis IN	1903-1909

Q

None

R

Name	Company of Manufacture	Location	Period
Rae	Rae Electric Co.	Cleveland OH / Boston MA	1905- / 1909
Rauch & Lang	Rauch & Lang Electric Inc.	Chicopee Falls MA	1893-
Raulong	Baker-Rauch & Lang	Cleveland OH	1928
Riker	Riker Electric Vehicle Co.	Elizabethport NJ	1896-1913

S

Name	Company of Manufacture	Location	Period
Scott Electric	Scott Automobile Co.	St. Louis MO	1901
Searchmont Wagonette	Searchmont Motor Co.	Philadelphia PA	1901
Silvervolt	Electric Fuel Propulsion	Detroit MI	1969-1980
Skene	Skene Amer. Auto Car Bldg. Co.	Lewiston ME / Springfield MA	1900 / 1902
Solectria	Solectria Corporation	Arlington, MA	1989

Name	Company of Manufacture	Location	Period
Sportabout	Electric Fuel Propulsion	Detroit MI	1969
Standard Electric	Standard Electric Car Co.	Jackson MI	1912-1915
Stanhope	Hewitt Lindstrom		
Stearns Stanhope	E. C. Stearns & Co.	Syracuse NY	1900-1902
Steinmetz	Steinmetz Electric Motor Car Co.	Baltimore MD	1922-1927
Storm	William E. Storm	Detroit MI	1915
Strong & Rogers	Strong & Rogers	Cleveland OH	1900-1901
Studebaker	Studebaker Wagon Co.	South Bend IN	1902-1903
Sturgis Surrey	William Morrison Co.	Des Moines IA	1890-1906
	Sturgis Electric Motocycle Co.	Chicago IL	1892
Syracuse	Syracuse Automobile Co.	Syracuse NY	1899-1903

T

Name	Company of Manufacture	Location	Period
Tate	Tate Electric Ltd.	Windsor, Ontario	1912-1913
TEVan	Chrysler	Detroit MI	1988-
Thunderbolt 240	Linear Alpha Inc.	Evanston IL	1962-1976
Thresher Electric	Thresher Electric Co.	Dayton OH	1900-1903

U

Name	Company of Manufacture	Location	Period
Urban Electric	Kentucky Wagon Mfg. Co.	Louisville KY	1912
U. S. Electric	U. S. Automobile Co.	Attleboro MA	1899-1901

V

Name	Company of Manufacture	Location	Period
Vanguard	Vanguard Vehicles Inc.	Kingston NY	1972-1973
V.E.C.	Vehicle Equipment Co.	Long Island City NY	1903-1904

W

Name	Company of Manufacture	Location	Period
Ward Electric	Ward Motor Vehicle Co.	Mount Vernon NY	1914
Ward-Leonard	Ward-Leonard Electric Co.	Bronxville NY	1901-1903
Watterman	C. H. Waterman Industries Inc.	Athol ME	1972
Waverly	Waverly Electrical Vehicle Co.	Indianapolis IN	1898-1916
White Electric	White Sewing Machine Co.	Cleveland OH	1902
Woods Electric	Woods Motor Vehicle Co.	Chicago IL	1900-1919

Name Table of American Electric Cars

Name	Company of Manufacture	Location	Period

X
None

Y

Yare	T. P. Laboratories Inc.	La Porte IN	1975

Z
None

APPENDIX D
Nostalgia

The following articles are reprinted from *The Horseless Age*.

Runaway Automobiles

Runaway automobiles have been quite numerous of late, two being reported in the present issue. In one case a mischievous boy was responsible for the trouble, having placed his hand on the lever while the chauffeur was occupied underneath the machine. In the other case the owner had stopped his vehicle and applied the brakes. No sooner had he entered a house than the machine is said to have started down the street. Reports have it that, but for the efforts of a policeman, who turned the machine into a trolley pole, it would have passed through the plate glass window of a store.

Automobiles, being inanimate, do not take fright and dash down the street. We must, therefore, look into the causes that bring about this accidental starting and try to remedy it while we also take measures to prevent the small boy from playing such costly pranks.

Street gamins soon learn that thrusting the throttle lever of a steam carriage forward will cause the engine to run. If the automobile belongs to a physician who employs it to make professional calls the boys of the neighborhood are all the more likely to learn how to produce a sensation at his expense. We would therefore advise users to attach some form of locking device which requires a key to open it.

If the motor is of the hydrocarbon type and the control devices are such that applying either the foot or the hand brake automatically relieves the main clutch, it requires but the release of the brake lever to start the vehicle. Here it would be wise to lock the brake lever, and, if the application of a suitable device presents difficulties which the user cannot overcome, he should stop his motor and remove his switch plug. All gasoline vehicles should be fitted with such a plug, which is preferable to the ordinary switch for this and other reasons.

July 23, 1902

Automobile War on the North Shore, Chicago

The mayors of the towns along the North Shore above Chicago are resorting to still more extreme measures to put a stop to auto scorching. The mayor of Glencoe has stretched a wire cable across the road and stationed deputies with stop watches at marked intervals along the way. By prearranged signals the automobiles are timed, and if the speed is found very excessive the rope is made taut and escape is barred.

Hemp rope was formerly used, but some of the more determined offenders are reported to have fitted scythelike cutters in front of their machines, which made short work of such ropes.

Still another mayor throws cord wood or even logs in the road to bring offenders to a standstill, so the Chicago papers say.

July 30, 1902

Charging Stations for Electric Tourists

Through the efforts of the touring bureau of the Automobile Club of America it is now possible for electric car owners in New York City to make long distance tours with perfect contentment of mind as far as recharging stations are concerned. Convenient stations are now located at various points along the route from New York to Buffalo and from the metropolis to Philadelphia. A list of the charging stations follows:

NEW YORK TO BUFFALO

o.o New York	Intermediate	Total
Yonkers	13.5	13.5
Peekskill	28.2	41.7
Poughkeepsie	32.3	74.0
Schenectady	92.1	166.1
Amsterdam	15.7	181.8
Utica	64.6	246.4
Syracuse	48.6	295.0
Auburn	27.6	322.6
Geneva	26.5	349.1
Canandaigua	16.2	363.3
Rochester	37.2	402.5
Lockport	63.5	466.0
Buffalo	25.0	491.0

NEW YORK TO PHILADELPHIA

	Intermediate	Total
Newark	12.6	12.6
Elizabeth	6.4	19.0
New Brunswick (proposed station)	18.4	37.4
Princeton (proposed station)	19.1	56.5
Trenton	11.0	67.5
Philadelphia	35.5	101.0

Aug 21, 1912

Cost of Scorching in France

Le Velo publishes the following itemized account of costs to a chauffeur who was condemned for furious driving to a fine of 10 francs and three days of prison:

Fine	francs,	10.00
War tax on same	francs,	2.50
Justice's fee	francs,	12.03
Legal notice	francs,	4.90
Cost of arrest	francs,	0.25
Stamp for receipt	francs,	0.25
Commutation of the three days' prison	francs,	31.25
Total	francs,	61.18

If we add to this the lawyer's fees, it will be seen that only the well-to-do class can afford to indulge in automobile scorching in Paris.

Dec 12, 1900

Doctors and the Speed Laws

The doctors of Buffalo, N.Y. who use automobiles in their practice have come into collision with the anti-speed law. Three of them were arrested the other day for exhibiting too much professional zeal in the effort to reach their patients quickly and were brought before a magistrate and fined. The president of the Buffalo Automobile Club, who is himself a physician, has interested the club in the matter, and it is more than likely that the pressure thus brought to bear may influence the police to relax the law to some extent in favor of the physicians.

In Detroit recently a physician who had been arrested for running his automobile at illegal speed was discharged by the magistrate when he explained that he was answering a hurry call. Elsewhere similar lenity has been shown. Surely a reasonable latitude must be allowed in such cases. A physician who habitually ran his automobile about the streets at dangerous speed would unquestionably be classed as a lawbreaker, but one who only occasionally and on urgent need took this liberty would be classed as a law abiding citizen and a humanitarian.

July 23, 1902

Track and Road Vehicles

It seems very hard for some newspaper writers to form a rational idea of the relationship which automobile and railway traffic will bear to each other in the future. The railroad is already at or near the highest perfection to be expected of it, while the automobile is yet in its infancy. Still, railroad service, especially in out-of-the-way places, is far from ideal, and the visionary who forgets that the facilities of transportation must necessarily be affected by local conditions has no difficulty in "seeing the finish" of local railroads as a result of the perfection of automobiles whenever some specially flagrant defect in railroad accommodation annoys him or when some particularly striking performances are made by automobiles.

Thus, a Kansas City man "believes it entirely probable that * * * all local traffic—that is, trips from 200 to 300 miles—will be made by automobile, for within the next year or two automobiles in common use will travel from 20 to 40 miles an hour. * * * Local traffic thus being taken from the railway, all local lines of railway will be abandoned. Only trunk lines will remain, and they will be used only for very heavy freight on long hauls, for travel and the mails."

Such superficial statements as the above are easily made when no evidence is required for their support. But they will not bear a close investigation. Let us take as an example the suburban railroad service of a large city. Could that be profitably replaced by a service of road vehicles equally perfected with the rolling stock of the railroad? The question is of no great difficulty to the engineer familiar with the commercial aspect of traction problems. Even on the finest pavements the traction effort and the wear and tear on the vehicles are very much greater than on a railway, and, as road vehicles cannot possibly be built with as large a capacity as track vehicles, the factor in the operating cost representing the wages of operators must be greater in the case of the former. The speed of a road vehicle must necessarily be considerably lower than the speed of a track vehicle, partly in order to minimize wear and tear in the road vehicle and partly because road vehicles run on public thoroughfares while track vehicles are confined to their own private way. And in suburban transportation speed is of great importance. The only thing in favor of road vehicles in suburban transportation is that each passenger could be set down at the front of his house, but even this advantage is inseparably linked with such a serious disadvantage that we fear few passengers would appreciate it.

The conclusion, then, is that in commercial transportation, where the volume of business is sufficient to pay for the fixed charges of a railroad and leave a surplus for other items, the track vehicle will meet no competition from road vehicles. It is not very difficult to arrive at this conclusion by a preliminary investigation, but present developments seem to indicate that a certain class of the public will not be convinced of it until they have learned it by sad experience.

Jan 22, 1902

Horse Breeding in England

Signs are everywhere apparent that the demand for high class harness horses has seen its best days, and reports of recent auction sales show that about 50 percent of the animals offered have been unsold. This happened on the occasion of the Brookfield stud sale, and that fate alone would be significant even if it stood alone. Royal persons have become adapts as well as enthusiasts in motoring; fashionable folk go to the opera in automobiles; society runs to Waterloo en route for Ascot by electric cabs, and the motor car is regarded as the "proper thing." Hence horse breeders will shortly turn their attention to hunters and horses for riding in preference to the high class harness horse, the demand for which seems to have sadly fallen off. But the popularity of the motor car is not wholly responsible for this state of things; increased rating and taxation have caused economies in many directions—a fact not to be overlooked by those who denounce the automobile for the changes it is causing in our national life.

July 23, 1902

Automobile Accidents — 1902

The rear axle of an electric automobile broke in Jersey City last week while it was crossing the car tracks. No one was hurt.

At Huntington, W. Va., a boy thirteen years old was run over by an automobile September 4 and severely injured, probably fatally.

A fire said to be of unknown origin consumed the steam machine of Dr. Kirby, Grand Island, Neb., recently. The doctor had just housed his machine in his barn for the night.

At Reading, Pa., the automobile of Dr. Bropst was struck by a trolley car and considerably damaged on September 3.

By a failure of the steering apparatus or the operator thereof, three persons were injured in turning a corner at New Haven, Conn., recently.

At Oakland, Cal., last Friday, while riding with her nephew in an automobile, which became unmanageable, the wife of United States Senator W. M. Stewart, of Nevada, was thrown out violently against the curb and killed.

The steam machine built by Harry Sharpe, of Omaha, Neb., is reported to have been destroyed by fire while standing at the curb in that city recently. It was unoccupied at the time and no cause is assigned by the press for the accident.

A heavy delivery automobile broke an axle in Pittsburg, Pa., September 2, and delayed traffic for some time. While the vehicle was being driven up Wood street the wheels lurched against a rail, which caused the axle to break.

1902

Judge Dixon's Righteous Charge

In charging the Bergen County (N.J.) grand jury recently in the case of the People vs. Blum, whose automobile scared a horse attached to a lawn mower in front of Mrs. Poor's house at Hackettstown, and thereby caused the death of John Henches, an employee of hers, Judge Dixon declared that it was matter of common knowledge that automobilists were abusing the common rights of the highway, that anyone driving an automobile at the speed alleged in this case was guilty of a public nuisance, and if it could be shown that the excessive speed was the cause of death the parties guilty should be charged with manslaughter.

"We all have a right," he concluded, "to the highways in our vehicles and on foot just the same as we did before these machines came upon the roads. It is not a question of municipal ordinance; it is the law of the State. It does not depend on a statute; it is the common law which we inherit from our ancestors. Everybody who so conducts himself as to endanger persons who are in the exercise of the common right is guilty of creating a common nuisance and should be indicted for the same."

Chronological Events in Development of Electric Vehicles[1]

BC	Ancients	Early manifestation of electricity: electric fish, rubbed amber, lodestones.
1600	Gilbert	*De Magnete*: Early explanation of magnetics.
1660	Von Guericke	First electricity machine (friction of glass and hand).
1680	Newton	Mathematics of the calculus, inverse square law.
1729	Grey	Non-electric material.
1733	Du Fay	Attraction and repulsion of unlike and like electric charges.
1745	Von Kleist	Charge from electric machine stored in glass bottle and delivered an electric shock.
	Musschenbroek	Electricity in a Leyden jar. Shock kills small animals.
1752	Franklin	Kite and key used to charge Leyden jar from lightning; identity of lightning and electricity proved.
1780	Priestley	Inverse square law conceived.
1786	Galvani	Discovered electricity may result from chemical action.
1800	Volta	Electricity generated by dissimilar metals; first battery.
	Nicholson & Carlisle	Decomposition of water into hydrogen & oxygen.
1812	Poisson	Mathematics applied to electric & magnetic fields.
1820	Oersted	Deflection of compass by an electric current.
1821	Ampere	Force relation between two circuits carrying current.
1821 - 1825	Faraday	Early direct-current electric motor.
1824	Arago	Rotation of compass needle by rotating disc of copper.
1825	Sturgeon	First electromagnet.
1827	Pecquer	Differential gearing system invented.
	Ohm	Ohm's law; $E = IR$
1828	Green	Potential function in mathematics.

---

[1] George Schwartz and Philip W. Bishop. *Moments of Discovery*, Basic Books, NYC, 1958, and others.

1831	Faraday	First rotating DC motor.
	Dal Negro	Vibrating motion made rotary by rachet action.
	Henry	Self induction, basis of transformer.
	Faraday	Electric current changing in time induces an emf in an adjoining circuit. Principle awaits 55 years.
1832	Pixii	First commutator DC generator.
1835	Faraday	Dielectric and capacitive studies.
	Davenport	First application of electric motor.
1837	Kelvin	Electromagnetic and CGS system of units.
1843	Goodyear	Discovery of vulcanization of rubber.
1845	Joule	Inter-relationship of mechanical and heat described.
	Wheatstone	First electromagnet on DC generator.
	Thomson	First pneumatic tire, but forgotten.
1847	Helmholtz	Conservation of energy.
1852	Kelvin & Clausius	Laws of Thermodynamics.
1856	Weber & Kohrbausch	Ratio between electromagnetic and electrostatic units is 3×10^{10}, approximately the speed of light in meters/sec.
1859	Planté	First lead-acid battery.
1860	Pacinotti	Inventor of ring DC machine.
1870	Mendeleef	Periodic Table of Elements.
	Gramme	DC generator and motor, first over one kilowatt.
	Crompton	Commutator improvement.
1873	Maxwell	Maxwell's equations on electric and magnetic fields.
1877	Thomson	Electric welding.
1881	Faure	Oxide of lead added to lead plates of a battery.
	Brush	First compound-wound generator.
	Trouvé	First electric vehicle, a tricycle. Paris.
1882	Edison	First electric central station.
	Edison	Edison effect, electron conduction through a vacuum.
	Stanley	Electric transformer.
	Hall	Commercial process for smelting aluminum.
1885	Jeantaud	Paris-Bordeaux-Paris 705-mile race. Electric car.
1888	Julien	Mercury alloyed to antimony-lead battery grid. Significantly increased specific energy.
	Shallenburger	Induction meter.
	Dunlop	Re-invention of pneumatic tire.
	Edison	Improved DC generator and motor.
	Tesla	Invented induction motor, modern transformer.
1890	Hollerith	Punched card, data processing.
	Riker	First American electric car.
1894	Carli	First multi-powered car.
1895	Michelin	Pneumatic tires for motor cars.

1897	Pope & Maxim	Largest early electric car maker. Discovery of touring (to tour).
1899	Many	America produced 1575 electrics & 936 gasoline-powered cars.
	Jenatzy	World speed record of 62 mph for any motor car; it was electric.
1900	Many	America's first auto show: 6 electrics, 7 steam, 19 gasoline.
	Riker	American electric car speed record of 57.1 mph.
	Woods	Publication, *The Electric Automobile: Its Construction, Care, and Operation.*
1900 - 1910	Edison	Iron-nickel battery.
1902	Many	Automobile assumes present configuration.
1907	Baekland	Phenolic plastic.
1908	Ford	Mass production technique applied to automobiles.
1909	Millikan	Electron existence proved.
1910	Steinmetz & Dey	Motor with armature and field rotating in opposite directions.
1912	Many	Early peak production of electric vehicles.
1925	Hilliard	Circuit Breaker.
1935	Carothers	Synthetic fibers used in tires.
	Detroit Electric	Last commercial production of early electric cars.
1950	Bardeen Brattain Schockley	Invention of transistor; led to solid state electronics.
1955	Holonyak	Invention of thyristor, used in motor current control.
1958	Kilby	Integrated circuit.
1965	Wakefield	Concept of frequency & pulse width modulation from DC to 3-phase AC for induction motor applied to EV.
1968	MIT-Cal Tech	USA cross-country electric car race.
1969	Agarwal	High-performance AC induction motor drive in EV.
1970	Murphy	Electronic transmission using frequency & pulse-width modulation of induction motor.
1972	McKee, Norberg, Borisoff, Lawn	First modern compleat electric vehicle, *Sundancer*.
1975	Wouk	First modern petro-electric hybrid.
1976	U.S. Congress	The Electric Vehicle Act of 1976.
1981	Garrett	Flywheel-electric dual-powered car.
	Freeman	English solar-powered vehicle.
1983	Larry & Gary Perkins	Paper: *The Quiet Achiever, With Solar Power Across Australia.*

Chronological Events in Development of Electric Vehicles

1984	Electric Utilities	Established The Electric Vehicle Development Corp.
1985	Muntwyler	Introduced solar-powered car racing in Europe.
1987	Tholstrup	Established World Solar Challenge Race in Australia.
	General Motors	*Sunraycer*, winner of the trans-Australia Race with solar-power.
1986 -		
1990	Ford/General Elec.	The ETX-I & II. Possibly the first modern viable electric vehicles.
1990	General Motors	*Impact*. First compleat EV designed for high production.
1991	Big 3 Autos	Established United States Advanced Battery Consortium.

APPENDIX F

Table 1. <u>Cal-Tech - M.I.T. Electric Car Race - August 19/23, 1968</u>[1]
The First Cross-Country Electric Car Race

<u>Route</u>	<u>Preferred Charging Location</u>	<u>Electric Utility Company</u>
I-90	Ludlow Service Plaza, Springfield, Mass.	Western Mass. Electric Co.
I-90	Iroquois Service Plaza, Albany, N.Y. (Indian Castle Service Plaza eastbound)	Niagara Mohawk Power Corp.
I-90	Service Plaza No. 30, Mohawk, New York	Mohawk Municipal Commission
I-90	DeWitt Service Plaza, Syracuse, N. Y. (Warner's Service Plaza eastbound)	Niagara Mohawk Power Corp.
I-90	Sececa Service Plaza, Rochester, N. Y. (Scottsville Service Plaza eastbound)	Rochester Gas & Electric Corp.
I-90	Clarence Service Plaza, Buffalo, N. Y.	Niagara Mohawk Power Corp.
I-90	Junction N.Y. 17, Westfield, New York	Westfield Board of Public Utilities
I-90	Junction Ohio 7, Conneaut, Ohio	Cleveland Elect. Illuminating Co.
I-80	Service Plaza #12, Cleveland, Ohio	Ohio Edison Company
I-90	Service Plaza #7, Sandusky, Ohio	Ohio Edison Company
I-90	Service Plaza #4, Toledo, Ohio	Toledo Edison Company

---

[1] Courtesy: Commonwealth Edison Company.

491

Route	Preferred Charging Location	Electric Utility Company
I-90	Service Plaza #10, Vistula, Indiana	No. Indiana Public Service Co.
I-90	Service Plaza #7, La Porte, Indiana	No. Indiana Public Service Co.
I-80	Junction I-94, Chicago, Illinois	Commonwealth Edison Co.
US 66/ I-55	Dwight, Illinois	Commonwealth Edison Co.
US 66	Junction I-74, Bloomington, Illinois	Illinois Power Company
US 66	Junction I-55, Springfield, Illinois	Central Illinois Public Service Co.
US 66	Litchfield, Illinois	Illinois Power Company
US 40	East St. Louis, East St. Louis, Mo.	Union Electric Company
I-44	St. Claire, Missouri	Union Electric Company
I-44	Rolla, Missouri	Rolla Municipal Utilities
I-44	Lebanon, Missouri	Lebanon Municipal Light & Power
I-44	Junction US 65, Springfield, Missouri	Springfield City Utilities
I-44	Junction I-44, Joplin, Missouri	Empire District Electric Co.
I-44	Vinita, Oklahoma	Public Service Co. of Oklahoma
I-44	Tulsa, Oklahoma	Public Service Co. of Oklahoma
I-44	Stroud, Oklahoma	Oklahoma Gas & Electric Co.
US-66	Oklahoma City, Oklahoma	Public Service Co. of Oklahoma
US-66	Weatherford, Oklahoma	Public Service Co. of Oklahoma
US-66	Erick, Oklahoma	Public Service Co. of Oklahoma
US-66	McLean, Texas	Southwestern Public Service Co.
US-66	Amarillo, Texas	Southwestern Public Service Co.

Route	Preferred Charging Location	Electric Utility Company
US-66	Vega, Texas	Southwestern Public Service Co.
US-66/ I-40	Tucumcari, New Mexico	Tucumcari Power & Light Dept.
US-66	Santa Rosa, New Mexico	Farmers' Elect. Cooperative Inc.
US-66	Clines Corners, New Mexico	Central New Mexico Cooperative
US-66	Albuquerque, New Mexico	Public Service Co. of New Mexico
US-66	Grants, New Mexico	Continental Divide Elect. Coop.
US-66	Gallup, New Mexico	Gallup Electric Power Dept.
US-66	Sanders, Arizona	Arizona Public Service
US-66	Winslow, Arizona	Arizona Public Service
US-66	Flagstaff, Arizona	Arizona Public Service
US-Alt. 89	Prescott, Arizona	Arizona Public Service
US-89/ Ariz.71	Aguila, Arizona	Arizona Public Service
US-60/ I-10	Quartzite, Arizona	Arizona Public Service
US-60	Desert Center, California	So. Calif. Edison Company
US-60	Thousand Palas, California	
US-60	Riverside, California	Riverside Public Utilities

Congressman Mike McCormack
Reports on the 1976 Electric Car Act

Reprinted from *Lead Power News,* Nov. 1976, No. 6, p. 5.

During the 1973 Arab oil-embargo Americans termed the long lines at local gas stations the 'energy crisis.' However, the real crisis began long before with our steadily increasing imports of foreign oil and the alarming depletion of our domestic supplies of finite resources, both oil and natural gas.

The crisis has been perpetuated by the complacency with which we have accepted both the escalation of imports and the cavalier usurption of our own supplies.

The words 'energy crisis' and 'energy conservation' have progressively become part of our contemporary rhetoric. Energy philosophy and policy have been espoused by scientists, educators, politicians and consumers. Much of the discussion and debate has finally coalesced and we have now begun to see some serious and practical legislation emerge from the U.S. Congress. Of this legislation the most recent and broadly supported has been the Electric and Hybrid Vehicle Research, Development and Demonstration Act which passed the 94th Congress in September. This bill is only the 89th in the history of the American Republic that has been enacted over a presidential veto. It has had the diverse support of business, labor, the public and public interest groups.

The program authorized by the bill is directed toward the realization that any national energy policy must have a substantial component that addresses the energy consumption of our highway vehicles in America today.

Transportation now accounts for about 50% of our petroleum consumption and we presently have to import 40% of all the petroleum we use from foreign countries. By appreciably reducing transportation's use of gasoline for propulsion we will be able to stem the flow of petrodollars from America, lessen our dependence on foreign oil supplies and help this nation reach its goal of energy independence.

Electric vehicles are not an innovation of the 70's; they appeared on this nation's roads before World War I, but soon lost out to the more powerful automobiles powered by internal combustion engines that used cheap abundant gasoline for fuel. However, gasoline is no longer cheap and will become increasingly more expensive, and the petroleum from which it is made is no longer abundant. Thus we must seriously reconsider electric automobiles as viable alternatives to today's cars.

The Members of Congress have clearly understood that in order for electric vehicles to gain acceptance by the consumer public, the present state of the art must be greatly improved and, in addition, there must be a concerted effort to place these new cars in service on the American scene where people can drive and evaluate them.

The program mandated by the Electric and Hybrid Vehicle Research, Development and Demonstration Act is designed to do this.

Over a six-year period the Energy Research and Development Administration (ERDA) will conduct a three-phase program outlined in the bill. In the first phase, the ERDA Administrator will canvass the field and buy a sufficient number of present technology electric cars to test and analyze them in order to establish some performance criteria. Using these criteria as guidelines, ERDA will then purchase 2,500 cars for lease across the nation to local, state and federal government agencies and individuals for both personal and business use. The cars in phase two would probably be a composite of a conventional auto body retrofitted with electric driving components.

The use and evaluation of the phase two cars will provide the data needed for phase three which will commence approximately four years into the program. In this last phase ERDA will establish revised performance standards based upon the advanced technology resulting from the ongoing research and development program during the previous four years. The ERDA Administrator will then purchase up to 5,000 additional cars of the most advanced state of the art which meet the new criteria.

This demonstration program will put present and future state-of-the-art electric vehicles at the disposal of people who will eventually provide a market for them when they are commercially manufactured. By making the consumer vehicle visible and testable, the Congress hopes to promote an awareness and acceptability for electric vehicles as 'second cars.'

The statistics of American driving patterns substantiate the usefulness of these cars. More than half of the total automobile driving in America consists of trips of 5 miles or less, driving conditions under which internal combustion engines operate least efficiently.

Two additional provisos of the bill further insure the intent of the Congress. The first mandates that at least $10 million of the authorized $160 million will be spent during 1977 (the first year of the program) for battery research and development. The extension of battery operation between charges is critical to the acceptability and usefulness of electric cars. By conducting intensive research in this area at the beginning of the program we can insure a progressively advanced state of the art for the phase three vehicles.

The second provision authorizes the Energy Research and Development Administration to provide loan guarantees to qualified borrowers primarily small business concerns, for research and development related to electric vehicle technology. Loan guarantees will permit the active participation of small firms whose limited capital investment would ordinarily preclude them from taking part in a program that might require using more funds than they could normally allocate for one specific project. By backing a portion of the loan that these qualified borrowers find it absolutely necessary to apply for, we will be granting them the security that the investment community demands when considering priorities for loans.

In the final analysis electric cars can have a far-reaching effect on the American scene. Because their power supply will be derived from coal and nuclear, they will reduce oil consumption. They will alleviate both air and noise pollution by their clean, quiet operation and they will help to balance utility loads by off-peak hour battery charges. They will make a unique contribution by simultaneously forwarding our economic, conservation, environmental, and national security goals.

A Critique of The Electric Vehicle Act of 1976

There was some venture capital for electric vehicles in the late 1960s and to the middle 1970s. By the decade's end it had largely disappeared. The unrealistic statements of some utility spokesmen, and government transportation planners for the "$2000 electric car," and the "millions" expected on the roads in the 1980s: time was exposing these numbers for the dreams they represented. Henry Ford II was far more astute when he reportedly related in the early 1970s, "The Ford Motor Company will not offer an electric car while I am associated with it." His grandfather, starting the company in 1902, as the reader is probably aware, had a more difficult choice.

Expostulation of the Act

If, indeed, electric cars were to be placed on the roads of America, as a national policy, government assistance appeared vital. No matter the persuasion of one's economic thought, like the military procurement of aircraft in their infancy, the early 1900s, state pump-priming in encouraging electric vehicles appeared desirable to a growing number of congressmen and senators. With road transportation assuming almost half of America's petroleum consumption,[1] a sizable fraction of personal transportation could be fueled by electric energy derived from coal, nuclear, and hydro sources. The Stanford Report had indicated that the impact of electric vehicles on national resources would be almost insignificant.[2] The electric utility industry, which had in the early 1970s appeared as the most natural[3] conduit to visibly place electric vehicles into the economy, failed to follow through, as chronicled in Chapter 24. Into this void Congressman Mike McCormack of the state of Washington stepped. It was another classic example of an ever ready, aggressive government moving when private industry was

---

[1] *Mike McCormack Writes on the Electric Vehicle Bill, Lead Power News*, Nov. 1976, No. 6, p. 5.

[2] Patrick J. Hartin, *Electric Vehicles in America's Future*....SRI, 1975.

[3] The high incidence of electric appliances in the American home is no accident. The marketing departments of the electric utilities plus the sales effort of the manufacturers were most effective.

reluctant to go forward. It represents a typical case why America has Big Government. After public hearings,[4] and much debate, Congress passed, over President Ford's veto, the Electric & Hybrid Vehicle Research, Development, and Demonstration Act of 1976.

The Act described above by Congressman McCormack is one bead on a necklace now nearly two centuries old since Volta's first battery, an event which eventually enabled the first electric vehicle to be assembled by Trouvé some four score and one years later. During this period the private and public sectors have intertwined and unwound a multiple number of times, occasionally to the benefit of the citizens, sometimes to their detriment. To the reader the evidence must be overwhelming that in the last two hundred years cited, it was the individual who was the initiator. Not a committee. Not a government. And this entrepreneur taught others, and from the whole, wealth was created, and the nation moved ahead. What of the Act's influence on America today?

A Retrospective View

At this writing more than ten years have passed since the enactment of a program to accelerate by legislation the introduction of electric vehicles upon the roads of America. The meager 'pulse-taking' of informed citizenry by the author indicates that the Act is not all bad, but neither has it lead the private sector to place many unsubsidized electric vehicles on the road. And the few driving, when 5000 mile annual use of electric vehicles is considered,[5] *total costs* per mile have probably been double the mileage cost annually cited by the Hertz Corporation for subcompacts.[6] The electric vehicle in its total concept is complex, and the in-place gasoline automobile's totality is highly viable, and furthermore, is being improved. Many writers on electric vehicles have a veneer thickness in their understanding of them; *neither have they personally maintained them.* Such intimacy enhances respect for petro-cars, and mutes ardor for electrics.

Congressman McCormack's hopes of 1976 were deflated in 1982, and the Washington State representative's views were rejected on the hustings. The substantial strides made in improving the energy efficiency of the IC vehicle created a moving target, and one difficult to overtake. Further, the higher energy capacity batteries failed to yield easily to development, or possessed insufficient cycle life, or were too expensive. In addition, electric rates, constantly falling for many years, began with inflation and too often poorly designed, sleazily constructed and ineptly managed nuclear power plants to increase substantially.[7] For the second time in a century few electric vehicles were newly being assembled.

---

[4] *Hearings Before the Subcommittee on Energy Research, Development & Demonstration of the Committee on Science and Technology, U.S. House of Representatives, 94th Congress, H.R. 5470*, U.S. Government Printing Office, 1975.

[5] The author too often reads biased or incomplete data on electric cars.

[6] *Typical U.S. Subcompact Costs 44.6¢ a mile, The Wall Street Journal*, November 16, 1981, 4:4.

[7] Mathew L. Wald, *Nuclear Plant Drain Put at $100 Billion for U.S., The New York Times*, February 1, 1988, pp. 21 & 27.

While the Act encouraged development in high-energy batteries as outlined in Chapter 11, established a number of test vehicle fleets based on pick-up trucks and vans illustrated in Chapter 20, probed the petro-hybrid car, and indeed assembled the flywheel assisted battery-powered automobile, a growing number of the citizenry viewed the Act as a legal means of financing government laboratories established for other tasks in which interest had waned.[8] As a result reports compounded, many tests were made of unlikely long term benefit, and dissemination of findings appeared profligate. Increasingly many believed the new Department of Energy was a fruit with too generous a husk and too large a pit, and unworthy, as presently constituted, of further taxpayer support; that the electric vehicle need stand by itself in the marketplace. Under the present system surely government bureaucracy was encouraged, and little funding trickled down to the entrepreneurial class, the area of traditional innovation, and the womb wherein jobs are most effectively nurtured.[9] By the late 1970s there appeared a growing disenchantment with the Vehicle Act of 1976.

In April 1982 the U.S. General Accounting Office, in a report to Chairman Richard L. Ottinger, New York Democrat in the Congress, wrote in part: "The government electric vehicle program has been a failure and will stay that way until a better battery is developed and at least one major auto maker is committed to make and sell electrics...."[10] One long-term observer, extremely well informed on electric vehicles, told the author: "With the exception of the high energy battery program, all money expended by the Department of Energy on electric vehicles after the General Electric's 1978 *Centennial*, which was perceived as inadequate, has been wasted."[11]

Had President Ford in wielding his veto on the Electric Vehicle Act been correct, and the Congress with its generosity in overriding his restraint been wrong? Presently the near term optimism for electric vehicles is declining: European countries have scaled back their effort, Japan's program is of a lowered profile, the General Motors Corporation announced "indefinitely delaying the introduction of a battery-powered passenger car."[12] Ford, too, as recently as March 1988, has stated, "Although the Ford Motor Company currently does not have any plans for the commercial production of the ETX-II or any other electric powertrain, we are trying to bring the technology to a point where such production would be feasible if a suitable market were to develop for (electric vehicles)."[13] Moreover, constriction of Federal funds will almost surely pare electric vehicle subsidies, for Secretary of Energy James Edwards has currently said, "in recent years some of the (Federal) laboratories have lost their identities."[14] G. A. Keyworth II, Science Advisor to the President, paints a somber outlook for national laboratories for having usurped the traditional areas of industrial and university research and development.[15]

---

[8] *U.S. To Spend $160 Million of Research & Development, Electric Vehicles*, Vol. 62, No. 4, December 1976, pp. 10-11.

[9] *The Wall Street Journal*, June 24, 1982, p. 1, column 3, and earlier issues. Also: *Small Business Innovative Research Act* was passed by the House and by the Senate as of June 29, 1982, *The New York Times*, June 29, 1982.

[10] Helen Kahen, *Electric Car Program Called a Flop, Automotive News*, April 1982, p. 62.

[11] Personal communication, April 20, 1982.

[12] *The New York Times*, June 3, 1982, p. 33.

[13] Personal communication, Ford Motor Company, March 4, 1988.

[14] R. Jeffrey Smith, *Edwards Defends Budget Cuts at DOE, Science*, 216 May 14, 1982, pp. 716-717.

[15] G. A. Keyworth II, *The Role of Science in a New Era of Competition, Science*, 217 4560 August 13, 1982, pp. 606-609.

Adding to the pessimism above, incrementally some believe the American people are perceiving the nation, like a family, has been living beyond its means for some four decades; that a greater discipline is required for husbanding opportunities for later generations; and for more than two centuries under the American system that coercion was provided by the market place. Now, and for more than one hundred years, the pursuit of the electric automobile has been a noble quest. Phoenix-like, will personal electric transportation arise in the 20th century from the ashes of an earlier period, or must its rebirth await the 21st when pollution control will be its prod?

Early Electric Car Races

The following are articles on early electric car races reprinted from various publications.

Times-Herald Contest – 1895 – The Horseless Age.

Through Snow and Slush Contestants Struggle on —
A Severe Test and a Signal Triumph

Notwithstanding that Chicago had been visited by a severe snowstorm the day before the date set for the motor vehicle contest, and the snow and slush lay from six to eight inches deep over the course, the judges were true to their word and ordered the contestants to the starting point at Midway Plaisance and Jackson Park.

On the previous evening eleven inventors had signified their intention of engaging in the race, but at 9 o'clock the next morning only six wagons had put in an appearance. The others being deterred by the terrible condition of the roads, or by the incompleteness of their machines.

The wagons which appeared at the starting point were: The electrobat of Morris & Salom; the gasolene wagon of the Duryea Motor Wagon Co.; the Benz wagon of the H. Mueller Manufacturing Co., Decatur, Ill.; the Benz wagon of the De La Vergne Refrigerating Machine Co.; the Roger wagon, owned by R.H. Macy & Co., and the electric wagon of Harold Sturges.

Morris and Salom were unable to make arrangements for supply stations over the entire length of the course, and announced that they would simply make a short run to show that the electric wagon could make satisfactory headway through deep snow. They made the run to Lincoln Park and part of the way back, when their supply of batteries gave out and they were compelled to stop. Henry G. Morris conducted and Hiram Percy Maxim acted as umpire.

The Duryeas came to the scene of the race, and returned after the finish by their own power. They were unable to complete the new and improved wagons on which they have been engaged for about two months, and were obliged to enter the old experimental wagon, which was built two years ago, has been run several thousand miles over ordinary roads, and was forced into the ditch with such disastrous consequences during the Consolation Race, November 2nd. The Duryea company were aware of its weakness, and scarcely dared hope that it would carry them over the course. But it did, and brought them first to the winning post.

At 8:55 the judges gave the word to the Duryeas, and the wagon passed out through the crowd at a lively pace. The occupants being J. Frank Duryea, and Arthur W. White the umpire appointed for the vehicle.

Shortly afterward the Benz wagon of the De La Vergne Co. was sent off under the guidance of Frederick C. Haas, with James F. Bate as umpire, but the wheels slipped in the deep snow, and Mr. Haas decided to withdraw from the competition.

The Macy wagon started at 8:59 with J. O'Connor as operator and Lieutenant Samuel Rodman, Jr., as umpire. The deep snow of the Midway Plaisance proved too much for this wagon as it had for the Benz wagon, and it had to be assisted over the bad spot by Mr. O'Connor.

The Sturges electric wagon started at 9:01, carrying Harold Sturges, the owner, and T.T. Bennett, the umpire, but the Mueller wagon owing to a delay in reaching the starting point, did not get off until six minutes past ten. Oscar Mueller conducted, and Charles B. King acted as umpire.

The speed of the wagons varied according to the condition of the roads. Where snow was deep or slush was plenty they toiled through the mess as best they could, but on certain stretches, conditions were more favorable for speed, and some lively sprinting was witnessed by the thousands of spectators who lined the way, and cheered heartily as each contestant passed.

As this was the first opportunity motor wagon inventors had had of testing the operation of the rubber tire in snow, some misgivings were felt, and an odd device was resorted to to prevent slipping. The tires of the Mueller and Duryea wagons were wound with twine under the impression that this would give a firmer grip on the snow. The occupants of the Duryea wagon soon dispensed with this makeshift as it appeared to them unnecessary. One of the occupants of the Mueller wagon also busied himself in sanding the belt from time to time to prevent its slipping.

The Sturges wagon reached Lincoln Park at 12:15, and soon afterward abandoned the race, the deep snow of the midway having proved so great a tax upon its motor that the conductor had to make frequent stops to keep it from burning out.

The Duryea wagon led from the beginning of the race, but the steering apparatus broke, necessitating a delay during which the Macy wagon passed the competitor. The Macy wagon led until Evanston was reached, where the Duryea again took the lead. The trip of the Macy machine was spiced with adventure. The vehicle collided with a street car in the city, and not very long afterwards it disputed the way with a heavy coach, and came out of the encounter with a broken steering gear and other infirmities, which speedily became chronic, and brought the machine to a standstill finally at 6.15 P.M., twenty-five minutes behind the Duryea.

The Duryea machine arrived at the finish at 7:18, ten hours and twenty-eight minutes from the time of starting. Taking into account the delays for repairs, etc., the Duryea wagon made an average of about 7 1/2 miles an hour, the actual time the vehicle was in motion being 7 1/2 hours. Some time was also lost by losing the course at Lawrence Avenue on return.

The Horseless Age

The Trial and Postponement

Brief Review of the Preliminary Tests and the Consolation Race

Owing to a general feeling among those who had entered in the Times-Herald Contest that insufficient time had been allowed them for preparation, the judges wisely decided to postpone the event until Thanksgiving Day, November 28th. Only eight vehicles could be mustered on the Washington Driving Park on Friday, the day before the race, and one or two of these were in an unfinished condition. They were: The Benz wagon, imported from Mannheim, Germany, and owned by the H. Mueller Mfg Co., Decatur, Ill.; the Duryea wagon, of the Duryea Motor Wagon Co., Springfield, Mass.; two electric wagons built by Morris & Salom, Philadelphia, Pa.; a motor bicycle and two victorias entered by Thos. Kane & Co., Chicago, Ill., and an unfinished electric wagon exhibited by the Columbia Perambulator Co., Chicago, Ill.

A large crowd of experts and curiosity seekers gathered around these vehicles as they were put through their paces on the track, some of those present having come from remote points to witness the exhibition.

The Testing Apparatus

A unique testing apparatus had been set up at the Park and it was stipulated in the rules of the contest that each vehicle should be subjected to this test before being allowed to compete in the Race. Three vehicles only were put through the ordeal, the Benz wagon, the Duryea, and one of the victorias of Thomas Kane & Co. The figures of these tests were not given out however, the judges having decided to reserve them until the publication of the complete tests, which are to be made previous to the Thanksgiving Day event.

The machine adopted consists of a raised platform with an incline leading to it, permitting the motorcycle to be run upon the platform without difficulty. Immediately in the rear of the platform is a shaft containing two revolving drums and a friction brake. The friction brake is a standard dynamometer and registers accurately the power consumed by the revolving drums and shaft. The vehicle is also attached to the platform through a dynamometer, which registers accurately the pull it exerts.

The Providence Race

The motor carriage races advertised to take place Sept. 7th to 11th inclusive, at Narragansett Park, Providence, R.I., in connection with the annual Rhode Island State Fair, commenced on schedule time, but the programme was so seriously interfered with by two days of violent storm that only three out of the five heats proposed were run, the result being a victory for the electric carriages.

Out of the twelve original entries only eight materialized. These were the Duryea Motor Wagon Co., J. Frank Duryea, George Henry Hewitt, Fiske Warren, George H. Morrill, Jr., William M. Ashley & Son, Riker Electric Motor Co., and the Electric Carriage & Wagon Co. The last two were electric vehicles, the first being an entirely new one, and the second the "Electrobat," which received the gold medal at Chicago last fall. All the remaining wagons were of the Duryea model, one being entered by the Duryea company and the rest by private purchasers.

The electric carriages arrived several days before the opening of the fair, whereupon their owners began a search for charging facilities on the grounds. No provision for current having been made by the management, arrangements had to be made with a local electric light company, and the only place where the proper connections could be made was a cow shed some distance from the main entrance. Here the electric carriages took their stand, while the gasolene contingent occupied a number of stalls nearly half a mile away. The separation of the vehicles caused great inconvenience to the hundreds who came with the single object of seeing the motor carriages.

No space in any of the buildings had been fitted up for an exhibition and no exhibition of any kind was held, the management claiming that separate entry was required in order to qualify for the exhibition, and that the requisite number of entries had not been received. Consequently no prizes were distributed under this head.

On Monday, Sept. 7th, about 5:30 p.m., the carriages were called upon the track and numbers were assigned to them, as is customary in horse racing.

Each carriage being required to carry a weight of at least 165 pounds in addition to the driver all preferred to take this in the form of an extra passenger, who was either an employee or friend of the owner, or some well-known student of the subject.

The Riker carriage had the pole, the vehicle of the Electric Carriage & Wagon Company secured next position, and the gasolene wagons filled out the row.

All the contestants were sent back some distance behind the post for the start and came up in good order. At the word the electric carriages shot ahead, followed by the entry of the Duryea Motor Wagon Company. The other Duryea wagons were road wagons not geared for high speed, and they fell back from the start. Throughout the five-mile dash the electric carriages gradually increased their lead, finishing close together, the Riker carriage first.

The first Duryea wagon was about three-quarters of a mile behind the winners.

A very strong wind was blowing, and the track, while fast for horses, was too rough and lumpy in parts for motor carriages. The time of the four leading vehicles for the first heat was as follows:

Riker Electric Motor Company .... 15 min. 1 sec.
Electric Carriage & Wagon Company .... 15 min. 14 sec.
Duryea Motor Wagon Company .... 18 min. 47 sec.
William Ashley & Son .... 20 min. 59 sec.

As this was the first heat ever run on a track between motor vehicles it is reasonable to suppose that the contestants felt new and strange, and could not do themselves full justice. On the second day, however, they gained courage, and determined to improve on the time of the previous day. Both electric and gasolene wagons were carefully prepared for the second event. That of the Electric Carriage & Wagon Company received an accession of batteries, and the cells of both the electric wagons were thoroughly saturated with the powerful fluid.

The Riker vehicle again took the pole on account of its victory in the first heat. The Electric Carriage & Wagon Company were given the second position, the Duryea Motor Wagon Company the third, William Ashley & Son the fourth and so on.

At the word the Riker vehicle took the lead as on the first day, maintaining it to the finish, closely followed by the Duryea wagon and the wagon of the Electric Carriage & Wagon Company.

This heat was closely contested by the three leaders and evoked great enthusiasm from the spectators. The time was a considerable improvement over that of the preceding day:

Riker Electric Motor Company .... 13 m. 6 s.
Duryea Motor Wagon Company .... 13 m. 13 s.
Electric Carriage & Wagon Company .... 14 m. 33 s.
William Ashley & Son .... 16 m. 31 s.

On Wednesday and Thursday a violent northeasterly storm prevailed throughout that section of New England. Rain fell in torrents and the wind played havoc with the shows and with the plans of the management. All races were declared off on these two days, and hundreds of persons who had come from distant parts not touched by the equinoxial gale and could not remain for pleasanter weather, went back disappointed. During the continuance of the storm many showed their interest in the new vehicles by wading through mud and water to the sheds where they were quartered.

On Friday the weather cleared, and by afternoon the track was in good condition. The strong wind which had impeded the racers in the two previous heats had died away, and fast time was predicted. A vast assemblage, estimated at nearly 50,000, had collected in the grand stand and around the track by the time the motor race was called.

Riker took the pole in the third heat; Duryea, second position; the Electric Carriage & Wagon Co., Wm. Ashley & Son, fourth; and so on.

The electric carriages dashed off at a two-minute pace, closely followed by the Duryea wagon. A little beyond the half-mile the Duryea wagon was pulling up with the two electrics, when a tire punctured and the wagon gradually lost headway. The Riker carriage maintained its lead until the homestretch was reached, when the other electric spurted ahead and crossed the line a second ahead of its rival. Much better time was made by all the entries in this third heat, scarcely one falling below the 15-mile-an-hour limit. The time of the four winners was as follows:

Electric Carriage & Wagon Company	11 m. 27 s.
Riker Electric Motor Company	11 m. 28 s.
Duryea Motor Wagon Company	11 m. 29 s.
William Ashley & Son	15 m. 47 s.

The Riker carriage was conducted by A.L. Riker...; the carriage of the Electric Carriage & Wagon Company by Henry B. Morris in the first two heats, and by Adams in the third.

The blood of the contestants was now up, and all were bent smashing records on Saturday, the last day of the fair. It was announced that two heats might possibly be run, but owing to the large number of postponed horse races, which had to be run off, darkness closed on the track before the motors could be called, and the management announced that the three heats already run would constitute the race. There was considerable grumbling among the contestants, and some of the occupants of the grand stand, when this decision was made known, but no appeal could be made.

The Duryea wagons went overland to Worcester on the following day, and from there were shipped by train to Springfield. The wagons belonging to Fiske Warren and Geo. H. Morrill, Jr.. were both run on their own wheels to the residences of their respective owners, the first to Harvard, Mass., and the second to Norwood, Mass.

One of the Duryea wagons made the run to Worcester in three hours, a distance of 47 miles by the road.

The electric wagons were shipped to their destinations as soon as possible.

The race was conducted by the association under the general rules applied to trotting races, and the awards were made upon this basis. The conditions called for a 25-mile race of five heats of five miles each, one on each of the five successive days of the fair.

As unfavorable weather prevented the completion of more than three heats three-fifths of the purse only was divided, the following proportions: First money, to the Riker Electric Motor Co., of Brooklyn. N. Y., $900; second, to the Electric Carriage & Wagon Co., Philadelphia, Pa., $450; third, to the Duryea Motor Wagon Co., $270; fourth, to Wm. Ashley & Son, Springfield, Mass., $180.

According to the precedent in uncompleted track events two-fifths of their entrance fees were refunded to all contestants not disqualified by failure to attain the required average rate of speed.

Public interest in the motor races in Providence and vicinity was very keen, and quite a number of students of the new method of locomotion came from distant points to witness the trial of speed.

The management of the fair stated that they feel amply repaid for their venture.

The electric carriages weighed from 2,200 to 2,500 pounds in racing trim, including passengers, the heavier of the two being that of the Electric Carriage & Wagon Company. The leading Duryea wagon weighed about 1,200 pounds all on.

The fastest mile was covered by the Riker electric carriage, the time being 2.13.

It was quite generally commented on by the audience that the electric vehicles made as much or more noise than the gasolene at high spccd.

Prof. W.H. Pickering, of Harvard University, acted as Chairman of the Board of Judges, being assisted by Prof. Alonzo Williams, of Brown University D.M. Thompson, president of the Corliss Steam Engine Company, Richards Howland, editor of the Providence Journal, and ex-Governor D. Russell Brown.

From the Chairman of the Judges

Cambridge, Mass., Sept. 20, 1896

Editor Horseless Age:

Now that the Providence races are over, and we have had an opportunity to examine and weigh the results, I think we must conclude that some very valuable information has been obtained. Unlike the Chicago and New York competitions, this was a speed contest pure and simple. Only eight vehicles were entered for competition, and therefore, according to the published rules governing the races, no other points were considered by the judges. The comparison between the electric gasolene carriages was particularly interesting, and the results were quite different from those obtained at Chicago. No electric carriages were entered in the New York contest. While at Chicago the electric carriages were badly beaten at Providence both of these entered came out with flying colors, distinctly in advance of the best gasolene vehicle.

The reasons for this difference are obvious. In Chicago the race lasted several hours, and the course lay over a rough and very difficult track. In Providence, on the other hand, the race lasted but a few minutes, and the course lay over a hard and perfectly level road. Both vehicles, doubtless, have been much improved since the Chicago race; but were it to be tried over again tomorrow we cannot doubt that the result would be the same.

Another point that seemed to me to be of interest was the comparatively low speeds that were at first obtained — low, that is, in comparison with what was claimed for the vehicle before the race, and the rapid improvement made in the successive heats. On the first day but four of the vehicles recorded a speed in excess of 15 miles an hour and none reached a speed of 20 miles, although as compared with common roads the course was an excellent one. Later, much better figures were scored, one of the electric carriages completing a mile in 2 m. 23 s., and one of the gasolene carriages accomplishing it in 2 m. 26 s. One of the electric carriages ran the whole five miles at an average speed of 25.2 miles per hour, while the gasolene carriage reached an average speed of 25.0 miles.

Much public interest was manifested in the races, especially upon the second day, when the competition was very close, and it appears certain that for racing as well as for practical purposes the motor vehicle has come to stay. That before long much higher speeds will be obtained upon the track, as soon as it becomes an object to construct vehicles especially for that purpose, also appears reasonably certain. In the meantime the motor vehicle has conclusively demonstrated that under favorable conditions an average speed of 15 miles an hour is perfectly practicable for ordinary purposes of pleasure travel.

Report of the Board of Judges at the Providence Race

Entries	Order Sept.			Time Sept.			Result
	7,	8,	11,	7,	8,	11,	
				m. s.	m. s.	m. s.	
Riker Electric Motor Co.	1	1	2	15 01	13 06	11 28	1
Electric Carriage Wagon & Co.	2	3	1	15 13	13 33	11 27	2
Duryea Motor Wagon Co.	6	2	3	20 59	13 14	11 59	3
Wm. M. Ashley & Son	3	5	4	18 47	16 31	15 47	4
Geo. Henry Hewitt	4	4	5	19 31	16 12	15 49	5
Fiske Warren	5	0	8	20 03		19 00	Disqualified
J. Frank Duryea	7	6	7	21 23	17 52	18 07	7
Geo. H. Morrill, Jr.	0	7	6		18 19	17 19	Disqualified

APPENDIX J

William H. Shafer Letter
Re: Electric Vehicle Costs

FOX VALLEY ELECTRIC AUTO ASSOCIATION, Inc.

William H. Shafer, Secretary

308 South East Avenue / Oak Park, Illinois 60302

(708) 383-0186

Dr Ernest Wakefield
2300 Noyes Court   29 February, 1992
Evanston, IL 60201

Dear Ernest:

       I enjoyed today's telephone conversation concerning electric
vehicle costs. As agreed, this response will provide information
about the experience of the FVEAA regarding these costs.

       Costs need to be considered in two categories; purchase and
operating. The first attachment covers FVEAA experience on the
probably project cost to recycle and repower a conventional car for
electric drive. Our latest figures indicate $ 4000 should be allowed.
Once the conversion project is complete, we find that there are no
future capital costs. My DAF, converted 17 years ago, is still
running fine, but the body is rusting and this is one item that will
send any car to the crusher. The electrical components could be
recycled into another electric conversion.

       In terms of operating costs, our experince indicates the
per-mile costs for an electric car driven a modest 10 miles per day for
300 days per year (well within the performance capability of our
converted cars) have been:

Battery amortization		
(Lead-acid, 5-yr life, @ $55)	10	cents/mile
Insurance ($ 200/year)	7	"
Electric Power (1/2 Kwh/mile @ 10 cents)	5	"
License and Fees	2	"
Miscelleaneous costs	1	"

Total	25	"

Costs are well below comparative figures for conventional cars which
must include finance and depreciation items which our electrics do not
require. We believe it is economically advantageous for an individual
to do a conversion project which can be completed with 3-5 months work
and use a vehicle which has proven to be a useful transportation tool
for urban driving trips.

atch.

Sincerely

Bill Shafer

Wilʹliam H Shafer

Declaration of Energy Independence

A Declaration by the Fox Valley Electric Auto Association

The freedom of any United States citizen for unrestricted travel anywhere within the USA is an essential part of our liberties. With this freedom comes the obligation of each citizen to act in a responsible manner during his journeys. Laws establishing vehicle construction and performance have been adopted, together with standards and regulations governing vehicle orderly operation, by the States.

External events and technological developments make necessary a review of our personal transportation. The universal ownership of affordable cars has caused us to become ever more dependent on the personal vehicle. With it, the driver can go anywhere he desires, be accompanied by anyone he chooses, feel secure, and travel at any time. Suburban development has been based on the travel freedom provided by the personal auto.

For six decades the availability of reasonably priced petroleum fuels has been a vital part of this transportation. Gasoline supply has been interrupted only three times during this period, in 1941-44 during wartime rationing, in 1973 in the first OPEC embargo, and in 1978 in the second OPEC embargo. Each of these events restricted our travel freedom.

We are becoming more aware that use of personal cars for travel has exacted an environmental price. The pollution associated with growing automobile use in urban areas is becoming more acute, despite advances in anti-pollution technology. The larger effects of burning the world's accumulated store of fossil fuels becomes more evident with each new investigation. The future supply of petroleum based fuels obtained from foreign sources is a matter of both supply and economic concerns.

We the members of the FVEAA do therefore today declare our energy independence from petroleum use for urban personal transportation. The vehicles we construct utilize the electrical energy that, in the Chicago Area, is 83% obtained from nuclear sources and 15% from low-sulfur coal. Nuclear fuel adds nothing to air pollution, and low-sulfur coal does not contribute to acid rain.

We invite our fellow citizens to join us and build their own electrically powered cars, and to support our call for accelerated development of mass produced cars using electricity as their power source.

Presented this 22nd Day of April, 1990
On the 20th Anniversary of Earth Day

FVEAA Electric Car Conversion Manual

Part I, Getting Started - Budgeting and Car Selection

This series of papers is intended for the person who wishes to enjoy the benefits of electric car ownership but is unwilling to await the time when they may be purchased commercially, or who wishes to recycle a conventional car at a modest cost. Since its founding in 1975, over 20 FVEAA members have converted various conventional cars to electric power and have 15 years of construction and operating experience to share with persons who have recently become interested.

The first step in the project is to establish a budget so you will not be surprised midway thru the work. The major components in a conversion are listed below:

Item	Cost Range
Car Purchase	$ 200– 400
Electric Motor	300–1800
Machine Shop Work	500– 700
Controller	600–1200
Batteries (72-volt system)	600– 700
Charger	200– 700
Cables & Miscellaneous	300– 500
Total	$ 2700–6000

Your car can save you money. I converted a DAF and drove it for 16 years and kept a record of expenses. The total annual cost for this car was $392, less than 7% of Runzheimer's 1991 annual cost of $5820 in Chicago for a new conventional car.

The car selected will have a major effect on the final outcome of the project. The best conversions have used a lightweight subcompact car, preferably one that has an inoperative engine. These can usually be purchased from a salvage yard or disgruntled owner for a few hundred dollars. Scan your local newspaper ads. If you buy the car from a salvage yard and receive a salvage title, be prepared for some extra work to get it licensed by the Secretary of State. The better shopper you are, the less your project will cost.

Remember that RUST is the single item that will eventually send your electric car to the crusher. The drivetrain components may be in good operating shape and reinstalled in another vehicle, but rust will not only cause you a lot of extra work initially; it will also impair your enjoyment of the car. Select a car with a body in good shape.

Avoid cars where replacement parts for brakes, shocks, steering components, suspension members, and accessories such as taillight lenses will be are hard to find and expensive. Select a car where these components will be available at reasonable cost. It can be a frustrating experience to search for some small but vital component that needs replacing.

The car you select will determine what you can do with a conversion. Table I lists representative subcompact cars with their original specifications:

Table 1. Cars Suitable for Conversion to Electric Power

Car	Weight	F/R	Net HP @	RPM	Ratio	RPM/Mile	
Geo Metro (88)	1640	47/53	55	5700	3.95		4.15
Honda Civic (1300)	1760	62/38	63	5000	3.30	3060	4.1
(88)	2138	60/40	92	6000	4.16		3.6
Ford Festiva (87)	1713		58	5000	3.78	4.1	
Fiesta	1800	63/37	66	5000	3.15	3070	4.1
Dodge Colt	1800	62/38	70	5200	2.97	2750	
Renault LeCar	1830	59/41	60	6000	3.72	3480	
Yugo (87)	1832	64/36	54	5200	3.76		4.8
Chevy Spectrum (86)	1874	63/38	70	5400	3.58	3.58	3.9
VW Rabbit (84)	1930	63/37	71	5800	3.78	3455	3.0
Alliance (86)	1960		77	5000	3.56		3.8
Mazda GLC	1980	55/45	66	5000	3.73	3405	
Datsun 310	2000	62/38	65	5600	3.46	3170	
Subaru (84)	2050	64/36	67	5200	3.81	3480	
Audi Fox (87)	2070	61/39	78	5500	3.70	3380	3.6
Ford Escort (86)	2080	62/38	80	5400	3.73		
Chevette	2110	53/47	70	5200	3.70	3390	
Hundai Excel (87)	2150	63/37	68	5500	3.47		4.2
VW Dasher	2160	61/39	78	5500	3.74	3420	
Dodge Omni (85)	2200	62/38	70	5200	3.37	3105	
Toyota Corolla (88)	2242	60/40	90	6000	3.72	3645	3.8
Honda Accord	2240	59/41	72	4500	3.05	2785	
Nissan Sentra (84)	1855	55/45	67	5600	3.36		
(87)	2326	-	70	5000	3.89	-	5.4

The original curb weight listed in Column 2 will determine how many batteries you can expect to put into the car. You will remove 200-300 pounds of engine-related parts from the car. Each golf-cart type deep discharge battery you install will weigh about 70 pounds, including rack. Motor weight will add about another 100 pounds. To stay within the original car specifications, the passenger load must be reduced. You will be in for extensive modifications if you exceed the gross vehicle limit (GVW) for your car. Check this parameter carefully. Table I DOES NOT list GVW.

The third column lists the weight distribution between the front and rear wheels of the car. This will determine WHERE you can locate batteries. The ideal ratio of 50-50 is seldom found in front-wheel drive cars. Too much weight in the front may cause difficult steering. Too much weight in the rear may cause difficulty with emergency braking. Your converted car should keep the same weight distribution as the original spec. Battery placement requires individual attention and ingenuity.

The fourth column lists the horsepower developed by the original car engine and the rpm at which it is achieved. The performance of your converted car will probably not match this number, but it is a factor to be considered.

Motor selection will be influenced by the data in the sixth and seventh columns which show the final drive ratio and the RPM per mile of travel.

The battery weight ratio is one of the early and most important EV decisions. A converted car realistically will end up with 25-30% of its curb weight made up of batteries. The curb weight of the EV will probably be 20-30% above the original value listed in Table I.

Early in the project you should define how you intend to use the car. An electric can be tailored to your expected use. The factors to be considered are:

1. What is the desired acceleration rate?
2. Top speed?
3. Single-charge operating range?

You must set realistic expectations. Faster acceleration will require additional batteries or sacrifice of battery life and efficiency. Higher top speed will increase battery weight. The further you want to go before recharging the more batteries will be needed. Based on FVEAA experience, a converted car can accelerate from 0-30 in 6 seconds, have a top speed of 50 MPH, and go up to 30 miles without recharging. An EV with this performance will be a useful urban transportation tool.

A VW Rabbit will be used to illustrate how the preceding information can be utilized. A passenger weight of 150 lbs each will be assumed. The curb weight listed in Table I is 1930 lbs. The GWV for this 4-passenger car would be 1930 + (4) (150) = 2530 lbs. The net weight after engine removal would be 1930-300 = 1630 lbs. Carrying one passenger makes the pre-conversion car net weight 1780 lbs. Subtracting this from the GWV yields a conversion parts weight of 750 lbs.

When the 100 lbs of motor weight is subtracted, we find that 9.28 batteries can be accommodated. Rounding up to the next integer would say that based on these assumptions, a 60-volt system with 10 deep discharge batteries can be considered. At 700 pounds, the power batteries would make up 27% of the EV curb weight. The 63/37 weight distribution requires 6 of the power batteries be located in the front and the remaining 4 in the rear of the car. Fitting them in poses an interesting challenge. The curb weight of the converted car is 2430 lbs.

W.H. Shafer   (8/21/1993)

Glossary

A glossary for electric vehicles and multi-powered electric vehicles is an assembly of specialized terms from physics, chemistry, aerodynamics, electrical and mechanical engineering, computer science, and automotive lore. Additions are sought for future editions. Credits are in the Acknowledgement.

Absorption: When light strikes a surface, some of it penetrates into the material and is trapped. This trapped energy is called absorption. Transformation into other forms suffered by radiant energy passing through a material substance.

Aerodynamic Drag: Force proportional to frontal area, drag coefficient and speed squared, measured in pounds or kilograms as determined in a wind-tunnel. See Drag Coefficient.

Air Dam: Barrier beneath the front bumper used to divert the flow of air beneath the car. Usually intended to reduce lift and drag.

Air gap voltage: Voltage across a gap or equivalent filler of nonmagnetic material across the core of a choke, transformer, or other magnetic device.

Alternating-current (A-C): Current in which the charge-flow periodically reverses, as opposed to direct current, and whose average value is zero. Alternating current usually implies a sinusoidal variation of current and voltage.

AM-air mass or atmospheric mass: This is a measure of the absorption and scattering of light by the Earth's atmosphere. AM 0 indicates no atmosphere in the path of light. This is the condition in space where the power density of light is about 1.36 kilowatt/square meter. AM 1 is the condition at the surface of the Earth where the light passes through one atmosphere. Power density is about 1.0 kilowatt/square meter.

Ampere: A transfer of one coulomb per second, where a coulomb is the quantity of electricity which must pass through a circuit to deposit 0.0011180 grams of silver from a solution of silver-nitrate.

Ampere-hour meter: An instrument that monitors current with time. The indication is the product of current in amperes and time in hours.

Ångström: The Ångström is a measure of the wavelength of light. One Ångström = 10^{-10} meter. Yellow light from a sodium street-light is about 5500 Ångströms.

Anti-dive: Front suspension design that counteracts front-end lowering under braking.

Anti-roll bar: An anti-roll bar yields low roll centers with the attendant advantage of minimum jacking effect due to lateral loading and minimum lateral wheel deflection on the bump - without the disadvantage of large roll angles and consequent camber change.

Anti-squat: Rear suspension design that counteracts rear-end lowering under acceleration.

Aspect ratio: In tires the ratio between the sidewall height and the overall width. A 50-series tire with a width of 8 inches, for example, has sidewalls 4 inches high.

Battery: A direct-current voltage source made up of one or more cells to convert chemical energy into electric energy. A Primary Cell delivers electric current as a result of an electrochemical reaction that is not efficiently reversible, so the cell cannot be recharged efficiently. A Secondary Cell is an electrolytic cell for generating electric energy, in which the cell after being discharged may be restored to a charged condition by sending a current through it in the direction opposite to that of the discharging current.

Belt line: In an automobile the line where the top of the body and bottom of the windows meet.

Blocking diode: A semiconductor connected in series with a solar cell or cells and a storage battery to keep the battery from discharging through the cell when there is no output, or low output, from the solar cell.

Bump stop: A condition of driving when the vehicle support springs are fully compressed.

CAD-CAM: Computer aided design, computer aided manufacturing implies integrated use of the computer in the conceptualization, design, and manufacture of a product. Included are design and simulation, redesign, materials handling, maintenance, process control, quality control, and inventory management.

Camber: Angle between the plane of the wheel and a vertical. Most cars have slightly negative camber; the tires tilt in at the top.

Capacitance: The ratio of the charge on one of the conductors of a capacitor (there being an equal and opposite charge on the other conductor) to the potential difference between the conductors. Symbolized C.

Capacitor: A device which consists essentially of two conductors (such as parallel metal plates) insulated from each other by a dielectric and which introduces capacitance into a circuit, stores electrical energy, blocks the flow of direct current, and permits the flow of alternating current to a degree dependent on the capacitors capacitance and the current frequency.

Carbon fiber: Threads of pure carbon used to reinforce resin in a composite.

Center of gravity of a vehicle: That point in a vehicle from or on which the body can be suspended or poised in equilibrium in any position. The distance the center of gravity of a vehicle is above the ground is a limiting factor in roadholding.

Charge (electrical): A basic property of elementary particles of matter.

Chassis: Frame with all mechanical systems in place; in other words, everything except the body and interior. Race car chassis types are: multitubular, space, twin tube, and unitary or monocoque frame.

Circuit breaker: An electromagnetic device that opens a circuit automatically when the current exceeds a predetermined value.

Coast-down test: To determine dissipative losses associated with on-road travel such as aerodynamic drag and rolling resistance losses a coast-down test may be performed before testing a vehicle on a chassis dynamometer. The key to successful coast-down testing is to carefully measure and monitor as many variables as possible and to eliminate all that cannot be measured or controlled, viz., wind speed and direction must be continually recorded. No testing should be performed with wind speeds greater than 2 mph (3 km/h). The tire temperatures should be recorded after every other run. In order to minimize other uncertainties half-axles and disc-brakes should be removed from the vehicle so rolling losses result only from the tires and wheel bearings. The vehicle is then towed up to approximately 60 mph (100 km/h) and released to coast over a carefully surveyed segment of track. Data reduction by formulae developed by Jet Propulsion Laboratory of the California Institute of Technology yields the coefficient of aerodynamic drag and rolling resistance.

Composite: Material made from two or more dissimilar components. Most commonly used to refer to reinforced plastic resins such as glass-fiber reinforced resin, commonly called fiberglass.

Controller: An element which restricts the flow of electric power to an electric motor for the purpose of controlling torque and/or power output. Controller, Three Phase: An electronic circuit for controlling the output frequency and power from a 3-phase inverter.

Corner point speed: The transition between constant torque and constant power operation in an electric motor or an engine.

Coulomb: A unit of electrical charge, defined as the amount of electric charge that crosses a surface in 1 second when a steady current of 1 absolute ampere is flowing across the surface. One electron has a charge of -1.602×10^{-19} coulomb.

Concentrator cell: A solar cell designed for power densities much greater than the normal power density of sunlight at the surface of the earth. Concentrator cells can be used with focusing arrangements that increase the power density of sunlight hundreds of times.

Concentration ratio: The amount light is magnified by a focusing system. For example, if a lens or reflector system increases the power density of sunlight from the normal 1.0 kilowatt/square meter to 3.0 kilowatt/square meter, a magnification of three times, the concentration ratio is 3 to 1.

Contact patch: Hand-size area of a tire that is actually touching the road surface and which provides all acceleration, braking, and turning friction.

Curb weight: Weight of a vehicle less the expected load expressed in pounds or kilograms.

Current: The rate of transfer of electricity. The unit is the ampere.

Demand charge: A surcharge levied by an electric utility for unusual, short term energy use.

Diamagnetic: Having a magnetic permeability of less than one; material with this property are repelled by a magnet and tend to position themselves at right angles to magnetic lines of force.

Differential: Allows torque to be applied to two different gears that can turn at different speeds. In negotiating a corner, the outside wheel of a car must travel farther than the inside wheel in the same amount of time.

Diode: A two-electrode semiconductor device that utilizes the rectifying properties of a pn junction or point contact.

Direct current motor: An electric motor which is energized by direct-current to provide torque. There are several classes of direct-current motors. The designer chooses the type to yield the desired characteristics.

Disc brake: Flat disc or rotor that rotates with the wheel and is stopped by pressing on both sides with a caliper. Bicycles use caliper brakes that press the tire rim (a rotor).

Down force: Aerodynamic force that presses the car body closer to the road.

Drag coefficient: A measure of how easily a fluid, usually air, will flow around an object. Often abbreviated "Cd" or "Cx". If D is the drag of a body in a uniform stream of density p and velocity V, the drag coefficient is $Cd = 2D/p \, V^2 \, S$ where S is a representative area of the body, usually taken as frontal area. A teardrop has a Cd of 0.05, a barn door about 1.15, a Toyota Previa minivan 0.33, a Porsche about 0.30, the GM Impact 0.19, the GM Sunraycer 0.12.

Drivetrain: Motor, transmission, driveshaft, differential, and axle shafts.

Drum brake: Cast iron drum that rotates with the wheel and is stopped by pressing against the inside of the drum with a curved brake shoe.

Eddy current: An electric current induced within the body of a conductor when that conductor either moves through a nonuniform magnetic field or is in a region where there is a change in magnetic flux.

Efficiency of a solar cell: The ratio of the electrical power output of a solar cell to the solar power that it intercepts. For example, a solar cell 3 inches (7.6 cm) in diameter intercepts about 2.39 watts of solar power under full sun conditions. If the electrical output of this cell is 0.34 watt, the efficiency will be

$$\frac{0.34}{2.39} = 0.14, \text{ or } 14\%$$

Electrode: Either terminal of an electric source.

Electrolyte: An electric conductor in which passage of current is accompanied by liberation of matter at the electrodes.

Four-wheel steering: Steers the rear wheels as well as the front wheels.

Frequency and pulse-width modulation circuit: A circuit for varying the current into a motor and therefore the torque output. Sometimes called a variable frequency inverter.

Fuel cell: A cell that converts chemical energy directly into electric energy, with electric power being produced as part of a chemical reaction between the electrolyte and a fuel such as kerosene or industrial fuel gas.

Full sun: The full sun condition is the amount of power density received at the surface of the earth at noon on a clear day — about 1.0 kilowatt/square-meter. Lower levels of sunlight are often expressed as 0.5 sun or 0.1 sun. A figure of 0.5 sun means that the power density of the sunlight is one-half of that of a full sun.

Fuse: An expendable device for opening an electric circuit when the current therein becomes excessive, containing a section of conductor which melts when the current through it exceeds a rated value for a definite period of time.

G: One gravity, or 32.2 feet (9.80 m) per second per second. In an automobile used to measure acceleration, braking and cornering force. High-performance passengers cars can brake and corner at about 1 G, racing cars can corner at 4 G, and an F-16 airplane corners at well over 8 G.

Gate: A circuit in which one signal, generally a square-wave, serves to switch another signal on and off.

Gauss: A measure of magnetic flux density. In the centimeter- gram-second electromagnetic system: one maxwell per square centimeter, where a maxwell (line) is a unit of magnetic flux. The magnetic flux density at the surface of the earth is about one-half gauss. At a magnetic pole of an electric motor the magnetic flux density is about 8000 gauss.

Greenhouse: Everything above the beltline of an automobile, essentially the windows and roof.

Ground effect: Air squeezed between the bottom of a moving car and the road can be directed to produce downforce or other useful aerodynamic effects.

Horsepower: One horsepower (hp) equals the power required to lift 550 pounds 1 foot in 1 second. Equals 0.746 kilowatts. A well designed two-place electric car will require about 8-10 hp in traveling 50 miles per hour on a level concrete road.

Hybrid electric vehicle: A multi-powered electric car. With a series hybrid an alternate source of power charges the battery which in turn drives a motor providing torque to the wheels. In a parallel hybrid vehicle the alternate source of power directly applies torque to the wheels. There have been petro-electric, solar-assist, flywheel, capacitive, spring, and hydraulic hybrid vehicles.

Hysteresis: An oscillator effect wherein a given value of an operating parameter may result in multiple values of output power or frequency.

Independent suspension: The movement of one wheel does not affect the movement of the opposite wheel.

Inductance: That property of an electric circuit or of two neighboring circuits whereby an electromotive force is generated (by the process of electromagnetic induction) in one circuit by a change of current in itself or in the other.

Induction motor: An alternating-current motor in which a primary winding on one member (usually the stator) is connected to the power source, and a secondary winding on the other member (usually the rotor), carries only current induced by the magnetic field of the primary. The magnetic fields react against each other to produce a torque. One of the simplest, reliable, and cheapest motors made.

Incident light: The amount of light reaching an object.

Insolation: The amount of sunlight reaching an area. Usually expressed in milliwatts per square centimeter.

Jounce: Compressing the suspension; the opposite of rebound.

Joule: A unit of energy. The work done by one newton acting through a distance of one meter. A joule is one watt-second.

Kelvin temperature scale: A temperature scale developed by Lord Kelvin (William Thomson) in England in the 1860s now used in physics. With the Kelvin scale at zero degrees, symbolized K, the molecules of a material do not vibrate from their stable lattice position according to classical physics. To provide a temperature range the Kelvin scale is established to have a difference of 100 degrees, like the Centigrade scale, between the freezing and boiling points of water under standard conditions. With this arrangement absolute zero temperature is 0°K, or -273.2°C, or -459.7° F.

Kevlar: Synthetic fiber produced by DuPont, popular as a reinforcing element for resin composites.

Kilowatt-hour: Is 1000 watt-hours of energy. Equals to 1.341 horsepower-hours.

Live axle: Usually a solid rear axle as opposed to an independent rear suspension.

Magnetic field: The region around a magnet or an electric current-carrying wire is a volume of special properties. The most familiar is the torque experienced by a small magnet when placed in such a region.

Magnetic permeability: Is a factor, characteristic of a material, that is proportional to the magnetic induction produced in a material divided by the magnetic field strength.

Maximum power point tracker (MPPT): An electronic circuit which assures the delivery of peak power from a solar cell to its load. A solar cell normally delivers peak power when operated at about the knee of its characteristic current-voltage curve.

Maxwell: A centimeter-gram-second electromagnetic unit which produces an electromagnetic force of 1 abvolt in a circuit of one turn linking the flux, as the flux is reduced to zero in 1 second at a uniform rate. (1 abvolt = 10^{-8} volt in the absolute meter-kilogram-second system). Abbreviated aV.

Monocoque: Also called unit or unitized construction. The body and chassis are structural and there is no separate frame.

Motor: A machine that converts electric energy into mechanical energy by utilizing forces produced by magnetic fields on current carrying conductors.

Multi-powered Electric Vehicle: A vehicle with two or more power sources for propelling it, sometimes known as a hybrid vehicle.

Nanometer: A unit of measurement of the wavelength of light. One nanometer = 10^{-9} meter = 10 Ångström units. Yellow light is about 550 nanometers.

Newton: A unit of force. One newton is the force that will impart an acceleration of 1 meter per second per second to a mass of one kilogram.

Oersted: The unit of magnetic field strength in the centimeter-gram-second electromagnetic system of units, equal to the field strength at the center of a plane circular coil of one turn and 1-centimeter radius, where there is a current of 1/2 abampere in the coil. An abampere is 10 times an ampere.

Ohm: The unit of electrical resistance in the meter-kilogram-second system of units. Equal to the resistance through which a current of 1 ampere will flow when there is a potential difference of 1 volt across it. In direct-current a constant of proportionality of voltage divided by current, viz., V/I.

Oversteer: When rear tire slip angles are higher than front tire slip angles; i.e., if you go too fast into a corner, the car will leave the road tail first.

Pascal: A unit of pressure equal to the pressure resulting from a force of 1 newton acting uniformly over an area of 1 square meter. Symbol, Pa. Also known as torr. Rough: 15 psi (pounds per square inch) equals 100 pascals.

Peak sun hours: While the amount of sunlight is latitude, seasonal, and time dependent, the over-all amount of sun may be expressed as peak sun hours per day. There is also an average annual peak sun hours for any locality. In Los Angeles with the yearly average of 5.5 peak sun hours per day, the GM Sunraycer solar array, delivering 1500 watts, would provide $1500 \times 5.5 = 8250$ watt-hours of electrical energy to the battery and motor-drive system.

Phonon: A quantum of an acoustic mode of thermal vibration in a crystal lattice.

Photon. A photon is a quantum of electromagnetic radiation which has zero rest mass and an energy which is the product of h (Planck's constant) and the frequency of the radiation. Photons are generated in collisions between nuclei or electrons and in any other process in which an electrically charged particle changes its momentum. Conversely photons can be absorbed (i.e. annihilated) by any charged particle. Planck's constant is 6.6252×10^{-27} erg/second, where an erg is an energy unit equal to 10^{-7} watt-seconds.

Photovoltaic cell: A photovoltaic cell generates electrical power when light falls on it. This term distinguishes it from photoconductive cell (photoresistor), which changes its electrical resistance when light falls on it.

Photoelectric effect: Changes in the electrical characteristics of a substance due to radiation causing the emission of bound electrons following the absorption of photons. The two laws are: 1) electrons are emitted with a maximum energy proportional to the frequency of the radiation, and 2) the number of electrons released per unit time is directly proportional to the incident light.

Pinion: The smaller of a pair of gear wheels or the smallest wheel of a gear train.

Pitch: Rotation about a horizontal axis.

Planck's Constant: The fundamental constant of quantum mechanics expressing the ratio of the energy of one quantum of radiation to the frequency of the radiation is approximately equal to 6.625×10^{-27} erg/seconds, its symbol the letter h with a slash.

Plugging: Braking an electric motor by reversing its connections, so it tends to turn in the opposite direction; the circuit is opened automatically when the motor stops, so the motor does not actually reverse.

pn-junction: The interface of a boron-doped silicon (P-type material) block on which a thin layer of phosphorus-doped silicon (N-type material) is deposited. Across this interface a barrier potential occurs. Sunlight piercing the N-type layer cause hole- electrons pairs to form. The electric field which exists at the junction will prevent the holes and electrons from recombining, with the results the cell is a source of energy. The N-type material is the negative pole and the P-type material is the positive pole with current flowing to the load from the positive pole.

Power factor: The ratio of the average (or active) power to the apparent power (root-mean-square (rms) voltage time the rms current) of an alternating-current circuit. In a balanced 3-phase a-c circuit the cosine ø in the equation $P = \sqrt{3}\ VI \cos ø$, where ø is the angle in electrical degrees between the current and the voltage. The power factor may be leading or lagging depending on whether the load is capacitive or inductive, respectively.

Pressure (P): The force (F) or thrust exerted on a surface divided by the area of the surface (S). $P = F/S$. Here: tire gauge pressure measured relative to atmospheric pressure taken as zero. Unit, see **pascal**.

Quantum yield: A technical parameter from quantum physics. For practical purposes the quantum yield of a solar cell is the spectral response of the cell, that is, the relative output at different wavelengths of light.

Rack and pinion: Compact steering gear in which a toothed bar, a rack, linked to the steered wheels is moved side-to-side by a pinion gear turned by the steering wheel.

Random access memory (RAM): A data storage device having the property that the time required to access a randomly selected datum does not depend on the time of the last access or the location of the most recently accessed datum.

Read only memory (ROM): A device for storing data in permanent or nonerasable form; usually a static electronic or magnetic device allowing extremely rapid access to data.

Rebound: Extending the suspension; the opposite of jounce.

Recirculating ball: Steering gear in which a toothed block, a rack, linked to the steered wheels is moved by a worm gear turned by the steering wheel. Recirculating ball-bearings reduce friction between block and gear.

Redline: Maximum safe revolutions-per-minute; traditionally shown by a red line or area on the tachometer face.

Reflected light: When light reaches an object, some of it may be absorbed, and some may be bounced off the surface. The light which is bounced off the surface is called reflected light.

Regenerative braking: A system of dynamic braking in which the electric drive motor is used as a generator and returns the kinetic energy of the motor armature and load to the electric supply system.

Rheostat: A resistor constructed so that its resistance value may be changed without interrupting the circuit to which it is connected. Also known as a variable resistor.

Rigid axle: Solid axle which connects a pair of wheels left to right and causes the movement of one wheel to affect the other.

Roadholding: The maximum road holding of any car may be defined as the highest degree to which cornering force can be developed without the driver losing control.

Roll: Rotation about a longitudinal axis.

Roll angle: The angle in degrees the vehicle rolls while cornering.

Roll center: The longitudinal axis around which the vehicle rolls while cornering.

Rotating electromagnetic field: A poly-phase electrically wound stator, when energized, establishes a coaxially rotating electromagnetic field. The rotational rate of the field is proportional to the frequency of applied power, and inversely proportional to the number of pole-pairs in the stator winding.

Shock absorber: More properly called a shock damper. Dampens unwanted natural spring oscillations by converting motion into heat.

Silicon controlled rectifier: A four-layer semiconductor device that normally acts as an open circuit, but switches rapidly to a conducting state when an appropriate gate signal is applied to the gate terminal. The element is easy to turn on and difficult to turn off. Abbreviated SCR.

Sliding pillar: A suspension in which each wheel is mounted on a vertical sliding member that acts on a coil spring controlled by a telescopic damper.

Slip (electrical): In an induction motor the difference between the speed of rotation of the stator electromagnetic field and the speed of the rotor is known as slip. For an induction motor to provide torque there must be slip.

Slip angle (mechanical): Difference between the direction the wheel is pointing and direction the tire is rolling caused by deflections of the tire tread and sidewall during cornering.

Solar cell: A pn-junction which converts the radiant energy of sunlight directly and efficiently into electrical energy.

Solar constant: Rate of power flow per square-meter received from the sun at the outer edge of the atmosphere; considered to be 1.36 kilowatts per square-meter. Due to absorption and scattering, the amount received at the earth's surface is about 1.0-kilowatt per square-meter.

Solar panel: A collection of solar cells connected in series, in parallel, or in series-parallel combination to provide greater voltage, current, or power than can be furnished by a single solar cell. Solar panels can be provided to furnish any desired voltage, current, or power. They are made up as a complete assembly. Larger collections of solar panels are usually called solar arrays.

Specific energy: The energy density of a battery expressed in watt-hours per kilogram. World class solarmobiles often use expensive, high specific energy batteries developed for torpedo or satellite use offering typically 100 watt-hours/kilogram. A lead-acid battery has a specific energy of 40-50 Wh/kg.

Specific power: The rate at which a battery can dispense power measured in watts per kilogram. The greater the specific power of a battery, the greater the rate of acceleration of an electric vehicle, all else being equal. A lead-acid battery has a specific power of 80 W/kg; a silver-zinc battery 200 W/kg.

Spoiler: Small wing or lip fitted to the rear of the car to increase aerodynamic downforce.

Spring: Supports the chassis and flexes to absorb road shocks.

Superconductivity: A property of many metals, alloys, and chemical compounds at temperature near absolute zero by virtue of which their electrical resistivity vanishes and they become strongly diamagnetic. The phenomena was first discovered by Heike Kamerlingh Onnes of the University of Leiden in 1911. Bardeen, Cooper, Schrieffer (BCS) theory of superconductivity: A theory developed in 1957 by John Bardeen, Leon N. Cooper, J. Robert Shrieffer, all then of the University of Illinois, to explain superconductivity. This theory describes quantum mechanically those states of a system in which conduction electrons cooperate in their motion so as to reduce the total energy appreciably below that of other states by exploiting their effective mutual attraction; these states predominate in superconducting material. High temperature superconductivity: A phenomenon discovered by Karl Alex Müller and Johannes Georg Bednorz of IBM-Zurich in 1987 in which a compound containing copper, oxygen, barium, and lanthanum exhibited superconductivity at temperatures as high as 35°K. Subsequently in 1987 C. W. Paul Chu and Maw-Kuen Wu at the Universities of Houston and of Alabama-Huntsville respectively, developed a compound which was superconducting at temperatures as high as 90°K, a temperature above that of liquid nitrogen, a low cost substance. Several other compounds have been found to yield similar results. A number of theories have been proposed to explain this phenomenon. Meissner effect: The expulsion of magnetic flux from the interior of a piece of superconducting material as the material undergoes transition to the superconducting phase.

Suspension frequency: In a chassis the oscillation frequency of the sprung mass, generally 70 - 80 per minute.

Swing axle: A suspension pivoted at or near the center-line of the car in front elevation, usually with fore-and-aft linkage.

Synchronous motor with permanent magnets: In a synchronous motor the stator is wound to carry poly-phase alternating-current. When energized the stator establishes a coaxially rotating electromagnetic field. In synchronous motors for electric vehicles the rotor bears pairs of permanent magnets whose pole-pairs equal the pole-pairs of the rotating field. Inasmuch as opposite poles attract, the poles on the rotor are magnetically coupled to the rotating poles of the stator thus providing torque to the load.

Temperature coeffient of a solar cell: The amount by which the voltage, current, or power from a solar cell will change with changes in the temperature of the cell.

Three-phase inverter: An electronic circuit capable of receiving direct-current and efficiently converting it into 3-phase alternating-current whose frequency and power may be controlled by the operator. Achieved by frequency and pulse-width modulation.

Three-phase power: Power (P) is the time rate of doing work. A three-phase power three-wire system is an alternating-current (I) supply comprising three conductors between successive pairs of which are maintained alternating differences of potential (V) successively displaced in phase by one-third of a period. In the general case in a balanced 3-phase system $P = \sqrt{3}\ VI \cos \phi$, where ϕ is the electrical angle between current and voltage. Household power is generally-single phase power requiring at least two wires. For electric motors larger than about three-kilowatt, 3-phase power is usually employed.

Toe in: In automotive use, the amount the left and right wheel deviate from the parallel. Most rear-drive cars have slight toe-in, while front-wheel drive cars often use toe-out.

Torque: That which produces or tends to produce rotation or torsion; the product of the tangential force and the radius of the part which rotates. One-kilogram-meter of torque equals the force of 1-kilogram applied to the end of a 1-meter lever. An energy unit.

Torque converter: A device for converting the torque from the drive shaft to the torque required by the driven shaft.

Traction control: Computerized control that prevents wheelspin under acceleration.

Transel (transportation-super-conducting-electric): A proposed superconducting magnet-levitated automobile equipped with a battery-powered, motor-driven air-screw capable of maintaining forward motion while soaring a few centimeters above a non-magnetic, electrical conducting roadway.

Transaxle: Transmission and differential combined in one unit. Commonly, but not exclusively, used in front-wheel drive cars.

Transformer: An electrical component consisting of two or more multiturn coils of wire placed in close proximity to cause the magnetic field of one to link with the other; used to transfer electric energy from one or more alternating-current circuits to one or more other circuits by magnetic induction.

Transistor: An active component of an electronic circuit consisting of a small block of semi-conducting material to which at least three electrical contacts are made, usually two closely spaced rectifying contacts and one ohmic (non-rectifying) contact; it may be used as an amplifier, detector or switch.

Tumblehome: When the greenhouse is narrower at the top than at the bottom, the car's body is said to have tumblehome.

Turn-In: Transition between driving straight and cornering.

Understeer: When front tire slip-angles are higher than rear tire slip-angles; i.e., if you go into a corner too fast, the car will leave the road front first.

Volt: A Unit of potential difference or electromotive force in the meter-kilogram-second system, equal to the potential difference between two points for which 1 coulomb of electricity will do 1 joule of work in going from one point to the other. Symbol V.

Voltage-current characteristic: A plot of the current output of a solar cell versus its terminal voltage. Usually several curves are given for different amounts of sunlight reaching the cell.

Watt-hours per mile: Energy consumption per mile at a particular speed or condition of driving. A convenient overall measure of a vehicle's elegance of design. The GM Impact is reported to use 113 watt-hours per mile at 55 miles per hour (71 watt-hours per km at 85 kph), while the GM Sunraycer is stated to require only 30 watt-hours per mile (19 watt-hours per km) for the same speed.

Weber: The unit of magnetic flux in the meter-kilogram-second system, equal to the magnetic flux which, linking a circuit of one turn, produces in it an electromotive force of 1 volt as it is reduced to zero at a uniform rate in 1 second. Symbol Wb.

Wheel stiffness: The rigidity of a wheel. A wire-spoked wheel is less stiff than a pressed-steel wheel which is less stiff than an cast-aluminum wheel.

Wheelbase and track: Respectively the distance from front and rear axle centers, and the right-angle distance between tire marks. Front and rear tracks may be different.

Wishbone: A type of vehicle suspension which serves to minimize wheel-to-wheel interference as well as to reduce the effect of body roll on wheel camber change.

Yaw: Rotation about a vertical axis.

Index